MICHELANGELO: SCULPTOR

CRISTINA ACIDINI LUCHINAT

Michelangelo sculptor

Photographs by Aurelio Amendola

24 ORE Cultura

Front cover
Michelangelo, *Pietà*, detail
Vatican City, Saint Peter's
© Aurelio Amendola, Santomato (PT)
Courtesy of the Fabbrica di San Pietro in the Vatican

Acknowledgements
I wish to thank my colleagues, and all of the conservators and scholars who shared their knowledge and opinions with me. I also wish to thank Elena Capretti for her assistance in this undertaking (as in others in the past), which she carried out with outstanding skill and admirable devotion. Thanks also go to the Publishers and the members of their superb editorial staff, with whom I worked while conducting research and writing the book, and who were always willing to satisfy my requests, always responsive to my concerns, understanding when I was late, over and beyond anything I could reasonably have hoped for. *C.A.L.*

Aurelio Amendola wishes to thank the Publisher for having given him the chance to see his Michelangelesque dream take shape.

Translated from the Italian by
Sylvia Adrian Notini

First edition in the "Le Gemme" series
October 2010

ISBN 978-88-7179-640-6

TABLE OF CONTENTS

To dedicate a book to Michelangelo Buonarroti the sculptor: a "terrible" challenge, like the man himself and his entire oeuvre. And yet it is also an irresistible challenge, one which signifies and foreshadows a good many things. It means following a well-trodden path that has seen the tracks of eminent scholars at times becoming indistinguishable from those of wreckless popularizers.
It means confronting a titanic bibliography whose monumental cornerstones are documents produced during Michelangelo's time and day – first among which the Ricordi, *the* Carteggio diretto, *and the* Carteggio indiretto *– for centuries published in no particular order but ultimately pieced together with masterly skill under Paola Barocchi's supervision; no fewer than two biographies in the artist's own lifetime, one published in 1550 by Giorgio Vasari, the artist at the Medici court, and one in 1553, a sort of response to Vasari's words, by Michelangelo's assistant Ascanio Condivi, in which the master, by then nearing his eighties, poured forth memories, clarifications and objections. And this was followed by Vasari's second edition of the* Lives, *published in 1568, with additional information and counter-deductions.*
*Writing this book means examining archival data, literary sources and writings on art, which have grown over the centuries and become, from the late 1800s and through the 20th century until the present day, a measureless tide of critical contributions founded on a diversity of methods, expressing the most disparate viewpoints, written in a variety of languages. And this has been followed by both filmic expression and the digital image, now rightly included among the critical tools available, so that any approach to Michelangelo's work cannot overlook the "critofilm" by Carlo Ludovico Ragghianti commemorating the fourth centenary of the artist's death (*Michelangiolo, *1964), the short made by Michelangelo Antonioni four years afterward (*Lo sguardo di Michelangelo, *2004), the* Digital Michelangelo Project *initiated at Stanford University, the* Virtual Model *of the Florence* Pietà *designed by Jack Wasserman in a joint effort with IBM (1997-2002); nor can Carol Reed's popular film adaptation of Irving Stone's biographical novel* The Agony and the Ecstasy *(1965) be neglected, for many Americans (and not only them), the sole source of information on Michelangelo.*
That Michelangelo chiefly considered himself to be a sculptor transpires from many passages in his own biography, and is confirmed by one piece of writing in particular which, as it is both private and autograph, has all the requisites of a reliable source: namely, the words – "Mich[e]lagniolo Schultore" – which the artist himself wrote in Vittoria Colonna's Tutte le rime, *a volume published in 1558, after the poet's death.*[1] *And yet by that time, Michelangelo had already painted his major works on wood and frescoes, and was chief architect at a number of important building sites.*
So the question is this: how do we go about approaching one single aspect of a man who excelled in all the arts, in the three Arts of Disegno *– Painting, Sculpture, Architecture – and even Poetry? To his contemporaries, Michelangelo's death was not the passing of one man, but of four, his fourfold creative potential symbolically expressed by the image of four crowns, or four different fronds.*[2]
What right do we have to dismantle, dissect, and treat as a separate argument one part – magnificent and immense, albeit a part – of the creative output of a figure who excelled in every single expressive form? And as soon as we have come to terms with the intrinsic complexity of our task, which critical method should we use to get our bearings in the midst of such a great wealth of information and commentaries? Which literary tools can we use to express them, without forgoing their multiform richness, but also without lapsing into verbosity, and without waiving the chance to humbly put forwards a personal viewpoint? How can we ensure that readers are given a complete array of information, as verifiable and objective as possible, addressing their intellectual curiosity and at the same time accompanying and, why not, perhaps even engendering an emotional reaction in them?
This flurry of questions ought to be enough, I hope, to show that what might have seemed like marginal issues at the start of the journey have become demanding, insistent and at times awkward travelmates.
Fortunately, I have been able to count on other companions for their constant support. Aurelio Amendola's photographs, for instance, many of which are firmly a part of the history of 20th-century art photography. Taken by an artist who has become a great expert on Michelangelo's statuary, Amendola's black and white images offer a gallery of sculptural and architectural shapes, familiar yet surprising for the way in which the chiaroscuro is distributed, the choice of perspective, the sensitivity towards the marble's volume and surface. The contours that Amendola's pictures bring out from these sculptures make manifest the ideas that Michelangelo secretly kept inside, but that cannot be found on any drawing, as they were transferred directly from the artist's mind onto the material itself, under the pressure of the creative drive channelled by supreme technical mastery.

The artist's relationship with the marble

One of the many reasons for the impact of Michelangelo's sculptures, both in the past and in the present, is that no other sculptor – certainly not in the Renaissance, but perhaps ever before – carries us "inside" the artist's own quest the way this artist does, enabling us to follow what most inspired him, accompanying us through the stages of the creation, sharing with us his many difficulties and frequent concerns as well as his rare moments of self-satisfied pride. The sculptor's trade, especially if he works with marble, is an art that requires, indeed demands, an intimate knowledge of the material. For Michelangelo, it meant hand-to-hand combat, as violent as waging a war, and as gratifying as love, envisioning the struggles and facing disappointments. A relationship that had begun far away, amidst the wilderness lying between the Apuan Alps and the coast, with his visits to the quarries and his familiarity with the mining veins; settling legal issues and taking risks, handling money, dealing with treacherous quarrymen, go-betweens, cart drivers and bargemen, and no less important was his need to conduct high-level business with local governments and the pope in Rome. Michelangelo never shirked these duties, but rather became totally immersed in them, taking on enormous and (to use a modern expression) stressful responsibilities, which would at times even distract him from his work as an artist. During all this time, he would go to great pains to describe the months spent on the Tuscan coast, giving us detailed information about the statues that we have today, outlining the dense and multifaceted network of relationships and dealings whereby these pieces were actually sculpted, confirming the full or partial expression he sought for each work, but also the historical and personal conditions that weighed more on the final outcome than has previously been thought, and which warrant a more thorough evaluation. Nor ought we to overlook the lasting impact of Buonarroti's lengthy periods of residence at the Carrara quarries, which not only brought economic prosperity to the area, but also irreversibly affected the evolution of the marble quarrying trade, an art that with the arrival of modern technology has changed its practices but not its essence.

On the other hand, it is precisely on the grounds of an appreciation of the material, the tools and the techniques that considerable progress has been made in recent years,[3] along with (not surprisingly) an educated, humble abandonment to the great philosophical visions, especially based on Neoplatonic readings of the master's work, directing, and to some extent influencing, the interpretation of Michelangelo's art throughout the 20th century. The new, direct knowledge as to how and where the marble was transferred has recently prompted more searching stylistic study. So that – to provide one of the most extraordinary cases in point – the fact alone that the block of marble destined to be used for the Saint Matthew in Santa Maria del Fiore was not delivered to Michelangelo, as was believed, between 1503 and 1505, but after a long layover at the port awaiting shipping, in March 1506,[4] all at once cleared up one of scholarship's most lingering doubts: whether or not the intense pathos of the figure of Saint Matthew, condensed in a sudden upward twist, was indeed inspired by the Laocoön Group. The renowned Hellenistic sculptural group was dug up in a vineyard in January 1506, and for as long as the block of marble for the Saint Matthew was believed to have arrived two years earlier, so as to justify the similarities between the two sculptures, it was necessary to postulate a coincidence, or a reworking of the modern one after the discovery of the antique one. But as the marble did indeed arrive in 1506, and Michelangelo began to work on it when he returned to Florence in mid-April, the chance that he may have drawn inspiration from the Laocoön is not just greater, but, on the back of a fresh emotional experience – Michelangelo had himself seen it emerge from the ground where the excavation was being made in the vineyard on the Esquiline Hill – necessary. Likewise, information about a block of marble stationed at Vicopisano has cleared up a critical doubt, previously believed to be insoluble but immensely significant, i.e. whether or not Michelangelo was capable of responding both immediately and enthusiastically to the appearance of one of the most spectacular groups that had survived from Antiquity. Though the Gordian solution of this untractable critical knot has not fully dispelled the visionary hypothesis (greatly convenient to media-seekers) that attributes the Laocoön directly to Michelangelo.

Misleading simplicity pervades the few but meaningful comments Michelangelo himself made on the art of sculpting marble, considered to be a higher form of art than the mere shaping of materials and the casting of bronze statues. "By sculpture I mean the taking away: the same as one does in painting by adding", were his words to Varchi. Removing material, as it cannot be put back again in the event of error, was the highest mastery, and required the sureness of judgement that the artist himself – taking the words of Leon Battista Alberti – expressed through a metaphor: that he had a "seste", or compass, in his eyes. It was a precept that Giorgio Vasari would repeat in his Preface to the Lives of the Artists.

Carving was none other than laying siege to one of the faces of a block of marble, to two or more if an angular view was required, and releasing the figure that lay within it, gradually making the forms emerge like water allowed to drain from a basin, according to the analogy made by Vasari; an analogy, I believe, whose literary inspiration, of a figurative nature, is Dante's description of the damned sealed inside the limpid and transparent ice of Antenora, each one visible "like straw in glass" in a wide variety of poses, some even unnatural and twisted: "Some are lying, some are erect, this with the head, that with the soles uppermost; another, like a bow, bends his face to his feet".[5] Words especially echoed in the lines Michelangelo uses to begin his bitter, ironic reflections in the tercets of poem 267: "I'm locked up here like pulp within the ring / or like a genie trapped inside a bottle; / I live like this, poor, lonely and confined". Two strikingly different similes follow one after the other here, and both denote a sense of claustrophobic confinement: the former image of pulp confined within an opaque rind ("scorza" was also the word used to describe the rough "skin", or surface, of marble) alludes to the plant world, while the image of a genie trapped inside a transparent glass prison is of alchemical origin. Sculpting simply meant chipping away the marble that was superfluous to attain the wanted shape hidden within, as the artist noted in his famous Sonnet 151: "The best of artists can no concept find".[6] It seems that the French diplomat Blaise de Vigenère (who would later become famous in the field of cryptography) saw him doing just that when he went to visit him between 1549 and 1551; the Frenchman described Michelangelo as he toiled away at the very hard marble, with an impetus and a rage that one would not expect from a seventy-five-year-old, surrounded by the sparks made while his hammer broke away splinters so large that no blunder could every be remedied.[7]

If we bear in mind the poetic and incisive metaphors Michelangelo used to describe the figure that emerged from the marble like a body from water, and the superfluous material that flew away un-

der the skilled hacking of the point and hammer, when we look at the drawings preserved in the Archive in the Casa Buonarroti showing the heaps of marble lying on Tyrrhenian sandstone – little more than the dry recording of bureaucracy – by making the sculptor's inner vision our own, we can picture in those simple contours of shapeless masses the figures described above, each one encapsulated in its stone prison yet visible like "straw in glass" or a "genie trapped inside a bottle".

But as concerns the linearity of the method of Neoplatonic inspiration weighed down by the formula "the hand that obeys the intellect", the works tell a very different story as they relate to the clear-minded certainty of the project that is translated into the frenzied energy of the action. Stories about regret, abandonment, mutilation which make of the statues – especially the later ones – "palimpsests" of gradually modified thought, whose traces overlap, intersecting, like the layers of different relics. In the two later Pietàs, *the approach to the marble becomes paradoxical, surpassing and contradicting the very nature of the material, and with it, of the Michelangelesque precept: the block of marble is forced by the artist, who is perennially dissatisfied with accepting changes in the design put before him: so that it is written and overwritten in the manner of a sheet and modelled in shapes incompatible with one another.*[8]

Michelangelo has enabled us to decipher and reconstruct the sequence of tools he used as he worked: many of his sculptures were indeed left unfinished (and rarely manipulated by others),[9] *and as such they reveal different ways of dealing with the volumes and surfaces, which correspond to marks left by different work-tools: the chisel, the claw-tool, chisels with one, two or more teeth, the pitching tool, the point, the scraper. This is not the case for the great majority of statues made before the 19th century: having reached the level of refinement sought by the artist, these show only rare signs of intermediate reworking. Moreover, even in Michelangelo's finished works, executed between the days of his youth and his maturity, the execution stage has been completed and surpassed by a final polishing that erases any trace at all: a foremost example of this is the Vatican* Pietà, *which is also memorable for the "supreme and luminous finishing of the skin, which is not something extra but a form of expression".*[10]

The "non-finito" and other characteristics

And now we come to the core issue of the "non-finito", or unfinished, a characteristic so personal and a phenomenon so specific to Michelangelo's statuary,[11] *that it has become an art term in itself, and printed in any one of the forms in use in the international literature: in roman characters, in quotation marks or in hyphenated form.*

Giorgio Vasari and Benedetto Varchi, both responsible much before that crucial 1564 for the first biographical and critical evaluation of Michelangelo the man, an immense and difficult figure, the glory of Italy and the pride of the small Tuscan Grand Duchy before all of Europe – sought admirably to find ways to aesthetically justify this Michelangelesque "non-finito", so that none of the master's works would be without some positive evaluation, which they felt was an indispensable ingredient for an overall evaluation of an artist revered universally and without reserve. Had Vasari perhaps noticed the problems some artists had had before the "non-finito", like Battista Franco (Venetian, not Florentine), who in a drawing from 1536 had converted the indistinct shape of the face of Day *into a cloud of beard and whiskers? We'll never know, but one thing is certain, that already as early as 1550 Vasari insisted on the conceptual completeness and therefore the aesthetic dignity of the* Medici Madonna, *reserving his positive opinion for the perfect work which, not without critical audacity, he distinguished from the imperfect model in which it was enclosed: "and although the figure is not equal in every part, and it was left rough and showing the marks of the claw-schisel, yet with all its imperfections there may be recognized in it the full perfection of the work".*

For his part, Varchi legitimated the "non-finito" in the funerary oration (1564), and Vasari kept insisting on it in the second biography of the artist (1568). What is so much praised in the unfinished statues that were still in Florence, the Saint Matthew *and the* Captives, *is their educational value in the training of young sculptors at the recently founded Accademia delle Arti del Disegno. But one generation later, what was "non-finito" in the* Captives *was given a completely different interpretation – though not in the pages of the literature – when Bernardo Buontalenti brilliantly came up with the idea, undoubtedly shared by the Grand Duke Francesco I de' Medici, of positioning them in the four corners of the entrance to the Boboli Garden's Grotta Grande (1585-1588). Set within that architectural and figurative system, which alluded to metamorphosis in the primordial genesis of bringing inanimate material to life, the* Captives, *blending into corners amidst walls encrusted with rustic decorations, became the visual sign of the struggle of the human form that yearned to set itself free from the grip of rough stone. In taking over the critical evaluation of modern art in Florence at the end of the century, Francesco Bocchi was able to provide a refined interpretation in a mythological key, with reference to the Ovidian interpretation of the myth of Deucalion and Pyrrha, that is, the creation of humanity from stone. Bocchi defined the statues of the* Captives *"full of subtle intuition: for they are roughed out with such astonishing artifice that they appear determined to break free of the marble to escape the ruins about them".*[12]

Moreover, whether it was because of the superficial but enchanting resemblance between the more rustic features of Michelangelo's "non-finito" and the natural and artificial rock formations in the garden, ever poised somewhere between form and formlessness, or the fact that they blended in with the rough, discontinuous ancient statuary in a state of ruin, a number of his marble works were positioned outdoors for a certain period of time. The first Minerva Christ *in the garden of Metello Vari; the* Florentine Pietà *in the Bandini vineyard on the Quirinal Hill, the two* Slaves, *which had been taken to France and moved from one castle to another before reaching the Louvre; the* Crouching Boy *in the Carskoe Selo*

Grotto, the tzars' former residence. And in numerous 16th-century engravings Michelangelo's statuary is set in open landscape used as a backdrop or in the shelter of derelict caverns.

The debate over the "non-finito" began when Michelangelo was still alive – something that the early critical covens of Florentine literati and artists wisely decided was to be cherished, thus sweeping aside any chance of appraisal being reductive or negative – and continued, we might say, for centuries, to include interpretations and commentaries of all kinds with full-scale analyses of the matter throughout the 20th century.[13] *This is not the place, however, to go over arguments so complex and numerous that Raphael Rosenberg, in his study on the reception of Michelangelo's New Sacristy in the church of San Lorenzo, Florence, was able to devote a whole, lengthy chapter to the critical concept of the "non-finito": but his methodical classification alone of the motivations adopted is worth translating and, if necessary, reporting, to give an idea of the sheer breadth of the reflections of scholars from various cultures, languages, nations and periods.*[14]

For the sake of drastic simplification, the gamut of interpretations is very broad and ranges from the more philosophical, which according to Neoplatonic doctrines sees in the unfinished figure an adequate manifestation of the idea, to the more pragmatic, which takes into account, one statue after another, the circumstances surrounding the abandonment: the sudden appearance of a vein in the marble, the artist's loss of interest in the project, an excess of commissions, his transfer from Florence to Rome, and ultimately his death. In one chapter, entitled "Unfinished Works", of the Dictionary of Art, *Anthony Hughes became the spokesperson for this line of thought (which sounds very much like the Anglo-Saxon empirical tradition) to the extent that he excludes the idea of considering the Michelangelesque "non-finito" as a bona fide means of expression, also in light of the artist's own words as reported in Condivi, that what he failed to appreciate in Donatello's sculptures were the less finished parts; Hughes instead insists on identifying a deliberate differentiation of "texture" and consistency to the touch within each sculpture.*

As concerns the artist's voluntary abandonment of some of his sculptures, while not excluding possible uncontrollable circumstances (changes in the project itself, defects in the marble, his death) I continue to be of the mind that Vasari's words are a precious key to interpretation, he being both a living witness and a highly perspicacious critic, although his writings have been plagued with futile rereadings since the mid-20th century; Vasari explained the other abandonments as an offshoot of the fact that Michelangelo was very hard to please; he would be exasperated with the "dismisura", or disparity, between the excellence of the concept and the supposed inadequacy of the results. Delving inside Michelangelo's multifaceted psychological make-up may, however, also open up broad dizzying prospects of excess: suffice it to recall that the biographies all speak of episodes of sudden intolerance (but alternating with solicitude, bonhomie and generosity) and not just towards the outside world,[15] *but towards himself and his own conditions too.*

As for the different ways of treating the surface, I agree that within Michelangelo's sculpture they are a means of expression, sometimes linked to final effects that have since been lost or thwarted. One example is the outcome of the closer examination and diagnostic testing conducted on the David *prior to its restoration, which ended in 2004, and showed that the rough grain of the two-striped sling and striated bark of the trunk is due to the surface preparation with bolus for subsequent gilding. And I might add that it is neither improper nor reductive, but rather in line with a canny tradition of saving work and material, to suggest that some of the parts of the statue were deliberately simplified or left roughed-out because they were not intended for viewing.*[16] *Difficulties arise when one surmises – as has indeed been done on occasion – that certain areas were intentionally treated with less refined tools with the purpose of eventually receiving and capturing dust so that they might darken over time and highlight the chiaroscuro effect. But this hypothesis is yet to be proven, although scientific experts and restorers discuss it repeatedly each time any kind of cleaning of the marble, however minimal, and especially when it concerns one of Michelangelo's works, is undertaken.*

In this regard, I cannot fail to underscore the fact that restoration of Michelangelo's statuary over the last ten years has provided the immensely valuable opportunity to delve deeper into a direct knowledge of the marbles, the signs legible within them, of their material vicissitudes; a universe of new knowledge accessible through the eyes, the mind, the hands of the restorer and the field researcher, which I have attempted to make my own, and to whom I am greatly indebted, for I have been able to extend my own skills and chances for a hands-on approach through them.

This close-up scrutiny of the marbles once again prompts us to reflect – without particularly expecting to find a solution – on the question of Michelangelo's collaborators and their actual contribution to the statues: from the sbozzatori *from Carrara in the quarries to professional sculptors like Raffaello da Montelupo, Giovannangelo Montorsoli, Niccolò Tribolo; from masters of the arts like Antonio da Pontassieve and Jacopo del Duca to more modest executors like Pietro Urbano, Tommaso Boscoli, Tiberio Calcagni. And even down to the humblest rough-hewers from the hills of Fiesole, the workers from Settignano whose art Michelangelo learned by drinking the milk of his wet-nurse; workers whose clanging of hammers on iron and cricket-like chattering provided an endless soundtrack to the artist's life, from his childhood experiences in the* pietra serena *quarries to his work at the head of the building site for Saint Peter's, Christianity's supreme workshop.*

Different sculptures

This emphasis on the marble itself is necessary, given that it is upon Michelangelo's statuary that his fame as a sculptor rests. But this is only because the statues in bronze have been lost, and those sculpted in wood have only relatively recently – about forty years – come to the attention of the critics; whereas the figures in terra-

cotta, wax, or other materials have only been included in an analysis of the master's output in the past five years. While I am personally convinced of the excellence of the work carried out and leading up to the attribution of the Crucifix *for the church of the Santo Spirito, which – it has been suggested – takes its place amidst the recent ascriptions of smaller wooden* Crucifixes, *I am less comfortable with the treatment of the material itself, by definition polychrome wood. Once the layers of primer and paint are removed, together with the added impastos of mixed material (hair, for instance), what's left rarely shows signs of Michelangelo's distinctive handling of the tools. A more interesting comparison can be made with the small* Christ *figure executed later, now housed in the Casa Buonarroti (inv. 195), whose vibrant "non-finito" state evinces the tight texture of cuts and passages compatible with the master's autograph.*
Those few sculptural bozzetti, *or preliminary models, that have revealed to criticism the principal features of Michelangelo's craftsmanship, thus providing autograph works and indicating their preparatory function,*[17] *also raise some intriguing new questions. Perhaps prepared to show someone, a rough-hewer or other assistant, the volume and the orientation of the figure, their nervous modelling denotes the artist's confident but also rapid use of the flat chisel and fingers. Furthermore, the fact that they lack extremities, if not the limbs and at times even the head, confirms what the statues themselves and certain study drawings would seem to suggest: Michelangelo's growing interest in the middle portion of the human body, where the pelvis and torso join but allow for rotation in directions that would seem to be unrelated, and therefore the* contrapposto, *forming a powerful architecture of bone connected to the support muscles. The rest of the figure – the bends in the arms and legs, the turn of the neck, angle of the head – is governed by and stems from the unleashing of the dynamism that lies within that densest part of the human anatomy in which the vital organs throb: it becomes even clearer how the* Belvedere Torso, *the highest possible* exemplum *of antique statuary, owes its concentrated physical expression to its mutilated physique. Hence, in his statuary Michelangelo appears to have first resolved and conducted with exclusive concentration the theme of the trunk and of its inherent angles and torsions, giving rise to that powerful inner thrust which in Michelangelo's own advice renders the human figure "serpentinata", or serpentine. The extremities (which, however paradoxically, included the head) were thus sculpted last of all, and were merely blocked out in the unfinished statues.*[18]
The sheer power of Michelangelo's thinking was such that he gave rise to sculpture fashioned by other hands, as testified to in his drawings.[19] *Proving the point is the example of Michelangelo's great assistance to the ever-faithful Daniele da Volterra, who had been commissioned, in 1559, with the bronze casting of the* Equestrian Monument to Henry II, *as requested by the king's widow Caterina de' Medici, daughter of Lorenzo, duke of Urbino.*[20]
Further evidence comes from the case of Leone Leoni, who received from Michelangelo the project for the funerary monument to Gian Giacomo and Gabriele Medici to be placed in the Cathedral in Milan, commissioned to Leoni by Pope Pius IV, thanks to the good offices of the Florentine artist.[21]

This book

I have decided that the most appropriate approach to this book would be a basically biographical narrative, including – possibly chronological – comments on the statues, individually, as a series and as a group: to use the language of cinema, it is like panning the artist's oeuvre with close-up views.
Special attention has been dedicated to Michelangelo's early period, which is dense with many of the as yet unsolved issues, such as his training in the art of sculpting, a period that still leaves room for some stimulating albeit hazardous guesswork on possible attributions. Among the few recent examples are: the Young Archer *(New York) which after much (unnecessarily acrimonious) debate has been added to the master's corpus of works, almost by surprise, after the appearance on the market of a drawing from Michelangelo's circle published by Joannides. Or the wooden* Crucifixes *in a private collection, attributions which will continue to kindle discussion, but whose real merit is the fact that they have channelled studies in less familiar directions.*
Further knowledge on the work is contained in the forty-six entries at the back of the book, one for each work that I have judged to be truly autograph (based more on exclusive than inclusive criteria), or worthy of discussing alongside those of certain attribution. In these brief explanatory texts I have mainly noted the material history such as the ownership sequence, the changes in exhibition venue, any restoration work carried out, all the stages of the long life of the works that enable us to overcome the distance of centuries that separates us from the time of their creation.
A great many arguments have been condensed, others omitted.[22] *Likewise, the bibliography is a painstaking selection, limited to those cited here, and giving priority to more recent contributions to the debate.*

Cristina Acidini Luchinat

Notes

[1] London, British Library, C. 28.a.10, p. 392, Cf. *Vittoria Colonna e Michelangelo*, 2005, no. 64, p. 190.

[2] The portrait by Pompeo Caccini entitled *Michelangelo in his Study* (1595), now at the Casa Buonarroti, portrays a garland lying on the artist's table, and of the four fronds the artist just touching the olive sprig.

[3] I refer briefly here to the studies carried out by Giovannini (1998) and Rockwell (2003).

[4] Amy, 2000.

[5] Dante Alighieri, *The Divine Comedy*, I (*Inferno*), XXXIV, 12-15.

[6] The first complete quatrain reads: "The best of artists can no concept find / that is not in a single block of stone, / confined by the excess; to that alone / attains the hand obedient to the mind". A similar image is found in the madrigal to Vittoria Colonna (no. 152) with precise reference to the soul as spiritual essence imprisoned in the superfluous body: "By what we take away, lady, we give / to rugged mountain stone / a figure that can live / and which grows greater where the stone grows less; / so, hidden under that excess / which is the flesh, the trembling soul / still contains some good works / that lie beneath its coarse and savage bark. / You alone can extract them still / and free them from this outer shell / for in myself I find no strength or will".

[7] An anonymous 16th-century engraving portrays him in heroic nudity *all'antica* as he throws himself upon a block of marble that has been lain on the ground, and from which the *Dawn* (identified by Steinmann 1913, pp. 15-16) is taking shape, destined for the *Tomb of Lorenzo de' Medici* in the church of the same name: the sculptor was about fifty years old at the time. The engraving was published in Sigismondo Fanti (doc. 1514-1527), *Triompho di Fortuna*, Venice, 1527, dedicated to Clement VII, under the title *Spera de Iove*, from the most eminent architect from Antiquity Vitruvius (c. XXXVIII). This is the first printed representation of Michelangelo (cf. P. Ragionieri, in *Michelangelo tra Firenze e Roma*, 2003, pp. 20-21, no. 2.)

[8] It is virtually inevitable and a recurring critical *topos* to link together the torment Michelangelo inflicts on the marble with his personal trials in the search for spiritual balance, which through meditation on the Redemption and other religious themes distances the aging artist from his own creations, particularly those of a more profane or sensual nature. Much has been written on the relationship between Michelangelo, the Catholic Counter-Reformation, and the spiritual circle in Rome that bordered on heterodoxy.

[9] Some of the works manipulated by assistants and pupils include: the *Brutus*, the *Florentine Pietà*, the *Victory*, and the first *Risen Christ* at the Minerva (Giustiniani). Interference has been hypothesized for the early works now at the Casa Buonarroti in Florence, but without definitive proof. Upon its arrival in England, the *Taddei Tondo* risked being reworked. Vasari was the first to speak of the common belief in the intangibility of Michelangelo's sculptures, however incomplete they might appear to be.

[10] Paolucci, 1997, p. 9.

[11] In the attempt to relate the phenomenon of the "non-finito" to Michelangelo's complex psychological relationship with his patrons and with money, Hatfield, 2002 (*Unfinished Work*, pp. 197-200), stresses the fact that the phenomenon affects the sculptural works alone; however, the idea holds only if we don't count the *Manchester Madonna* and the *Entombment* at the National Gallery, London – both unfinished works acknowledged to be autographs by Michelangelo the painter.

[12] Bocchi, 1591, 1677 ed., p. 138.

[13] For the sake of providing an example, let us recall among these: Körte, 1995; Barocchi, 1958, pp. 221-235 and *eadem*, 1962a, III, pp. 1175 and ff.; Schulz, 1975; Elam Hughes, 1996, pp. 440-441; Rosenberg, 2000, the latter especially but not exclusively as concerns the marbles in the New Sacristy.

[14] The chapter is divided into *Le circostanze avverse* (including the sections *La morte del committente*; *Le "difficoltà" dell'artista*); *Il complemento da parte dell'osservatore* (including the sections *Il completamento virtuale*, *Il processo creativo*); *La "mano del maestro"* (including the sections *Lo svelamento della tecnica*; *L'intimità con il creatore*; *"Nessun altro poteva finirla"*); *L'effetto della superficie* (including the sections *L'impressione ottica*; *I valori espressivi*); *Il non-finito come programma contenutistico*; *Il non-finito, un discorso complessivo*.

[15] Exemplary was Michelangelo's loathing of the use of Latin, attested to from the early years in Rome in the testimony of Jacopo Galli and in that, not without amazement, of Galvano Parlanciotto, a notary from Carrara, who was forced on November 1, 1516 to draught a contract in Italian: "Hoe scripto in vulghare questo contracto perché lo excelente homo m.o Michelangelo non po soferire che qui da noi d'Italia s'habia a scrivere non chome se parla per tractare le cose pubbliche" (note in the margin of another contract (lost?) transcribed by Frediani (reproduced in Rapetti, 2001, p. 31). Sarcasm has always been considered a typically Florentine way of expressing intolerance towards the limits and errors of others, and Michelangelo poured forth his own version in many cutting words; but the subject would lead us astray from our work.

[16] The rear parts of many statues are unfinished, but so are the candelabra on the *Tomb of Julius II*, the hidden arms of the *Captives*, and the left side of the head of the vanquished figure in the *Victory* now at the Palazzo Vecchio in Florence.

[17] Among the many enthusiastic reactions in the 19th century to the *bozzetti* held to be autograph work, one case in particular is offered by Ernst Hähnel, who purchased some terracotta models from the market in 1842 attributed to Michelangelo, and made some plaster casts of them (sold in 1938, some of which since lost, and others now housed in different museums). In 1875, he exhibited his set of models at the exhibition in the Accademia, with great success; when the exhibition closed in September, Hähnel donated a number of them to the Casa Buonarroti. See S. Corsi, in *Michelangelo nell'Ottocento*…, 1994, pp. 60-65, nos. 48-57.

[18] If we take the Minerva *Christ* in Santa Maria we see that not surprisingly Michelangelo made in-depth studies of the rotation of the bust around the hips (see the drawing in the Brinsley Ford Collection); and not surprisingly Pietro Urbano devoted his clumsy finishing job *in loco* to the statue's feet, which were evidently left incomplete.

[19] Among the "indirect" sculptures, worth noting are: the high-relief of Francesco di Simone Mosca (called Moschino; Carrara marble, 125 x 96 cm, Berlin, Staatliche Museen, Preussischer Kulturbesitz, Skulturensammlung; cf. D. Gasparotto, in *Magnificenza*…, 1997, pp. 44-45, no. 14) taken from the drawing of the *Fall of Phaeton* (Windsor, Royal Library, inv. 12766; engraved by Nicolas Beatrizet in the mid-16th century). The marble figure by Bartolomeo Ammannati (Florence, Bargello, no. 73 S; cf. E.D. Schmidt, in *Leonardo*…, 2001, pp. 166-167, n.IV.6) from *Leda and the Swan*, a lost painting for the Duke of Ferrara, known from an engraving by Cornelisz Bos made in the sixties, and other derivations. Jacopo del Duca made a terracotta tile now at the Biblioteca Vaticana, and another at the Galleria Nazionale dell'Arte Antica (inv. 2028, Donazione Dusmet, 1949) after a drawing of the *Pietà composition for Vittoria Colonna* (Boston, Isabella Stewart Gardner Museum, inv. 1.2.o/16.0, repeatedly copied and engraved by Bonasone in 1564). And not least, a sizeable set of bas-reliefs in wax, plaster and ivory from the red-pencil drawing of the *Deposition* (Haarlem, Teylers Museum, inv. 25°), for which see the catalogue *Daniele da Volterra*…, 2003, pp. 76-77 (entry for the one in the Bargello, Florence, inv. Cere 1914, no. 420).

[20] By September 1565, Daniele had only completed the casting of the horse, which was immortalized in an engraving by Antonio Tempesta (*circa* 1606/07); the artist died one year later. In 1586, the horse was ceded to the banker Orazio Rucellai for his Roman residence on the Corso; after Richelieu had it sent to France, it was used in 1639 as an equestrian monument to Louis XIII, portrayed by Pierre II Biard, in the Palais Royal. During the French Revolution (1793) it was destroyed because it was considered an emblem of the monarchy. See entry in the catalogue *Daniele da Volterra*..., 2003, n. 49, pp. 158-159.

[21] In 1561, Leoni returned the kindness with four examples of the renowned medal featuring his profile view on the *recto*, and as a pilgrim on the *verso* (see the entry by P. Ragionieri, in *Michelangelo grafia e biografia*..., 2001, no. 60, p. 81), with the short verse "*Docebo iniquos vias tuas et impii ad te convertentur*" (Psalm 51:15, from the *Davidic Psalter* included in the ancient offices of the dead). This is not the place to go into the still unanswered question of Michelangelo's portraiture, but I should note that several details (legs apart, dog, and the emblems of pilgrimage) suggest that the artist is identified here with Saint Roch, who offered not only protection from disease, especially contagious ones, but also the ability to tolerate infirmity, difficulties and mishaps, trusting in the knowledge of celestial succour. Michelangelo's paternity in Leoni's Milanese project is neither mentioned nor discussed in Repishti, 2000.

[22] Just to provide a few examples: an analysis of bronzes derived from models by Michelangelo or indirectly from his designs; an appraisal of the preparatory or related drawings for sculptural works, which have only been consulted where deemed indispensable since the quantity and density of the folios that have reached us (in the likely estimate of Joannides, only a fraction of the total number generated in eighty years of continuous output) would have occupied too much space otherwise needed for the discussion of Michelangelo's statuary oeuvre; the use of sources and documentary evidence with relative commentaries in printed form and themselves copious, but without overlooking Vasari (1550 and 1568 editions) and Condivi (1553); the immense "critical success" of Michelangelo as an artist, not to mention the Freudian psychoanalytical commentaries; the diffusion through copies of every possible kind, either partial or whole, of the master's works, which for centuries have offered study material in the art academies and especially for sculptors in training; the presentation of Michelangelo Buonarroti the man, in terms of his complex relationships with family, patrons, collaborators and friends.

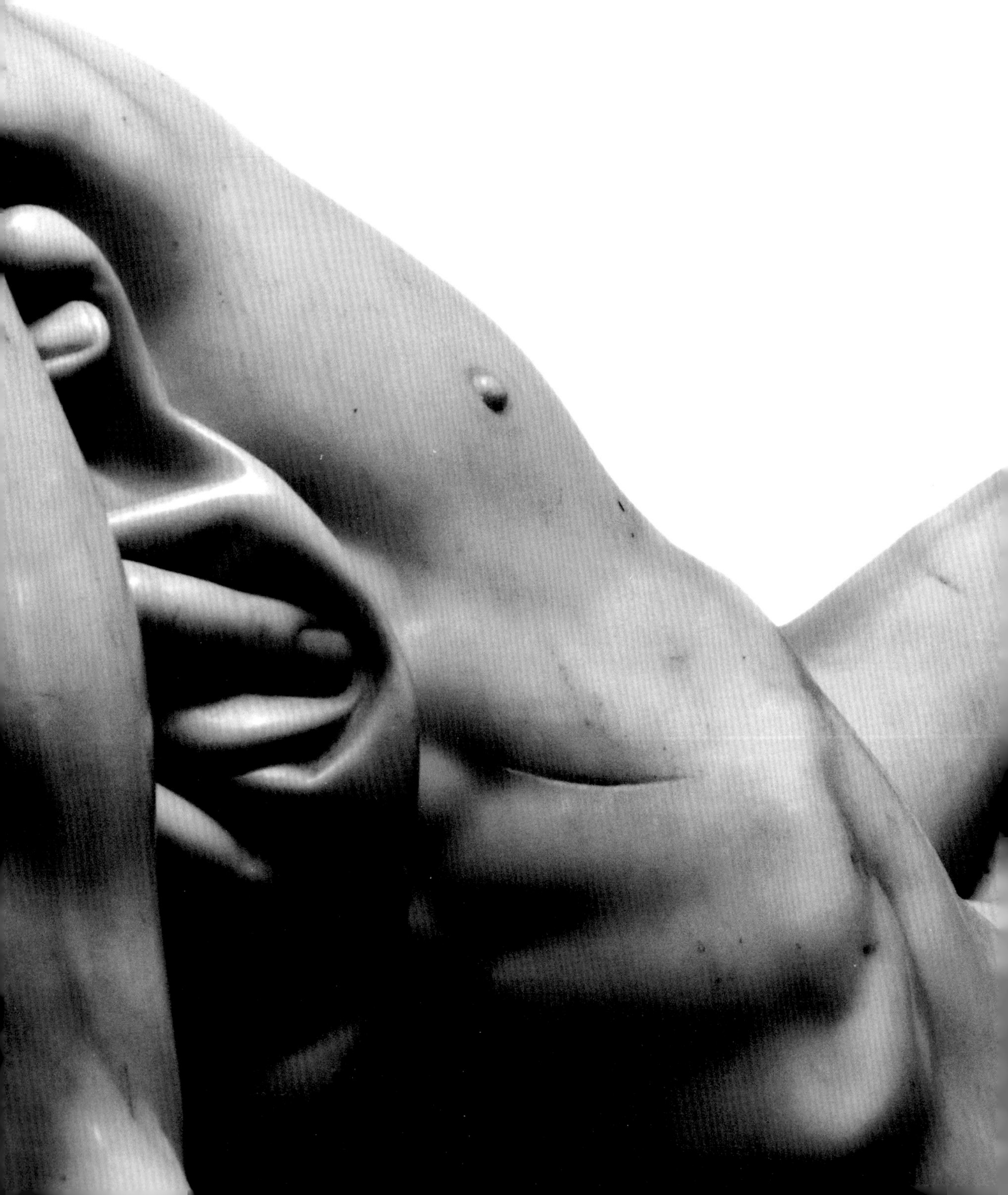

The very young sculptor

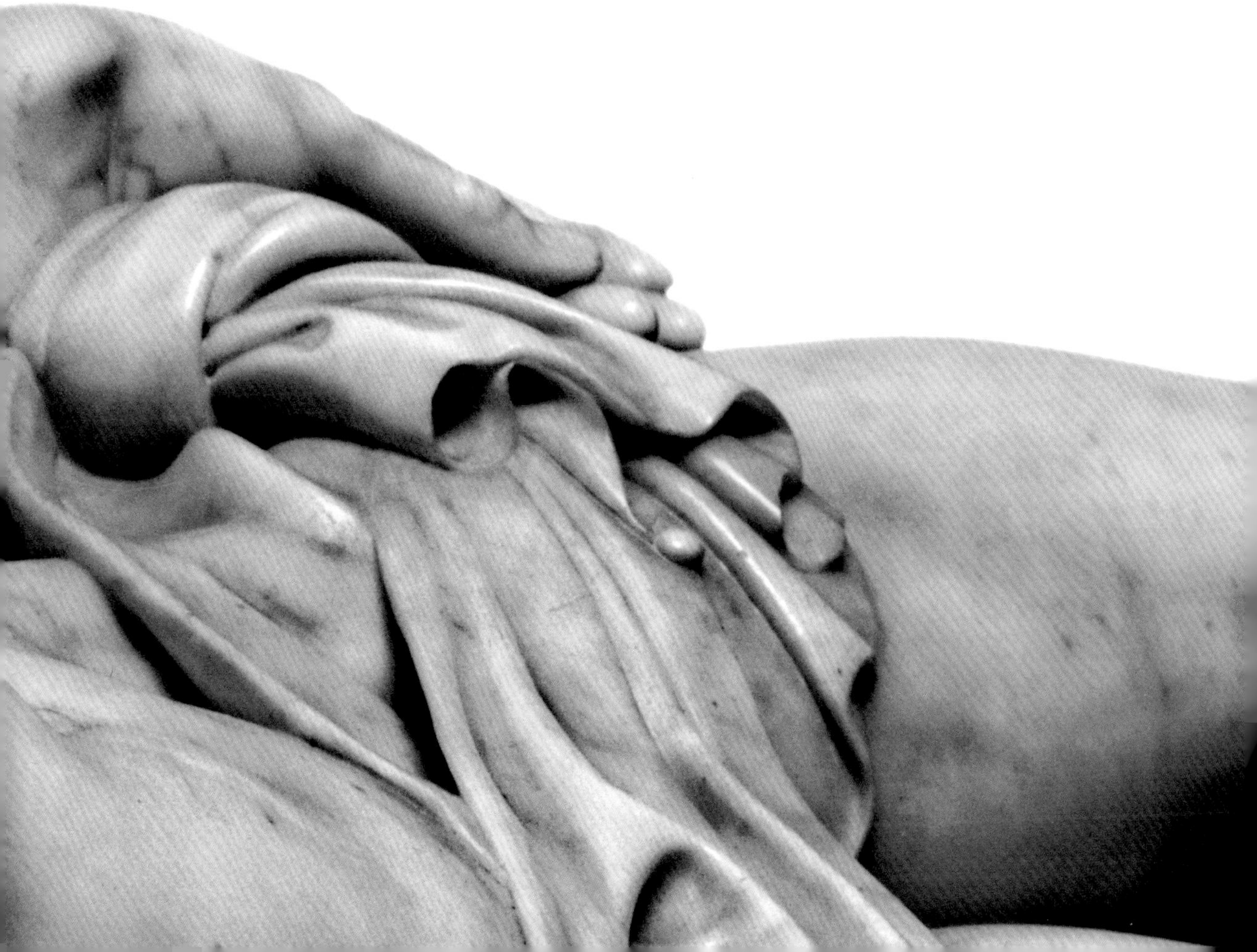

The beginnings

Michelangelo Buonarroti was born on March 6, 1475 in Caprese at Anghiari near Arezzo (now called Caprese Michelangelo), where his father Ludovico was serving a term as mayor (*podestà*) of the Florentine Republic. Michelangelo was very proud of the fact that his family belonged to the Republic's minor nobility, and would often boast their social status, saying that they descended from Matilde di Canossa. Nonetheless, at the time, the double-barrelled Buonarroti Simoni household was not that well off. Michelangelo was the second eldest of five children.[1] His mother, Francesca di Neri di Miniato del Sera, died in 1481 when he was just six: an early loss for the artist, and one which has over time led to countless analyses and a great deal of conjecture on the part of art critics and psychologists.

When the family moved back to Florence, a very young Michelangelo was entrusted to a wet-nurse living at his father's villa in Settignano – a fact of considerable importance to his artistic biography. In this hillside town northeast of Florence, but also in the nearby village of Maiano and in the River Mensola valley, fine-grained grey sandstone marble, called *pietra serena*, was quarried. This material was typically used in Florentine constructions and above all was a feature of religious and civil architecture from Filippo Brunelleschi onwards. As the wet-nurse's father and husband were both stonemasons, Michelangelo spent his earliest childhood years in the midst of skilled craftsmen, and he soon became familiar with the sites where stone was extracted and worked, as well as the techniques used for doing so; in the last years of his life, he would say that he had imbibed the hammer and chisel of the sculptor's trade along with his milk – partly in jest, but also on the grounds of what was believed to be true at the time concerning physiology: "the nurse's milk is so powerful in us that often, by altering the temperature of the body which has one propensity, it may introduce another, quite different from the natural one".[2] Although the importance of this anecdote should not be overstated, it has recently been observed that Michelangelo's statue-making, tools and techniques reveal an approach to the stone material that is closer to the methods of the stonemason than to that of the sculptor.[3]

To determine a second phase in Michelangelo's approach to sculpture we need to move forwards to the year 1490 when the artist, then fifteen and still undergoing his education, was invited to study at Lorenzo de' Medici's Sculpture Garden near San Marco. Michelangelo's inclination towards the arts was already apparent, also thanks to the encouragement of his friend Francesco Granacci, six years his senior, and despite the firm opposition of his father, who wanted him to study letters instead and had pledged him to instruction by the grammar master Francesco da Urbino. The artist's decision to pursue a trade that, at the time, was considered to be a contamination of the "mechanical" arts – the social ascent of the figure of the artist, which Michelangelo himself would help encourage, was still very far-off – clearly disappointed his father, who preferred an intellectual profession more suited to an aristocrat. Michelangelo's first formal apprenticeship actually took place in painting, when he joined the busy Bigordi workshop run by Domenico del Ghirlandaio; that was in June 1487 and Michelangelo had just turned twelve:[4] he would, as an elderly man, try to deny that such an apprenticeship had ever taken place, using Condivi's writings to refute Vasari's words in the 1550 edition of the *Lives*; but Vasari would continue to insist on this fact in the second edition of his work, quoting documentary evidence that he knew about to prove it, to which present-day criticism would also eventually contribute.[5] Likewise, the copies the artist made from frescoes by his great predecessors – Giotto, Masaccio – proven by the drawings he left behind, were also a part of his apprenticeship as a painter, and helped him forge an image of himself as being self-taught. The same may be said for his study of engravings from across the Alps, which impassioned him to the point that he was inspired to make a coloured copy of Martin Schongauer's *Temptation of Saint Anthony*.

It was indeed thanks to Ghirlandaio – who, if we accept Vasari's report,[6] it seems informed Lorenzo de' Medici about the promising young artist – that Michelangelo had become a part of the Medici Sculpture Garden, marking his transition towards the genre that he would always consider to be "his", i.e. sculpture. But there is still some uncertainty as to what the garden actually consisted in, along with Michelangelo's experience there in the two-year period from 1490 to 1492 before the death of Lorenzo il Magnifico, and perhaps prior to his departure for Venice before October 1494 when he could still be dubbed "ischultore dal giardino".[7]

The Garden near San Marco, whose existence and role are no longer cast in doubt,[8] was the site of a number of activities commissioned by the Medici,[9] but most importantly it was the ideal location for an encounter between "Antico" and modern, a place where sculptures and antique pieces belonging to the family were undoubtedly preserved. Their arrangement, however, is still a matter of debate, as the most important testimonies available to us are dated later and are, more importantly, of a celebratory kind. Inherited reliefs and statues, alongside those Lorenzo himself had purchased or received as gifts, were put on display in the palazzo in Via Larga, but less valuable pieces or those needing restoration work were probably scattered throughout the garden area and were, in any event, made available for study, through drawing, to promising, handpicked young artists. Albeit only partially reliable, the passage devoted by Vasari in his biography of Michelangelo to this unique mixture of antiquity, art and schooling, is a memorable one: "At that time the Magnificent Lorenzo de' Medici kept the sculptor Bertoldo in his garden on the Piazza San Marco, not so much as a custodian or guardian of the many beautiful antiques that he had collected and gathered together at great expense in that place, as because, desiring very earnestly to create a school of excellent painters and sculptors, he wished that these should have as their chief and guide the above-named Bertoldo, who was a disciple of Donato".[10]

Leonardo was one of the first to be associated with the Garden, in around 1475. Painters included Giuliano Bugiardini, Lorenzo di Credi, Niccolò Soggi; sculptors, Pietro Torrigiano, Giovan Francesco Rustici, Baccio da Montelupo, Andrea Sansovino. All these artists worked under the guidance of the elderly Bertoldo di Giovanni, Donatello's last assistant before his death. It goes without saying that Bertoldo, a specialist in bronzes and medals and in general a modeller rather than a sculptor, could hardly have trained Buonarroti in the art of marble: the biographers indeed say that at the beginning, Michelangelo, like the young Torrigiano, imitated his clay figures. But it is quite likely that through Bertoldo, no less by observing Donatello's sculptures in Florentine churches and houses, the very young Buonarroti would be the successor to the greatest sculptor of the Florentine Quattrocento.

Not only was Michelangelo invited to spend time in the Giardino, and even given a key that he could keep "di continuo",[11] that is, all the time, because of his exceptional talent he was a guest of the Magnifico in the palace itself,[12] sat at the same supper table with his children and received from him a monthly compensation of five ducats. Lorenzo even appointed the artist's father Ludovico as excise officer in the customs house. Michelangelo's patron would receive the artist in his study, where he could contemplate the very private collection of precious stones and medals there. Glyptic art was especially a source of extraordinary prestige for Lorenzo, and it was also an inspiration for the artists. This fact concurs with Lorenzo's well-known tendency to offer artists vocational as well as informative opportunities.[13]

This is what would seem to have inspired the author of a larger-sized marble relief[14] of the famed gem depicting *Apollo and Marsyas*; after its successful life on the antiquarian market due to its Michelangelesque attribution, the relief finally became a part of the Kress Collection, and is now judged to be a fake, crafted in the 18th-century Roman workshop of Bartolomeo Cavaceppi.[15]

To complete the picture of the many and varied opportunities for learning that stimulated and honed Michelangelo's natural talent in that short period of time, the fact that stonemasons also worked in the Giardino is worth mentioning. Their task was to prepare the stone *conci* for the "library" being built for San Lorenzo: one of many projects interrupted by the Magnifico's premature death, resumed by his descendants in the following century.

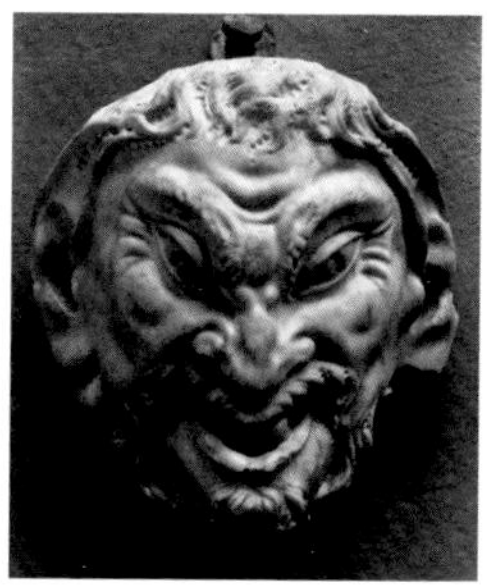

Author unknown, at times attributed to Michelangelo, *Head of a Faun*
Formerly in Florence, Museo Nazionale del Bargello; current location unknown

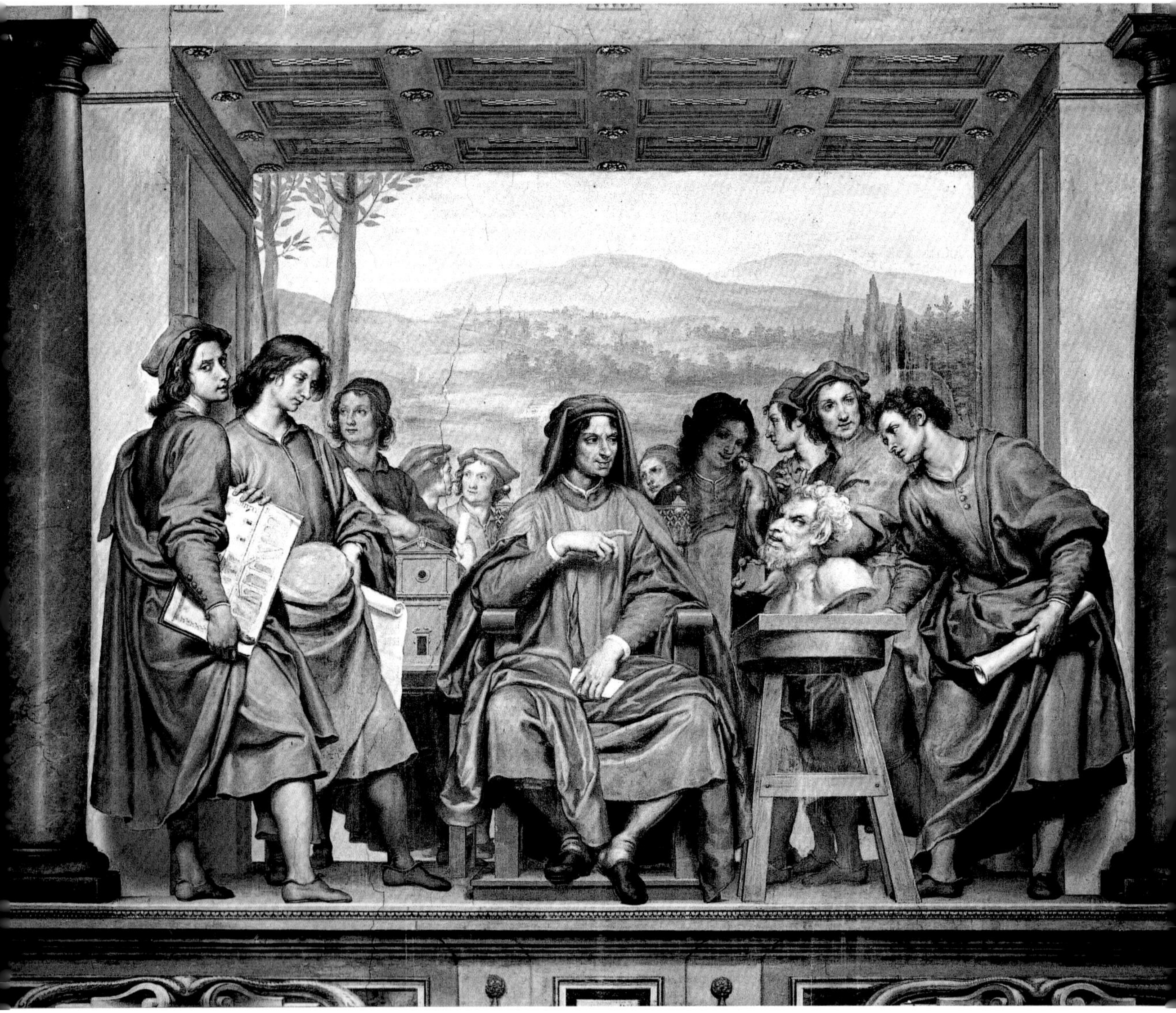

Ottavio Vannini, *Michelangelo Presenting the Head of the Faun to Lorenzo the Magnificent, Surrounded by the Artists of the Sculpture Garden*
Florence, Pitti Palace, Giovanni da San Giovanni Hall
(Museo degli Argenti)

The *Head of a Faun*

A favourite episode among biographers of the young Michelangelo, also celebrated in later artistic representations, concerns the *Head of a Faun*,[16] which Michelangelo sculpted from a piece of marble after an ancient model of an old, bearded faun-like face. Michelangelo had drawn upon his imagination to add on the features that were missing in the antique model, that is, the nose and "the open mouth as of a man laughing".[17] Lorenzo il Magnifico both praised the young man's work, and good-heartedly criticized it, pointing out that it was unlikely that a man that age would have all his teeth. Inspired by the Magnifico's observation, Michelangelo hastened to remove one of the teeth by drilling into the gum, and it pleased his patron to see how quickly he was able to modify the sculpture. The *Head* is now said to be lost, but a lively debate went on concerning a similar marble and mask, believed until 1860 to be the original one; at first displayed at the Uffizi Gallery it was then transferred to the Museo Nazionale del Bargello in 1865, after which it was stolen during World War II, and therefore cannot at the present time be fully evaluated.[18] The piece, recalled by Filippo Baldinucci in 1681 as just having arrived from the collection of the Grand Duke's secretary Apollonio Bassetti, is referred to in copies and derivations.[19] The original would have had a label to prove it was an autograph.[20] The attribution was dismissed in the 20th century, but it was again taken up on the basis of style when the plaster was displayed in 1999,[21] which resulted in the renewed and insistent suggestion that it was dated from the late 15th century, and that it had all the features of a work by a young sculptor as gifted as Michelangelo must have been when he made his first attempts at carving. Moreover, some of the physiognomic findings, such as the resemblance to features in later statues (the three *Statuettes* in Bologna, the *Bacchus* at the Bargello and especially the panther's head on the animal skin) as well as technical observations concerning the artist's use of the drill, led Frommel, in the catalogue entry, to again suggest that the object, now lost, was in all likelihood made by Michelangelo. The fact that it looks flat, so that it appears to be more like a mask than a head when viewed in a photograph, is because it was made with a thin piece of marble.
The *Head* now in the Casa Buonarroti may have inspired 17th-century painter Ottavio Vannini for his fresco for the Giovanni da San Giovanni hall in the summer Quarters of Pitti Palace portraying *Michelangelo Presenting the Head of the Faun to Lorenzo il Magnifico, Surrounded by the Artists of the Garden.*
Two marble sculptures both currently in Casa Buonarroti in Florence, the *Madonna of the Stairs* and the *Battle of the Centaurs* are dated from the time of the Sculpture Garden.

The *Madonna of the Stairs*

The earliest mention of the marble relief the *Madonna of the Stairs* may be found in the second edition of Vasari's *Lives*: "a Madonna of marble in low-relief by the hand of Michelagnolo, little more than one *braccio* in height, in which when a lad, at this same time, wishing to counterfeit the manner of Donatello, he acquitted himself so well that it seems as if by Donatello's hand, save that there may be seen in it more grace and more design".[22] Although 20th-century criticism has doubted the chronology of the work, establishing the date of execution to be as late as 1495 if not later, as well as its autography, suggesting Vincenzo Danti or the circle of Baccio Bandinelli, scholars now tend to concur that the relief, dated *circa* 1492, is the earliest extant work by Michelangelo.
The scene, which is set in an irregular, rustic frame carved all around directly into the material, is unquestionably original from the iconographic and compositional standpoints. The Virgin sits in profile on a slightly foreshortened cube of stone and offers her breast to the Child under her mantle. To the left, appearing from a flight of stairs with a balustrade that rises up in a steep perspective, is a chubby putto. In his hand is one end of a cloth, while the other end is in the hands of a companion, who is squeezed right up against the frame to the far

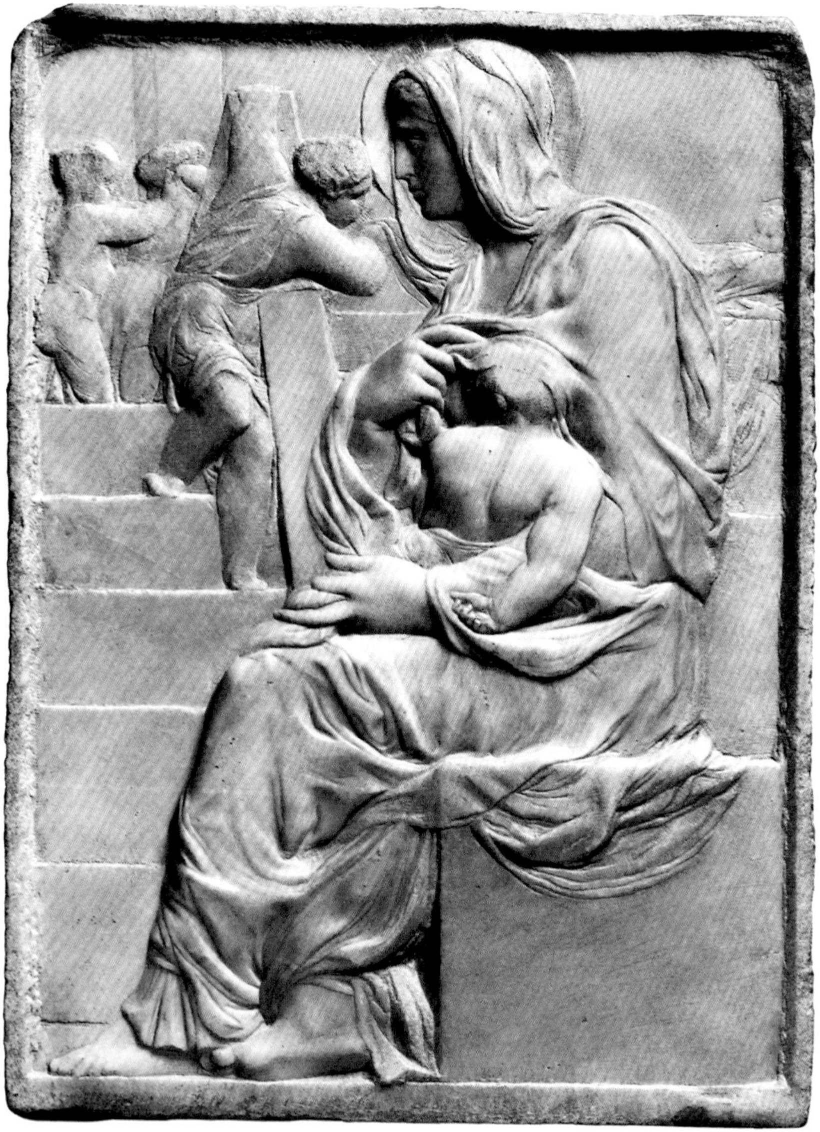

Michelangelo, *Madonna of the Stairs*
Florence, Museo di Casa Buonarroti

p. 19
Michelangelo, *Madonna of the Stairs*, detail of the Child sleeping at his Mother's breast, as muscular as a small Hercules
Florence, Museo di Casa Buonarroti

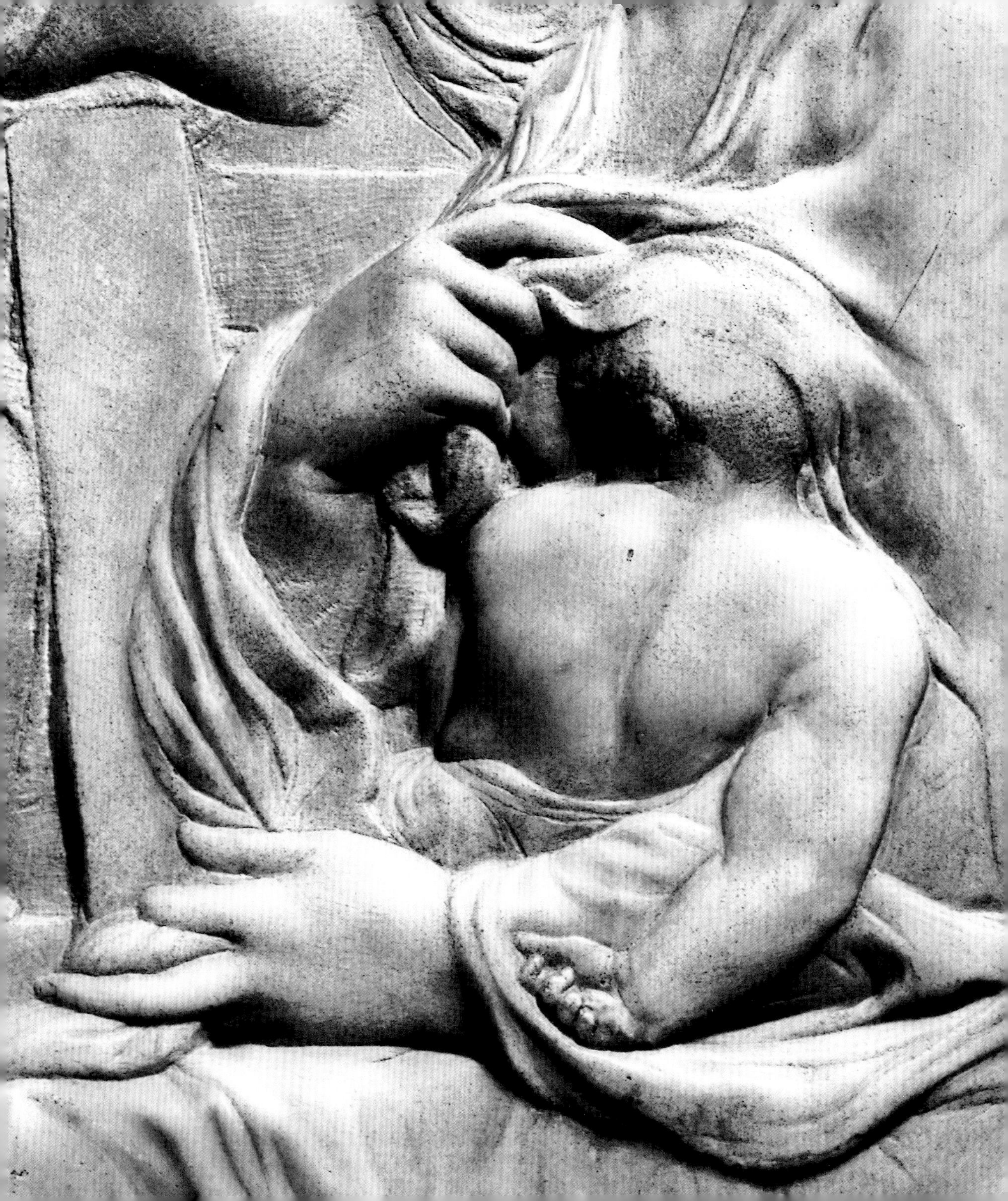

right. On the landing, considerably foreshortened from bottom to top (perhaps) and "stiacciati" (literally, squashed) so that they're very shallow, two putti seem to be engaged in a scuffle. An indistinctly architectural pilaster or door-jamb is visible in the background.
The relief has more than one point in common with Donatello's motifs and inventions: the *Del Pugliese-Dudley Madonna* in the Victoria and Albert Museum in London, who likewise sits in profile on a cubic seat; *Herod's Banquet* in the Musée des Beaux-Arts in Lille, which also features an oblique flight of steps. And the gradation of the relief, which is more pronounced in the foreground and shallow, almost graphic in the areas farther back, reinforces the idea – which pervades the relief – of the artist's having worked "in the manner" of Donatello. Also visible however, are the distinctive embryonic signs of Michelangelo's approach to marble, which confirm that this is an autograph: especially the shift from shiny, polished volumes touched by the light to rough surfaces suggestive of shadow, for a chiaroscuro effect that I believe is a very personal addition of pictorial sensitivity to the sculpture.[23] The features of the working would also seem to indicate the left-handedness of the sculptor, who would grasp the chisel with his right hand and powerfully hammer it using his left hand.[24]
The particular, if not outright peculiar, elements in the composition have been underscored by the critics and often overwhelmingly interpreted as expressing the psychological state attributed to the artist. The setting is indistinct. The Virgin's halo (the only one here) bends up against the frame. The steps are very steep, the shapes of the putti drastically foreshortened. The Mother looks away into the distance, paying no attention to the Child, who has fallen asleep, one arm uncomfortably twisted on his back, instead of suckling the breast offered to him. This tiny Jesus has the muscles of an infant Hercules.
Maria does not gaze upon her Son, but stares away into the distance instead, and this is seen to be her ability to foresee the future, also in light of the beliefs expressed by Fra Girolamo Savonarola, the Dominican who in the 1490s dominated the conscience of the Florentines with his reformist and visionary preachings: "Do you not believe that she [the Virgin] knew of all of Christ's passion from beginning to end?".[25]
There are also those who interpret the rectilinear, slanted element populated by children (wingless angels) to be a cross, and the composition to be a reference to Jacob's ladder of angels reinterpreted by Savonarola as a prefiguration of Christ's cross as link between Heaven and Earth.[26] Persuasively, Weil-Garris Brandt has hypothesized that in order to express the Virgin's sense of mournful anticipation concerning the death of her adult Son, adumbrated here in the baby's deep sleep, Michelangelo was inspired by antique funeral reliefs.

The *Battle of the Centaurs*

Despite authoritative past opinions to the contrary, this high-relief marble sculpture is considered to be the second earliest extant sculpture by Michelangelo,[27] again conceived of and realized while he was an apprentice in the Medicean Garden near San Marco, and left unfinished. The marble block appears to have been taken up and worked on by the sculptor on two different but simultaneous registers of depth: a level strip with an irregular profile that serves as a frame, and a taller strip all along the top perhaps meant for some kind of architectural element (or perhaps, once smooth, intended for a *titulus*), and a rectangular field sculpted in depth, with humans and centaurs strapped together in a furious throng.
The relief was first mentioned in a letter written in 1527 by the agent of the Gonzaga in Florence, Giovanni Borromeo, to Federico Marquis of Mantua, who was looking for a work by Michelangelo, now over fifty and very famous: a "certain picture of naked figures, in combat, made of marble, which he has begun at the request of a great lord [Lorenzo il Magnifico?], but is not finished. It is one and a half *braccia* on each side and so to see it is a beautiful thing, and there are more than twenty-five heads and twenty different bodies, and they adopt various attitudes".
Two 16th-century biographers indicated different subjects for the work: "A Battle between Hercules and the Centaurs" (Vasari, 1550)

and "The Rape of Dejanira and the Battle of the Centaurs" (Condivi, 1553). Modern criticism has suggested a number of different subjects taken from the Classics (Hyginus, Ovid) but Dante, too. In particular, and most likely with reason, the rape of Hippodameia by the centaur Eurytus has been suggested (Ovid, *Metamorphoses*, Book XII). Truthfully, as is often the case with Michelangelo, although the action is efficiently described, the subject remains elusive, or rather so implicit as to identify with the action itself. The figures (males and one or several females) are naked, with the exception of a few cloths, and lacking in attributes, but episodes and roles can be discerned in the composition, enlivened by a dynamism that involves each of the muscular bodies to a different degree.[28] In this struggle between men and centaurs, the defeated, which include a pair of male and female centaurs (Cyllarus and Hylonome?), collapse in the foreground. The centaur in the middle draws attention as he lifts his arm, and is aimed at by a naked man portrayed in three-quarter view bearing a huge stone. The primordial violence of the battle is heightened by the weapons that prevail here: stones and wooden clubs. A man seen from the back grabs a shapely woman by the head – who struggles to break free – and attempts to drag her away while another centaur embraces her to hold her still. Another man is either abducting or rescuing a figure of uncertain identity by lifting him or her onto his back. Mixed in with the rest are figures duelling, shouting, balancing a stone before tossing it. A combatant holds his arms out straight as if drawing a roughly made bow. The man (or woman?) next to him who has just been hit by a stone has his (or her?) hands over his (or her?) temples; likewise the naked figure to the lower left was hit before he had a chance to throw the stone he is holding, and his body now falls forwards from the pain in his head.

The mixture of genres, personalities and poses here would suggest that the subject is indeed the *Battle between Centaurs and Lapiths* or the *Rape of Hippodameia* according to Ovid: that is, the disruption of the wedding banquet of Perithoos and Hippodameia by the centaur Eurytus and his drunken followers, transposed into a painting by Piero di Cosimo in the panel at the National Gallery in London, in a period of time close to Michelangelo's relief.[29]

Agnolo Poliziano, previously a tutor in the Medici household and at the time holder of the chair of Latin and Greek eloquence in the Studio Fiorentino, has been identified as the author of the invention. The cultural background for the relief may to some extent be found in Poliziano's humanistic poetry replete with reverent love for the "Antico", where the pagan theme – whatever the subject may be – is rendered in artistic forms inspired by the legacy of antique Roman sculpture, although not that alone. In their search for the iconographic and figurative sources of the work, critics have suggested the Roman sarcophagi of the Camposanto in Pisa; but reliefs by Pisano, sculptures by Donatello, Bertoldo's *Battle Relief* now in the Museo Nazionale del Bargello, Pollaiolo's copper engraving with the *Battle of the Nudes*, and others still may be added to these, each suggestion providing useful albeit not exhaustive elements for analysis. In fact, the scene, which with only apparent irreverence could be reduced to a ferocious and noisy skirmish between primitives, stands out for its absolute originality in taking the classical myth in the direction of an ambitious exploration of the various poses of the naked bodies submitted to strain and violence: which is what would occur twelve years later with the group of *Soldiers Climbing Out of a River* for the cartoon of the *Battle of Cascina*, where Michelangelo would elevate the weak historical idea to a stunning declaration of mastery in proposing the male nude, the main theme of the drawing and the anatomy, in a variety of expressive poses each of which portraying a different reaction to the same alarm.

Another indication of the young sculptor's maturity is the way he approached the relief, using the thickness of the marble to try out the greatest amount of spatiality possible not just by gradating the volumes, from free-standing in the foreground to the shallow, nearly pictorialness of the rear plane, but also by balancing out the clear-cut and the indistinct to achieve the effects of illusionistic dilation. The three-quarter nude figure on the left might appear to be detached from the rear plane, but he is instead absorbed there by way of spread out feet and legs. The frontal nude figure on the right that is being grabbed by the neck by the figure jumping onto his back has one leg which disappears in indefinite profundities behind the bent arms of the two contenders below. The unfinished state of the middle and rear planes allowed the artist to make corrections while the work was in progress.[30]

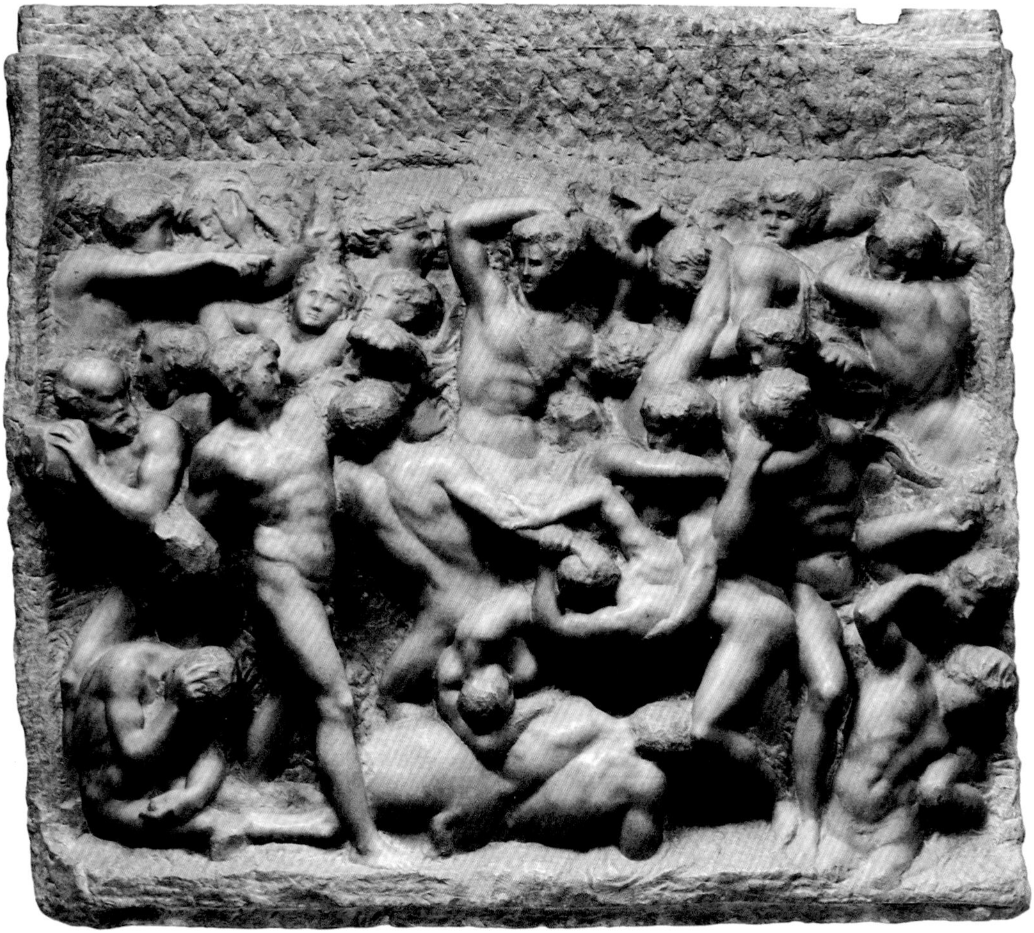

Michelangelo, *Battle of the Centaurs*
Florence, Museo di Casa Buonarroti

p. 23
Michelangelo, *Battle of the Centaurs*, detail of the central portion with the abduction of a woman (Hippodameia?)
Florence, Museo di Casa Buonarroti

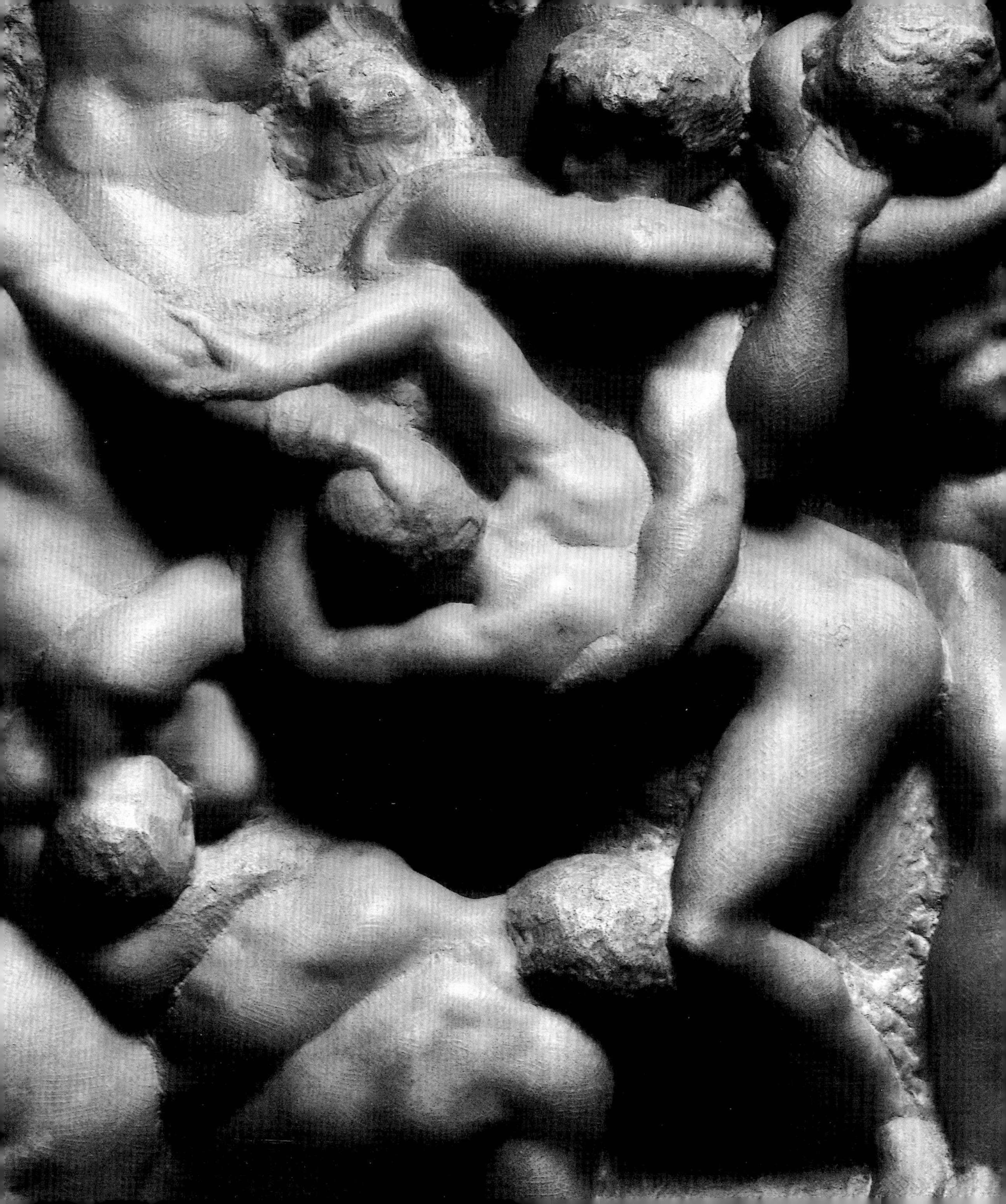

Like for many Michelangelesque sculptures, the issue of multiple and differentiated stages in the work (prevalently using a chisel and range of claw-tools) is entwined with the critical evaluation of the "non-finito" and its meaning in historical and aesthetic terms. Michelangelo himself dubbed the slab of marble to be "imperfect".[31] This is evident, for example, in the frame left rough, where the strip at the top is roughed-out by hacking while holding the chisel at a slant, in a direction indicating the sculptor's left-handedness, but becomes more difficult to determine for the summarily achieved portions with the figures, as well as for the rough rear plane. Reworking of portions by the sculptor himself and, perhaps, later modifications have been hypothesized.[32] Despite some errors and inconsistencies, the outcome of excessive boldness in approaching the block in terms of compositional layout, the *Battle* reveals intellectual wisdom and skill in a sculptor who was not much more than a beginner, and this would help explain the master's fondness for this early work, along with the fact that it contains a series of models and poses that he sought out and *contrapposti* that he would go back to and develop in his later work.[33] There are "types" and poses here that anticipate the colossal *David*, the *Apollo/David* the statues for the New Sacristy (including the figure crouching with pain in the Hermitage *Crouching Boy*), and on up to the figures of the *Last Judgement* on the Sistine Chapel wall, a work undertaken more than forty years later. Despite its naïveté and harshness, Michelangelo was the first to understand the *Battle*'s great potential and considered it to be early proof of his truest calling. Condivi remembered having heard the artist's own opinion on the work: "when he saw it again he recognized how much wrong he had done to his nature in not following promptly the art of sculpture, judging by that work how well he might have succeeded". Tiberio Calcagni added that considering the relief in his home in Florence "art's labours, for one who falls in love with it, are very light".[34] Since its presence in the Casa Buonarroti, the relief was studied by Peter Paul Rubens, who was in Florence at the start of the 17th century, as witnessed by two drawings attributed to his circle.[35]

Some thoughts on his education

The experience in the Sculpture Garden was crucially important to the young sculptor's training, as it was there that he reinforced his familiarity with a stonemason's approach to marble, and was introduced by Bertoldo to the art of modelling plaster, terracotta and bronze. It was Vasari who mentioned the "clay" statues that Michelangelo would model to emulate "some figures in the round", executed by Pietro Torrigiani under Bertoldo's guidance. The terracotta and wax models of his later years are proof that he was familiar with such techniques.

But if our purpose is to imagine the whole path taken by the young Michelangelo as sculptor, other experiences must be hypothesized, perhaps ones he was having at the same time, with marble and wood, for instance, techniques he had already mastered halfway through the 1490s. Lisner reasonably hypothesizes his closeness to Benedetto da Maiano, from whom he would appear to have borrowed stylistic and typological ideas, also in accordance with a current of Florentine painting, led by Sandro Botticelli, in the last twenty years of the century. The period of time Buonarroti is thought to have spent with Maiano has repeatedly been linked to the putto to the right above the altar of the *Annunciation* in Sant'Anna dei Lombardi in Naples (1489-1492?); I am not certain, however, that the attribution to Michelangelo is a correct one.[36]

At the time, I was intrigued by the presence of a Michelangelesque foreboding in the relief for a baptismal font in the cathedral of Pistoia, a work by Benedetto, left unfinished when he died in 1497, and continued by his collaborators:[37] the young girl on the left in the *Birth of Saint John* relief, whose aloof pride has more to do with Buonarroti's Madonnas and Sybils to come than with the other soft and graceful female figures in the font. And while nothing prevents us from linking this relief to Michelangelo's presence in Tuscany over the four months between November 1497 and mid-March 1498 (common usage), with Andrea Ferrucci to replace the master, who died while the work was being done, I feel that it may be useful to once again point out Buonarroti's harking back, with a far different meaning, to the compositional and sentimental themes hinted at in Maiano's work.

Notes

[1] Leonardo, born on 16 November 1473; Buonarroto, 26 May 1477; Giovan Simone, 11 March 1479; Sigismondo, 21 January 1481.

[2] Condivi, *The Life of Michelangelo* (1553), 2006 ed., p. 7. See the comment in Weil-Garris Brandt, 1992.

[3] Giovannini, 1998.

[4] Bonsanti, 1992; Acidini, 1999, pp. 105-108.

[5] Cadogan, 1993, pp. 30-31.

[6] Vasari, 1550, 1986 ed., p. 883; Condivi, 1553, 1998 ed., p. 10; Vasari, 1568, 1962 ed., I, p. 10.

[7] This is how Michelangelo is defined by the clergyman ser Amadeo in a letter of October 1494 to his brother and sculptor Adriano di Giovanni, called Adriano Fiorentino (cf. Elam, 1992a, p. 169; Elam, 1992b, pp. 58, 73).

[8] Andrè Chastel was the first to question the role of this "school" for young artists which the Magnifico attributed to his Garden near Piazza San Marco (Chastel, 1952, pp. 159-167; Chastel, 1959, 1964 ed., pp. 13-31). Subsequently, further acquisitions of documents and a critical rereading of the sources allowed for a clarification and a more reliable definition of the issue of the "sculpture garden"; see: Borgo, Sievers, 1989; Elam, 1990; Elam, 1992a; Elam, 1992b, Baldini, 1999 (with previous bibliography).

[9] Elam, 1992a.

[10] Vasari, *The Lives* (1568), 1996 ed., II, 646.

[11] Vasari, "The Life of Michelangelo" (1550), 2007 ed., p. 154.

[12] Condivi (1553) says from 1490-1492; Vasari (1568) instead says for four years, until Pietro di Lorenzo was ousted in 1494.

[13] It may be recalled, for instance, how Lorenzo asked the Roman correspondent Giovanni Ciampolini to show Filippino Lippi, in Rome at the time, "the canvases and other things" in 1489 (in *Il Giardino di San Marco*..., 1992, p. 23).

[14] 41.2 x 31.4 cm. I wish to thank Nicholas Penny for kindly providing me with the information.

[15] Washington, D.C., National Gallery of Art. Originally in Florence, where it was installed on the wall of a garden in Lungarno alle Grazie, it was purchased in 1891 by Baron R. von Liphart and immediately published by von Bode (1891) as an autograph work. It became a part of the S. H. Kress Foundation in 1948, and was donated to the National Gallery in 1961. The attribution was shared by Mackowsky and Middeldorf (and an in-depth photographic campaign was carried out for the Kunsthistorisches Institut in Florenz), while Tolnay referred it to another author influenced by Michelangelo in around 1520 (cf. Baldini, 1973, no. 64, p. 110). Over the course of the twentieth century, it was on display in four different exhibitions. Any reference at all is dismissed in *Michelangelo e l'arte classica*, 1987, p. 40. Personally, in coming to the conclusion that on the basis of how it was carved (parts of which awkwardly) it has little or nothing to do with Michelangelo's autograph works, I nonetheless wish to point out that, intriguingly, the profile view of Marsyas' face resembles the wooden *Crucifix* in Santo Spirito, whose attribution to Michelangelo still hadn't been made in Cavaceppi's time. Nor to be overlooked is the 19th-century Florentine provenance of the piece, which further complicates attribution to the Roman counterfeiter.

[16] See, especially, the 17th-century fresco by Ottavio Vannini in the Giovanni da San Giovanni hall in what is currently the Museo degli Argenti in Pitti Palace (1638-1642) and the marble sculpture made by Emilio Zocchi in 1862 situated in the Galleria Palatina (inv. OA n. 453). Several replicas by the same author and the version by his cousin Cesare Zocchi now in the Casa Buonarroti are known of (inv. 695).

[17] Condivi, *The Life of Michelangelo* (1553), 2006 ed., p. 12.

[18] Height 26 cm., white marble (?) not identified, inv. 124. This piece with other works of art was in the castle in Poppi, and was stolen during the night between 22 and 23 August 1944. According to a recent reconstruction of the facts (P. Vagheggi, "Il fauno rubato", in *La Repubblica*, 26 August 2004), a detailed report on the theft would seem to exist in the archives of the allied services in Washington D.C.

[19] On the subject, see the recent entry by P. Ragionieri in *Vita di Michelangelo*, 2001, p. 33. A copy of the head that appeared in the 1699 inventory for the Medici property may be viewed in the Casa Buonarroti.

[20] In 1746, Mariette published the engraving of the marble with the words: "M.A. BONARROTAE PUERI PRIM. OPUS E MARM FLOR IN MUSEO CAESAR", on the basis of an inscription with the same contents. The marble mask with plaque is reproduced in the engraving for the printed edition of Condivi's *Life*, edited by Anton Francesco Gori (Florence, 1746).

[21] C.L. Frommel, in *Giovinezza*..., 1999, pp. 226-227, no. 15.

[22] Vasari, 1568, 1962 ed., I, p. 12. To Vasari is also due information on the location of the work. For the critical success of the work, see E.D. Schmidt, in *Giovinezza*..., 1999, pp. 170-173, no. 1.

[23] A subsequent reworking of the marble to smooth portions which had remained unfinished has been hypothesized by Weil-Garris Brandt, 1999, pp. 69-75. I, however, accept this hypothesis with some caution, considering that Michelangelo's sculptures, venerated everywhere precisely for their obvious incompletion, must have been especially safe, in the family home, from awkward work to finish them off.

[24] Weil-Garris Brandt, 1999, p. 69.

[25] G. Savonarola, Sermon of 1 April 1496. With the purpose of strengthening the relationship between Savonarola's sermon and this work, an unnecessary shift forwards to the period between January (1495 Florentine usage) to June 1496 (Guerra, 1999) has been suggested.

[26] Calì, 1967 and 1980; Guerra, 1999.

[27] Roberto Longhi dated it after the statues in Bologna and the Vatican *Pietà*, and hypothesized that Michelangelo had reworked the relief at a later date (1958, 1976 ed., p. 7).

[28] See the related graphic representations in Weil-Garris Brandt, 1999, pp. 78-79.

[29] E. Capretti, in *Giovinezza*..., 1999, pp. 230-233, no. 17.

[30] This is why, and I agree, the resemblance between the *Battle* and the same subject by Bertoldo is believed to be only partial. While exasperated poses and dramatic *contrapposti* that may have inspired Michelangelo indeed existed, in the bronze relief the medium itself means working "per via di porre" (by adding) so that the figures denote their individual origin and final aggregation: on the contrary, in Michelangelo's marble the working "per forza di levare" (by taking away) unifies the different planes and the rear plane.

[31] Recollection by Tiberio Calcagni in a note to Condivi's *Life*, 1553, 1998 ed., p. XXI, no. 2.

[32] See the stimulating observations in Weil-Garris Brandt, 1999, pp. 75-84.

[33] "The bas-relief is an extraordinary gathering of physical situations: a veritable vocabulary that in a nutshell contains every possible development in Michelangelo's future work" (U. Baldini, in *Michelangiolo*..., 1989, no. 17).

[34] Remembered by Tiberio Calcagni in a note to Condivi's *Life*, 1553, 1998 ed., p. XXI, no. 1.

[35] Cf. R. Rosenberg, E.D. Schmidt, in *Giovinezza*..., 1999, pp. 200-203, nos. 6a and 6b.

[36] The attribution, advanced by Lisner, 1958, pp. 141-156, was favourably reconsidered by D. Carl in the catalogue *Giovinezza*..., 1999, pp. 276-279. See also Caglioti, 2000a, p. 126, figs. 2, 6, 10, 12.

[37] Andrea di Piero Ferrucci, called Andrea da Fiesole, with Jacopo di Andrea di Matteo, called del Maza or del Mazza (cf. Acidini Luchinat, 2003, pp. 97-99).

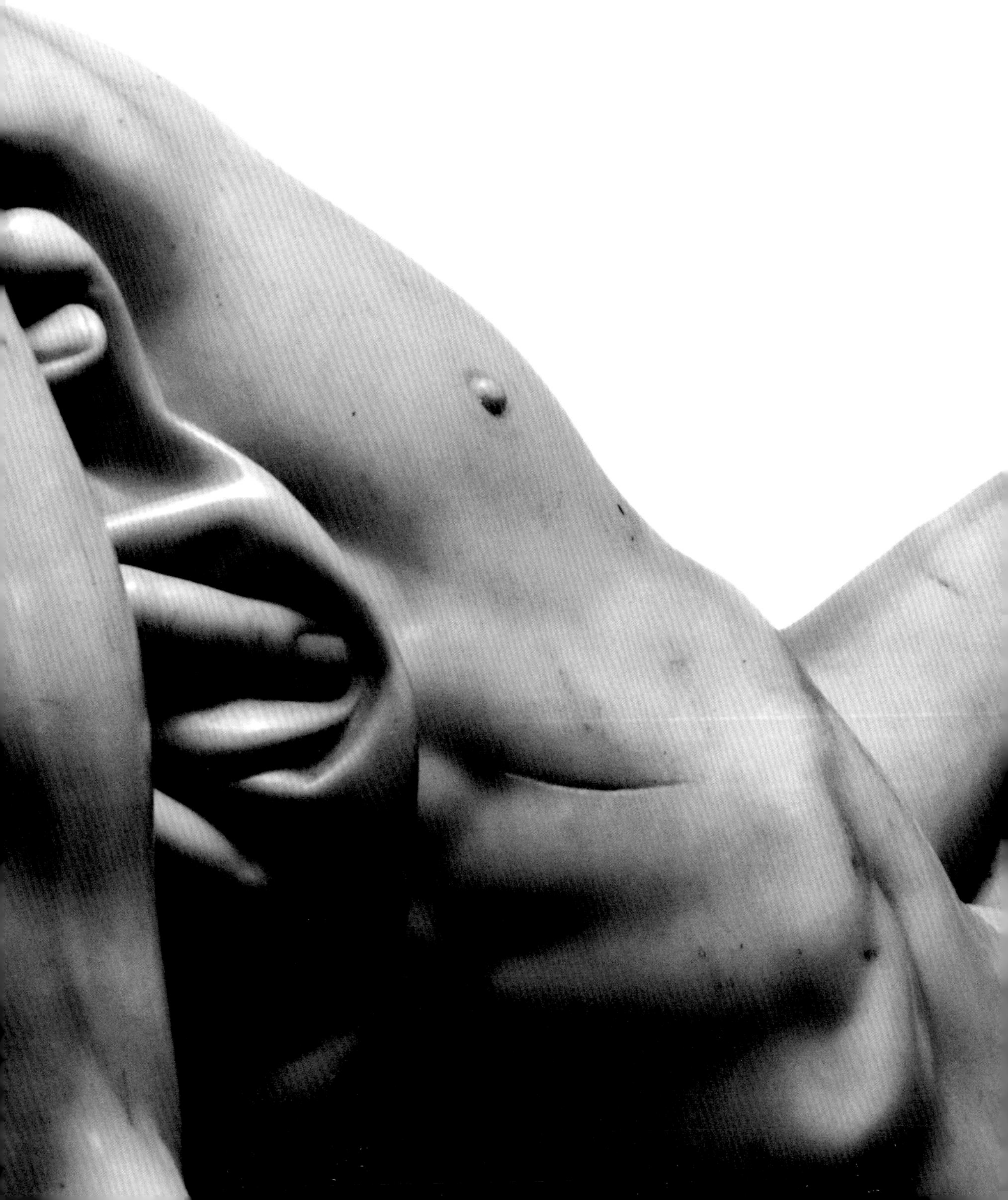

From the death of the "Magnifico" to departure for Rome

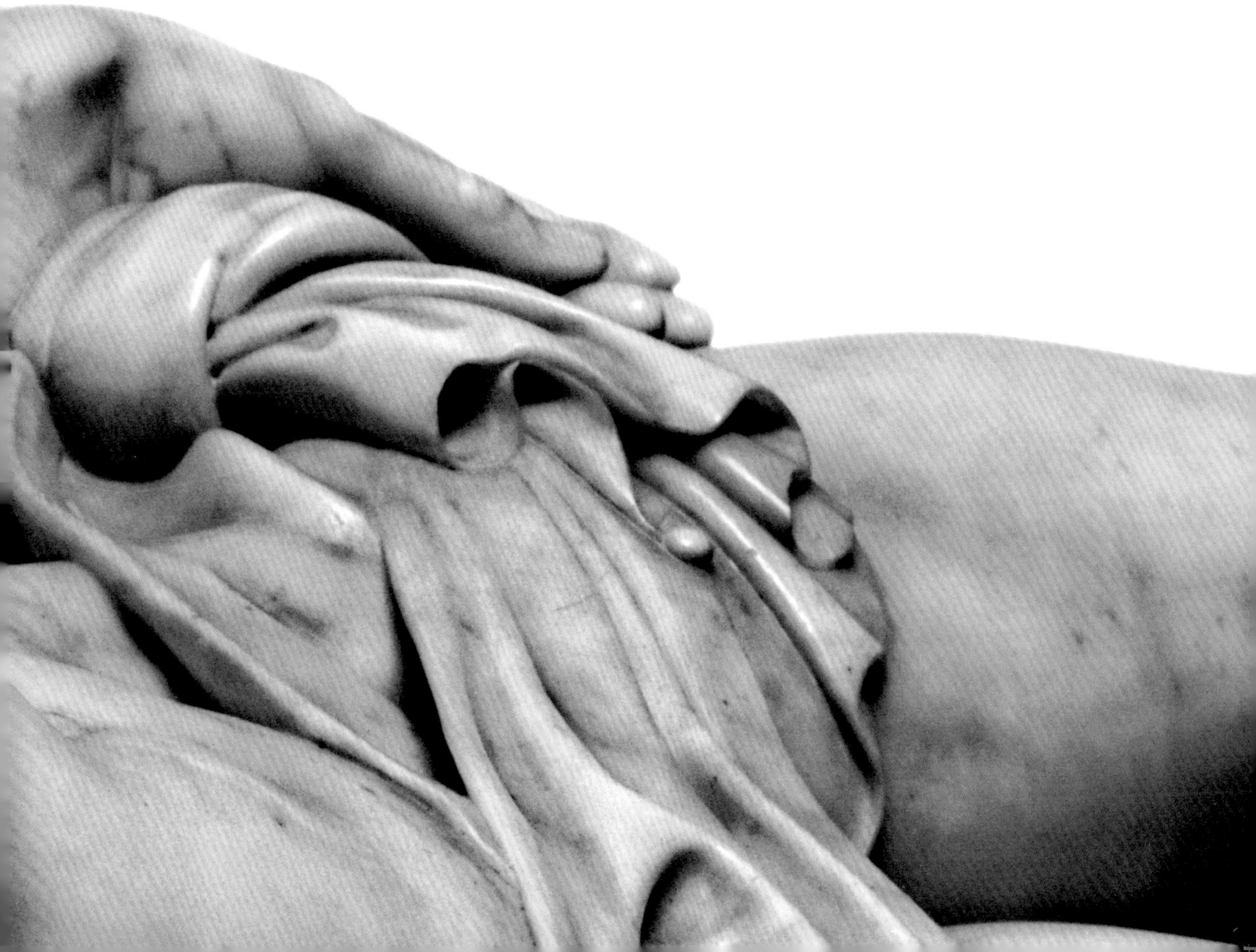

A period of uncertainty

When Lorenzo il Magnifico died on 8 April 1492, Michelangelo lost his patron and point of reference, but not his ties with the Medici family. At first he went back to his father's house, but was then summoned by the young Piero de' Medici and – as before – began spending time in the palace in Via Larga, living there once again as if he were a member of the "family", in the oldest, most all-embracing sense of the word.

If we are to agree with the sequence of events reported by Condivi, his return there must have taken place after 20 January 1494 (common usage) when, on the occasion of a exceptional blizzard, whose date was recorded by the diarist Luca Landucci, Piero "wanted a statue of snow made in the middle of his courtyard. He remembered Michelangelo, sent for him, and had him make the statue; and he wanted him to stay in his house as in his father's time".[1]

It would thus appear that Michelangelo stayed away from the Medici household for about one year and nine months, enough time for a young artist, by then skilled at both painting and sculpture, to produce some work; but facts in this regard are few and far between in the sources and the documents.

The *Hercules*

It was perhaps indeed for Piero de' Medici and again in the Sculpture Garden that between 1492 and 1494 Michelangelo worked on a block of marble 4 *braccia* (more than 230 cm) high, from which in subsequent years he carved out a *Hercules*.[2] The artist had the work with him in 1495, after which it went to the Strozzi. Finally, in 1529, through Giovan Battista della Palla, Filippo Strozzi the Younger gave it to Francis I, King of France, who installed it in the gardens at Fontainebleau. All trace of the work was lost after 1725.[3] The work's preparatory phase has been linked to a drawing now housed in Munich, which shows a study of a robust male torso with his head covered by something resembling a lion's skin and, most convincingly, holding a club.[4] If it is true, and it probably is, that the figure was over life-sized, then for the first time Michelangelo was testing his skill at making something very large, and he chose to devote his efforts to the hero of Greek and Latin myth who, in Medieval and Renaissance moralization, was believed to be a bearer of Pre-Christian values and even a pagan metaphor for Christ.

The wooden *Crucifix* in Santo Spirito

Michelangelo's work on a wooden *Crucifix* for the Augustinian convent of Santo Spirito is reported to have taken place around this time. The first source is Giorgio Vasari's biography, in which the object is described as a way for the artist to thank the prior who was allowing him "to study the secrets of anatomy" by assigning him rooms where he could dissect the corpses from the Hospital. Again according to Vasari, the *Crucifix* was installed "above the lunette of the high-altar", that is, on the central arch of the 15th-century wooden choir, replaced in 1600 by the current marble ciborium.[5] Condivi, who remembered it as being "slightly less than life-size", went on to speak about the relationship between the artist and the prior Niccolò (or Nicholaio, in 15th-century diction) di Giovanni di Lapo Bichielli, to whom the *Crucifix* was presented: "He was very intimate with the prior, from whom he received much kindness and who provided him both with a room and with corpses for the study of anatomy, than which nothing could have

Michelangelo, polychrome wooden *Crucifix*, including the original *Titulus Crucis* in three languages
Florence, Santo Spirito

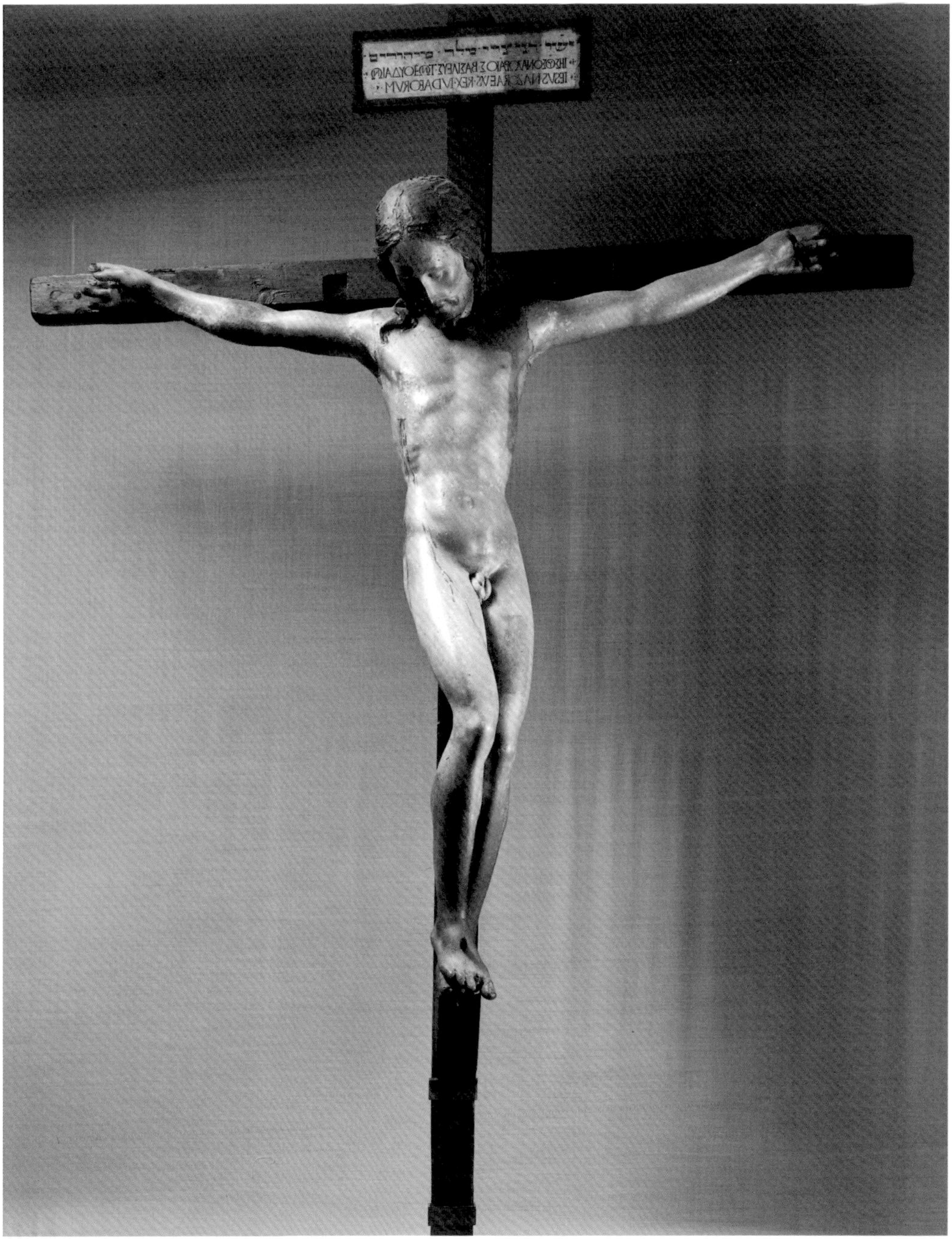

given him more pleasure".[6] It is likely that the corpses Michelangelo allegedly dissected rather secretly to improve his knowledge of the human skeleton and muscular system did indeed come from the hospital inside the Augustinian complex, and that the room he worked in was located on the convent premises. It seems the artist got into trouble for having dissected the body of a member of the Corsini family who had died prematurely.[7]
Although the prior no doubt played a key role in all this, we mustn't overlook the fact that the Medici family still very much controlled Santo Spirito, Piero having taken over his father's office as *operaio* (Overseer of the Committee of Works), and that before his death Lorenzo had made many important decisions for the church, for example, one concerning the construction of a Sacristy featuring a vestibule and a façade with three entrances. Believed to be lost until 1962, the wooden *Crucifix* now ascribed by most critics to Michelangelo[8] was identified by Margrit Lisner in a convent, despite the fact that it had been greatly overpainted and situated very high up. Its height, 139 cm, is compatible with the measurements recorded by Condivi: "slightly less than life-size". Linden wood was used: pieces were added along the perpendicular plane – front and back – of a main block of wood to achieve the volume required. A wood chisel and different-sized corner chisels were likely used, resulting in a very high degree of finishing; the work was then coated with a thin layer of plaster and glue primer and painted using leaner oil paints.[9]
In spite of the number of wholehearted supporters of attribution of the Santo Spirito *Crucifix* to Michelangelo, there are a number of authoritative deniers as well.[10] One of the problems put forth is that it is difficult, even impossible, to find suitable terms of comparison in the rest of the artist's corpus of works, as wood carvings are practically nonexistent (the Turin *Crucifix* and others are discussed later on); and there is also the question of the scant number of extant youthful works by the artist. If we are in favour of the attribution, we must accept the idea that at hardly twenty years of age Michelangelo was already capable of expressing delicateness and downright fragility, visible in the Christ's slender, longilineal body type, and fine, minute facial features. Halfway through the 18th century, upon seeing it after it was removed from the choir, Bottari noticed how it lacked "that grand, proud manner perceived in the other works made [by Buonarroti] afterwards".[11]
This would be an unheroic interpretation of Christ, inspired, rather, by the compassion with which the physical appearance of the Saviour was evoked, with figurative visual power, by the Dominican Girolamo Savonarola, precisely at the time he was writing his treatise on *The Love of Jesus Christ*, in 1492, in other words: a "candid" body, "of noble, tender and delicate complexion".
Michelangelo's well-known sensitivity to the friar's preaching renders the hypothesis a particularly likely one; nor is the hypothesis ruled out, as concerns style and historical verisimilitude, by the association often suggested between the Santo Spirito *Crucifix* and the one attributed to Benedetto da Maiano, and housed in the Museo di San Marco, believed to have belonged to the Dominican friar. A large production of wooden crucifixes in various shapes and sizes, and from large to small, is indeed attributed precisely to Benedetto, whom we tend to include among those sculptors who were points of reference, if not actual masters, for Michelangelo.
A Michelangelesque autograph may also be backed by exclusively historical-artistic evaluations, for instance, the sensitive features and studied pose of the thin body permeated by slight but dynamic torsions beginning from the reclined head and the gently spiralling bust, the spatially uneven buttocks, the relationship between the legs, with the left leg in a slightly more forwards position with one foot overlapping the other. The pointed face, whose features seem to gather in an expression of dignified sorrow,[12] is preceded by some of the heads in the *Battle of the Centaurs*, such as that of the combatant who throws himself onto the centaur in the lower right corner: inclined forwards and connoted by the quietly classical profile, his nasal bone descends straight down from his forehead, his eyes are small, swollen and almond-like in lowered eyelids, his closed mouth is soft. Similar features, furthermore, may be discerned in the face of the later *Apollo/David* in the Museo Nazionale del Bargello, absorbed in sleep.
While the anatomical precision of Christ's overall build and muscles is such that it has been judged to be extremely impressive by the specialists,[13] the proportions of the adolescent body, apparently that of

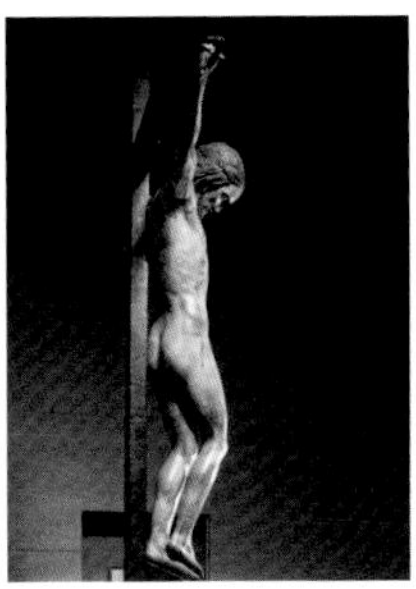

Michelangelo, polychrome wooden *Crucifix*, profile view showing torsion of the body
Florence, Santo Spirito

p. 31
Michelangelo, polychrome wooden *Crucifix*, detail of face with thin, dignified features
Florence, Santo Spirito

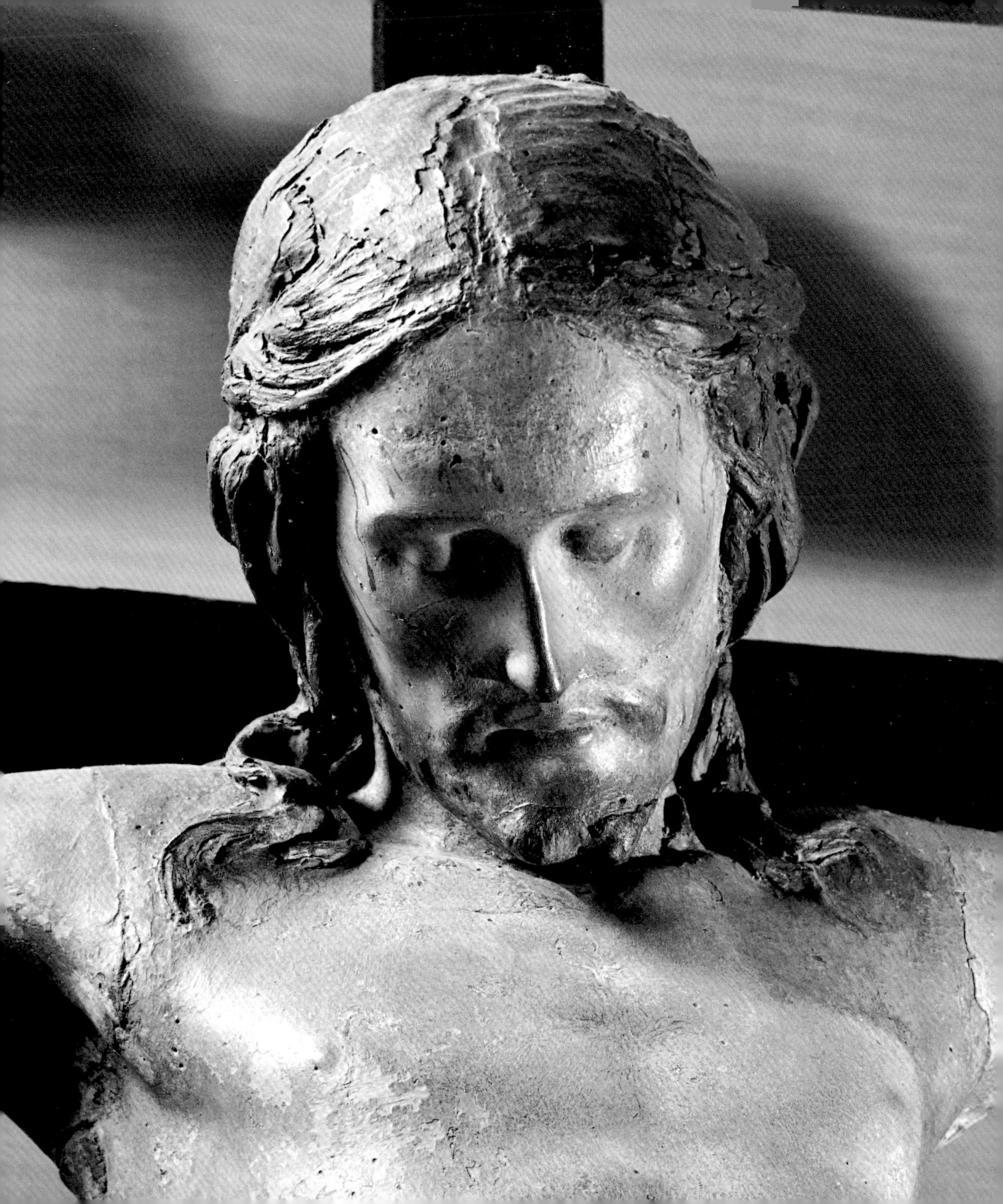

a fourteen-year-old, seem to be lengthened. But not to be overlooked is the fact that the midsection of the figure, which is at present naked, must have been covered with a loincloth, which would have interrupted it and shortened it visually. Furthermore, as the work was designed to be installed high up above the choir, a foreshortening effect had to be accounted for. The body's elongation would thus be an optical device used to achieve the correct proportions for the figure when clothed and viewed from below. We need to imagine the lost loincloth as having been a stiff piece of cloth, modelled and painted, like in many 15th and early-16th-century crucifixes, using a mixed media technique; the same may be said for the hair, finished with straw and stucco primer, which likely included a crown of thorns, also lost.
Lastly, the polychrome reveals an instance of painting style that, even if it weren't an autograph, would come very close to Michelangelesque intentions. Extremely accurate details are painted onto the warm, amber-coloured flesh: the wound in the side, the blood trickling down the body, a hint of hair under the armpits, on the chest and in the pubic region, the locks of hair that continue onto the skin.[14]
The wooden cross was made at a later date, and on it is the original scroll with the *Titulus Crucis* in Hebrew, Greek and Latin, also ascribed to Michelangelo. All three texts are written from right to left, just like the relic in the Santa Croce in Gerusalemme in Rome, and were rediscovered in a niche on 1 February 1492, indicating the rapid updating and significant reflection on the trilingual *titulus*' religious and humanistic theme, as was to be expected in the theological citadel of the Augustinians.[15]
The chronology of the *Crucifix* has settled at around 1492-1493, during the months that the artist was farthest from the Medici household. Not to be overlooked, however, is the chronology suggested by the Anonymous Magliabechiano with his mention of Pier Soderini's office as *gonfaloniere* of Florence; this would move the time Michelangelo spent in Santo Spirito for his anatomical studies up to 1498, and provide a broader time span for a date. As for the other crucial element, that is, the period of time Bichielli was prior, it can be stated that in 1513 he was still empowered to make important decisions for the Church.[16]
After the *Crucifix* was discovered and restored in 1963-1964, it was put on display in the Casa Buonarroti until 2000; it was then brought back to Santo Spirito where it can be admired in the Barbadori Chapel in the Sacristy.

Other wooden crucifixes: suggestions for attribution

The *Crucifix* theme, so dear to 15th-century Florentine sculptors starting from the striking opposition between the crucifixes by Brunelleschi and Donatello in the first twenty years of the century, had introduced the motif of perfect human proportions, expressed in the ideal canon for the nude male body, into art; Leonardo and Francesco di Giorgio conferred visibility to this canon in the early 1490s by creating the famed icon of the *Vitruvian Man*. On the other hand, Savonarola had founded his own personal devotion and that of others on the image of Christ on the cross, stimulating the multiplication of medium to small size crucifixes for chapels or for domestic use. Michelangelo, whom we know was also the author of many artworks destined for private use,[17] at the time and in those circumstances might have made other wooden crucifixes, not unlike what was commonly being done in a number of Florentine workshops and especially by Benedetto da Maiano and Baccio da Montelupo.
A suggestion has relatively recently been put forth attributing to a twenty-year-old Michelangelo, in around 1495, a linden wood *Crucifix* which is now part of a Turinese collection, small enough to fit into a room.[18] Viewed from the front, with Christ's head bent forwards and right, and his right leg flexed slightly and jutting out as if in reaction to the overlapping of the foot, he has a slender and delicate figure that recalls the *Christ* on the cross sculpture painted by Perugino, completed in April 1496 and placed in Santa Maria Maddalena de' Pazzi. The figure was carved from a wood block comprising pieces glued together. The purpose of a small wedge made

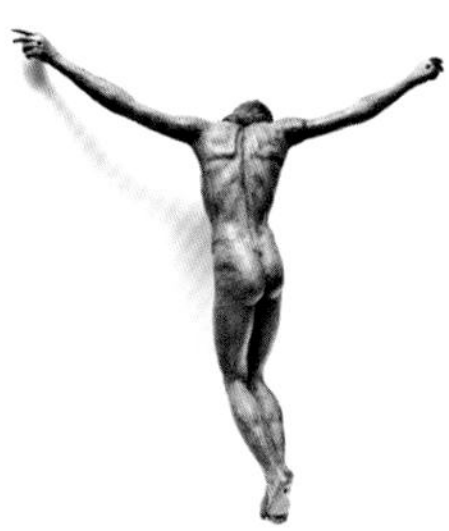

Attributed to Michelangelo, polychrome wooden *Crucifix*
Paris-New York, private collection

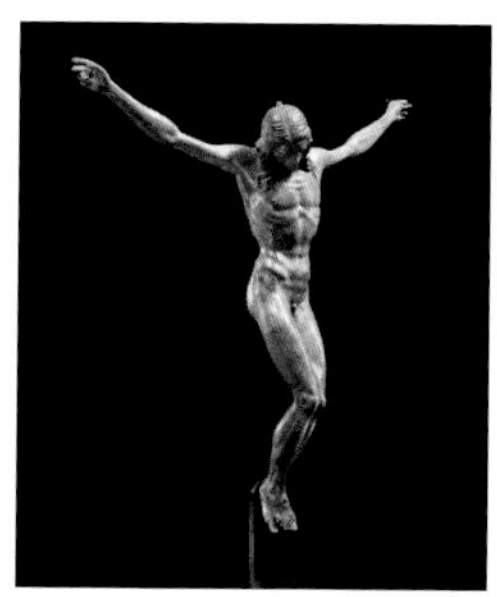

Attributed to Michelangelo, polychrome wooden *Crucifix*
Paris-New York, private collection

in the left side of the head is to accentuate the extreme inclination:[19] it is an original "pentimento" or structural rethinking which, in forcing the verisimilitude of the natural element, reveals a preference for pathetic expressiveness.
The frontal pose of the naked body does not exclude a slight rotation, punctually reflected by the anatomical modulation of the volumes, once again responding to the substantial correctness of both the structure and the surface.[20] Like in the Santo Spirito Christ, the longer proportions are visually compensated for by the loincloth, whose purpose is to interrupt the figure halfway. If the "compression of the hips" and the "delicately stretched twisting of the limbs" foreshadow some of the features of the *Pietà* in the Vatican Basilica, begun in 1497 and completed in 1499,[21] the animation of the torso by way of cavities and projections, creating vibrant planes and boldly chiaroscuroed features, suggests anticipations of the later and much larger marble *David*.[22]
The polychrome consists in considerably worn amber-hued flesh, and in the red-and-chestnut hair colour.
Critics who disagree with the attribution include Margrit Lisner (2004), who instead sees the author of the Turin *Crucifix* as being Andrea Sansovino when he was working in the Corbinelli Chapel in Santo Spirito, accounting for the similarities to Michelangelo's work by way of the experiences common to both young sculptors: an apprenticeship with Benedetto da Maiano, work in Santo Spirito, the study of anatomy. Nonetheless, the comparison between this work and the *Christ in Compassion* in Sansovini's marble altar is not very convincing from a stylistic viewpoint, due to the inertia in the distribution of volumes in latter work; nor is it advisable from a methodological point of view, because of the limits involved in comparing a polychrome wooden sculpture with a marble relief.
Other wooden crucifixes, which may be dated from the end of the 15th and the first decades of the 16th centuries, have recently been described as belonging to a kind of "family", whose typology is significantly consonant with those in the Santo Spirito and the Turinese collection on display at the Horne Museum.[23] Among these is a model similar in size to the previous one, despite the fact that it is privately owned, naked, and its anatomy is tested and rendered with precision as well as sensitivity, to the extent that it may be associated with the *Christs* in Santo Spirito and Turin, although not all the critics agree.[24]
On the other hand, as I stated in my introduction, it is the polychrome wood medium itself that complicates the question of attribution, because of the difficulty if not the impossibility of perceiving therein that distinctive way of working, and that we're used to recognizing in Michelangelo's marble statuary. What does remain possible and valid, however, is the acknowledgement of an inner impulse animating and innervating the flawless anatomies of these Christs, and this is transformed, for the sculptor, into a challenge to experiment with inclinations in every direction in space, occupying the third dimension with slender and subtle *contrapposti*: in the sculpture of that time, a likely starting point was the *Battle of the Centaurs*, and an equally likely arrival point was the *Bacchus* for Jacopo Galli.
The distance in time between this restricted nucleus of wooden sculptures (whose autograph continues to be debated) and the only other wooden sculpture we know Michelangelo to have made, the small *Crucifix* in the Museo di Casa Buonarroti,[25] which was as yet unfinished when he died, limit and eventually nullify any chance for a comparison. The subject of Buonarroti's early wooden sculptures is thus a research thread that leads to lively debate and the hope of making discoveries, also in relation to the continuous critical adjustments that become necessary as restoration work is carried out on works related by chronology, typology, attribution.[26]

From snowfall to flight

The artist's return to the Medici palace, whether or not strictly related to the execution of an ephemeral statue made of snow in January 1494, common usage (a commission which actually may have been less frivolous than it seems),[27] lasted only a few months. Michelangelo's attitude towards his new patron Piero can only be inferred from what Condivi wrote down. He "had taken his father's place but lacked the

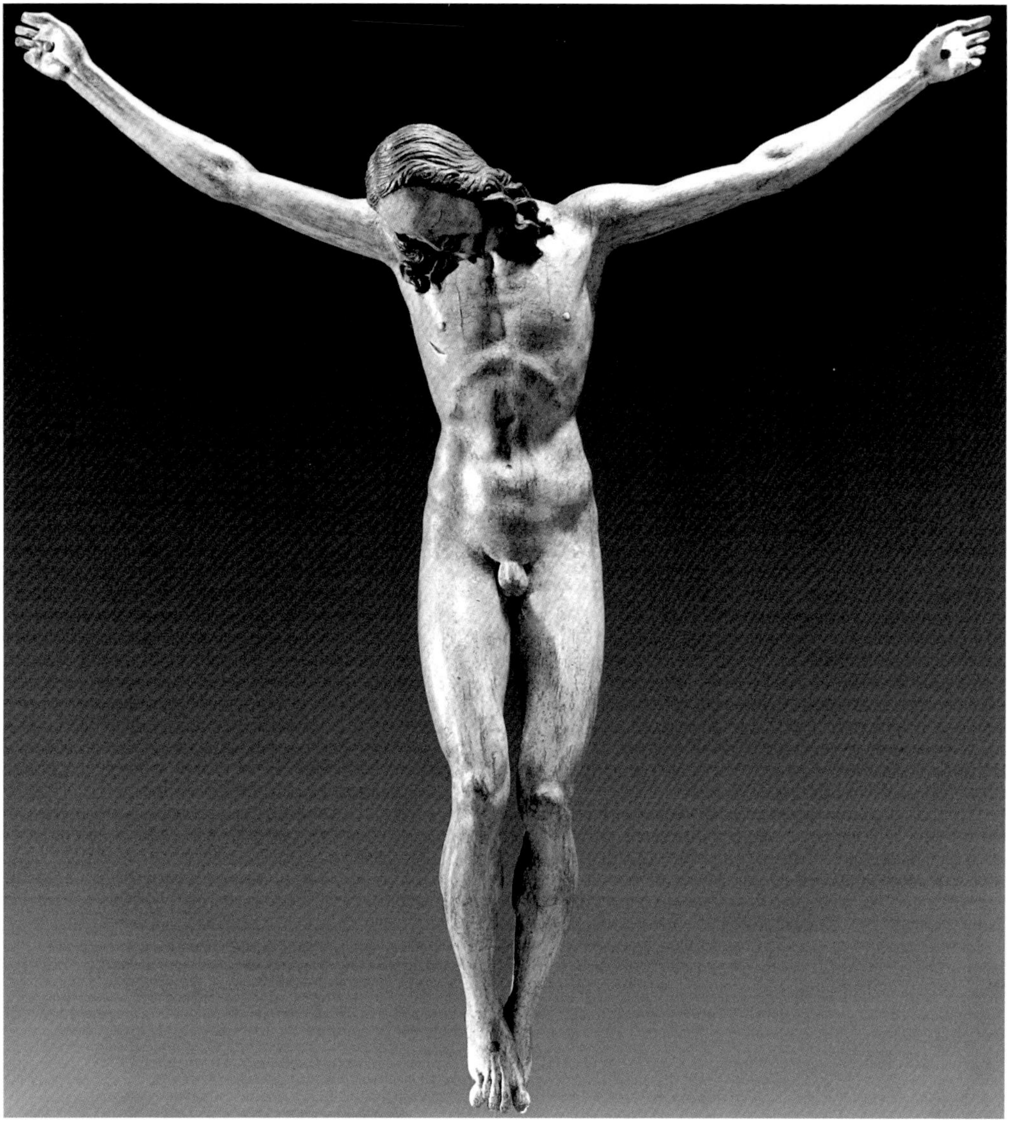

Attributed to Michelangelo,
polychrome wooden *Crucifix*
Turin, private collection

p. 35
Attributed to Michelangelo,
polychrome wooden *Crucifix*,
detail of anatomical rendering
of the torso and pelvis
Turin, private collection

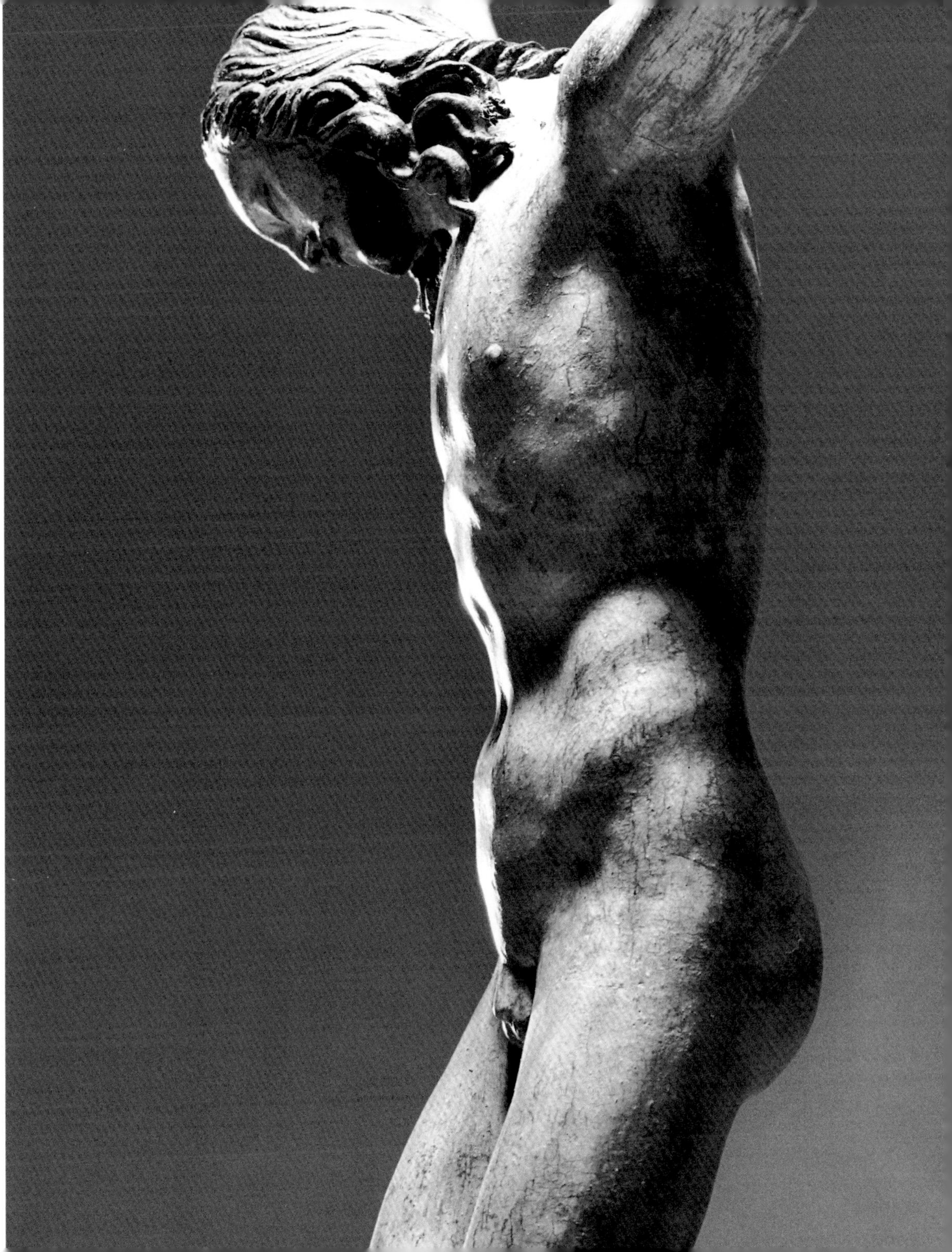

grace of his father" were Condivi's words about Piero. Michelangelo's note to the text reads that he never said such a thing",[28] but soon after, Piero was described as "insolent and intemperate".[29] Of course, Michelangelo couldn't have been pleased at the idea of being "much caressed by him" and hosted in a home where the head of the family thought of him as a "remarkable" person on the same level as a good-looking, nimble, Spanish groom.

Tormented by nightmares and sinister omens brought to him by Cardiere, a musician who had been dear to Lorenzo il Magnifico, and, of course, like everyone in Florence, on the one hand attentive to talk about the king of France's meddling in Italian affairs, and on the other to the increasingly fervent preachings of Fra Girolamo Savonarola, Michelangelo heeded his tendency to be cautious if not fearful,[30] and by mid-October 1494, left town with two unidentified companions, the three of them heading northwards. Just before leaving, he may have started working on a marble *Young Saint John* – destined for Lorenzo di Pierfrancesco, a member of a collateral branch of the Medici family whom Piero had exiled in May of that year – and a marble *fanciullo*, by some identified as the *Sleeping Cupid*; both of the statues were completed when he returned to Florence, and both are now lost. As his patron, Piero de' Medici took the artist's exit badly.[31]

Hardly a month had gone by when, on November 9, Piero and his family were banished from Florence; Charles VIII of Anjou was on his way and Piero had been unable to stop him. The palace on Via Larga and the Sculpture Garden near San Marco were siezed and ransacked by the people of Florence, and the valuable family collections stolen or confiscated.

In Bologna

After travelling through Bologna, Michelangelo continued on to Venice where he stayed a few days; he then went back to Bologna where he found the hospitality and patronage of Giovan Francesco Aldrovandi. Aldrovandi was serving in the government there and was the right-hand man to the Bolognese aristocrat Giovanni Bentivoglio, a friend to the Medici and, according to Condivi, the person who helped the young sculptor solve his problem with the Ufficio delle Bullette, which intended to fine him for not having the red wax thumbnail seal required to be able to enter the city.

But precisely because Aldrovandi had contacts with Florence and the Medici[32], it is likely that upon learning of the excellent youth's flight from Florence, he did all he could to intercept him and make sure he came to Bologna where sculpture and sculptors had been assigned a great deal of importance from the 15th century, as had the major commissions given to both Jacopo della Quercia and Niccolò dell'Arca.[33]

And as Piero de' Medici had himself turned to Bentivoglio asking for help against the French, and had stopped off in Bologna, with his family, on his way to exile in Venice in November 1494, a link between Michelangelo's presence in the city and the Medicean-Bentivoglesque alliance has been hypothesized;[34] but Buonarroti himself, in recalling the facts more than half a century later through Condivi, continued to express his amazement at what had taken place.[35]

Michelangelo stayed in Bologna just over a year, living a dignified life in Aldrovandi's home; every evening, Aldrovandi would ask his guest to read aloud passages from Dante, Petrarch or Boccaccio; there is speculation that he enjoyed the reader's very fitting Florentine accent.

While there, Michelangelo closely studied Ferrarese painting, especially such masterpieces as Ercole de' Roberti and Francesco del Cossa's *Gryphons*, a polyptych in the church of San Petronio, and the Garganelli chapel by the same two artists in San Pietro.[36] It is also likely he went to Ferrara to see Cossa's *Months* at the Palazzo Schifanoia (1469-1470).

Thanks to his Bolognese patron the young artist had the opportunity to carry on with his sculptural work and secure a commission for a monument of unquestionable prestige: a marble *arca* for San Domenico in the church of the same name.

Nicola Pisano and his collaborators (Fra Guglielmo da Pisa, Lapo, Arnolfo di Cambio), Niccolò dell'Arca, Michelangelo, Alfonso Lombardi, the *Shrine of Saint Dominic* Bologna, San Domenico

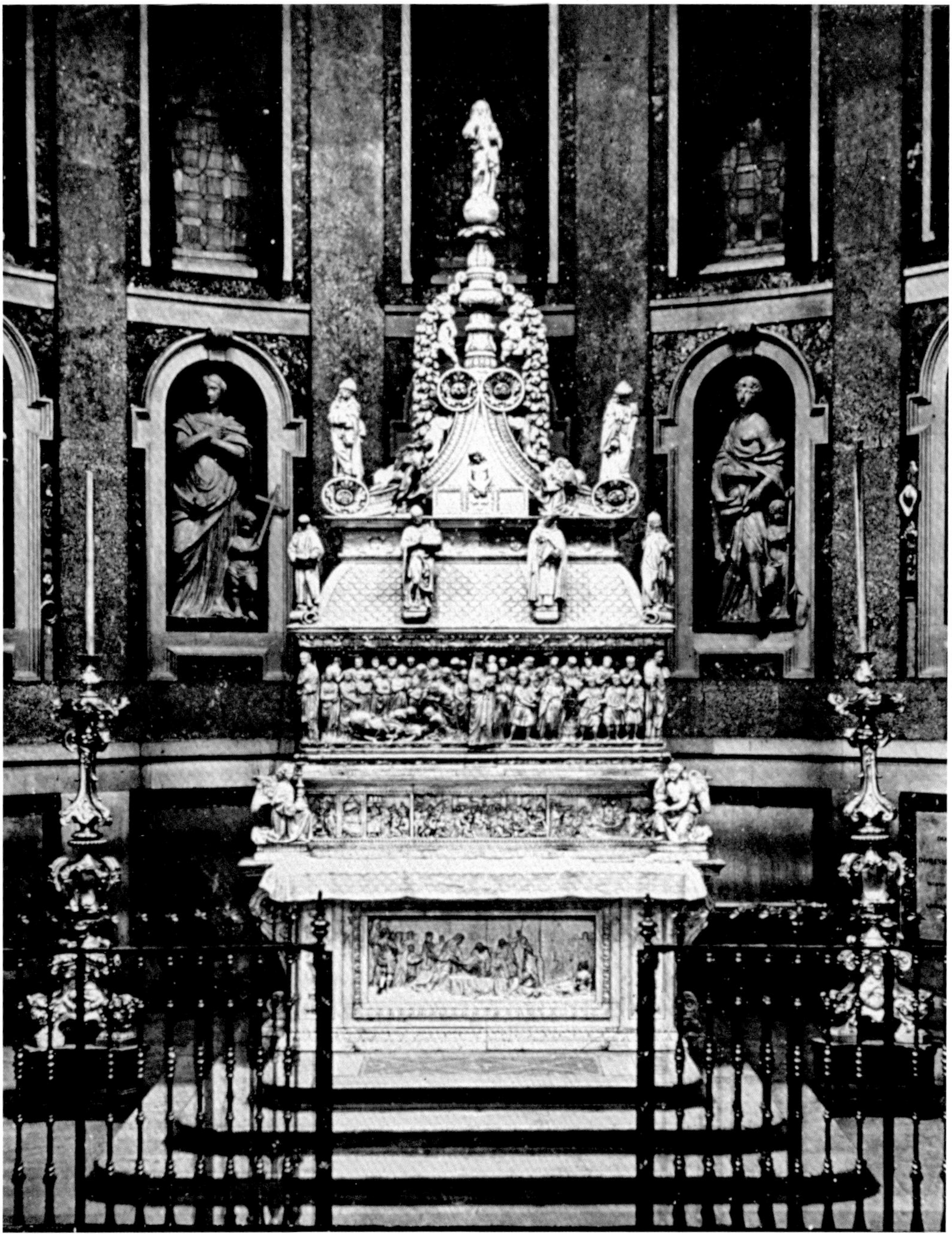

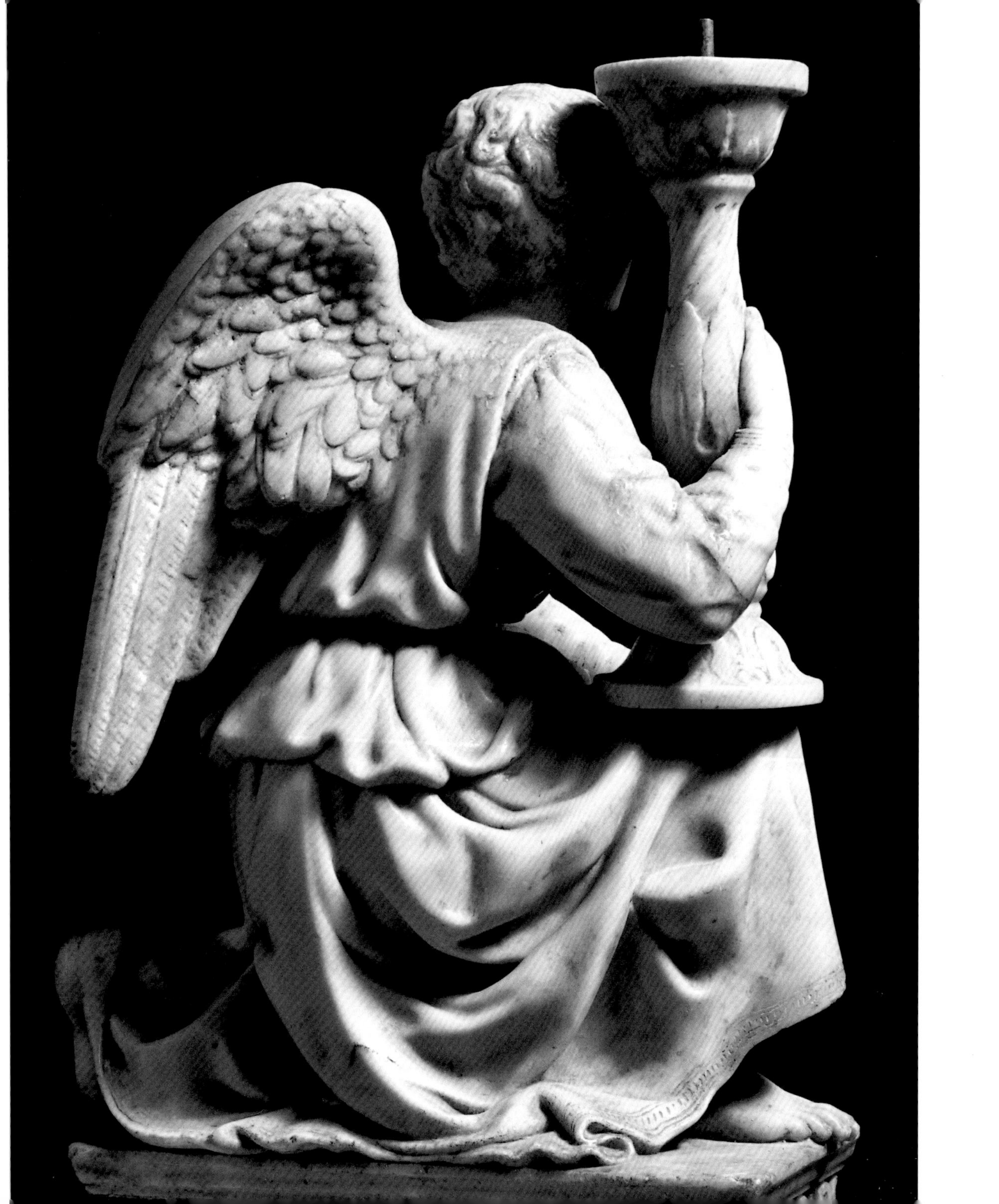

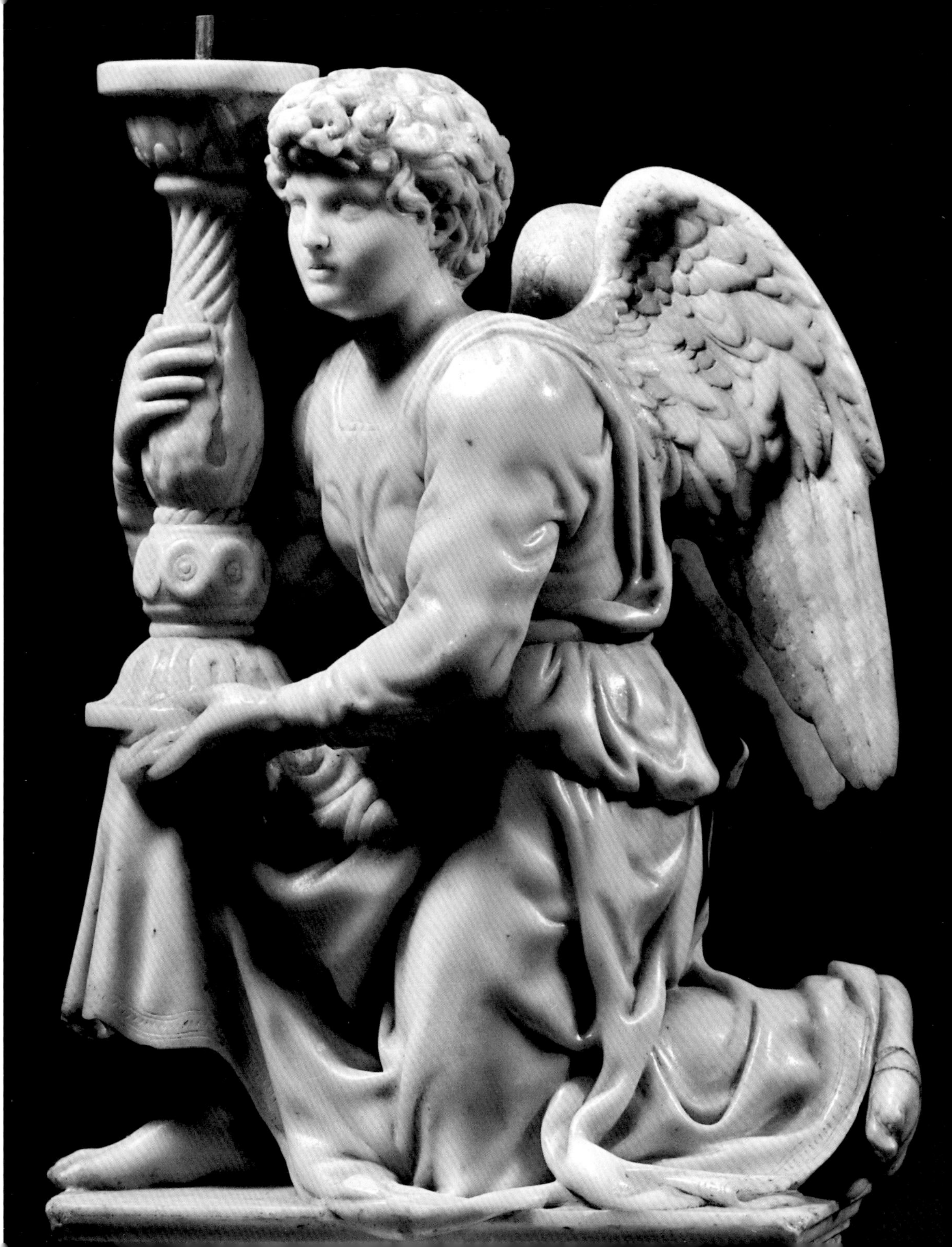

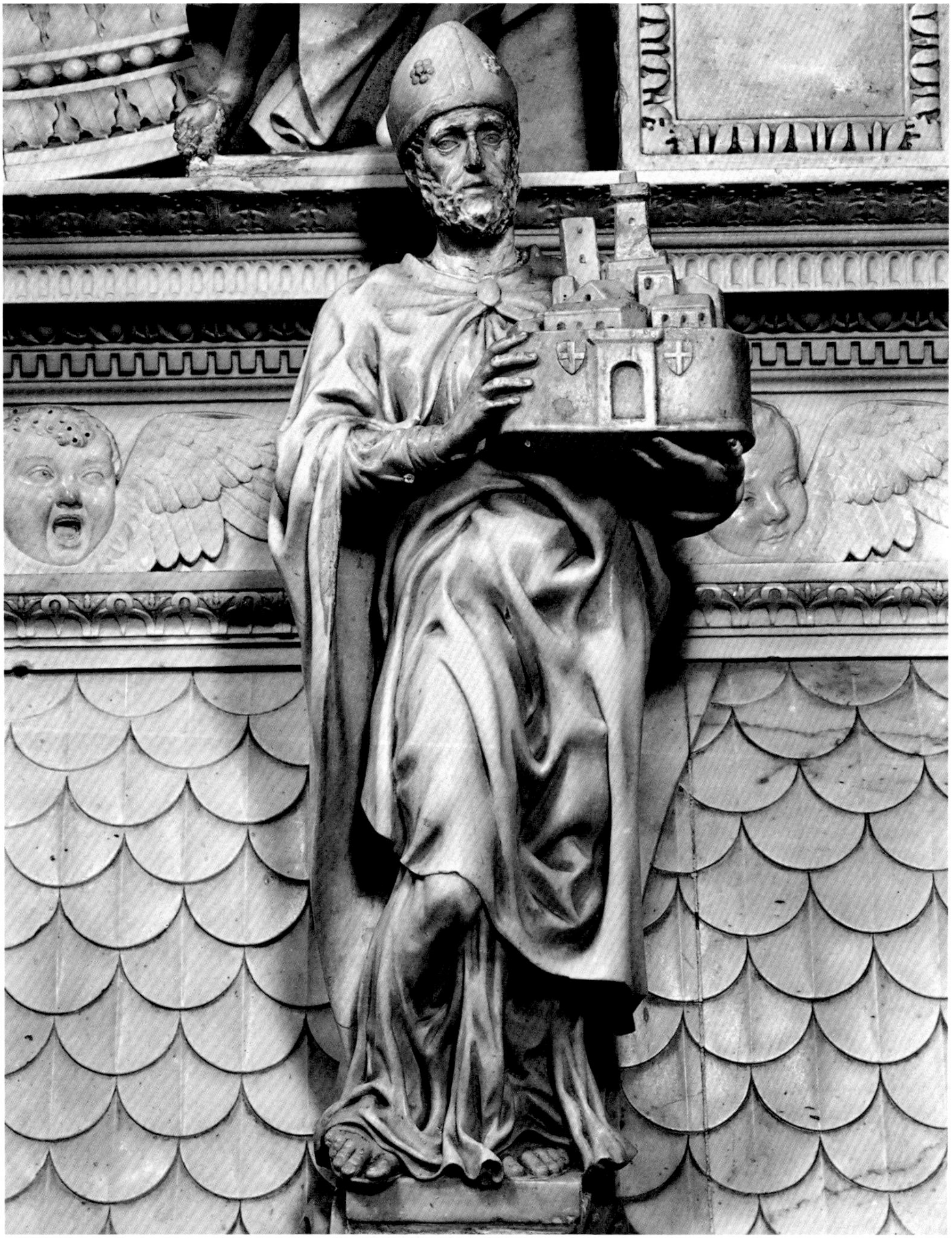

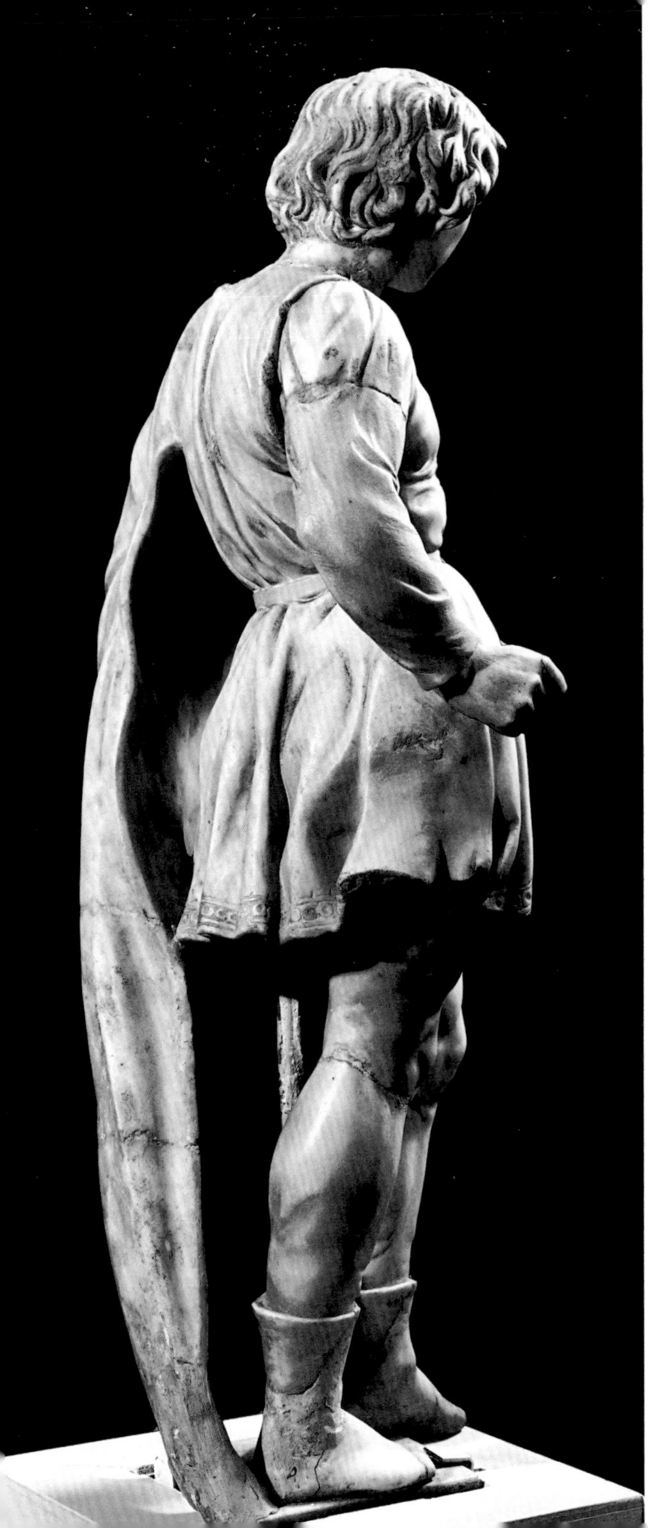
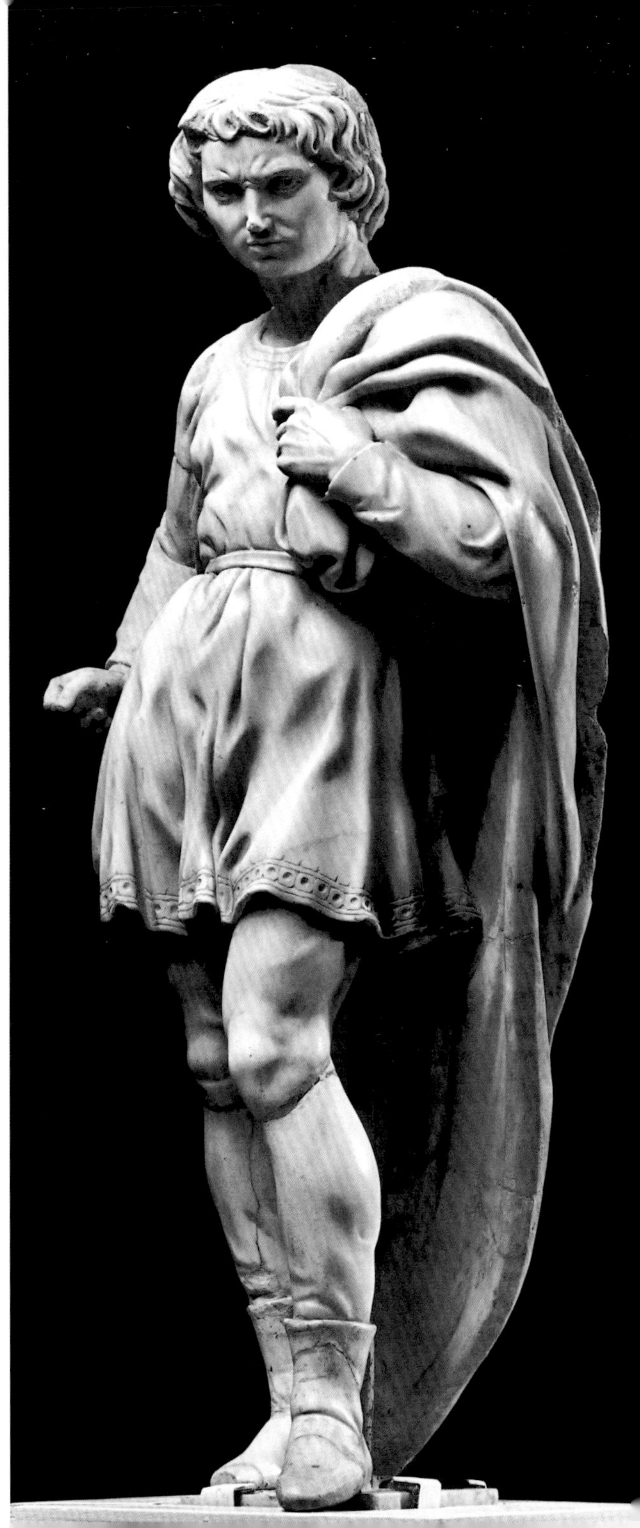

by the way the parts and inclinations are counter-positioned in space, reveals a quivering tension, which achieves *pathos* in the frowning face. It is a range of "perpetual rotations" of the body, culminating in the way "the young saint turns his head almost suddenly, as if obeying some unexpected order".[48] The intense expression leading to the angry mouth and especially the sullen forehead above eyes with daggers in them and in a sideways glance, anticipates one of the traits in the colossal marble *David* (1501-1504). Echoes of Ercole de' Roberti's painting, disclosed by Longhi,[49] and the suggestions borrowed from Cossa's *First Decan of Aries* in Palazzo Schifanoia,[50] without considering what has until now never been mentioned, that is, the probable influence of some other sculpture,[51] are all absorbed in an original energy, interwoven with emotions that transcend the ironwork of the Ferrarese artists.

And if the likeness to the scowling face of Verrocchio's Bartolomeo Colleoni is suggestive (Michelangelo must have viewed it while in Venice),[52] it is not the great strain, in terms of the severity and authority, of the bronze *condottiero* that *Proculus* the soldier must express, but rather the vigil state of alarm of someone reacting to a sudden danger – his executioners moving in from the side perhaps – and ready to fight. The hand that spasmodically grasps the folds of the cloak is actually letting it fall to the ground in order to free his body, proven by the inaccurate position of the hollow in the cloak collar, visible only from behind, but indicating Michelangelo's search for verisimilitude, something which lacked the necessary intensity. Fra Ludovico da Prelormo recalled that in 1572 the statuette was knocked down by a falling ladder and considerably damaged. Displayed in the exhibition *Giovinezza di Michelangelo* in 1999-2000, the work was then transferred to the Opificio delle Pietre Dure and submitted to conservative analysis, which revealed cracks, hinges and past additions of missing parts. Michelangelo introduced a very high-quality standard in the local artistic environment with his statues for the *arca* of San Domenico, what would seem to be the only works produced by the artist in that year he spent in Bologna, and this was something that didn't pass unnoticed.

While there, he was able to do something for Baccio da Montelupo, who had been a companion of his in the Sculpture Garden, and who, present in Bologna in 1494-1495, made a *Lament over the Dead Christ* in the church of San Domenico for the Bolognini. A member of the Buonarroti family was also present in the summer of 1495, in Bologna.[53] We cannot rule out the possibility that while in Bologna he may have met with Giovanni and Giuliano de' Medici, Piero's younger brothers, who stopped off there on 14 November 1495 on their way to Milan. The Garden in Florence had been confiscated a few days earlier and then sold to the Bolognese aristocrat Giovanni Bentivoglio: Aldrovandi may have played a role in the transaction.

Michelangelo's return to Florence, which took place around Christmas 1495, may have been hastened by the ill-will of a rival sculptor,[54] but it was more likely inspired by the artist's feeling that he was wasting his time in a foreign city. The political situation in Florence had calmed down, despite the fact that Savonarola was getting increasingly carried away, with his preaching becoming more and more visionary, making a deep impression on Michelangelo, among others.[55]

A *Sleeping Cupid* "all'antica"

Upon returning to Florence around Christmas 1495, or soon afterwards, Michelangelo was once again in touch with the collateral branch of the family of his patrons, the Medici. Lorenzo and Giovanni di Pierfrancesco, invited to the border by their cousin Piero, had returned to Florence one year earlier with Charles VIII of Anjou, and taken the name of Popolano. For Lorenzo, Michelangelo sculpted a *Young Saint John* (he may have been working on it when he fled his native city), and although it is known to have existed, it is now believed to be lost.[56]

Also dated in that period is the creation of a *Sleeping Cupid* made of marble, recalled by Condivi as "an Eros, six or seven years old, lying in the position of a man asleep", also lost.[57] Michelangelo worked on it in a room believed to have been inside the Sculpture Garden.[58] Although a thoughtless piece of advice from Lorenzo concerning the work did end up causing Michelangelo's discontent, in the final analysis, what it eventually led to was a great leap forwards in his success as an artist. What happened was that because the Medici found it to be a work "of great beauty", they advised the sculptor to age the object so that it could be sold as an antique and for a better price. In those days, fake antiques were being sold all the time in Rome, and were more sought after and expensive than "modern" ones. Michelangelo had, after all, begun his work as a sculptor by copying the antique head of a satyr or faun, and as a painter by counterfeiting the manner of the ancient masters, artfully using lampblack to age his sheets.[59]

The *Cupid* was probably sold in March 1496 (common usage) for thirty ducats to Baldassarre del Milanese, a Florentine banker in Rome, who in turn sold it to Raffaele Riario, cardinal of San Giorgio, for two hundred ducats. By early May the cardinal knew that the statue was a "fake" made by a young Florentine sculptor and succeeded in getting his money back from the mediator. But Riario was now interested in the artist, and sent a gentleman he trusted, Jacopo Gallo or Galli, to Florence, to find him. Michelangelo confessed that he was indeed the author of the *Cupid*, and to convince him, right before his eyes drew one of the hands: this is what the master told Condivi in the early fifties, his intention being perhaps to create a kind of legend, one about a portrait improvised by "his own" hand, a hand that those who wrote about the arts at the time were already referring to as divine.[60]

The artist, who was intent on getting back the sum of money he had been defrauded of and introducing himself to them, after the Feast of Saint John, on June 25, the artist went to Rome taking with him letters from Lorenzo de' Medici to show the Florentine bankers and Cardinal Riario. He stayed with Jacopo Galli[61] and quickly familiarized himself with antique statuary, of which he particularly appreciated Apollonius' vigorous, mutilated piece called the *Belvedere Torso*. Though he begged the cardinal to keep the "story about the fake" to himself, it soon spread, and even Paolo Giovio wrote about it in his *Vita di Michelangelo*, 1525-1530.

What happened after that as concerned the *Cupid* was very complex. Michelangelo attempted to buy it back but the Milanese had put it up for sale for two hundred scudi in Palazzo Sforza, where Pico della Mirandola saw it and described it as sleeping while "resting upon one hand" adding that it was "intact, measured about four *spanne* in length, and was very beautiful".[63] By the end of 1496, Cesare Borgia, son of Alexander VI, had offered it to Guidobaldo da Montefeltro, but he then took it back in 1502 when he captured the territory of the Duchy of Urbino. That same year the statue found its way to the Isabella d'Este's *studiolo* in Mantua, where it was placed on display right next to another *Cupid* ascribed to Praxiteles, in order to demonstrate the superiority of past artists over modern ones. After that, Michelangelo's work, along with the collections of the Gonzaga, migrated to England, and was subsequently lost, perhaps destroyed in the 1698 fire at Whitehall.

But as time went by, and beginning in the 18th century, attempts were made to identify the original work or its derivations in the countless marble *Cupids*, whether modern or of unknown period, in European collections, also on the grounds of three sleeping putti drawn on a sheet in the illustrated catalogue for the Gonzaga collections. One of the most recent critical appraisals is founded upon the hypothesis that the Michelangelesque *Cupid* was the model for the stocky *Child* by Fernando Yáñez in the painting in the church of San Nicolás in Valencia; if this were so, it would come close to the "type" of *Cupid*, now on British soil, in the Lord Methuen Collection in Corsham Court, Wiltshire.[64] But the Methuen *Cupid*'s right arm is raised above his head, and his left extends along his body and holds still a torch[27], and his pose does not fully correspond to a figure sleeping "resting upon one hand" as described by Pico, a gesture which instead appears in other ancient and modern putti.[65]

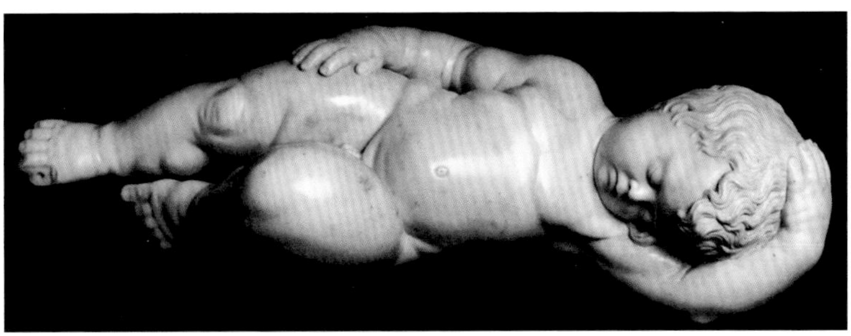

Unknown 16th-century (?) sculptor, *Sleeping Cupid*
One of the countless interpretations of a classical iconographic motif, perhaps inspired by Michelangelo's lost *Cupid*, sold as an antique in Rome
Modena, Galleria Estense

Notes

[1] Condivi, *The Life of Michelangelo* (1553), 2006 ed., p. 15..

[2] See Châtelet-Lange, 1972 and Châtelet-Lange, 1977. After that Elam (1993, pp. 59-61) and Hirst (1985, p. 155 and again in Hirst-Dunkerton, 1994, Ital. ed. 1997, p. 16) have suggested that Piero de' Medici commissioned the work. Elam and Hirst's hypotheses were later confirmed by documentary research conducted by Caglioti (2000b, pp. 262-265). For a summary of the issue, cf. P. Ragionieri, in *Vita di Michelangelo*, 2001, p. 34, no. 7.

[3] *Carteggio indiretto*..., 1988-1995, II, pp. 325 and ff. Thereafter, all the information available may be found in the catalogue *Vita di Michelangelo*, 2001, p. 34, no. 7. The *Hercules* was viewed and described as being in the Jardin de l'Estang by Père Dan in *Trésor des merveilles de la maison royale de Fontainebleau*, 1642, and represented by Israel Silvestre in an engraving of 1649 (an exemplar of which is now in Casa Buonarroti, inv. 783). It may have been lost after the Jardin de l'Estang was destroyed (1725).

[4] The drawing was discovered on the *verso* of a sheet (Munich, Staatliche Graphische Sammlung, inv. 2191) when its double bottom was removed in 1977; on the same side is the study of the hand of a skeleton, which confirms the date as being the early 1490s, when the artist was studying anatomy in Santo Spirito. The drawing was on display at the exhibition, and is included in the catalogue, *Il disegno fiorentino*..., 1992, p. 36, no. 19, with an entry by A. Natali. It was again presented critically by Harprath [1994], supported by images with special lighting and reliable graphic reconstructions. After that, a marble *Hercules* ended up on the market (Sotheby's New York, 1999), for which a Michelangelesque paternity was hinted at. Some resemblances to the torso in the sheet in Munich do exist, but from the opposite view. See Rèpaci, 1999. In the past, Tolnay (1964) suggested that a sheet at the Louvre attributed to Rubens was a copy of the front view of the *Hercules*, because of the typically Michelangelesque wasy the body had been carefully studied, so that it inclined and rotated on legs spread apart, with an animal skin (or drapery) close to the left thigh like in the *Bacchus* at the Bargello.

[5] Vasari, *The Lives* (1568), 1996 ed., II, p. 649.

[6] Condivi, *The Life of Michelangelo* (1553), 2006 ed., p. 17.

[7] According to the Anonymous Magliabechiano, Michelangelo "studied the anatomy of numerous bodies here, which he cut and dissected; and by chance one of these belonged to a Corsini, and a great fuss was made by the members of the Corsini family; the incident was reported to Piero Soderini, at the time Gonfalonier of Justice, who laughed it off, as he understood that he had done it for his art". Cited in Baldini, 2001, p. 28. Up until now no mention has ever been made of the fact that the anecdote should be dated not before 1498, when Soderini was appointed Gonfalonier of Florence (from 1502, for life), which tells us that Michelangelo must have studied anatomy in Santo Spirito for about six years, from 1492 to 1498 at least.

[8] Alessandro Parronchi is one of the strongest opposers of the attribution, on several occasions indicating the early wood en *Crucifix* by Michelangelo to be the one in the church of San Rocco in Massa (1961, 1968 ed., pp. 49-84; 1981, pp. 39-45; also see the scholar's testimony in Acidini Luchinat, Weil-Garris Brandt, 1999, pp. 165-166).

[9] Schleicher, 2000, pp. 69-97.

[10] For those favourable to the attribution, see the summaries in Lucchesi, 2000 and recently Gentilini, 2004, pp. 13-14, with previous bibliography. Those against include Ragghianti, 1974; Middeldorf, 1978; Parronchi, 1968, 1975, 1981, 1996; Beck, 1998. An interesting reconstruction of the debate may be read in *Il Crocifisso*..., 2001, pp. 38-49.

[11] Bottari, 1759-1760, I, 1760, p. 358, note 3. Bottari also wrote that Ignazio Hugford had told him that after leaving the Barbadori chapel (sacristy) it had ended up in the convent and "having examined it carefully, although it appeared to be beautiful and devout, he said, it has no Michelangelesque features; this is why he believes it is by a past sculptor".

[12] "...a Sufferer who resigned himself to pain, death, marked by the virile sweetness of a face that carried out a mysterious mission"; thus were the words of Padre G. Ciolini, introduction to the catalogue *Il Crocifisso*..., 2000, pp. 17-18.

[13] P.A. Bernabei and M. Gulisano emphasize "the absolute precision with which the anatomical details are reproduced, even the most insignificant ones, to the extent that they appear to be a mold cast from a fresh cadaver". The belly reveals the deformities typically occurring in the hours after death has occurred, in a subject who was in good health and must have died suddenly.

[14] Underneath the poor 18th- to 19th-century overpainting, the polychrome was discovered during an intervention in 1963 by the Gabinetto di Restauro della Soprintendenza at that time at the Galleries in Florence, under the direction of Umberto Baldini. A delicate cleaning of the work, including removal of the remaining lampblack and of the different retouchings, was carried out prior to the display of 1999. On recent restoration work, see Schleicher, 2000.

[15] See Lisner, 2000, pp. 31-68, synthesis and development of previous contributions by the same author over a thirty-six-year period.

[16] In 1513, Bichielli was appointed the patronage of the third chapel to the right, whereupon he dedicated it to Saint "Nicolao" of Tolentino and had an impressive altar made, the work of Nanni Unghero perhaps to a design by Baccio d'Agnolo (attribution by Alessandro Cecchi), with a wooden statue of the saint by Nanni himself and painting by Franciabigio; he died in 1518. See A. Cecchi, in *L'Officina*..., 1996, pp. 180-18, no. 52.

[17] "Innumerable other things", Condivi reported, "which are not to be seen and which would take time to describe", some of which he gave to private citizens out of friendship and generosity (Condivi, *The Life of Michelangelo* [1553], 2006 ed., p. 90).

[18] The attribution of the piece, owned by G. Gallino (Turin), is by Giancarlo Gentilini, with the support, among others, of Umberto Baldini and Luciano Bellosi. See the catalogue for the exhibition held at the Horne Museum, *Proposta*..., 2004.

[19] See Baldini, 2004 and Fioravanti, 2004.

[20] Bernabei, Gulisano, 2004. The artist's knowledge of human anatomy is judged to be mature and coherent in his reproduction of the corpse of a man aged between twenty and thirty, who had been dead at least a day.

[21] Gentilini, 2004, p. 25.

[22] Bellosi, 2004, pp. 33-39.

[23] *Appendice III. Una nuova famiglia di crocifissi fiorentini*, in *Proposta*..., 2004, pp. 77-87.

[24] 42.7 x 42.7 cm, the proportions of a perfect *homo ad circulum*. The polychrome consists in brownish flesh (probably modified) with blood trickling and chestnut-coloured hair. I wish to thank the property for having made the images available to me, and Andrew Butterfield for having shared his considerations. Critical debate continues, especially as concerns oral communications, and cannot be said to be settled as yet.

[25] My opinion is that despite the very high quality of the work, the reliefs in the polychrome wooden frame for the *Doni Tondo* in the Uffizi Gallery cannot be attributed to Michelangelo, which A. Cecchi (1987, p. 435) suggested were designed by Michelangelo but probably carved by Marco and Francesco del Tasso.

[26] See among the most recent episodes restoration of the polychrome wooden *Crucifix* in Badia a Passignano, published in *Il Crocifisso di Badia a Passignano*..., 2004.

[27] The creation of artistic objects made of ephemeral or short-lived material such as ice, sugar and butter as rather widespread in court banquets in this period of time. As for Piero, to whom by using the expression "come giovane" Condivi attributed the carelessness that the nickname "il Fatuo" (the Fatuous one) would seem to assign, was twenty-two years and had been married for four; therefore, it is difficult to imagine that he acted out of mere amusement. The snow statue may have been a small-scale reproduction of the marble *Hercules* which the sculptor was executing at the time, and ended up in France.

[28] Condivi, 1553, 1998 ed., pp. 14, XXI.

[29] Condivi, *The Life of Michelangelo* (1553), 2006 ed., p. 17.

[30] As concerns Michelangelo's premonitions, his fear of omens and his anxiety related to personal behaviour, family, city politics, especially see the essay by Spini, 1999, pp. 7-55.

[31] These were the words of the clergyman *ser* Amadeo in the famed letter to his brother the sculptor Adriano Fiorentino in October 1494 where Michelangelo is referred to as the "sculptor of the garden". Michelangelo had received 30 ducats from Piero as a down payment for a work he never executed, telling his father in 1497 that Piero had not kept his promises (*Il Carteggio*..., 1965-1983, I, p. 4, no. III) and gave it back in March 1498 (Hatfield, 2002, pp. 7-8).

[32] Giovan Francesco had been the mayor (*podestà*) in Florence in 1488. No doubt a man of humanistic culture, his favourite authors were Dante, Petrarch, Boccaccio. He had a very great collection of books, and he was also interested in ancient Bolognese memoirs. For a more complete profile, see Ciammitti, 1999, pp. 139-141.

[33] On sculpture at the time and how it was used by the Bentivoglio, see Perini, 1999.

[34] Elam, 1992a, p. 165.

[35] "... thus Cardiere's vision or diabolical delusion or divine prediction or powerful imagination, whatever it was, came true. This is truly remarkable and worth recording, and I have related it just as I heard it from Michelangelo himself"; Condivi, *The Life of Michelangelo* (1553), 2006 ed., p.18.

[36] See Holmes, 1907, pp. 235 and ff.; Longhi, 1940, 1956 ed., and Idem 1958; p. 61; Fiocco, 1937, p. 173 and Idem, 1941-1942, p. 7; Marongiu, 2000.

[37] Condivi, *The Life of Michelangelo* (1553), 2006 ed., p. 19.

[38] Precious testimony consisted in the manuscript of the Dominican from Bologna Leandro Alberti, who after having taken the tunic in 1495, in 1535 recalled that the statues "divi Petroni, Proculi et alteris Angeli" were the work of Michelangelo. The Dominican Ludovico da Prelormo agreed with him in his Memorie, halfway through the 16th century, providing interesting specifications. The two sources were published in 1875, so that the *Saint*

Proculus was not introduced into the artistic literature until later (cf. Emiliani, 1999, pp. 127-137).
[39] Tolnay, 1963; the statue of *Saint Proculus* was said to be located where the *Saint Florian* can now be viewed. The hypothesis was not accepted by S. Bottari (1964, pp. 61-62).
[40] The hypothesis that Michelangelo received a block of marble that had already been prepared seems neither verifiable nor necessary. Hirst, Dunkerton, 1994, p. 19.
[41] Emiliani, 1999, p. 131.
[42] G. Bonsanti, in *Giovinezza*..., 1999, p. 294.
[43] I agree with Bellosi's observations, 2004, p. 33.
[44] Bottari, 1964, pp. 74 and ff.
[45] Pope-Hennessy, 1963, 1966 ed., p. 306, followed by such authors as Emiliani, 1999, p. 130.
[46] Longhi, 1940, 1956 ed., p. 136, recently returned to in Emiliani, 1999, p. 132.
[47] Pini, 1999: "... there seems to be no record in Bologna of the memory of a Saint Proculus for the entire Middle Ages and until midway through the 11th century. The analysis began with [...] Vittricio di Rouen in his *De laude sanctorum* (396), and Paolino di Nola in a *Carmen* (492). [...] Proculus may not have been a second martyr, but an apposition of Agricola, defined <da Vittricio> *proculus* because far from his companion in martyrdom Vitale".
[48] G. Bonsanti, in *Giovinezza*..., 1999, p. 294.
[49] Longhi, 1958, confirmed by Emiliani, 1999, p. 132.
[50] See the *First Decan of Aries* as proposed by Marongiu, 2000.
[51] I am thinking of the marble *Saint Maurilius*, suggested to be the work of Paolo di Luca to the project attributed to Cosmé Tura, dated midway through the 15th century, in the Museum of the Cathedral in Ferrara. See the recent entry by R. Stemp in the catalogue for *Gli Este a Ferrara*..., 2004, no. 133, p. 353.
[52] Lisner, 1967, pp. 79-80.
[53] Cousin Francesco Buonarroti's son, who is said to have been away from Florence and busy in Bologna on 11 August 11 1495. See the "Cronologia ragionata...", in the catalogue *Giovinezza*..., 1999, p. 441.
[54] Condivi, 1553, 1998 ed., p. 17.
[55] The relationship often discussed between Michelangelo and Savonarola is solidly founded on the recollections of the artist himself as reported in Condivi: "he has always been very fond of him, and in his mind can still hear his strong voice" (Condivi, 1553, 1998 ed., p. 62). Also see Spini, 1964.
[56] For an overview of suggestions for identification, see Baldini, 1973, no. 10, p. 90. The most recent criticism includes the indication that the *gradivo Young Saint John* at the Museo Nazionale del Bargello in Florence, previously ascribed to Donatello and then shifted to Michelangelo by Parronchi (1960 and 1968), was confirmed to be by Francesco da Sangallo by B. Paolozzi Strozzi (entry in *L'Officina*..., 1996, pp. 366-367, no. 137, and dated 1520-1525), as had been proposed by Kauffmann (1931-1932, p. 4). As for the statue in the church of the Salvador in Úbeda in Spain, the studies carried out and now underway at the Opificio delle Pietre Dure are headed towards excluding the idea of its being a Michelangelesque autograph.
[57] Condivi, *The Life of Michelangelo* (1553), 2006 ed., p. 19.
[58] Vasari, 1550, is the only one to mention the room. Cf. Weil-Garris Brandt, 1999, p. 315.
[59] Condivi, 1553, 1998 ed., p. 17.
[60] Barolsky, 2001a.
[61] After careful reading of the sources and papers, this would seem to be the most likely hypothesis (cf. "Cronologia ragionata...", in *Giovinezza*..., 1999, p. 442); others believe that he was in a palace owned but not inhabited by Riario at the Cancelleria (cf., for instance, Hatfield, 2002, p. 2).
[62] Condivi, 1553, 1998 ed., p. XXI, note no. 7.
[63] The letter by Pico of 27 June 1496, addressed to his sister-in-law Isabella d'Este in Mantua. That was about the time of the stormy meeting between Michelangelo and the Milanese, who, as reported in *Il Carteggio*..., 1965-1983, I, 1965, pp. 354-355), rather than sell it back to author was willing to break it into "a hundred bits", perhaps irritated by Lorenzo de' Medici's criticism of him in his letters to the bankers and to Riario.
[64] K. Weil-Garris Brandt, "Sogni di un Cupido dormente smarrito", and entry by E.D. Schmidt, in *Giovinezza*..., 1999, pp. 315 and ff. According to the two authors 4 *spanne* would correspond to 92 cm, and not 80 as in Tolnay, 1943, p. 201 and in other writings; furthermore, the Methuen *Cupid* resembles the statue made of antique black marble at the Uffizi Gallery, which is believed to have been donated to Lorenzo the Magnificent by King Ferdinand of Aragon and brought to Naples by Giuliano da Sangallo. It is interesting to examine this piece of information alongside that – courtesy of James Methuen-Campbell – which speaks of his statue as having perhaps been painted black with tar until 1875, when the sulptor Boehm removed the paint without following the instructions of the then Lord Methuen, and damaged the marble.
[65] Giorgio Bonsanti expressed his favourable opinion as concerns a different "type" of sleeping cupid, much closer to the Child of the *Madonna of Bruges*, and presented the version at the Galleria Estense in Modena as a possible direct derivation from the Michelangelesque original by Prospero Sogari, viewed in Mantua (1985). But there are those who object that the putto could be a 19th-century reelaboration.

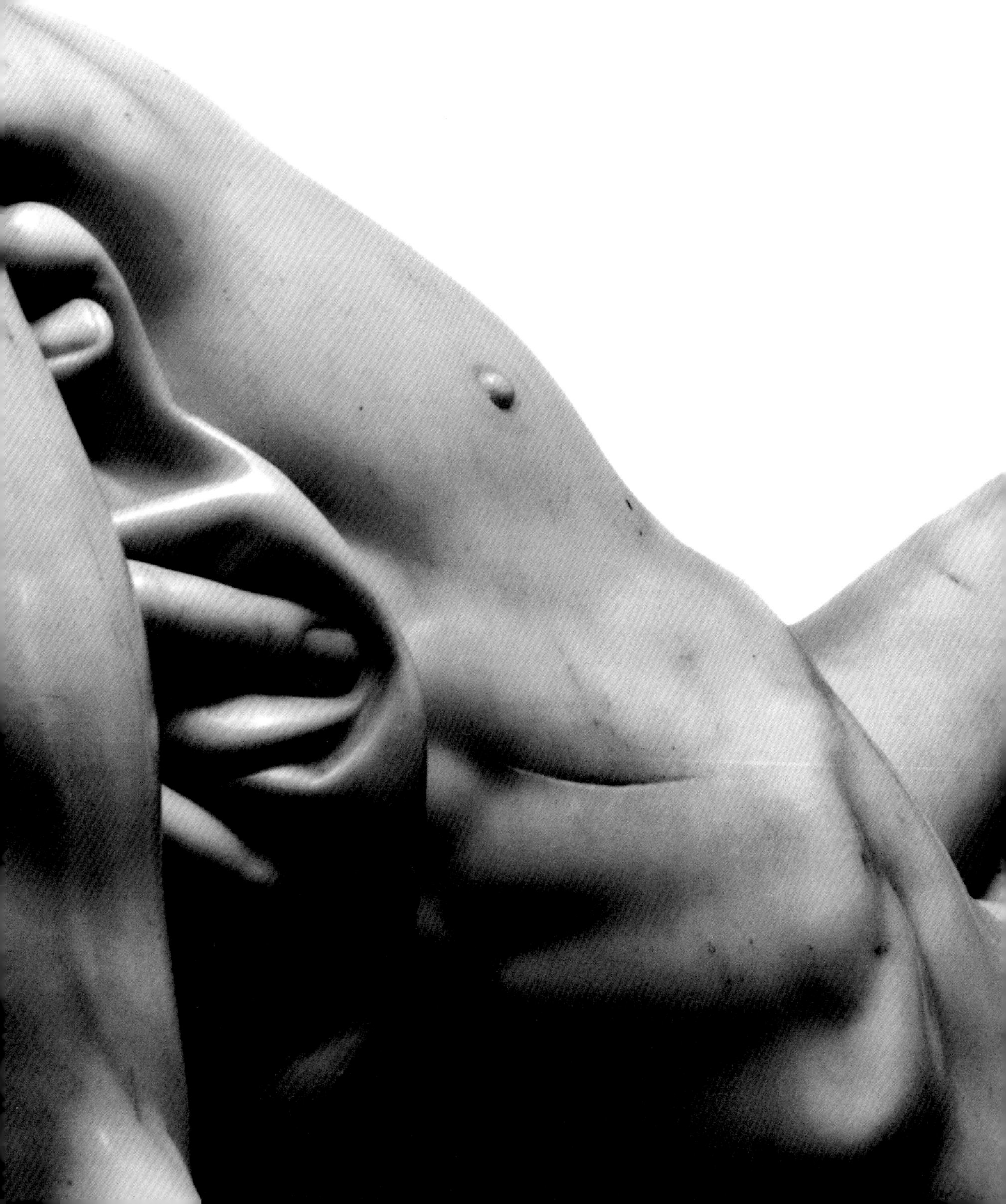

The first masterpieces in Rome

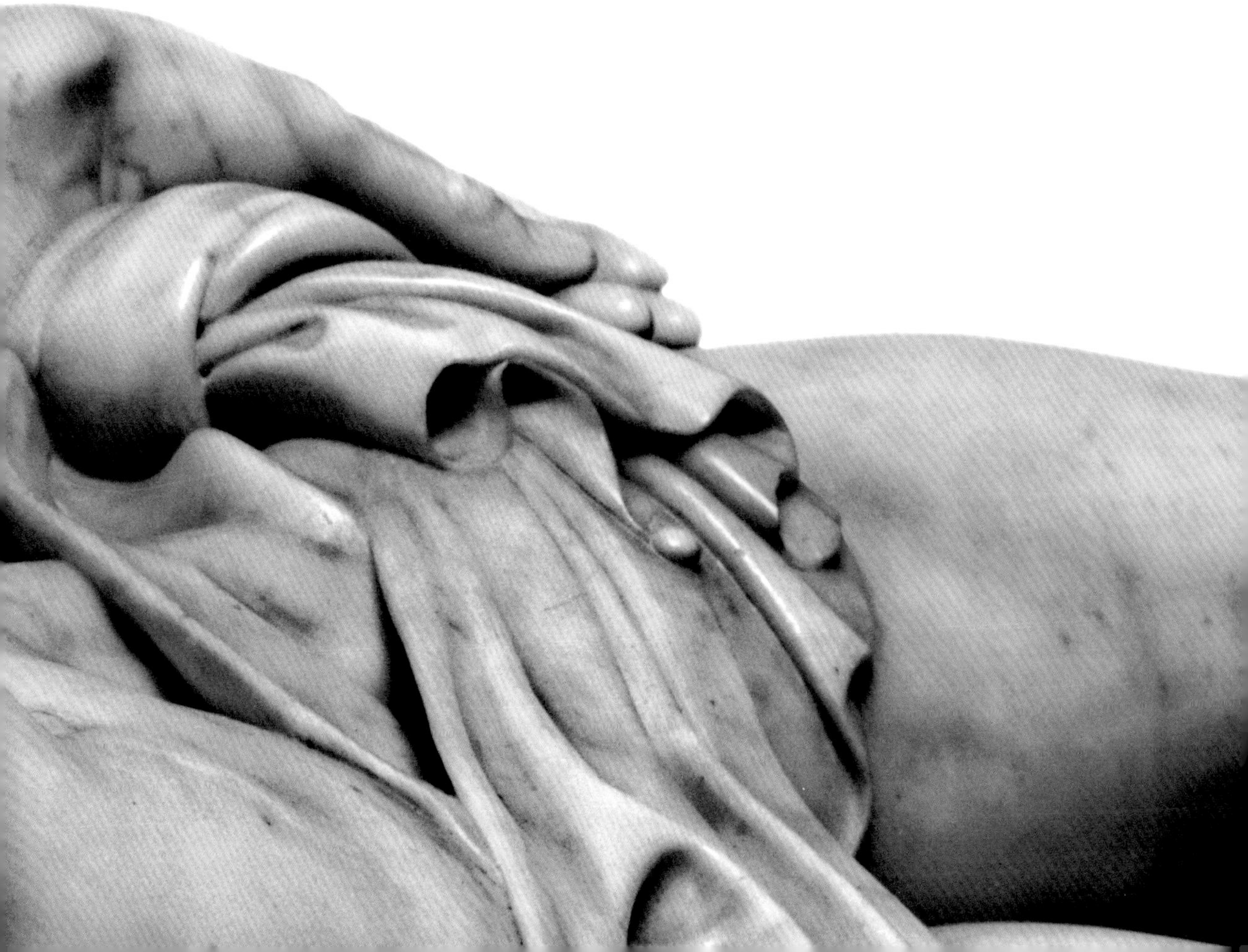

The *Bacchus*

Our reason for dwelling on the missing or, worse still, lost *Cupid* by the young Michelangelo is due to its importance – including the rapid rise in international gossip – in the artist's life: it took him to Rome where he was able to study the "Antique"; because of it his name became famous in various courts on the peninsula. It also secured the artist to the world of the cardinals and the community of the Florentine bankers in Rome, where power, culture and wealth all resided.
Early in July 1496, Michelangelo had already purchased a block of marble large enough to make a life-sized figure, probably the *Bacchus*. Michelangelo had a young helper with him, Piero d'Argenta from Ferrara, who has been identified by some of the critics as the painter called "Maestro della Madonna di Manchester", the author of modest paintings in Michelangelesque style (whose name-piece, the Madonna of Manchester, can now be removed, however, as this work has solidly been ascribed to Michelangelo).
A year later, on 1 July 1497, Michelangelo had finished with his "labour" for Cardinal Riario and was waiting to be paid the balance, which arrived two days later – an impressive one hundred fifty gold fiorini d'oro larghi without counting reimbursement for expenses. Both Michelangelo and Piero were paid through the bank of the Florentines Balducci, Baldassarre and Giovanni, who it seems were associated with Galli.[1] For reasons that are still unknown, Cardinal Riario never collected his marble statue of the *Bacchus*: after it was – in all probability – carved in the Galli home,[2] it stayed there for more than seventy years, before arriving at the Uffizi in Florence as one of Francesco I de' Medici's acquisitions.
Of the *Bacchu*s, Vasari wrote, "[i]t is clear that here Michelangelo wanted a striking combination in the limbs, and especially the male slenderness of a youth together with a female fleshiness and rotundity – a splendid thing that showed how he surpassed all previous modern sculptors".[3] The androgyny that Vasari so appreciated is confirmed by the observations of experts on anatomy, who point out the abundance of subcutaneous "panniculus adiposus" incompatible with the structure of the average male body. Moreover, the tenderness of the figure's shape had since antiquity been considered one of the lascivious god of wine's attributes, and in Condivi's words Michelangelo made his own version so that "[his] form and appearance correspond[ed] in every particular to the intention of the writers of antiquity".[4]
A naked young Bacchus is portrayed as he lurches forwards with the unsteadiness of a drunken man finding it difficult to keep his balance. With his right hand he raises a cup, with his left he clasps to himself a panther skin from which, like a loosened purse, two large bunches of grapes tumble out. A child-satyr nibbles on them and laughs, ready to whisk them away from the god's uncertain hold as he unknowingly moves through a wooded plain, briefly alluded to by the tree stump on which the satyr is sitting and the uneven rocky trail. The expression on the figure's full, sensual face bears the kind of focus that comes with drunkenness, intent as it is on the cup. The wavy hair interwoven with a sturdy wreath of vine leaves and grapes, and many other details in the group, like the satyr's tightly-massed curls and goatskin, or the loose layers of animal skin, allude to a mimetic carnality. Just as the inclination of the figure nearly throws the body off-balance, the twist of the torso introduces a further reason for instability, and accompanies the forwards movement of the arm with the cup, and a symmetrical drawing backward of the left shoulder, from which the sequence including the arm brought backward, the hand with the animal skin and grapes all the way to the avid little satyr, begins, its purpose being to resolve with circular dynamism the side and back views of the group. The two formal themes of utmost originality, Bacchus's sought-after physical sweetness, and the group's multiple angles, were soon praised by the fine connoisseur of sculpture Francesco Bocchi, appraiser of the "delicate, but all the same gently nimble body, with much beauty from every angle, requiring unprecedented skill".[5]
While the marble is smooth and polished in the front view, there are rougher areas on the side and back, which show signs of the drill (or pointed chisel) between the left thigh and the panther skin.

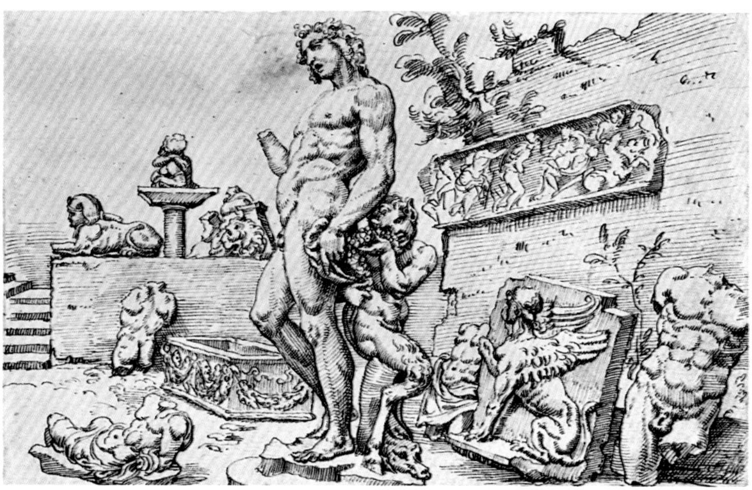

Maarten van Heemskerk, *Michelangelo's Bacchus in the Garden of Jacopo Galli's House* Berlin, Kupferstichkabinett

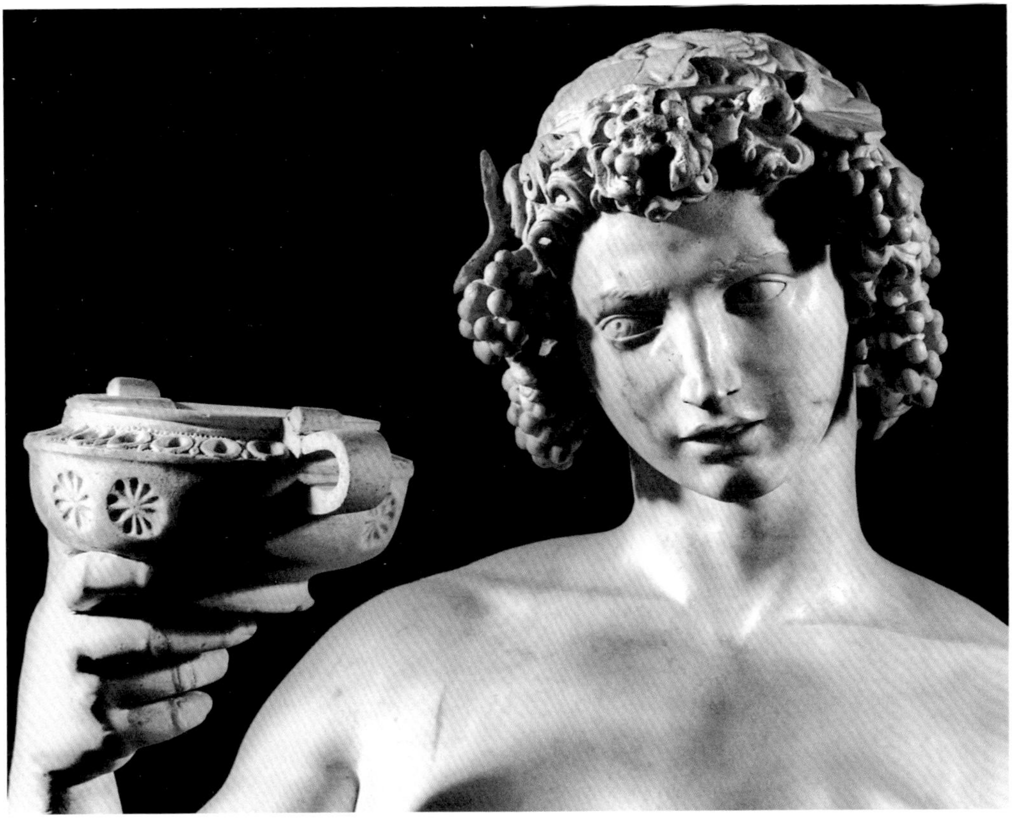

Michelangelo, *Bacchus*
The god's gaze stops short, replete with desire, on the cup of wine
Florence, Museo Nazionale del Bargello

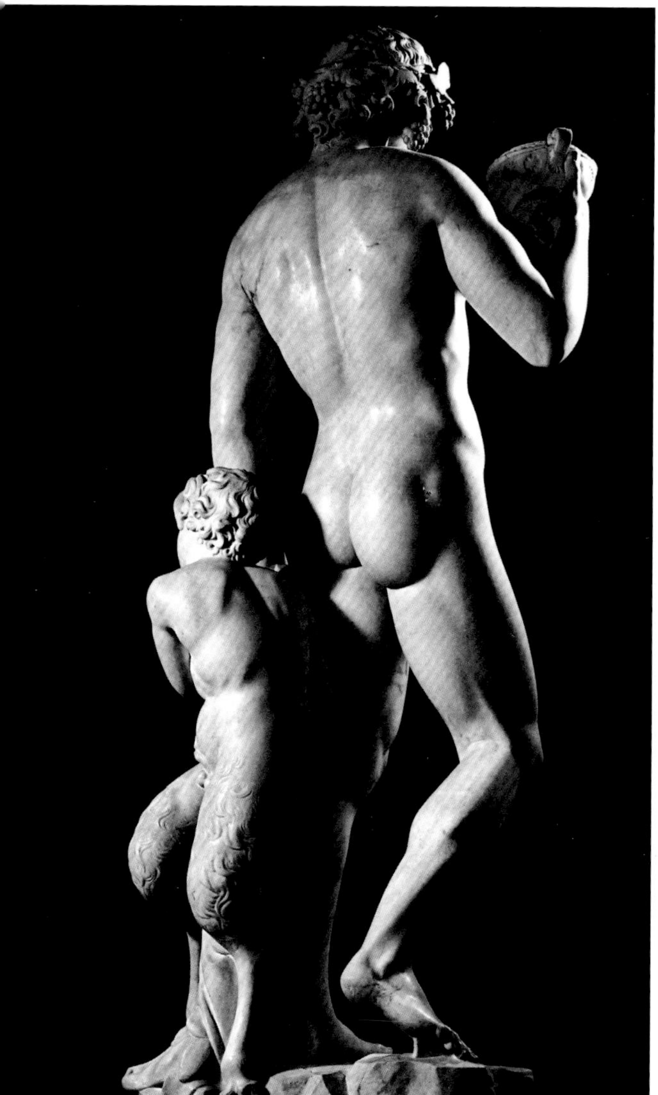

Michelangelo, *Bacchus*.
The effeminate roundness of the body had already been noted by 16th-century commentators
Florence, Museo Nazionale del Bargello

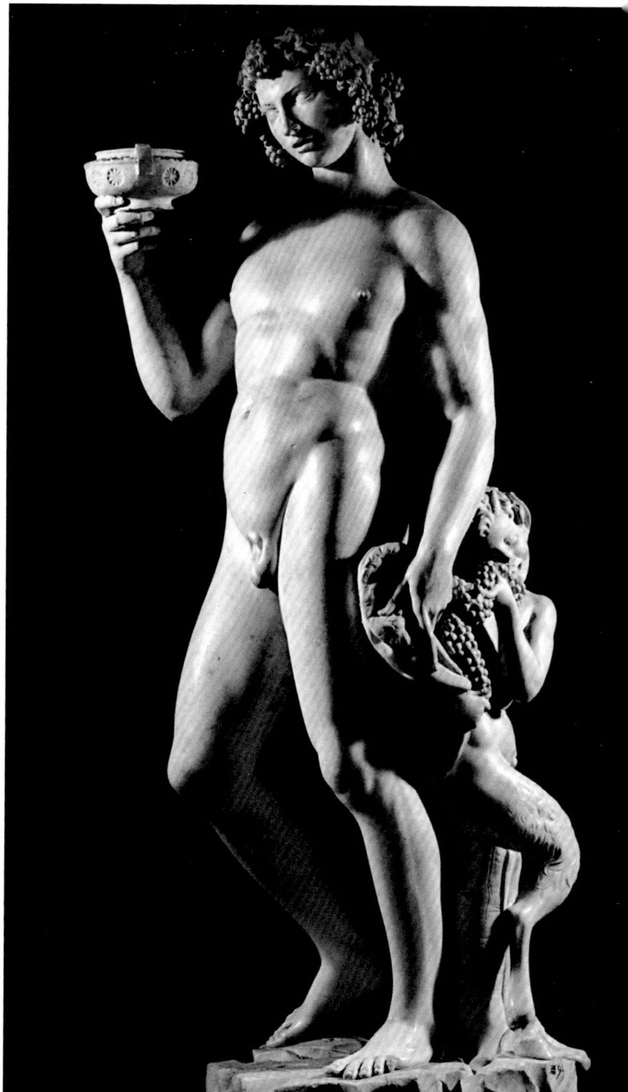

Michelangelo, *Bacchus*. The drunk god's unsteady movement causes the forwards imbalance of the sensual figure, while the child-satyr laughs as he nibbles on the grapes that tumble out of the soft animal skin
Florence, Museo Nazionale del Bargello

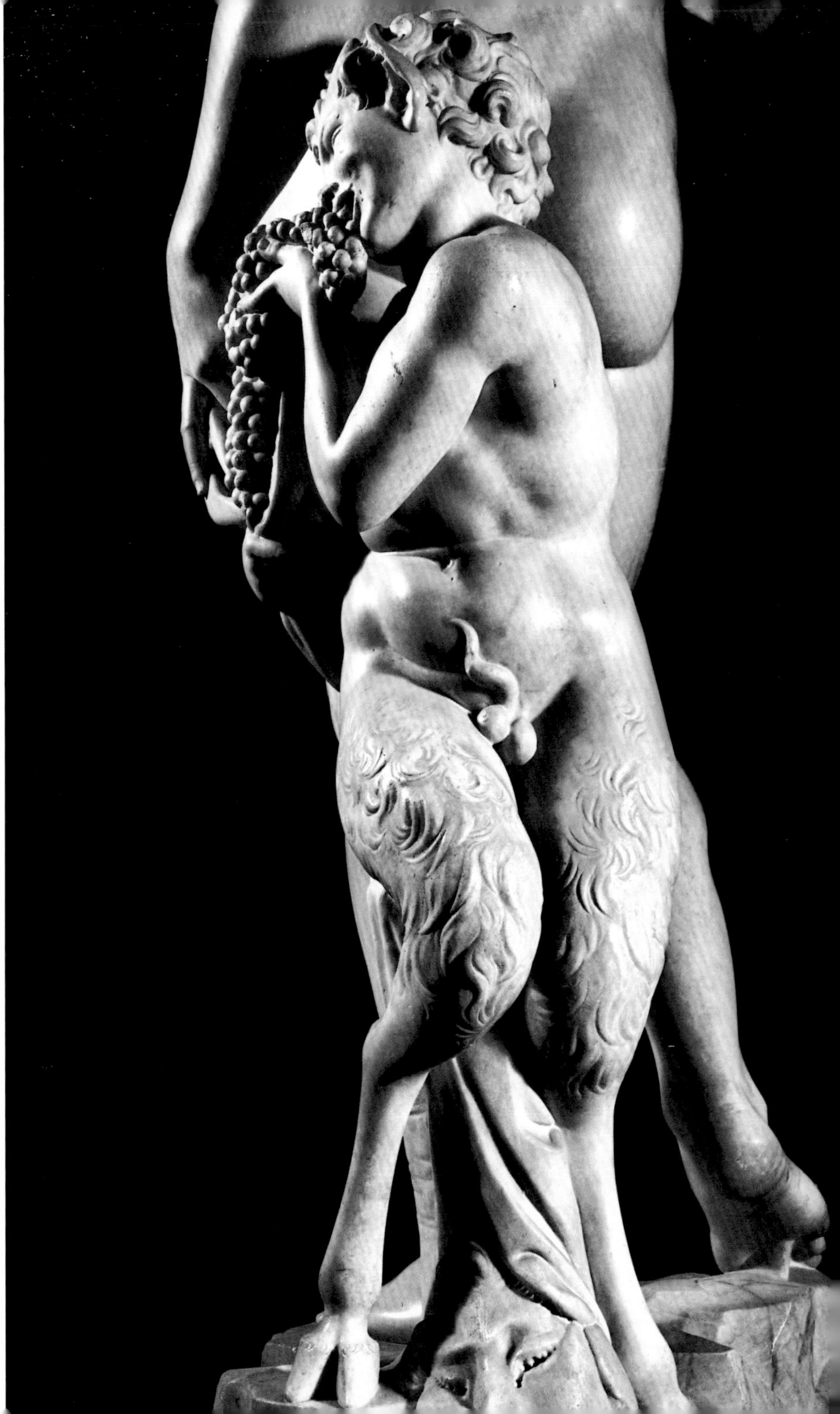

Michelangelo, *Bacchus*,
detail of child-satyr
whose torso boldly twists
above the hips
Florence, Museo Nazionale
del Bargello

Although a specific classical prototype for the *Bacchus* has never been identified[6] – the artist's challenge of antique art was pushed to the limit of a manipulation which was never made explicit, but was implied by the details and circumstances. From the vestibule in the Galli home, where the statue was located in 1505, it was transferred to the garden and placed amidst the ancient pieces in the collection; torsos, sarcophagi, reliefs, proven by a famous drawing made by Maarten van Heemskerk (1532-1535), in which he misunderstood or reinterpreted the tree stump attributing to it the face of an animal.[7] Despite its pagan nudity, the sculpture was saved from the Sack of Rome in 1527. Contributing to the statue's aura of antiquity were the "archaeological" details: the missing right hand (invented)[8] and penis of the god, the damage to the satyr's genitalia, damage which it is believed was deliberately produced by the sculptor to imitate "the intentional mutilations of pagan statues",[9] so that, not surprisingly, in the *Codex Cantabrigensis* (1550-1556), the label for the drawing of the *Bacchus* reads that it is an excavated relic.[10] The illusion of antiquity (encouraged more by the statue's owners than by Michelangelo) did not, however, deceive the Portuguese painter Francisco de Hollanda who, upon seeing the *Bacchus* in 1548, classified it as a modern sculpture founded on the criteria of a true connoisseur.[11]

Condivi's comment, dated between 1550 and 1553, reflected Michelangelo's desire – the Council of Trent had been hard at work for more than five years – to moralize the group by seeing it as a kind of warning: that he who is "overcome" by his love of drink, and gives in to the "senses" and to his "appetites", will ultimately lose his life, the same way the gluttonous feline loses its skin.

The *Young Archer*

Michelangelo also sculpted an *Apollo* for Jacopo Galli, which Ulisse Aldrovandi saw in around 1550: "a life-sized naked Apollo with quiver and arrows to the side and a vase at this feet: it is a work by the hand of Michael Angelo".[12] It was probably the same statue that was a part of the estate inherited by Galli Giuliano and Paolo, and that Condivi referred to as "Cupidine" (1553), Benedetto Varchi as "God of love" (1564) and Vasari as a life-sized "Cupid of marble" (1568).

It has been suggested that a connection can be made between the *Young Archer* in New York, a problematic work beginning with its autograph, and that period of time, or just before, and Galli's patronage.

The mutilated marble statue of a *Young Archer* (whose identity has ranged from Apollo to Cupid to Ganymede)[13] has an ancient and illustrious provenance: the Borghese collections, where evidence for the work can be found in the 17th and 18th centuries. Research is currently being carried out on the idea that Cardinal Scipione Borghese acquired the Galli collection. The statue went from the Borghese to Stefano Bardini, and from him to the architect Stanford White, who, in 1905, placed the statue in the atrium of his home on Fifth Avenue, New York, now the Cultural Services of the French Embassy. The work is a pastiche reminiscent of antique style mounted on a triangular base, and crowns a fountain designed by White. After Alessandro Parronchi went back to the idea of a Michelangelesque attribution, ventilated by Bardini, identifying it as being the Galli *Apollo/Cupid*, Kathleen Weil-Garris Brandt submitted it again on the basis of new ideas of a technical and critical nature, as well as documentary findings.[14] After some lively debate, some of which negative, and two exhibitions (Florence in 1999-2000, Paris in 2000),[15] a contribution of crucial importance emerged from the appearance on the market and subsequent publication of a drawing that reveals the stages in which the statue was developed, thus, as we shall see, reinforcing the attribution to Michelangelo.[16]

The *Archer* has a slender body with very elongated proportions; the fact that his legs are missing from the knees down limits the viewer's perception, while the way the statue is currently mounted changes the tilt of the pose, originally off-balance in a backward direction. A leftover fragment near the left leg might be interpreted as a piece of the "vase" described by Aldrovandi. The movement of the missing arms, in the act of taking an arrow from the quiver shaped like an animal's

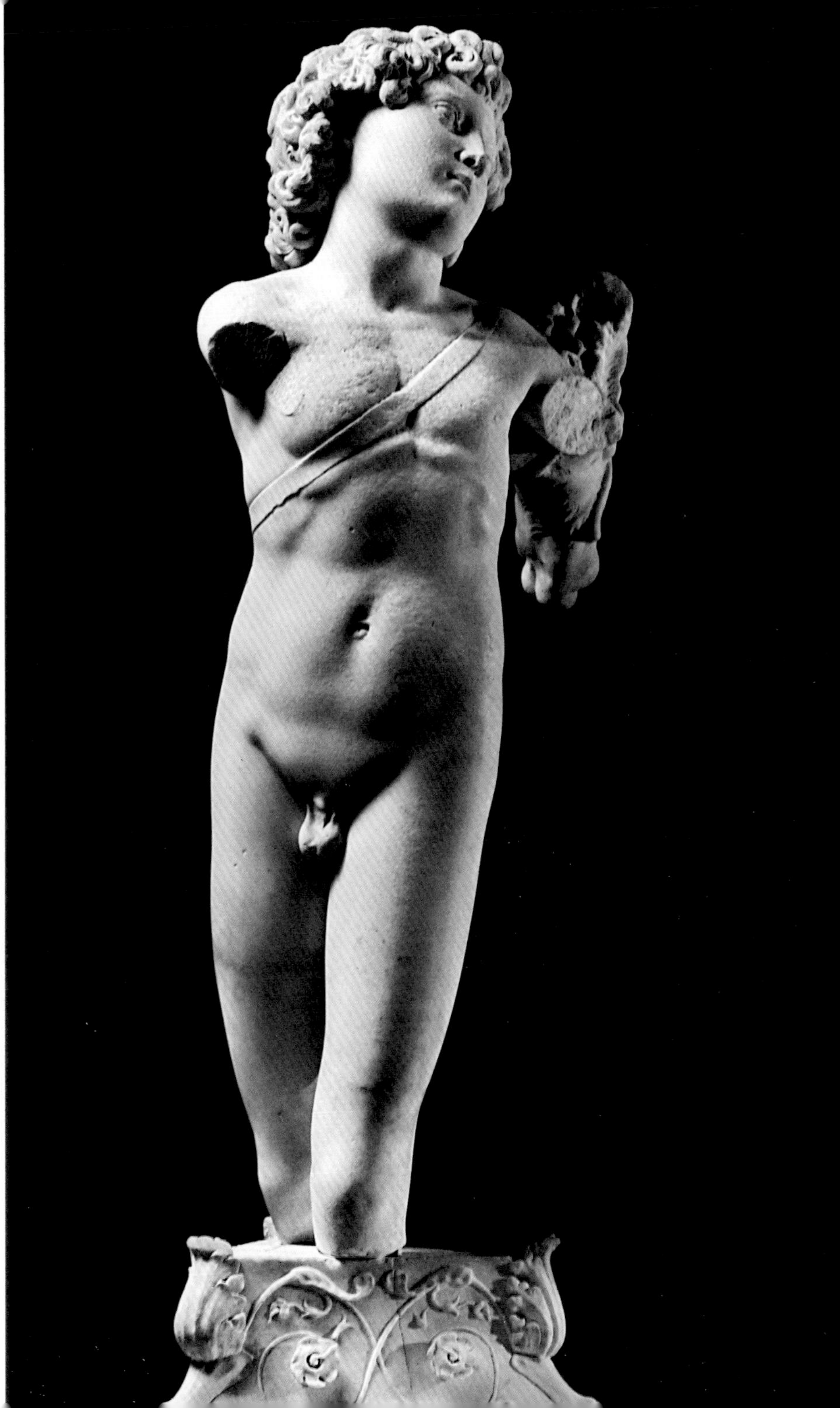

Michelangelo, *Young Archer*
Now mutilated and mounted on a base that is not the original one, the adolescent at one time extracted an arrow from his quiver
New York, Cultural Services of the French Embassy

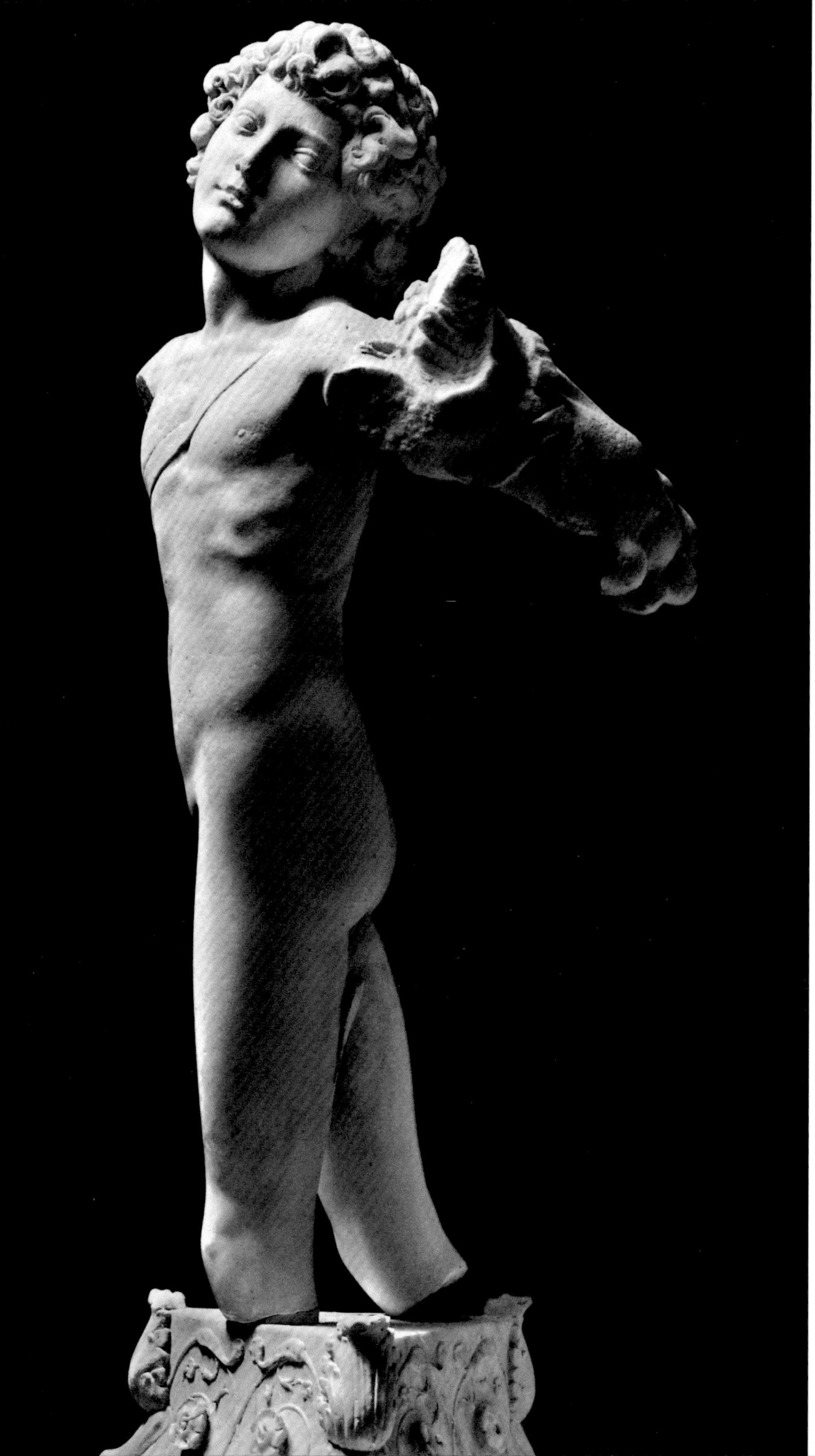

Michelangelo, *Young Archer*
His curly head is distinct from the slender body tipped backwards
New York, Cultural Services of the French Embassy

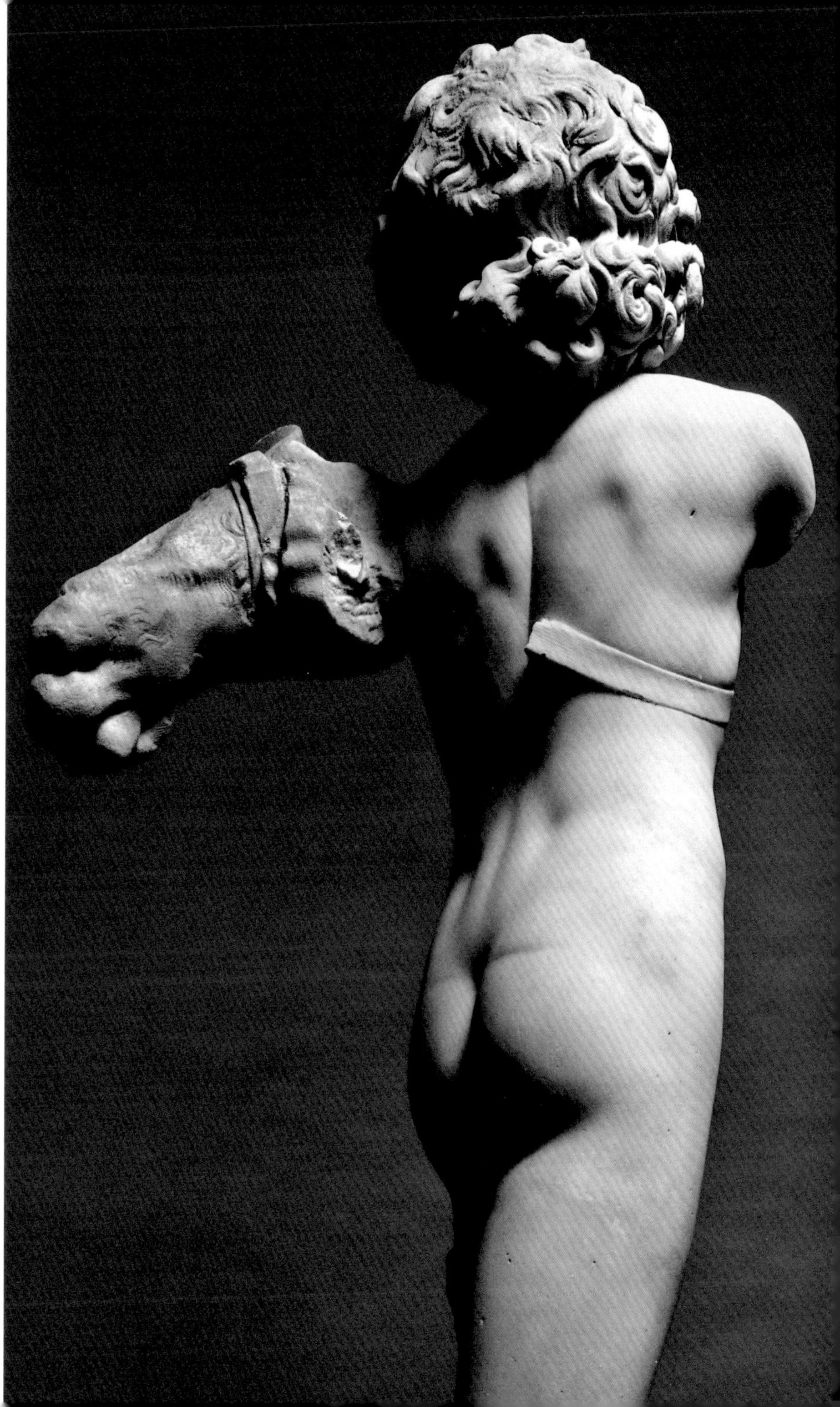

Michelangelo, *Young Archer*
The quiver tied to the baldric
pressing the soft body
is shaped like an animals's
paw and foreleg
New York, Cultural Services
of the French Embassy

paw and foreleg, accompanies the twisting of the adolescent torso, and culminates with the oblique rotation of the upturned head. There is some lack of harmony in the relationship between the full face under the cap of compact curls and the figure's slender torso. Signs of erosion due to atmospheric agents and, perhaps, traces of later interference have altered the face, especially on the right side. The connection between this work and the nude bronze statues by Bertoldo might explain the exotic and primordial suggestions, for instance, the protruding leonine quiver, as well as an interest in the adolescent body – with several awkward passages – in disequilibrium. But some of the features of the image, which are obviously a nod to antiquity, point to Michelangelo's juvenalia: the tightly-massed curls in a compact dome reminiscent of the hair of the Bolognese *Angel,* the modelling of the torso, which undulates with increasingly uneven reliefs that visualize the tender anatomical structure as it accompanies the rotating movement, not unlike what can be seen in the wooden *Crucifix.* The way the baldric tightly encircles the soft flesh, from which it had to be distinguished halfway up the figure's back, will again be seen in the straps and ribbons the artist uses to fasten his statues, beginning with the colossal *David.* By looking at the *Young Archer* from up close, touching it in the Conservation Laboratory of the Metropolitan Museum in 1997,[17] and repeating the experience on the occasion of the exhibition *Giovinezza di Michelangelo* held in Florence in 1999-2000, I became convinced that attribution of the work to a young Michelangelo should not simply be cast aside, but rather required very close critical assessment. Indeed, the sculpture, although inadroitly discontinuous, reveals passages of high-quality invention and successful technique, whose consonance with episodes in the artist's variegated youthful corpus of works – and with those alone – is not to be underestimated.

Joannides' discovery and subsequent publication of a drawing by one of Michelangelo's draughtsmen, unidentified, provides some interesting elements. The *recto* of the sheet shows four studies for or perhaps after the archer from different angles.[18] The most finished of the four depicts the figure from the front, standing, with his arms pulled backwards towards the left shoulder: the clearly visible baldric suggests that there's a quiver. A back view features a variation: the youth's left leg is bent and perhaps broken (like in ancient statuary), his knee rests on a large vase, the quiver is just outlined as though it were a large protruding object. In each of the studies the *Archer*'s body is a more mature one, muscular and proudly structured in *contrapposti* as compared to the Manhattan marble, despite the fact that the same figure is represented. The unidentified draughtsman may thus have heightened the master's original studies through his own interpretation, providing them with a more mature figure. Alternatively, Michelangelo may have translated his original plan into a more elongated, slender marble version, after certain models from Hellenistic statuary,[19] the idea being to make it radiate an adolescent aura. One thing is for sure: whatever the future critical developments may be, the *Young Archer* in New York cannot be separated from the corpus of Michelangelesque statuary.

The Vatican *Pietà*

The relationship between Michelangelo and the Balducci-Galli bank, which grew closer when the artist opened his own "bank account" some time before 23 March 1497, offers a richer historical scenario in terms of the circumstances surrounding some of the artist's most important early commissions. Light is also shed on the genesis of what is considered to be his masterpiece, the group referred to as the Vatican *Pietà*: in November 1497, the French cardinal Jean de Bilhères-Lagraulas deposited 133 and 1/3 "fiorini di Reno" (perhaps a third of the agreed upon total of 500) in the artist's account in view of the future purchase and working of the marble, while the actual contract was not drafted until 27 August 1498; the contract was a private one between the influential cardinal of Santa Sabina (previously a diplomat at the service of Louis XI, abbot of Saint-Denis, Charles VIII's ambassador to the court of Pope Alexander VI) and Jacopo Galli, who wrote the document and declared himself to be the sculptor's guarantor.[20]

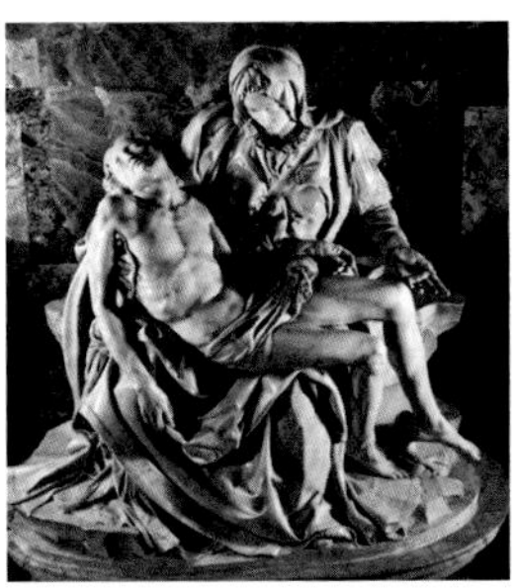

Michelangelo, *Pietà*,
view from above
Vatican City, Saint Peter's,
Pietà Chapel

p. 59
Michelangelo, *Pietà*, The Virgin sits on the rock of Golgotha and holds the Son's body in her lap
Vatican City, Saint Peter's

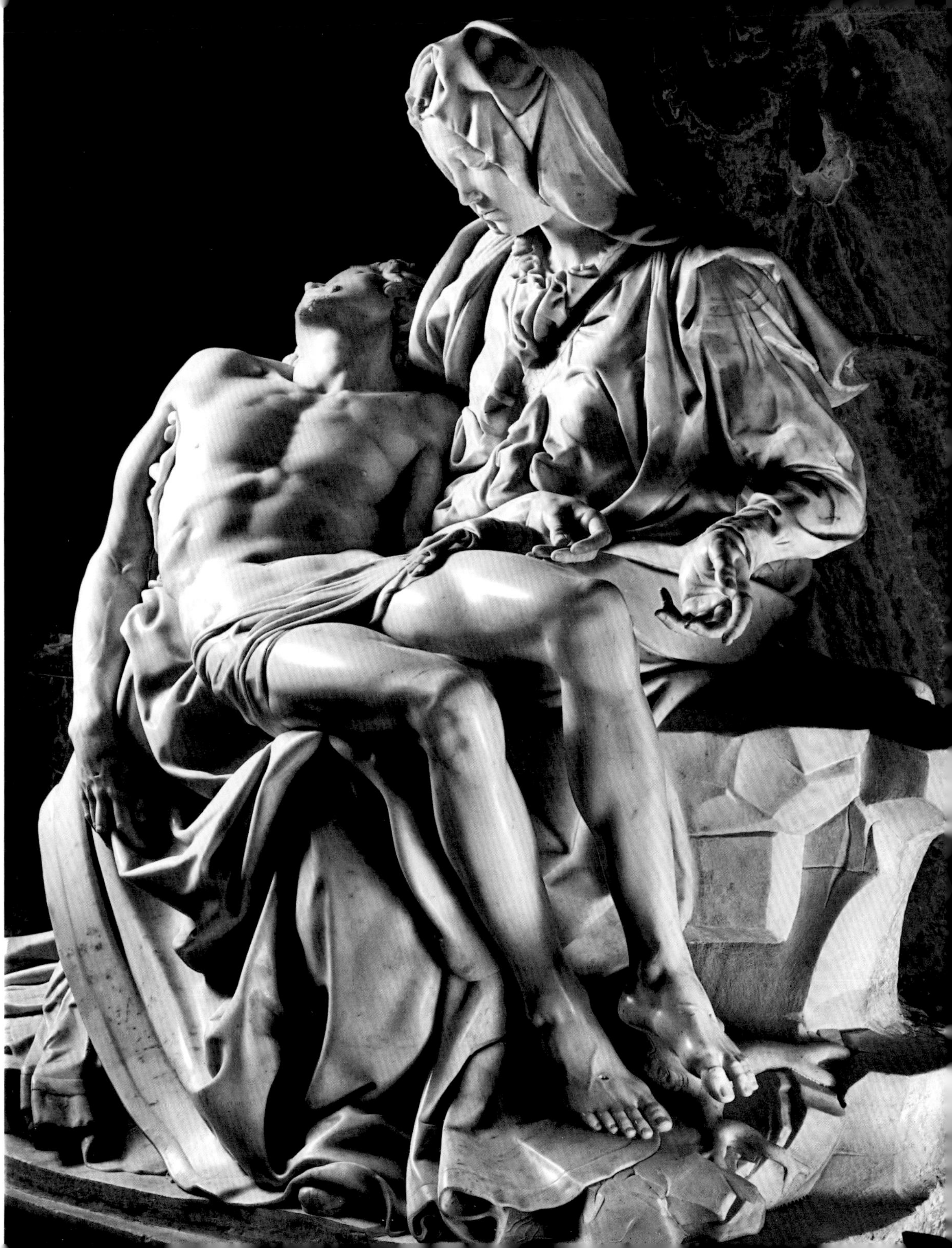

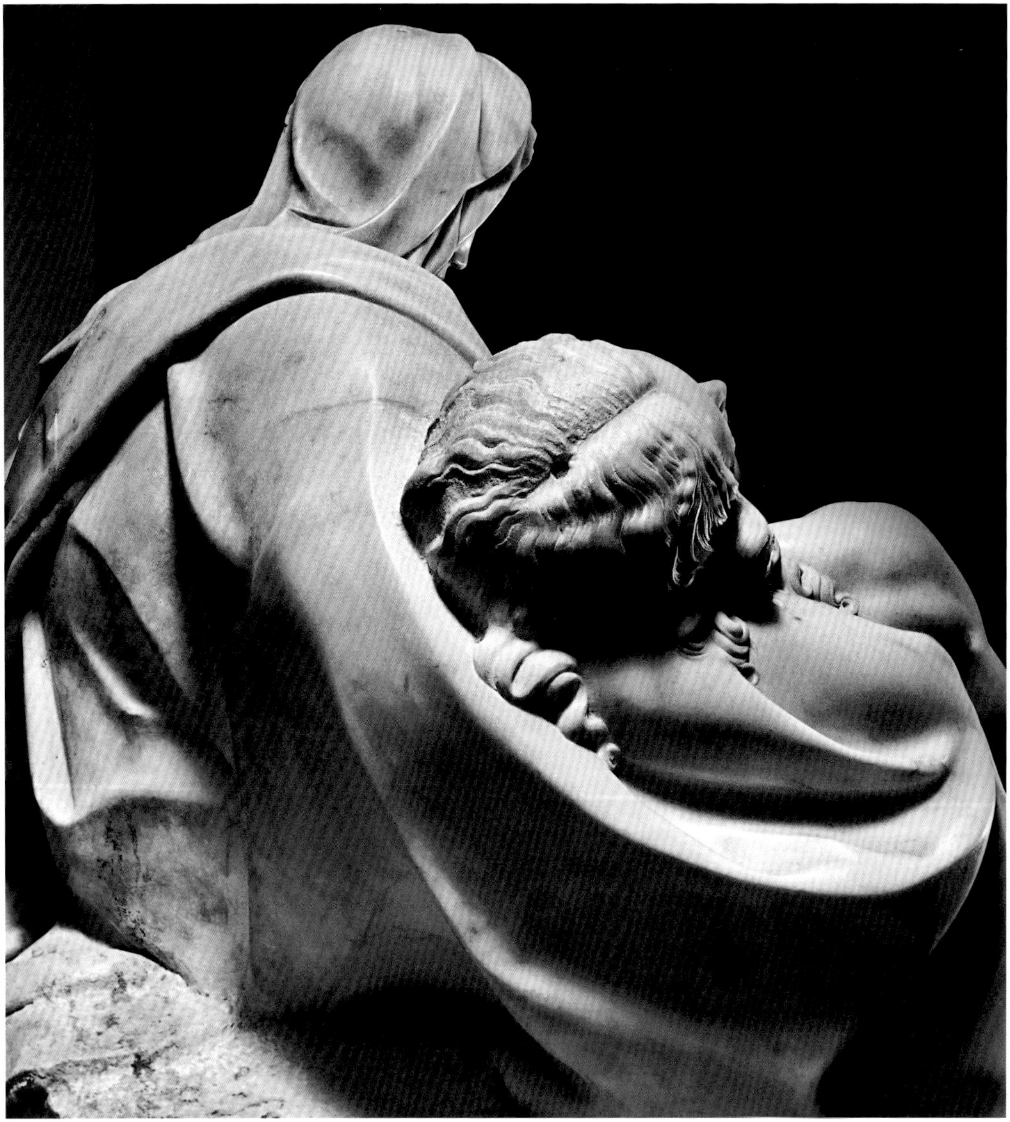

Michelangelo, *Pietà*,
back view detail of the simple,
monumental
fold in the Virgin's cloak
Vatican City, Saint Peter's

p. 61
Michelangelo, *Pietà*, detail
of the Virgin's profile, resonant
with Florentine recollections,
above the garment's
close-knit ruffle
Vatican City, Saint Peter's

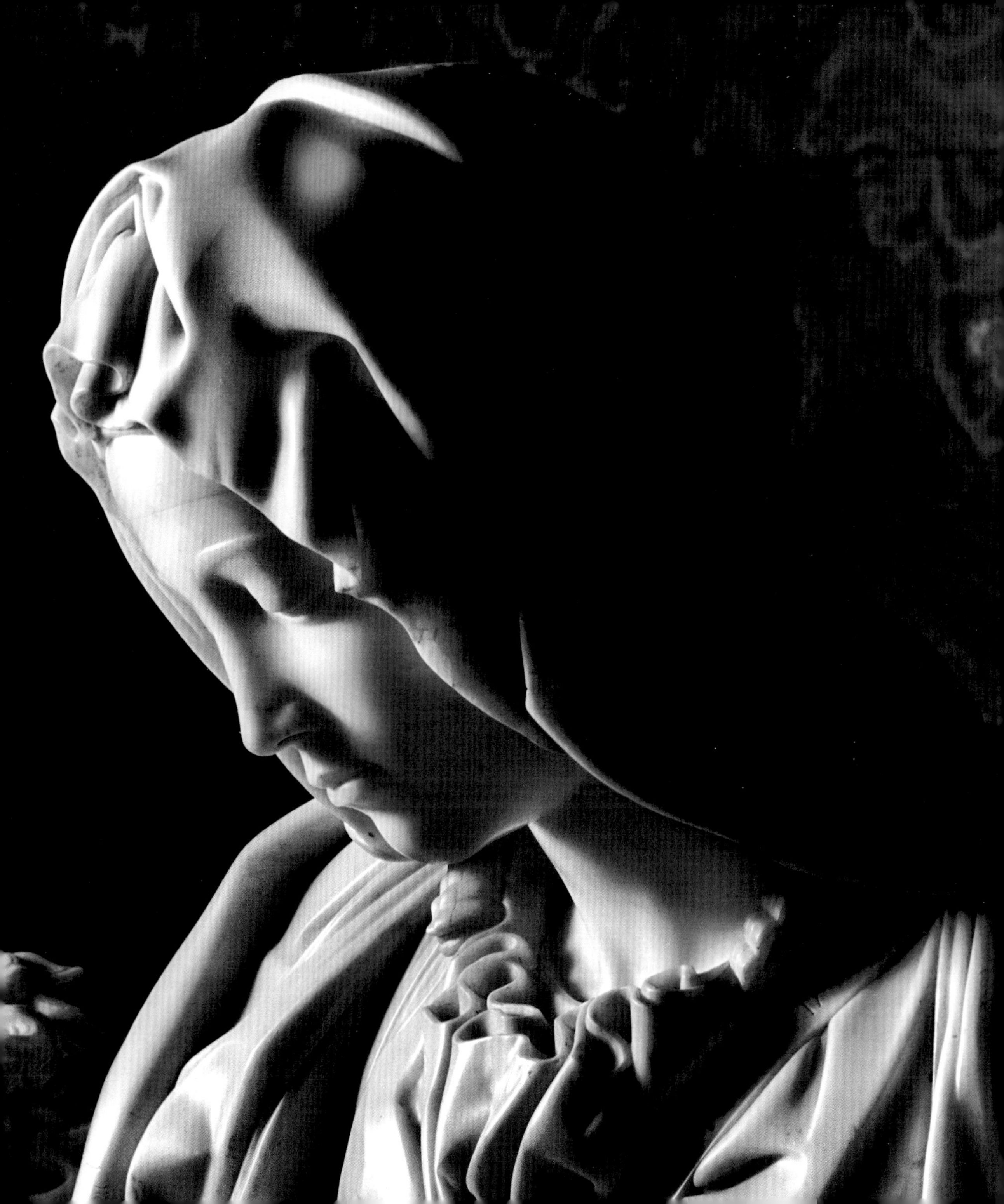

With the advance payment he had received, and preceded by a recommendation from the cardinal to the Anziani of Lucca, Michelangelo left for Carrara, where he personally supervised the extraction of a block of white Apuan marble of the finest quality and probably blocked out the piece right there on site before it was shipped.[21] It was also an opportunity for the artist to pass through Florence.

Carving of the *Pietà* had already been completed when, on 3 July 1500, the executor of the cardinal's will, who had in the meantime died, deposited the outstanding balance in Michelangelo's bank account: the year to complete the work as stated in the contract had not been long enough for the artist to execute that "marble *pietà* in the round",[22] which would eventually become one of the greatest symbols of Western artistic civilization.

It is impossible to approach the Vatican *Pietà* without hearing Giorgio Vasari's words in the 1550 edition of his *Lives* echoing with amazement, reverence and emotion as if it were the first time he had set eyes upon it: "No artist or sculptor, however gifted, could hope to surpass the design and grace of that figure; nor, however hard he toiled, could he cut and polish the marble with the skill of Michelangelo, for the work displays all the worth and power of sculpture. Among its many beauties (apart from the wonderful drapery) is the figure of Christ where the beauty of the limb and the moulding of the body are such that no one could hope to see such a marvellous nude figure, or a dead man that looked so dead. The lovely expression of the head, the harmony of the muscles in arms, legs and body, and the delicate tracing of veins and arteries leave one astounded that an artist's hand could make something so admirable and inspired in such a short time; for it is certainly a miracle that what was once a formless stone should ever be brought to that perfection which Nature can hardly attain in the flesh".[23]

For once, the biographer, who goes on to speak of the artist's "great effort" as well as his "love" for the work, is so bewildered and amazed at the sight of the masterpiece that while he briefly mentions parts of it, he forgets to describe it in full.

In comparison, Condivi is brief but descriptive, calling the group the "statue of Our Lady" who is "seated on the rock in which the cross was fixed, with her dead Son across her lap".[24]

What is immediately evident in the Michelangelesque group is in fact the iconography of the dead Christ on the Madonna's knees, rare in Italy but common beyond the Alps, to the extent that the Germans have a composite word for it: *Vesperbild*, a serotine image, because of the gloomy sadness it calls forth, and no doubt requested by the patron, whose meditation must have been familiar with that essential image of death and pain, "elaborated in Northern Europe in the Rhineland's atmosphere of mysticism and *devotio moderna*",[25] whereas in the Italian tradition it was more often staged as the choral event of the *Lamentation over the Dead Christ*, which included the presence of John, Mary Magdalene, the Pious Women, Nicodemus or Joseph of Arimathea, on occasion also some of the apostles.

From that Apuan block of marble Michelangelo sculpted the pyramidal composition, transferring to sculpture studies that Leonardo was conducting in paintings such as the *Virgin of the Rocks* and, later on, in compositions devoted to the *Virgin and Child with Saint Anne*, which would deeply impress Raphael in Florence in the first decade of the century. From the head of the Madonna, through the sequence of layers and cascading of the cloak amplifying the sweeping gestures of the arms in the act of embracing and revealing the body of the Son, the composition expands until the sudarium suddenly drops down onto the virginal garment's effusion of folds, without, however, completely concealing the summit of the Calvary, which is at once chair, step and rock foundation. In the plentiful volume of the drapery, where Mary's physical consistency is lost until it vanishes completely, Michelangelo seems to have searched for a feasible support for the body of Christ which, unmoving, weighs heavily and lengthens, tending to slip. Carved and polished with great care in all of its parts, except for the rough finish of the back of the rocky throne, achieved with slanted chiselling, the *Pietà* is one of the few sculptures by Michelangelo that features the "supreme and luminous polishing of the skin".[26] The artist's attention to detail is not just expressed in the chiselled richness of Christ's hair and beard, but in the tiniest, nearly imperceptible details as well, so imperceptible that it is difficult to appreciate them fully, for example, the "tiny knot" that stands out at the corner of Christ's loincloth, which, I believe, might be the only visible sign of a hem that was not sewn in place, but held still by

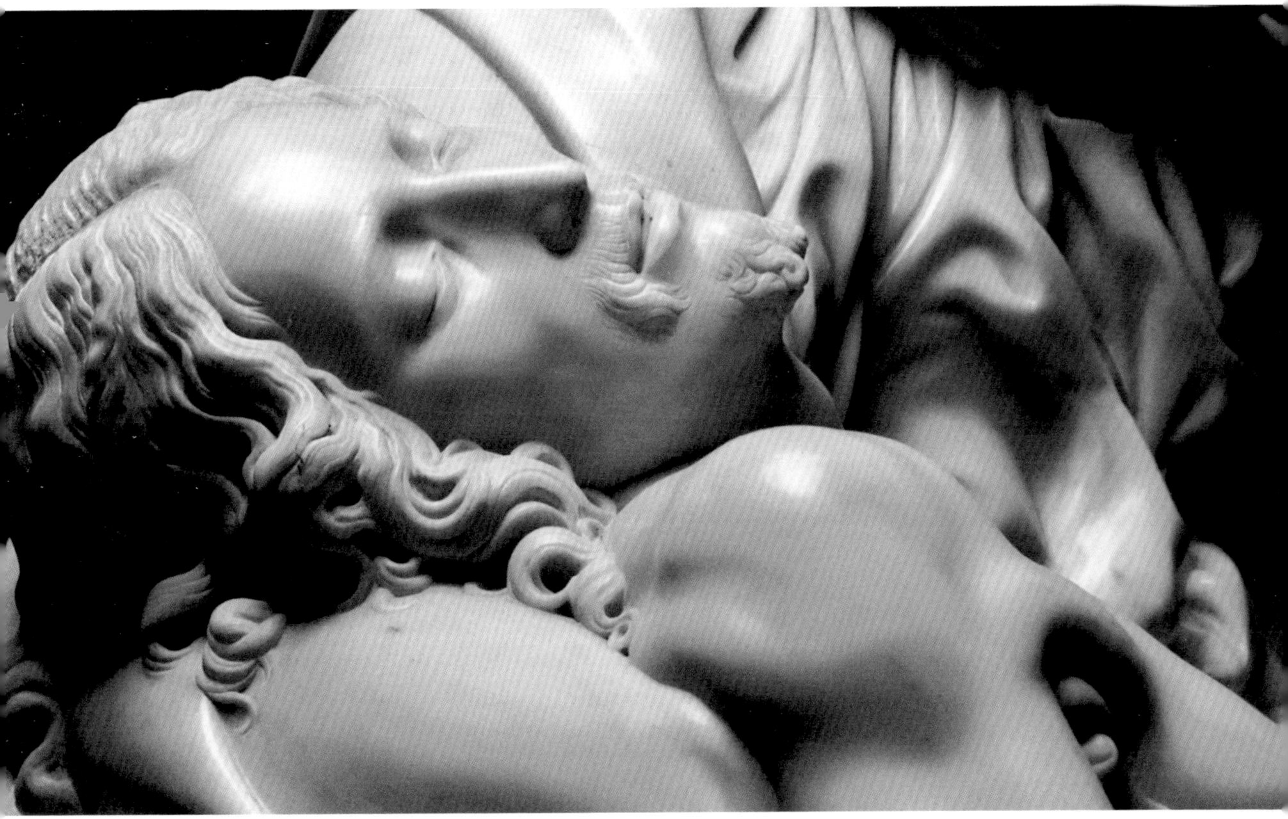

Michelangelo, *Pietà*, detail
of Christ's head tilted back
Vatican City, Saint Peter's

p. 64
Michelangelo, *Pietà*
Giorgio Vasari admired the
"harmony of the muscles
in arms, legs and body,
and the delicate tracing
of veins and arteries"
Vatican City, Saint Peter's

p. 65
Michelangelo, *Pietà*, detail
of the Virgin's hand, which
draws attention to the Son's
sacrifice to redeem humanity
Vatican City, Saint Peter's

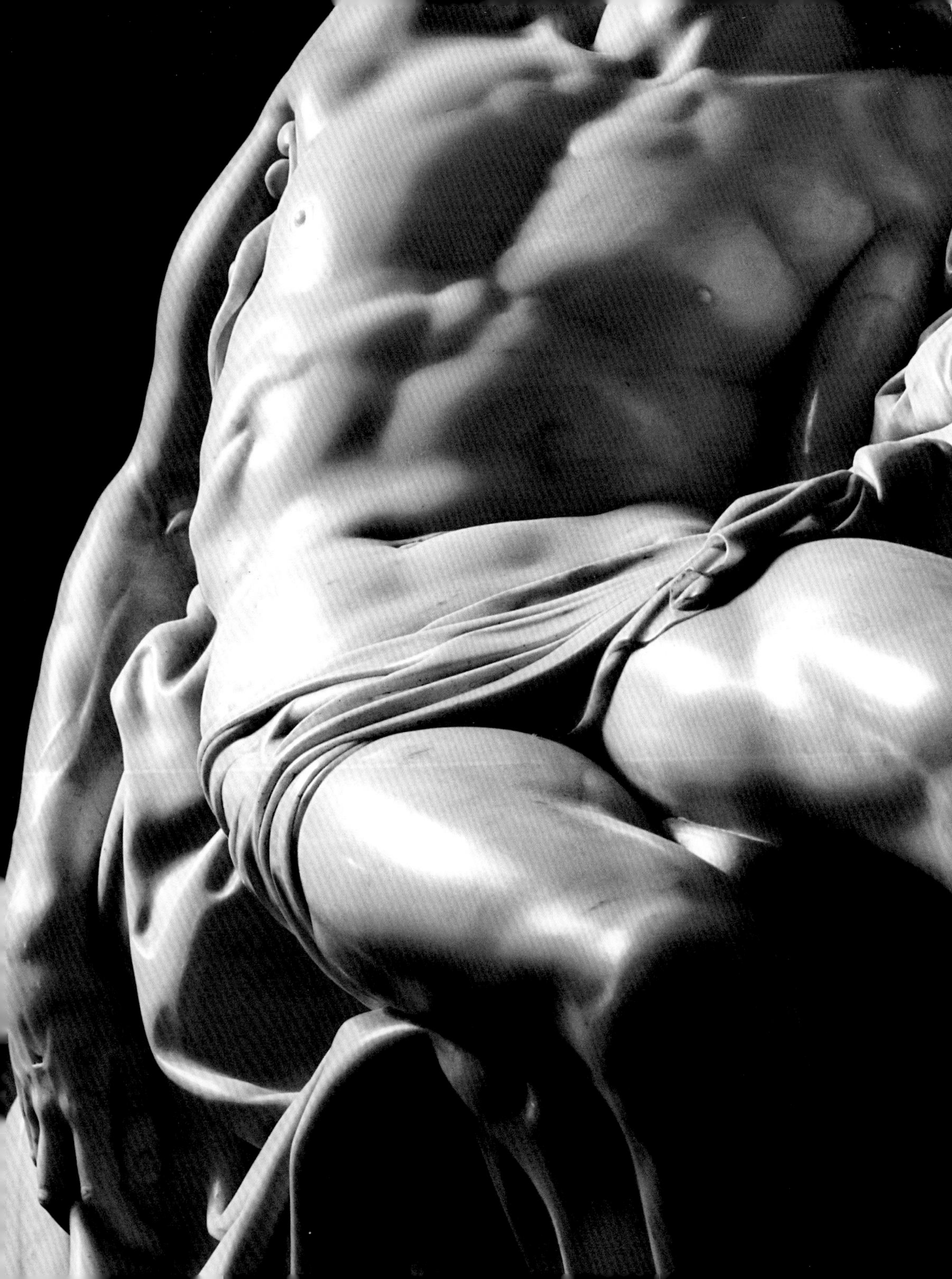

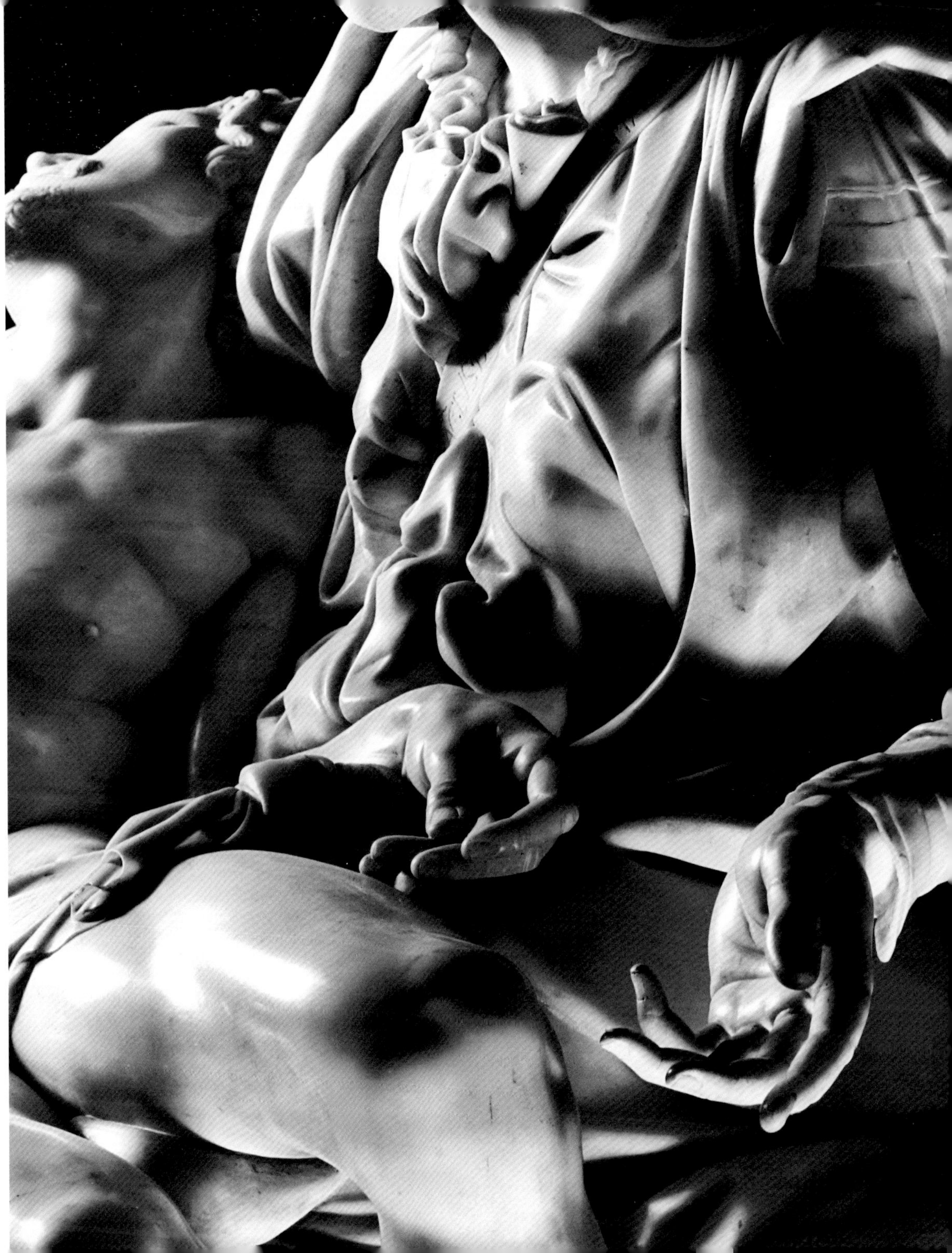

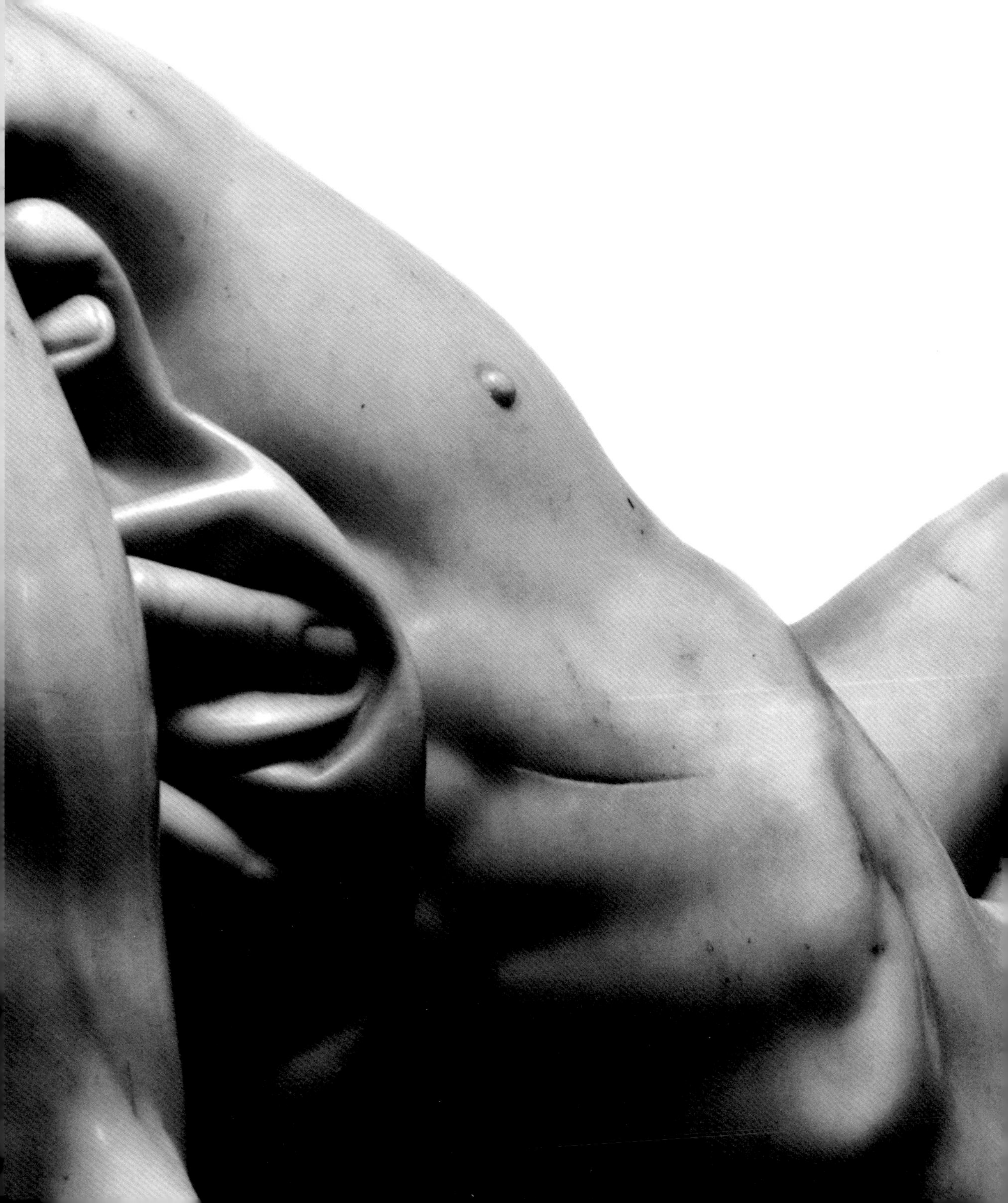

The *David*

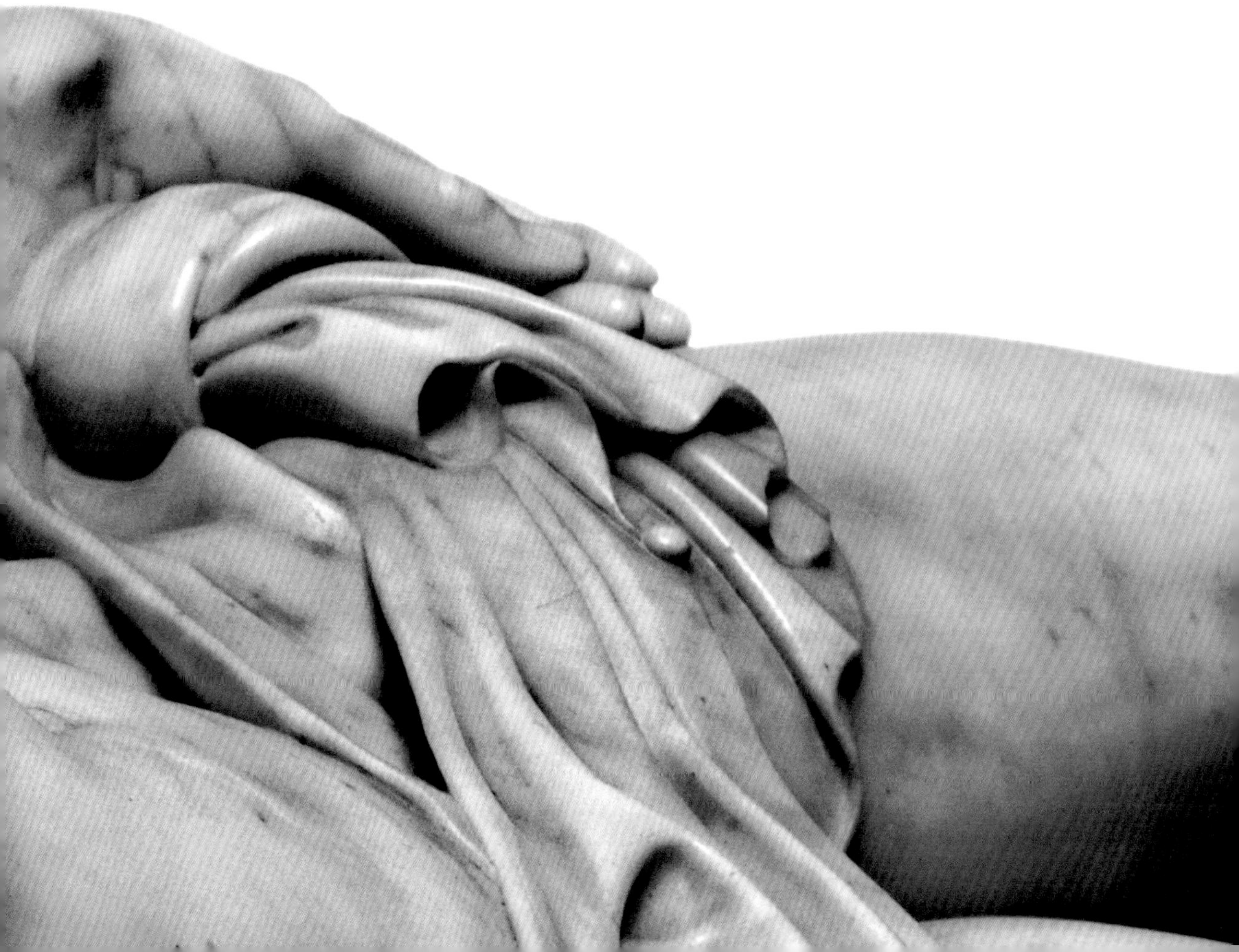

The block of marble

Michelangelo's return to Florence in May 1501 was accounted for by both of his biographers as being his opportunity to make a statue out of a very large piece of marble that had been badly blocked out, for decades lying in the courtyard of the Opera del Duomo. According to Vasari "some friends" had informed him that the cathedral officials were on the verge of entrusting it to a sculptor; Condivi believed that the *operai* were about to give it to Andrea Sansovino, and that only after they learned of Michelangelo's project did they offer it to him. Doubt has been cast on this explanation as being the real one as prior to underwriting the contract with the Opera for what was to be the *David*, the sculptor had signed an agreement with Cardinal Todeschini Piccolomini for the statues in the family chapel in Siena: but a simpler explanation might be that the contract for the job in Siena was drafted sooner than the one with the Florentine institution, a board comprising several members, whose procedures were lengthier, perhaps also restricted by solemn events such as the Feast of the Assumption on 15 August.
The block from which Michelangelo hoped to create a colossal statue most likely came from the quarry of the Fantiscritti in the Miseglia district of Carrara, which is what was presumed in the 19th century[1] and confirmed by recent petrographic analysis.[2] As for the marble itself, the artistic literature reports that it had already been carved on two different occasions by Agostino di Duccio in 1464, and by Bernardo Rossellino in 1476, for the purpose of making a gigantic figure to be installed on one of the buttresses between the "tribune morte" of the apse of Santa Maria del Fiore.[3] The original length of the block must have been about 9 Florentine *bracci*. From what Buonarroti could remember, both of the "stone-cutters who had made it" were still alive in 1501.[4]
It seems that both sculptors had stopped carving the marble owing to its poor quality and brittleness, but in the meantime they had done some work on its parallelepiped shape, so that when Michelangelo got it, certain binding decisions may already have been made (although this has never been proven): the space where the legs were to spread apart, the notching or partial depression in the shoulder area.[5] The block must have had some recognizable anthropomorphic trait as it had already earned itself the name of "giant" even before Michelangelo began working on it. Besides the intrinsic weakness of the marble, there were other elements which interfered with its aesthetic aspect: the veins running throughout the block and countless "taròli", or pinholes, riddling the surface.

From the project to the finished work

Not much has survived of Michelangelo's preparatory work for the subject, which we can easily imagine – on the grounds of the chronological overlap – must have coincided with that dedicated to the other *David*, the bronze commissioned to the artist and meant to be a gift to the marshal of Gié Pierre de Rohan. Scholarship concurs on the idea that the artist's study of the right arm, including the shoulder and connection to the chest, now at the Louvre, was a preparatory drawing for the marble giant; also at the Louvre is a drawing for a full figure of a triumphant David with Goliath's head at his feet, believed to be preparatory for the bronze statue, which contains the scholia "Dauicte cho-lla fromba e io choll-archo", "Michelagniolo" and "Roct-e l-alta cholonna e -l verd[e lauro]", the *incipit* for sonnet CCLXIX, for Laura's death, from Petrarch's *Canzoniere*.[6] Echinger-Maurach indicated another drawing at the Louvre as being a frontal view study of the *David*'s stance: with the finished statue in mind, the drawing especially matches the way the artist dealt with the torso, characterized by visibly detailed rib cage muscles.[7] A third drawing at the Louvre, with a male figure in a bent and twisted pose has also been related to the design for the *David*;[8] but although there may be some similarities in the

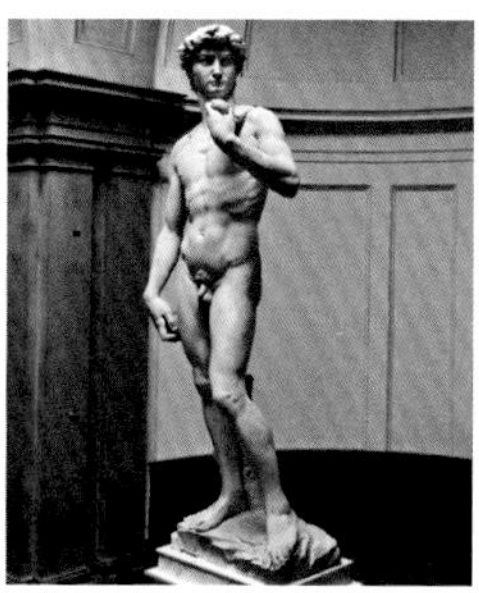

Michelangelo, *David*
Florence, Galleria dell'Accademia

p. 71
Michelangelo, *David*
Florence, Galleria dell'Accademia

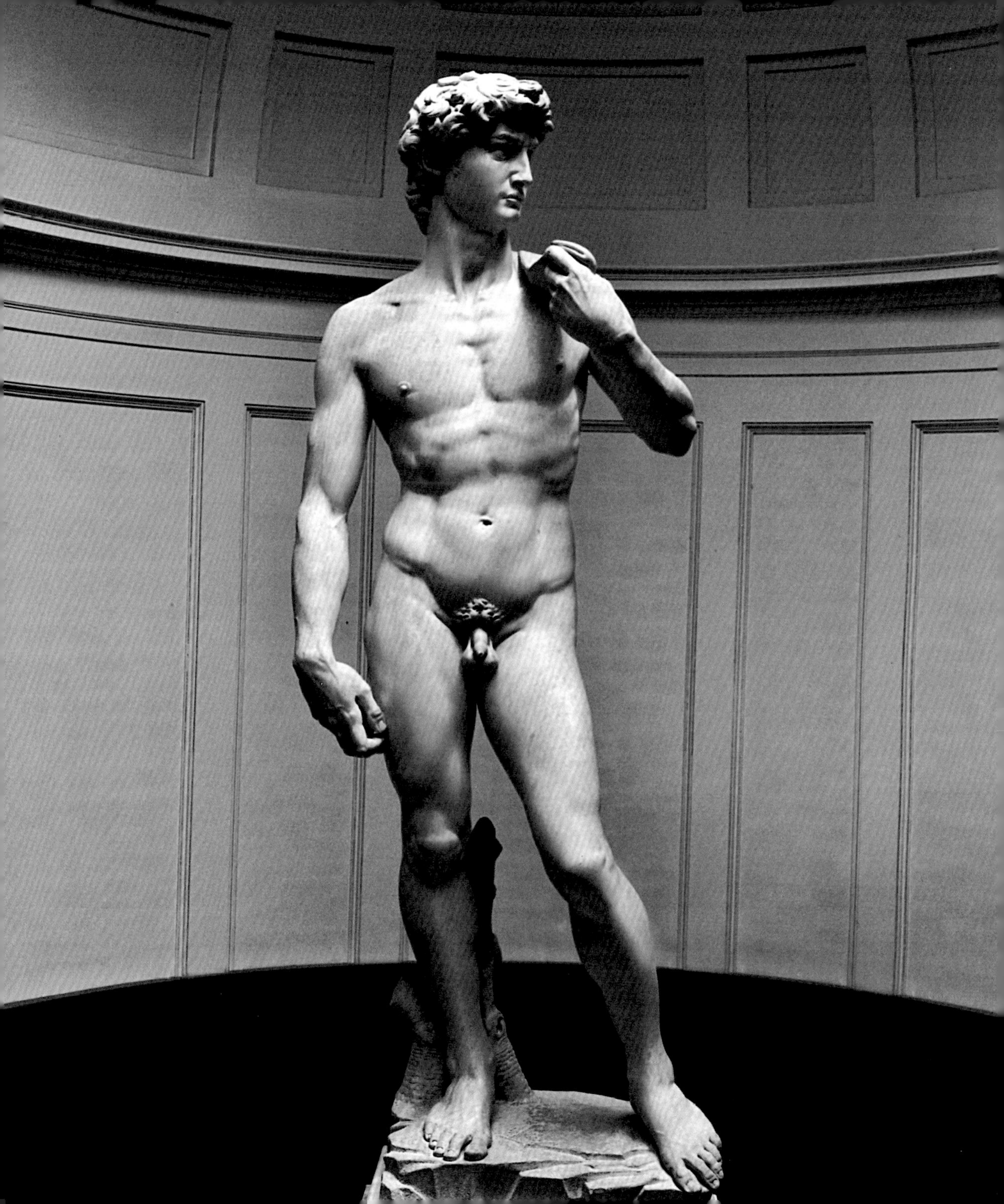

position of the arms, the considerable differences render the hypothesis a doubtful one, not to mention the fact that David is left-handed in the drawing.
Less certain results have been achieved as concerns possible preparatory models. Although Frederick Hartt's suggestion that one of these might be a headless terracotta figure of presumed Medicean provenance is in-depth and persuasive, it has not been followed up by criticism.[9] Michelangelo started working on the *David* in September 1501, after receiving the commission from the Opera del Duomo on 16 August 1501, the day after the great Feast of the Assumption: but the Opera had had the marble raised up at the beginning of July, perhaps to make it easier to evaluate it and set the terms for the contract after due consideration. The records show that the first thing Michelangelo did right there on the spot was to strike off a "knot"– with a couple of blows of the chisel – in the area where the statue's breast was to be. The contract stated that the *David* was to be made in two years. In February 1502 [1503 common usage], the *David* was described as "iam semifactum". A first, unofficial inauguration took place on 23 June 1503, on Saint John's Eve, when the doors to the fenced off area of the work site were opened to the public who were allowed to see the "giant". By the winter of 1503, Florentine usage (i.e. by 25 March 1504) the colossal statue was completed.[10]
The technique Michelangelo used to carve the *David* was studied on the occasion of the diagnostic survey that ended in 2003, which involved a close-up observation of the signs left on the surface of the statue by the different tools.[11] There are traces that different types of percussion tools were used; these would be held in one hand and hammered on with the other, requiring confidence and accuracy. At the outset, the pointed chisel was used to make holes in the block by way of what is known as "taglio a calata", a technique typically used by quarrymen and stone-cutters. Then, by combining the scraper, claw-tool and claw-chisels with two, three or five teeth, the sculptor defined the volumes for the subtly graduated passages that required only a few sharp cuts, and planed the surface to obtain the utmost smoothness, if necessary using abrasives. The figure's hair and down are the only areas where signs of the drill and graving tool can be observed, both of which requiring the direct application of muscular strength.
It appears that the carving was planned to obtain different degrees of finishing on the figure, sling, tree trunk and rocky base, and therefore different chiaroscuro effects. These range from the careful polishing of the skin, originally smooth and taut over the entire body (as proven by the areas that have been protected and are therefore almost intact) to the deliberate attempt to obtain a rough or rustic effect in the sling and tree trunk where gilding was to be applied, and traces of which have been discovered. A chiaroscuro effect was achieved in the full and thick head of hair with sharp reliefs and deep cavities. Not only did Michelangelo bestow the hair with a rich distribution of volume alongside more subtle passages, but he probably had to find a way to incorporate some of the features from the "old rough surface",[12] left over from the original marble surface, which he resolved with a "non-finito" effect. The variety of surface treatments the artist used foreshadows the growth in his technical and expressive register, but there is no trace here of the true "non-finito", which instead characterizes the unfinished statues made by the sculptor when he was an elderly man; therefore, there is no need to interpret it as being a deliberate aesthetic component.

Placing the statue in the city

Although the marble was originally part of a project by Santa Maria del Fiore, it had not been decided from the outset that the statue would be included in the cathedral ornamentations; in fact, its final destination was decided in the spring of 1504 by a committee that was made up of the most eminent artists in Florence at the time: Leonardo da Vinci, Sandro Botticelli, Giuliano da Sangallo, Cosimo Rosselli, Piero di Cosimo, Filippino Lippi, Andrea della Robbia, Pietro Perugino. While Botticelli was the only one who wanted to locate the *David* in the vicinity of the cathedral, all of the others agreed that it should be installed in Florence's most representative

p. 73
Michelangelo, *David*
The young hero stares off into an imaginary space where he "visualizes" his enemy, the Philistine giant Goliath
Florence, Galleria dell'Accademia

p. 74
Michelangelo, *David*
For the back and chest volumes the sculptor was limited by the dimensions of the block of marble
Florence, Galleria dell'Accademia

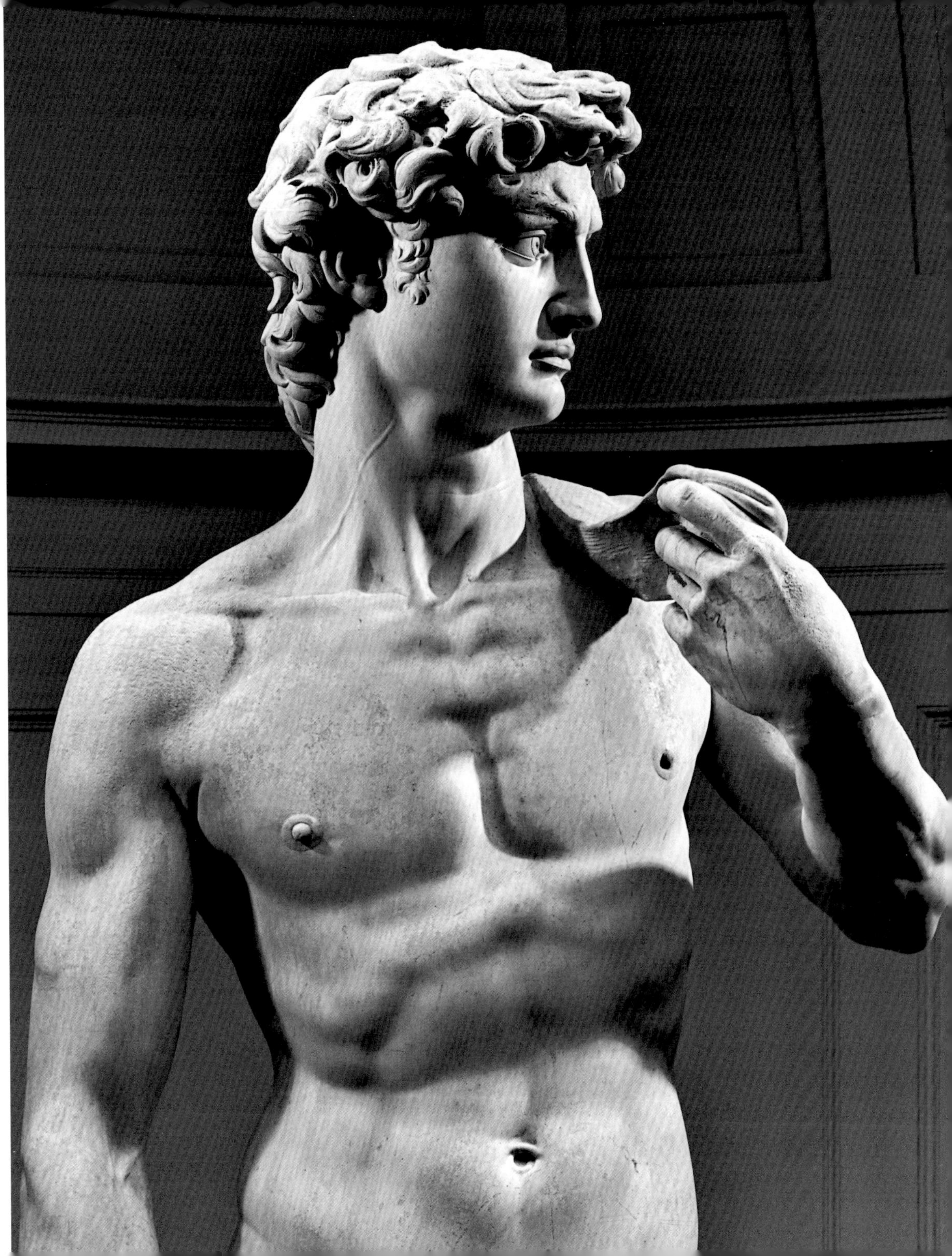

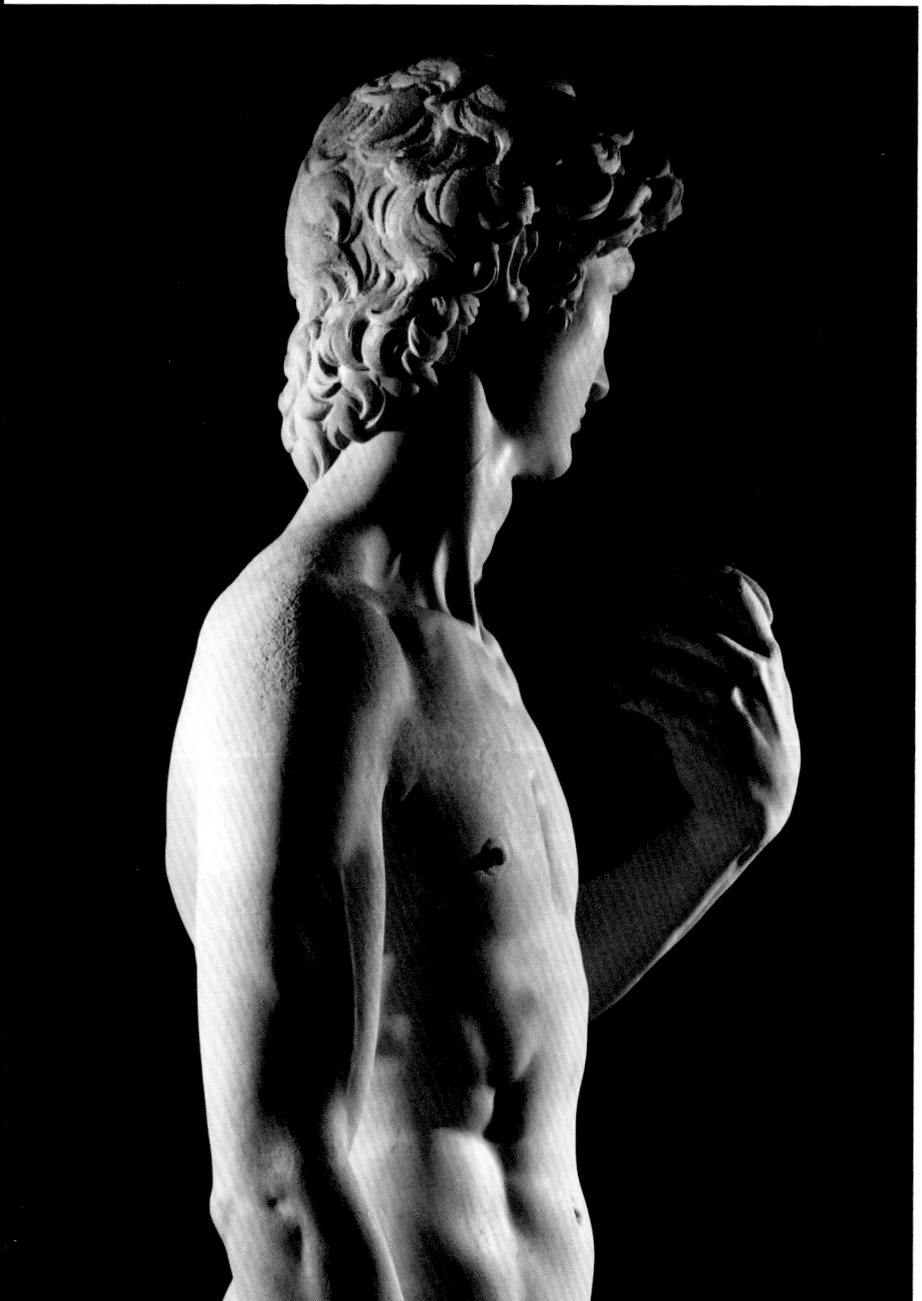

p. 75
Michelangelo, *David*, detail
of the sling in the shape
of a long double leather strip
Florence, Galleria dell'Accademia

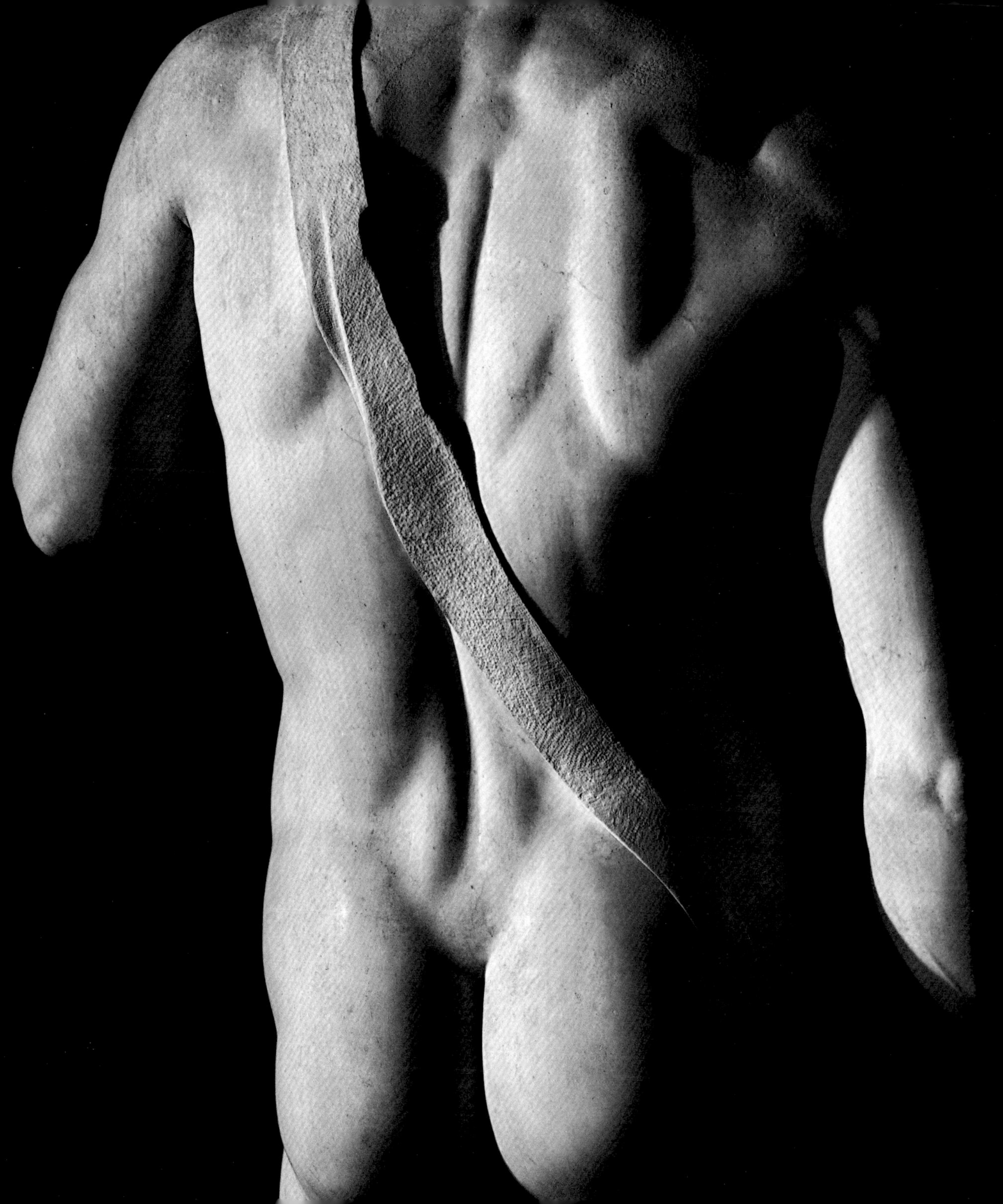

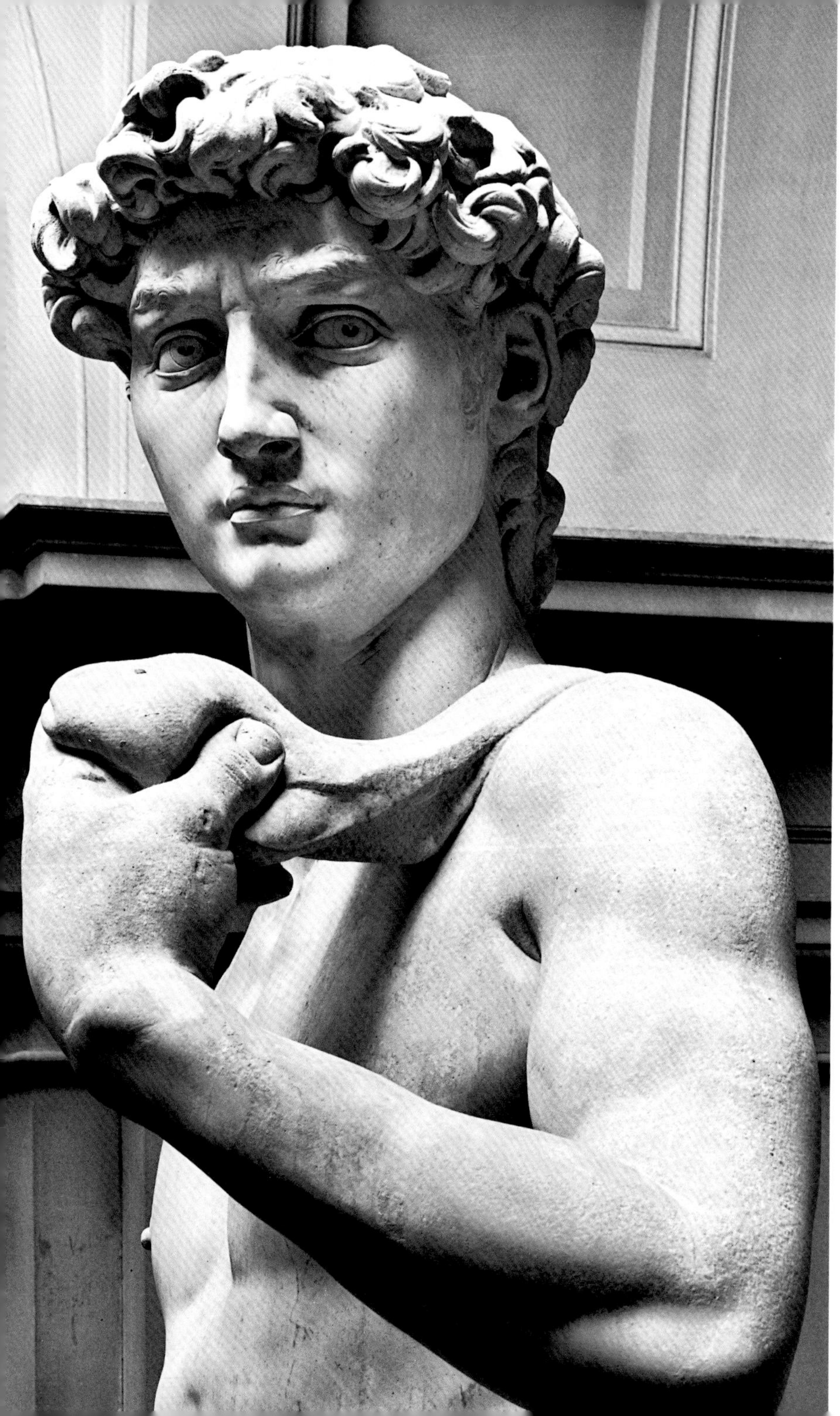

Michelangelo, *David*
With his left
hand he sizes up the stone
inside the sling as he gets ready
to toss it
Florence, Galleria dell'Accademia

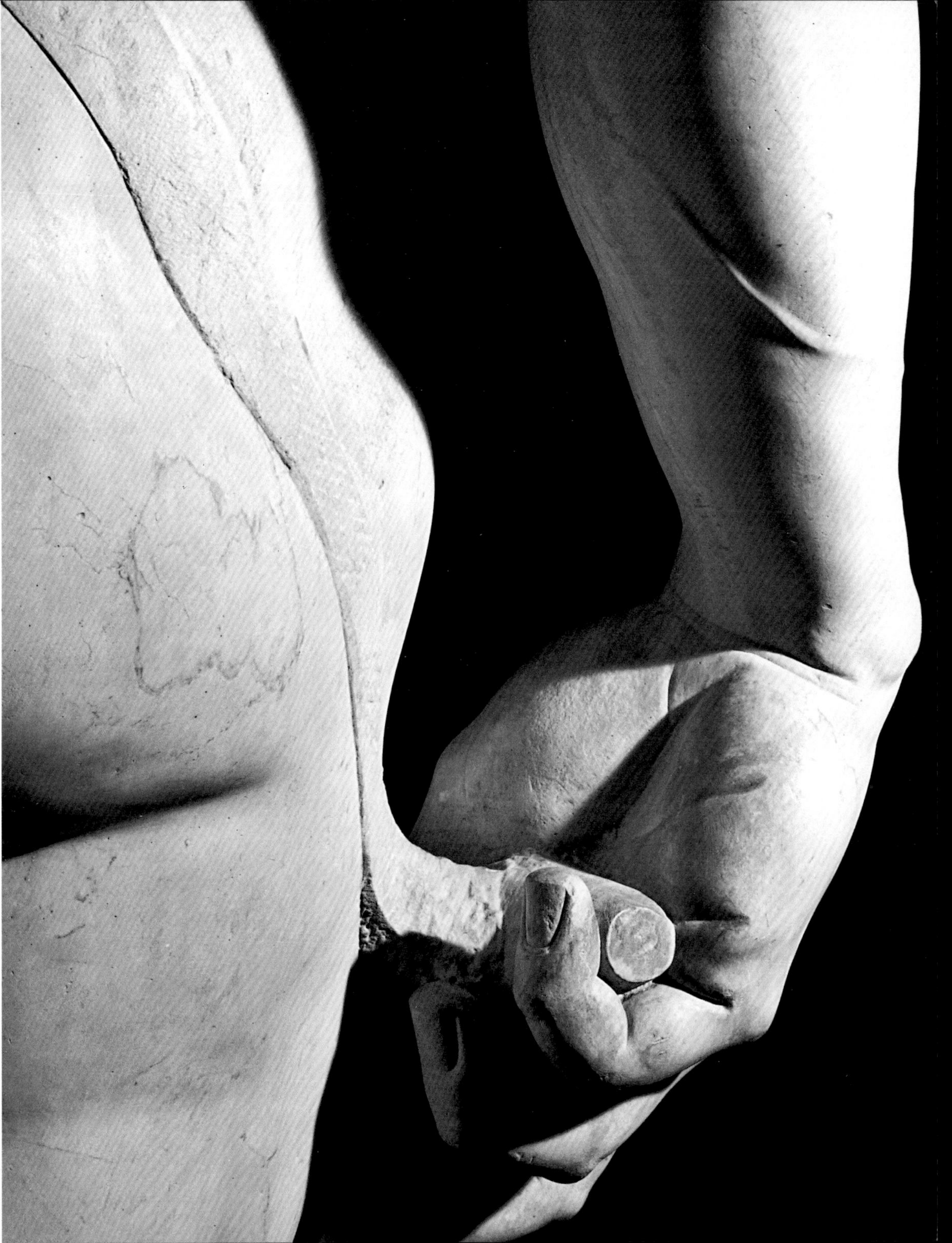

piazza, in front of the Palazzo della Signoria (now called Palazzo Vecchio), where, to cite the Signoria or parliament's first herald master Francesco, it would serve as an "insegna", or sign. The civic meaning of the statue, in relation to a long-lasting Florentine tradition, as we shall see further on, prevailed over its religious iconography. There were two proposals for the statue's placement in the piazza: out in the open, or in a sheltered area, the Arengario, at the foot of the building, or the Loggia dell'Orcagna, later to be called dei Lanzi. Giuliano da Sangallo substantiated his choice of the loggia by saying that the marble was "tenero e cotto" (weak and brittle),[13] a negative assessment from a technical standpoint, and one which is essentially backed by testing done today, and it seems this location was the first to be chosen.[14] Only after the meeting held on 25 May 1504 was the site at that time occupied by Donatello's bronze *Judith* on the Arengario chosen instead. About eighty years later, Raffaello Borghini wrote that Michelangelo would have preferred to see it inside a niche, as this would have meant one fixed view.[15] The statue's gruelling transfer took place between 14 May and 8 June 1504, and it required the work of more than forty men and the use of a complicated cart on rollers, designed by the architects and engineers Antonio da Sangallo, Simone del Pollaiolo called il Cronaca, Baccio d'Agnolo and Bernardo del Cecca. During the first night of the journey, four young citizens threw stones at the *David* – whether the reason for this was political dissent or just plain vandalism is still unknown[16] – the first of many attempts to damage the work.
With a resolution dated 11 June Antonio da Sangallo and il Cronaca were assigned the task of designing a marble base for the statue, still visible today underneath the *David* in a revised and perhaps smaller version: a white marble plinth in classical style with red Maremma marble panels.[17] Once the *David* was actually on the support, the statue was given a final finishing by Michelangelo himself. Whether or not he applied some kind of protective layer to it is not known for sure (he probably did, at least to fill in the very evident and dangerous pinholes); what we do know from the documents and traces discovered is that he had the "cigna", or long sling, and the "broncone", or tree trunk up against which the right leg leans, highlighted with gilding.[18] A garland with twenty-eight gilded metal leaves was ordered and paid for, but doubts remain as to whether it was ever placed on the head, or around the hips, or whether it was at all applied to the statue. The well-known anecdote told by Giorgio Vasari fits right in here. It seems that Pier Soderini, *gonfaloniere* of the Republic at the time, criticized the *David*'s nose from below as being "too thick", at which point Michelangelo pretended to touch the nose up with his chisel, but the marble dust that fell was really some he was holding in his hand. When he had finished, he asked the Soderini to look at it again: "'I like it better' – said the Gonfalonier – 'you have given it life'. And so Michelagnolo came down [...] he had compassion on those who, in order to appear full of knowledge, talk about things of which they know nothing".[19] The statue was unveiled and inaugurated on 8 September 1504, which was also the date of one of a number of Marian feast days in Florence.

Iconographic issues

The *David* for Michelangelo meant occupying a place in the midst of the long and splendid artistic tradition in Florence, but it also meant profoundly revisiting, perhaps even twisting the biblical account of the story.[20] The episode in the First Book of Samuel, which the figure of the young David is based upon, tells the story of when Jesse's youngest son David, a brave boy whose job was to tend sheep, accepted the challenge of the gigantic Philistine and chief of the enemy troops Goliath. Saul, king of the Israeli people, knew David from the time the boy had played his harp to alleviate the suffering that had been inflicted on him by an "evil spirit", and now offered him his cuirass and sword. But the boy – who couldn't move as he was unaccustomed to so much weight – got rid of them and advanced against the Philistine armed solely with his great faith in God, his sling and "five smooth stones" from the river which he carried in

p. 77
Michelangelo, *David*
Grasping an object with his right hand, perhaps a horn, he uses it as an end or grip for the sling
Florence, Galleria dell'Accademia

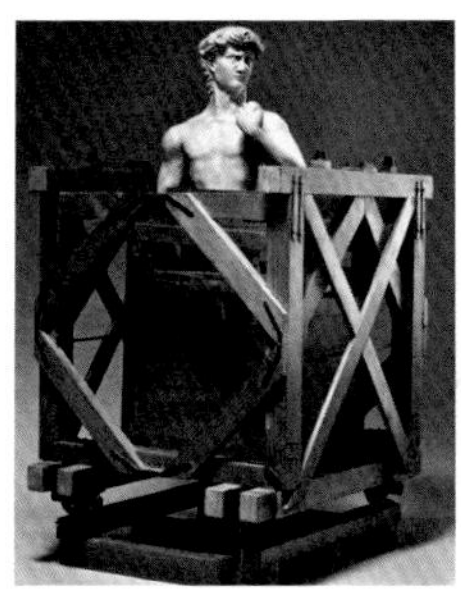

Model of the wooden framework used to protect the *David* while it was being transported on rollers from Piazza della Signoria to the Galleria dell'Accademia
Florence, Casa Buonarroti, inv. 697

p. 79
Michelangelo, *David*
The left foot is raised, as if he were about to make a sudden twisting movement in order to toss the stone
Florence, Galleria dell'Accademia

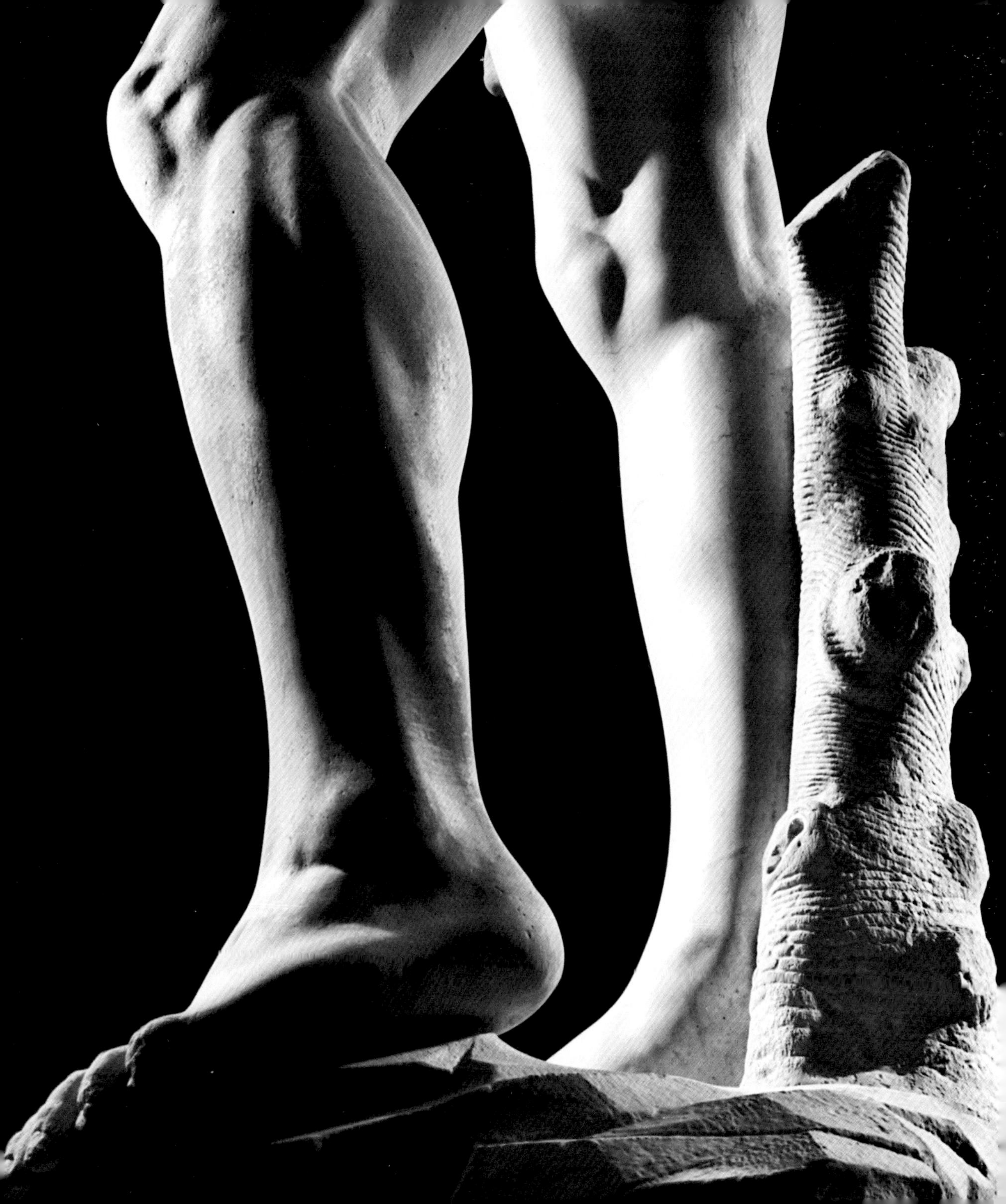

his pouch. When the duel began, David hit Goliath on the forehead with one of the stones, knocking him unconscious. The boy wasted no time and with the giant's own sword slew and beheaded him. A symbol of what is just, of vulnerability that prevails over what is strongly unjust, David is the biblical hero represented most in Florentine art, from Gothic to Renaissance, where the figure from the Old Testament rises up to become a civic icon of the defence of one's country and of divine aid against one's enemies.
Such masters as Lorenzo Ghiberti, Donatello, Andrea del Castagno and Verrocchio – not to mention miniaturists and painters of *cassoni* (wedding chests) – strove to represent the figure and the description of this particular event. In painting, the slain giant's huge body would be placed right next to David, while in sculpture the amount of space the dead Philistine took up was, for obvious reasons, reduced to just the chopped-off head. David's attributes varied and were often contradictory, and included either shepherd's clothing or light armour, boots or bare feet, a sling with stones or Goliath's sword, the giant's body or head. A more explicit sort of nudity, with the exception of the hat and boots, is the prerogative of the unique bronze *David* by Donatello (Florence, Museo Nazionale del Bargello), whose chronology is anything but settled, ranging from the 1410s to the 1440s. Most of the 15th-century celebratory and non-narrative images of David show him standing with his legs slightly apart, and the absorbed look of reflection or quiet triumph over the accomplished victory, proven by the slain enemy's head close to or between his legs. It would seem that the only portrayal of the young hero in the dynamic pose that precedes the throwing of the stone is the one by Andrea del Castagno on a leather shield (Washington, National Gallery of Art), despite the fact that Goliath's head, as though it were the exhortative epithet of his person, is already at his feet.
Michelangelo infringed on the consolidated artistic customs bound to an adolescent image of David. Where his predecessors in the arts showed predilection for some specific elements from the Bible, for example, the fact that he was the youngest of Jesse's eight children, a shepherd and not a warrior like his elder brothers, "ruddy, and withal of beautiful countenance, and goodly to look at"[21] as well as a harp player, it seems Michelangelo's glance fell on other lines: "a mighty valiant man, and a man of war";[22] "... and there came a lion, and a bear, and took a lamb out of the flock; and I went out after him, and smote him, and delivered it out of his mouth; and when he arose against me, I caught him by his beard, and smote him, and slew him. Thy servant slew both the lion and the bear",[23] images more suggestive of a young Hercules than a defenceless shepherd boy. If Saul's armour gets in the way, it is not because it's heavy, but because the boy is not used to wearing a helmet and cuirass.
So Michelangelo's interpretation of the young hero as athlete, exalted by his colossal size, is really not so arbitrary. Similarly, his total nudity carries to extreme consequences what is implicit in the line that refers to his armour: "And David put them off him".[24]
And as for the situation in which David is portrayed, it is neither an instant in which he celebrates his victory nor one of reflection on his actions (because Goliath's sword and head are both missing); but nor is it an ideal state, abstracted from the chronology of the biblical telling and projected into a timeless dimension. To my mind, Michelangelo catches David in the very instant – and no more than that – when he sets his gaze on his adversary, ready to cast the stone that will strike him on the forehead: right in the middle, under the bronze helmet that the text describes together with the monstrous coat of mail.[25] The sling, in this case a long doubled up strip presumably made of leather, is a simple weapon, dating from way back and typically used by shepherds.[26] The *David* holds the two ends in his right hand, one end of which is anchored to a grip, temporarily described as being shaped like the segment of a horn; it is important to recall that Saul had already anointed the boy, chosen by the Lord as Saul's successor to the throne of Israel, with oil that he kept in a horn.[27] The right hand, which holds the sling upwards and just a short distance away from the shoulder, seems to be in the act of placing at least one stone, whose volume slightly swells the folded strip, where it is meant to be. There are also some who believe the sling is actually empty, and that any swelling is simply due to the thickness of the leather. But as the projectile is a pebble from a stream and thus not particularly large, it is more likely that the roundness visible in the sling between the thumb and index finger of the left hand is the stone itself, which the daring shepherd expects will hit

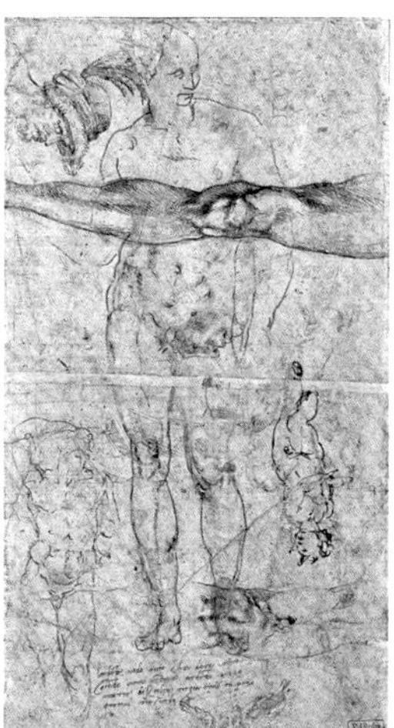

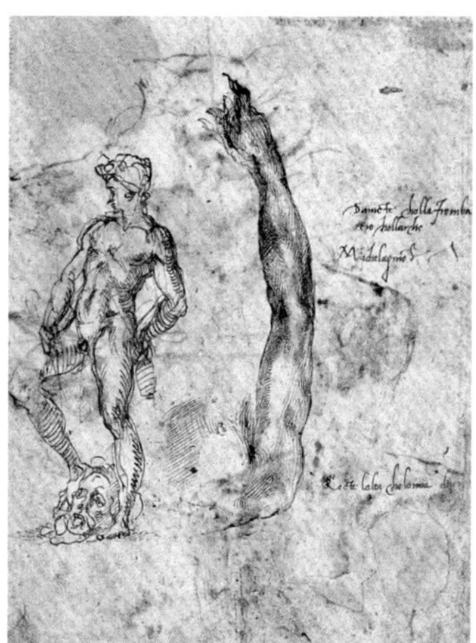

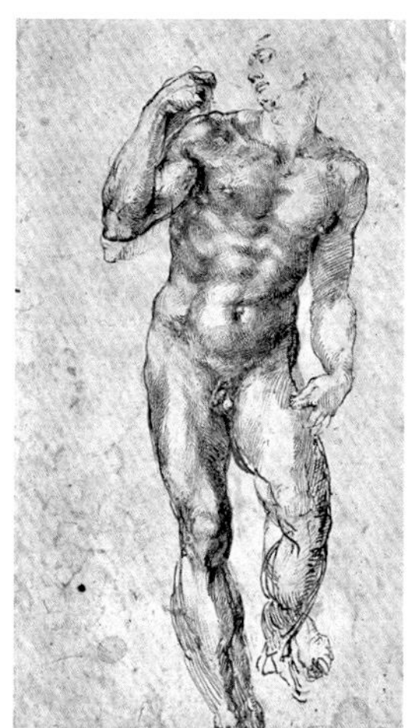

the mark, although it will not necessarily slay the giant: the weapon used to kill will actually be the sword. The only inconsistency, if there is one, is in the view from the back, where the thickness of the strip, at first double, is very much reduced: but this was not the only drawback that Michelangelo was forced to deal with; that block of marble was shallow, and insufficient for the artist to be able develop the giant's back.

The *David*'s stance is so painstakingly studied and described that the viewer is able to imagine the instant that comes right afterwards: the left hand lets go, the sling slips down along the figure's back, his stretched out right arm starts to swing the sling around in large circles until, by releasing the end, the strip undoubles and the pebble is hurled to strike Goliath in the forehead. The position of the pupils indicate that the *David* glances furtively, and we can assume that Goliath is to the side; if this is true, the statue's body will have to turn on itself, pivoting on its left foot which is already in a forwards position. The pose is so closely entwined with the gesture (one wonders how there could be any doubt) that in Hans Christian Andersen's delightful tale *The Metal Pig,* set in Florence in 1842, the poor little boy, who is also the main character, in his nighttime flight atop Tacca's magically animated Porcellino, sees the *David* amidst the crowd of statues in Piazza della Signoria that comes to life under his eyes, as the giant tosses his sling.

If we accept this interpretation of the *David*'s pose, then what follows is that his expression is not so much one of threatening pride upon seeing the enemy, but of deep concentration in calculating the amount of force needed to rotate the sling and take aim so that the projectile will hit the target. As a defender of his life and country, Michelangelo's *David* does what the artist himself did in his profession, he measures things up at a glance. The artist invented this moment, he stole this instant from the ardour of the biblical tale and, so to speak, introduced *ex novo* a "frame" in the frenetic sequence that shows David running, sticking his hand into the pouch, taking the stone out and slinging it with his weapon to hit Goliath.[28]

It is an instant of sheer intensity, balanced between instinct and reason: infinitesimal fear between two movements.

The calculation will be accurate because the thrower has "the compass in his eyes", as famously stated by his inventor. So the identity between the two, hinted at in the famous and previously mentioned hendecasyllable – "David with the sling shot and me with the bow" – in the drawing marked DAG inv. 714 at the Louvre, could take on a slightly different meaning from what is commonly underscored by the critics. While the bow, or in this case the bow-drill, is interpreted to be the sculptor's weapon by symmetry with the sling, which is David's weapon, the exact opposite might instead be true: the sling is an instrument for David, in the same way that the drill is for the artist: an instrument guided by the intellect as well as by the hand, a *conditio sine qua non* allowing the weak to prevail over the strong, the oppressed to defeat the oppressor; an instrument that, in shaping a precise trajectory to reach the desired point, traces an incorporeal if magnificent design. The obsession with the straight shot was to return in the years of the Sistine ceiling: "show me the crooked barrel that shoots straight" (sonnet 5, l. 17, *circa* 1508-1512).

Half a millennium of fame

The succession of events that open-air display as well as human intervention (even with the best of intentions) have inflicted on the *David* over the course of its existence until it was moved to the Galleria dell'Accademia in Florence in 1873 are summed up in the brief entry at the end of this book. The entry also contains notes on its state, diagnostic testing dedicated to its structure and surface, as well as the conservation work which ended in 2004. There is one complex phenomenon, which goes beyond any historical and artistic approach to the work and warrants multidisciplinary analysis. This concerns the current international fame of the *David*, an authentic icon of our times, capable of arousing the kind of admiration that comes close to idol-worship, but also of trou-

Michelangelo, *Various studies of figures, inscription after sonnet CCLXXI by Petrarch.* The studies for the legs are believed to relate to the *David.* Paris, Musée du Louvre, Département des Arts Graphiques, inv. 688 *verso*

Michelangelo, *Sketch for the bronze* David *and for an arm of the marble* David, scholia (Davicte cholla fromba... and Petrarchan sonnet CCLXIX) Paris, Musée du Louvre, Département des Arts Graphiques, inv. 714 *recto*

Michelangelo, *Male nude, frontal view*, by some related to the marble *David*, by others to the project for the *Ten Thousand Martyrs* Paris, Musée du Louvre, Département des Arts Graphiques, inv. 689 *recto*

bling individual and collective sensibilities. Since the very beginning in a position of the utmost visibility, praised in the artistic literature even before Vasari, it was in the 19th century that the *David* began its rise to fame, reaching a high point in 1873-1875, first when it became a part of the museum, and then with events related to the centennial celebration of Michelangelo's birth.[29] The statue's image was reproduced and diffused in two-dimensional terms, from photography to today's virtual rendering, but also in three-dimensional versions, in different sizes and in a variety of media.

The mould cast by Papi (1847) was followed by plaster copies, one of which is now in the Gipsoteca (plaster cast gallery) of the Istituto d'Arte located at Porta Romana, while others are housed in the collections of European and world academies. Papi's own bronze copy (1866) was installed in 1873 at the centre of the square named for Michelangelo, designed by Giuseppe Poggi to complete the panoramic view of the Viale dei Colli: the base of the statue was decorated with copies, also in bronze, of the New Sacristy statues *Night*, *Day, Dawn* and *Dusk*. In addition to paying tribute to Michelangelo four hundred years after his birth, the monument was historicist proof of Florence's supremacy in the arts, in support of the city that had just, and not without consequences, come out of a five-year period as the capital of unified Italy. In 1910, a faithful marble copy by Luigi Arrighetti was installed at the foot of Palazzo Vecchio, thus restoring completeness to the piazza. Since that time it has been impossible to actually count the number of copies made, life-sized or reduced,[30] or the disparate categories of souvenirs: miniatures made of artificial material of the whole figure or of parts, various-sized busts, magnets, postcards, and other by-products. The image is also often used in advertising illustrations.

As one of the statue's strongest features is the affirmative and full physicality of the male figure, whose total nudity is just one aspect, although one of the most perturbing, it has inevitably led to censorship in the past and fuels intolerance today. Despite its attraction for art lovers, the magnificent male nude seems to disturb those who (especially for ethnic or religious reasons)[31] know nothing of ancient Greco-Roman art and its countless reinterpretations beginning from the Italian Renaissance, within which the beauty of the human body was idealized to be the supreme fruit of Nature and the glory of Creation.[32]

To dispel the fears expressed by 19th-century Florentine artists, that reproduction of the image would generate boredom and indifference, the spread of the *David*'s image through numerous media does not seem to lessen the subjective and unique experience of actually seeing the original.

Notes

[1] Gotti, 1875, II, p. 45.
[2] Attanasio, Rocchi, Platania, 2004.
[3] For a summary and critical discussion on the history of the *David*, see Falletti, 2004.
[4] Condivi, 1553, 1998 ed., note no. 8, p. XXI.
[5] Moreni, 1813, p. 119; Giovannini, 2004, pp. 105-115.
[6] Paris, Musée du Louvre, DAG, 714*r*. See Echinger-Maurach, 1998b, pp. 302-323; Joannides, 2003a, no. 45.
[7] Paris, Musée du Louvre, DAG, inv. RF 1068*v*. See Echinger-Maurach, 1998b; p. 324ff; Joannides, 2003, no. 11r.
[8] Paris, Musée du Louvre, DAG, inv. 689*r*. See Echinger-Maurach, 1998b; p. 326ff; Joannides, 2003, no. 12*r*. There's a chance that this study (like the one cited in the previous note) was preparatory for one of the *ignudi* in the "ten thousand martyrs".
[9] Hartt, 1987.
[10] For the most recent discussions on the documents and subsequent reconstruction of the chronology, see Echinger-Maurach, 1998b, and especially Hirst, 2000.
[11] Cf. Giovannini, 2004.
[12] Condivi, *The Life of Michelangelo* (1553), 2006 ed., p. 28..
[13] Gaye, 1839-1840, II, 1840, pp. 454-468 (especially p. 458).
[14] Deliberation of the Opera di Santa Maria del Fiore dated 30 April, 1504, cf. Hirst, 2000, p. 490.
[15] Borghini, 1584, p. 164.
[16] These were Vincenzo di Cosimo Martelli, Filippo di Francesco de' Spini, Gerardo Maffei de' Gherardini, Raffaello di Agostino de' Panciatichi, arrested by the Otto di Guardia and then released. Although "political" motives for the gesture have been investigated, because the families of the youths involved were not particularly known as being anti-republican, it is likely that it was simply an act of vandalism.
[17] Weil-Garris Brandt, 1983, pp. 384-393.
[18] Weil-Garris Brandt, 1983, p. 385; Ristori, 1986, pp. 77-97; Caglioti, 2000b, pp. 334-336.
[19] Vasari, *The Lives* (1568), 1996 ed., II, pp. 654-655.
[20] Radke, 2004.
[21] *1 Samuel*, 16,12.
[22] *1 Samuel*, 16,18.
[23] *1 Samuel*, 17, 34-36.
[24] *1 Samuel*, 17, 39.
[25] *1 Samuel*, 17, 5.
[26] For a history of the weapon, including practical instructions for fabrication and use, see the website *Shepherd's sling* (www.fact-index.com/s/sl/slig.html).
[27] *1 Samuel*, 16, 13.
[28] *1 Samuel*, 17, 48-49.
[29] See *Michelangelo nell'Ottocento...*, 1994.
[30] A life-sized copy made from Apuan marble still adorns the city of Marseilles, a gift from its author Jules Cantini (1903). Others, specially made in the marble quarries of Carrara and Pietrasanta, have been sold worldwide, or await sale. One curious fact included in one of the many websites on the topic concerns a private garden in Los Angeles (CA) where as many as twenty-three versions of the *David* in all sizes are there for the viewing.
[31] While we may smile to hear the sad story of a copy of the *David* from 1939 in the Forest Lawn Cemetery in Glendale (CA), moralized by a fig leaf, undressed thirty years later and then destroyed in the earthquake of 1987, less amusing are the reasons behind refusal of the statue by communities where religious and moral values prevail that differ from those of Catholics. An embarrassing but exemplary case is that of Jerusalem's refusal in the 1990s to accept the city of Florence's gift of a copy of the real *David* so that it could be installed in David's Fortress. In 1969, in Sydney, a shopkeeper was taken to court and tried for gross indecency after putting up a poster of the *David*; he was eventually found innocent, also thanks to the help of the director of the New Wales Gallery who came to his defence.
[32] See Clark, 1995.

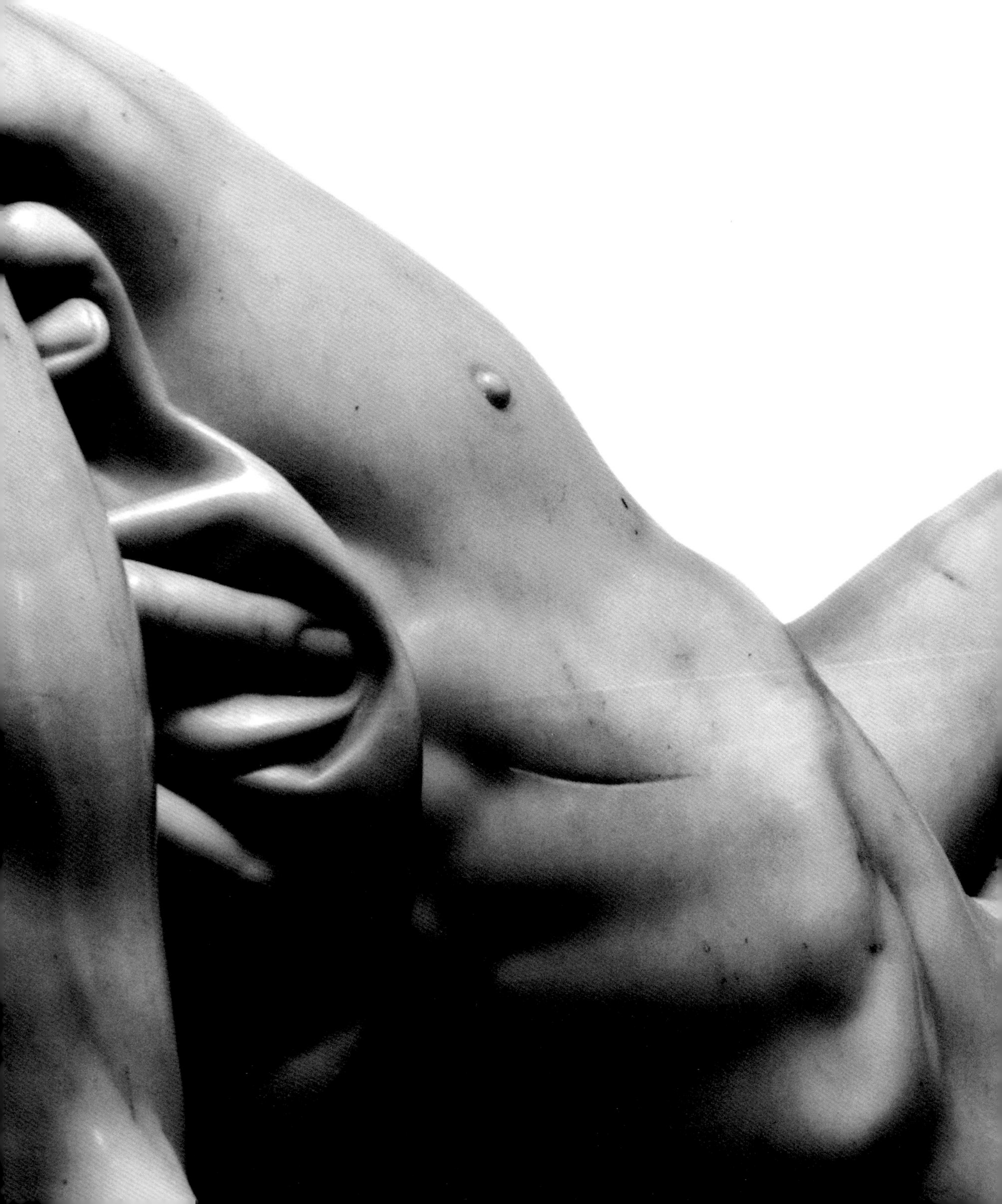

Sculptures and contracts in Florence

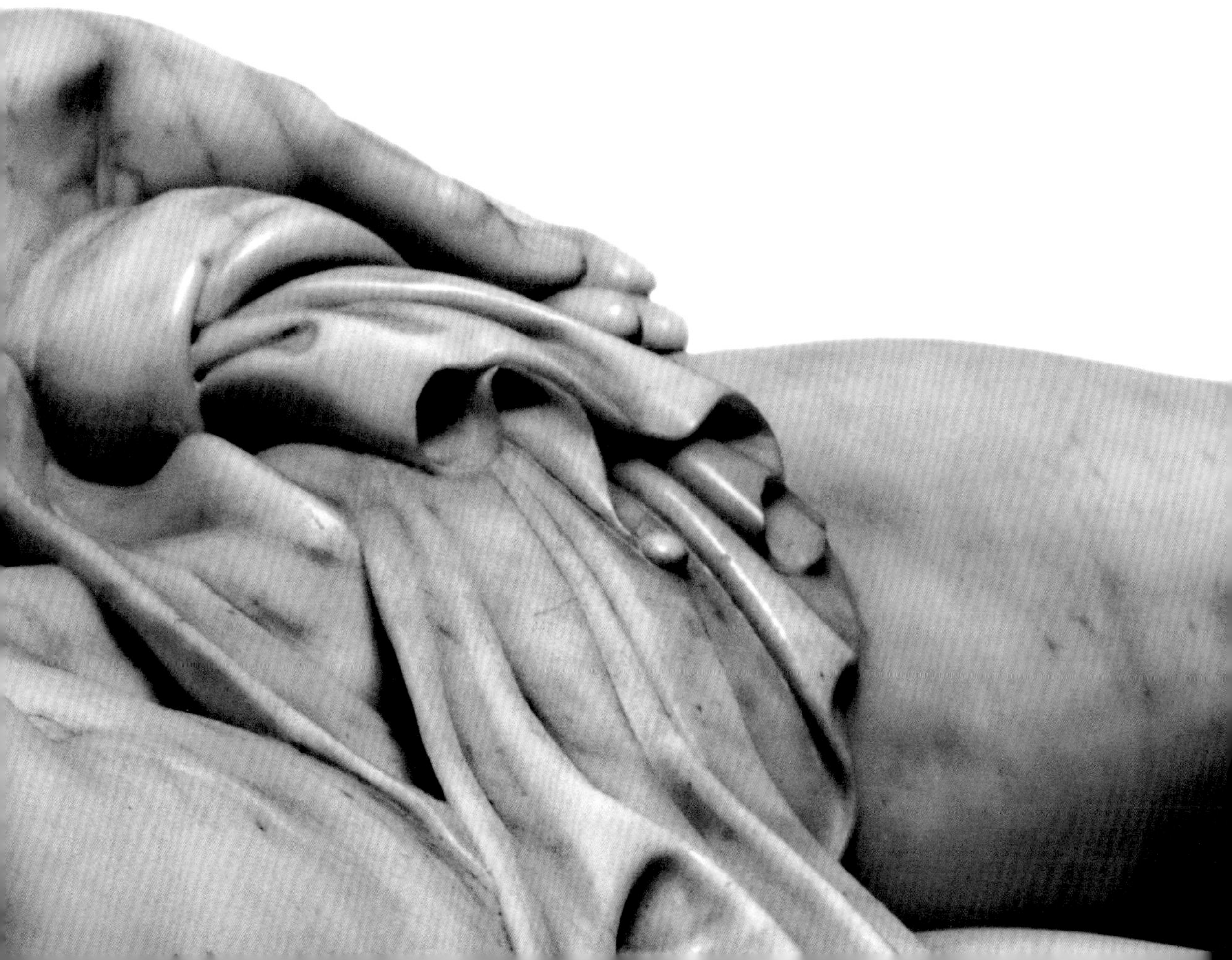

The commission for the Piccolomini chapel

Before, during and after the *David*, in those frenetic years from 1501 to 1505 in Florence, Michelangelo accepted a number of commissions, prevalently involving sculpture, but not just that, which he was able to complete only in part. He had come back from Rome with a commission from a Sienese patron, the only one he would ever have, with Jacopo Galli again acting as intermediary. The patron was Cardinal Francesco Todeschini Piccolomini, nephew of Pope Pius II, who, with the new century underway, was preparing magnificent examples of his patronage in Siena Cathedral: the Piccolomini library to house illuminated manuscripts, where Pinturicchio would fresco the walls with the *Stories of Pius II*, as well as the family chapel (commonly but reductively called "altar") situated along the wall of the left nave near the library entrance. Andrea Bregno, the most famous Lombard sculptor in Rome, had begun to work on the majestic marble façade sometime between 1480 and 1485.[1] The chapel was already inspired by ancient Roman architecture and harmoniously adjoined to one of the side arches. The lower storey, resembling the barrel vault of a triumphal arch, featured at its centre a niche with an altar and altarpiece, and to the sides two pairs of niches one on top of the other framed by fluted pilaster strips whose capitals were decorated with dolphins below, and carved candelabra with vegetal motifs above. The Attic storey featured a central niche that culminated in a triangular tympanum and two side niches with curvilinear tympana. In the spring of 1501, Michelangelo agreed to carve fifteen statues for all of the empty cavities and perhaps for some other parts, for example, the reins in the arches, and to do the job had Carrara marble that was "new, pure and white and without veins" brought there.[2]

The difficult assignment did not stop him from accepting other commissions, however. On 16 August of that same year, probably after lengthy discussion, he underwrote a contract for the "giant" to be made from the marble block entrusted to him by the Opera del Duomo, and set out to create the *David*, discussed in the previous chapter.

The bronze *David*

Buonarroti was perhaps already or on the point of carving the marble *David* when, in August of 1501, he received an offer he could not turn down from the Signoria in Florence: a bronze statue of *David*, a diplomatic gift to Pierre de Rohan, Maréchal of Gié, a way of guaranteeing the city's favour with France. What the Maréchal had in mind as a possible model was a bronze *David* he had seen in Florence in 1494, believed to be the one by Donatello, at the time still situated in the courtyard at the Medici palace.[3]

Lorenzo di Pierfrancesco Medici was given the task of assisting Michelangelo and finding the material he needed; his role as a garantor for the artist, by then an adult, has also been hypothesized, as there is no evidence to show whether or not he had specific experience in the casting of a bronze statue despite the fact that he had been guided by Bertoldo.[4] The contract was formalized a year later, on 12 August 1502, and in it Donatello's *David* is mentioned as being in the same location it had been since 1495, in the apartment of the "Signori" on the second floor: "apud Catenam scalarum dictorum Dominorum". But since the statue is now lost we have no way of knowing exactly how Michelangelo faced his twofold task – to follow in the steps of his great ideal master Donatello, and to cast bronze. To imagine what the statue must have looked like, we do, however, have the preliminary drawing on the same sheet at the Louvre with a study for the marble *David*'s arm, proof of the simultaneous development, in Michelangelo's project, of two rather different versions of the same subject.[5] True to Donatello's work and Florentine tradition in general, the *David* destined to the French – probably modelled after a young member of the workshop asked to pose naked while wearing a turban – has Goliath's head at his feet: he holds the sling in one

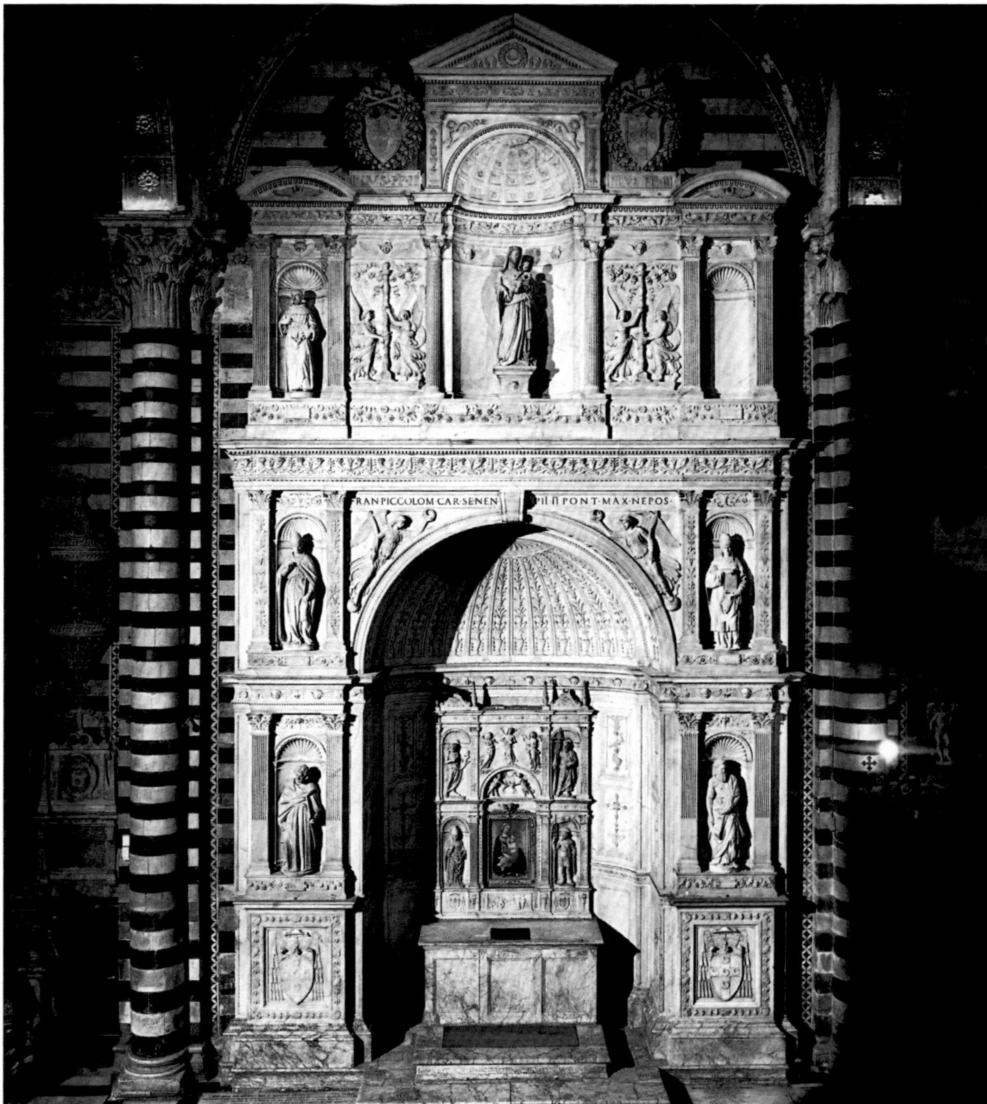

Architecture by Andrea Bregno,
Piccolomini chapel
Siena Cathedral

hand, in the other, the pouch with stones hanging down at the hip. The figure, solidly pivoting on the left leg he stands on, is off-balance in a forwards position, with his right knee farther forwards still while he crushes the severed head of the enemy; his elbow, which sticks out proudly and leads up to his upturned hand is preceded by the post-Donatellian development of the iconographic motif. As much as Donatello's young biblical hero gently gazed in contemplative absorption, Michelangelo's figure is, on the contrary, vigorous and aggressive in his triumph. Likewise as concerns size, the artist, by then in search of the monumental,[6] had not just shifted away from the model but from the instructions he had been given as well: he had been asked to make a statue two and one-quarter *braccia* in height (equal to more or less 131 cm), but the documents say he made it over life-sized, measuring 3 *braccia* or about 180 cm. It seems he never finished it:[7] it is perhaps the only instance where the artist abandoned a sculpture which was completed by another hand, for it was Benedetto da Rovezzano who finished it in 1508-1509.

Donated to Florimond Robertet, the *David* arrived in France and was installed in the Hôtel d'Alluye, prior to a series of other locations, until it vanished.[8]

The *Four Saints* for the Piccolomini chapel

In November 1502, Michelangelo still had to purchase the marble he needed to make the Piccolomini statues,[9] but in April 1503, he was given the commission to execute twelve marble *Apostles* for Santa Maria del Fiore. During that time, and in the two-year-period that followed, he was to work on other sculptures as well: the *Pitti Tondo*, the *Taddei Tondo*, the *Bruges Madonna*, a cartoon for the *Battle of Cascina*. So it is quite likely that he worked on the Sienese commission only very marginally, also due to the fact that the cardinal – who, on 30 April 1503 was still binding the artist to the contractual clause that stated that he was to make the statue "cum omni pulchritudine et perfectione"[10] – was elected pope with the name Pius III on 22 September 1503, and died on 18 October, bequeathing his complex relationship with the artist to his heirs.[11]

In a recently published letter of 1508,[12] Francesco da Sarteano, an agent for the Piccolomini family in Siena, invited the archbishop Giovanni (nephew of Pius III) to Rome in order to patiently renew the contract with Michelangelo: "I ask that your Lordship be patient and disregard the delay for neither here nor in any other place that I have heard speak of is there anyone capable of mastering the art of *disegno* better than Michelangelo".[13] The Piccolomini agent's impassive prose expressed a clear-sighted and not especially indulgent opinion of the artists of his time, attributing "disegno", that is, the complete intellectual and manual mastery of the arts to Michelangelo alone.

Also in the spring of 1510, Matteo Cuccarello, a supplier of Carrara marble, had four blocks for the Piccolomini statues shipped to Florence, but as Michelangelo rejected them, for reasons unknown they went to Baccio da Montelupo.[14]

The four statues for *Saint Paul*, *Saint Peter*, *Saint Pius* and *Gregory the Great*, installed in the lower side niches, are the only ones by Michelangelo decorating the Piccolomini chapel in Siena Cathedral, which also houses Pietro Torrigiano's 1501 *Saint Francis*, reworked by Michelangelo, and the preexisting *Madonna and Child* up above, by the hand of Giovanni di Cecco (1371). The statues were executed in Florence, and represent what Michelangelo managed to deliver between 1501 and 1504 in compliance with the contract. As time went by, the artist himself seemed to put the works at the back of his mind, and neither Condivi nor Vasari reported them; only the very erudite and informed Sienese Fabio Chigi, the future Pope Alexander VII, took note of "one" statue by Michelangelo in 1625-1626. More than one critic has cast doubt as to whether or not the statues are autographs. Even recently, Baldini shifted the authorship for the *Saint Paul* to Baccio da Montelupo,[15] to whom all four had been attributed;[16] along the same lines Lisner suggested that Baccio was the executor of the designs and models provided by Buonarroti.[17]

Recently reconsidered to be autograph sculptures, whose rank as minor works nonetheless includes inventions and an approach to

the marble equal to those we acknowledge to be masterpieces,[18] the four statues reflect the young artist's experimental and expressive manifoldness, not devoid of uncertainty and discontinuity. The *Saint Paul*, which is set on a molded circular base, is the most coherent and resolved figure of all of them. His pose is articulated in *contrapposti* and subtle torsions amplified by the richness of the folds in the tunic and mantle. The saint's serious, concentrated mien is said to be the artist's first self-portrait, for set in the intense expression lined with the early signs of aging is a nose that was broken and permanently deformed.[19] The working of the marble, whose more visible parts are finished, gradually leads to the rough-hewn back view, revealing the frequent use of the claw-chisel in all of the intermediate passages, true to the Michelangelesque touch.
The *Saint Peter*, whose ponderated pose tilts the figure while he at the same time holds still the vertical plumb-line of the robe he wears, bends his head downwards as if gazing at a faithful follower, and in doing so there is a mild torsion of the shoulders. The face, modelled with serene classicism, could be influenced, in its benevolent and remote expression, by the illustrious example of the antique bronze statue of *Saint Peter,* visible, then as now, in the Vatican. The circular base here is wider and lower, and entirely expressed in molding. For the *Saint Pius* and even more so the *Saint Gregory the Great*, we have to admit "a certain loosening up of [Michelangelo's] inspiring tension and faculties of invention".[20] The postures for the two sainted prelates show minimal inclinations in and flexions of the figure and, contrarily, a dropping of heavy linear drapery for the former, just slightly more clustered in folds and flaps in the latter. The regular features of those piously bent heads reveal a limited expressiveness. This does not mean, however, that the faces aren't fully Michelangelesque, as Kriegbaum's observation that the Madonna in the *Pitti Tondo* could be "the pope's sister" is indeed substantiated.[21] A certain brevity of execution in some of the features in the *Saint Gregory the Great*, such as the Triregnum and the hands, have suggested that this was the last of the four to be made, when Michelangelo was preparing to give up the commission. Nonetheless, a few more words do need to be said about the width and shape of the bases, as well as their relationship with the depth of the niches. The base for the *Saint Paul* somewhat protrudes, although very carefully, from the niche bottom: *Saint Peter*'s, lower down, advances even more into the empty space. The statue of *Saint Gregory the Great* is set on a thin (broken) disc with the same protruding effect. Lastly, the *Saint Pius* is on a base that is the same height as *Saint Paul*'s but because of its oval shape, it just manages to fit into the cavity of the niche. Without overstating our deductions, it seems we could claim that Michelangelo had no idea of the exact size of the niches before making the *Saint Pius*; that he probably had nothing to do with the preparation of the niches themselves, as has instead been suggested;[22] that the *Saint Pius* was the last statue he made; that, in view of the disorderliness and inconsistency of the bases, he worked for long intervals of time or hired others to deal with certain less important procedures, such as the completion of the support bases for the figures.

The Florentine Tondi

For a long time, but without ever reaching any conclusions, scholarship has debated over the dates for the *Pitti Tondo* and the *Taddei Tondo*, or at least their respective positions in the chronology of Michelangelo's corpus of works, either accepting or refuting the chronological priority of the *Taddei Tondi*, which would seem to be suggested in Vasari where it is the first to be mentioned. Nonetheless, since the time of the biographies written during the artist's lifetime, the two high-reliefs have always been considered together, first, because they date back to the same years, and second, because they both belong to the unusual typology of the round marble composition, or "tondo". Although the painted tondo, preferably including iconographic motifs that focused on the *Madonna and Child*, was a frequently used format in Florentine workshops in the second half of the Quattrocento and Cinquecento, its use in marble was instead much rarer. Unsurprisingly, examples of marble medallions are found among the late works of Benedetto da Maiano, who died in 1497.

p. 90
Michelangelo, *Saint Paul*, where the artist's self-portrait, about thirty years at the time, is clearly visible
Siena Cathedral, Piccolomini chapel

p. 91
Michelangelo, *Saint Peter*, inspired by the bronze effigy of the first pope in the Vatican Basilica
Siena Cathedral, Piccolomini chapel

p. 92
Michelangelo, *Saint Pius*
Siena Cathedral, Piccolomini chapel

p. 93
Michelangelo, *Saint Gregory the Great*
Siena Cathedral, Piccolomini chapel

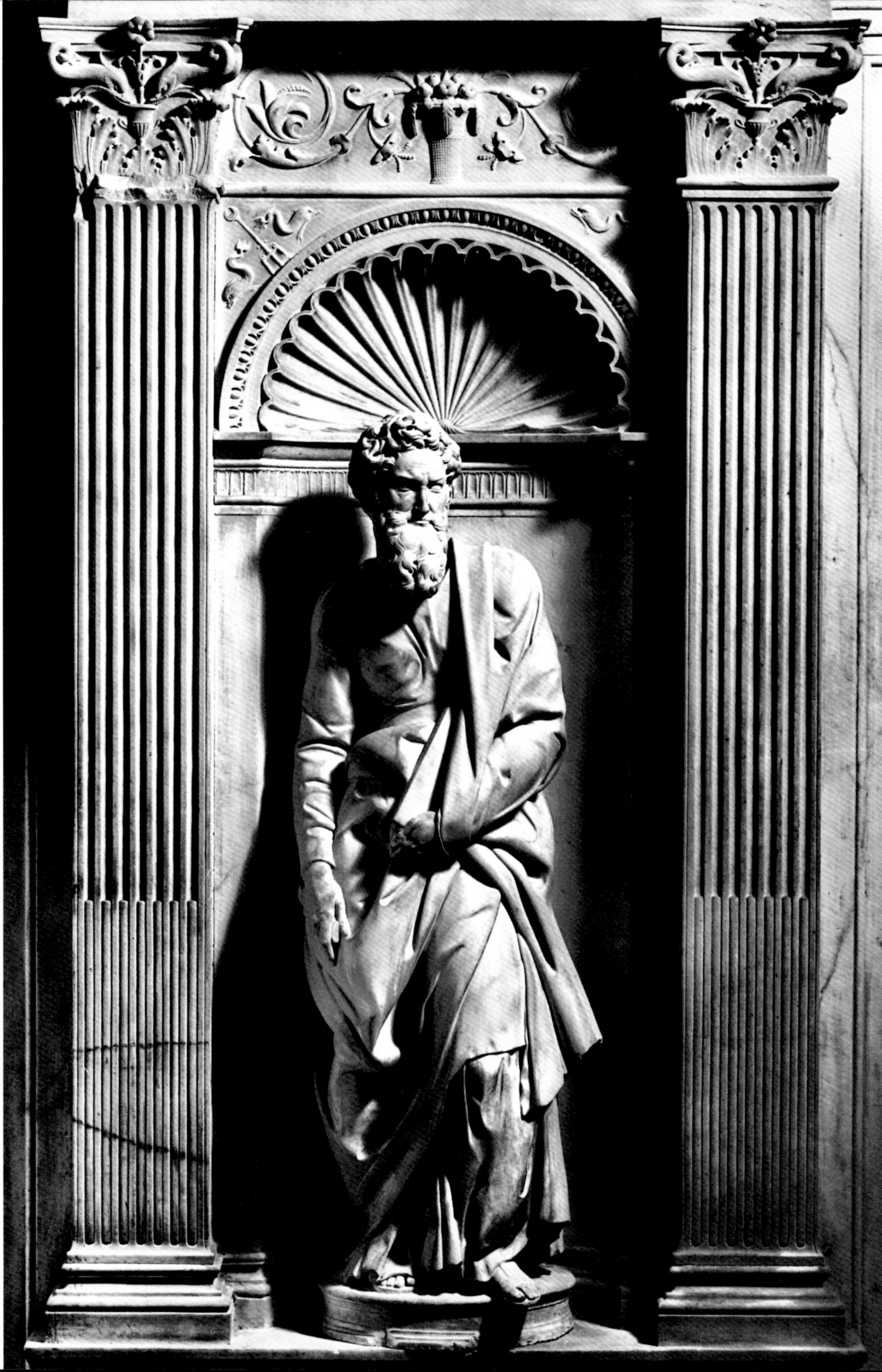

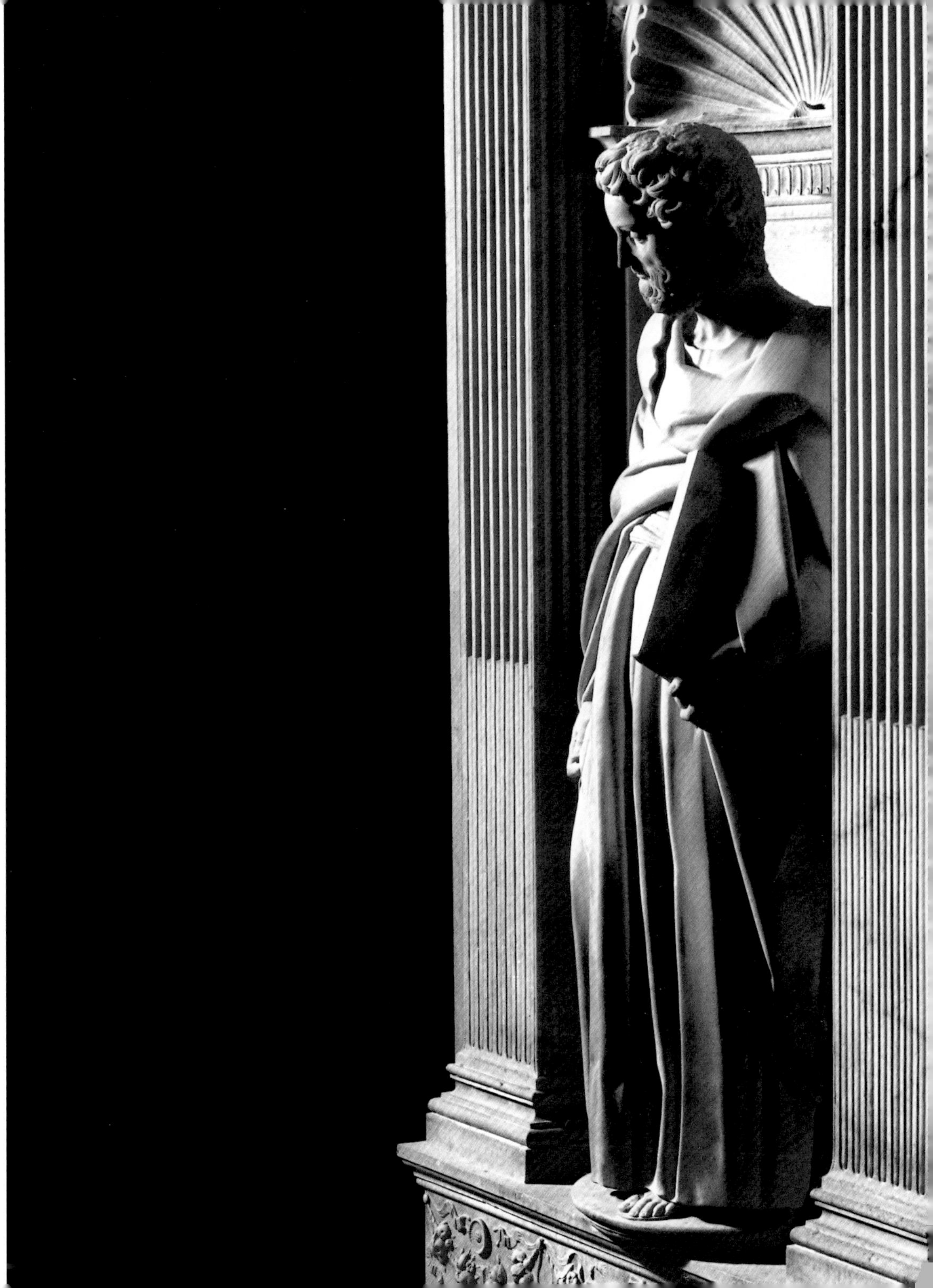

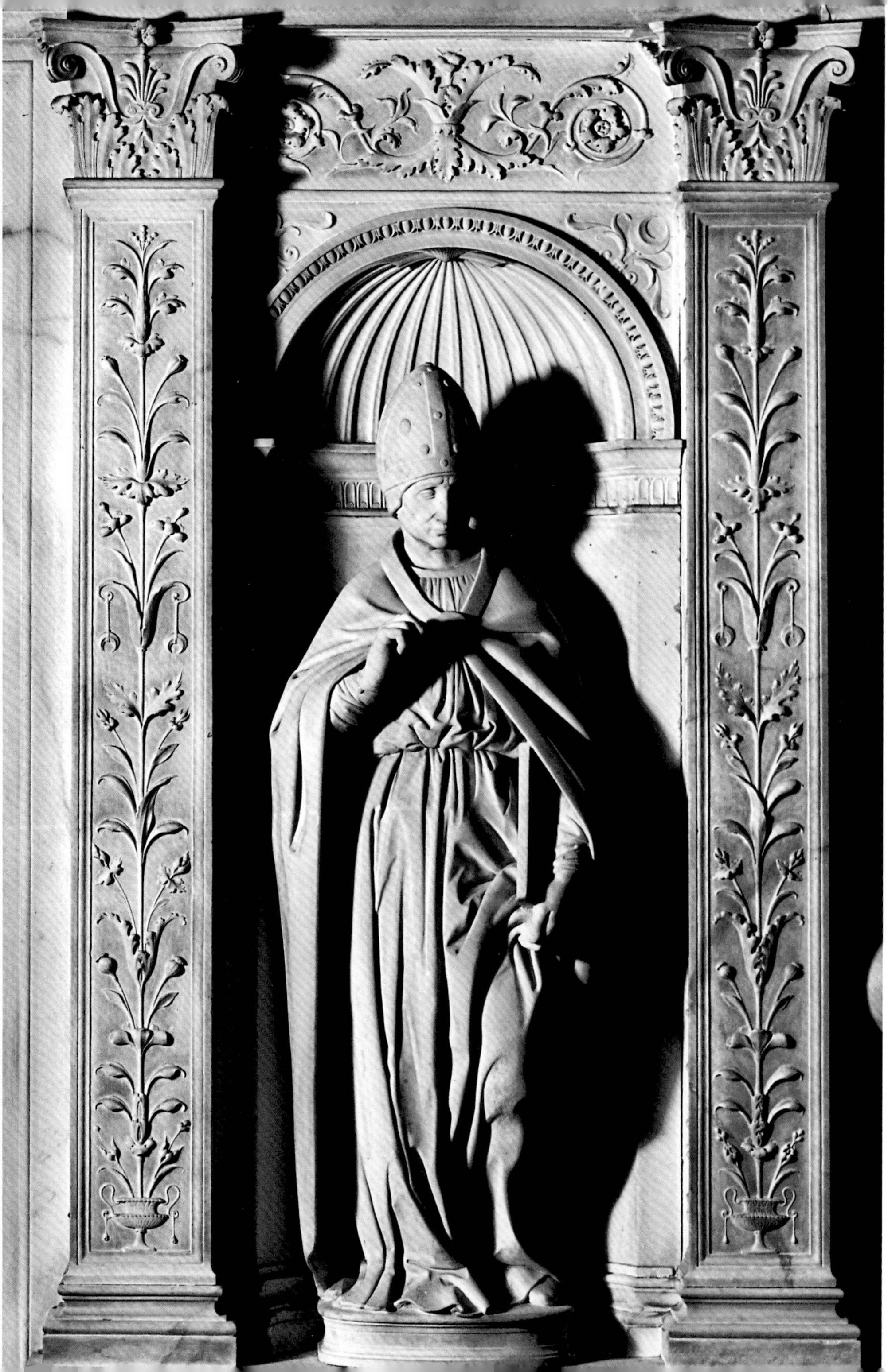

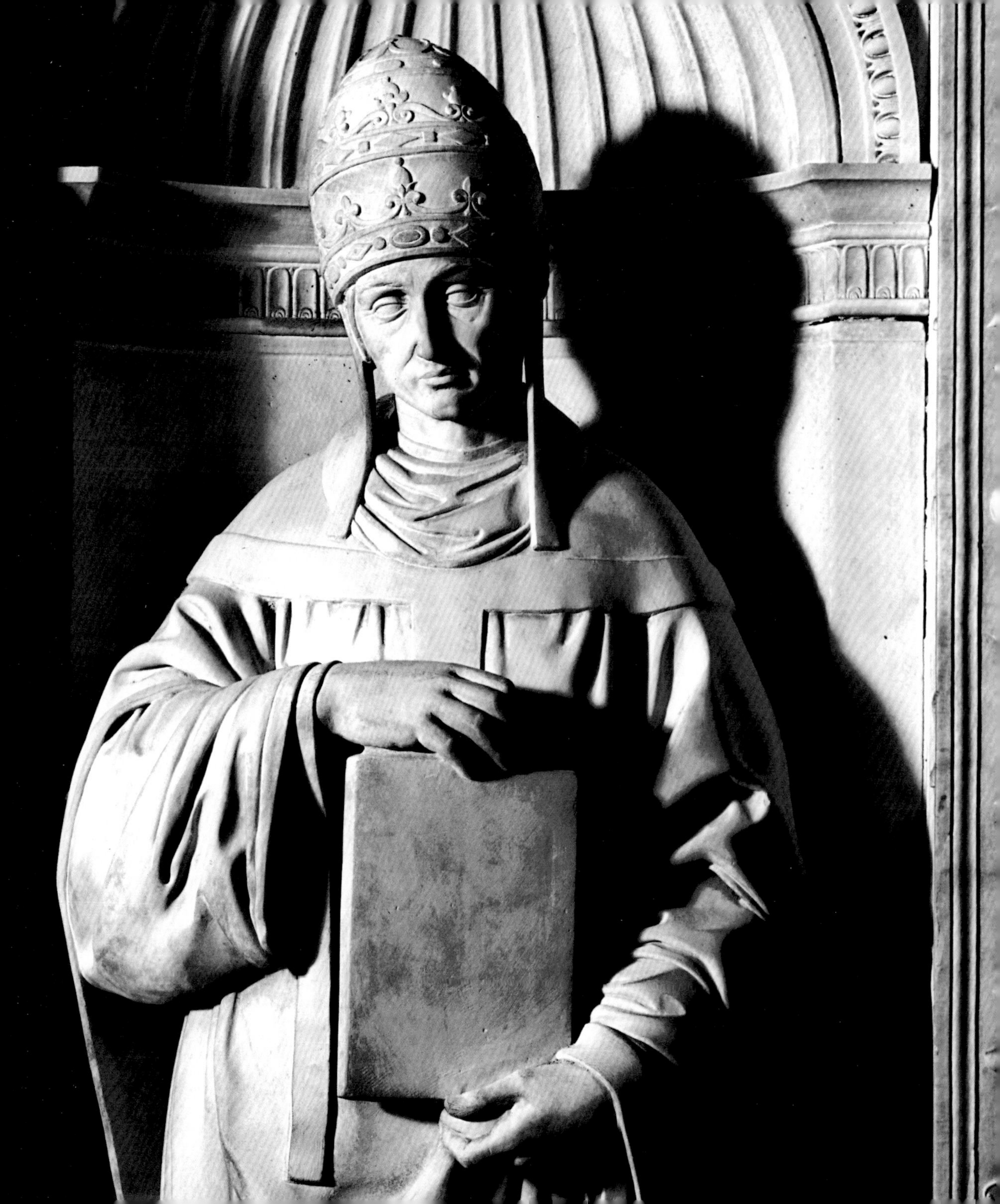

But Michelangelo was the first to introduce the portrayal of a full-sized Madonna and children in his marble tondi - and continued to do so in his painting with the *Madonna Doni*.[23] And in combining the holy image with the *ratio* of composition, he chose the example of the "Madonna of Humility", squatting on a low seat, or even sitting on the ground, again drawing inspiration from the work of Donatello.
Also common to the two Michelangelo tondi is the state of incompleteness: he "roughed out (but did not complete)" them, in the words of Vasari, rather, he only "began" the Pitti Tondo.[24] Due to the different degrees of carving visible, from rough-hewing to surface polishing, the works are an instructive demonstration of the marble-carving tools and techniques that were familiar to Michelangelo; tools and techniques that, as has been observed, so greatly relied on the art of chiselling stone. The dynamism that animates the relationships between the holy protagonists – the Madonna, Child, the Infant Saint John – reveal a Michelangelo who was very much involved in an intense confrontation with Leonardo da Vinci's ideas regarding composition, the author, at the turn of the century, of studies that in Florence would be accessible in the second (lost) cartoon of *Saint Anne*, visited by artists and admirers at the Servite convent of Santissima Annunziata, where Leonardo was a guest in 1501.[25]

The *Pitti Tondo*

For the *Pitti Tondo* now at the Museo Nazionale del Bargello in Florence, there is a likely connection as concerns its patron and chronology with the unfinished work of the *Apostles*, as the person to whom it would eventually go, Bartolomeo di Silvestro di Roberto Pitti, even recalled by Vasari, became an *operaio* of Santa Maria del Fiore on 1 July 1503.[26]
The profile of the marble disc reveals marked irregularities, particularly in the lower portion: in the upper portion, a raised lip hints at a frame effect, which is, however, interrupted in the middle by a high-relief made up of the Madonna's head. The veiled head, turned to the viewer's left, protrudes and turns simultaneously on the Madonna's neck, as she sits on a low parallelepiped (perhaps the cornerstone of the Mother Church), and takes up the central portion of the space. Right up close to her low-seated figure, between her rightward pointing knees, the Child leans up against the open book; both Mother and Child have stopped reading as if to lend their ears, in a moment of prescient and melancholy concentration, to the Infant Saint John, who nestles in the very small amount of space just behind the Madonna. Generally speaking, the iconographic motif for an interpretation of the work pertains to the theme – a very popular one in Florentine artistic tradition – of the Child's early training in the scriptures. But in Michelangelo's version the peacefulness of the domestic scene is upset by a number of omens: the Madonna's absorbed and tense face, whose gift of prescient knowledge seems to be symbolized by the cherub situated at the front of her hairstyle;[27] the Child's physical exhaustion, abandoned to a drowsiness anticipating his death;[28] the effusion of his mother's cloak, which, as a part of it lies between his hand and cheek, and between his torso and Mary's hand, suggests the subtle and merciful protection of the sudarium.
The composite garments worn by Mary, which consist in a robe with close-knit folds and a broad bordered overgarment, and the luxuriant locks of hair crossing the brow indicate similarities with the much more finished *Bruges Madonna*, while, as mentioned before, her full face with very regular features resembles that of *Saint Gregory the Great* in Siena. Other comparisons may be made with antique statuary, while at the same time the great 15th-century sculptural work of Jacopo della Quercia and Donatello also springs to mind. The suggestion of devout archaism seems to radiate from the Virgin's head, the curved top of which breaks free of the frame like in 12th- and 13th-century painted icons of "pittura delle origini", a venerated Florentine example being the *Madonna* in Santa Maria Maggiore, among others.
The medallion's relatively flat rear plane reveals marks left by a point-

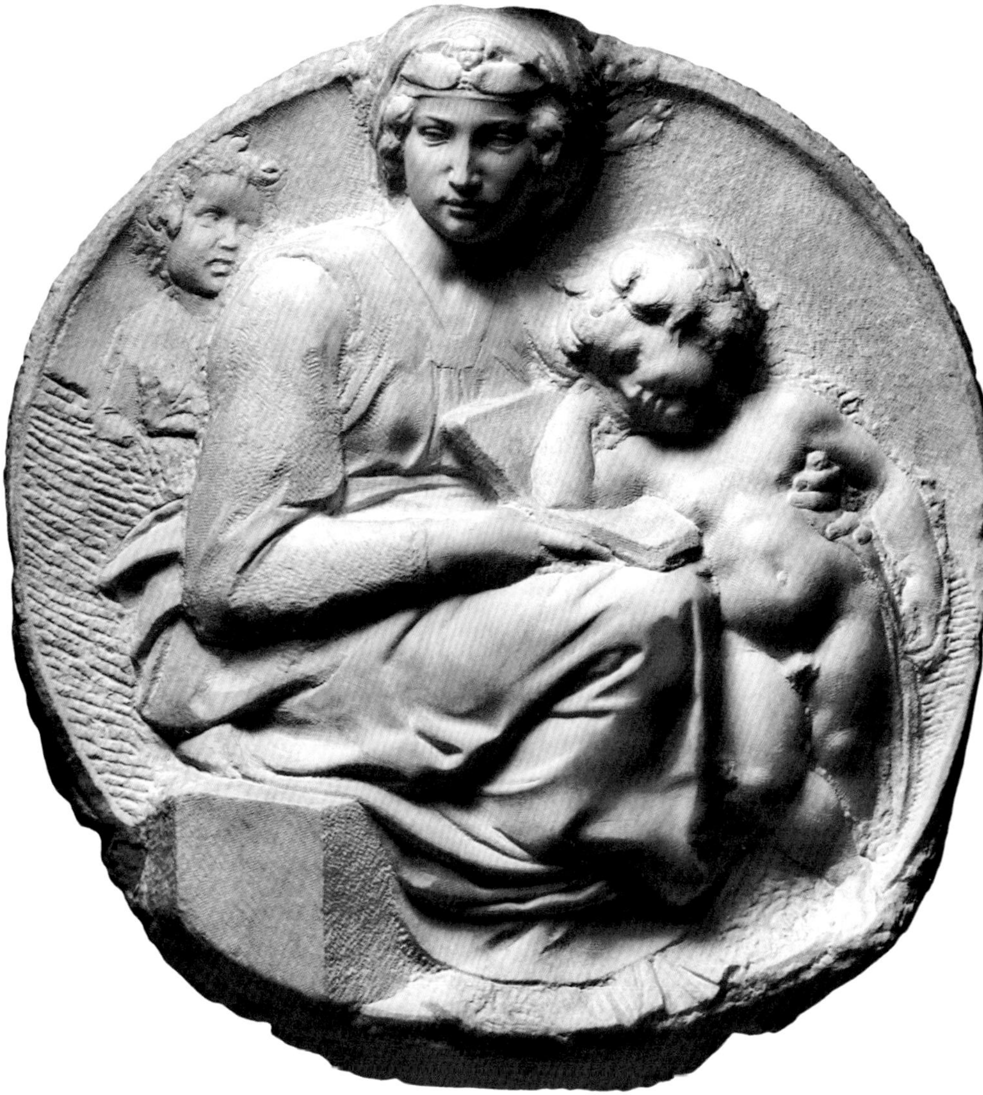

Michelangelo, *Pitto Tondo*
(*Madonna and Child with the Infant Saint John*)
The child seems to abandon himself to a drowsiness filled with prescient knowledge during a reading of the holy scripture
Florence, Museo Nazionale del Bargello

ed chisel to the left, while the claw-chisel was repeatedly used in the depth of the material. In the catalogue of sculptor's marks, the volumes reveal carefully sought out chiaroscuro effects, especially evident in the two sides of the block-seat. The neat sequence of parallel grooves show how Michelangelo achieved his shapes by regularly and controlledly sinking his carving tool across the whole surface: an example of this is the way he achieved the relief for Mary's breast. Another enlightening detail is the residual presence of irregular depth of the marble thickness all around the figures, for an effect ranging from blurred to sharp: this was obviously superfluous marble that was to be eliminated in subsequent stages.

Like for other apparently unfinished works by Buonarroti, we have always wondered about the reasons for this state of incompletion. While some write it off as simply an interruption ("left incomplete"),[29] for others it constitutes an expressive device, and was at any rate deliberate.[30]

The *Taddei Tondo*

The *Taddei Tondo*, now at the Royal Academy in London, was carved for Taddeo Taddei, as recalled by both Vasari (1550, 1568) and Benedetto Varchi (1564). Similar to the *Pitti Tondo* as concerns subject and perhaps chronology, the work depicts a very different moment of reflection on the subject of the Madonna and Child with the Infant Saint John: as much as the Florentine composition expresses the subject in terms of dignified and prescient knowledge, the London work animates it with reciprocal tensions between the sacred players. The Infant Saint John to the left, who already wears the animal skin and bow[1] of his future hermitage as Precursor in the desert, crosses his wrists as he holds his arms out to Jesus while offering him a little bird (the robin or goldfinch symbolizing the Passion) and another object, left unfinished and only implied in the residual marble. Although a crown of thorns has been suggested,[32] I believe it was more likely meant to be a scroll with the words "Ecce Agnus Dei". Faced with the multiple prophetic signs of his own destiny, the infant Christ bounds forwards in fear and hides in his mother's lap, whereupon Mary, whose pose is that of "humility", gathers him up, placing her right hand on the infant Saint John's shoulder to stop him from advancing any further.[33] The scene appears to feature the credible liveliness of a domestic episode, where the naughty child frightens his little cousin and is gently but firmly reproached by his aunt,[34] if it weren't for the deep-seated and subtle theological implications that accompany it, and that critics at the time had no difficulty interpreting. A fitting recollection here is of the letter written by Isabella d'Este's agent who, while commenting on the mutual fleeting attitudes of Anne, Mary, Jesus and the Infant Saint John in Leonardo's first *Saint Anne* cartoon (*circa* 1498), interprets them in light of the Church's disapproval of the Madonna's efforts to save her Son from the Passion. To go back to Michelangelo, the sacred intangibility of the body of Christ, who has no contact whatsoever with his Mother's flesh, is respected here once again.

Like in Leonardo's cartoon (as well as Verrocchio and Lorenzo di Credi's *Madonna di Piazza* in Pistoia Cathedral and in other paintings from that time), the Child is half-reclined with his stomach turned upwards, a pose that, it has been noted, had at least one ancient precedent in the putto of the Medea sarcophagus in the Staatliche Museen in Berlin.

Athough doubt has been cast on the medallion's autograph, it is now generally included in Michelangelo's corpus of works, although in some parts of the relief there is a lingering doubt as to further work having been done at a later date. Furthermore, the obvious "non-finito" condition of the work is visual proof of a sampling of typical treatments in Buonarroti's autograph style, which is totally compatible with those present in works that have been firmly attributed to him; the *pentimenti*, some of which are quite significant, in the area of the Virgin's left arm reveal a laboured creative process.

The medallion, characterized by an extremely irregular border, is carved very deep, to the extent that in some parts very little is left of the rear plane: a further sign of its fragility is the presence of a crack,

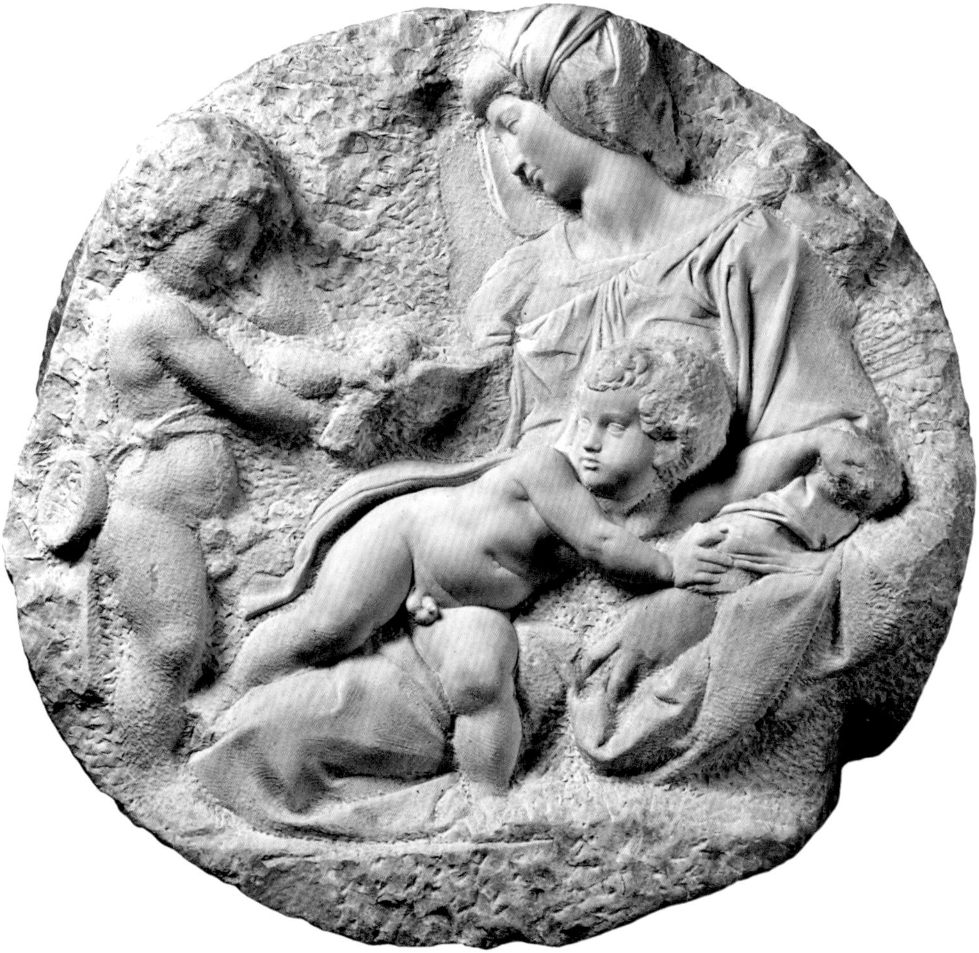

Michelangelo, *Taddei Tondo* (*Madonna and Child with the Infant Saint John*)
The infant Saint John frightens Jesus when he shows him a goldfinch, symbol of the Passion, while the Madonna seems to gently stop him
London, Royal Academy

or *pelo*, in the hidden profile of the Virgin. A symbol that reads "LA" has been identified on the *verso*.[35] Emerging from the penultimate skin of the marble left rough are the limbs and figures, outlined by rows of pseudo-holes that actually mark where the claw-chisel struck the marble. The most advanced parts may be seen in the busts of the Madonna and the Child, where the insistent work carried out by the different types of claw-chisel, which became increasingly finer, smoothed the areas of flesh and drapery, without, however, accomplishing a final lustre for the surfaces. The reasons for the "non-finito" state of the work are, as always, the topic of debate: departure for Florence, technical difficulties, occurring at the same time as the crack; or the artist's lack of interest in an invention that had by then been delineated; or his satisfaction with what he had been able to accomplish which, despite its incompletion, fulfilled its function as a sacred narrative.

No less controversial is the date of the tondo, which ranges from 1502 in Baldini[36] because of the sharp contrast with Leonardo, to *circa* 1508 in Venturi[37] because of the Madonna's similarity to the female figures in the Sistine ceiling. There are indeed quite a few similarities between the *Virgin* and the *Sibyls*, or the *Ancestors of Christ*; but there are other very evident similarities too: the exotic turban and the sharp profile, the way her cloak stretches out diagonally as it crosses her breast, and the salient knot on her shoulder.

Another fact (but one which is not determinative in terms of chronology) comes from Raphael who, as a friend of Taddei, saw the medallion in his patron's home during one of his stays in Florence, in either 1504-1505 or 1508. Fascinated by the composition, he took graphic notes and revealed the reworking of some of the motifs in a number of his youthful *Madonnas*.[38]

The *Bruges Madonna*

Among the contacts established in Rome through the Balducci-Galli bank, which developed positively even after the artist returned to Florence, there was one with the Flemish merchants Jean and Alexander Mouscron, referred to in Italian as "i Moscheroni", clients of the bank from 1501. Michelangelo was paid 4,000 florins to carve a *Madonna and Child* for them. This commission overlapped with others in the early part of the 16th century, but the exact years are not known; what we do know for sure is that in January 1506 (common usage) Michelangelo told his father to be sure to have the statuary group – which must have been finished – brought to his home, and not show it to anyone,[39] and that in August it was ready to be shipped to Bruges, to the heirs of the by then deceased Mouscrons.[40]

The site for the *Madonna and Child*, called the *Bruges Madonna*, Michelangelo's only marble located in the Netherlands, was determined by the Mouscron heirs. Although the circumstances surrounding the commission are not known, it is important to recall that at the end of the 15th century Bruges was an active trading centre, and that there was a steady presence of Florentine merchants and bankers there. The statue was destined to be placed in the family's funeral chapel in the Bruges church of Notre Dame (Onze-Lieve-Vrouwekerk), and that is where the great German painter Albrecht Dürer saw it in 1521. Its original site was an ornate tabernacle. The current one, which was made later, consists in a triumphal polychrome marble façade, where Belgian black marble prevails, whose central niche houses Michelangelo's *Madonna*, and whose lateral niches house two statues representing *Faith* and *Hope*: the way in which the Italian statuary group has been arranged confers the meaning of *Charity* to it.

Very few actually saw the Madonna before it left for Bruges, and for this reason Condivi and Varchi both recall it as being a bronze work, and Vasari, but not until 1568, as a "medallion".[41] The Virgin together with the Child form a sculptural group that corresponds to a pyramidal distribution of the body volumes when viewed from the front, but appears to be more articulated when observed from the sides, where the two figures obviously acquire greater individuality. Set on an oval base (reminiscent of the one for the *Saint Pius* in Siena), the Madonna sits on a rock in layers with her foot resting on one of them so that she can hold the naked Child between her knees in the space of her lap; the Child, in turn, uses both hands to hold onto his mother. Both the

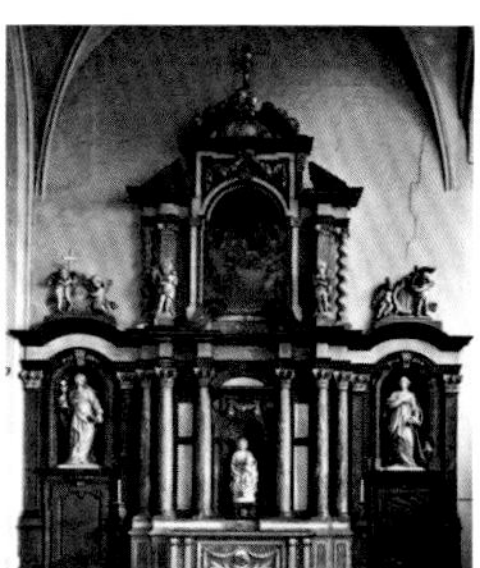

The Mouscron chapel with the monumental marble altar where Michelangelo's *Madonna and Child* was placed in the centre, to symbolize *Charity* amidst the later statues of *Faith* and *Hope*
Bruges, church of Notre Dame

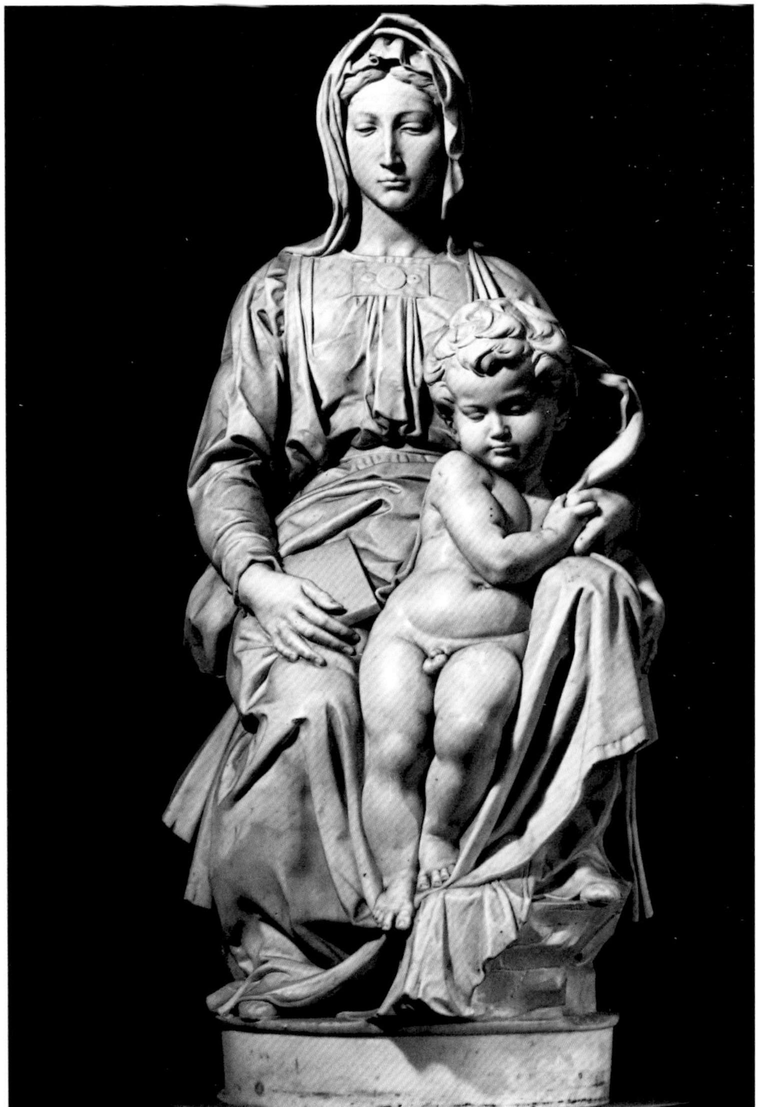

Michelangelo, *Madonna and Child*
Bruges, church of Notre Dame, Mouscron chapel

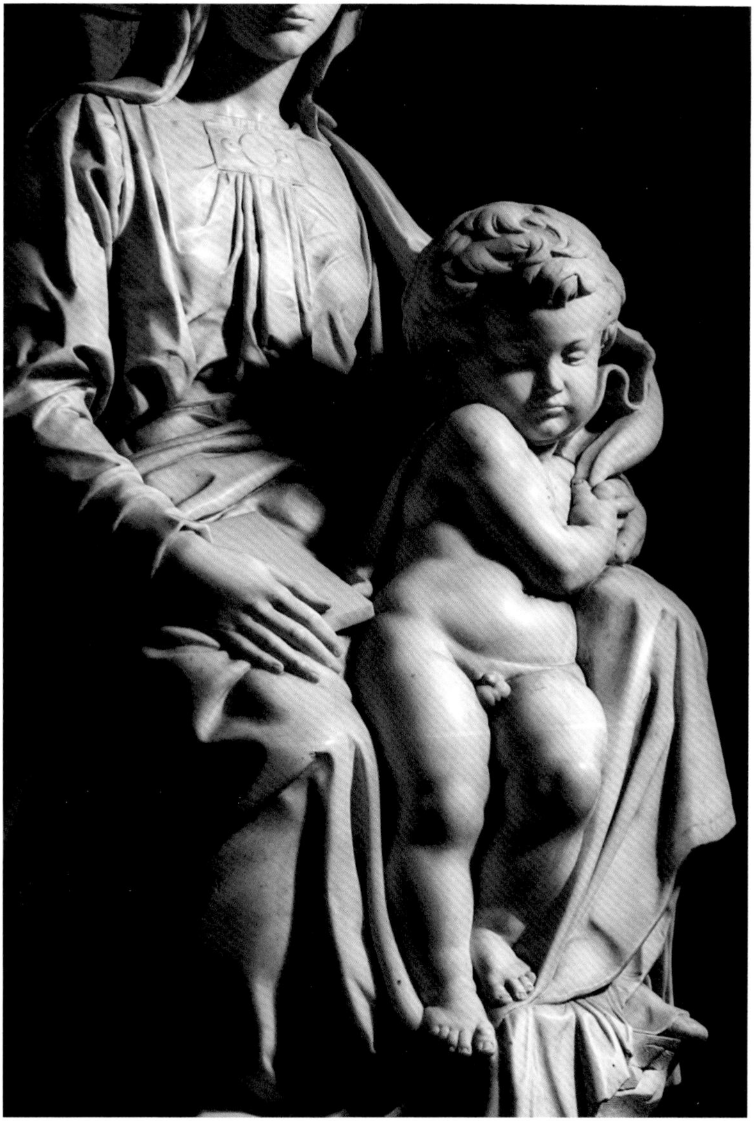

Michelangelo, *Madonna and Child*. Jesus is about to leave his mother's lap, as if to set out on the path towards sacrifice
Bruges, church of Notre Dame, Mouscron chapel

p. 101
Michelangelo, *Madonna and Child*. The clasping of hands seems to suggest Jesus' fear of facing up to his destiny, and at the same time his Mother's reluctance to let him go
Bruges, church of Notre Dame, Mouscron chapel

p. 102
Michelangelo, side view of the *Madonna and Child*, which reveals the complex relationship between Mother and Son
Bruges, church of Notre Dame, Mouscron chapel

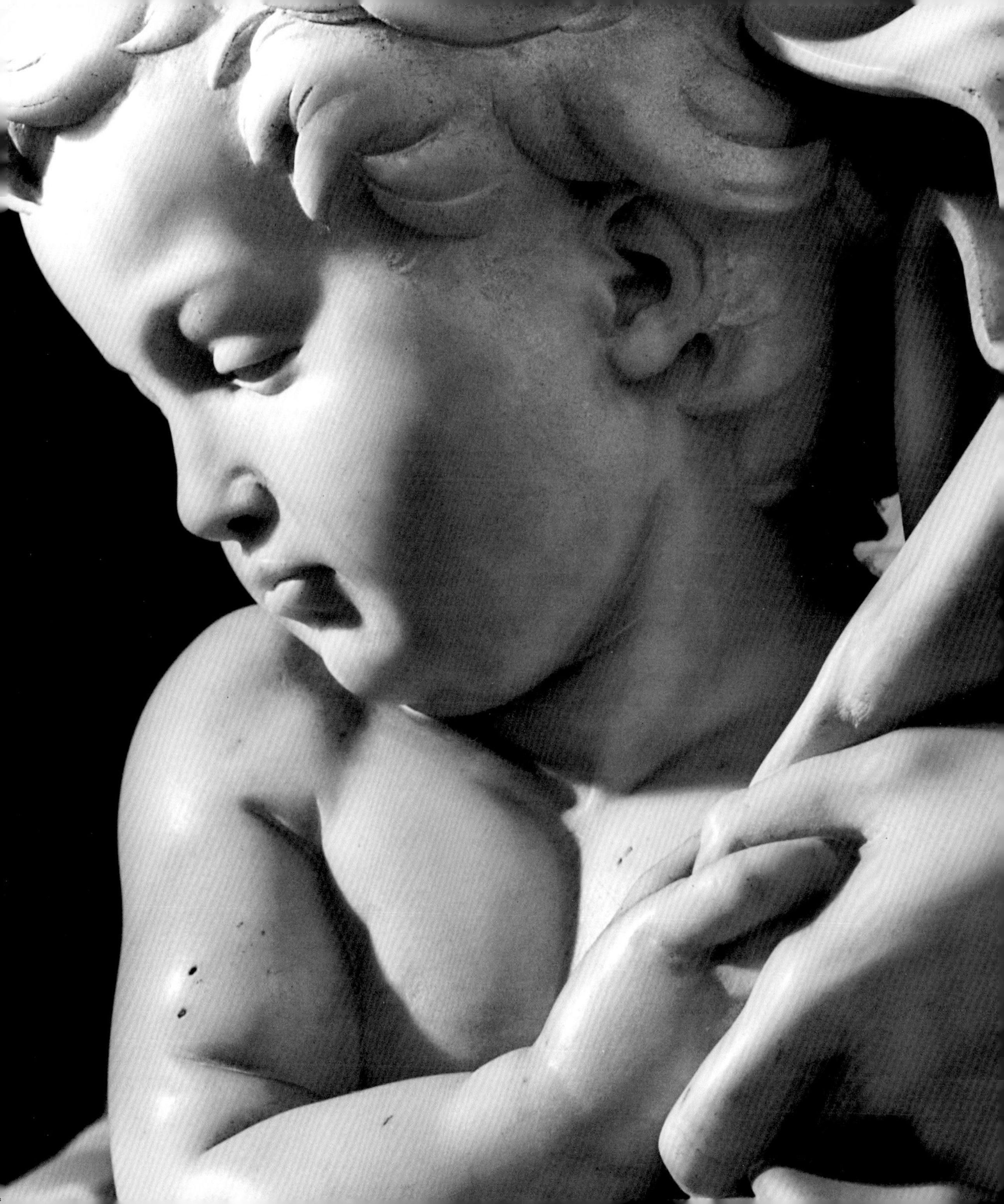

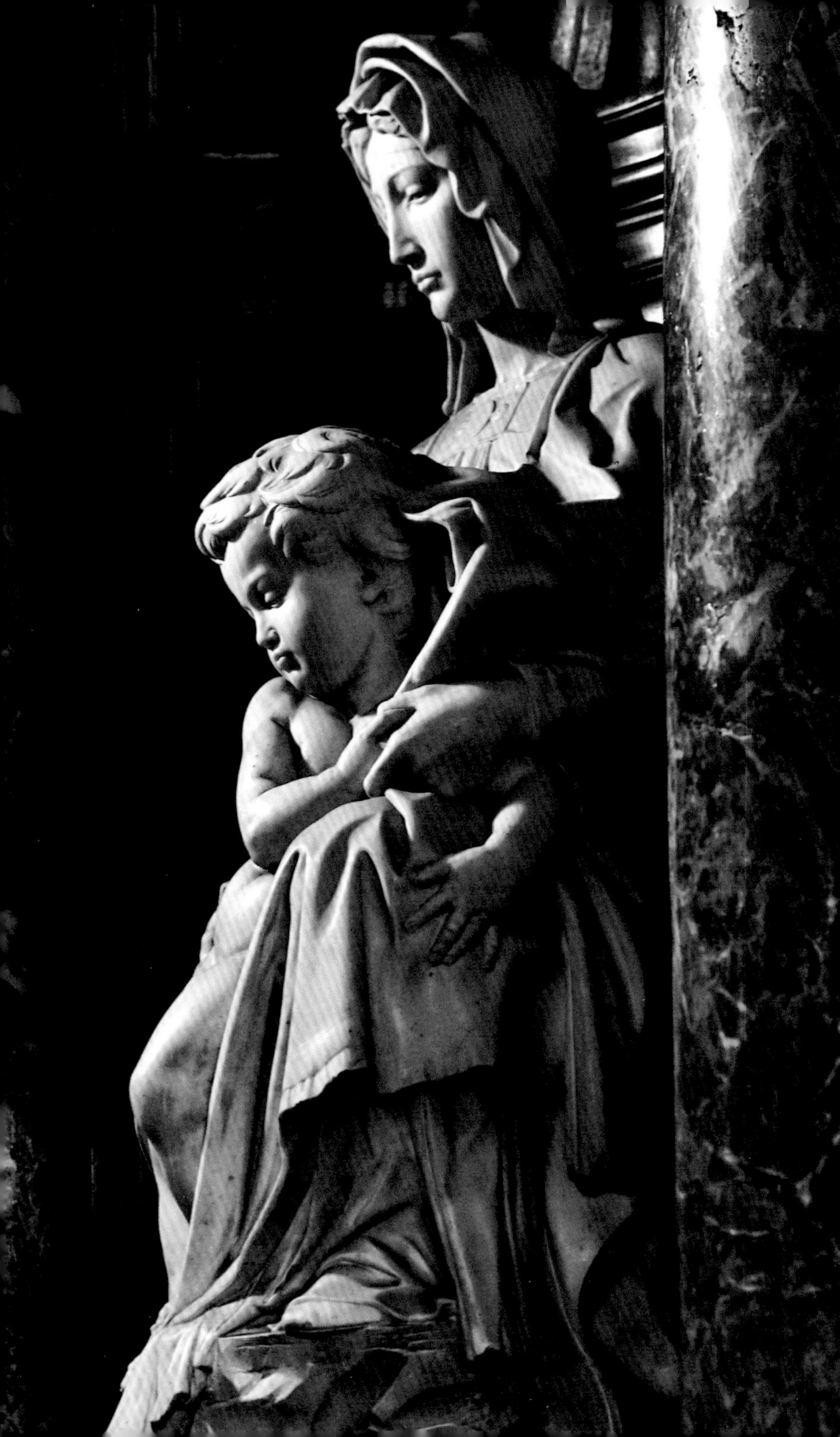

p. 103
Michelangelo, *Madonna and Child*, detail of the Madonna's sweet, melancholy face under the wavy folds of her veil
Bruges, church of Notre Dame, Mouscron chapel

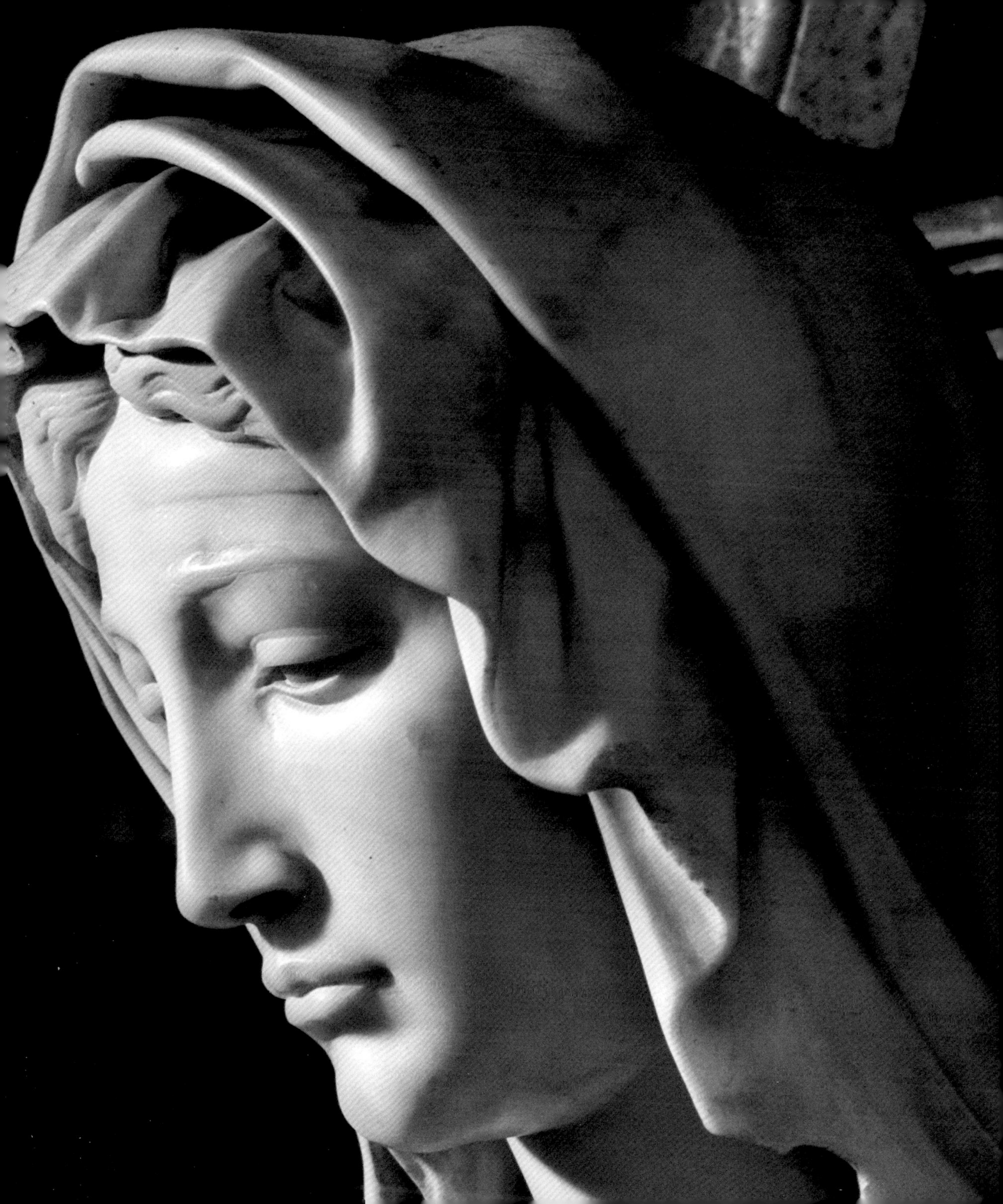

Virgin, whose face is made in extremely refined Botticellian-Maianesque style, and the chubby putto gaze forwards and downwards in the direction of an invisible point in space from which the start of Christ's journey through the world symbolically begins: the book of Scriptures, closed in the Mother's hand, has obviously been read, and the destiny of the Redemption understood. Here too, like in the medallions, the implicitly prescient vision generates very high emotional tension that is expressed in transfigured naturalism. The Child reveals his twofold inclination even as far as the most delicate torsions of his body which slips forwards and rotates in studied *contrapposti*: on the one hand, he is ready to leave the nest of folds in his mother's lap and descend towards the sacrifice he is destined for; on the other, he is held back by his refusal that renders his first step tentative, but his arm's hold on his mother's knee secure, to the point that it is completely enveloped in the drapery. After all, however much the expression on her face absorbed in thought may seem to be a peaceful one, Mary betrays her symmetrical reluctance to let her Son go with the gesture of her left hand: as she covers his naked shoulder with a wide piece of her cloak (also an anticipation of the sudarium), she intimately clasps his right hand. It seems that the complex pose, rich in dynamic spatial developments, was studied by the master in a drawing where the sitter was, of course, not a woman but a naked boy with a child.[42]

As in the case of the Roman *Pietà*, the Virgin's robe is plentifully draped, and her cloak drops down with large, supple folds gathering the figure into a sinuous sign. With just a shade of contradiction, on the Madonna's right side the cloak is adorned with a ruffled border, while on the left side it is irregularly cut to allow her forearm to emerge. The Virgin's robe is also fluted with ornamental stripes, an extreme citation from the precious painted fabrics of the end of the 15th century, while the unusual fibula, surrounded by a panel, that holds her robe still on her breast for a diaconal effect, is already in tune with the archaic and holy impression of the accessories worn by the Old Testament figures in the Sistine Chapel ceiling: see, for instance, the *Prophet Joel*. For the Child, Michelangelo suggested a sort of vigorous infantile attractiveness, which was commented on in reference to the Neoplatonic concept of God's beauty as the expression of his goodness.[43] The artist transformed the material into flawless translucence, the only rough areas with rustic effects being in the rocky base: like in the Vatican *Pietà*, the many folds of lavish drapery are accompanied by the minutest of details (such as the borders of the fabrics, the fine cords between the plates on her breast, the shoulder button); also visible is the artist's great skill at reducing the thickness of the marble, for example, in the scheme of crumpled folds visible in the space between the Child's head and Mary's arm. It would seem that Michelangelo forced himself to extract from the marble every description and expression possible.

The contract for twelve *Apostles* for the Florence Cathedral

In those hectic Florentine years from 1501 to 1505, Michelangelo also had the opportunity to prove himself in painting, by preparing, in 1504, the monumental albeit unexecuted cartoon for the fresco the *Battle of Cascina* in the Palazzo Vecchio, and probably also the *Madonna Doni* now in the Uffizi Gallery.

From 24 April 1503, the *operai* of Santa Maria del Fiore and the consuls of the Wool Guild contracted with him to carve twelve *Apostles* for the Florentine Cathedral. In addition to payment, the contract included permission for the artist to use a house that the Opera's master builder Simone del Pollaiolo, called il Cronaca, was to build for him near what is currently known as Borgo Pinti, in the "artists' quarter", where artists gravitated towards the Santissima Annunziata, just opposite the church at that time known as "del Cestello", now Santa Maria Maddalena de' Pazzi. As the exact period of time the artist worked on the *Saint Matthew* is uncertain, it has until now been assigned to the two-year period from April 1503 to March 1505, between the time of the contract and Michelangelo's departure for Rome. Nonetheless, further in-depth research into the shipping of the marble[44] has led to convincing evidence that the partial making of the apostle and evangelist, which would in fact be referred to after April 1506, should be brought forwards.

During those same years in Florence, Michelangelo is said to have completed a *Hercules* measuring more than two metres in height, commissioned to him by Piero de' Medici, and interrupted in 1494 (see Chapter Two).

A thirty-year-old Michelangelo was by now famous for his masterpieces in painting, but especially for his sculpture. In his *De Sculptura*, 1504, Pomponio Guarico included him in a roster of the most eminent living sculptors with Giovan Francesco Rustici and Andrea Sansovino, adding that he was "etiam pictor".[45] In 1506, Raffaello Maffei recalled three of his sculptures, the Vatican *Pietà*, the *David*, the *Bacchus*.[46] Vasari determined the three cornerstones of Michelangelo's fame, for that period of time, to be the *Pietà*, the "Giant" and the "cartoon".[47]

Notes

[1] This was be a funeral chapel as the cardinal was to be buried in the floor in front of the altar; but because he was elected pope with the name Pius III, he was buried in Rome in 1503. Cf. *infra*. Hirst has suggested that the two lowest flanking tabernacles are Michelangelo's own first work in architecture (1994, p. 81, no. 58).

[2] Mentioned in a letter by Michelangelo dated 22 May 1501, the request became formal with a contract signed by the cardinal on 5 June, by Michelangelo on the 19th and by Galli as guarantor on the 25th. The amount established was 500 ducats (cf. the catalogue *Giovinezza...*, 1999, p. 308). The artist was also asked to personally complete the statue of *Saint Francis* sent from Rome by Pietro Torrigiano.

[3] Siezed from the Medici after they were ousted in 1494, the bronze was moved to the Michelozzo courtyard at the Palazzo Vecchio. It is for this reason that in the request that had arrived by way of Lorenzo di Pierfrancesco and Pierfrancesco Tosinghi, Florentine goldsmiths at the French court, in a letter dated 22 June 1501, the *David* was to be "chome quello ch'è nella corte delle Signorie Vostre".

[4] For the supply of metal, Medici referred to the Capitani di Parte Guelfa, who resolved favourably on 26 August 1501. For more on this episode, cf. Gatti 1994, Caglioti 1996a, also as concerns what took place afterwards.

[5] Paris, Musée du Louvre, DAG , inv. 714 (cf. the entry by M. Hirst, in *L'officina...*, 1996, no. 23, p. 23, after that in Joannides, 2003a, no. 4).

[6] To this regard see Echinger-Maurach, 1998b.

[7] Reminders by Pierre de Rohan (letter from Niccolò Valori to the Dieci di Balia dated 23 February 1504, common usage), after he fell into disfavour with King Louis XII in April 1504 were followed by the reproaches of the French treasurer Florimond Robertet (letter by Filippo Pandolfini, French ambassador, dated 27 September 1504). The episode was at the centre of what was truly a diplomatic crisis.

[8] Corresponding to changes in ownership it was moved to the court of honour at the castle of Bury-en-Blésois, and then to the gardens of the castle of Villeroy, where its memory remained in poetic form (cf. Duchon, 1996; Echinger-Maurach, 1998b; Caglioti, 2000b, pp. 123, 291, 313-318, 321, 327, 404). If we consider the fact that Donatello's *David* was set on an elaborate column support, and that the *David* for Rohan was installed in Bury on a column, we may ask ourselves whether or not the transcription of the incipit of Petrarch's sonnet CCLXIX from the *Canzoniere* for the death of Lady Laura in the sheet at the Louvre is incidental: "Roct-e l-alta cholonna el verd[e lauro]" (Broken are the column and the green laurel).

[9] As stated in the documentary reconstructions by Hirst, 1994, 1997 ed., p. 85 and Hirst, 2000, where the Piccolomini statues are related to orders for marble from Carrara deliberated by the Opera di Santa Maria del Fiore on 28 November 1502.

[10] Mancusi-Ungaro, Jr., 1971, pp. 74-78.

[11] The first contract was ratified by Andrea di Vanni Todeschini Piccolomini on 15 September 1504. Soon after, on 11 October, Andrea and his brother Jacopo stipulated a new contract through Filippo di Niccolò d'Antonio, in which it would seem the sculptor had already delivered four statues and promised to make the other eleven. This would never occur, and his non-fulfilment worried him for the rest of his life, seeing that on 20 March 1561 (at eighty-one years) he wrote to his nephew Lionardo asking him to find and copy the contract for him. Payment of the balance only occurred after the artist's death, between his nephew Lionardo and the Piccolomini heirs.

[12] Jenkens, 2002.

[13] Jenkens, 2002, *Appendix*, p. 754.

[14] Mancusi-Ungaro, Jr., 1971, pp. 17-18.

[15] Baldini, 2001, pp. 36-37.

[16] Tolnay, 1943, and subsequent editions of 1947 (p. 29) and 1969. Not even Longhi (1940, 1956 ed., p. 137) believed that the statue was an autograph, although he did acknowledge it to have Ferrarese components compatible with Michelangelo's experiences; he also believed that, at least for the *Saint Peter*, the master's involvement was nothing more than a preliminary study drawing. Thereafter, Tolnay (1975, p. 11) stated that the *Saint Peter* and the *Saint Paul* were at least in part made by Michelangelo, while the *Saint Gregory the Great* and the *Saint Pius* by Baccio, after drawings by Buonarroti, instead.

[17] Lisner, 1967.

[18] G. Bonsanti, in *Giovinezza...*, 1999, p. 310.

[19] Kriegbaum, 1940.

[20] E. Carli, in *Michelangiolo...*, 1989, no. 46.

[21] Kriegbaum, 1940.

[22] Hirst, 1994, 1997 ed., pp. 78, note 58, pp. 84-85.

[23] Echinger-Maurach, 2000, p. 138.

[24] Vasari, "The Life of Michelangelo" (1550), 2007 ed., p. 158.

[25] The first cartoon for the *Saint Anne*, which was preceded by sketches and drawings, was made in Milan prior to 1500 (now in the National Gallery in London).

[26] Hirst, 2000, p. 489 and note 19.

[27] Tolnay, 1943, with irreprehensible reference to the cherubic diadem of the Madonna in the altar for Donatello's Saint in Padua.

[28] Scholarship generally agrees that the Child is an adaptation of the antique angel of death "type" (cf. Lightbrown, 1969, p. 25).

[29] A. Hughes, in Elam, Hughes, 1996, p. 435.

[30] The same may be found, for example, in M.S. De Salvia Baldini, in *Michelangiolo...*, 1989, no. 13. But in 1969, Lightbrown had already hypothesized that the sculptor had abandoned the medallion after making an irreparable mistake: "in his impatience sketched out the cherub [...] too low and then found the mistake impossible of correction", p. 26). What has gradually become the prevailing opinion, especially in Anglo-American studies, is a pragmatic view that would more or less relate the "non finito" to a series of material circumstances in the life of the artist or of his patrons.

[31] The gesture is repeated, with variations, in a drawing with studies of the Madonna and children (London, British Museum, 1887-5-2-117*v*.).

[32] This hypothesis was put forth by John Larson, who I wish to thank for having discussed it with me in depth, and showing me his digital renderings.

[33] Easton, 1969, pp. 391-393.

[34] Michelangelo's "secularization" of sacred subjects has been alluded to; cf. Echinger-Maurach, 2000, p. 139 and note 73.

[35] Also Larson, 1991. For the time being, neither quarrymen nor go-betweens with these initials have been identified, and in truth some reservations may be advanced as to its actually saying "LA".

[36] Baldini, 1973, no. 16.

[37] Venturi, 1936, p. 37.

[38] A drawing reproduces the bust of the Madonna and Child, except for the left leg (Paris, Musée du Louvre, DAG, inv. 3856; see Lightbrown 1969, p. 23); also referring to them is a sheet now in the Gabinetto Disegni e Stampe at the Uffizi in Florence, inv. 496 E, whose *verso* shows sketches for the *Madonna of the Goldfinch*. In another study for the painting, visible on a sheet at the Ashmolean Museum in Oxford, inv. P. II 517*r*, the figure of the Infant Saint John standing and seen from the side seems to be inspired by the Michelangelesque relief. Other works by Raphael from that period of time contain cues from and returns to the composition in the *Taddei Tondo*: Paris, Musée du Louvre, DAG, inv. 3586; Vienna, Albertina Graphische Sammlung, inv. 209, R.53, S.R. 250; London, British Museum, inv. 1902-8-22-4; Chatsworth, inv. 783 (cf. Knab, Mitsch, Oberhuber, 1983, nos. 133, 161-162; Joannides, 1983, nos. 93*v*., 111*v*., 180, 181*v*.); the *Bridgewater Madonna*, Edinburgh, Duke of Sutherland but at the National Gallery of Scotland in Edinburgh.

[39] Letter to Michelangelo while in Rome to his father Ludovico in Florence, 31 January 1506 (common usage), in *Il Carteggio...*, 1965-1983, I, 1965, pp. 11-12 no. VII. This suggestion has often been considered an indication of Michelangelo's jealous caution as concerned his work. Nonetheless, one website (www.isi.edu/~ hobbs/madonna.pdf, consulted in April 2005) refers to the donation of the monument by the Mouscron to the Bruges church of Notre Dame (Archive in Bruges), which contained the clause that the sculpture was not to be shown to anyone without the family's express permission; perhaps, therefore, Michelangelo's secrecy stemmed from the patrons' explicit request.

[40] Letter from Giovanni Balducci in Rome to Michelangelo in Florence, 14 August 1506, in *Il Carteggio...*, 1965-1983, I, 1965, p. 17, no. XI.

[41] Condivi, 1553, 1998 ed., p. 22; Varchi, 1564, p. 29; Vasari, *The Lives* (1568), 1996 ed., II, p. 656.

[42] London, British Museum, Department of Prints and Drawings, inv. 1859-6-25-564*r*. Cf. Wilde, 1953, no. 5; Echinger-Maurach, 2000, fig. 12.

[43] Echinger-Maurach, 2000, p. 132.

[44] Amy, 2000.

[45] Gaurico, 1504, 1999 ed., p. 251.

[46] Maffei, 1506 (*Raphael Volaterranus, Libri XXXVIII*, Romae MVI).

[47] Vasari, *The Lives* (1568), 1996 ed., II, p. 658.

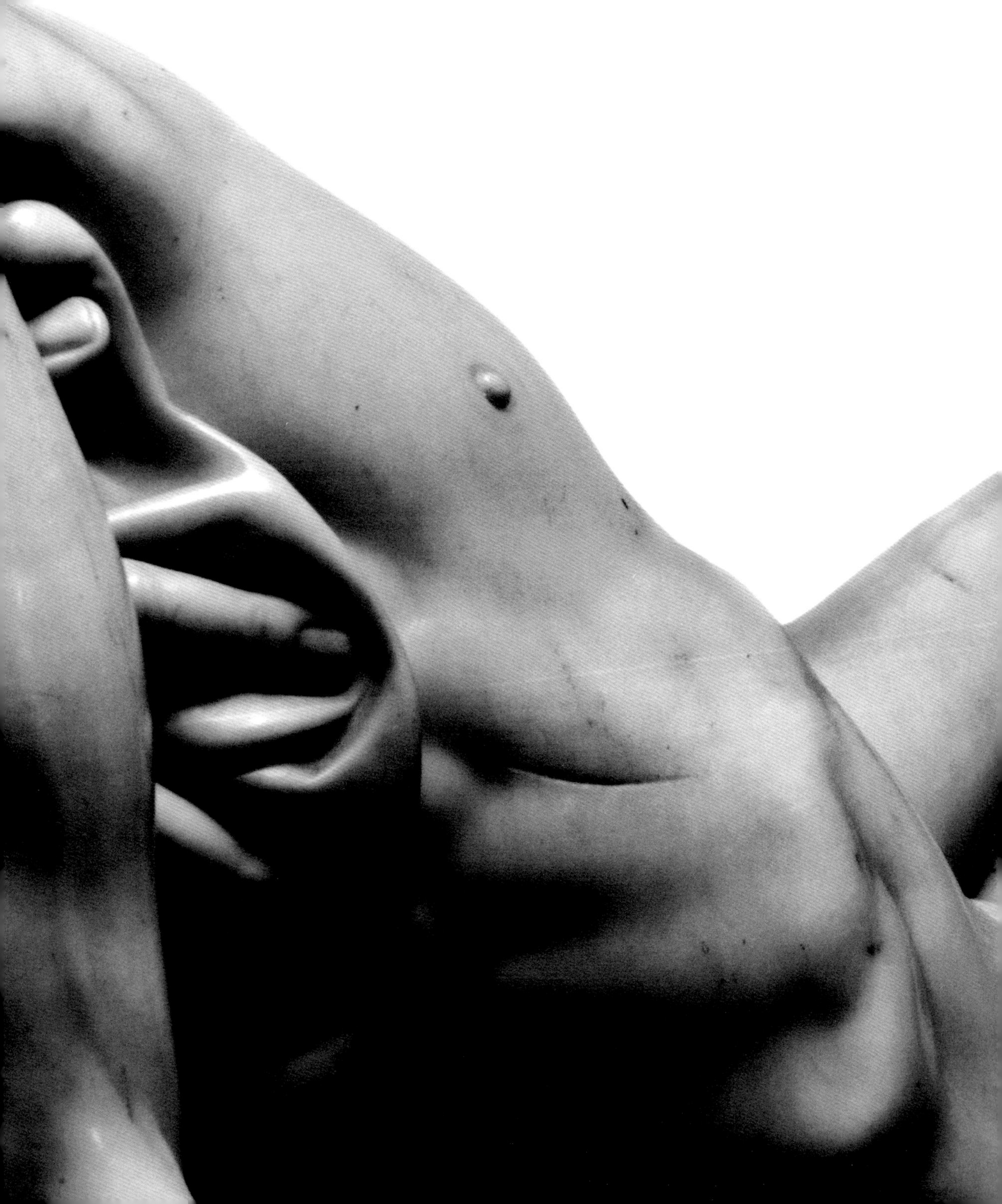

From Julius II to Leo X

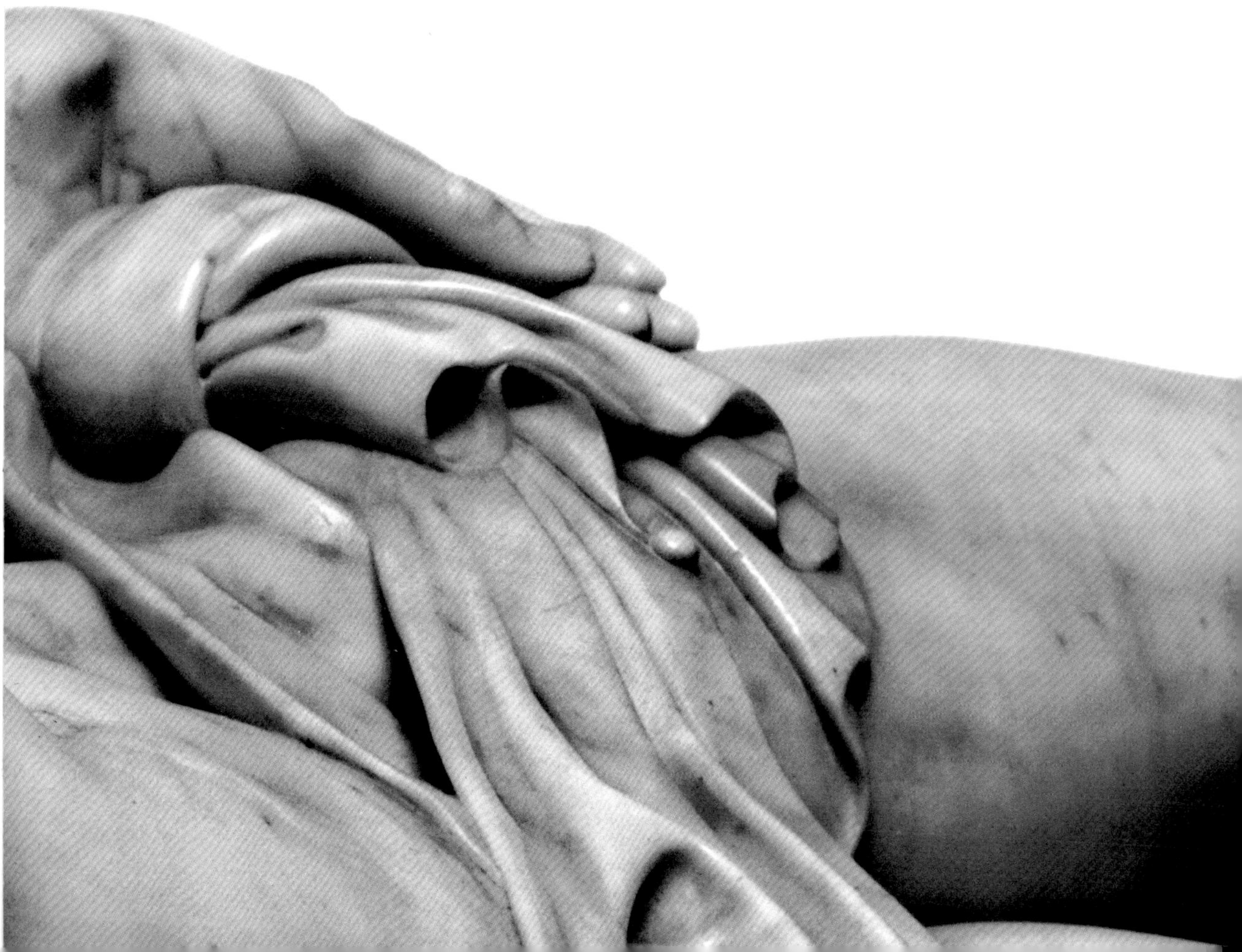

Battle of Cascina for the Great Council Hall in the Palazzo Vecchio, he resumed and finished the cartoon in the large hall of the Compagnia dei Tintori: this was the very cartoon that would eventually be studied and copied by artists who were so enthusiastic about it that it ended up being divided into several pieces.
Sometime in 1506 Michelangelo was commissioned by the *gonfaloniere* to make a marble *Hercules*, to be situated opposite the Palazzo della Signoria as a companion piece for the *David*. But the artist never got past the design and rough-shaping stages, and in 1534, Baccio Bandinelli would use the block to make his *Hercules and Cacus*, still today located to the viewer's right of the west entrance to the palace, leading into the Michelozzo courtyard.[16] That same year, although not for long, Michelangelo worked on a project that he had totally neglected.

The *Saint Matthew*

When Michelangelo had left for Rome slightly less than a year before, in March 1505, he was still the head of a demanding commission to produce a series of sculptures: the twelve *Apostles* for the Florentine Cathedral, commissioned by the Opera di Santa Maria del Fiore and the Wool Guild. It has often been said that the artist soon received the marble required for the work,[17] and began to carve only one statue, the *Saint Matthew*, without completing it. Again according to the most widely accepted reconstruction of the facts, his numerous assignments and trips to Rome and Bologna were what convinced the patrons that he would go no further; so on 18 December 1505, the contract was cancelled and the concession of the house, at least on paper, revoked. It is, after all, commonly known, and reported by Vasari, that the remainder of the *Apostles* were commissioned to other masters: Andrea Ferrucci, Benedetto da Rovezzano (not da Maiano), Jacopo Sansovino, Baccio Bandinelli. As the exact period during which Michelangelo worked on the *Saint Matthew* is not certain, it has generally been established as having taken place from April 1503 to March 1505, between the time of the contract and Michelangelo's departure for Rome.
In-depth research into the shipping of the marble[18] has clarified that the first block of marble did not arrive in Florence until December 1504; it was definitely transferred, in January 1505, to Michelangelo's home "prope Cestellum", that is, in Borgo Pinti, but soon after, as deliberated by the Opera, it was relocated to Andrea Ferrucci's house nearby so that he could carve out "his" apostle, the *Saint Andrew*. Three more blocks arrived in Florence in March 1506, and it is likely that one of these was for Michelangelo, who was in Rome, however, and who would not be back until April after severing all ties with Julius II. If, therefore, as seems to be the case, the short period of time that Michelangelo worked on the *Saint Matthew* indeed stretched from April to late November 1506 (before he moved to Bologna), a troubling critical issue would finally be resolved, which arose at the end of the 19th century and seemed to be destined to remain forever unanswered: the similarities between this statue and the *Laocoön* of the eponymous Hellenistic group.[19] The monumental marble group of the Trojan priest strangled together with his adolescent sons by monstrous sea serpents was discovered in Rome in January 1506 in a vineyard on the Esquiline Hill, and Michelangelo himself was one of the first who rushed to see it.
In the entire corpus of works by Buonarroti, the *Saint Matthew* is correctly considered to be the unfinished work that best illustrates artistic conception through the sequence of workings obtained by using different tools.[20] Moreover, it is especially effective in conveying to the viewer the artist's vision of the figure as something already contained in the marble, gradually emerging thanks to the removal of the "superfluous" – that is, of the excess material that imprisons and hides the image – by the artist. It is also the perfect example of the gradual emergence of the figure that, as reported in Vasari, Michelangelo believed became visible like a body immersed in a basin from which water is slowly drained. Vasari was really the first to interpret the informative and actual pedagogical value of the statue, observing that "rough as it is, [it] reveals its full perfec-

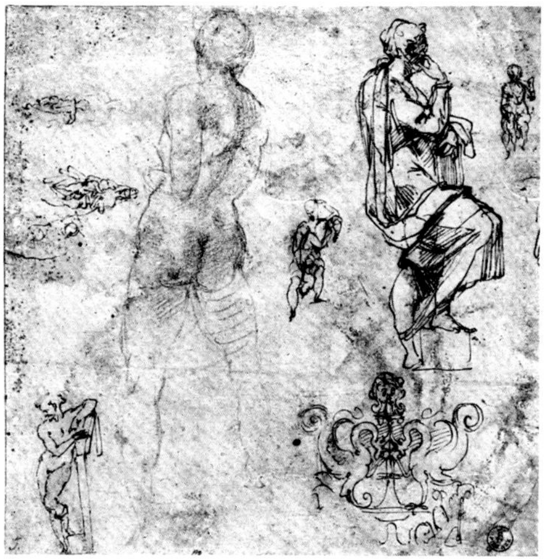

Michelangelo, *Studies for a figure and decorations, including the studies for the apostles*
Florence, Gabinetto Disegni e Stampe degli Uffizi, inv. 233 F *recto*

p. 111
Michelangelo, *Saint Matthew*
Florence, Galleria dell'Accademia

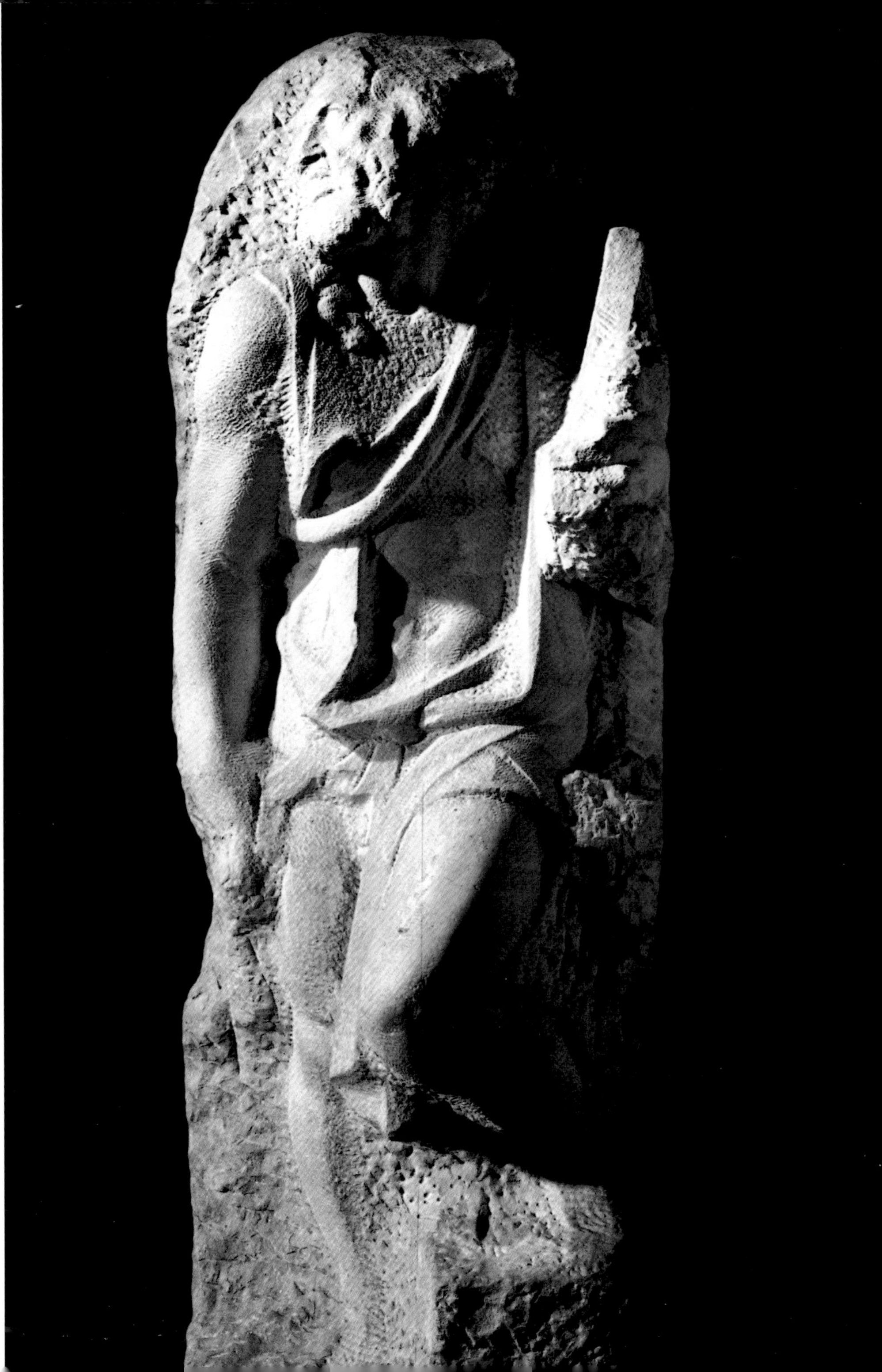

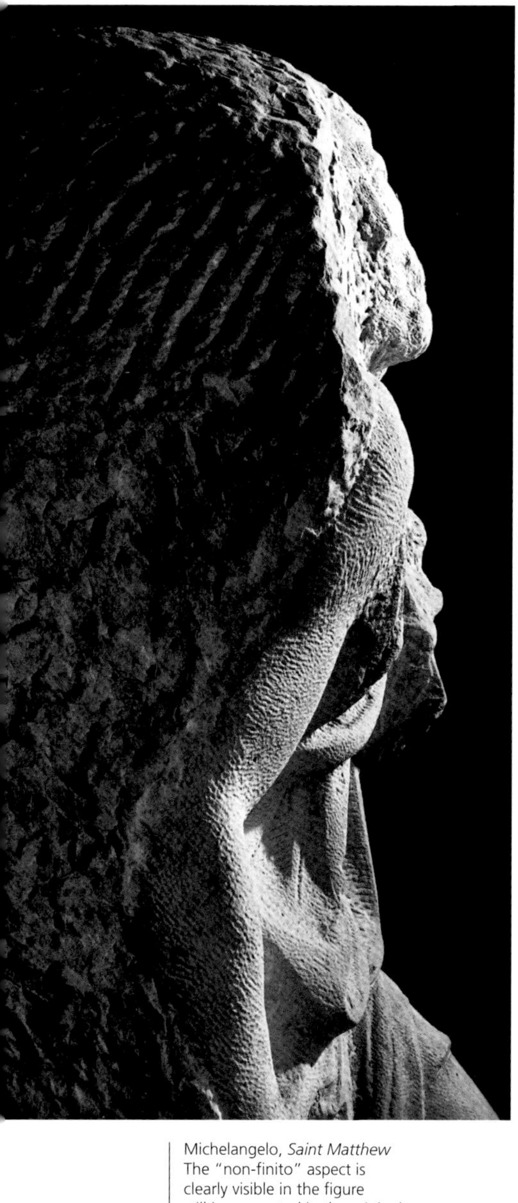

Michelangelo, *Saint Matthew*
The "non-finito" aspect is clearly visible in the figure still incorporated in the original block
Florence, Galleria dell'Accademia

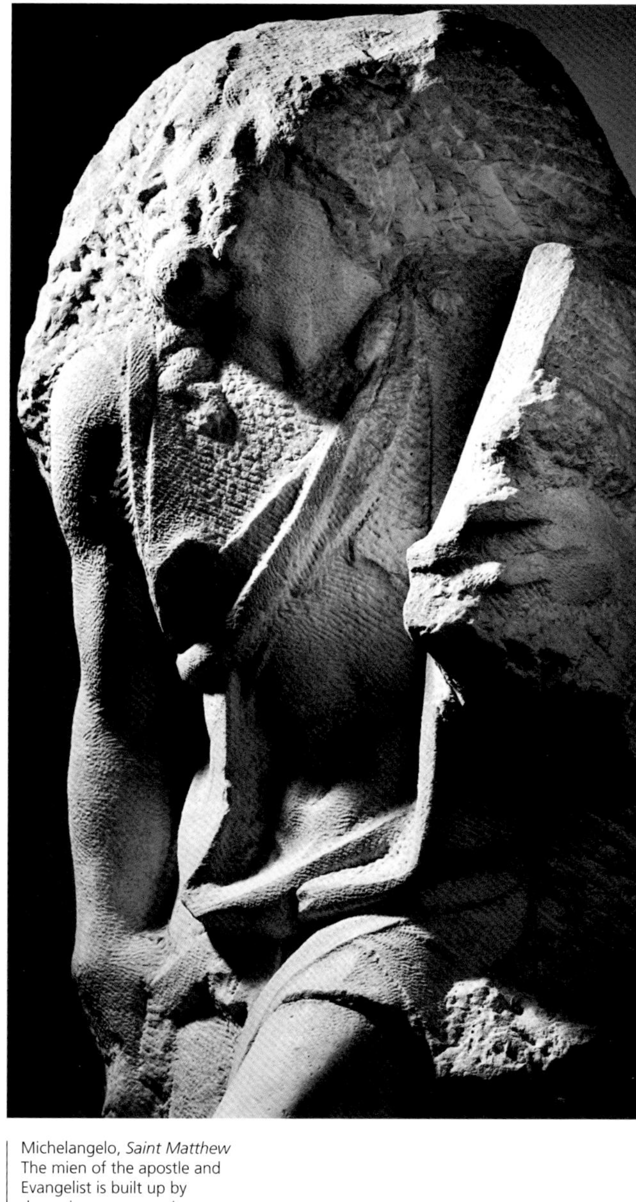

Michelangelo, *Saint Matthew*
The mien of the apostle and Evangelist is built up by dynamic *contrapposti*, as he turns his head upwards for the kind of pathos that recalls the ancient *Laocoön*
Florence, Galleria dell'Accademia

tion and teaches sculptors in what manner figures can be carved out of marble without their coming out misshapen, so that it may be possible to go on ever improving them by removing more of the marble with judgement, and also draw back and change some part, according as the necessity may arise".[21]
Emerging from the marble block still visibly roughed out is half of the potentially three-dimensional development of the figure of a mature man characterized by a powerful body clad in a tunic but with all four limbs in sight, and the particular leaning position of the right hand, whose thumb inside a fold in the fabric keeps it still.
The standing pose includes a cube-shaped base on which the figure's left foot is raised forcing the knee to protrude; this results in the unusual spiralling that passes into every part of the anatomy, *in fieri*, of the Evangelist apostle, all the way up to the upwards turn of his head towards divine inspiration – at once the calling[22] and the source of the book he holds in his left hand. The daring *contrapposto*, the dynamism pervading the saint's body in every direction, a body that is tense and distressed as it harks the divine inspiration, the sudden turn of the head, all justify the intriguing comparison between the *Matthew* and an agonizing *Laocoön*. Although reliable documents are still missing, a number of authoritative critics have expressed themselves in favour of the comparison, one of them being John Pope-Hennessy.[23]
The unfinished statue was much-appreciated by the artist's biographers, although the chronological and critical coordinates all varied.[24] While it was located at the Opera di Santa Maria del Fiore, the *Saint Matthew* remained on view, and was a powerful inspiration to the artists of the time. Raphael studied it, copied it, in part enlarging the unfinished image on the *verso* of a drawing now at the British Museum dedicated to the Baglioni *Deposition* at the Borghese Gallery in Rome, dated 1507.
Besides the complex and richly pathetic pose, the details of the *Saint Matthew* also seem to have influenced the artist's contemporaries. I personally find it feasible, for example, to perceive in the divisions of folds, just squared out in simple geometries, one of the sources of inspiration for the essential drapery featuring sharp, jagged edges in the work of the so-called "early Mannerist" painters, such as Rosso Fiorentino and Domenico Beccafumi.
The work remained on the premises of the Opera di Sant Maria del Fiore until 1834, whereupon it was transferred to the Galleria dell'Accademia in Florence, and it now stands at the head of the parade of Michelangelesque marbles leading up to the tribune of the *David*.

Michelangelo and the *Laocoön*

There have been numerous, different comments on the relationship between Michelangelo's sculpture and the dramatic Hellenistic group, the work of Hagesander, Athenodorus and Polydorus, discovered in January 1506 in a vineyard near Sant Maria Maggiore and immediately acquired by Julius II for the statuary collection of the Vatican Belvedere. As previously said, thanks to the information that has resurfaced and has been interpreted concerning the shipping of marble blocks from the shore to Florence it was possible to remove the resemblance, or better still the reliance, of the *Saint Matthew* on the Trojan priest and victim of Poseidon from a limbo of conjectures,[25] finally transporting the work to a level of certainty. Michelangelo, like many other artists in his day, was inspired by the extraordinary discovery and became very involved in the strong emotional temperature of the sculptural group, expressed in anatomical distortions and stylistic virtuosity, whose monumental size confers further pathos on the work. Invited by Giuliano da Sangallo, Michelangelo went to see the work right after it was discovered.[26] Both he and Giovan Cristoforo Romano, also a sculptor and expert in antiquity, identified it as being the group mentioned by Pliny, although executed in pieces and not monolithic. He defined the sculpture "a unique miracle of art", but to be admired more than imitated,[27] and he made drawings of it. The relationship between Michelangelo and the *Laocoön* has recently been reread in an unusual key, i.e. considering the group as the skilful forgery by Buonarroti's hand, who is to have made it in pieces (seven) reassembled on site and then buried,

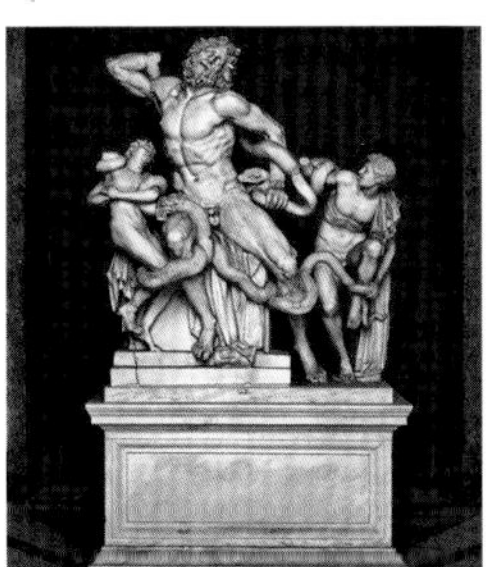

Hagesander, Athenodorus and Polydorus, *Laocoön and His Sons*. The extraordinary Hellenistic group, unearthed in January 1506, was an inspiration for countless artists including Michelangelo
Vatican City, Vatican Museums

after which he hastened to certify its discovery.[28] The provocative theory, which has up to now aroused consent as well as bewilderment, has a number of weak points, the most evident of these being the secrecy of the entire, gruelling operation. Surrounded by fellow-artists, assistants, literati, officials, friends and enemies, not to mention malicious stone-cutters, it would have been very difficult for Michelangelo to carve, transport, assemble and bury the heavy pieces of marble with no one knowing: his minor deceit of Cardinal Riario with the falsely antiqued Cupid (cited as being an earlier work) lasted about two months, this colossal deceit would have lasted five centuries.

Reconciliation with Julius II in Bologna

While Michelangelo was in Florence, some three letters from Julius II were sent to the Signoria requesting his return. Even Soderini, unwilling to cross the pope, began pressuring the artist, who now seriously contemplated accepting the offer from the sultan of Constantinople, Bajazet or Bayazid II, who had visited Rome at the time of Alexander VI and hoped to employ him.[29]

A reconciliation with the pope finally did take place in Bologna, conquered when Giovanni Bentivoglio was exiled in November 1506. In a very agitated scene, which Condivi wrote along the lines of the other stories where Michelangelo's fear is described, Julius II was indignant when he received the artist but after venting his anger on a monsignor who had bungled an attempt at mediation, he forgave the artist and took him back into his service. Before leaving for Rome he commissioned him to make a bronze statue with his portrait for the façade of San Petronio, to be paid one thousand ducats: he was just in time (by 22 February 1507) to see the "clay" model that showed him with his right hand raised in blessing in a "forceful gesture", but with a menacing air, and in a short amusing conversation he had with the artist ordered him to place a sword in his left hand.[30]

The statue for *Julius II* was cast (twice because the first time, in June, it came out wrong)[31] and raised up to its niche above the portal of San Petronio on 21 February 1508 at 3 p.m. Opinions on its exceptional size varied, but what is certain is that it was no less than and perhaps over 3 metres in height. Vasari recalled (but without having personally seen it) that "[t]here was great art in the posture, for everything conveyed majesty and grandeur; there was richness and magnificence in the draperies, and in the face courage, strength, resolution and awesome severity".[32] His right hand was raised in the act of blessing while his left held the keys. The statue's life span was short: when Annibale Bentivoglio returned to Bologna it was pulled down and cut up into pieces on 30 December 1511; all that is left to prove what it was like is a drawing with a portion of the façade of San Petronio, where the statue can be seen, seated in the act of blessing as described in the sources, in the high triangular tympanum decorated with "gattoni", or floral ornaments, atop the main portal.[33] The Bentivoglio family's rule of the city only lasted until 1513 when they were expelled for good. Duke Alfonso d'Este had the bronze fragments of the statue brought to Ferrara, in exchange for a supply of artillery for the people of Bologna, and had them cast into a culverin ironically dubbed "Giulia". He did save the head, however, which weighed 600 *libbre*,[34] and which in Vasari's day was kept in the ducal apartment.

The incident recounted by Vasari that involved the painter Francesco Raibolini, known as il Francia, took place towards the end of Michelangelo's stay in Bologna; it seems that that painter asked and was allowed to see the statue that had already been cast. His comment, "that it was a most beautiful casting" sounded to Michelangelo as though "he had praised the bronze rather than the workmanship", so he answered il Francia with harsh words, making him feel mortified.[35]

Michelangelo had spent several months in Bologna, which he described as "a miserable existence".[36] In July 1507, the *operai* of Santa Maria del Fiore had gone looking for him, to ask him for a model or drawing for the marble finishing on the drum at the base of Brunelleschi's cupola. Other artists had also been invited to this sort of competition of ideas, and in November 1507, the choice fell upon the mod-

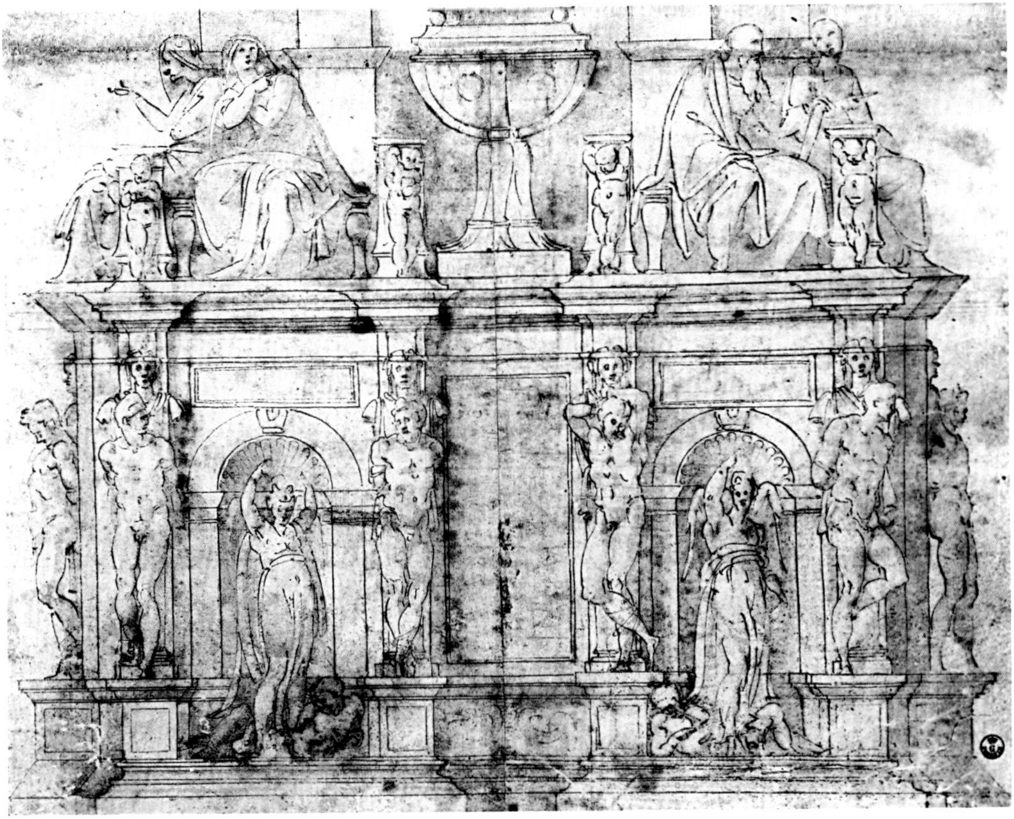

Michelangelo, *Partial project for the Tomb of Julius II*
One of the first to be executed, visible on the lower storey are the *Slaves* and *Terminal Figures* on the projecting part,the female *Victories* in the niches
Florence, Gabinetto dei Disegni e delle Stampe degli Uffizi, inv. 608 E

el by il Cronaca, Giuliano da Sangallo and Baccio d'Agnolo.[37] There is no evidence of Michelangelo's immediate involvement with the events of the drum's completion; but his opinion on the subject did arrive in 1516, followed by a plan for it in 1519.

The Sistine Chapel ceiling

Once the bronze statue of Julius II was completed, Michelangelo went back to Florence in February 1508 (common usage), but, after celebrating the New Year with his family, he returned to Rome, where on 27 March he again opened his account with the Balducci bank. Nonetheless, although he was once again at the service of the pope he did not resume work on the tomb.
From the spring of 1506, when Michelangelo had left Rome in a hurry, Julius II had been thinking about having the ceiling painted in the chapel his uncle Sixtus IV had had built and whose walls had been magnificently frescoed with *Scenes from the Old and New Testament* and the series of *Popes*, by Pietro Perugino, Sandro Botticelli, Domenico Ghirlandaio and Cosimo Rosselli together with their assistants in the 1480s. The Sistine Chapel ceiling had been painted with gold stars against a blue background by Piermatteo d'Amelia. Despite the fact that Michelangelo knew of the pope's intentions,[38] he once again began to order marble, also to make up for the loss of some of the pieces that had remained in Piazza San Pietro at the mercy of the people. It is likely that when commissioned to paint the Sistine ceiling, formally on 10 May 1508, he hoped to carry out both of these huge undertakings with the help of an adequate number of assistants, seeing that in April Francesco Granacci was already recruiting helper-painters for him in Florence.
But the events took a very different turn. Forced to put aside his project for the tomb, Michelangelo practically worked on the Sistine ceiling by himself, and in January 1509 even ended up dismissing his only assistant Jacopo, perhaps the Jacopo di Sandro mentioned by Vasari.[39] The artist's monumental undertaking ended on 31 October 1512, on the eve of All Saint's Day. By inventing and mastering an extremely complex scheme, based on the illusionistic relationship between the multiple figurative planes of the flat portion, the groins and the lunettes, Michelangelo transposed into "buon fresco" painting – whose technique he was familiar with despite his lack of experience – facts and figures from the Old Testament, starting with the Genesis, to proceed towards the advent of Christ. The cycle includes the soothsayers, that is the Hebrew prophets and the pagan Sibyls who announced the Redemption, Christ's forbears, and a series of athletic telamons, the Ignudi, that bear medallions and festoons made of oak branches (rovere), alluding to the pope's heraldic "cerquata".

Leo X and the second contract for the Tomb (1513)

Michelangelo was unable to resume work on the tomb until the winter of 1512-1513. But Julius II's death on the night between 20 and 21 February 1513 (common usage), marked a change in the relationship between the artist and this great undertaking, as Vasari drastically summed up, "on the election of Pope Leo X",[40] solemnly celebrated with the "ceremony of possession" held on 11 March 1513. Condivi's words are vaguer, his biography replete with his desire to exonerate Michelangelo from the accusation of negligence in the Della Rovere project: "[b]ut he had not get very far with it before he was interrupted, to his great distress [...] Michelangelo, who had begun to work on the tomb of Julius with great devotion, put up all the resistance he could".[41]
The pope, who would soon divert Michelangelo from the Della Rovere tomb, was Giovanni de' Medici, Lorenzo il Magnifico's second son, just a few months younger than the artist, and with whom he had eaten at the same table in the palace in Via Larga. Until the

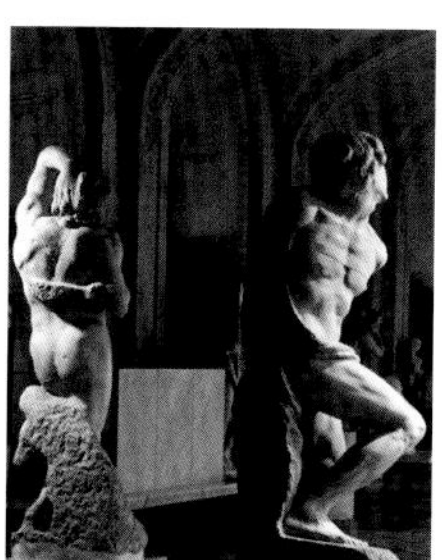

Michelangelo, the *Two Slaves*, originally destined to the *Tomb of Julius II*
The present-day arrangement of the Michelangelo gallery (formerly the Galerie Mollien) dates from 1994
Paris, Musée du Louvre

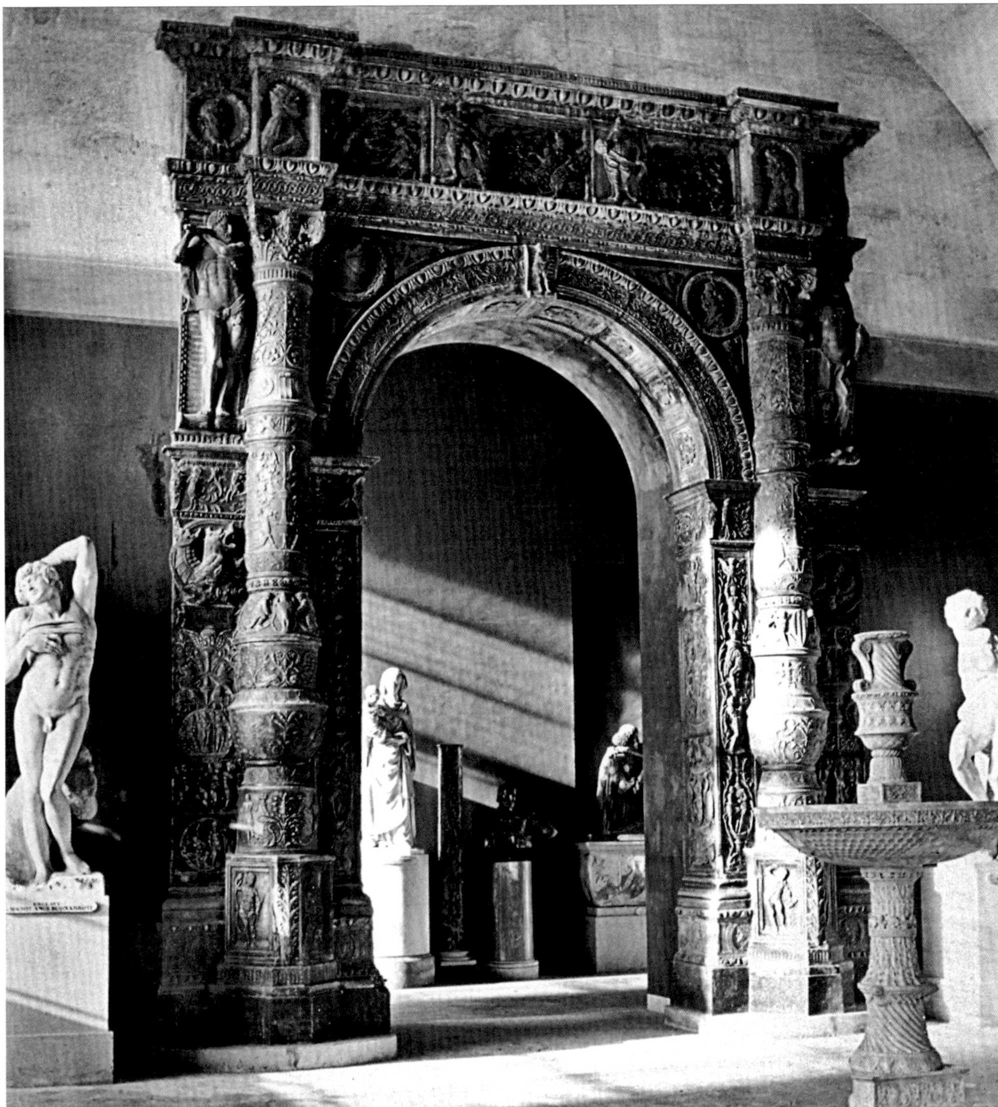

Michelangelo, the *Two Slaves* as they were in the Galerie Mollien, late 19th to early 20th century
Paris, Musée du Louvre

election, Giovanni's life had been more worldly than spiritual: secretly a cardinal at the age of thirteen, then officially at sixteen, after the Medici were expelled from Florence he had travelled through the courts in Italy and Europe along with his brother Giuliano and his cousin Giulio, to eventually settle in Rome in the family residence in the Palazzo Madama, true to Medicean tradition a patron of artists and intellectuals, but also at the service of Julius II in his politics of war. And it was precisely with the support of the Spanish-papal troops that he had been able to re-establish the Medicean *Signoria* in Florence (1512-1513), where he governed together with his brother Giuliano. He was ordained a priest and elected bishop only after the election, during the ten days before the coronation.

Over the two-year period from 1513 to 1515, Michelangelo was able to devote himself to sculptures for the Julius Tomb, but within a frame of a different kind of relationship with his patronage, now taken over by the executors for the tomb, Cardinal Santiquattro, called Datario because of the office he held, and Leonardo Grosso Della Rovere, cardinal of Agen, thus called Cardinal Aginense, who was also the pope's nephew, and as such a representative of family interests.

Michelangelo stipulated a new contract with them on 6 May 1513, where the description of the new tomb was based on a small wooden model that the artist had prepared. Hirst is due credit for the link between an autograph drawing and this particular phase of the project.[42]

A first significant change concerned the structure of the monument, which would be free on three sides with the fourth (one of the two heads) attached to the wall. This meant a series of prescriptions for its two-tiered arrangement, alternating niches with pilasters, the presence of pairs of figures, standing, sitting – i.e. the *Victories*, *Slaves*, *Moses* and a *Saint Paul* with the various *Allegories* – and the deceased *Julius II*, for a total of six pairs of figures, twenty-eight single figures and three historiated bas-reliefs in marble or bronze.[43]

On 9 July 1513, Michelangelo signed a private document, which was undersigned by witnesses, entrusting the "cutting and carving of the marble" for the architectural frame to master Antonio da Pontassieve.[44] By subcontracting (to use a modern term) some of the work, Michelangelo got rid of the less creative part of the undertaking, which concerned the marble finishing chiselled "a quadro", i.e. with level slabs that featured moulded cornices, and "a intaglio", i.e. decorative motifs in relief: plant candelabra, antique mascarons, satyrs, harpies, plant volutes with acorns from the Della Rovere coat of arms. Executed by the subcontractor with great diligence, the marble decorative apparatus would seem to be very closely bound to Florentine ornamental expressions at the time, for example, the painted and graffito grotesques by Andrea Feltrini, or those in carved form by Andrea Sansovino and Benedetto da Rovezzano.[45] The refined and lively quality of the sharp reliefs, when placed in an architectural view that was further redesigned thirty years later, does not keep them from appearing to be expressive of a minutious ornamental attitude of antiquarian inspiration that had run its course. By the end of the summer of 1513, the marble that had been ordered from Carrara had not as yet arrived, despite the good weather and, therefore, easier transportation, and the artist bitterly complained of this to Baldassarre di Cagione.[46]

This was the period of time when the two *Slaves*, referred to as the *Dying Slave* and the *Rebellious Slave*, now on display in the Louvre in Paris, were produced in the artist's Roman home in Via Marcel de' Corvi. Six sketches for the *Slaves*, together with studies for cornices and the *Lybian Sibyl* on the Sistine ceiling may be seen in a drawing at the Ashmolean Museum in Oxford.[47]

The *Dying Slave*

The *Dying Slave* is one of Michelangelo's most harmonious and sensual male statues. The youth, characterized by a strong but also delicate body balanced in a standing pose brings his right hand to his chest while he raises his left arm to his curly head, sinking his fingers into his hair. His face tilts towards his shoulder, his eyes and mouth are closed. Cloth fetter-like bands left rough and encircling the torso and left wrist are all that he wears. Carved from the rough mass that acts as a backdrop and support for his legs is an ape, at the time classified as a *cynocephalus*, holding an indefinable object in its hand. The frontal pose suggests that, for the purposes of the tomb, the figure was to occupy an intermediate position between two niches. This would explain the surface treatment, finished in the front part, approximate elsewhere, rough to the extent that it is a mass of rough-hewn material at the back. A relationship has been suggested with the light-coloured terracotta model entitled *Male Torso* in Casa Buonarroti, attributed with some doubt to Michelangelo, which features delicate bodily proportions, and a similar stance and arrangement.[48]

It was Hans Grimm who first dubbed the figure with the word "dying",[49] obviously inspired by its pathetic abandonment, which has often encouraged a comparison with the typology of Saint Sebastian.[50] While most scholars interpret the figure's sleeping state as anticipating death,[51] there have also been those who have interpreted it as close to awakening, a rousing to a superior life in contrast with the natural brutality expressed by the ape.[52] Numerous other allegorical interpretations have been offered, at times relying on Condivi's version (the death of the arts) at times on Vasari's (the subjugated provinces) and expanding it in the most disparate directions, and also as related to Michelangelo's personality. If I were to trust Condivi, who is closer to the artist's recollections, I would accept the interpretation of the *Slaves* as the arts, rendered – for laudatory purposes – afflicted and enslaved after the pope's death. Especially important in symbolic terms here is the ape, which does not necessarily express Painting in the sense of *simia naturae*; because it is actually a cynocephalus (now simply called "ape"), according to an antique and authoritative source like the *Hieroglyphica* of Horapollo it alludes to literary knowledge: the commentator Piero Valeriano added that it is seated amidst books and holds a tablet and stylus in its hand to write in the manner of the Egyptians (1556).[53] Not until the end of the 16th century would the animal, provided with the instruments of the arts, become the symbol of the artistic Accademia.[54] It is thus possible that Michelangelo's ape, by perhaps holding a rolled up scroll in his hand, was meant to imply that the *Slave* was one of the humanities condemned to painful oblivion because of the pope's death.

Whatever the real meaning may be, the *Dying Slave* achieves a peak of touching expressiveness that anticipates the very high notes of the *Times of the Day* in the New Sacristy in Florence: just like those figures, he bears witness to and is a victim of a loss that upsets the entire world, in the same way that *Night* – which we shall discuss further on – seeks merciful blindness in sleep, and finds, through contact with its own body, shelter and comfort in the chaos of the world.

The *Rebellious Slave*

The *Rebellious Slave* owes its sobriquet to the forced bodily posture that, restricted by the figure's arms tied behind his back, twists with a dynamic spiralling movement projecting his left shoulder forwards and tilting his head upwards, as if he yearned freedom. It must be observed that this pose, which is obviously typical of the antique representations of captives and the vanquished, had been used, however, in numerous variations in the *Ignudi* of the Sistine ceiling, who were not defeated, but instead triumphant in their youthful beauty.

Leaning up against a rocky spur, which also works as a base for his right foot, with the same effect that had previously been experimented with in the Florentine *Saint Matthew*, this slave with a muscular body structure was almost certainly meant to occupy a corner position of the monument, as the right shoulder is nearly nonexistent and that side of the statue is flat. Like his companion, some of the parts are at an advanced stage of completion: see the complex landscape of muscles in the back and chest, inspired by the celebrated antique *Belvedere Torso*.[55] In comparison the treatment of the face (crossed by a rather visible vein that continues down onto the shoulder), and even more so of the hair, is more superficial. Traces of some kind of hat or band might be an indication of the allegorical identity of the figure: an artificer wearing a band to hold his hair still?[56] Also of a coarse texture is the surface of the cloth that conceals his genitalia, and the rocky support is rustic. As always

p. 120
Michelangelo, *The Dying Slave*
Paris, Musée du Louvre

p. 121
Michelangelo, *The Dying Slave*,
detail of the torso where
the hand moves towards
the bands he is bound by,
abandoned to his suffering
Paris, Musée du Louvre

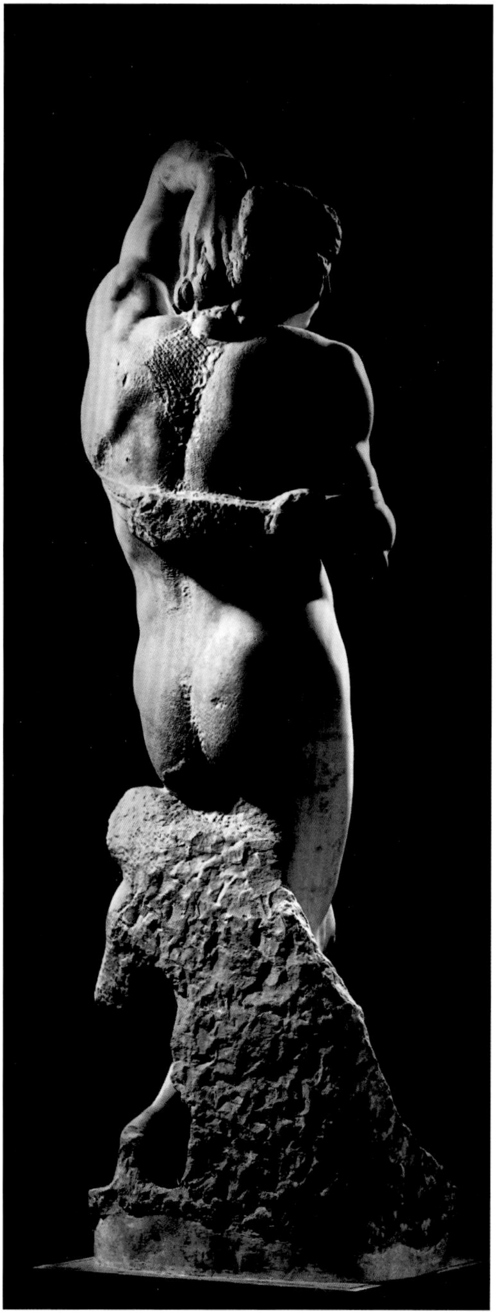

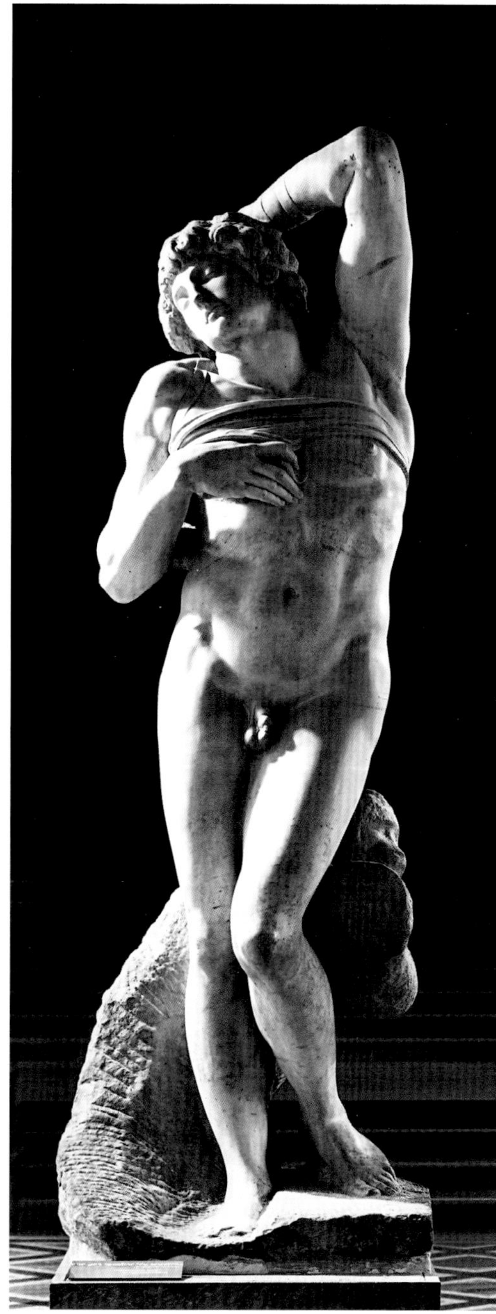

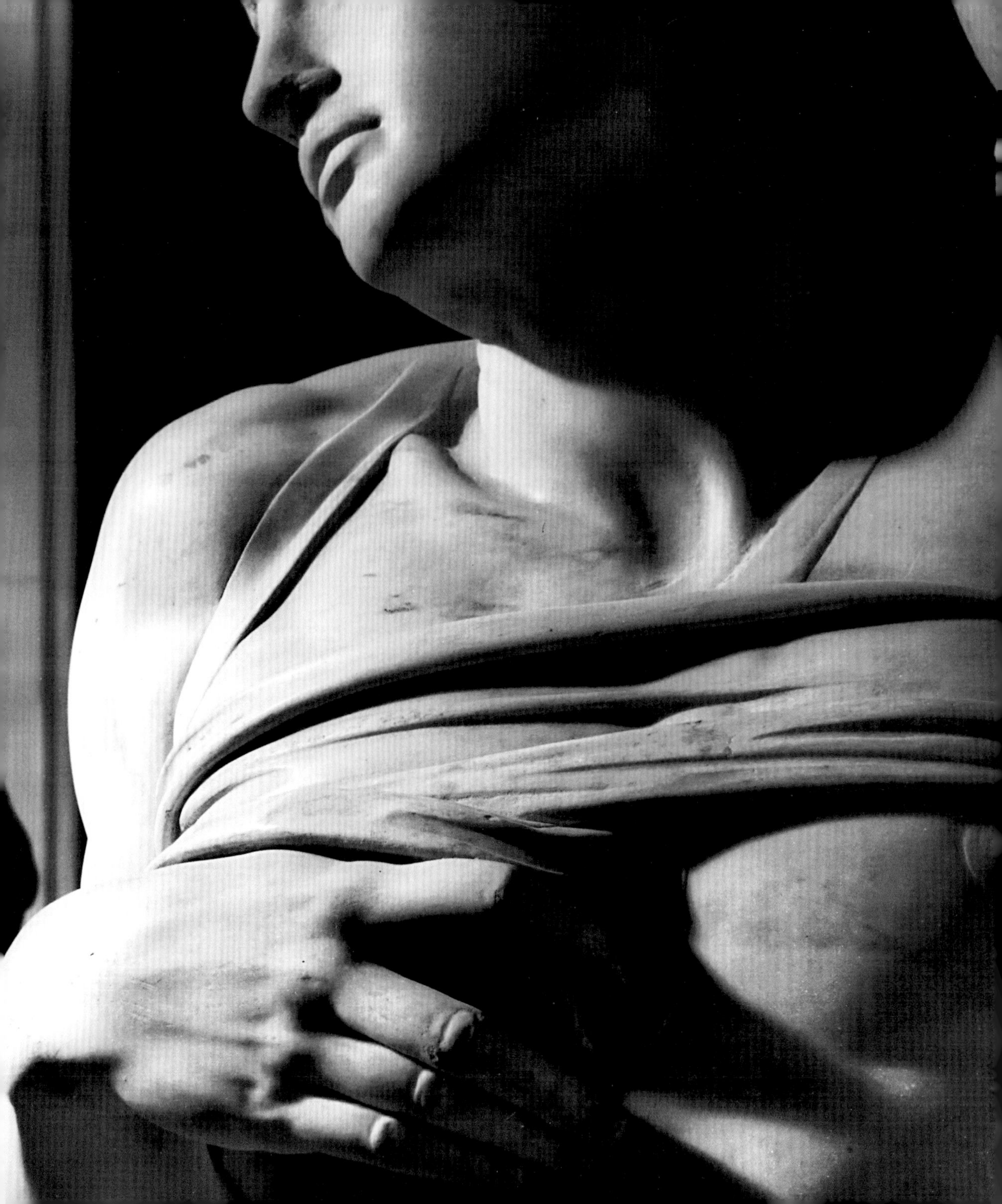

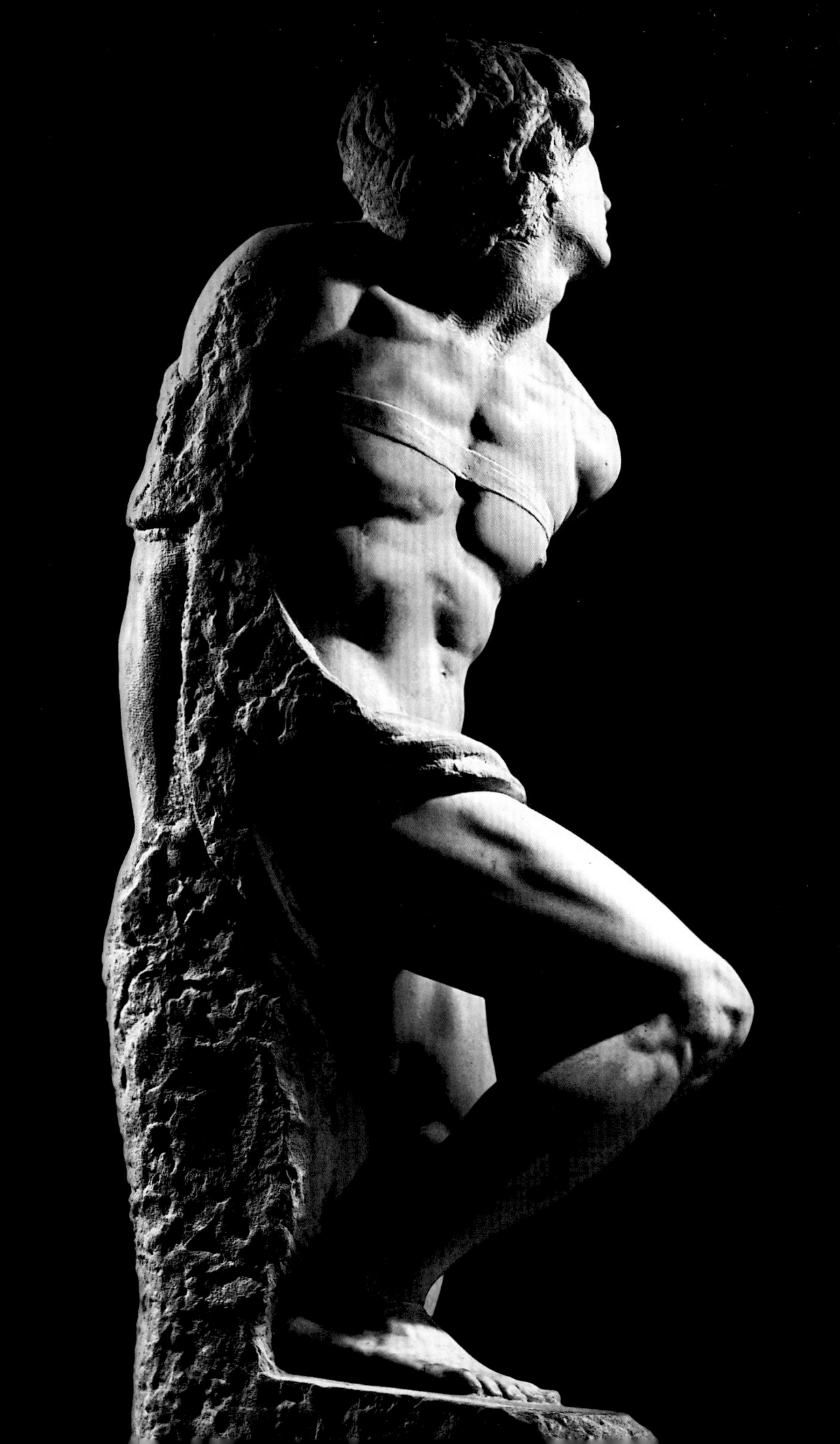

Michelangelo, *The Rebellious Slave*
Designed for a corner position the figure's right arm is retracted and restrained
Paris, Musée du Louvre

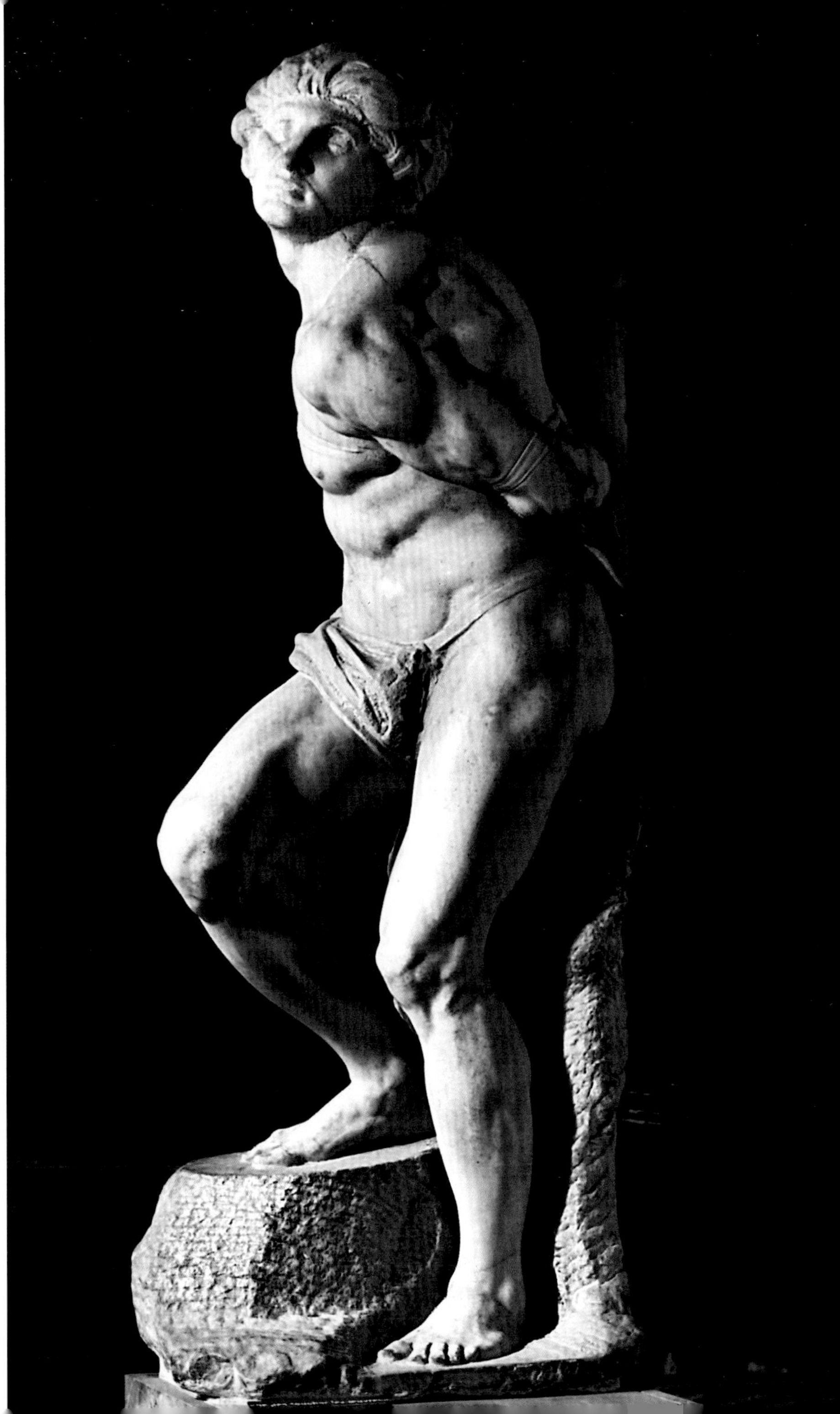

Michelangelo, *The Rebellious Slave*
A dark vein, clearly visible in the marble, crosses the figure from head to shoulder
Paris, Musée du Louvre

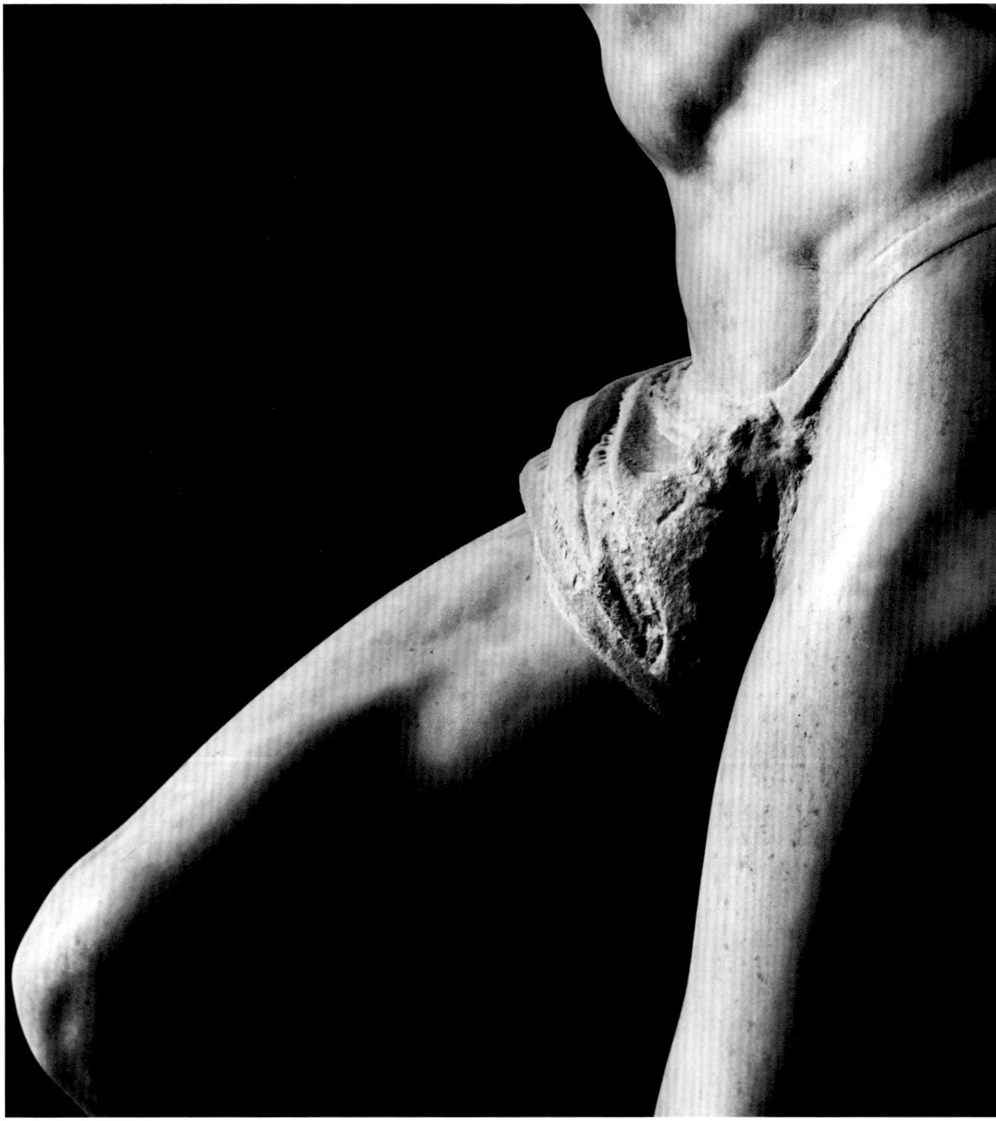

Michelangelo, *The Rebellious Slave*
As he moves his right leg forwards a small mass of marble just roughed out serves as a loincloth
Paris, Musée du Louvre

p. 125
Michelangelo, *The Rebellious Slave*
The muscular left shoulder brought forwards expresses all of the violent tension of the bound prisoner
Paris, Musée du Louvre

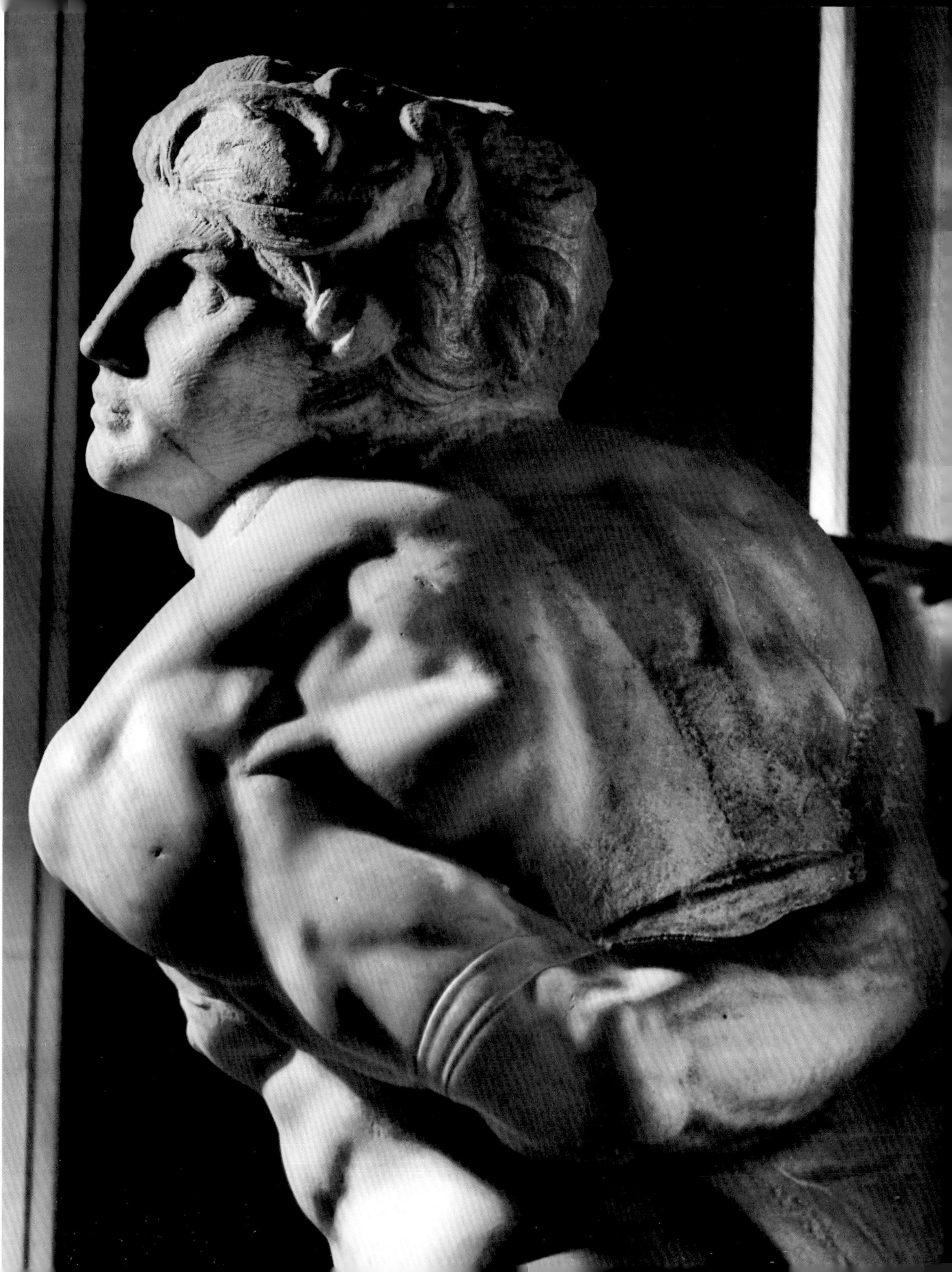

we are not really sure why the work is in a "non-finito" state, but we cannot overlook the fact that the presence of the vein in the face and shoulder may have discouraged the artist from continuing.
This is the only *Slave* figure for which proof exists from the time of its execution. Michelangelo indeed wrote that he had received a visit from the elderly painter from Arezzo Luca Signorelli while working "on a standing marble figure four *braccia* high with his hands behind his back".[57]

The *Moses*

It seems that during the period just after the Louvre *Slaves*, or perhaps even at the same time, Michelangelo worked on another part of the tomb: the large seated statue for the second storey of the tomb complex for Julius II, the celebrated *Moses*.
The figure of the biblical Lawmaker, which had been a part of the overall project since 1505, has survived in a copy of a drawing now in Berlin, and like the *Saint Paul*, *Active Life* and *Contemplative Life* he was to occupy one of the corners of the upper storey. He was also to have occupied a high niche position in the 1513 project. His final position was, however, in the central arch of the wall monument in San Pietro in Vincoli, assuming an unplanned hegemonic role and – to his disadvantage – situated lower down, where the sculptor's efforts to balance out the proportions through perspective foreshortening are lost.
Twice life-sized, the *Moses* is a unique masterpiece of Renaissance statuary and art in general. It is believed that Michelangelo was alluding to this very same statue when he wrote, on 16 June 1515, "I have to work very hard this summer to finish this work quickly".[58] The truth of the matter is that the statue remained in the room in Via Macel de' Corvi for almost thirty years, until it was installed in the church between 1542 and 1545, where it became the fulcrum of the monument to Julius II, a rather reduced version as compared to the original project. Most of the work was carved to a finished state, although some of the less visible parts, such as the neck, the back of the head and the seat, are rough.
Moses is seated, clad in a tunic, leggings and sandals alluding to biblical antiquity, and his legs are wrapped in a heavy cloak that cascades down to fill the space between his knees. His right foot is firmly set forwards on the ground, while his left foot is retracted and precariously balanced on the edge of the sculpture plinth; the pose is unstable perhaps to suggest that the figure is about to rise. With the torso in a frontal position the head sharply turns to look left. Both hands are occupied with the flowing, wavy ropes of Moses' long beard: the left hand grabs at the ends of the curls, the right moves the central mass over as if caught in it, at the same time holding still up against his side the two tablets of the Ten Commandments. From the top of his head, amidst the deep volutes of curly locks, two horns emerge from a striated surface, an allusion to the two beams of superhuman light that emanated from Moses when he came down from Mount Sinai. Situated behind the Moses are two relief slabs of unequal quality – now visible only in photographs – that represent two giants holding up a coat of arms.
The conservation work that ended in 2004 encouraged us to reconsider the figure's position (which is not the original one but rather the one decided on in the 19th century by a commission of the Accademia di San Luca chaired by Antonio Canova), also in light of the *pentimento* in the left leg. It is commonly known that a significant autograph *pentimento* while the work was underway involved the "turning" of the head.[59]
The exceptional might of the statue was immediately perceived by the artist's contemporaries, starting from the cardinal of Mantua who, upon seeing it in the study in Via Macel de' Corvi during a visit while in the retinue of the recently elected Paul III (1534), stated that the statue was "sufficient to do honour to the tomb of Pope Julius".[60] And Vasari dwells on expressions of admiration for what he considered to be a masterpiece unsurpassed by the ancients, and unsurpassable by the moderns, indicating that: "the hairs [...] are finely feathery, soft and so precisely drawn out that the chisel seems impossibly to have become a brush" and "[n]ot only is the face beautiful with its truly

p. 127
Michelangelo, *Moses*
Carved in 1515, it was not placed in the final version of the *Tomb of Julius II* until thirty years later
Rome, church of San Pietro in Vincoli

p. 128
Michelangelo, *Moses*, detail of the head, where the "horns" allude to the beams of light that sprang from the biblical hero's head
Rome, church of San Pietro in Vincoli

p. 129
Michelangelo, *Moses*
His powerful gaze expresses the strength of the "leader and duke", the words Michelangelo's biographer Condivi used in 1553
Rome, church of San Pietro in Vincoli

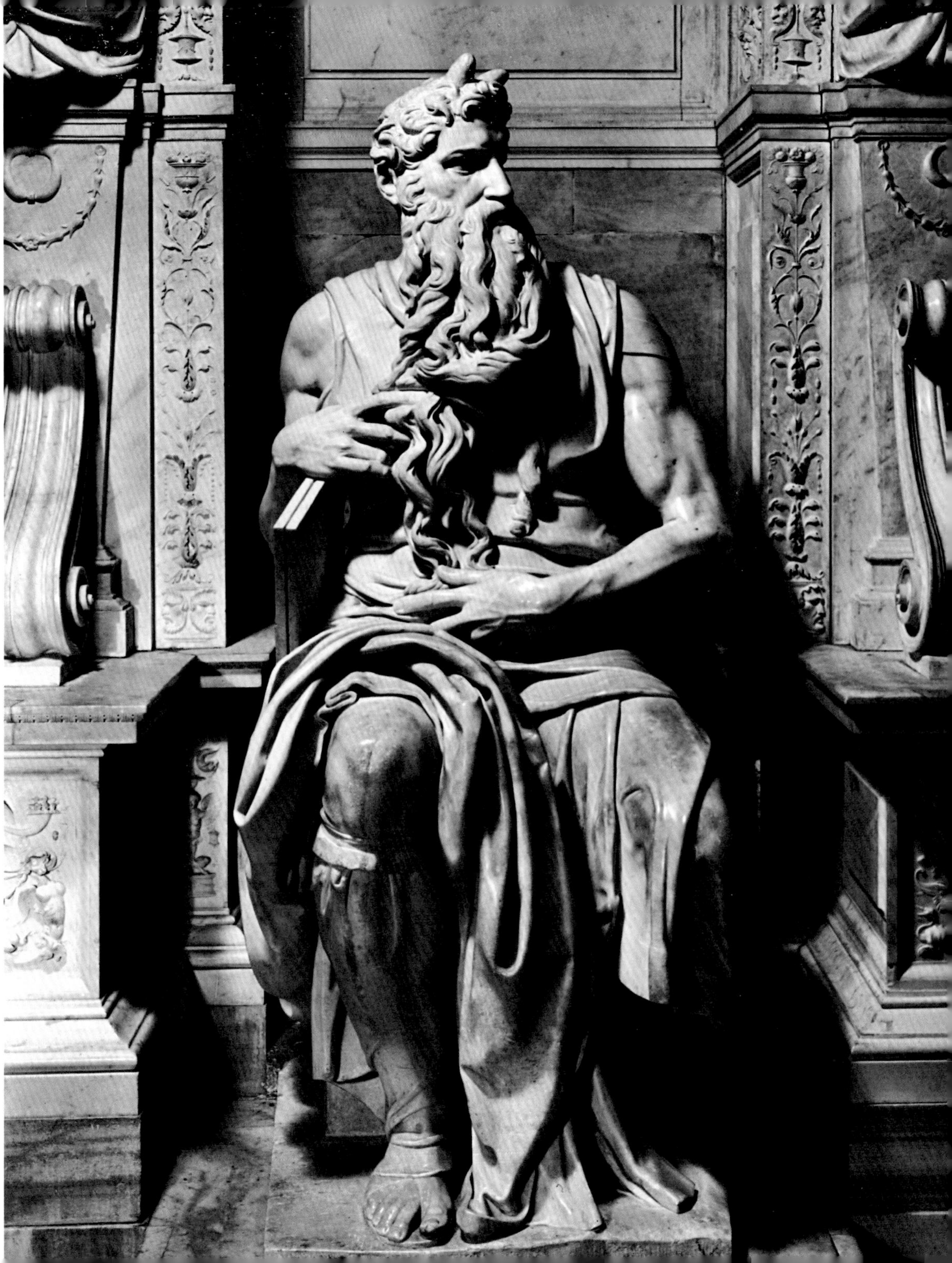

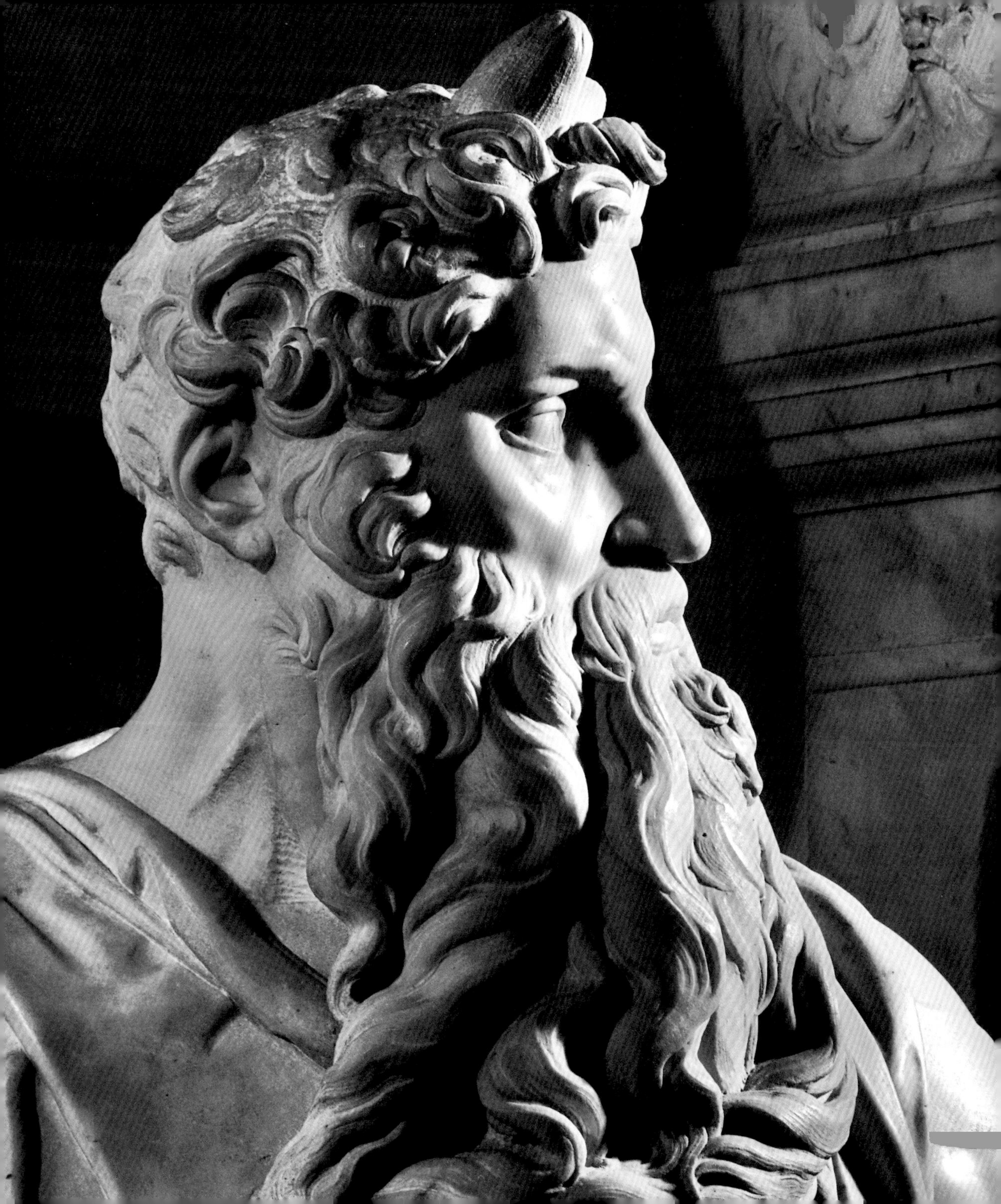

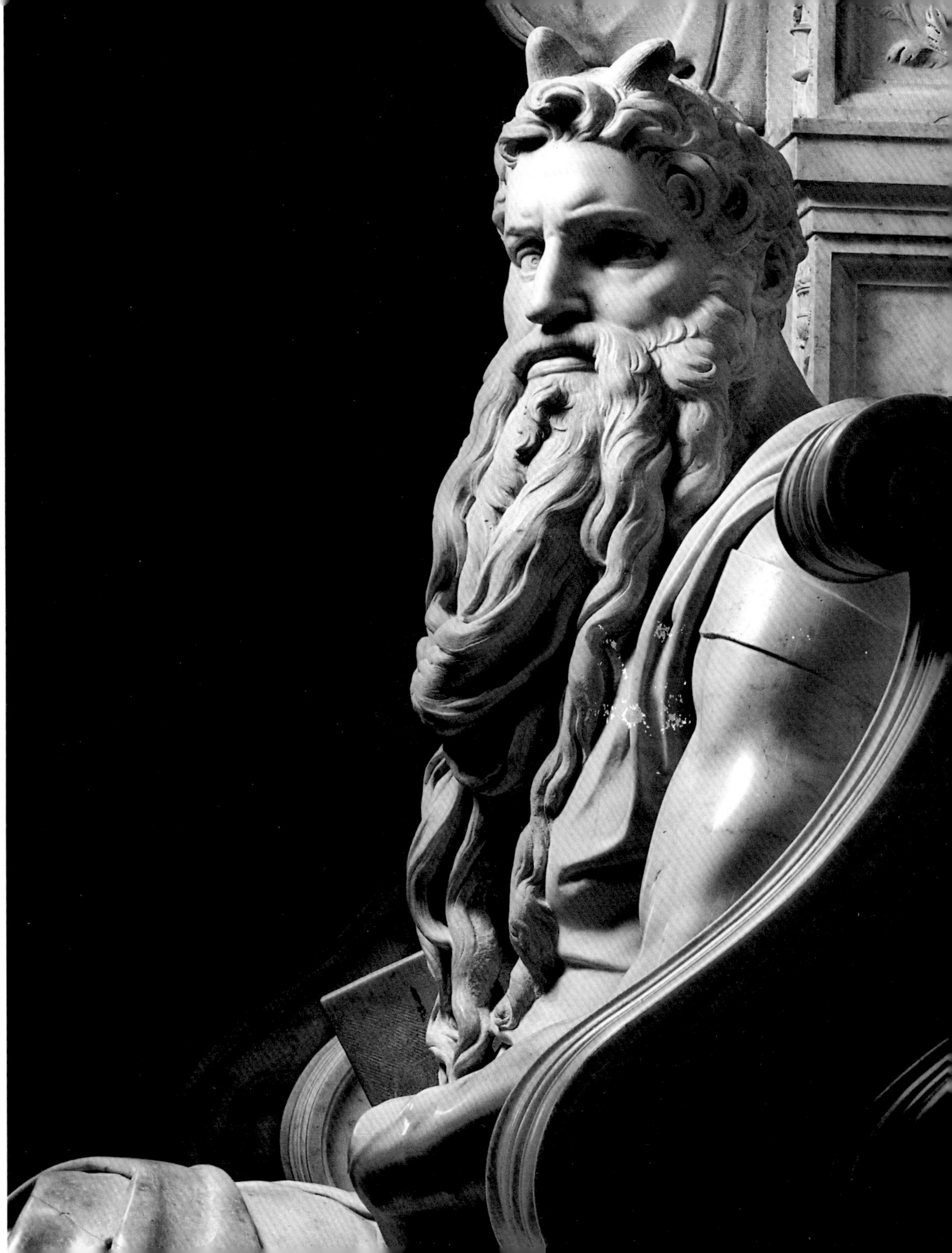

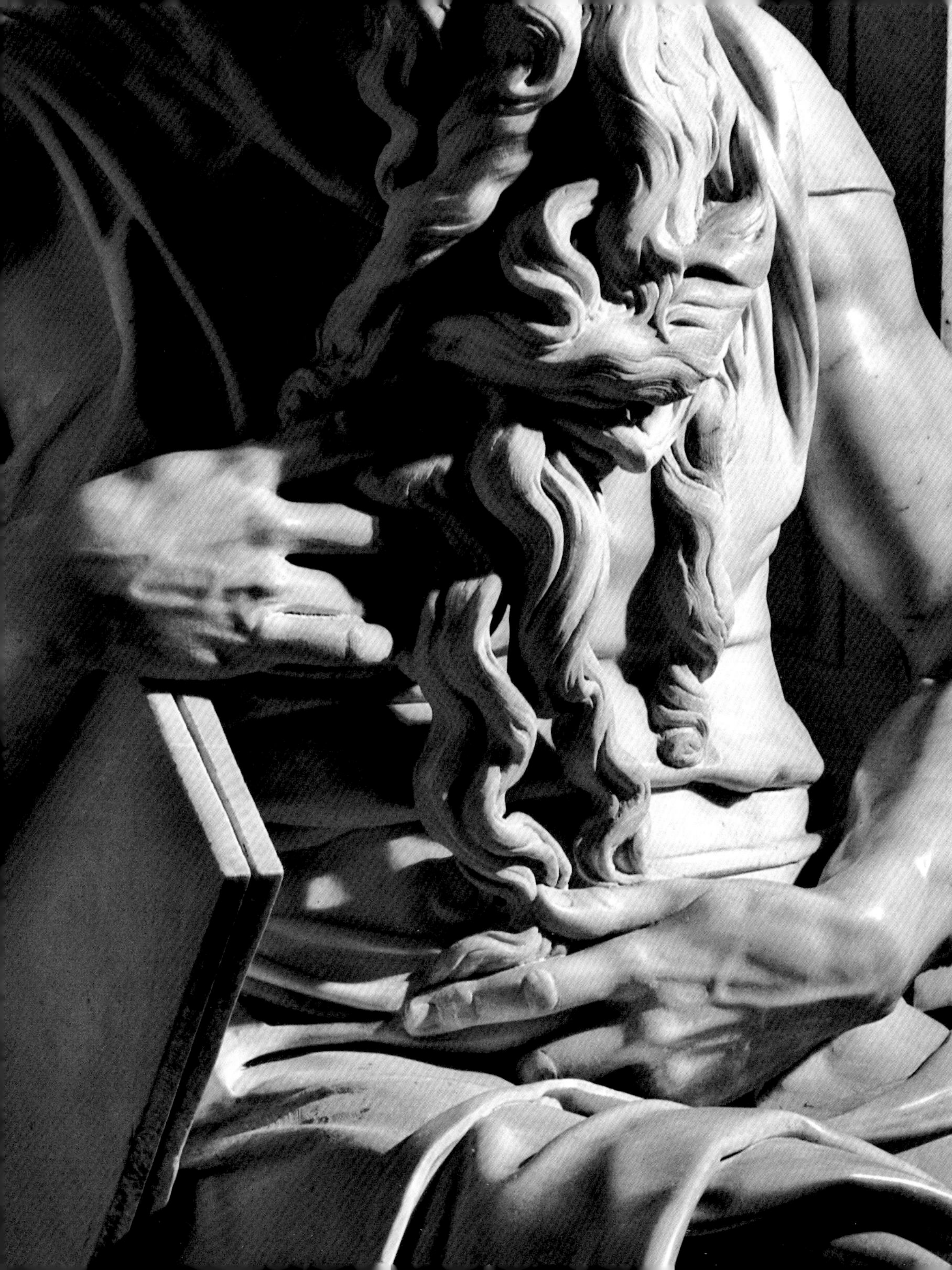

saintly and regal expression" but the "drapery is carved and finished with a lovely turning of the hem, and the arm muscles and the bones and nerves of the hands are finely wrought, and the legs, knees and feet are perfectly shod". Vasari concludes with a highly poetic image that contains the memory of a singular, rare moment of convergence between religions around the work of art: "Long may the Jews continue to visit and adore it, as they do in crowds every Sabbath, both men and women, like flocks of starlings; for they will be adoring what is not human but divine".[61] Condivi's comments, probably under Michelangelo's guidance, differ in tone: the *Moses* is dubbed "leader and captain [...] in the attitude of a wise and pensive man"; his face is said to be "full of animation and spirit, apt to inspire both love and terror, which was perhaps the truth", the figure is praised for the boldness of the anatomy, as below his garments is "a marvellous work and full of art, but all the more so in that the whole nude form is apparent under the beautiful draperies which cover him". With an unusual narrative twist, the gesture of the left hand is described as "supporting his chin [...] like a person who is weary and full of cares".[62]
Many are the figurative sources that scholarship has called into question as precedents for some of the features of the *Moses*: the antique river gods for the bearded elderly type, the characters of the Trajan Column for the Roman clothing, the statues of Emperor Tiberius but also 15th-century sculpture, especially Donatello for the solemn seated pose, and in particular the *Saint John the Evangelist* in the Museo dell'Opera of the Cathedral in Florence.
Since the 19th century, there has been a series of critical comments on the statue that have interpreted its features (moreover, already interpreted in two very different ways by the two biographers of his time!) in light of the most varied and not necessarily warranted interpretations. It was viewed in light of Savonarolian thought as an allegory for the papacy, as a self-portrait or projection of Michelangelo, as a cosmic being comprising the four elements. His frown and heedful expression has been justified as his reaction to seeing the Jewish people make offerings to the bronze serpent. A 19th-century psychological interpretation of his mien paved the road for Sigmund Freud who, in his essay *Der Moses des Michelangelo* (in "Imago", 3, 1914) analysed the artist's rendering of the Bible character in terms of an exceptional and rational power of self-control over the passions, considering it the image of a hero of spirituality, ready to sacrifice his individual affective life to defend the fate of the Jewish people.[63]
Rather than thinking of the *Moses* as an atemporal creation to which both legitimate and arbitrary suggestions may be linked, I believe it would be useful to bring out into the open those meanings that offer the best criteria for classification: time, the patron's expectations, the artist's vision, the project, the meaning of this biblical figure. Selected for the latter was the iconography established by medieval theologians, without forgoing such details as the horns, despite the fact that they were often a source of embarrassment for Christian writers aware of Saint Jerome's error in the *Vulgate* concerning Moses' face as he descended from Mount Sinai: the saint's use of the word "horn" to render the Hebrew word that also means "radiant".
Condivi was correct in recalling that the first meaning for Moses was the historical and secular one of "leader and captain": the commander of a people that he had reunited and led to salvation from the slavery of Egypt, the Lawgiver revealed, the winner of a conflict in which his sacred authority as head rejects the presumed right of the Jewish people to refuse his guidance. Moses, in a theological and doctrinary vision rooted in antiquity, is the founder of a heroic genealogy, which beholds the revelation and is in turn revelatory, which includes Christ (with whom the correspondences were underscored) and then the principles of Saints Peter and Paul the Apostles. And it was thus with complete congruence that the original iconographic programme for the Tomb of Julius II, who had been the vicar of Christ and successor to Peter, not to mention military commander, included the figures of Moses and Saint Paul: without overlooking the fact that the attribute for the latter, who was an apostle of the Gentiles, was the sword that Julius II had not disdained holding and wishing – in jest – for the bronze statue in Bologna. The Bolognese statue, so similar in size, was important to Michelangelo, as was the fruit of his pictorial experimentations on the solemn male figures of the *Prophets* on the Sistine ceiling.
As for the features for the *Moses* introduced by Condivi (not without some distortion), such as his pensiveness, wisdom, fatigue,

Michelangelo, *Moses*, detail of his long, wavy ropes of beard pulled to one side by his right hand, which at the same time holds still the two tablets of the Ten Commandments
Rome, church of San Pietro in Vincoli

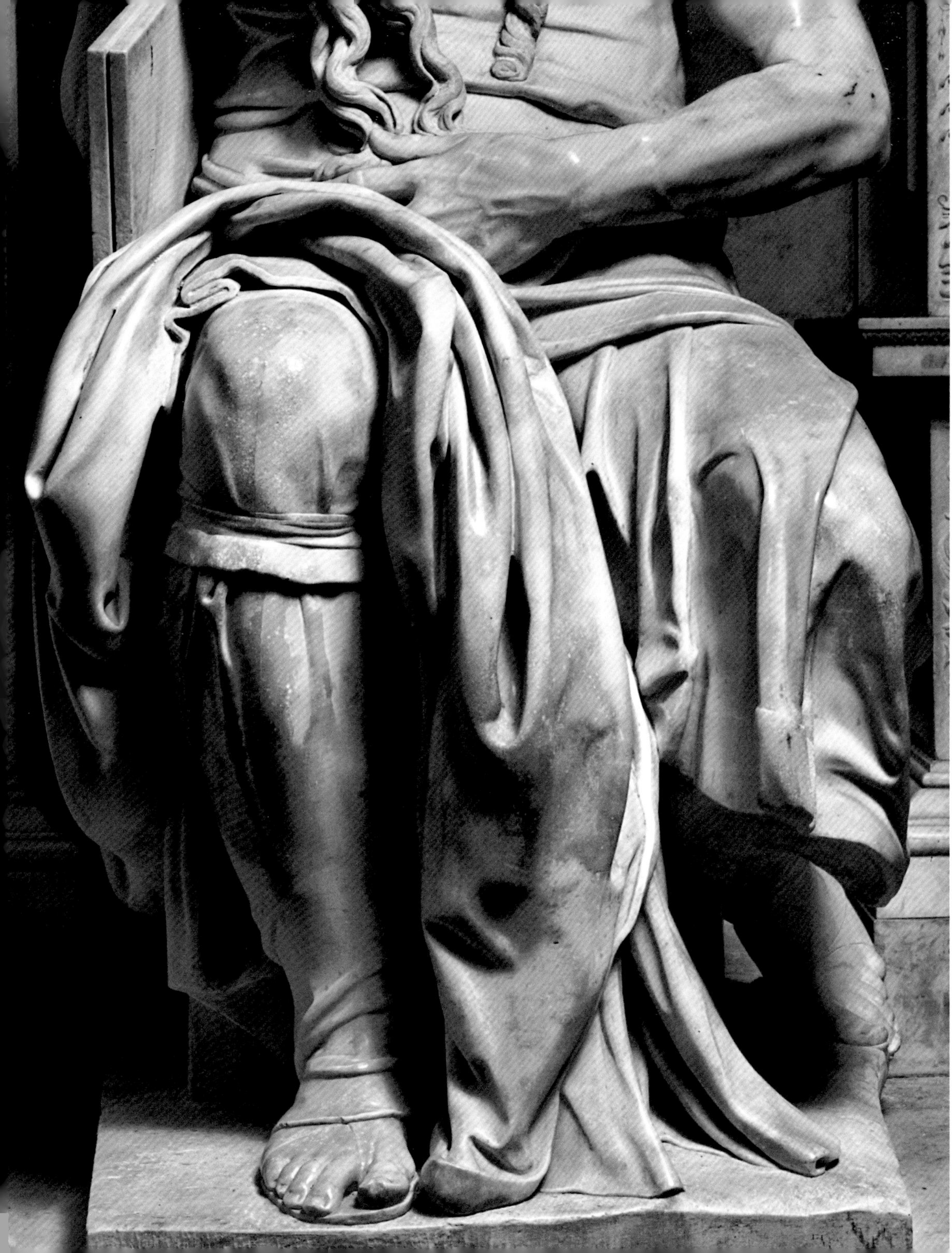

concerns, it is likely they were meant to express his acceptance of the *Contemplative Life*, which had been planned from the start along with the *Active Life*, even more suited to both the biblical hero and deceased pope. These thoughts, destined to be expressed in terms of composition and figure, were to be found years later in the "leaders and dukes" Lorenzo and Giuliano de' Medici, both of whom were commanders in this world and, artistically speaking, almost the separate filiations of two aspects reunited in a hendiadys in the Roman statue, and that would become semantic loan-words: Vasari would in fact characterize Lorenzo as being "pensive", borrowing from Condivi one of the adjectives used to describe the *Moses*.
The *Moses* has a considerable hold on both the scholarly and popular imagination. The story about the sculptor tossing his hammer at his new creation and shouting "Why don't you speak to me?" is one of the most famous. The *Moses* expresses the highest degree of convergence between a patron with an energetic personality and an artist anxious to test himself with grandiose challenges, in this case a biblical figure of superhuman dimension: these are, nonetheless, initial conditions, from and beyond which Michelangelo's exceptional artistic power would proceed to create a figurative presence that has no equal in Western art. Even the substantially unresolved mysteries, such as those concerning his mien and gesture, embellish the masterpiece with evocations that transcend the most accurate definition and profoundest exegesis.
Perhaps it is for this reason, among others, that the colossal statue has never ceased feeding into current creativity, as proven by the documentary by Michelangelo Antonioni *Lo sguardo di Michelangelo* (2004, presented at Cannes in June),[64] in which, for a full fifteen minutes, the great film director touches the statue, exalting its plastic and spatial dynamics.

The chapel in Castel Sant'Angelo

Leo X's attention was inevitably drawn to Michelangelo, a familiar figure from twenty years before and an artist who was by now celebrated both locally and beyond, and soon to be defined, with the clear-sightedness of critical judgement not devoid of citizen pride, as having no equal anywhere in Europe.[65]
In November 1514, Michelangelo began to work on the façade for the papal chapel in Castel Sant'Angelo that adjoined the 15th-century papal apartment: he completed the work in 1517. Although the project rigorously involved construction, Leo X's chapel in Castel Sant'Angelo made from pure white statuary marble can really be classified somewhere between architecture and sculpture. In the boldly articulated front, dominated by a triangular pediment with the Medicean emblems of the ring, the three feathers and the "breve" with the family motto elegantly fluttering to either side, two Tuscan orders are superimposed, one made up of pilaster strips alone, the other of semi-round columns and pilaster strips. The central span, separated from the pediment by a high frieze, is symmetrically organized to the sides by what is known as a "pieno in asse", an unusual structure made up of a minor pilaster strip topped by a bracket: two circular windows to let the light in are framed by minor apertures, also circular, for an effect that is reminiscent of the antique example of the nymphaeum at Gennazzano, closely studied by the architects of the time, and also an allusion to certain pictorial-plastic effects in the façades of 15th-century Venetian churches. In the side constructions, two tall and narrow scooped niches are each topped with a lion's head, the pope's personal emblems as well as citations from the "Marzocco", the heraldic lion symbolizing Florence. The boldly original architectural and plastic partition in the middle would seem to recall the apse area of Santo Spirito in Florence, a church that Michelangelo was familiar with and carefully observed,[66] for which Filippo Brunelleschi had designed an unusual central column separating two arches, and to which four doors on the façade were to correspond, reduced to three in the final late-15th-century project.
Michelangelo's architectural experience entertains a dialogue of

Michelangelo, *Moses*
After the original place for the statue in the first project for the *Tomb* was modified, Michelangelo reworked the figure's legs
Rome, church of San Pietro in Vincoli

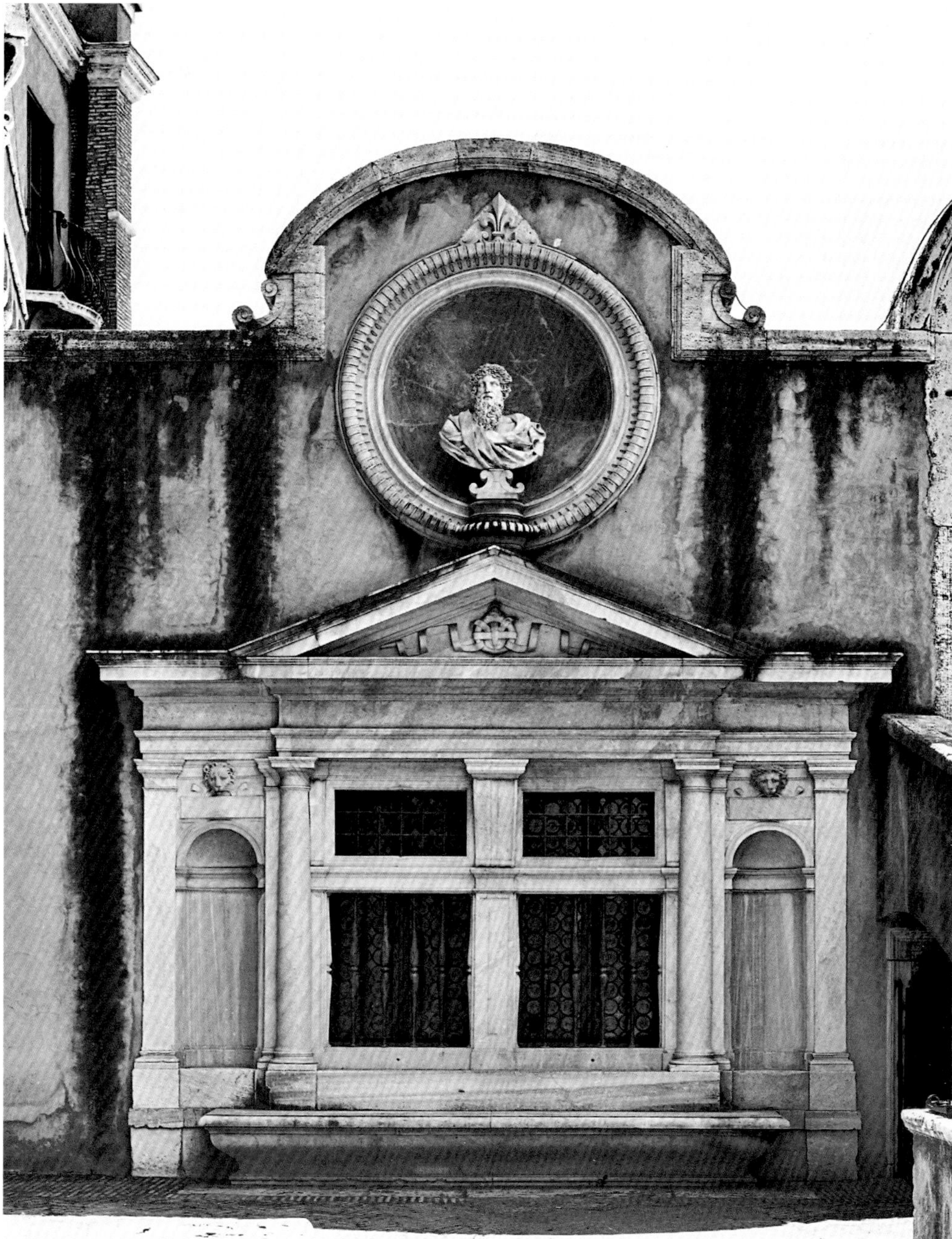

chronological and conceptual contemporaneousness with the projects that were gradually modified, to be exact reduced, for the Julius Tomb, whose original, small-scale temple layout was being transformed into a monumental wall shrine.

The Risen Christ (the "first Minerva Christ")

Despite the fact that he was working for the heirs of the deceased pope (they had even set limits on his activity) and expected to soon be employed by the ruling pope, as early as 22 May 1513, Michelangelo had made an agreement with the Roman aristocrat Metello Vari de' Porcari, together with Bernardo Cenci, a nobleman and Vatican canon, and Mario Scappucci of Roman origin, for a statue of the *Risen Christ* destined to be placed in the church of Santa Maria sopra Minerva in Rome. The contract was made official on 15 June 1514.[67] The three men, of which Vari was a client at the Balducci bank, were the trustees for the construction of a chapel in memory of a relative, Marta Porcari, but they instead destined the entire amount available to the statue they intended to obtain from the Florentine artist.

Michelangelo was to carve "a life-sized marble figure of Christ, naked, standing and holding a cross in his arms".[68] And this he did: the artist worked on the *Risen Christ* until 1516, when he stopped, as he himself recounted, because of the appearance of a black vein in the marble in the facial area. This unfinished version of the statue was followed by another one, completed and shipped from Florence in 1521. It is a well-known fact that Michelangelo gave the unfinished statue to Vari, who placed it in the garden of his family home in Rome, where Ulisse Aldrovandi saw it halfway through the century before its owner died in 1554.[69]

After a past proposal for identification,[70] recent research has suggested reconsidering a statue that – based on ownership history and location – shows features that are of particular interest to and highly compatible with the episode of the first Minerva *Christ*.[71] According to this reconstruction, the statue was offered to Francesco Buonarroti in 1607, but the potential buyer, upon the advice of Florentine painters Passigano and Cigoli, gave up on it: the work was incomplete, tampered with by another hand and too expensive.[72] A number of considerations, such as the Giustiniani patronage over Santa Maria su Minerva, one aspect of their strong presence in the Pigna *rione*, have led to the belief that the first Michelangelo *Christ* went to Vincenzo Giustiniani, a man of letters and art connoisseur, who would have had it finished and installed in the palace until, in 1644, it was placed on the high altar in the church of San Vincenzo Martire in Bassano Romani, where it can still be seen today.

The statue was on display at the *Caravaggio e i Giustiniani* exhibition in 2001 after the publication of several articles in the year 2000; given the importance of the attribution, the critical reaction was controversial. The Michelangelesque elements are such that the issue deserves careful consideration. The naked, standing figure leans up against a cross and trunk to its sides, with a frontal pose whose reflection is corrected by a slight *hanchement* and tilt of the head. The smooth, fleshy body (among other things, reworked by an unknown 17th-century sculptor) suggests its potential affinity with the *Dying Slave* at the Louvre, while one side of the head quite resembles that of the Christ in the Vatican *Pietà* on one side, and the other side the second Minerva *Christ*. The hand pressing the tunic up to the thigh resembles that of the *Bacchus* clutching the animal skin. As for the face, not only is the black *pelo* recalled in the letters visibly present, but also visible is the attempt to incorporate it into the features as a line of expression: the attempt failed, as the defect descends too far down and runs into the beard and neck, but it is nonetheless masterly. Furthermore, it is worth noting that works derived from or inspired by Michelangelo show traits that come from this *Christ*: the left hand is copied in a drawing at the Louvre,[73] the pose and even the details of the symbols of the Passion can be seen in Raffaello da Montelupo's *Christ the Redeemer* in the Cathedral of Orvieto (1563), all of which is proof of the resonance of this incomplete work by the master with his closest followers.

p. 134
Michelangelo, Façade of the chapel for Leo X
Rome, Castel Sant'Angelo

p. 136
Michelangelo and unknown sculptors of the 16th-17th centuries, the *Risen Christ* (the "first Minerva Christ")
Abandoned by the master, it was completed by other artists
Bassano Romano (Rome), church of San Vincenzo Martire

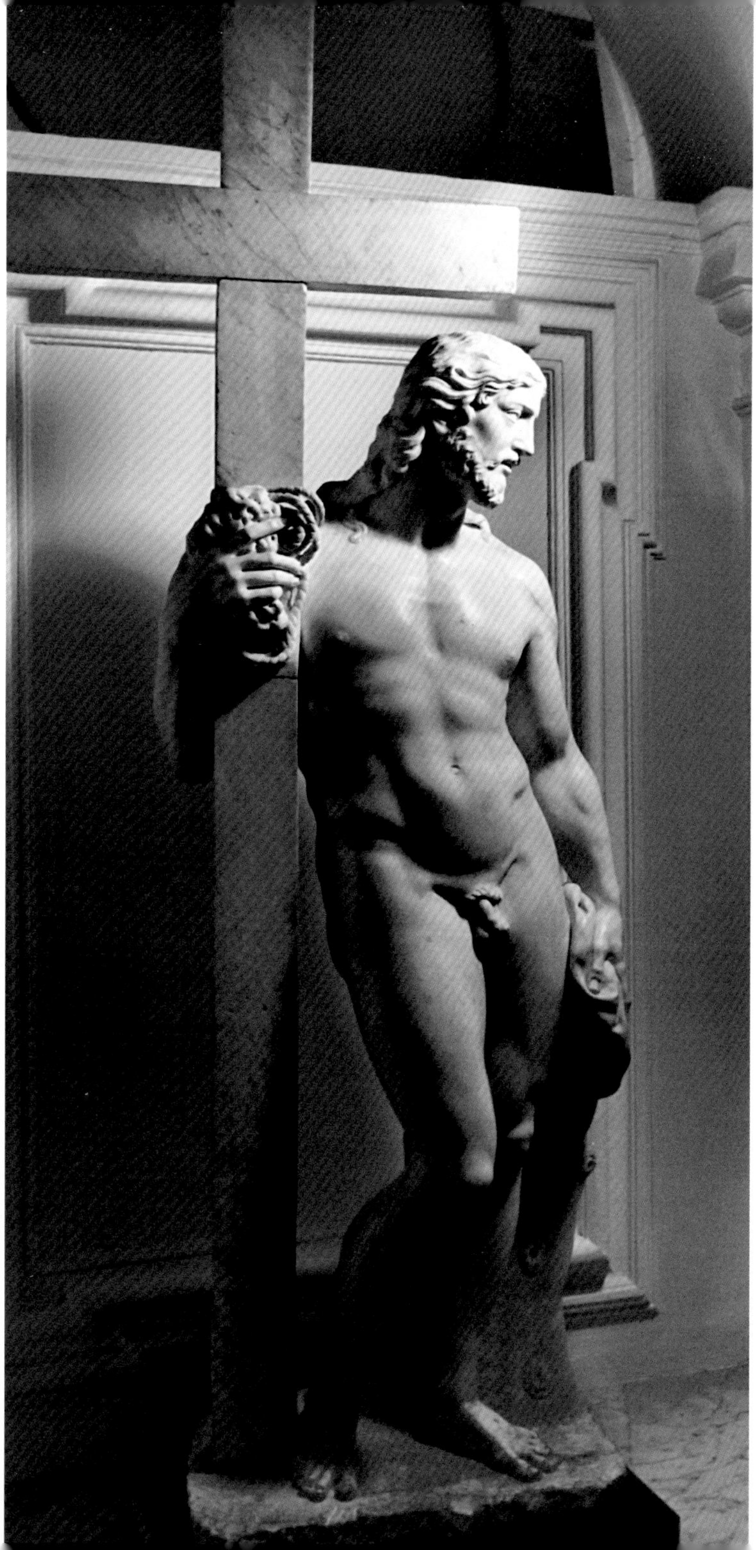

p. 137
Michelangelo and unknown 16th-17th-centuries sculptors, the *Risen Christ* (the "first Minerva Christ"). The instruments of the Passion are arranged in the artist's typical style
Bassano Romano (Rome), church of San Vincenzo Martire

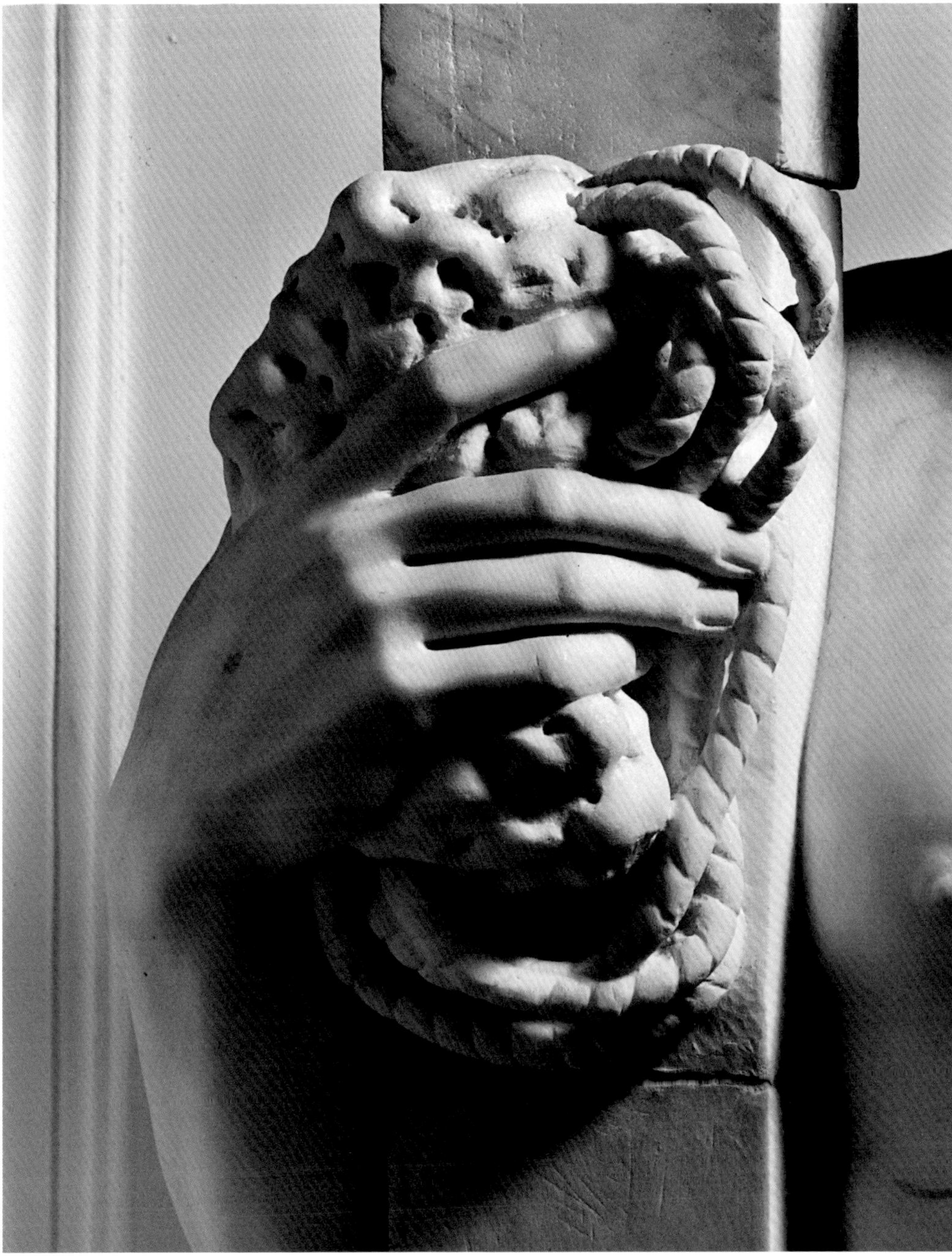

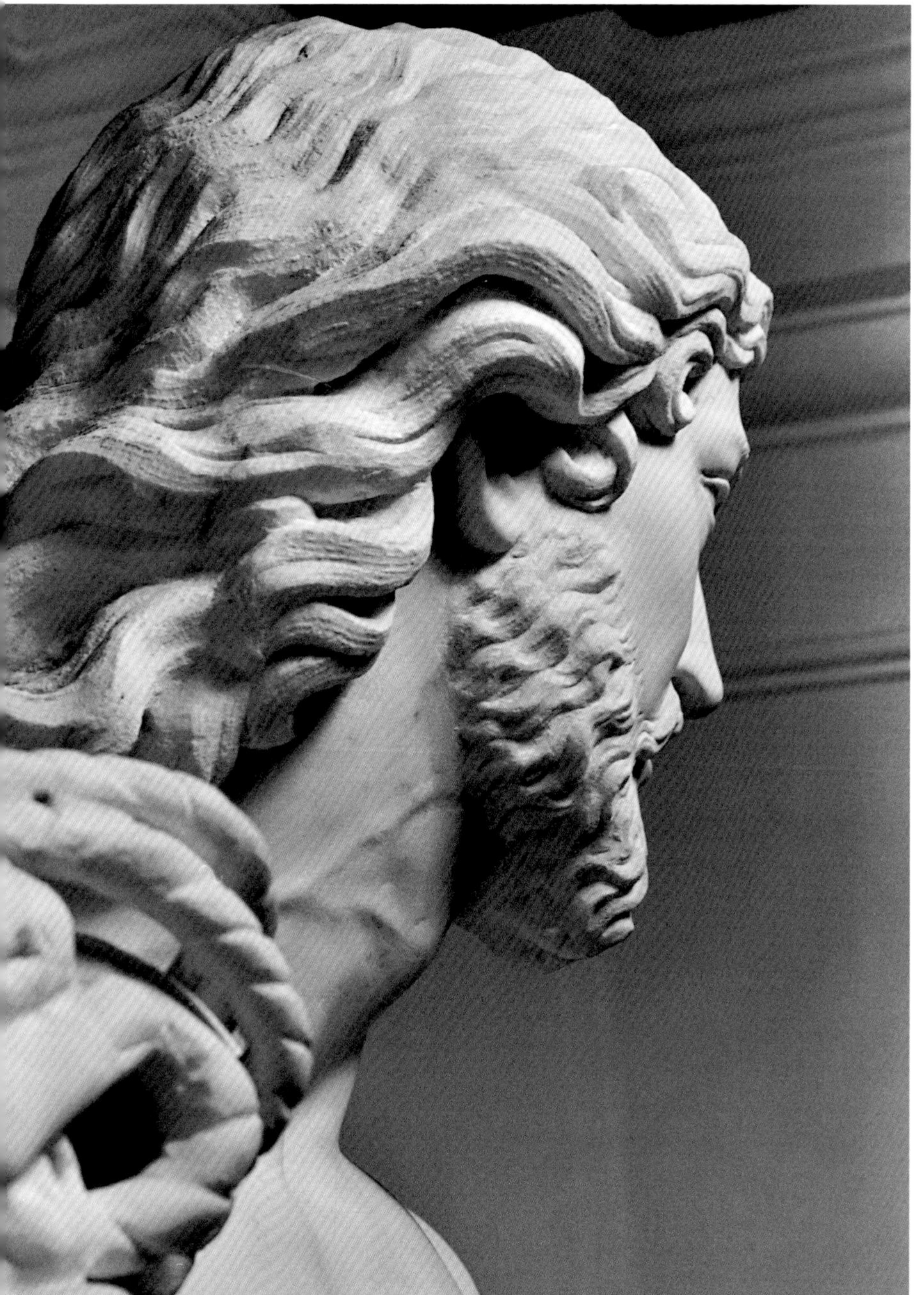

Michelangelo and unknown sculptors of the 16th-17th centuries, the *Risen Christ* (the "first Minerva Christ")
Michelangelo probably roughed out the hair and beard, but he was not the one to carve them
Bassano Romano (Rome), church of San Vincenzo Martire

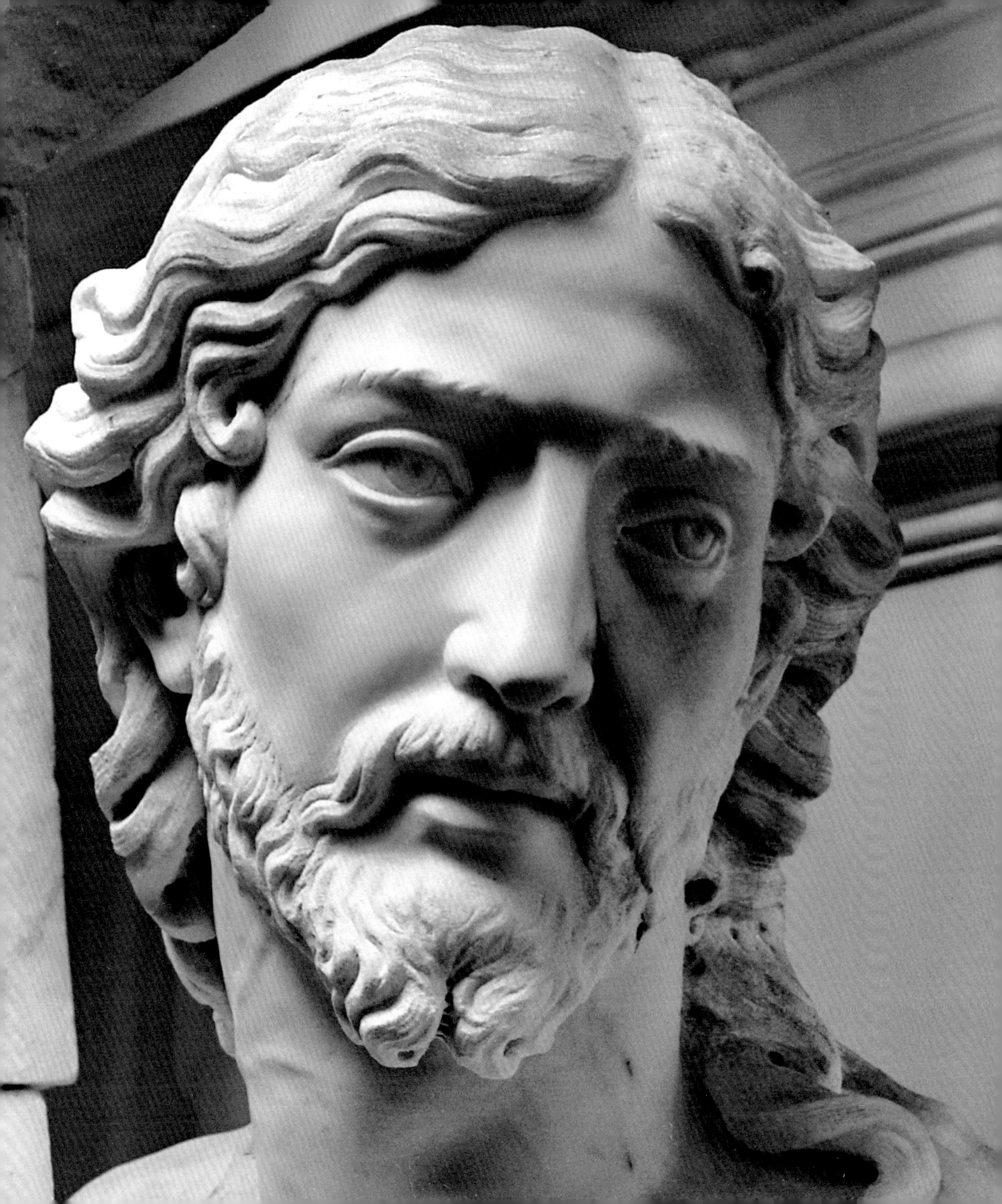

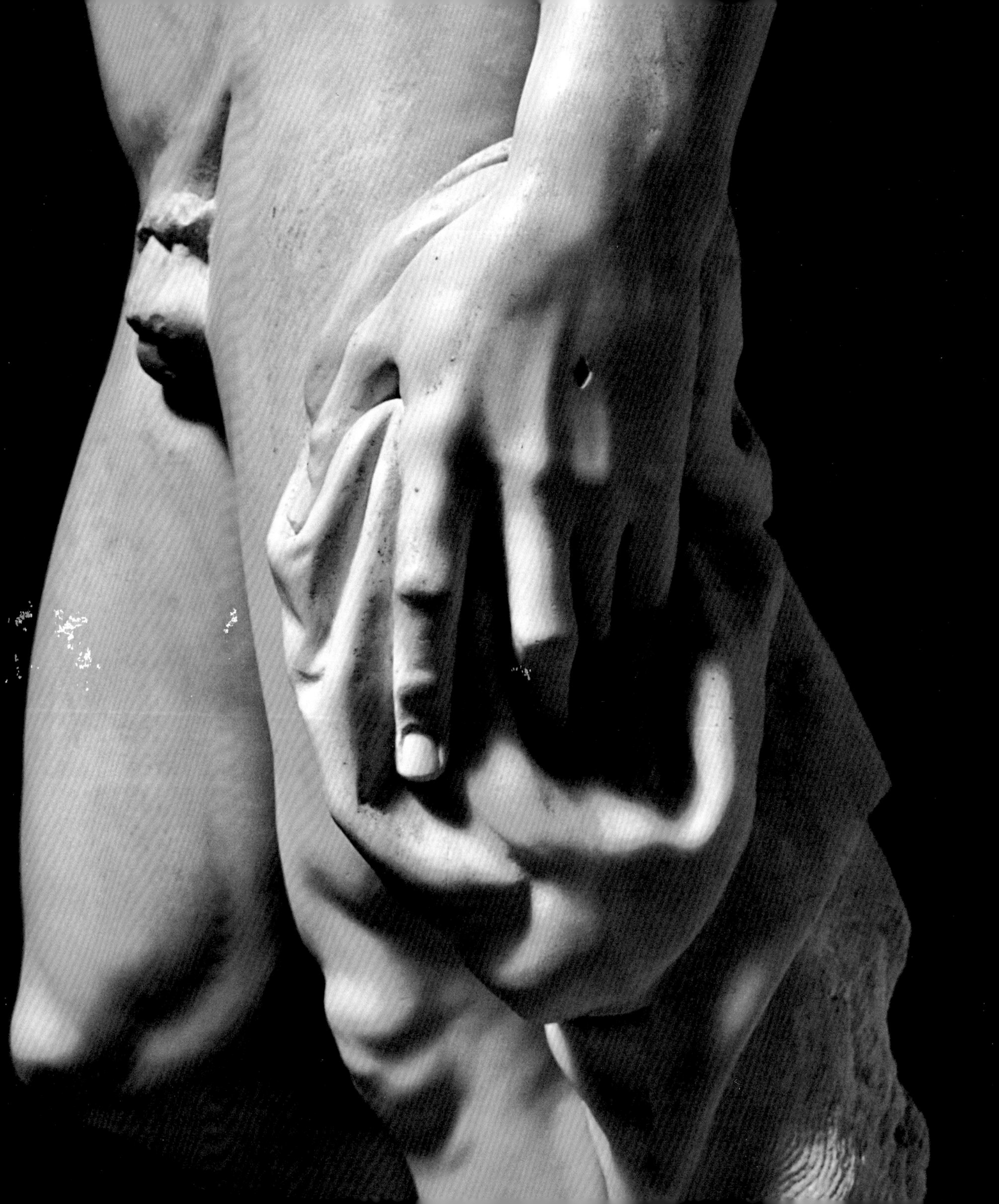

Between Florence, Carrara and Pietrasanta for the façade of San Lorenzo

Because of the political events underway in Rome and Florence Michelangelo's personal life and professional activity changed drastically. Until recently, we have always considered Leo X's short but triumphal stay in Florence from 22 December 1515 to 19 February 1516 (common usage) as the onset of a grandiose architectural and sculptural project on the pope's initiative: the realization of a façade for San Lorenzo, the original one being unfinished, and thus covered with an ephemeral façade whenever ceremonies were held in the pope's honour. But, as demonstrated by Michael Hirst, some of the events leading up to the task assigned are actually to be traced to the months before: halfway through June of 1515 Michelangelo expected that he would be called to the service of Leo X, and perhaps underwent a brief apprenticeship on the subject of architecture, copying Bernardo della Volpaia's notebook of drawings from the antique.[74] In Florence, in the month of July, there was already talk about redeveloping the piazza in front of San Lorenzo.
The way Vasari tells it the pope organized a sort of competition, entered by "Baccio d'Agnolo, Antonio da San Gallo, Andrea Sansovino and the gracious Raffaello da Urbino",[75] as well as Michelangelo. The information needs to be corrected, however, as it was not Antonio da Sangallo but Giuliano (for whom six design plans are housed at the Gabinetto Disegni e Stampe at the Uffizi) who was involved, and Jacopo Sansovino offered to make statues, not the entire façade.[76] It has been hypothesized that the pope may have intended to entrust Sangallo with the architecture and Michelangelo with the sculptures, but that as Sangallo died in 1516, Michelangelo's project prevailed; the artist's great desire to be the sole guide of the entire project, that is, for both the architecture and the sculpture, would soon lead to conflict and misunderstandings with the other artists.
In the meantime, Michelangelo's relations with the quarrymen from Carrara continued to be complicated: "because if they are not fools, they are knaves and rascals", he wrote to his brother Buonarroto in early July 1515, specifying that as he didn't personally wish to go to Carrara,[77] he would send intermediaries in his place instead. But the marble supply was of crucial importance to Michelangelo, and he had to be able to count on receiving top-notch materials that had been properly quarried on site. Any hostility had to be toned down, also in view of the artist's desire to be of service to Leo X for sculptural commissions.
Leo X in person, through his own brief, created the conditions for the artist to be relatively free from the task of making the Julius Tomb, and it was he who saw to any mediating required with the curators of the Della Rovere interests. On 4 July 1516, Lorenzo Pucci, a Florentine prelate whom the pope would soon nominate cardinal, also on behalf of Cardinal Aginense, revoked the contract of 1513. A third contract was drawn up soon after on 8 July.[78] In it the projection of the mausoleum was further reduced, this time to a deep wall façade. Nonetheless, the niches would still contain the *Victories* framed by terminal figures with *Slaves* on the lower storey, and other statues seated or standing around the deceased pope in the upper storey. The statues to be executed now numbered twenty, the bronze reliefs three; the artist was given nine more years. For his part, Leo X had promised the sculptor that he could work on the tomb in his Florentine studio. Also influencing the rewriting of the agreement was the fact that one month before Urbino had been taken over by papal troops, and the power of the Della Rovere family had weakened. Several drawings by Michelangelo are related to this phase, one of which contains the words: "This sketch represents a part of the frontal façade of the tomb which once completed, meaning by this the 'quadro' [basic structure] and the 'intaglio' [decoration], will measure 6 *braccia* in height from the ground to the first cornice, and 11 *braccia* from one end to the other [...]".[79] These measurements indeed coincide with the ones recorded in the contract of 1516 for the lower storey, and the works of "quadro" and "intaglio" were those completed by Antonio da Pontassieve. The panels with grotesques and the candelabra in the lower storey were copied in drawings by the artist's contemporary Giovanni Colonna da Tivoli.[80]
"So it came about that Michelangelo, weeping, abandoned the tomb

p. 139
Michelangelo and unknown sculptors of the 16th-17th centuries, the *Risen Christ* (the "first Minerva Christ") Michelangelo stopped when a dark vein appeared on the face
Bassano Romano (Rome), church of San Vincenzo Martire

p. 140
Michelangelo and unknown sculptors of the 16th-17th centuries, the *Risen Christ* (the "first Minerva Christ"), detail of the hand clutching the sudarium
Bassano Romano (Rome), church of San Vincenzo Martire

and went away to Florence"[81] in the summer of 1516. He had closed, this time for good, his bank account at the Balducci bank, using the Zanobi del Bianco and Bartolomeo da Empoli bank instead.[82]
Of the few but crucial facts related to Buonarroti's summer move to Florence, it is important to recall his highly critical opinion of Baccio d'Agnolo's gallery all around the south-eastern side of the Santa Maria del Fiore cupola, inaugurated on the Feast of Saint John a year before, on 24 June 1515: "a cage for crickets" were the artist's words.[83] With its cruel accuracy, like many of the quotations attributed to Michelangelo, it is the perfect definition of the elegant marble structure's only weak point, that is, its fragility and minuteness if compared with the vast and synthetic architectural divisions of the Gothic drum and Renaissance cupola.
Preceded by a letter of recommendation suited to the Malaspina marquises,[84] on 5 September Michelangelo was already in Carrara quarrying marble for the figures destined to the Della Rovere, actually welcomed by the quarrymen with whom any differences had more or less been patched up.[85] Michelangelo's stay in Carrara was fraught with all sorts of worries, however, from the news of his father Ludovico's ill health, to his horse's illness. In the meantime, he was receiving insistent requests from Pietrasanta, a walled coastal town under Florentine dominion located close by, that he go examine the marble being quarried there, and at the time he may have gone there to do just that. Through subsequent contacts with quarrymen and their intermediaries, from late 1516 to early 1517 (common usage), Michelangelo went ahead with the marble supply, requiring that it be white and veinless: not to be overlooked is the fact that in the past, veins that had surfaced in the marble blocks while work was underway had caused the artist to abandon the *Rebellious Slave*, and the *Christ* for Metello Vari.
However, in early December of 1516, he had taken an important trip to Rome, summoned by Leo X to evaluate the project for the façade of San Lorenzo.
Upon returning to Carrara on 31 December, Michelangelo resumed his hard and at times exasperating job to acquire marble, aided by Pietro Urbano from Pistoia, engaging in complex relationships with the quarrymen, stone-cutters, sculptors, go-betweens, shippers, bargemen, agents, bankers, all documented in both public and private writings; at the same time he kept up a great exchange of letters with Domenico Buoninsegni, secretary to Pope Leo X, from whom he learned of the desires and reactions of the pope and of Cardinal Giulio de' Medici, who was in charge of the work on the façade of San Lorenzo. Although highly esteemed – the respect he had earned was even expressed in the way the documents concerning his work were actually drawn up, for instance, in the contract of 17 April 1517, where is was dubbed "archimaestro scultore de la Sedia Apostolica" –, Michelangelo was nonetheless overwhelmed by problems of a practical nature, and somewhat tormented by a feeling of uncertainty. There was no shortage of money, and in early 1518 (common usage) he could already bank on 1,000 ducati d'oro larghi, the first quarter of a total 4,000 that he himself would later recall as having been allotted for the façade. But for a long time his assignment from the pope remained informal, and he lived in constant fear – drafted in a notarial document no less – of its being suddenly revoked. In May 1517, he still hadn't been officially commissioned to do the work,[86] despite the fact that he was taking personal risks in making very hard decisions about the marble, which was sometimes "cosa fallace", or imperfect, when it should have been the very finest. Accidents that occurred during the extraction phase, hidden flaws in the blocks visible only after they had been quarried and the negligence of the workers were often the cause of waste and delays, and Michelangelo was always in a state of dread and discomfort. On the other hand, as had happened before during his long periods of time spent in the quarries, his contact with the environment and the material gave him the energy to develop magnificent artistic visions, and this meant renewed enthusiasm. Gradually becoming impassioned with the work on the façade, he announced to Buoninsegni that it would be a work of "architecture and sculpture, the reflection of all of Italy".[87]
But in order to get the pope and the cardinal to make a decision about the commission, the artist had to show them a three-dimensional model, which would be more efficient than any drawing. Michelangelo had already given them one "di terra", but on 9 May he was asked to show them a wooden model, as well as to deal with

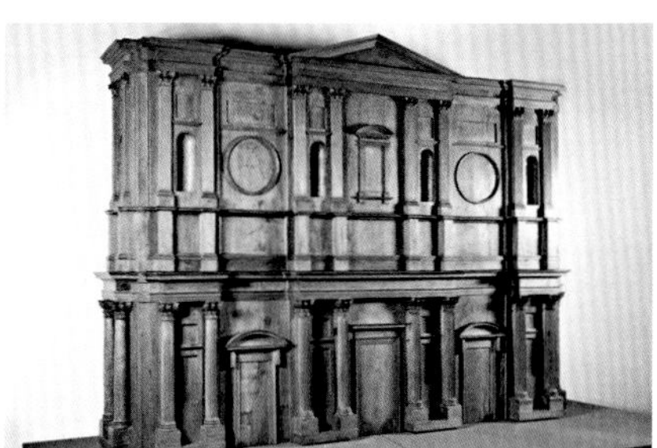

Project by Michelangelo, *Wooden model for the façade of San Lorenzo in Florence*, the only one to have survived of the two made for Leo X and Cardinal Giulio
Florence, Museo di Casa Buonarroti

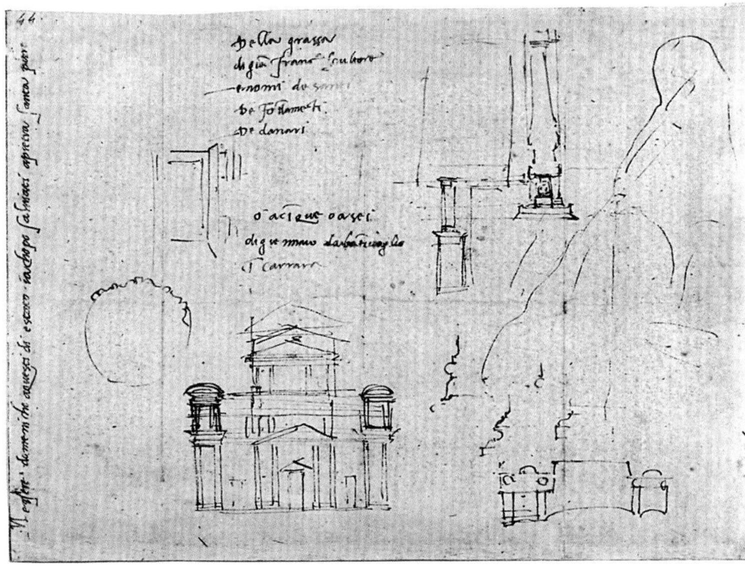

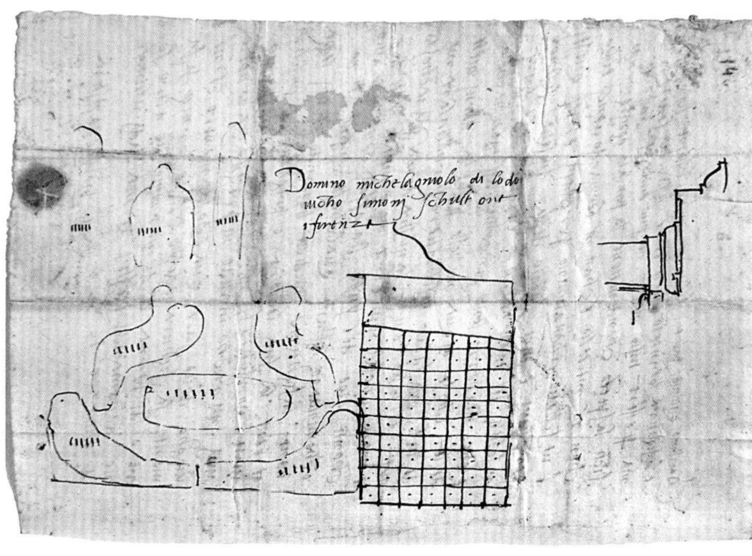

Michelangelo, *Various studies,* including a sketch of the façade for San Lorenzo
Florence, Museo di Casa Buonarroti, inv. 44 A *recto*

Michelangelo, *Various studies*, including outlines of marble blocks for the Medici tombs in San Lorenzo
Florence, Casa Buonarroti, Archivio Buonarroti, X, inv. 627 *verso*

the foundations of the façade in Florence.[88] The artist nonetheless stayed on to personally supervise the choice and extraction of the marble: this was too delicate and crucial a phase to simply be handed over to others. A precious notebook now preserved in the Casa Buonarroti, at first believed to be for the New Sacristy but then correctly related to the preparatory work for the façade and Julius Tomb,[89] records the sizes and shapes of the blocks, the letters and symbols for the suppliers carved into the marble, and it confirms Michelangelo's use of three intertwined circles, a mark made for practical reasons, but also of symbolic meaning. The notebook is not a personal item belonging to the artist, but a legal record signed by a notary.

Although he was immersed in the problems of transportation, with most of the marble in the port area or expected in September, Michelangelo decided to go back to Florence at the end of August to produce the wooden model that the pope had been wanting for some time. A wooden model was constructed with wax figure standing in for the intended sculpture, the iconography of the statues having already been decided on. The lower storey was to contain (from left to right) Saints Lawrence, John, Peter and Paul; the upper storey would instead show the Evangelists Luke, John, Matthew and Mark in a seated position; at the top the two patron saints of physicians and the Medici house Saints Cosmas and Damian in their professional garb. The list itself reveals the balance the artist sought out in choosing the saints that were worshipped in Florence, Princes of the Apostles that alluded to the papacy, the Syrian patron saints of the Medici family, and the Evangelists as the pillars of the Christian faith. The size of the statues can be calculated from the brief descriptions of some of the blocks to be quarried and rough-hewn for September: five *braccia* (almost 3 metres) for the standing figures, three and a half (1.75 metres) for those seated, thus quite a bit more than life-sized.

The pope was wholly satisfied with the model, his only doubt being that the magnificence of the undertaking might keep it from being completed; Michelangelo was thus invited to hire expert assistants, although he would personally make the main statues and oversee the preliminary models. But the liaisons between all those involved in the project would be anything but peaceful. On 30 June 1517, Jacopo Sansovino wrote a letter full of contempt accusing Michelangelo of having used hypocrisy and stealth with the intent of being awarded the entire commission for the undertaking.[90]

According to the contract, which was finally drawn up on 19 January 1518, the façade was to be executed by piece-work for a total of 40,000 ducati d'oro larghi, and made of "fini" white marbles from Carrara or Pietrasanta. Michelangelo probably had a larger wooden model of it made after the contract was signed, one that could act as a guide for future construction. Michelangelo gave both of the models to Duke Cosimo in 1555[91] and they could still be seen scattered about in the Grand-Ducal collections in the late 17th century. While the smaller of these is now lost, a large-scale model 1:12 made from a variety of woods and providing an example of the final project, preceded by drawing (43A*r*), are both currently in the Casa Buonarroti.[92]

The façade is majestic, featuring two Corinthian orders one on top of the other, and in between a high mezzanine with pilaster strips at regular intervals, whose rectilinear crowning (just rising up together with the central pediment) expands to become a large-scale version of the chapel in Castel Sant'Angelo, recalling a palace more than a church.

When he returned to the marble quarries on the coast, in 1518, Michelangelo abandoned Carrara for Pietrasanta, partially because of his difficult relations with the annoying and not very reliable Carraresi, and because of the pressure being made by the Medici to begin cultivating quarries in territories under Florentine rule. But continually faced with impediments, such as the slow progress being made to build a new road in the Serra Valley and the lack of experience of the stone-cutters brought in from Settignano (where *pietra serena* was worked), Michelangelo was soon forced to confess his disappointment and the fact that he missed Carrara. Columns and blocks were extracted and rough-hewn in Seravezza in a careless manner, and there was some bad luck as well: one column caused an accident and resulting death, in another a vein was discovered, a third one broke. In the meantime, the pope had personally intervened with a brief asking the Marquis Malaspina not hold up the complicated loading of the marble from Avenza, which the Marquis denied ever having done, attributing any misunderstandings to the shady, aggressive nature of the artist instead. Loaded onto carts, sometimes up to five in number, drawn by pairs of oxen, as well as on Pisan or Ligurian rented barges, the supplies of marble travelled from the quarries to the port area to the ports themselves, moving slowly and amidst countless difficulties (including drought which lowered the water level), to finally reach Florence and the studio Michelangelo had had built for himself in Via Mozza, the last stretch of what is now Via San Zanobi.

In 1519, with the pope's consent, Michelangelo once again began receiving supplies from Carrara, diminishing his commitment to Pietrasanta, where, in April, while it was being transported, a column fell into the river and was shattered into pieces. In September, he went back to Florence and eagerly began work on the marbles with the help of Domenico, called Topolino. But the façade for San Lorenzo, for which the foundations were laid between the end of June and 29 September 1517,[93] was never built, and the contract was revoked on 10 March 1520, to Michelangelo's bitter disappointment. When the first column arrived in Florence in 1521 the situation was already hopeless: for a long time the column lay in the piazza, eventually to be buried, it seems, under the church courtyard, where it apparently still is. Four others, ready to be carved, were still lying on the shore halfway through the century.

A lack of funds was said to be the reason for the interruption,[94] either that or the waning of the pope's interest.[95] It is also quite likely that Lorenzo Duke of Urbino's death in 1519 shifted the pope and Cardinal Giulio's attention to the construction of a funerary chapel. Here, in this appropriately monumental chapel, is where the remains of Lorenzo and Giuliano, who were the sons of Piero il Gottoso and referred to as "i Magnifici" (they died in 1478 and 1492, respectively, and for decades had rested in a temporary tomb) along with those of Giuliano, son of Lorenzo il Magnifico, and Lorenzo, son of Piero il Fatuo, leaders and dukes, were eventually buried.

Notes jotted down on the work carried out and expenses incurred for a façade that was never built still have the power to express Michelangelo's regret for the time wasted, his great effort – having been "on horseback for eight months" –, his disappointment. Stone-cutters from the Opera di Santa Maria del Fiore were sent to Pietrasanta to work the marble that had already been quarried and destined for the cathedral floor: the beautiful polychrome pavement polychrome that worshippers and visitors still walk on today are therefore the noble leftovers of the magnificent Michelangelesque project, which came to a halt even before it even began. Marble for the Julius Tomb continued to arrive from Carrara, while the blocks ready to be used to make the statuary were gradually sold in 1520 to others, including Jacopo Sansovino in Rome, Vittorio Ghiberti in Naples, Domenico Naldini in Florence. Michelangelo was kept informed as to the whereabouts of the marble, and it seems that to one of his informers, Francesco di Giovan Michele, he delivered a disenchanted opinion on go-betweens from Carrara: "they'd sell their own daughters to those who come to them with money".[96]

Notes

[1] Hatfield, 2002, p. 16.
[2] Vasari, "The Life of Michelangelo" (1550), 2007 ed., p. 160.
[3] Echinger-Maurach, 1991. After examining the subject of the tomb in the biographies, the author systematically discusses contributions by Springer, 1883; Schmarsow, 1884; Burger, 1904; Brinckmann, 1919; Panofsky, 1937 and 1964; Laux, 1943; Tolnay, 1951, 1954, 1970 ed.; Russoli, 1953; Wilde, 1954; von Einem, 1959 and 1973; Fasolo, 1965; Weinberger, 1967; Hartt, 1969; Frommel, 1977.
[4] Vasari, "The Life of Michelangelo" (1550), 2007 ed., p. 160.
[5] Condivi, *The Life of Michelangelo* (1553), 2006 ed., p. 33; Vasari, *The Lives* (1568), 1996 ed., II, p. 659.
[6] Florence, Gabinetto Disegni e Stampe degli Uffizi, inv. 608*r*. (Tolnay, 1975-1980, n. 56*r*.).
[7] Berlin Kupferstichkabinett, inv. 15305*r*.
[8] New York, The Metropolitan Museum of Art, Department of Prints and Drawings, Rogers Fund, 1962, inv. 62.93.1 (C. Echinger-Maurach, in *Giovinezza*..., 1999, p. 217).
[9] Condivi reports (1553, 1998 ed., p. 22) that Julius II paid him 1,000 ducats in Florence through Alemanno Salviati. Hatfield (2002, p. 19) corrects Alemanno to Jacopo.
[10] Contract of 12 November 1501 with barge owners Domenico di Pargolo and Giovanni Antonio del Merlo di Lavagna. One *carrata* corresponded to 2,500 Florentine *libbre*, equal to approximately 850 kg; the shipment was therefore close to 30 tons (Rapetti, 2001, p. 18).
[11] Agreement dated 10 December 1505 with the stone-cutters from Carrara Matteo Cuccarello and Guido di Antonio di Biagio, in Milanesi, 1875, p. 63. For further details on the supply see Rapetti, 2001, pp. 18 and ff.
[12] Annotation dictated to Tiberio Calcagni in a passage in Condivi, 1553, 1998 ed., no. 10, p. XXI.
[13] The famous anecdote is taken from Vitruvius; it was also recorded in Machiavelli in his *Discorsi sopra la prima deca di Tito Livio*, 1513-1519, 1-1: "Dinocrates the architect went to Alexander the Great, who wanted to have a city built for his glory, and showed him how he could build it at the top of Mount Athos, where, in addition to being strong, it could be carved so that a human form could be given to the city; this would be a marvellous and rare thing, and deserving of its greatness".
[14] Condivi, *The Life of Michelangelo* (1553), 2006 ed., p. 30.
[15] Hatfield, 2002, p. 22.
[16] Hirst, 1997. The project for a statue depicting *Hercules and Antaeus* was resumed by Clement VII in 1525, but Michelangelo averted the commission because he was very busy with the New Sacristy. Towards the end of the Republic, in 1528, the marble was proposed for use in a *Hercules and Cacus*. The latter subject is visible in an autograph sketch in Florence, Casa Buonarroti, inv. 63 F (Tolnay, 1975-1980, I, no. 63; Barocchi, 1962b, pp. 18-19, no. 10). See also Caglioti 2000b, I, pp. 221 (especially note 291), 246, 343. For the long story of the *Hercules and Antaeus* never executed see Joannides 2003c.
[17] The interpretation is based on Michelangelo's letter from Florence to Giovan Francesco Fattucci in Rome, end of December 1523, in *Il Carteggio*..., 1965-1983, III, 1973, p. 7 (thus, for example, in Rapetti, 2001, p. 14).
[18] Amy, 2000.
[19] Ollendorff, 1898.
[20] See Giovannini, 1998.
[21] Vasari, *The Lives* (1568), 1996 ed., II, pp. 655-656.
[22] Undoubtedly, Michelangelo kept the circumstances of Levi Matteo's "vocation", a publican by trade, in mind, before Christ summoned him to follow him.
[23] Pope-Hennessy, 1963, 1985 ed, p. 311.
[24] Vasari, 1550, 1986 ed., p. 888, 158 did not include it in the commission for twelve figures; Condivi, 1553, 1998 ed., p. 52, included at the last moment, but using very exact words ("who began by wanting to make twelve Apostles"); Varchi, 1564, p. 28 underscored its incompletion ("although it was not delivered"); Vasari 1568, 1962 ed., I, p. 23 appreciated it as a model of great pedagogical value for sculptural technique.
[25] Among the "questionable changes in the chronology of his artistic production" it was included in *Michelangelo e l'arte classica*, 1987, pp. 54, 56, no. 4.
[26] Francesco, son of Giuliano da Sangallo, recounted the episode to don Vincenzio Borghini sixty years later, clearly remembering that the pope sent his father to see the statue, with Michelangelo, who was at their home, in tow. No sooner did he see the group in the hole during the excavations than his words, it seems, were: "this is the Laocoön which Pliny writes about" (in *Michelangelo e l'arte classica*, 1987, p. 54).
[27] This is what Boissard reported, 1597-1602, 1627 ed., I, p. 7: "Hanc [statuam] Michael Angelus dicit esse miraculum artis singolare: in quo divinum artificum debeamus suspicere ingenium potius quam ad imitationem nos accingere".
[28] Lynn Catterson, conference at the Italian Academy at Columbia University in New York, April 2005.
[29] Through some Franciscans it seems he was asked to design a bridge from Constantinople to Pera. In the marginal note to the passage in Condivi (1553, 1998 ed., p. 27 and no. 13, p. XXII) Calcagni confirmed this piece of information: "It was true, and he told me he had already made a model for it". The bridge on the Golden Horn – still today the only one that joins Europe and Asia – was a magnificent challenge, with which Michelangelo would have measured himself up further on with his rival and senior Leonardo, who had also been asked for a design in 1502. Leonardo's design still exists in the Topkapi collection in Istanbul; studied and reelaborated by V. Sand, the bridge was made in Aas, Norway in 2001.
[30] Condivi, *The Life of Michelangelo* (1553), 2006 ed., p. 38. The allusion to the hand raised in an ambiguous gesture of benediction-malediction is related differently in Vasari (Vasari, "The Life of Michelangelo" [1550], 2007 ed., p. 162).
[31] Only half of the figure came out, to the waist, and the rest of the metal remained in the furnace. The work was, however successfully recast, and the other half completed.
[32] Vasari, "The Life of Michelangelo" (1550), 2007 ed., p. 161.
[33] Unidentified drawing from the 16th century (1510-1511), Paris, Musée du Louvre, DAG, Rothschild inv. 1466, published by Huse, 1965-1966.
[34] Milanesi, 1878-1885, VII, 1881, p. 172, note 1.
[35] In the first edition (1550, 1986 ed., p. 891) Michelangelo's answer was "You and Cossa go to the bordello, you're both solemn disasters in art". In the second edition (Vasari, *The Lives* (1550), 1996 ed., II, p. 664) the sculptor was attributed a more general comment: "I owe the same obligation to Pope Julius, who has given it to me [the beautiful casting and fine material], that you owe to the apothecaries who gave you your colours for painting" and the "goffo" was for Francia alone, probably because, as Marongiu (2000) notes, Cossa had been dead thirty years and Michelangelo appreciated his painting. Condivi (1553, 1998 ed., pp. 64-65) reported two other biting comments on sul bel figlio giovinetto del Francia ("Your father's living figures are finer than those he paints") is a play on words regarding the fact that Bolognese oxen are larger than Florentine ones, which Vasari then included in the second edition (1568).
[36] In a letter to his brother Buonarroto, Michelangelo stated that he was staying in a room and sleeping in the same bed with three assistants, Pietro Urbano and the Florentines Lapo d'Antonio sculptor and Ludovico del Buono foundryman. The latter two were fired by him while the work was under way, and the Milanese Bernardino d'Antonio dal Ponte was summoned, master of the artilleries for the Republic of Florence.
[37] See Corazzi, 1995.
[38] Letter from Piero Rosselli in Rome to Michelangelo in Florence dated 10 May in *Il Carteggio*..., 1965-1983, I, 1965, p. 16, no. X.
[39] Condivi and Vasari's comments on Michelangelo's loneliness have been disputed by the critics. One of the most recent contributions is by Hatfield (2002) and based on banking, and it tends to show that the artist fired his assistants because he couldn't afford to pay their salaries.
[40] Vasari, "The Life of Michelangelo" (1550), 2007 ed., p. 170.
[41] Condivi, *The Life of Michelangelo* (1553), 2006 ed., pp. 59-60.
[42] Hirst, 1976.
[43] Published by Milanesi, 1875, pp. 635-639, especially p. 637.
[44] Milanesi, 1875, p. 640, no. XI.
[45] See Acidini Luchinat, 1982.
[46] Letter from Michelangelo in Rome to Baldassarre di Cagione in Carrara after 20 August 1513 (perhaps September), in *Il Carteggio*..., 1965-1983, I, 1965, p. 144, no. CIX. Michelangelo reproached the quarrymen very harshly: "voi fate male a mancare della fede e a stratiare chi vi fa utile". From the artist's accounts we can see that on 9 August Baldassarre was paid some 100 fiorini d'oro larghi through the Balducci branch in Pisa (Hatfield, 2002, p. 31).
[47] Oxford, Ashmolean Museum, inv. P297*r*. (Tolnay, 1975-1980, I, no. 157).
[48] Model made of light-coloured terracotta, 22.5 cm in height. Florence, Museo di Casa Buonarroti, inv. 191. The relationship to the *Dying Slave* is in O'Grody, 1999. As part of a more in-depth reconsideration of the small models preserved at the Casa Buonarroti, attribution of this *bozzetto* of a male torso to Michelangelo was confirmed, which was deliberately left incomplete where the limbs would have been attached (*I bozzetti*..., 2000, no. 2, p. 32), while the head is instead missing. What it has in common with the *Dying Slave* is the accentuated pose of the neck and arm, and the tilt of the strong and yet sinuous body. Although it was not identified until Goldscheider's publication (1953), it was already believed to be a Michelangelesque "piece" in around 1585: it was in fact designed by Andrea Commodi, the author at the time of a series after drawings by Buonarroti, today in the Gabinetto Disegni e Stampe at the Uffizi, inv. 18538 F. Cf. *I bozzetti*..., 2000, no. 2, p. 32.

[49] Grimm, 1860-1863, II, pp. 29 and ff.
[50] The *Saint Sebastians* by Antonio Rossellino in the tabernacle at the Museo della Collegiata in Empoli, and Benedetto da Maiano in the church of the Misericordia in Florence have been used as examples (von Einem, 1959). But there have also been references to the *Laocoön* group.
[51] After Grimm, also Thode (1908-1913), Kriegbaum (1940), Janson (1952).
[52] G. Bonsanti, in *Michelangelo...*, 1989, no. 36.
[53] The first manuscript of the *Hieroglyphica* had arrived in Florence in 1423; Biblioteca Medicea Laurenziana, Cod. Laur. Gr. LXIX, 27. Also available in 1505, 1515 and 1517 were printed editions in Latin. Various statues of seated cynecephali of Egyptian provenance could be seen in Rome; furthermore, Leo X owned one or more apes.
[54] Zimmerman, 1991.
[55] For Michelangelo's relationship with the *Torso* by Apollonius, referred to as the *Belvedere Torso* because of its location, see *Michelangelo e l'arte classica*, 1987, pp. 54 and ff.
[56] In a first version of the figure, visible in the Oxford drawing (Ashmolean Museum, inv. P 297*r.*) it was originally a bearded warrior, perhaps an allegory for the Art of war.
[57] *Il Carteggio...*, 1965-1983, II, 1967, pp. 7-8, no. CCLXXXV (Michelangelo [in Florence] to the Capitano di Custodia in Cortona [first half of May, 1518]).
[58] *Il Carteggio...*, 1965-1983, I, 1965, p. 166, no. CXXVIII (Michelangelo in Rome to his brother Buonarroto in Florence, 16 June 1515).
[59] M. Forcellino, 2002, A. Forcellino, 2002a, Forcellino, 2003. Among the reviews: Smolizza, 2002, de Klerck, 2004. B. Agosti in the magazine "Alias" with *Il Manifesto*. Rapetti (2001, p. 73) indicated "a vertical microfracture through the right knee that continues into the cloak above", stating that the block was as flawed as the one for the *Pietà* in Florence.
[60] Condivi, *The Life of Michelangelo* (1553), 2006 ed., p. 77.
[61] Vasari, "The Life of Michelangelo" (1550), 2007 ed., p. 161.
[62] Condivi, *The Life of Michelangelo* (1553), 2006 ed., p. 79.
[63] Freud's essay has also led to numerous comments in timee, not all of which agree. See the most recent of these in Briefel, 2003.
[64] The film was made possible thanks to Lottomatica, a sponsor for the restoration.
[65] Letter from Argentina Malaspina (wife of Florentine *gonfaloniere* Pier Soderini) in Florence to her brother Lorenzo the Marquis of Fosdinovo dated 15 July, 1516, in *Il Carteggio...*, 1965-1983: "we believe that there is no man equal to him in Europe today".
[66] See chapter II. Also cf. Acidini Luchinat, 1997.
[67] Cf. Hatfield, 2002, p. 35.
[68] Milanesi, 1875, p. 641, no. XI, "given to Michelangelo for the marble figure of a Christ risen for the church of the Minerva in Rome".
[69] "In a courtyard or garden I saw a naked Christ with the Cross to the right side left unfinished because of a vein discovered in the marble of the face, the work of Michelangelo, & he gave it to M. Metello, & as well as another similar one, which is now in the Minerva, M. Metello had made at his own expense by Michelangelo" (Aldrovandi, 1556, 1562 ed., p. 247).
[70] Parronchi, 1975, pp. 157-190, identified it as being the *Saint Sebastian* by Nicolas Cordier for the Aldobrandini chapel in Santa Maria sopra Minerva; Salvini does not agree, 1978, p. 104.
[71] Baldriga, 2000, Danesi Squarzina, 2001.
[72] The statue was described in a letter written by Francesco Buonarroti in Rome to Michelangelo the Younger in Florence: "signor Passignano [...] wants me to go and see a marble model by the hand of Michelangelo of the Christ of the Minerva itself, but in a different pose, and he likes it, and he thinks that the price will be not much more than the value of the marble itself, the figure, you know, is life-sized" (Sebregondi, 1986). Because of its state of incompletion the work was compared to the *Slaves* and to the *Saint Matthew*.
[73] Paris, Musée du Louvre, DAG, inv. 717, in Joannides, 2003a, pp. 387-388, n. R 2. A further observation that, however, leads in the opposite direction is that the hand (for which the small hand in the act of drawing depicted next to it seems to indicate a colossal dimension) is not unlike what we might consider to have been the left hand of the lost Strozzi *Hercules* which was finished in France, the way we would see it – if we accept Tolnays' proposal in 1964 – in a drawing at the Louvre attributed to Rubens but also in the statue that passed through the antiquarian market (New York, Sotheby's, 13 October 1999, in Rèpaci, 1999).
[74] The notebook, known as the Coner Code (London, J. Sloane Museum) had just been completed in 1515. Cf. Hirst 2004b.
[75] Vasari, "The Life of Michelangelo" (1550), 2007 ed., p. 170.
[76] Barocchi, 1962b, II, pp. 662-678; Barbieri, Puppi, 1964, pp. 46-47; and Millon, 1988, pp. 5-8.
[77] Letter from Michelangelo in Rome to Buonarroto in Florence, in *Il Carteggio...*, 1965-1983, I, 1965, I, p. 170.
[78] Milanesi, 1875, pp. 649-650, no. XVII (transcription in the vulgar of the third contract for the Tomb of Julius II).
[79] London, British Museum, Department of Drawings and Prints, inv. 1859-5-14-824 (Wilde, 1953, pp. 41-42, no. 23; Echinger-Maurach, 1991, pl. 63). Other Michelangelesque sheets in the British Museum contain sketches for marble rough-hewn and finished for the blocks and a study of the capital decorated with mascarons.
[80] Echinger-Maurach, 1991, pl. 75.
[81] Condivi, *The Life of Michelangelo* (1553), 2006 ed., p. 60.
[82] Hatfield, 2002, p. 33.
[83] The other reason why Michelangelo did what Vasari defined "tanto rumore" was of a conservative order: to build the gallery "si tagliavano le morse che aveva lasciato that Filippo Brunelleschi" had left there deliberately (Vasari...). Michelangelo contributed to preparing another model of the finishing for the tambour and elaborated designs that can even be dated later, to 1519-1520. On the whole episode of the outside gallery, see Corazzi, 1995.
[84] Letter from Argentina Malaspina (wife of the Florentine *gonfaloniere* Pier Soderini) in Florence to her brother Lorenzo Marquis of Fosdinovo, dated 15 July 1516, in *Il Carteggio...*, 1965-1983, I, 1965, I, pp. 188-189. The various suggestions made include the idea of introducing him to the Marquis Alberico Malaspina.
[85] Rapetti, 2001, pp. 26-27.
[86] Letter from Michelangelo in Carrara to Domenico Buoninsegni in Rome [dated 2 May 1517], in *Il Carteggio...*, 1965-1983, I, 1965, pp. 277-279, no. CXXI.
[87] Letter from Michelangelo in Carrara to Domenico Buoninsegni in Rome [dated 2 May 1517], in *Il Carteggio...*, 1965-1983, I, 1965, pp. 277-279, no. CXXI.
[88] Letter from Domenico Buoninsegni in Rome to Michelangelo in Carrara dated 9 May 1517, in *Il Carteggio...*, 1965-1983, I, 1965, pp. 281-282, no. CCXXIII.
[89] Bardeschi Ciulich, 1994, pp. 100-105.
[90] Letter from Jacopo d'Antonio called il Sansovino in Florence to Michelangelo in Carrara, 30 June 1517, in *Il Carteggio...*, 1965-1983, I, 1965, no. CCXXXI.
[91] Letter to this regard, dated 28 September 1555, in *Il Carteggio...*, 1965-1983, V, 1983, no. MCCXV, p. 45.
[92] See the entry by A. Fara in the catalogue *L'officina...*, 1996, p. 228, no. 73. For the other drawings, in particular nos. 91A, 45A, 44A*r.*, 47A*r.*, cf. Millon, 1988, pp. 17-62 (nos. 2, 3, 4, 6, 7).
[93] Millon, 1988, p. 11.
[94] Vasari, 1568, 1962 ed., I, p. 57.
[95] Condivi, (1553), 1998 ed., p. 37.
[96] Letter from Francesco di Giovan Michele in Carrara to Michelangelo in Florence, 29 February 1520, in *Il Carteggio...*, 1965-1983, II, 1967, p. 217.

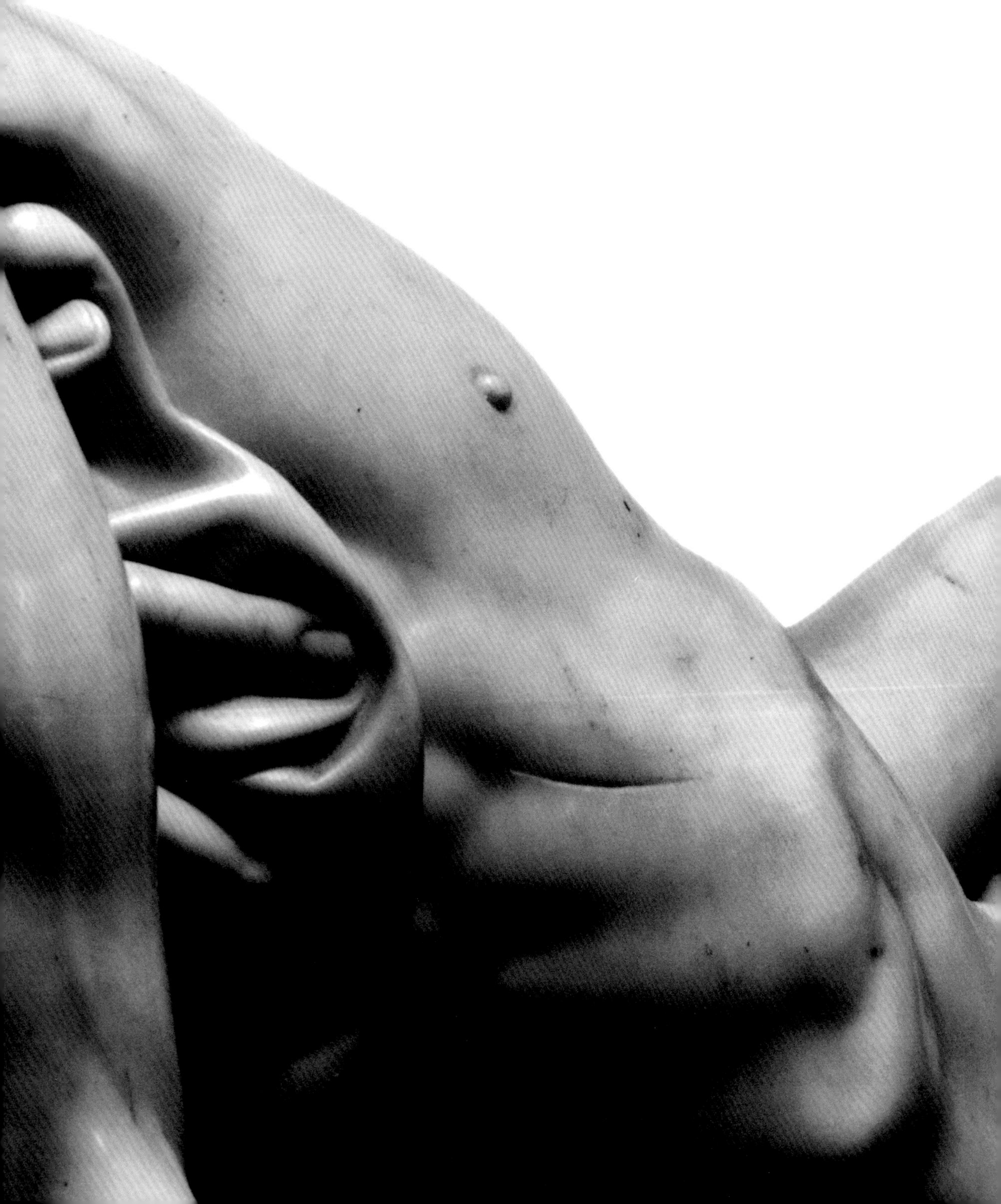

The tombs of the Medici at San Lorenzo

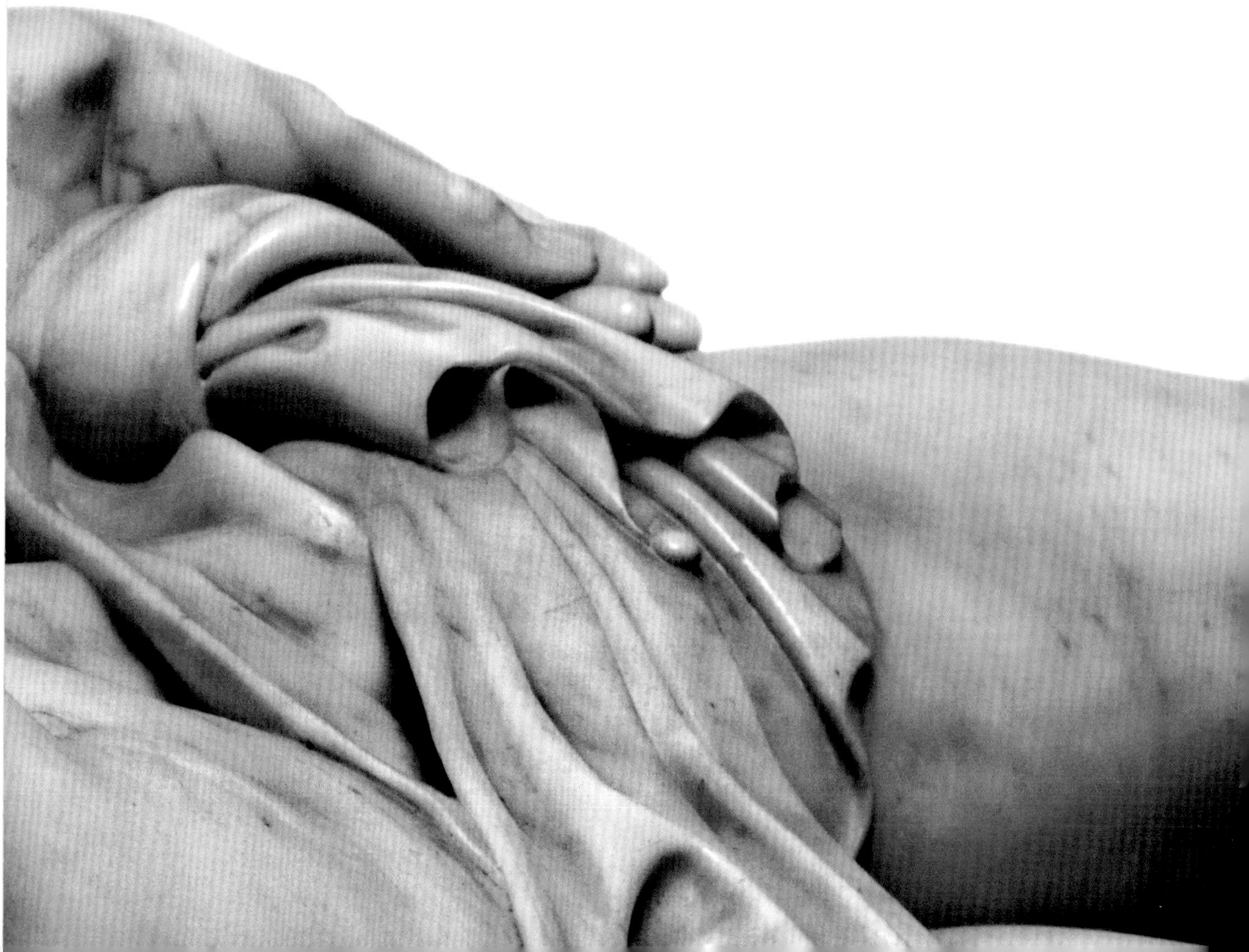

partitions are contours of different dimensions. The stone had been expertly chosen by Michelangelo himself in the Fossato quarry located in the valley of the River Mensola below Settignano, thus ensuring that it was "gentile di grana" and "azzurrigna" in colour.[8]
The artist wanted to personally oversee the choice of the marble. In 1521, with 200 ducats from Cardinal Giulio, he went to Carrara to have marble quarried for the tombs, for which he must have had at least a general idea in terms of structure and volume.[9] With his usual suppliers – il Pollina, Leone, il Bello, who would eventually become partners with Quindici – he agreed on the delivery of two hundred *carrate* of the finest marble from the Polvaccio quarry, to be used for the figures and the "opera di quadro", or architectural framing. The marble was still being delivered in 1526, what with the delays of the quarrymen, poor streets, a dry Arno, and the ensuing complaints of the artist who was busy in the Florentine site with heavy loads of work and much responsibility;[10] for this reason, in fact, he was represented in Carrara by his trusted assistants, who worked directly from the detailed instructions he had prepared that contained drawings and measurements for the pieces he needed. After the Sack of Rome in 1527, when the Medici were expelled from Florence and work on the project came to a halt, all of the marble required had actually already been delivered. Some of the pieces were not what the artist had ordered, either because they were the wrong size (he too had been making changes in the project),[11] or because the marble just wasn't beautiful or fine enough.

The architecture

The disposition of the masses in the great hall hosting the tombs consists of two orders. The lower order, which features fluted, cabled pilaster strips with Composite capitals crowned by a cornice, houses the dukes' tombs and the "cassone" for the Magnifici on three sides. It opens up behind the altar in a rectangular apse flanked by two narrow spaces referred to as "lavamani", for a revisitation of the Brunelleschian architectural scheme for the Old Sacristy, retrieved in its flagrant originality after the deductions that succeeded one another over the 15th century.[12] The upper order (separated from the lower one by a flat fascia of plaster wall) is supported by a deep, moulded string course where pairs of windows with triangular tympana, situated at the corners, alternate with lunettes corresponding to the tombs. In the altar wall, the stone contour of the lunette is actually the large arch behind which the small hemispherical cupola stands out against the pendentives, each of which marked by an oculo. The main area is also topped by a cupola, divided into five layers of coffers like in the Pantheon in Rome. Giovanni da Udine, who worked for the Medici for a short period of time, in 1532-1533, decorated it with white and gold stucco work that bestowed a note of elegance and mirth on the austere atmosphere: "beautiful foliage, rosettes [...] birds, masks and figures",[13] which in the final work done on the Sacristy were forever destroyed.[14]
The cupola is supported by pendentives that include round cornices, and the four lunettes located below are each crossed by a window with a semi-circular tympanum, whose side jambs converge to achieve stronger perspectival foreshortening.
In the cubic space of the room the angular constructs are particularly evident, formed by two sequences (at 90°) consisting in a door topped by a marble tabernacle, decorated inside with a patera on a festoon, in axis with the windows of the upper order: an element of unprecedented ambivalence is the pair of fluted brackets which, submitted to the shrine, become a part of the cornice around the door. This rich architectural page is framed by superimposed orders of pilaster strips. The quantity and quality of innovative elements in the architectural language were noted by Giorgio Vasari and commented on in an understandably famous passage: "but with another manner of ornamentation, he made in it an ornamentation in a composite order, in a more varied and more original manner than any other master at any time, whether ancient or modern, had been able to achieve, for in the novelty of the beautiful cornices,

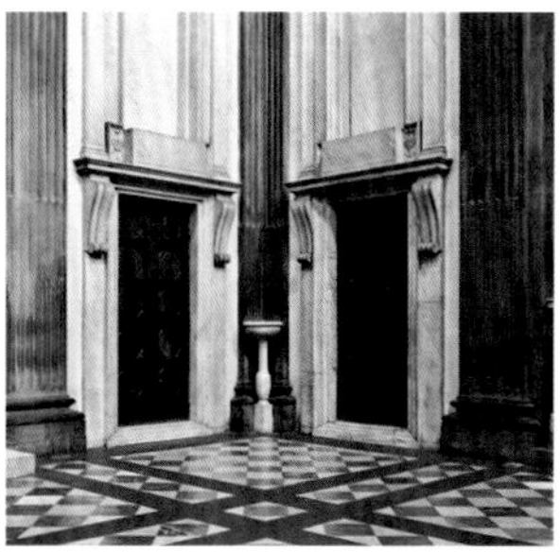

View of the New Sacristy with the corner construction including two doors crowned by tabernacles
Florence, San Lorenzo, Museo delle Cappelle Medicee

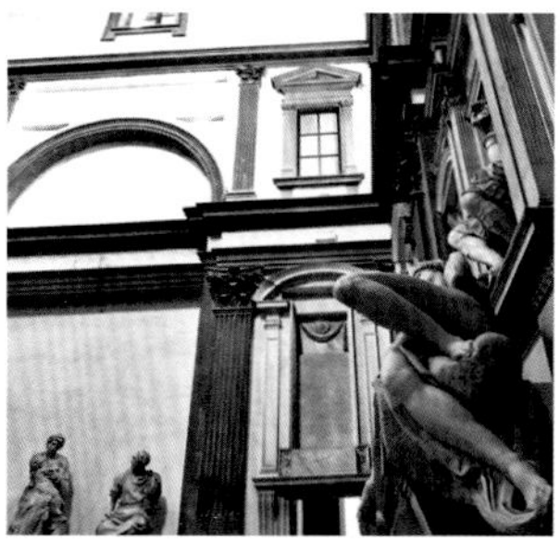

View of the New Sacristy, upper storey with lunette and window
Florence, San Lorenzo, Museo delle Cappelle Medicee

capitals, bases, doors, tabernacles, and tombs, he departed not a little from the work regulated by measure, order and rule, which other men did according to a common use and after Vitruvius and the antiquities, to which he would not conform. That licence has done much to give courage to those who have seen his methods to set themselves to imitate him, and new fantasies have since been seen which have more of the grotesque than of reason or rule in their ornamentation. Wherefore the craftsmen owe him an infinite and everlasting obligation, he having broken the bonds and chains by reason of which they had always followed a beaten path in the execution of their works".[15] Benvenuto Cellini would say that Michelangelo invented a new Composite order, one of Tuscan inspiration.[16]
In ascribing to Michelangelo the first, overwhelming manifestation of the originality of architecture, and in referring to the Sacristy for every subsequent development in architectural and decorative expression towards the conception of art often referred to as Mannerism or Maniera, Vasari lavished great praise on Buonarroti, essential to a teleological vision of the kind of art that identified him as being the highest possible aspiration without equal. But it is also true that the New Sacristy was the source of inspiration for generations of artists, who borrowed from it and reworked every single aspect of it, from the government of its complex spatiality to the transgressive imagination of the ornamental details. Niches, tabernacles, plinths, corbels, festoons, friezes of mascarons, candelabra, in short, all that it contained were studied[17] and reinterpreted in countless variations, in a long season of Florentine art that ended (but not without peripheral or vernacular exemplars) only with the advent of the Baroque from outside, in the 1630s.
Our attention was once again drawn to the candelabra after the discovery of a drawing – whose attribution to Michelangelo was very well-founded – of a monumental unexecuted candelabrum with structural and ornamental motifs similar to those of the Sacristy.[18]

Tombs for leaders and dukes

Between the niches in the lateral walls the dark reliefs of the double pilaster strips and the cornice made of *pietra serena* enclose the tombs, where architecture and sculpture, in their different treatments, respond to an identical sentiment of the material governed by the intellectual force of *disegno* and excellent technical skill.
Elaborated over the course of graphic experimentation combined with architectural and figurative elements datable from January 1524,[19] the marble wall that juts out from a platform which is also made of marble features a basement with cornices (simple or with mascarons) before which the sarcophagus is set on a parallelepiped; on the lids of the sarcophagi pairs of statues conventionally indicated as the *Times of the Day – Night, Day, Dawn* and *Dusk* – recline. In the register above the centre of each of the tombs a niche opens up with the statue of the deceased duke; to the sides, separated by binate fluted pilaster strips with "grotesque" capitals are two empty tabernacles with a curved tympanum supported by *loricate* brackets. Crowning the composition is a tripartite attic, with pairs of balustrades corresponding to the pilaster strips: the marble panels are carved with festoons, amphoras, bucrania and shells *all'antica*, except for the one in the middle whose only projecting element is a simple bracket at the top of the *mezzeria*.
Michelangelo had planned many more figures and orders for the tombs. Two *Trophies of Arms* commenced by Silvio Cosini are still to be found in situ, but they were never assembled on the attic atop the marble walls. Instead, a *Crouching Boy* is now housed in the Hermitage Museum in Saint Petersburg, where we can see proof of the onset of Michelangelo's first project. This had included two pairs of sorrowful figures (or vanquished ones, depending on the interpretation) huddling in the attic storey above the lateral tabernacles of the tombs.[20] It is also likely that other figures were to be added to the empty tabernacles, accompanied by epigraphs. This would be suggested by the famous sheet at the British Museum in London that bears these words: "Fame holds down the epitaphs. They go neither forwards nor

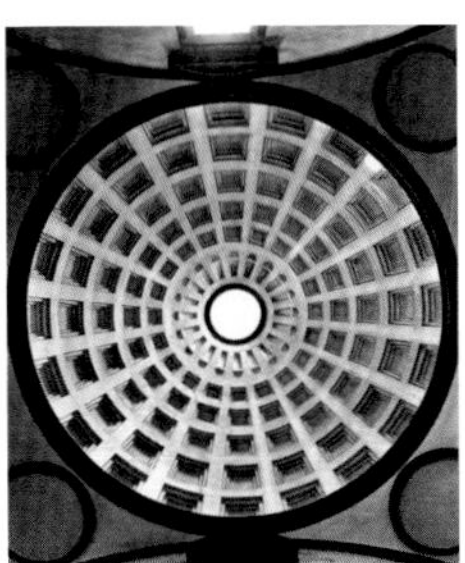

New Sacristy cupola with coffers, previously decorated with stucco work and paintings (now lost) by Giovanni da Udine
Florence, Museo delle Cappelle Medicee

p. 154
Michelangelo and collaborator, *Crouching Boy*, a vanquished or sorrowful figure, which was to be placed on the attic storey of the Medicean tombs in the New Sacristy
Saint Petersburg, Hermitage Museum

p. 155
Michelangelo and collaborator, *Crouching Boy*, detail of face underneath a cap of curls
Saint Petersburg, Hermitage Museum

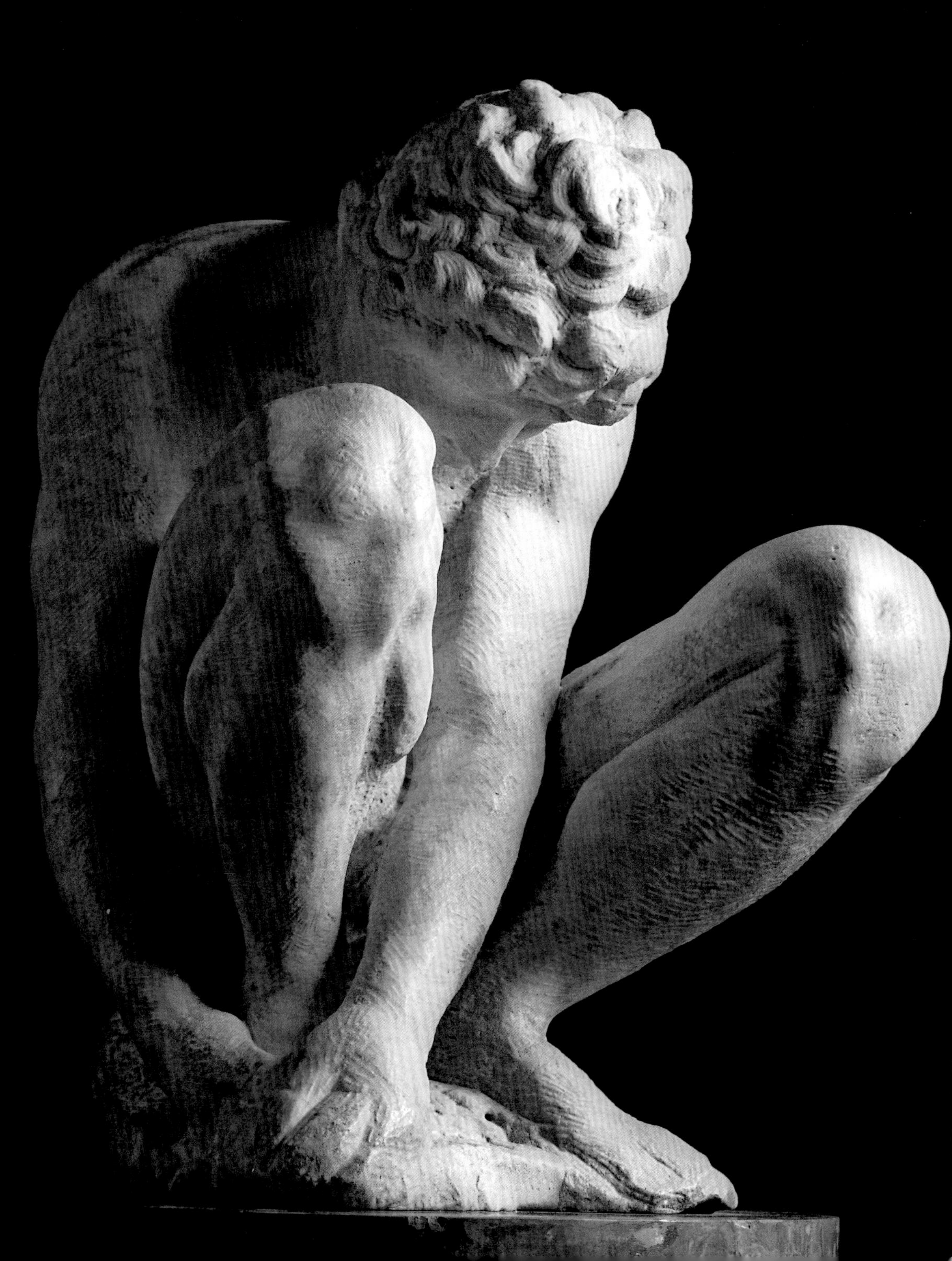

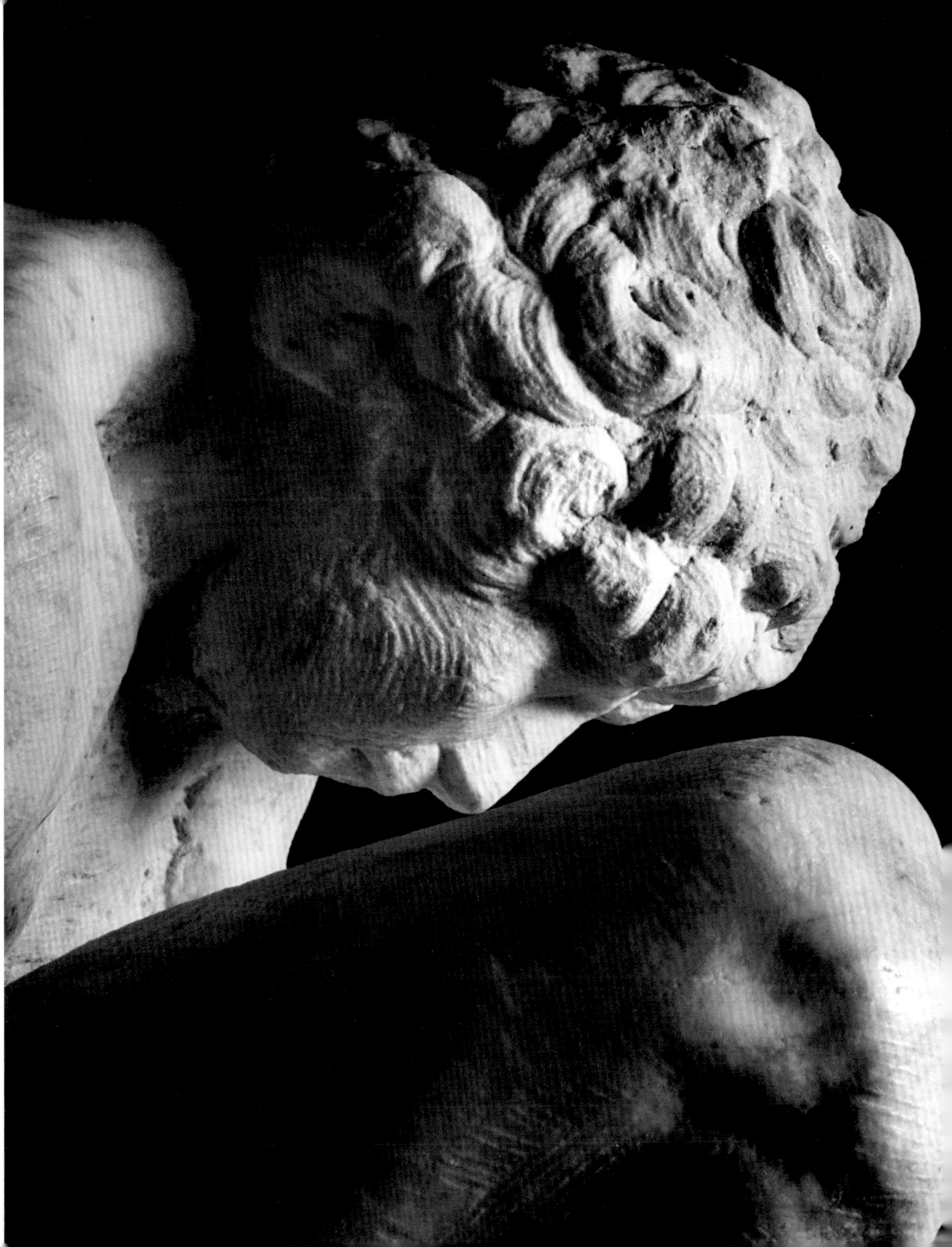

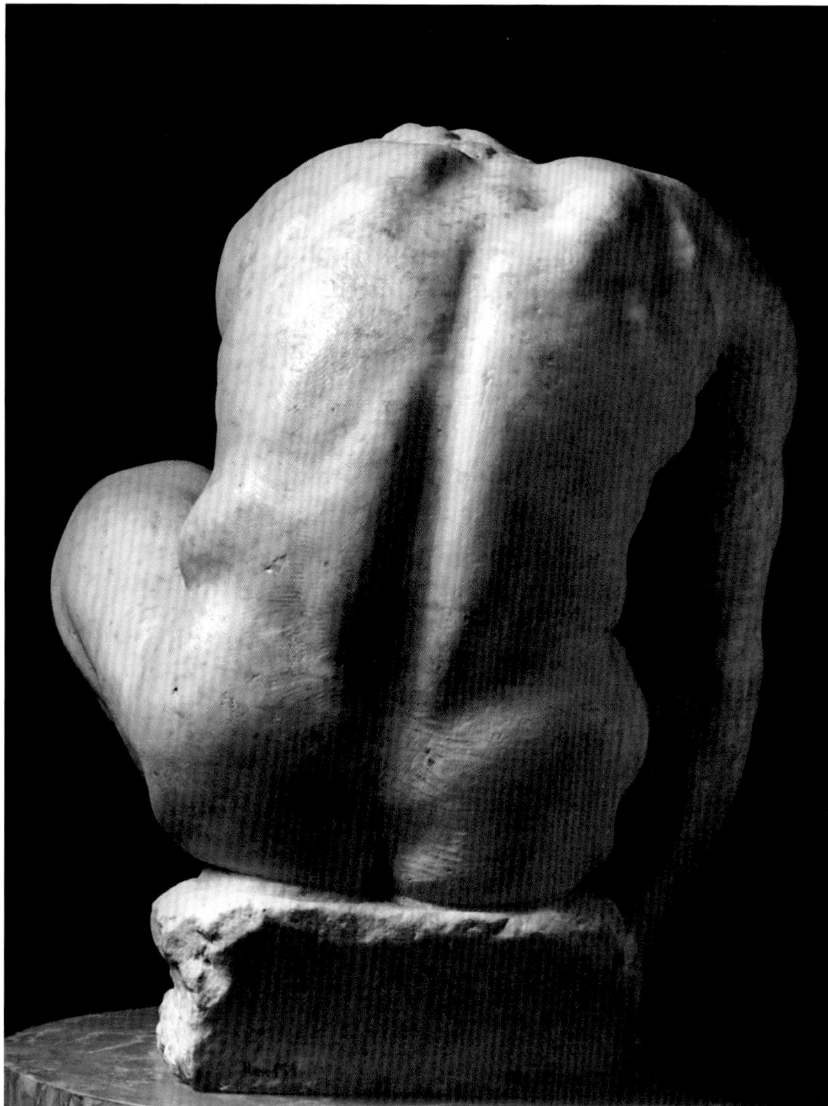

Michelangelo and collaborator,
Crouching Boy, back view
Saint Petersburg, Hermitage
Museum

p. 157
Michelangelo and collaborator,
Crouching Boy, the powerful,
articulated features indicate
Michelangelo's sculptural style
Saint Petersburg, Hermitage
Museum

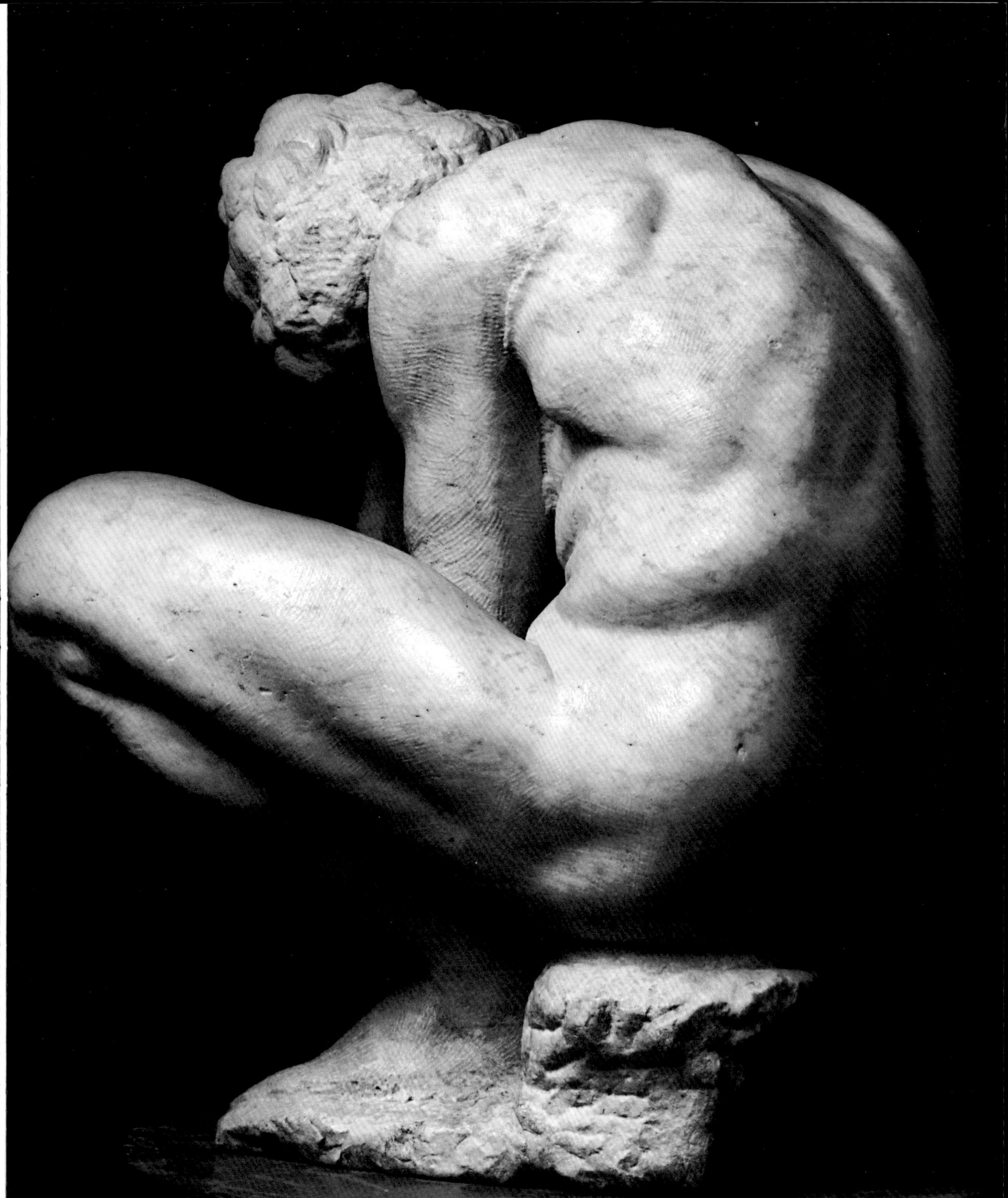

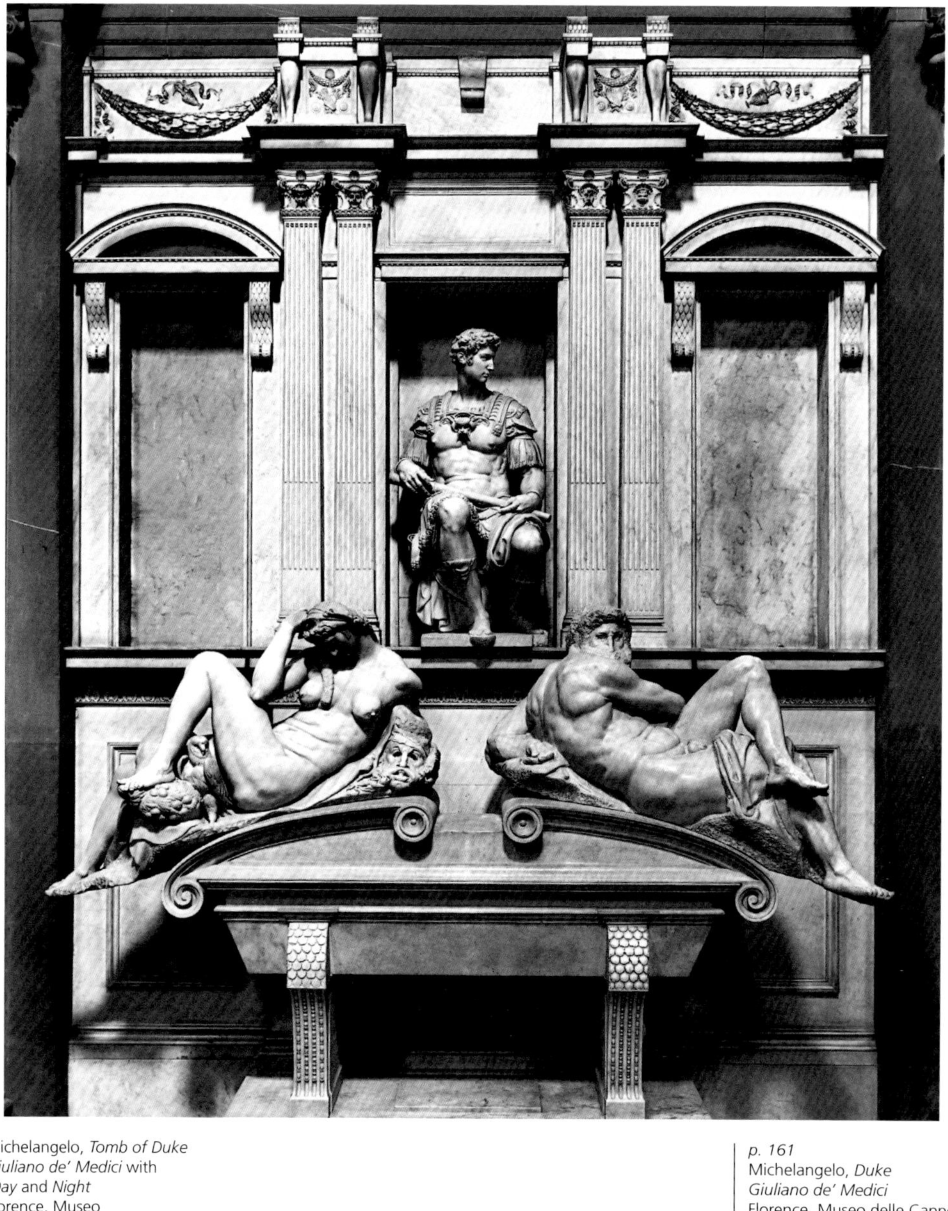

Michelangelo, *Tomb of Duke Giuliano de' Medici* with *Day* and *Night*
Florence, Museo delle Cappelle Medicee, New Sacristy

p. 161
Michelangelo, *Duke Giuliano de' Medici*
Florence, Museo delle Cappelle Medicee, New Sacristy

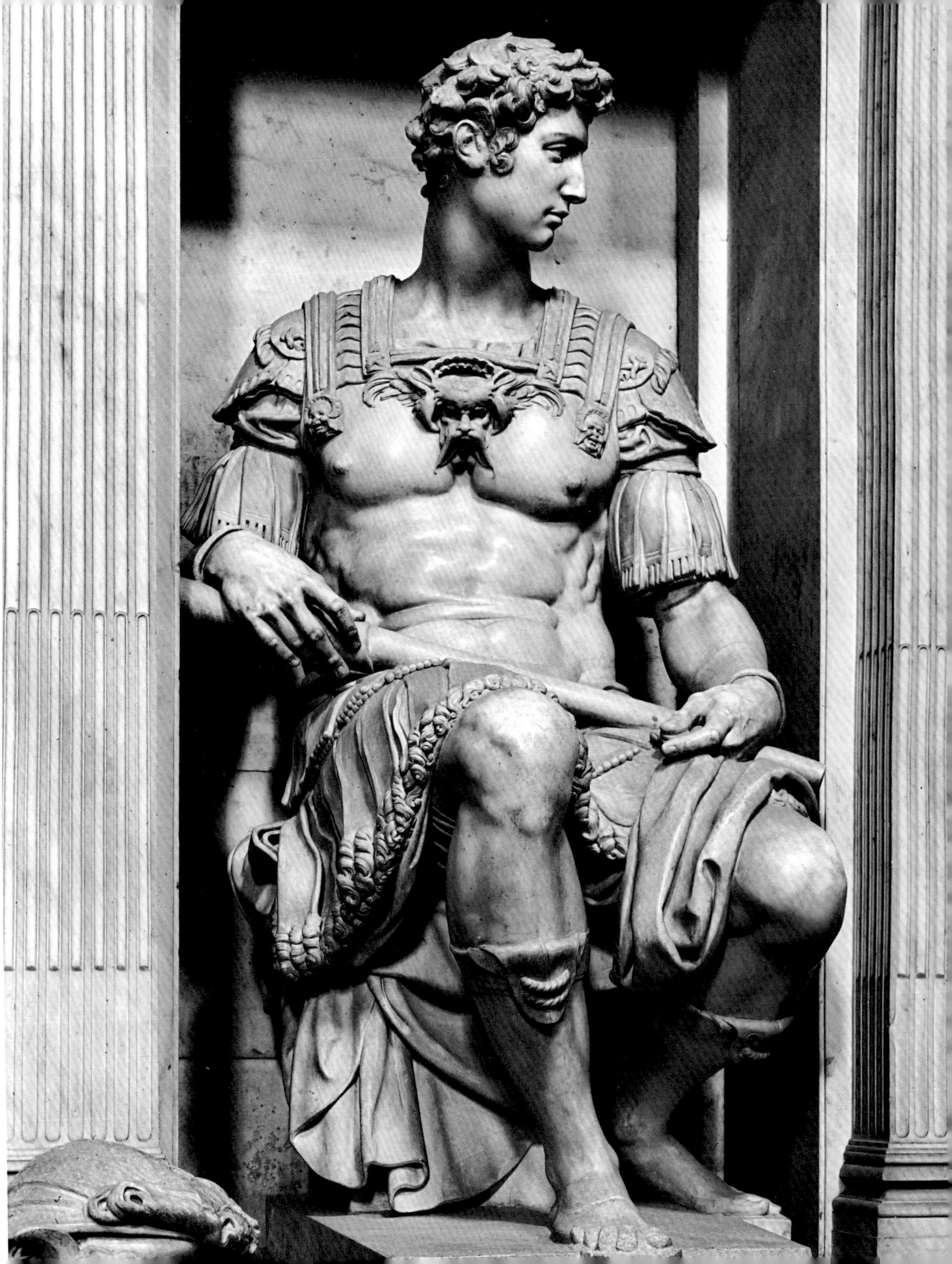

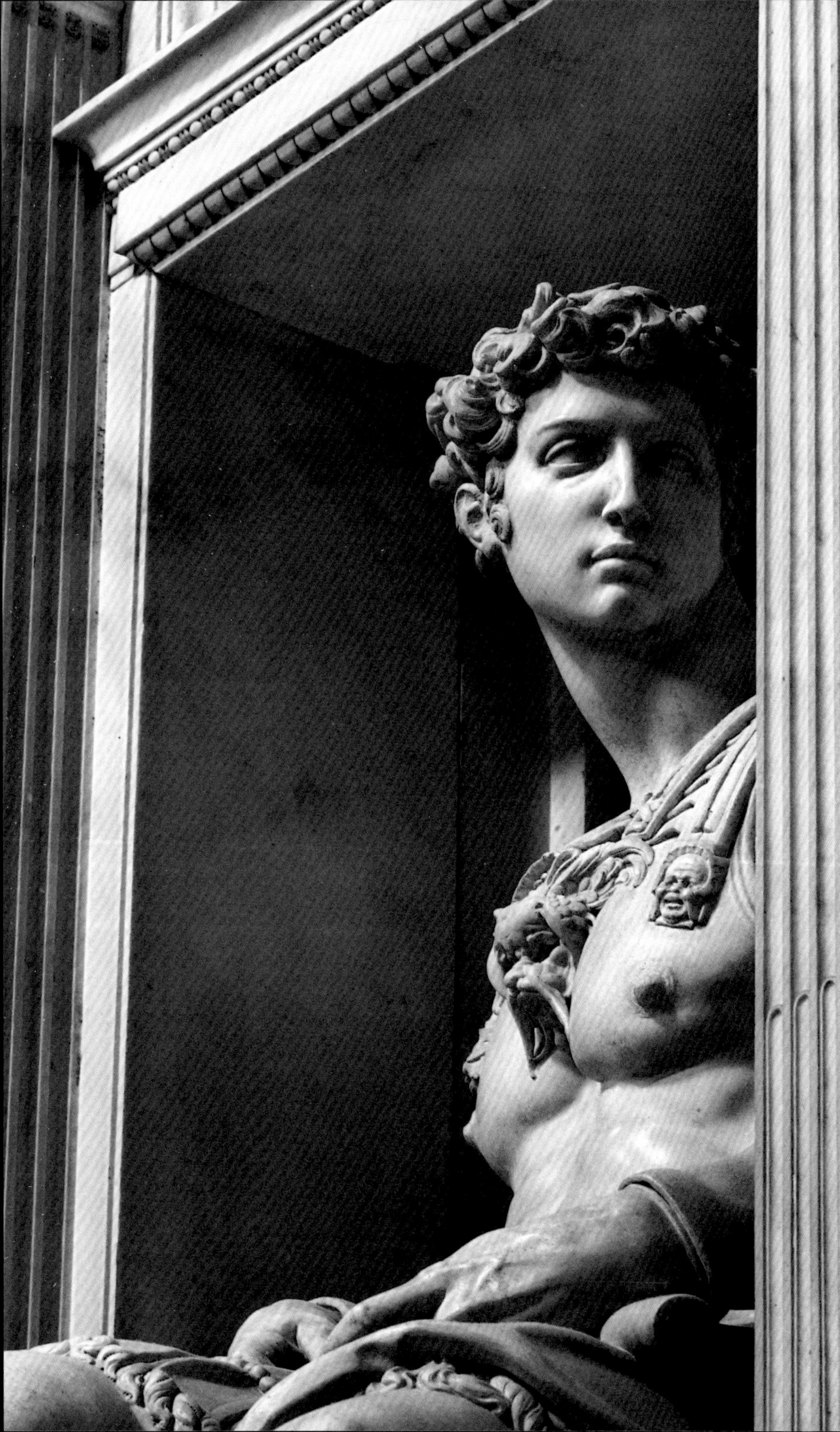

Michelangelo, *Duke Giuliano de' Medici*, detail
Florence, Museo delle Cappelle Medicee, New Sacristy

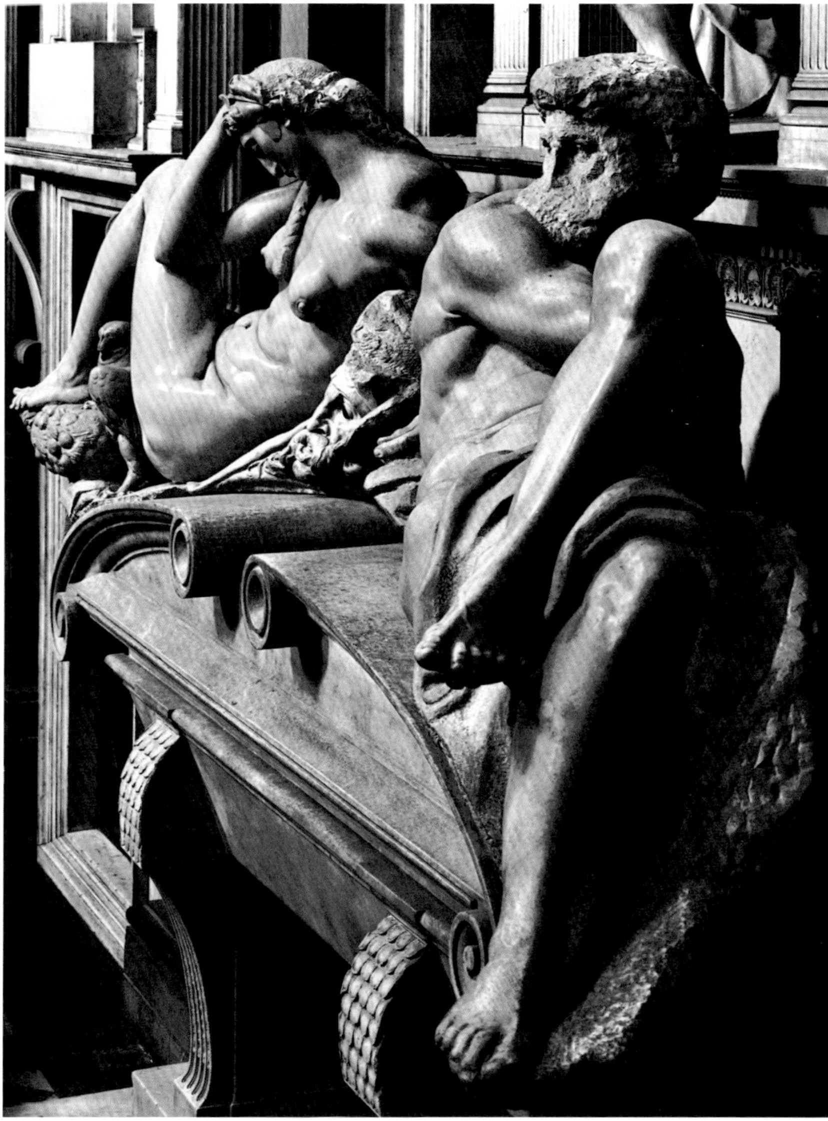

Michelangelo, *Day* and *Night*
on the sarcophagus
of Duke Giuliano de' Medici
Florence, Museo delle Cappelle
Medicee, New Sacristy

pp. 164-165
Michelangelo, *Day*
on the sarcophagus of Duke
Giuliano de' Medici
Florence, Museo delle Cappelle
Medicee, New Sacristy

p. 166
Michelangelo, *Day*, detail of
the arm twisted behind the
broad, muscular back
Florence, Museo delle Cappelle
Medicee, New Sacristy

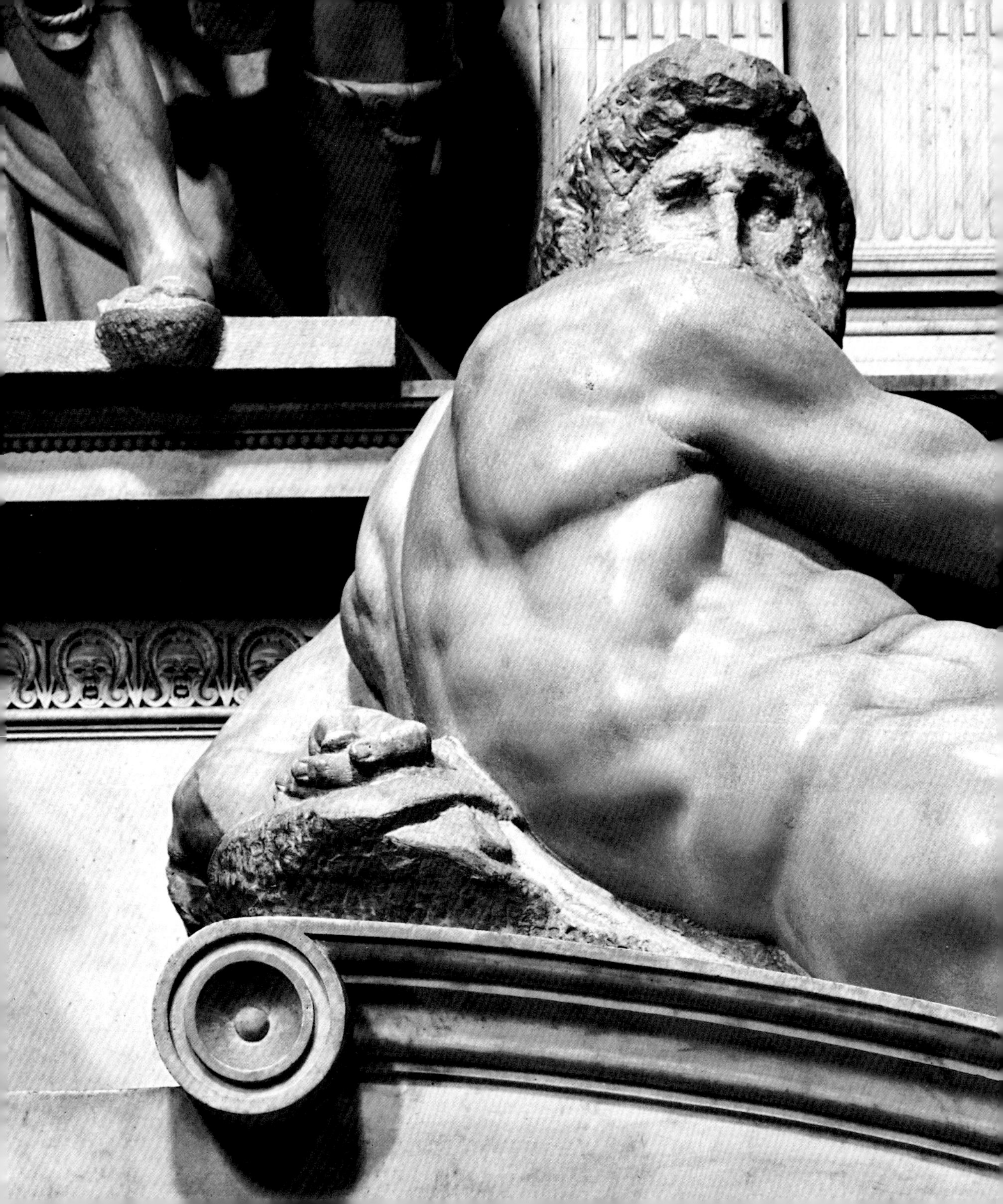

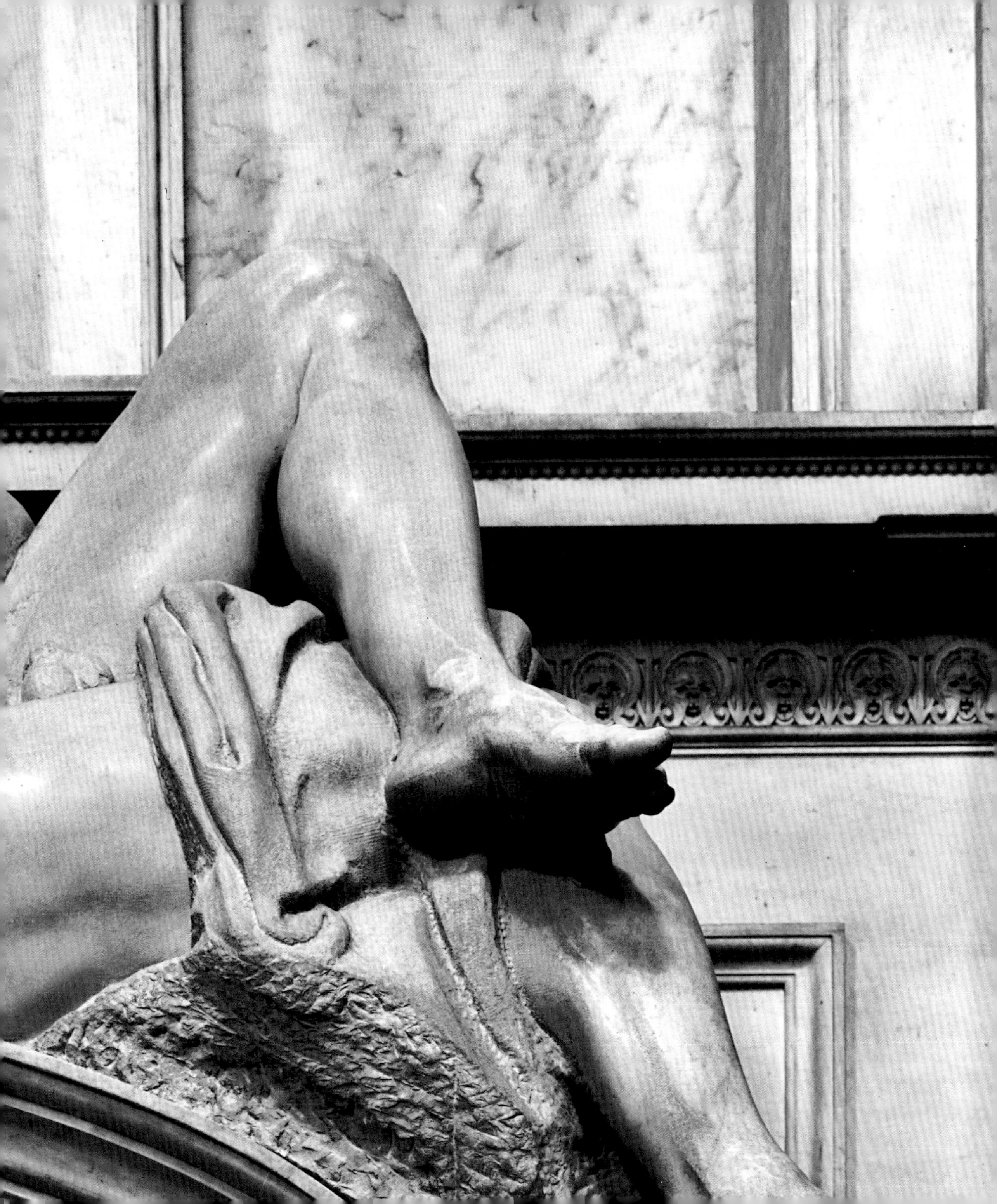

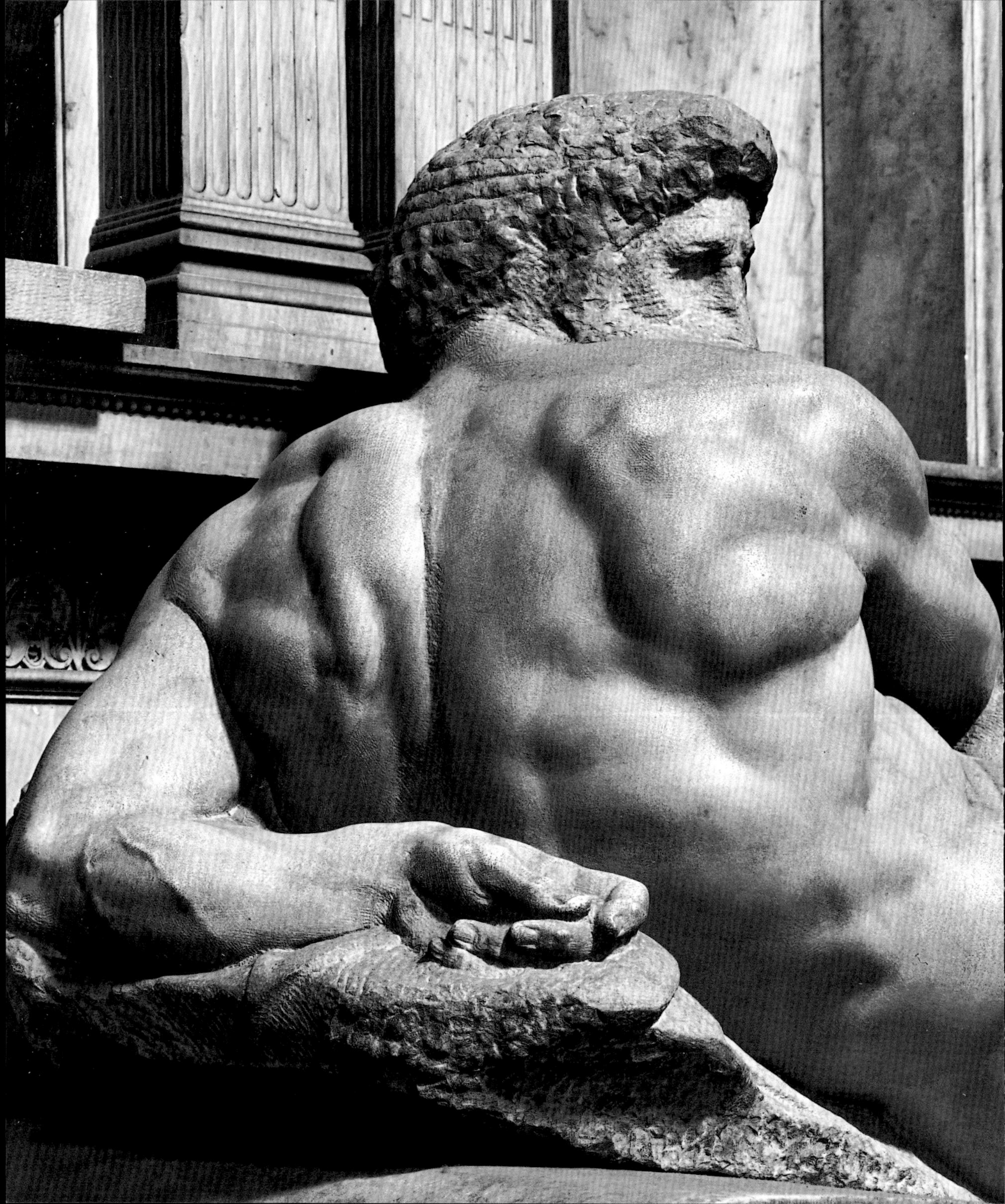

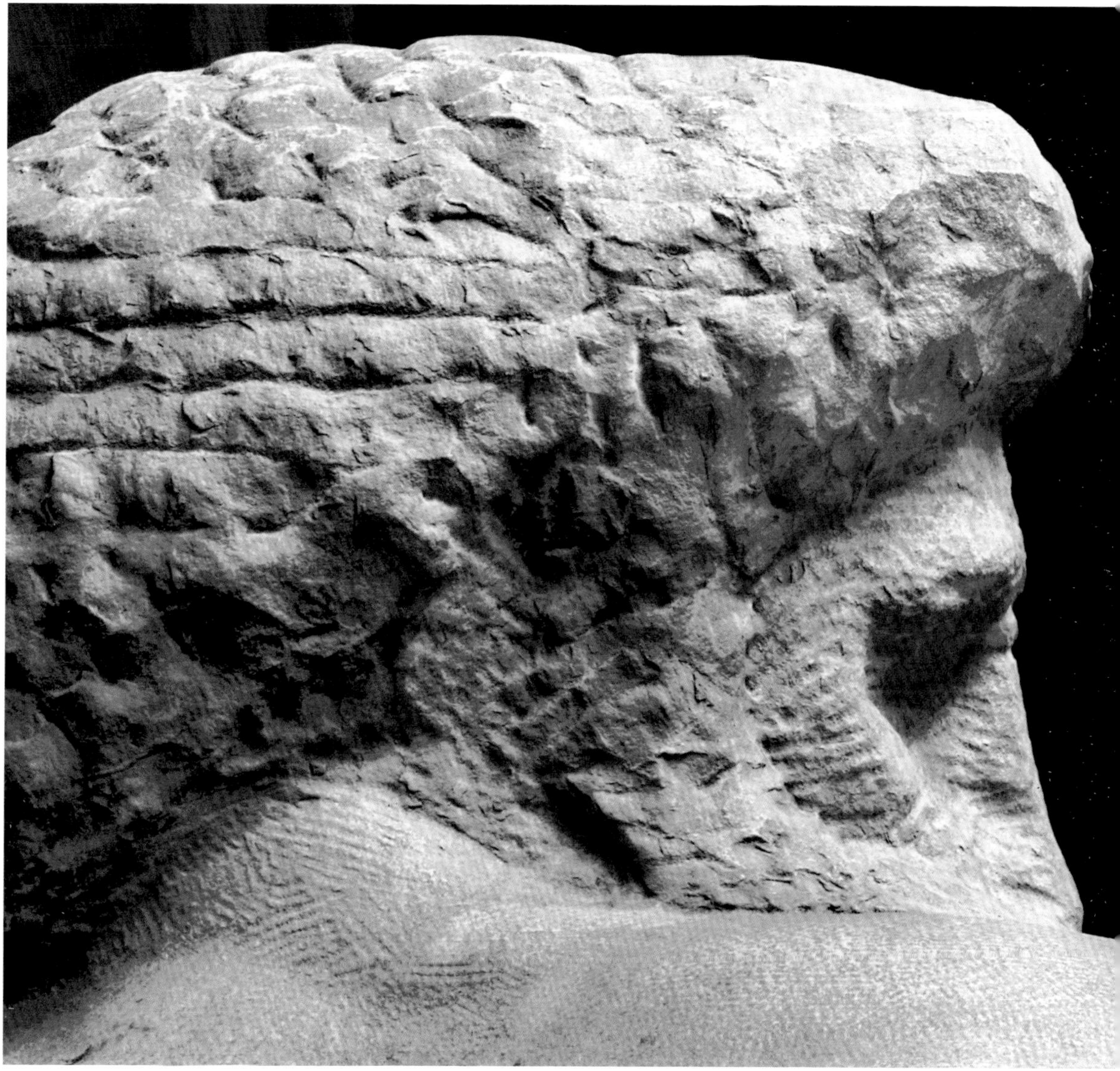

Michelangelo, *Day*,
detail of the head
just roughed out and
furrowed, with its
evident "non-finito" effect
Florence, Museo delle Cappelle
Medicee, New Sacristy

pp. 168-169
Michelangelo, *Night*
on the sarcophagus of Duke
Giuliano de' Medici,the only
statue of the four with attributes:
stars, an owl, the mask of sleep,
the poppy capsules
Florence, Museo delle Cappelle
Medicee, New Sacristy

p. 170
Michelangelo, *Night*,
detail of the forehead
decorated with a crescent
moon and star
Florence, Museo delle Cappelle
Medicee, New Sacristy

p. 171
Michelangelo, *Night*,
detail of the hairstyle
ending in a long, thick braid
Florence, Museo delle Cappelle
Medicee, New Sacristy

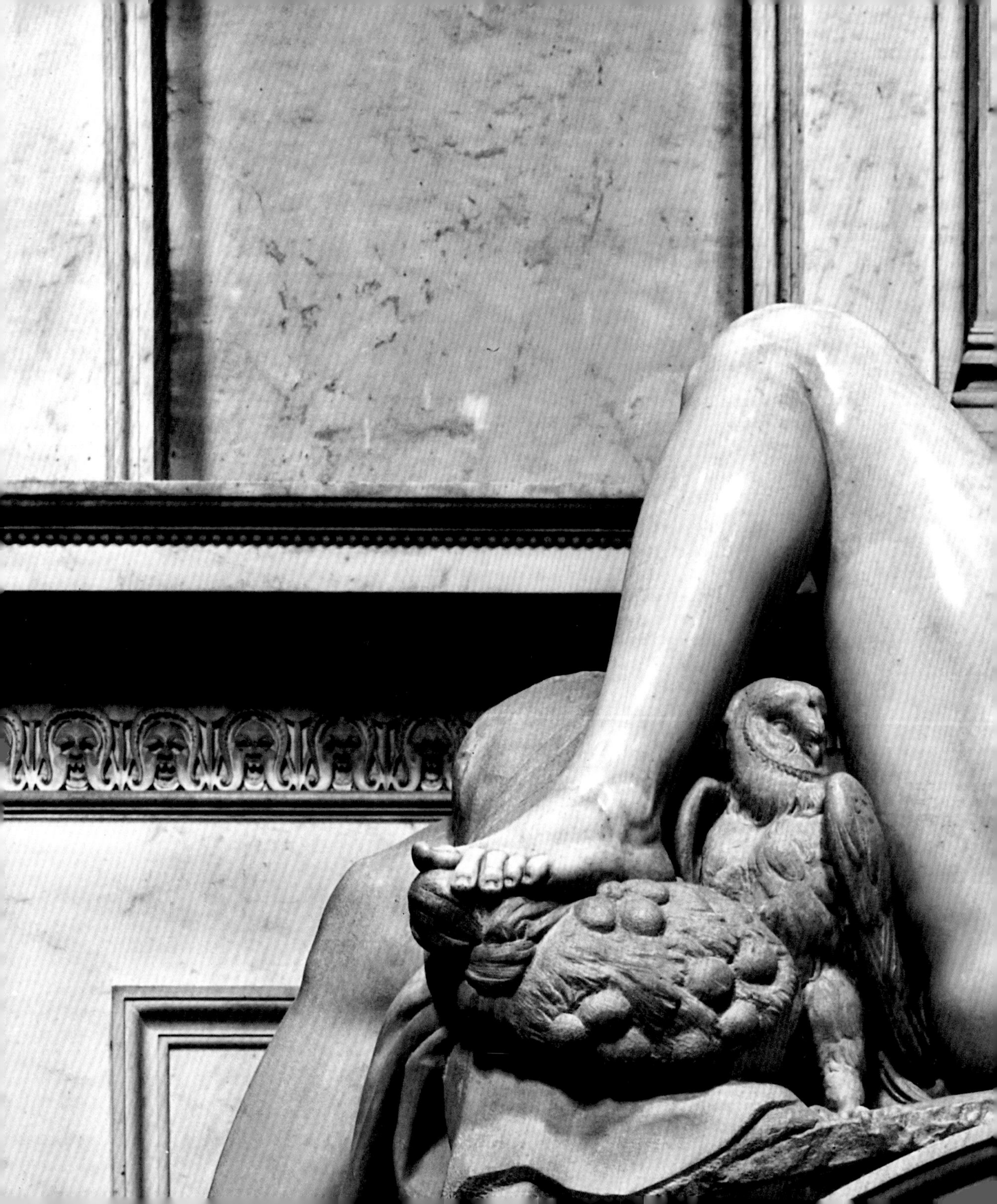

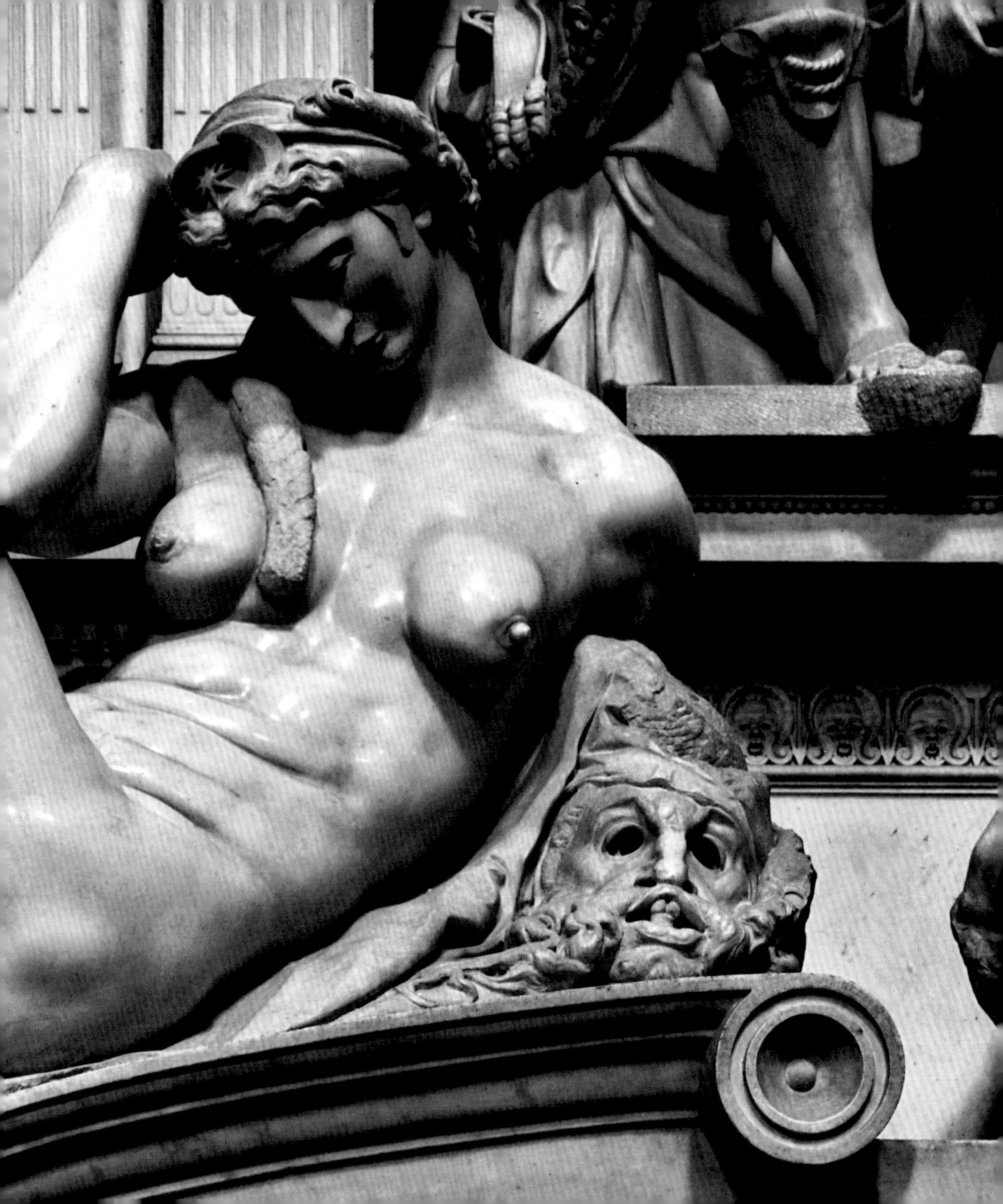

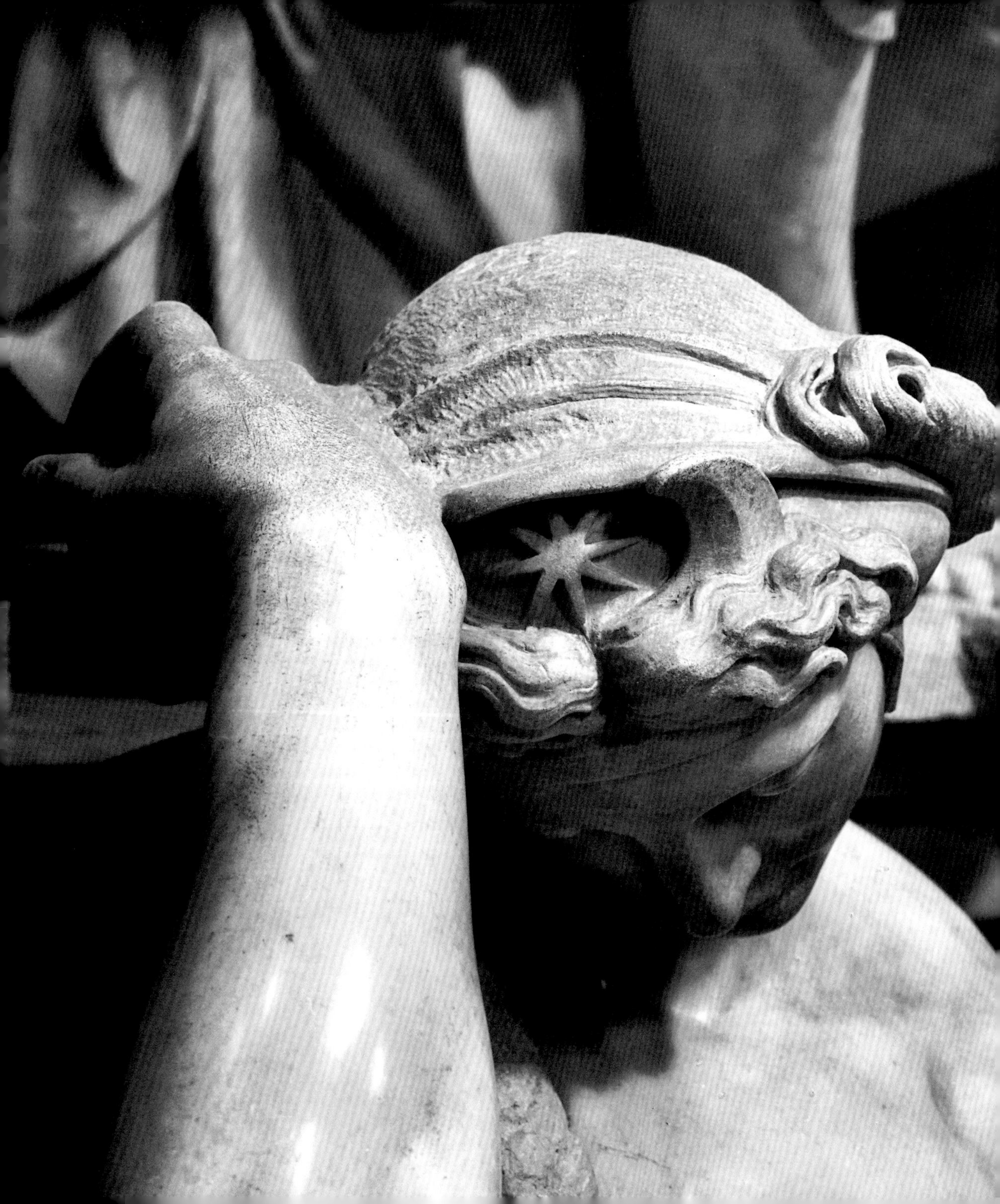

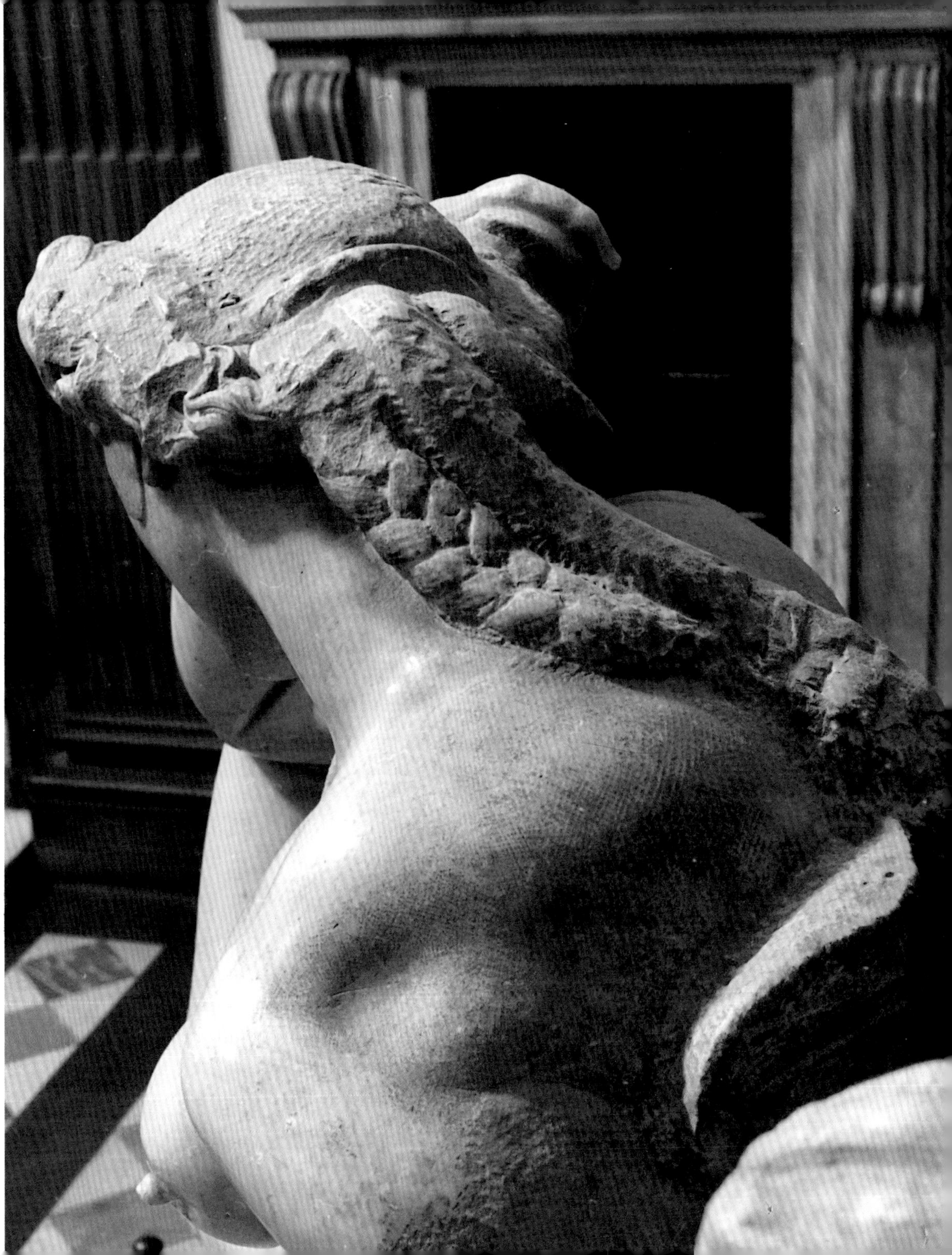

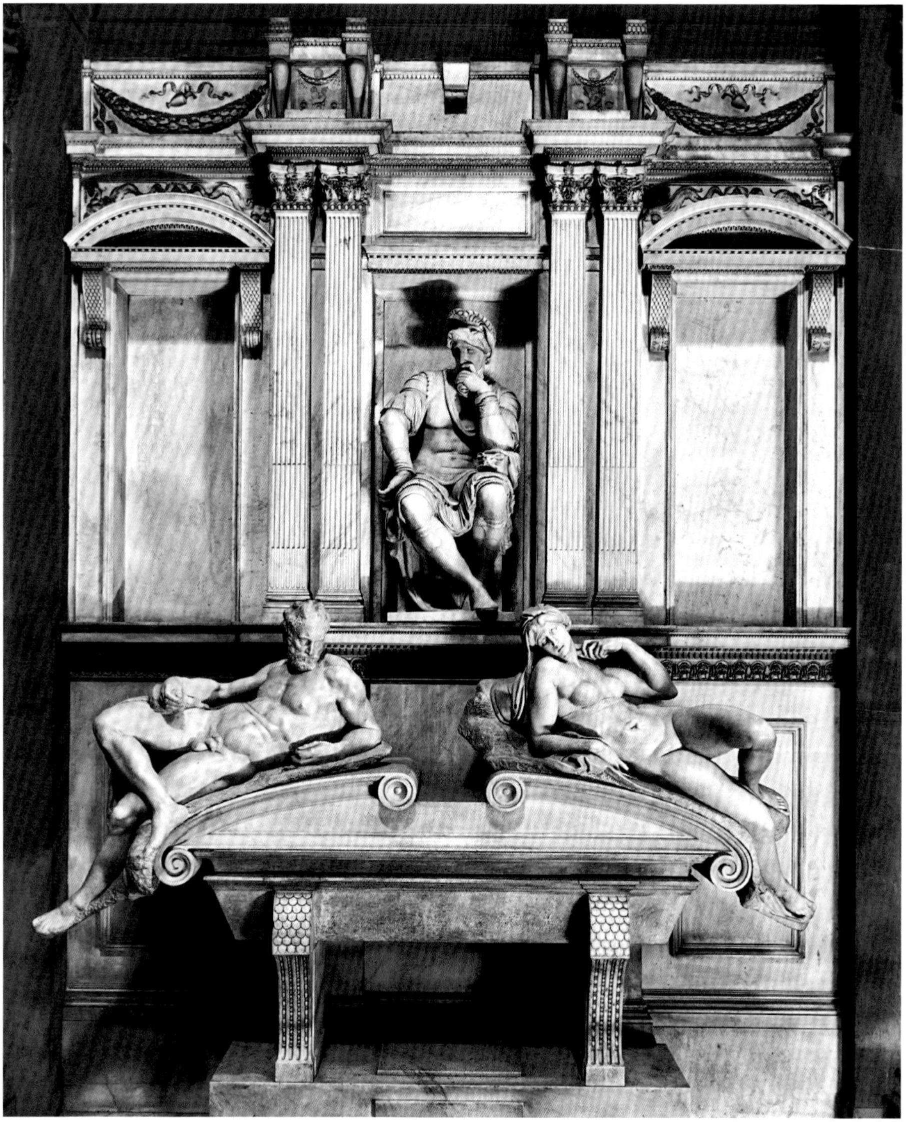

Michelangelo, *Tomb of Duke Lorenzo de' Medici* with *Dusk* and *Dawn*
Florence, Museo delle Cappelle Medicee, New Sacristy

p. 175
Michelangelo, *Duke Lorenzo de' Medici*, detail of the bust in a "pensive" pose, a rolled up kerchief in his hand
Florence, Museo delle Cappelle Medicee, New Sacristy

p. 176
Michelangelo, *Duke Lorenzo de' Medici*, detail of his hand pronated against his thigh with a coin (?) in his fingers
Florence, Museo delle Cappelle Medicee, New Sacristy

p. 177
Michelangelo, *Duke Lorenzo de' Medici*, profile, a fanciful wolf (?) helmet on his head,
Florence, Museo delle Cappelle Medicee, New Sacristy

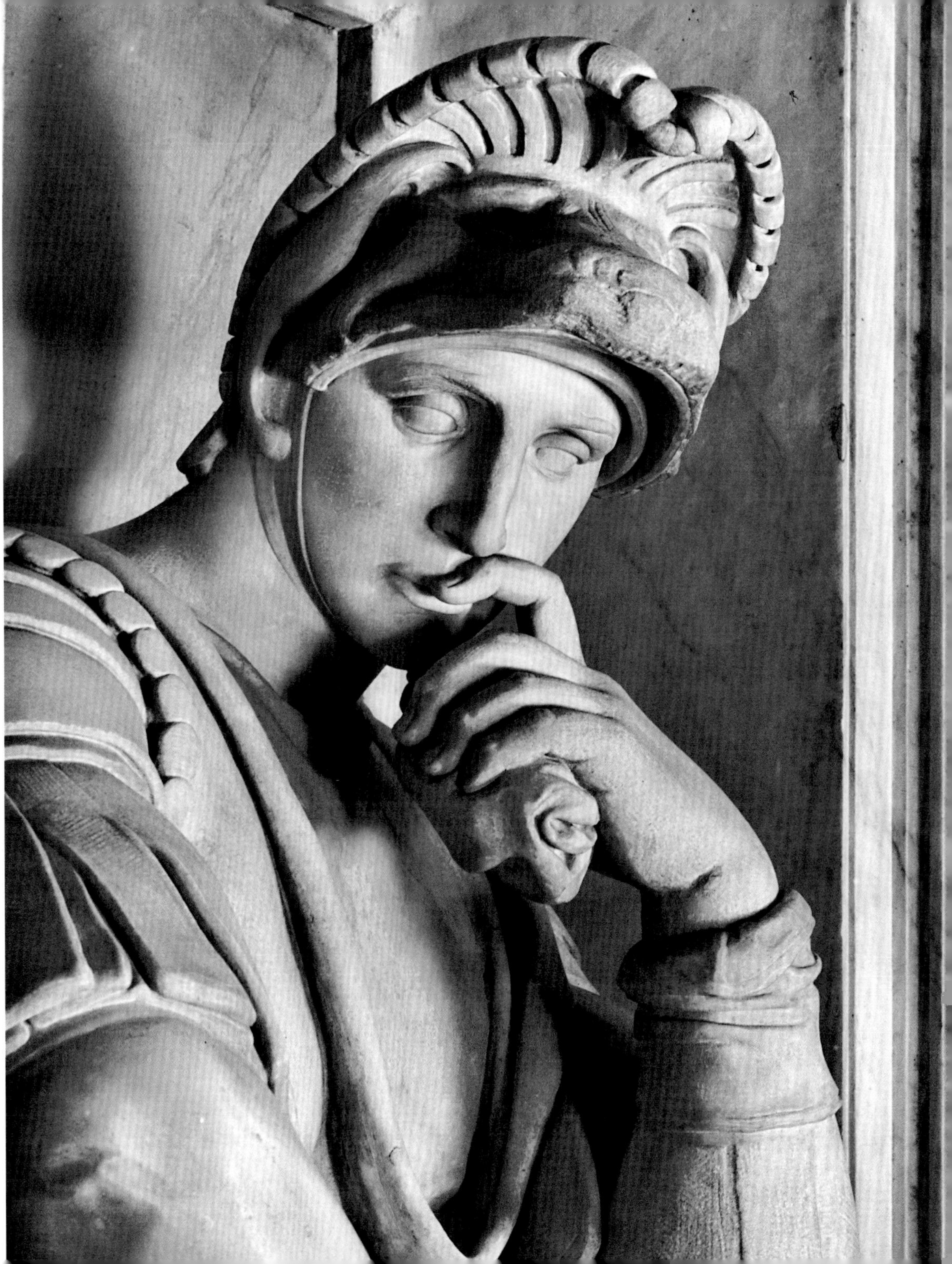

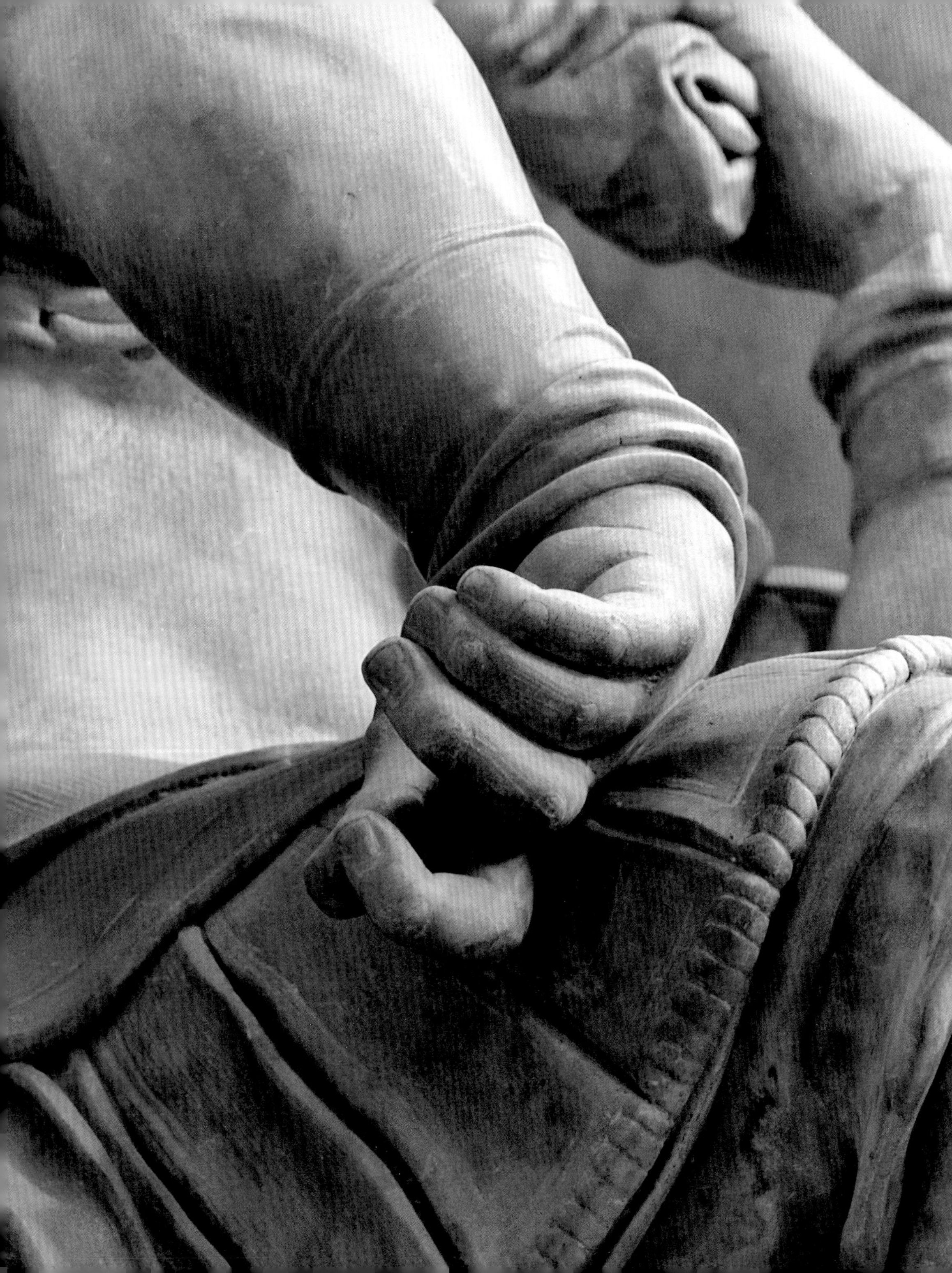

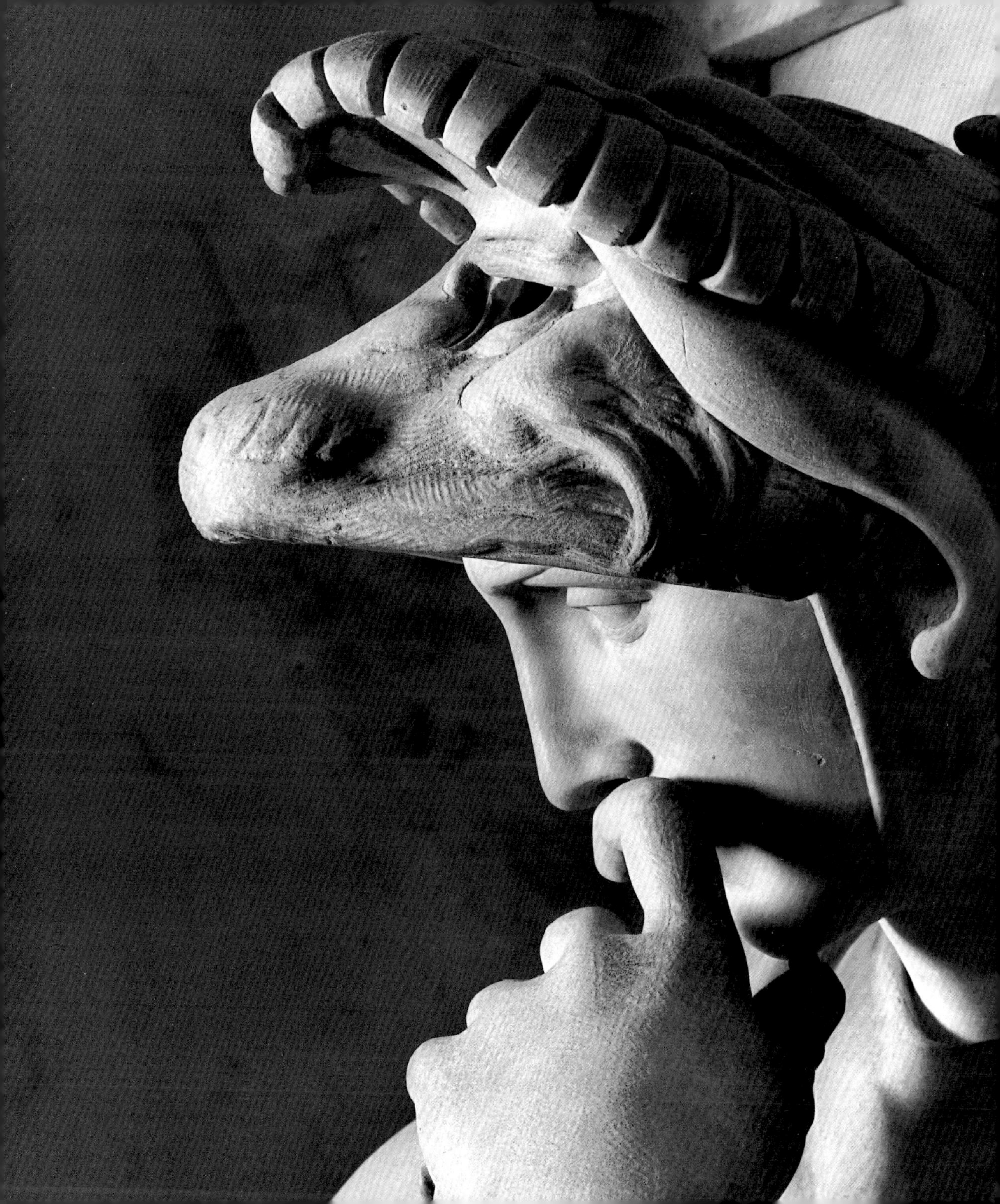

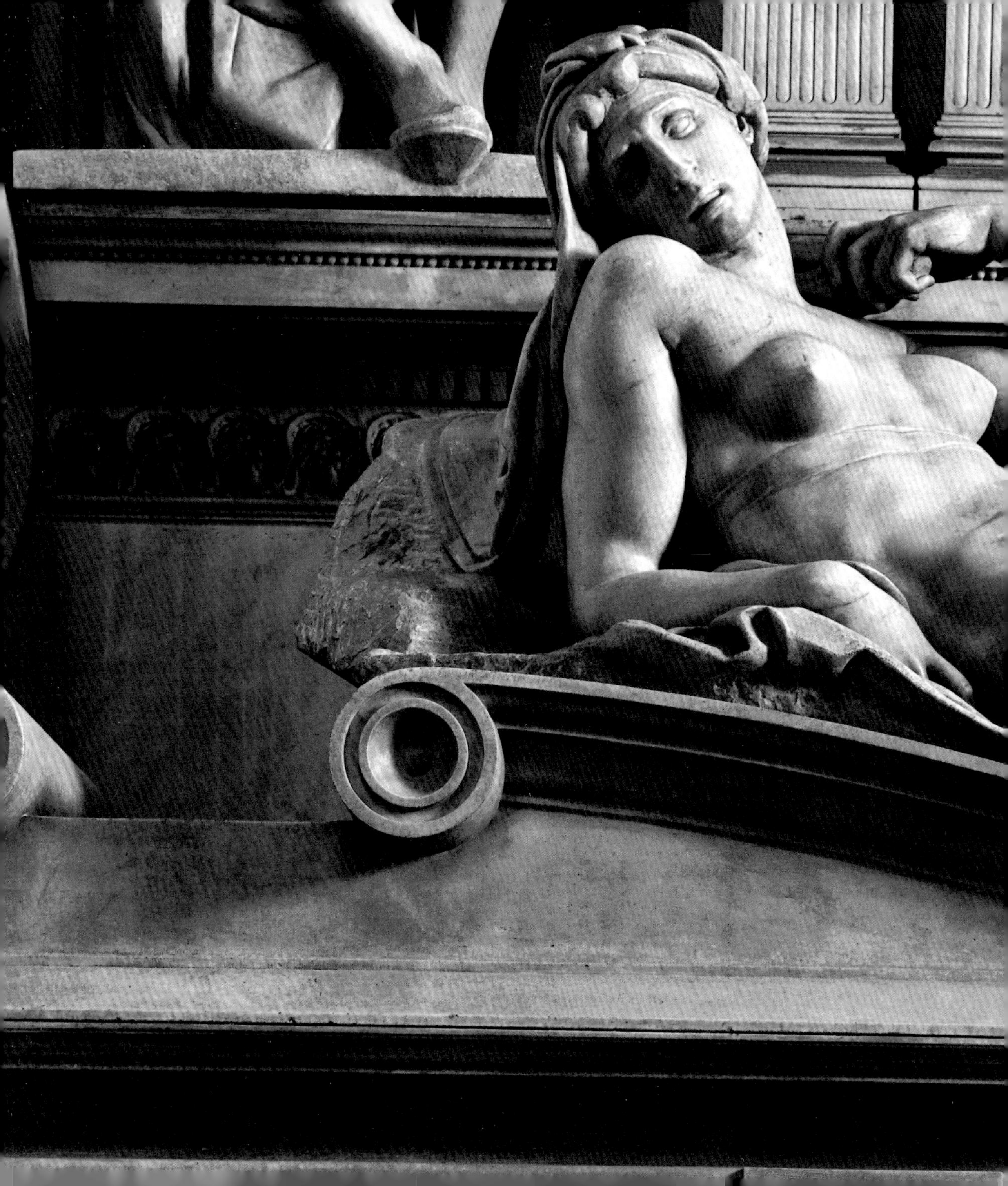

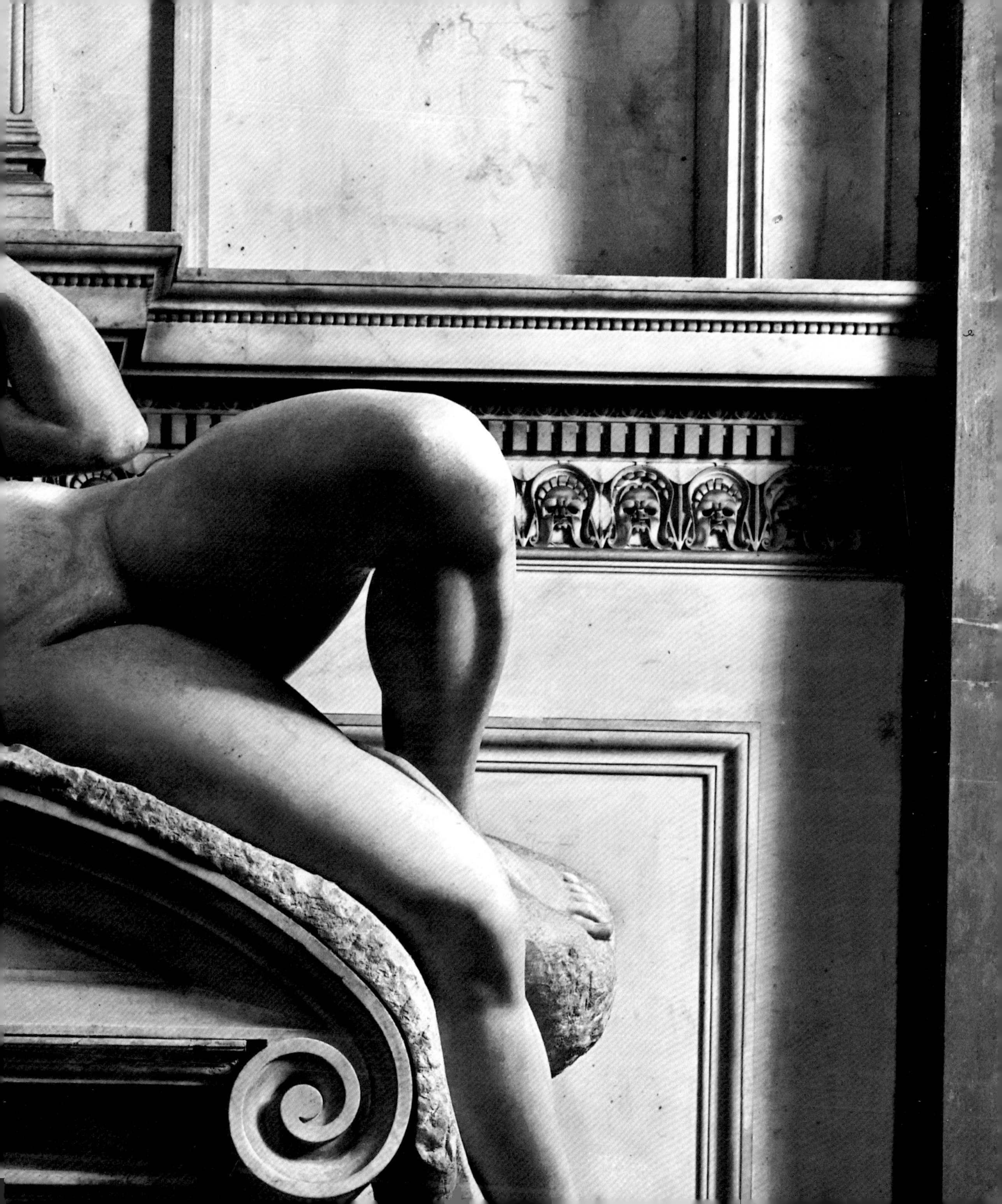

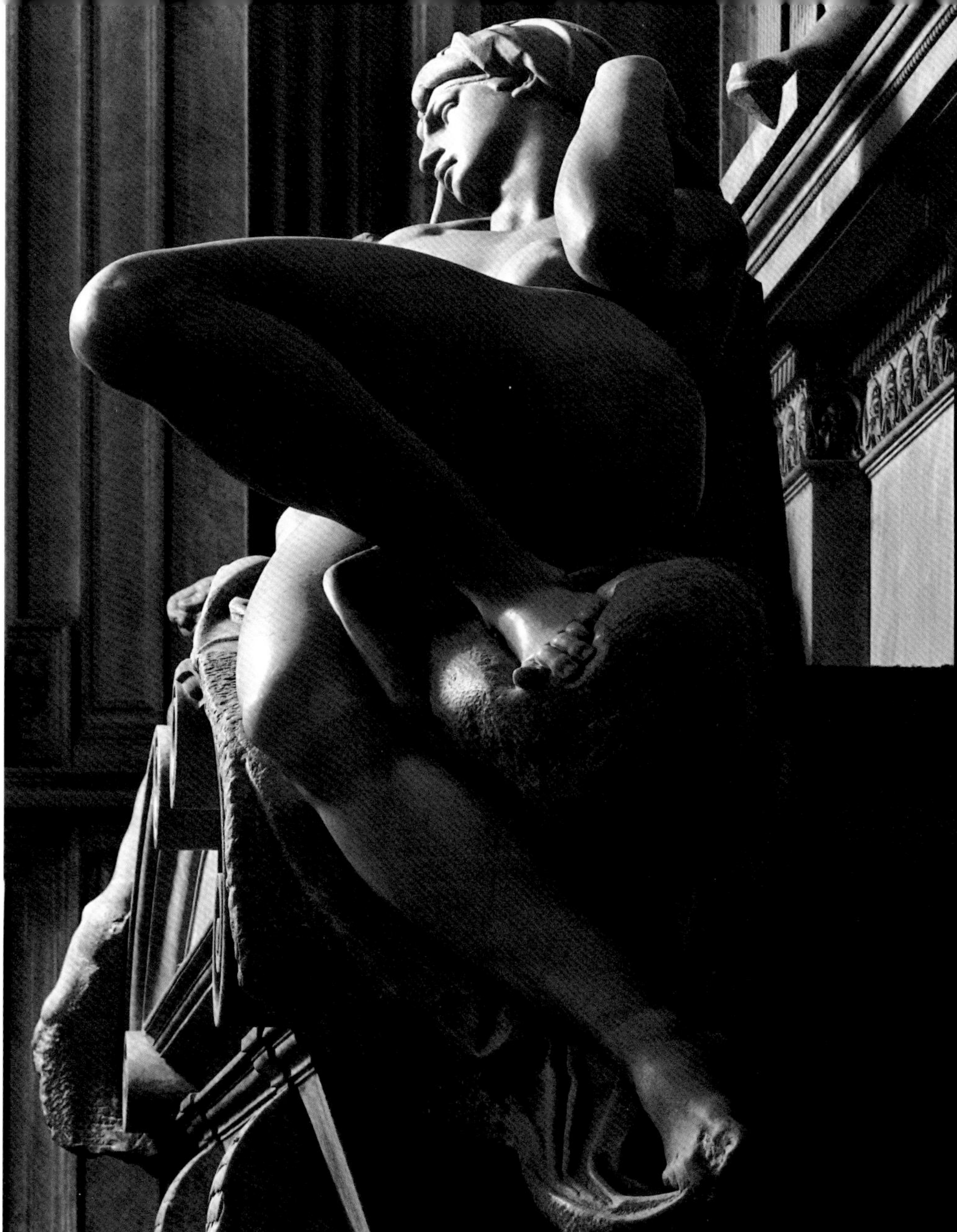

pp. 178-179
Michelangelo, *Dawn* on the sarcophagus of Duke Lorenzo de' Medici, praised for her beauty by all of the past commentators
Florence, Museo delle Cappelle Medicee, New Sacristy

p. 180
Michelangelo, *Dawn*, foreshortened view with her left foot on the clouds (?) and her right on the farthestmost part of the veil
Florence, Museo delle Cappelle Medicee, New Sacristy

p. 181
Michelangelo, *Dawn*, whose sorrowful expression and contorted pose reveals her bitterness at the death of the young Medici
Florence, Museo delle Cappelle Medicee, New Sacristy

pp. 182-183
Michelangelo, *Dusk* on the sarcophagus of Duke Lorenzo de' Medici
Florence, Museo delle Cappelle Medicee, New Sacristy

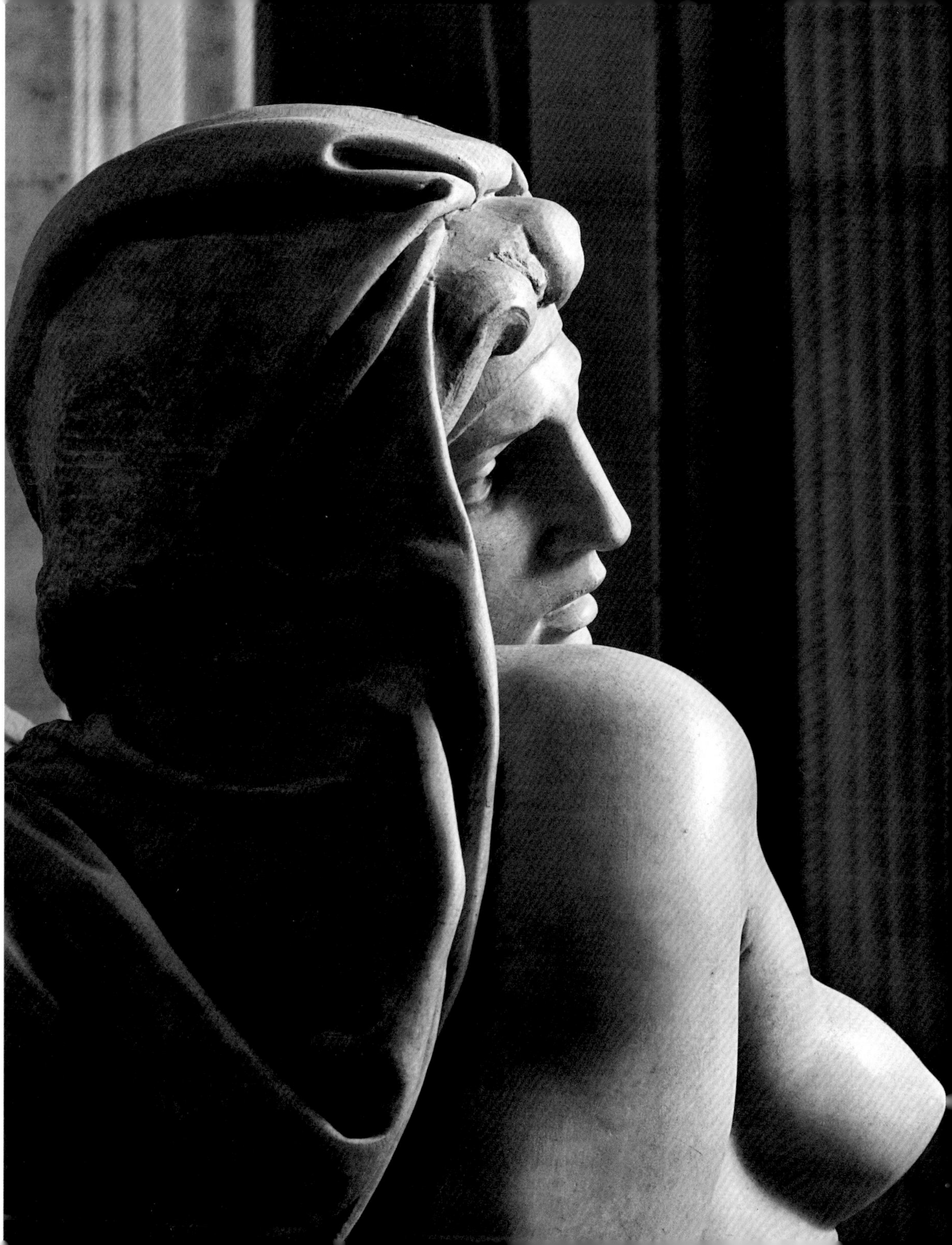

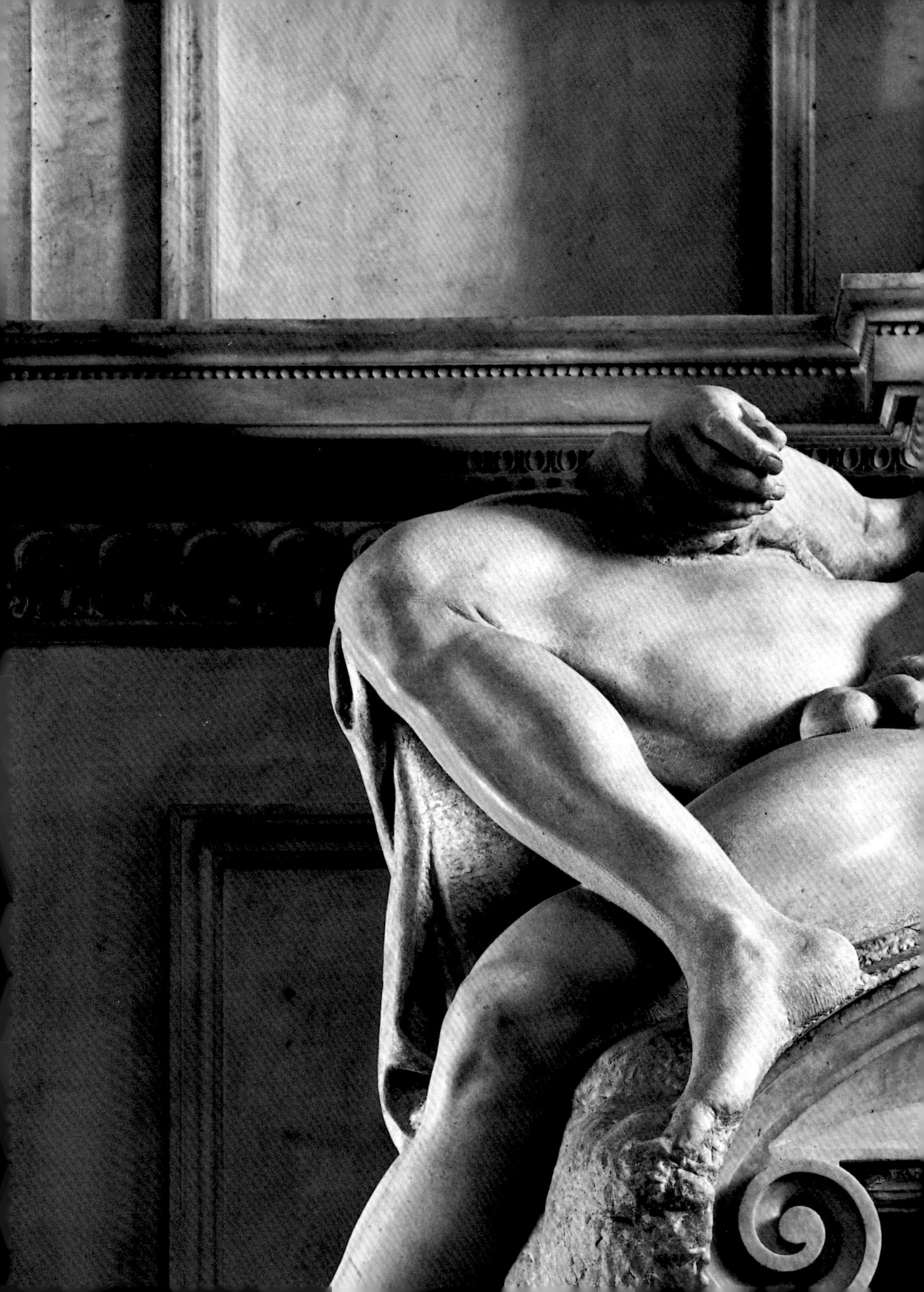

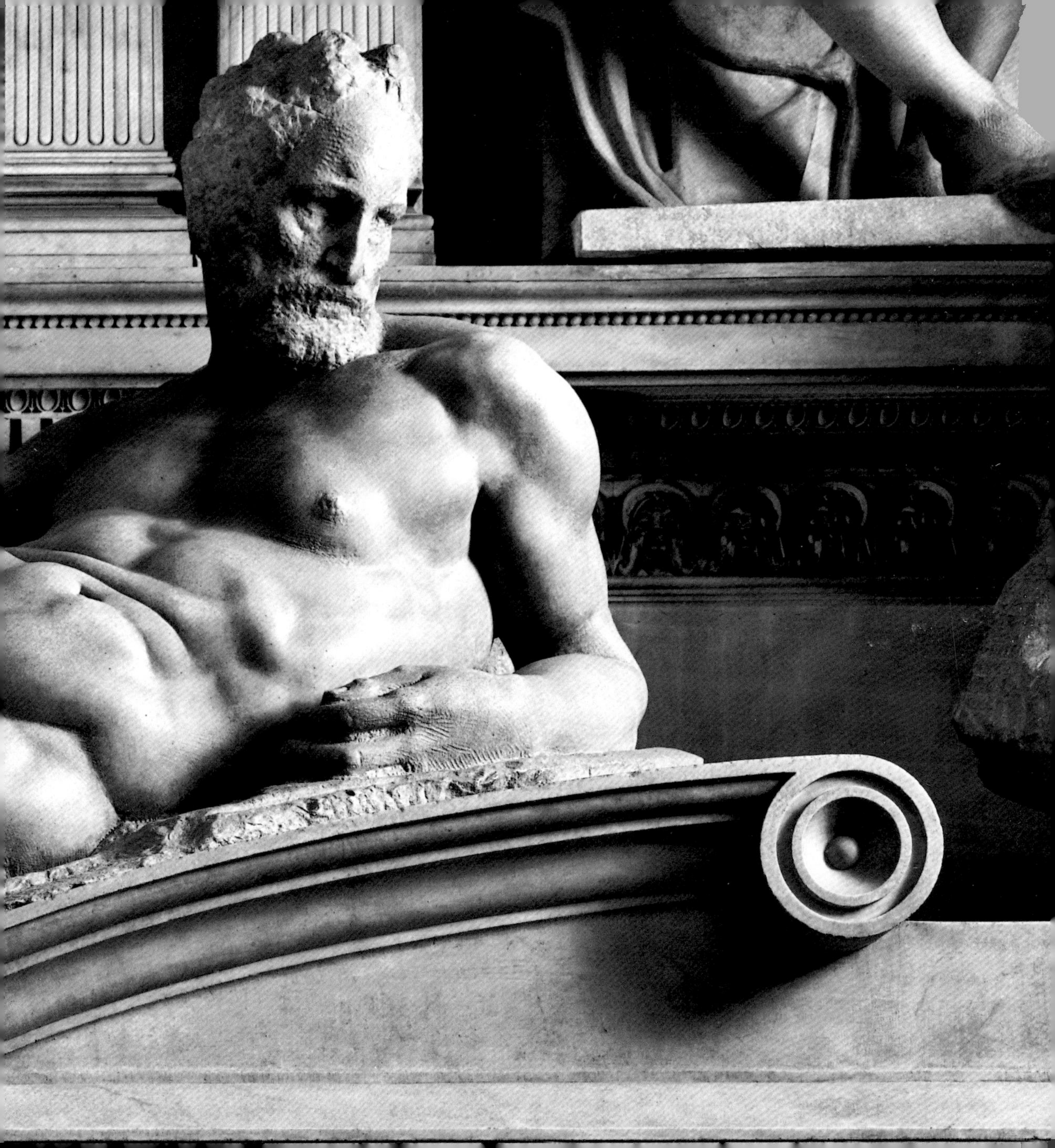

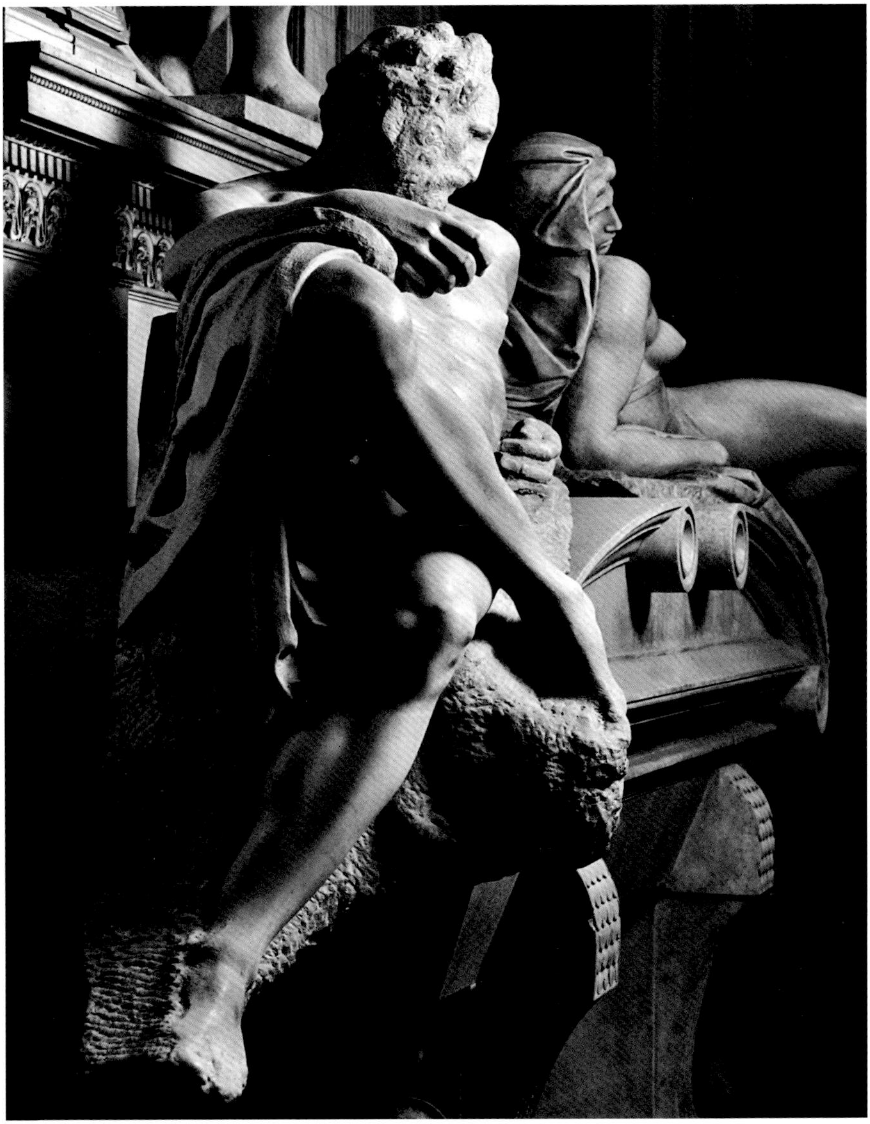

Michelangelo, *Dusk* and *Dawn* on the sarcophagus of Duke Lorenzo de' Medici
Florence, Museo delle Cappelle Medicee, New Sacristy

p. 185
Michelangelo, *Dusk* whose face shows the strokes of the claw-chisel
Florence, Museo delle Cappelle Medicee, New Sacristy

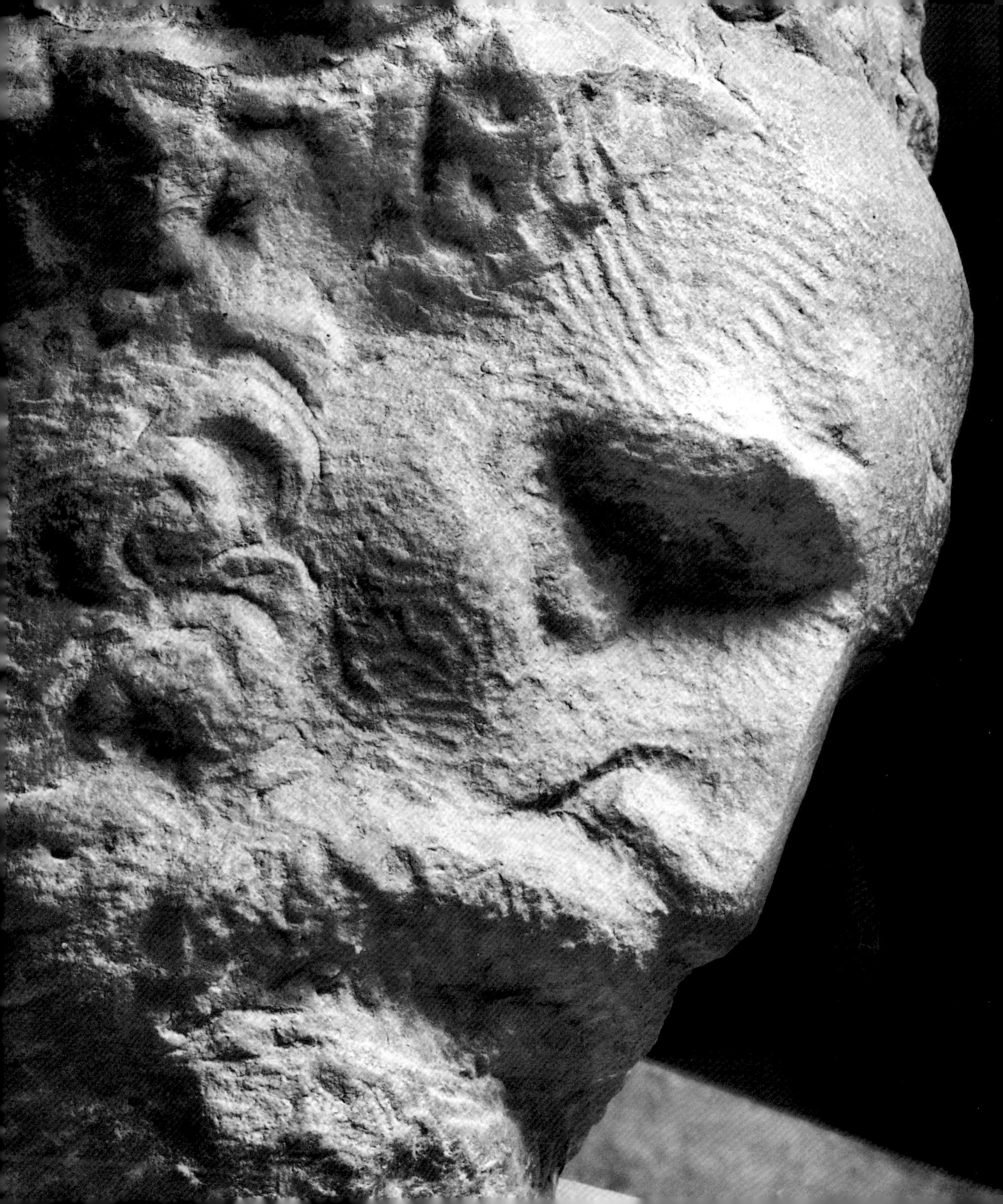

struction from the Greco-Syrian legend by Barlaam and Josephat, which Western writers had already taken up in the 13th century, was to be sculpted "on the work", perhaps on the figure of *Day*, cited by Condivi just prior to his reference to the mouse. An attack by the rodent on the diurnal allegory of the *Times of the Day* would have expressed the tragedy in all its magnitude: the end of the dynastic hopes of the Medici descendants of the *Cosimo Pater Patriae* branch of the family, and the weak entrustment of the dynasty's continuation on illegitimate progeny. Perhaps for this reason Michelangelo was "prevented" from portraying the animal. The person who prevented Michelangelo from sculpting the mouse remains anonymous, but to my mind, it was Ottaviano di Bernadetto, a Medici kinsman, the trustee for both of the branches of the house and a contributor to the plan for the Sacristy,[45] perhaps acting in the interest of his lineage by softening the harshness of the metaphor. One of the interpretations that digresses most from Neoplatonic- or dynastic-oriented scholarship is the one proposed by Balas who perceives *Night* to be Magna Mater, i.e. Leda, Cybele and Terrestrial Venus all in one, *Dawn*, the Celestial Venus, the male statues, the dark and the light Sky, the dukes, Jupiter and Saturn.[46]

The tomb of the "Magnifici"

Very different from the original project, the tomb of the Magnifici Lorenzo and Giuliano consists in the simple assembly of three statues, left behind in the vicinity of the Sacristy when Michelangelo departed for Rome, atop a 13th-century marble "cassone" with the remains of the two Medici. Of the three statues, the *Madonna and Child* is an autograph, known as the *Medici Madonna*. Michelangelo worked on in about 1526, but left it unfinished.
The Virgin's majestic figure, with the Child straddling her knee, presents the iconography of the Madonna *lactans*, widely revered and interpreted here under the sign of the powerful development of the distribution of the body volumes and internal dynamism that Michelangelo was working on, especially visible in the *Times of the Day*. The Virgin is unstably seated on a multi-level plinth carved out by the slanted use of the pointed chisel on a rustic base in relation to which it is slightly off-centre, perhaps explained by its possible, although unexecuted, corner arrangement in a niche of the tomb, to which the backwards lean of the right shoulder and arm would indeed correspond. She moves energetically towards the Child, who in turn twists to seek his mother's breast. The movement of the Virgin's body, despite the abundant criss-crossing folds and layers of her robe, can be discerned in the forwards rotation of the torso, followed by the curving projection of her veiled head, in the torsion of her pelvis that ensues from the unusual way she crosses her legs (which would leave her left foot dangling in the air if there weren't a connecting "bridge"), in the way she uses her right hand to hold onto her seat, while her left guides and pulls the Child towards her. The muscular Child, whom scholarship has often compared to the infant Hercules, turns away from us so that our frontal view is of his back, similar to the Christ in the *Madonna of the Stairs*. The uniqueness of the way the two figures engage was fully perceived by Vasari, who described it at length.
Many comments, some of which in a psychological and psychoanalytical key, have regarded the vacant expression of the Mother, whose face is beautiful, carefully defined in volume, although neither finished nor smoothed. Also evident is the ambiguous physical relationship between the pair, for neither does the Child (semi-worked and indistinct) touch his mother's breast, nor is it exposed for view: thus, the iconographic motif is treated allusively and not expressed in the figure of the mother, which is instead what occurs in the numerous portrayals of "Madonnas of the Milk" in sacred art from Gothic to Renaissance.
Over the years, many of Michelangelo's drawings revealed his interest in the motif of the Madonna seated with the Child in her arms; particularly evident is the long-lasting impression made in the early part of the century by Leonardo da Vinci's *Cartoon*. The particular image was the high point of the older master's numerous

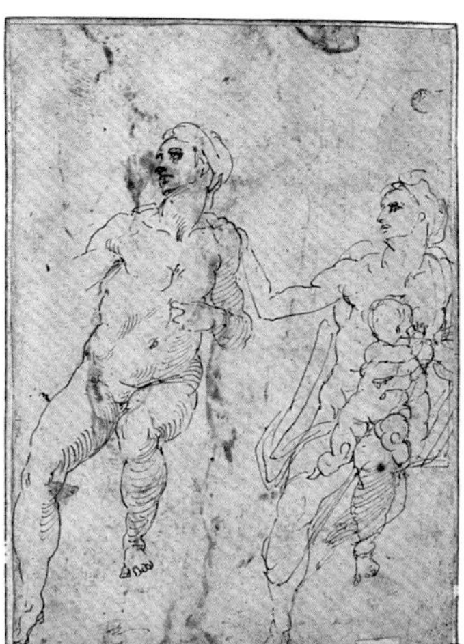

Michelangelo, *Two seated figures, one with a child*, the motif of the child who twists towards his mother's breast (1505), will return in the later *Medici Madonna*
Paris, Musée du Louvre, Département des Arts Graphiques, inv. 689 *verso*

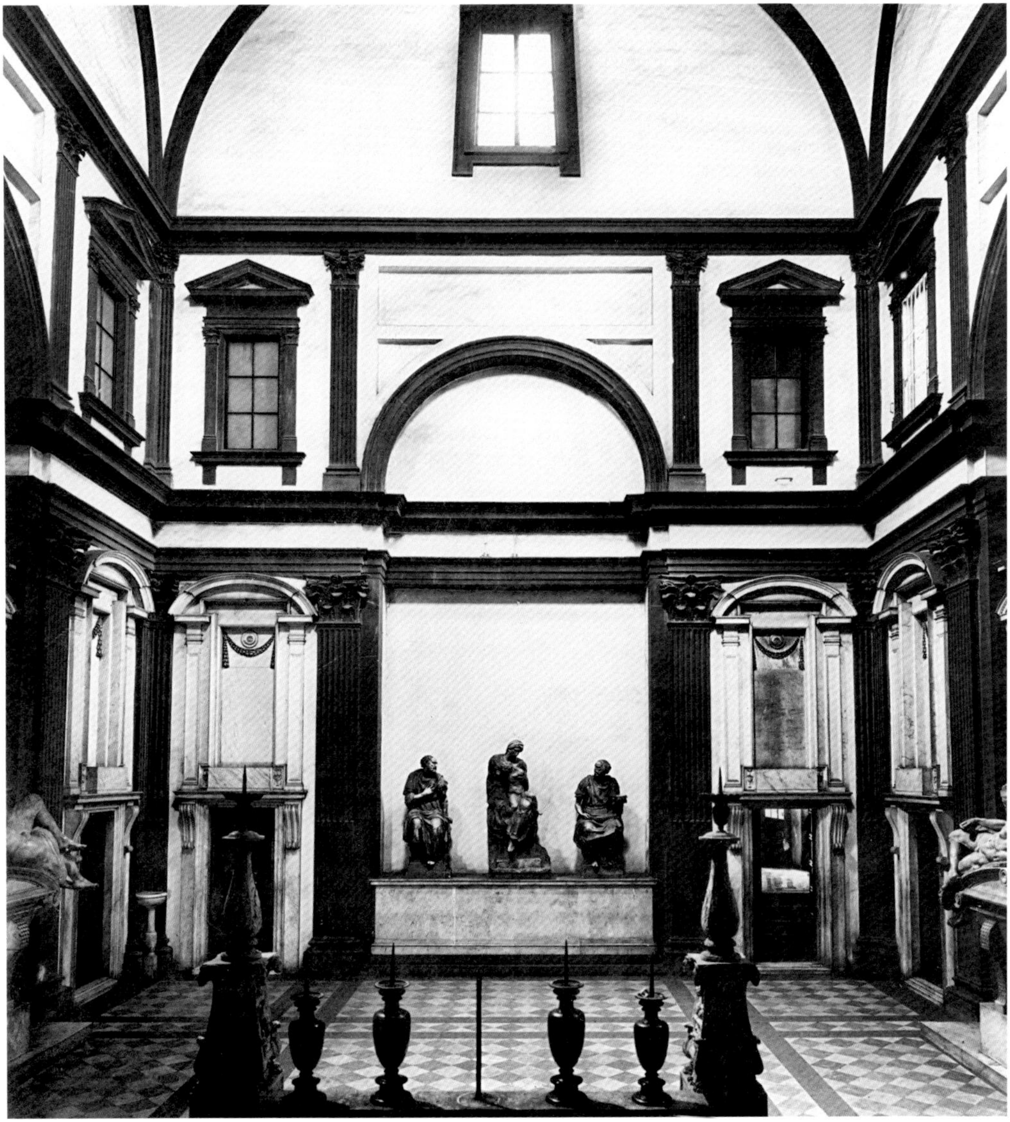

View of the wall of the New Sacristy with the tomb of the Magnifici
Florence, San Lorenzo, Museo delle Cappelle Medicee

p. 188
Michelangelo, *Madonna and Child* (*Medici Madonna*)
The iconography of the Madonna *lactans* expresses the religious theme of intercession for the deceased
Florence, Museo delle Cappelle Medicee, New Sacristy

p. 189
Michelangelo, *Madonna and Child* (*Medici Madonna*)
The infant Jesus turns to his mother's breast under the Virgin's distant gaze
Florence, Museo delle Cappelle Medicee, New Sacristy

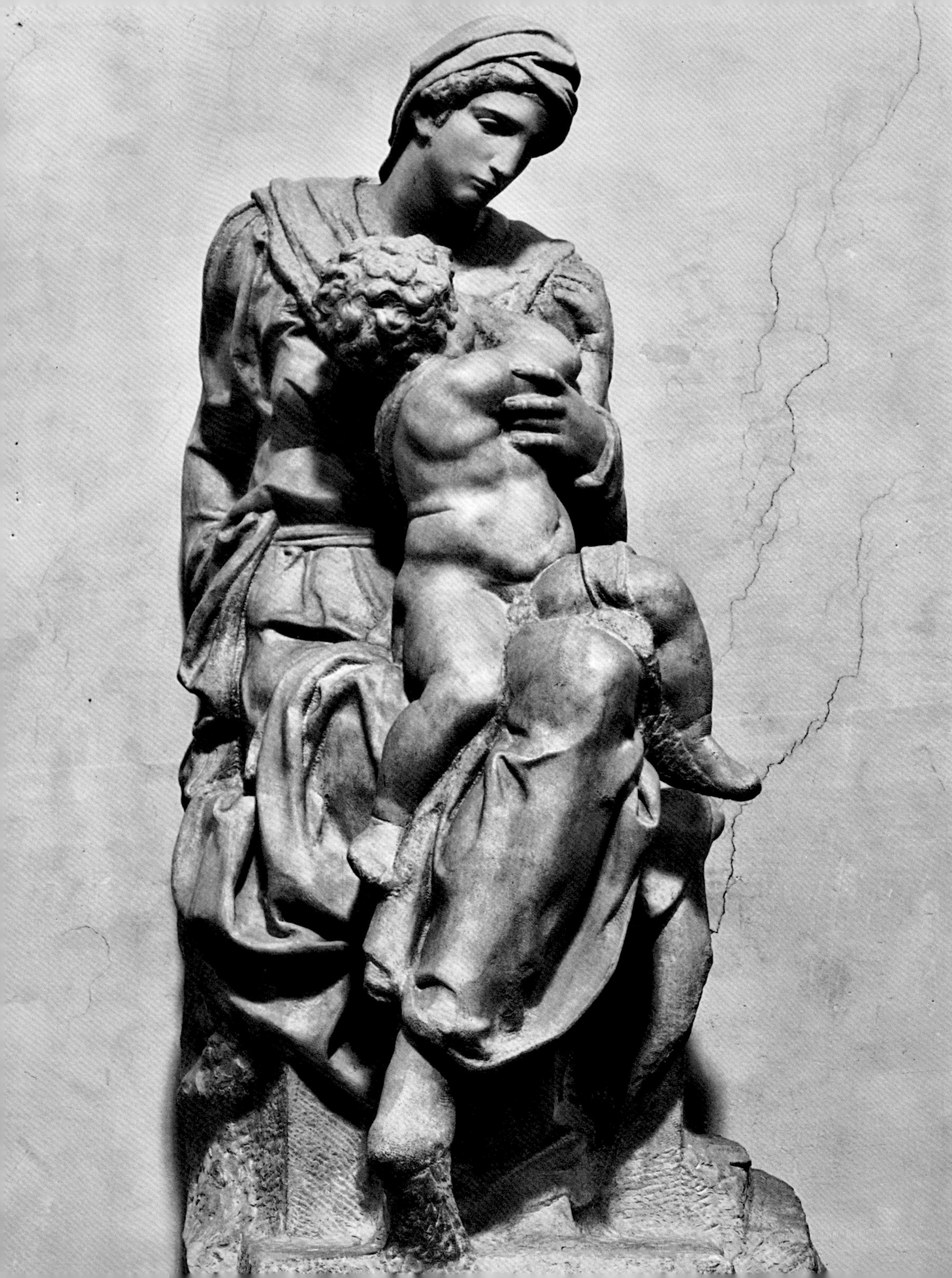

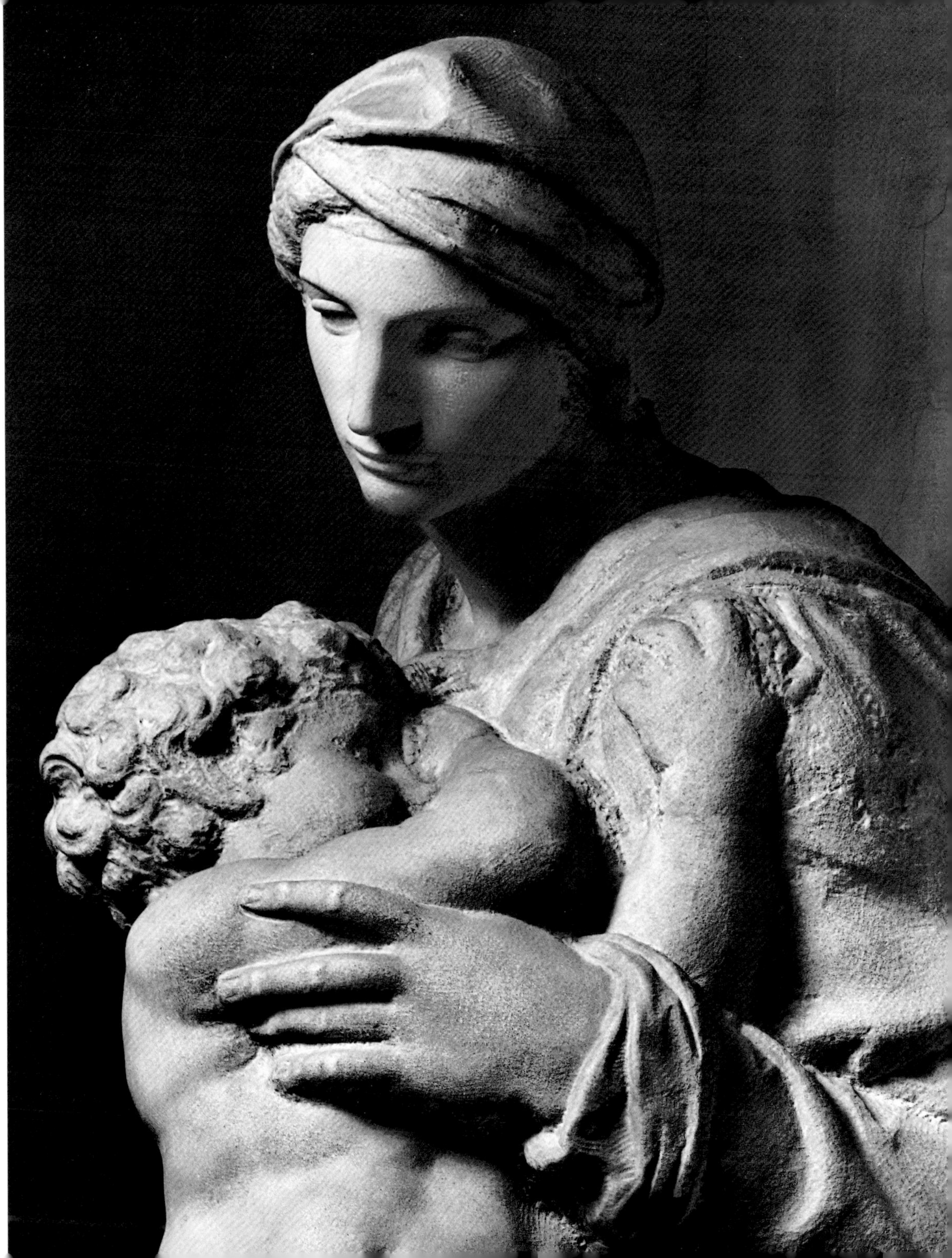

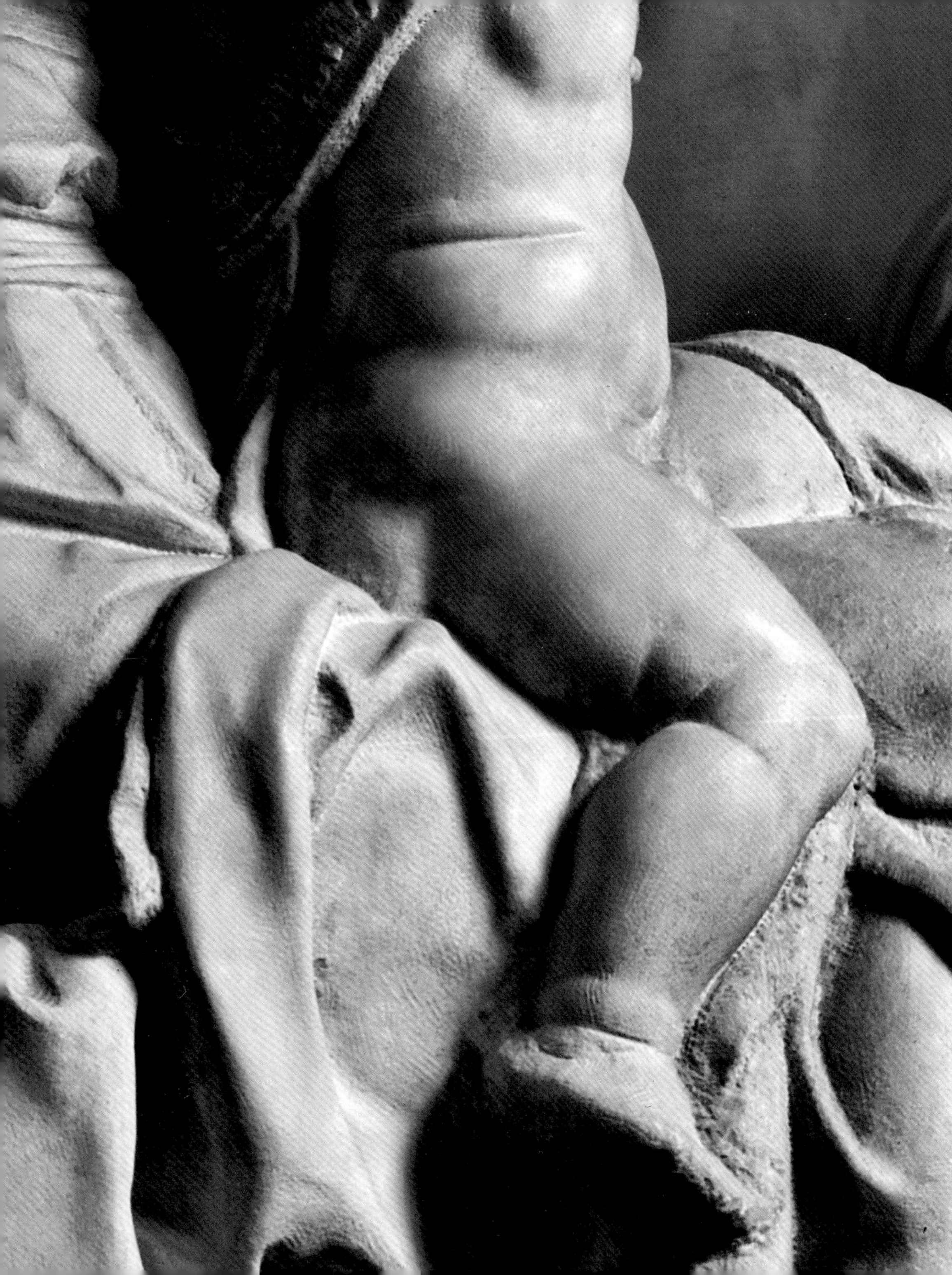

studies on the dynamics of mother-child relationships. While Michelangelo almost immediately responded in his painting with the *Doni Tondo*, he did not react sculpturally until he carved the *Medici Madonna*, and this was preceded by a number of compositive sketches where, by overturning the Mother-Child relationship of the *Tondo*, it is the Child who rotates and seeks the source of his desire backwards.[47] Michelangelo seems to have focused all of his attention on the infant Jesus' pose, using animated contours to define the chubby putto's unique movement as his body undergoes the effects of a sudden *contrapposto*: "with the thighs astride the leg, he turns", were Vasari's words.

Unreservedly admired from the time of the earliest commentators, the Madonna has often been considered the fulcrum of the Sacristy's complex iconographic programme because of the redeeming power of her milk, a symbol of the Redemption.

Seated to the sides of the *Medici Madonna* are the two patron saints of the Medici family, *Saint Damian* by Raffaello da Montelupo, and *Saint Cosmas* by Giovannangelo Montorsoli. These were the artist's most trusted sculptors, and he gave them other works to do as well. In 1526, as stated in a letter to Clement VII's representative Giovan Francesco Fattucci, Michelangelo had personally decided to work on eleven statues (the seven he actually carved, plus the four unexecuted *Rivers*),[48] assigning all of the others in the plan, as well as the decorative apparatuses, to his collaborators.

The two saints, undoubtedly carved by the two authors after models by Michelangelo,[49] show intense pathos in the way they turn to the Madonna, one with his hand over his heart, the other displaying his box of medicines. In light of the sacred iconography representing the double intercession, they turn to the Madonna as "advocate" of the humanity of sinners close to God, and the dispenser of redemption, interceding for the dynasty they protect.

Other materials for the Sacristy

We previously mentioned the *Crouching Boy*, now at the Hermitage, the only work actually commenced for the vanquished or sorrowful figures, which was intended to crown the entablature of one of the tombs of the leaders and dukes.

For the four reclining *River Gods*, planned for the base of the two tombs, Michelangelo personally made drawings and models, his belief being, in 1526, that they were to be carved. The *Rivers*, in the traditional iconography of reclining old men, appear in the drawings for the wall tombs datable to about 1521, just quickly sketched out in the London drawing,[50] more detailed in the one in Paris,[51] where we see them surrounded by aquatic plants amidst putti who help pour water from the heavy jugs. Especially evident in the latter version is Michelangelo's antiquarian inspiration, which is revealed in his close attention to the type of river god that was surrounded by the symbols of fertility; widespread in Hellenistic and Roman art, some of the most celebrated examples are the *Marphurius* or the *Tiber*, known of from the Middle Ages, and the *Nile*, discovered in 1513 and at once greatly admired.

A turning point in the project is attested to in a published sheet, on the basis of an autograph annotation, dated *circa* 1525.[52] It consists in the study from two angles of a figure that may be identified as one of the *Rivers*: lacking any attributes at all, the *God* is kneeling, semi-erect, and in the act of holding a weight on his shoulders.

The sculptor also made life-sized models, one of which has survived and is now in the Casa Buonarroti; it may have been made for his collaborators to be used as a guide for rough-shaping the blocks of marble.[53] When Anton Francesco Doni wrote *Marmi* in 1541-1542, two enormous "bozze di terra" (which had also been worked on by Niccolò Tribolo) were still lying on the ground.[54] In one of the engravings illustrating the volume, the Arno was obviously inspired by a model by Michelangelo. The design for laughing *Heaven* and weeping *Earth*, on which Tribolo must have worked, is from an even earlier preliminary stage.

p. 190
Michelangelo, *Madonna and Child (Medici Madonna)*, detail of the Child's muscular body: "with the thighs astride the leg, he turns" were Vasari's words
Florence, Museo delle Cappelle Medicee, New Sacristy

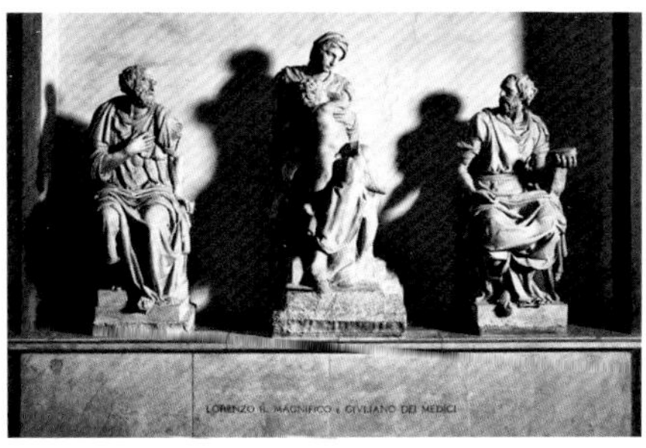

Michelangelo, *Madonna and Child*. On either side: Raffaello da Montelupo, *Saint Damian*, and Giovannangelo Montorsoli, *Saint Cosmas*, physician saints who interceded in favour of the Medicean dynasty
Florence, Museo delle Cappelle Medicee, New Sacristy

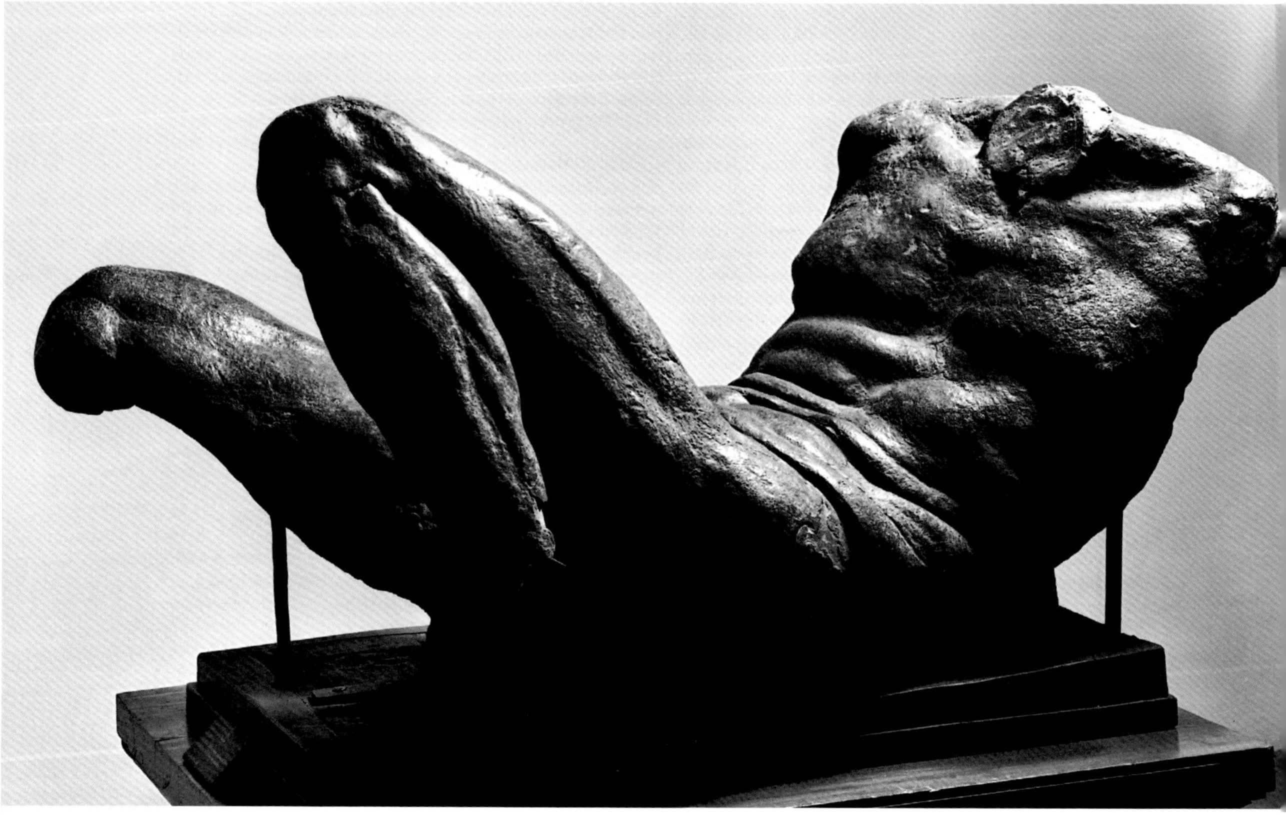

Michelangelo, model for a *River God*, designed to be placed on the Medici tombs Florence, Museo di Casa Buonarroti

The overall programme for the Sacristy traced out here, if programme is the right word for an unsteady string of excellent fragments, would be that of the spiritual redemption of the great men of the Medici house who died too soon, to the disconcertment of the entire universe, without forgoing hope in the dynasty's glorious continuation. A studied combination of mourning and exaltation, pain and hope, death and salvation, legible, from the point of view of the patron family, as a message by way of images which before the world celebrates the long life of the Medicean nobility: in history through their deeds, in eternity through their faith.

The success of the Sacristy: descriptions and derivations

What is generally referred to as the "success" of the New Sacristy, beginning with its origins, is so great that an exhaustively documented publication has been devoted to the subject and to that alone, which includes and analyses descriptions and derivations (drawings, engravings, small copies for statues, life-sized copies and plaster casts) from Michelangelo's day to the threshold of our time.[65] Of particular interest is the role the work played as a "gymnasium" for the apprenticeships of artists that were hired almost immediately after Michelangelo's departure, despite the fact that it was still difficult to actually visit the Sacristy, as it had to be specially unlocked by Ottaviano da Bernardetto de' Medici, a relative of Duke Alessandro. While Buonarroti was still present in the Sacristy, only his closest collaborators, such as Montorsoli, Raffaello da Montelupo, Cosini and Tribolo, in other words very few sculptors, actually shared its creation with him; later, many other artists took the time to study the Sacristy, even contributing through drawings and copies to the dissemination of its acknowledgement. For as long as the statues lay on the ground it was possible to view them from up close and admire the latent vitality in the carnal splendour of the figures, especially the female sculptures, as well as climb nonchalantly on the unfinished pieces and architectural reliefs. Visible from all angles, the *Times of the Day* were studied and drawn from perspectives that would no longer be possible once they were mounted on the sarcophagi. Sculptors, starting with Tribolo, made reduced copies or life-sized plaster casts from them.[66]
Already halfway through the century, even before the time when Pontormo painted in the choir (1546-1556), young people were routinely allowed into the area, including some of Buonarroti's early admirers such as Giorgio Vasari and Bartolomeo Ammannati. The Accademia delle Arti del Disegno that Vasari, in agreement with Borghini, had Duke Cosimo establish in 1563, actually held group sessions there for graphic study and criticism, as portrayed in two interesting drawings by the painter Federico Zuccari, academic from 1565.[67] Battista Franco, Francesco Salviati and Giovan Battista Naldini were among the first artists to study the statues, one of their goals being to make engravings of them. Franco set the statues (which had not as yet been mounted) in landscape settings, to make them look like ancient ruins that had been excavated. In 1570, Naldini, the author of masterful sheets, gave them to Cornelis Cort to be engraved. Passarotti, Tintoretto (who owned partial plaster casts of them) and then Cigoli, Boscoli, Rubens, and on up to Rodin and others all tested their ability based on these works.
Within its walls Michelangelo's legacy was assimilated by generations of Florentine and foreign artists, providing at first a direct personal experience but eventually becoming a legend. This was further and impressively developed in the artistic literature, which remained steady in time and intensified in the past century. Partial or total plaster casts exported the perception of the body volumes of the statues, and were included in the study materials of some of the finest Fine Arts academies in Europe; drawings, engravings, photographs and, lastly, virtual images have disseminated knowledge of the works worldwide. When the digital survey made by the Stanford University in California and Georgetown University in Washington, D.C. in 1998-1999 of the *Times of the day* is finally developed, it will provide accurate 3D digital models that will further facilitate viewing, appreciation and knowledge (like for the *David*).

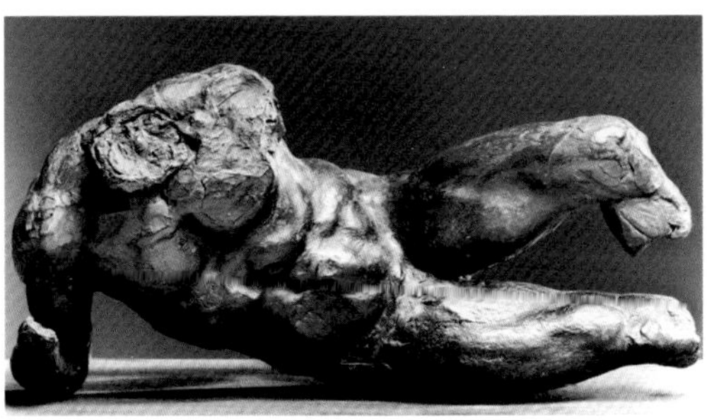

Michelangelo, model
for a *River God* (?)
Florence, Museo di Casa
Buonarroti

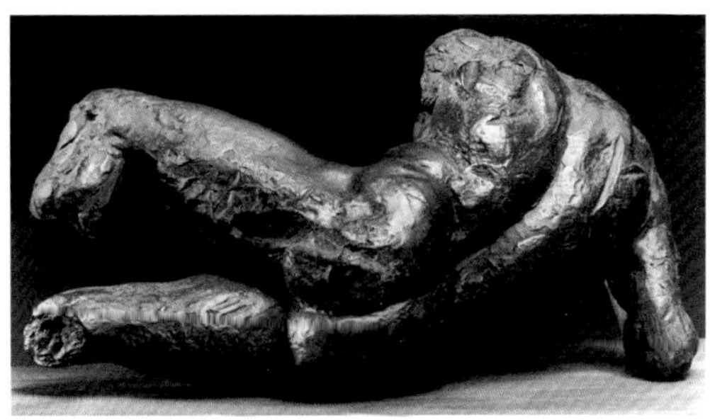

Michelangelo, model
for a *River God* (?)
Florence, Museo di Casa
Buonarroti

Notes

[1] For this site and possible preexisting ones, see Elam, 1979, pp. 155-186; Ruschi, 1993, pp. 119-120.
[2] Argan, Contardi, 1990, pp. 175-185, especially p. 175; Morrogh, 1992, pp. 567-570.
[3] Vasari, "The Life of Michelangelo" (1550), 2007 ed., p. 171.
[4] See the previous note. But a close-up study of the "ball" has revealed a different geometric configuration (Vincenzo Vaccari in an oral communication).
[5] The heraldic arms and mottos taken by the Medici from the 15th century include references to the cyclical nature of time and to its eternity: the *ouroboros*, the ring, the "broncone", or laurel branch producing or extinguishing flames, the mottos SEMPER and LE TENS REVIENT. Of the vast bibliography, see the various titles by F. Ames-Lewis (e.g. 1979) and, among others, Cox Rearick, 1984; Acidini Luchinat, 1991; Cardini, 1992. The Janus temple divides the long frieze of the Medicean villa at Poggio a Caiano, conceived prior to the death of Lorenzo il Magnifico, and associated with the theme of time and its eternal return. For additional considerations on the Michelangelesque citation of the Arch of Janus and its meaning in this context, see Gahtan, 2002.
[6] Morrogh, 1992.
[7] Vasari, "The Life of Michelangelo" (1550), 2007 ed., p. 173.
[8] Vasari, 1550, 1986 ed., p. 29. In 1545, the chapel was opened to the public and after four years "ammattonata" (clad in brickwork).
[9] Michelangelo was already very familiar with the quarrymen in Carrara and chose to avoid Pietrasanta, perhaps because of his negative experience with the marble for the unexecuted façade of San Lorenzo. For the marble of the Medici tombs, see Rapetti, 2001, pp. 79-94.
[10] For an idea of how hard Michelangelo worked, and how he organized his work, see the reconstruction of a typical week: from Monday, 24 July to Sunday, 30 July, 1525 (Wallace, 1998). On the same subject also see Wallace, 1994. For this, but also for other events in the artist's professional life, his *Ricordi* (1970 ed.) are of essential importance.
[11] We know that wooden models for the tombs were made by "Bastiano legnaiuolo".
[12] The same plan had been expressed by Brunelleschi, albeit with different proportions, for the Pazzi Chapel in Santa Croce. Michelozzo di Bartolommeo was inspired by the Sacristy for the chapel of the Magi in the Medici palace. The unknown author (perhaps Michelozzo himself) of the "chiesina", or small church, of the bishop Donato de' Medici near the Pistoia Cathedral had referred to it too, although the changes that took place later make it hard to identify it.
[13] Vasari, *The Lives* (1568), 1996 ed., II, p. 495.
[14] On the controversial date for this destruction, see Rosenberg, 2000, pp. 144-145. On the decoration, since lost, see: Cecchi, 1983, pp. 20-44; Dacos, Furlan, 1987, pp. 154-159. The testing carried out in the course of the 19th century to at least discover the vestiges of the decoration has been fruitless.
[15] Vasari, *The Lives* (1568), 1996 ed., II, pp. 679-680.
[16] Cellini, 1857 ed., p. 223, cited in Conforti, 1993, p. 41.
[17] For the so-called reception phenomena, see Rosenberg, 2000; *L'adolescente*..., 2000, pp. 172-198.
[18] Discovered by Sir Timothy Clifford in the Cooper-Hewitt National Design Museum, Smithsonian Institution, New York, inv. 1942-36.4 (Clifford, 2002).
[19] See Morrogh, 1992, pp. 587 and ff.
[20] A drawing generally believed to be an autograph by Michelangelo, with a trophy at the centre of the attic and pairs of "accosciati" to the sides, is in the British Museum, Department of Prints and Drawings, inv. 1859-5-14-823. Further details are visible in the crowded Louvre drawing for the tomb of Giuliano (DAG, inv. 838), whose attribution wavers from Stefano Lunetti to an unknown follower, with rare support for a Michelangelesque autograph. For the entire issue of the marble at the Hermitage, see the exhibition catalogue *L'Adolescente*..., 2000.
[21] London, British Museum, Dept. of Prints and Drawings, inv. 1859-6-25-543 (Wilde, 1953, n. 28*r*.).
[22] Trexler, Lewis, 1981; Trexler, 2000.
[23] Vasari, "The Life of Michelangelo" (1550), 2007 ed., p. 174. The poetic exchange is dated 1546.
[24] Vasari, "The Life of Michelangelo" (1550), 2007 ed., p. 173.
[25] Paris, Musée du Louvre, DAG inv. 838. See Joannides, 2003a, no. 27.
[26] Balas (1992 and 1995) has suggested that these are pomegranates; if this were so, it would influence the whole iconography, and if accepted, require a complete revision of the Sacristy's entire interpretation, as we shall see further on. Among painted replicas of Michelangelo's *Night* let us recall those by Francesco Brina (?) in the Casa Buonarroti with a series of four paintings also including *Dawn, Leda* and *Venus and Cupid* (Nelson, 2002, pp. 50-51); by Michele Tosini, *circa* 1565, Rome Galleria Colonna and by the circle of Michele Tosini, formerly Brescia, antiquarian market (cf. J.K. Nelson, in *Venere e Amore*..., 2002, pp. 166-167, cat. 13).
[27] Vasari, 1550, 1986 ed., p. 902; Borghini, 1584, pp. 65-66. See Rosenberg, 2000 for the question of the identifications.
[28] Florence, Casa Buonarroti, inv. 10A. For a recent entry, see the catalogue *L'Adolescente*..., 2000, pp. 129-131, no. 21. I believe that this text, like "Fame holds down..." etc., is likely the Italian translation of a proposed Latin epigraph.
[29] Letter from Anton Francesco Doni in Piacenza to Michelangelo [in Rome], 12 January 1543, in *Il Carteggio*..., 1965-1983, IV, 1979, pp. 160-163, no. MVI, especially p. 161.
[30] The disease is cancer, as has also been observed by art historians and oncologists, independently of one another.
[31] Nelson, 2002, pp. 30-40.
[32] Varchi, 1549-1550, 1998 ed., p. 47.
[33] Bocchi, 1584, 1962 ed., pp. 178-179.
[34] Lee, Anstruther-Thompson, 1904, pp. 101-110, where in particular it says: "the marble [in the Night] is worked to the highest pitch of brilliancy, and she is almost as elusive as the moonlight itself; the high lights are literally luminous, and the shadows are very dark".
[35] As for the deliberateness and other issues concerning the "non-finito" in Michelangelo, see the Introduction.
[36] Vasari, "The Life of Michelangelo" (1550), 2007 ed., p. 173.
[37] If it is a lion, which seems likely, it is the traditional symbol of courage, but also a tribute to Florence's Marzocco, and to the memory of Leo X.
[38] According to Trexler, Lewis, 1981 (emphasized in Trexler, 2000) it is the "mappa", the piece of cloth that Roman consuls dropped on the ground to signal the start of the games: this would explain its proposed identification with Duke Giuliano, captain general of the State of the Church (Lorenzo held the same role for the city of Florence).
[39] At times identified as a money "bag" (defined in the Vocabolario dell'Accademia della Crusca as "spezie di tacchetta, o borsa di cuoio, cucita a un ferro, per portarvi dentro danari"), but also as the armrest on the chair (Santi, 1993, p. 37; but the position of the back corner in relation to Lorenzo's chest is not compatible with this hypothesis), the box is morphologically similar to the beehives, placed one atop the other in the manner of a pyramid for a total of six, visible in one of the "heraldic arms" of Lorenzo il Magnifico, grandfather of Duke Lorenzo; it is also a recurring motif in his illuminated manuscripts.
[40] Vasari, "The Life of Michelangelo" (1550), 2007 ed., p. 173.
[41] Doni, 1552, 1928 ed., II, p. 21.
[42] London, British Museum, inv. MLA 1859, 7-19, 2, length 12.3 cm. It was acquired directly from the Casa Buonarroti, whose catalogue of 1648 listed it as a model by Michelangelo (Thornton, Warren, 1998). Similarities have also been observed with the *Awakening Captive* at the Galleria dell'Accademia. Rejected by Tolnay (1954) and Weinberger (1967), accepted by O'Grody (1999, no. 5), with the suggestion that because of its quality as a very small model without armour quickly modelled out of wax it may have been used to perform a demonstration for the quarrymen in Carrara.
[43] Tolnay, 1948, pp. 61-76 with a great following by scholarship.
[44] Condivi, *The Life of Michelangelo* (1553), 2006 ed., p. 67. To this regard it is also important to recall the sheet *Allegory of Death* by the Senese Giovanni Fortuna engraved by the Mantuan Andrea Andreani in 1588 (in *Rappresentazione del destino*... , 2001, pp. 72-73: a complex composition in the form of a sinister frontispiece, where the figure of *Night* wearing a mask and with a bird of prey, in contrast with bright-faced *Day*, is inspired by the Sacristy. At the centre a sort of macabre rose window where Death revolves, bearing along with the scythe the suffix *-mus*, which serves to complete maxims such as "Mortem vitare nequi*mus*", "De limo homo pri*mus*", "Cum nos Terra su*mus*", etc. And *mus* in Latin indeed means mouse. Not to be overlooked is the presence of the devouring mouse in the subject of *vanitas*, plague and devastation of the 17th century, especially across the Alps.
[45] Vasari reported that the Magnifico Ottaviano allowed him to go into the Sacristy while Michelangelo was in Rome in 1532 or 1533 (Vasari, 1568, 1962 ed., I, p. 282); he would also let Tribolo in, who gratefully presented him with a small model of the *Medici Madonna* (Vasari, 1568, 1962 ed., I, p. 248). Ottaviano commissioned Giuliano Bugiardini to make a portrait of Michelangelo. For his relationship with other artists, see Bracciante, 1984.
[46] Balas, 1992 and Balas, 1984.
[47] In particular, the *Three Sketches of a Madonna and Child* in the Gabinetto Disegni e Stampe at the Uffizi in Florence (inv. 233 *Fr.*), the *Seated Figure and Madonna Lactans* at the Louvre in Paris, DAG, inv. 689*v*., the *Madonna Lactans* at the Albertina Graphische Sammlunga in Vienna, inv. 118*v*. (cf. Echinger-Maurach, 2000).
[48] Letter from Michelangelo in Florence to Giovan Francesco Fattucci in Rome datable to 17 June 1526, in *Il Carteggio*... , 1965-1983, III, 1973, pp. 227-228, no. DCCLII.
49Nonetheless, they are different from the types and poses that Michelangelo had assigned the two lateral saints in a project of about 1521, known through a number of copies from that time (for example, Paris, Musée du Louvre, DAG, inv. 837), and that were more in-depth with studies of single figures like the sheet in Paris, Louvre, DAG, inv. 708.

[50] London, British Museum, Dept. Of Prints and Drawings, inv. 1859-5-14-823.
[51] Paris, Musée du Louvre, DAG, INV. 838.
[52] London, British Museum, Dept. of Prints and Drawings, inv. 1859-6-25-544.
[53] A small autograph model made from wax and other materials in the Casa Buonarroti (inv. 542) is currently believed to be a preliminary study for a *River God*, and thus displayed in a reclining position (*I bozzetti...*, 2000, no. 3, pp. 38-41); I would prefer, however, to set it in an upright position and consider it preparatory for a *Slave* (see Introduction). For the success of Michelangelo's inventions for river gods as represented in drawings and sculptures by a number of artists in his day, see O'Grody, 1999.
[54] Doni, 1552, 1928 ed., II, p. 22: "*Peregrino*: Che stupende bozze di terra son queste qui basse? *Fiorentino*: Avevano a esser due figuroni di marmo che Michel Angelo voleva fare".
[55] Rosenberg, 2000, p. 133, according to documents from the Archivio di San Lorenzo.
[56] Michelangelo apologized to the duke through the Florentine ambassador Averardo Serristori, and to Vasari through his nephew Lionardo.
[57] Di Domenico, Lippi, 2005.
[58] See Parronchi, Panichi, 1993, pp. 207-213.
[59] Panofsky, 1939, 1972 ed.
[60] Gahtan, 2002.
[61] In light of the 16th-century developments of the theme of the rivers as a strong element of territorial identity – the iconographies of Tribolo in the garden of the Castello and of Vasari in the Palazzo Vecchio, to mention two artists who were close to the Sacristy – I suggested that the river gods symbolized the rivers of the Florentine dominion (the Arno and its tributaries) or of the city of Florence alone (Acidini Luchinat, 2002, p. 27, note 43); but this hypothesis, which I worked out at a later date, seems to be more convincing.
[62] Although the iconography of the Madonna who reveals her breast in the act of interceding with her Son in favour of sinners is rare, it did have a number of precedents in Florence, including the most famous and visible of these which was the canvas (at that time believed to be a banner) from the 15th century in the Cathedral counterfaçade, and now in the Lehman wing of the Metropolitan Museum of New York. As for the two physician saints as intercessors, 15th-century examples in painting include tablets by Angelico and Gentile da Fabriano.
[63] Clements is due (1996) the observation of the repetition of the motifs of Time in terms of day, night, light, darkness, hours in Michelangelo's written work. By using a hendiadys for "Time" and "hours", Michelangelo seems to distinguish between the eternal physical flow from the way man instead beats out its rhythm. It is difficult to say whether these themes were congential to the artist, or instead solely developed in view of the Sacristy.
[64] The theme of Time in the Sacristy, among other things present in Renaissance culture in a large variety of versions, was especially used by Anton Francesco Doni, who, as previously stated, was a very interested visitor of the location, going there three or four times over a short period of time, to then write about it to Michelangelo himself in enthusiastic terms in a letter of 12 January 1543 (*Il Carteggio...*, 1965-1983, IV, 1979, no. MVI, pp. 160-163). In later writings, Doni further refined and expanded the representation of Time by placing alongside it the Sun-Apollo and the Moon-Diana as divinities personifying Day and Night, and then the Seasons, the elderly Past, the Future child, History symbolized by a book.
[65] Rosenberg, 2000; also see, more specifically, Rosenberg, 2003.
[66] For the sake of providing an example: right after 1534, Tribolo executed small-scale terracotta copies of the four *Times of the Day*, of which the *Night* went to Vasari, as well as of the *Madonna*, which he gave to Ottaviano de' Medici. In 1557, Daniele da Volterra made plaster copies of Michelangelo's statues. In 1573, Vincenzo Danti made casts from the original *Times of the Day* at the Accademia di Perugia, his native city.
[67] The two drawings by Federico Zuccari (Musée du Louvre, DAG, inv. 4554 and 4555) are datable to the artist's first stay in Florence in 1565 or less likely the second, between 1575 and 1579. The images show the young artists drawing as well as the arrangement of the Sacristy, with one of Cosini's *Trophies* test-mounted on the attic of the tomb of Lorenzo, subsequently removed.

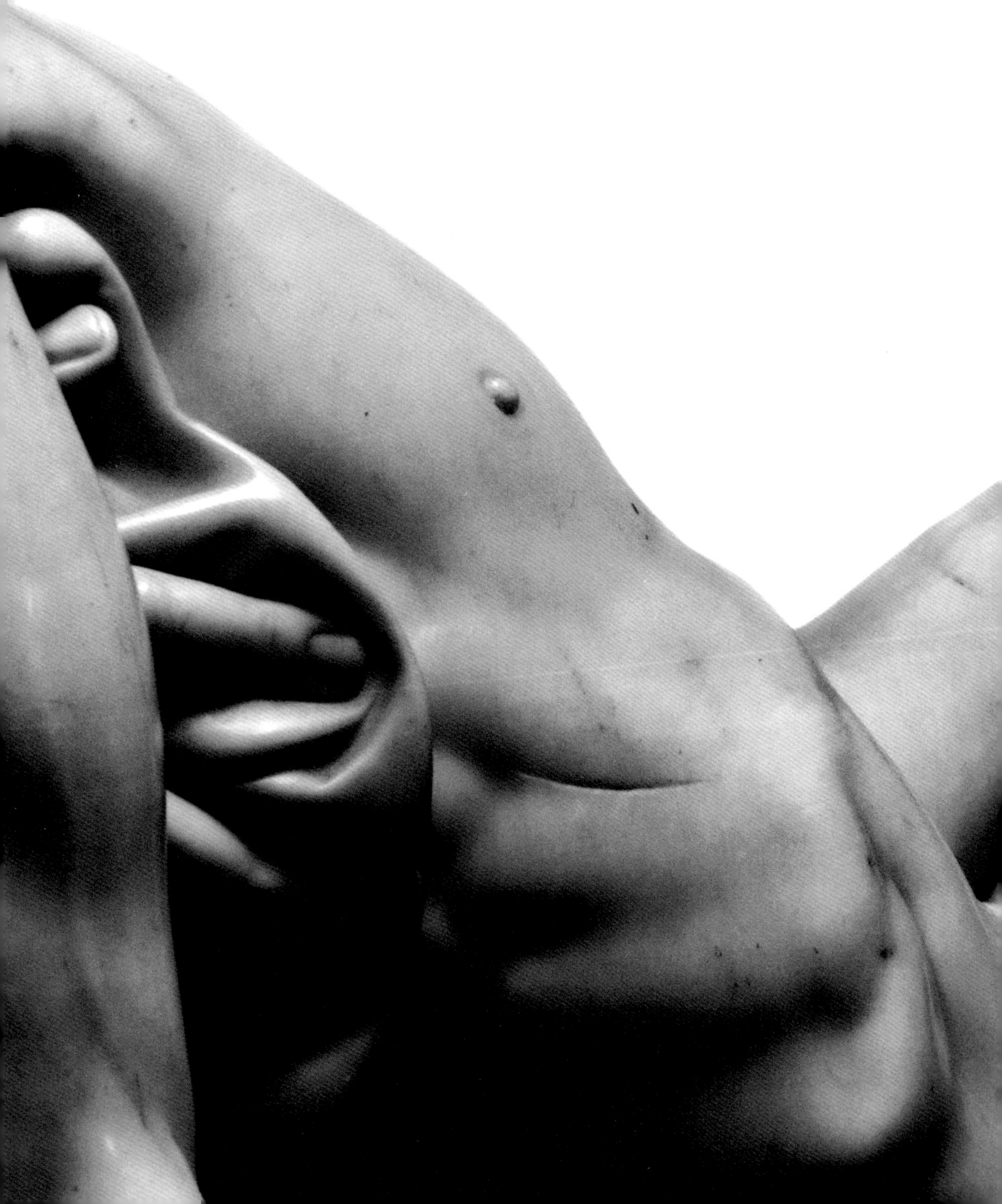

Between the Florentine Republic and the Rome of Clement VII

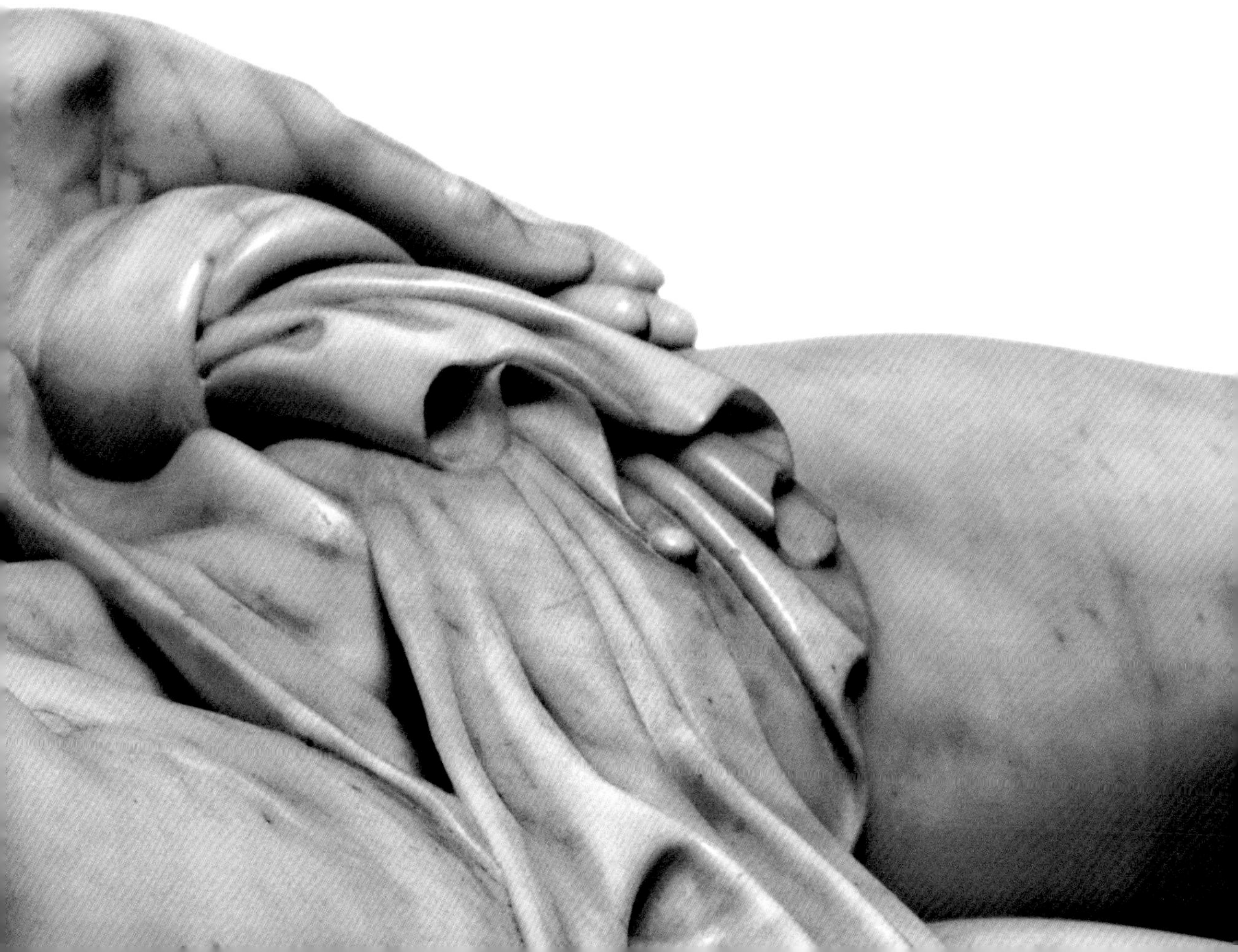

The republican hiatus

When the Medici were expelled from Florence in May 1527, the constrution site at San Lorenzo closed down and Michelangelo was deprived of his commission. The newly restored republican government resumed a project that had originally been engineered by *gonfaloniere* Pier Soderini to have Michelangelo execute a colossal statue for the Arengario at the Palazzo della Signoria. It even assigned him marble that had previously been given to Baccio Bandinelli. But Michelangelo would not complete the statue this time either, and Bandinelli eventually used the block to carve his *Hercules and Cacus* (1534).

In view of the imperial troops' arrival, on 6 April 1529 the Dieci di Balia appointed Michelangelo commissary-general for work to redevelop the city's fortifications. The post created especially for him was a way of acknowledging his by now consolidated fame as an excellent architect and artist. It was also a very good source of income. Datable to this period are extraordinary designs for bastions, most of which housed at the Casa Buonarroti in Florence. Only a small number of these were actually executed. Michelangelo is said to have supervised the construction of parts of the city walls along the Via dei Bastioni at the foot of the hill of San Miniato.[1] But after just over five months, Michelangelo abandoned the post as well as the city, which was under siege, and took refuge in Ferrara. His explanation would be that the dark threats of some unidentified figure had encouraged him to flee. The canon Figiovanni, who knew Michelangelo well, instead suggested that because he was now financially well off, he was afraid of being forced into "loaning" some of his money to help with the cost of war. Michelangelo gave up on his plans to emigrate to France: the Florentine government had declared him a rebel and this meant that his property was in danger of confiscation. When he returned to Florence he indeed had to pay 1,000 florins; the amount was never returned to him.[2]

When the Medici regained power in August 1530 and the city fell, Michelangelo hid for fear of the pope's wrath;[3] the pope pardoned him, however, and the artist resumed working on the Sacristy. But after the long interruption Michelangelo was much less devoted to the Medicean building site. His relationship with Duke Alessandro de' Medici, whom he recalled as being fierce and vindictive, was more strained than ever, and his plans for the future were more and more in the direction of Rome.

The *Risen Christ* (the *Minerva Christ*)

Neither his work for the New Sacristy, which began at the end of 1519, nor the political turmoil of the years from 1527 to 1530 stopped Michelangelo from continuing to work on the Julius Tomb as well as other architectural and sculptural projects.

One of these was the second version of the *Risen Christ* or the *Minerva Christ*, which Metello Vari and the others were still waiting for in Rome. The records suggest that Michelangelo carved a new block of marble between September 1519, when he returned from the Apuan quarries, and April 1520. This was perhaps the worst period in his difficult relationship with Pope Leo X and Cardinal Giulio de' Medici. At the same time his project for the façade of San Lorenzo continued to slow down and would eventually be completely put aside. When compared to the previous version, the majestic nude figure of the Redeemer who holds the symbols of his Passion including the cross showed that Michelangelo had gone further in the development of some of the statue's structural themes: especially as concerned the artist's construction of the figure by *contrapposti*, which he generated by rotating the figure's hips. This was the most delicate part of the figure's powerful anatomy; unsurprisingly, the artist studied the muscles in detail, proof of which may be viewed in

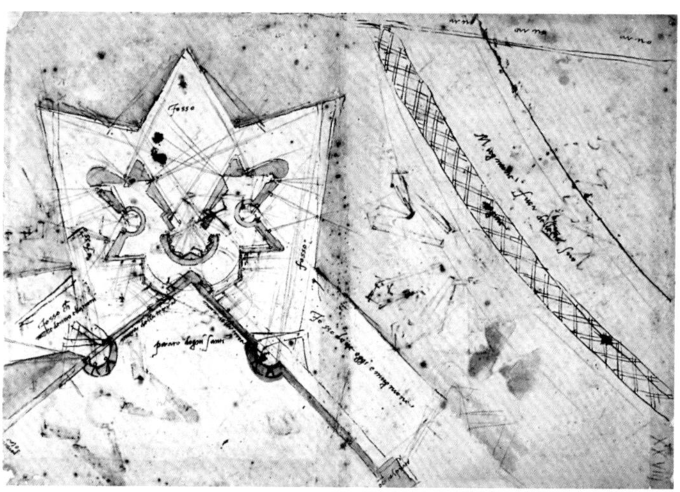

Michelangelo,
Design for the Bastion of the Prato di Ognissanti,
executed in view of the siege of Florence
Florence, Casa Buonarroti, inv. 13A

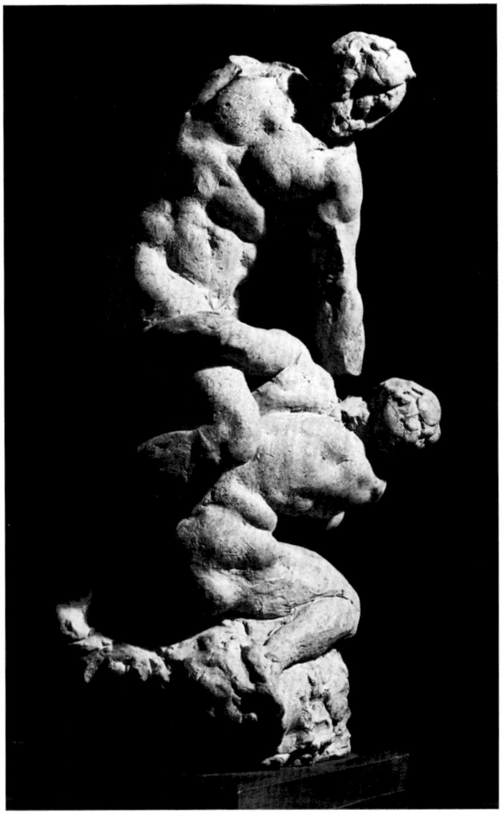

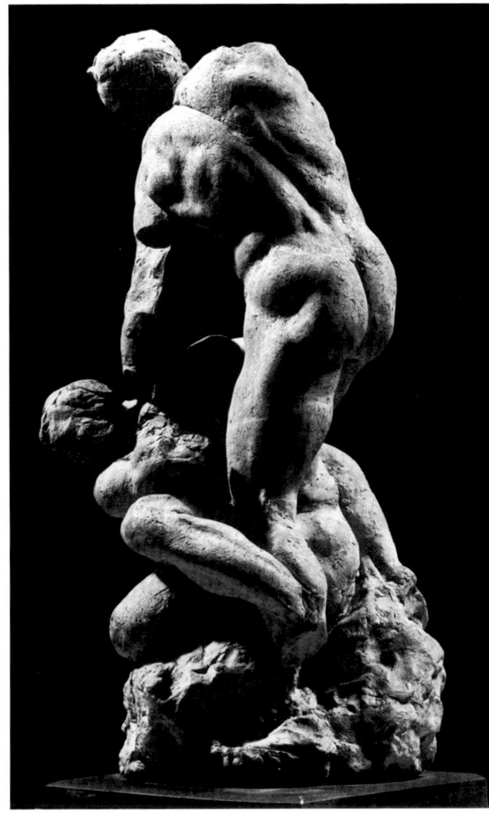

Michelangelo,
model for *Two Wrestlers*
Florence, Museo
di Casa Buonarroti

Michelangelo,
model for *Two Wrestlers*
Florence, Museo
di Casa Buonarroti

p. 202
Michelangelo, *Risen Christ*,
second and final version
of the statue commissioned
by Metello Vari
Rome, church of Santa Maria
sopra Minerva

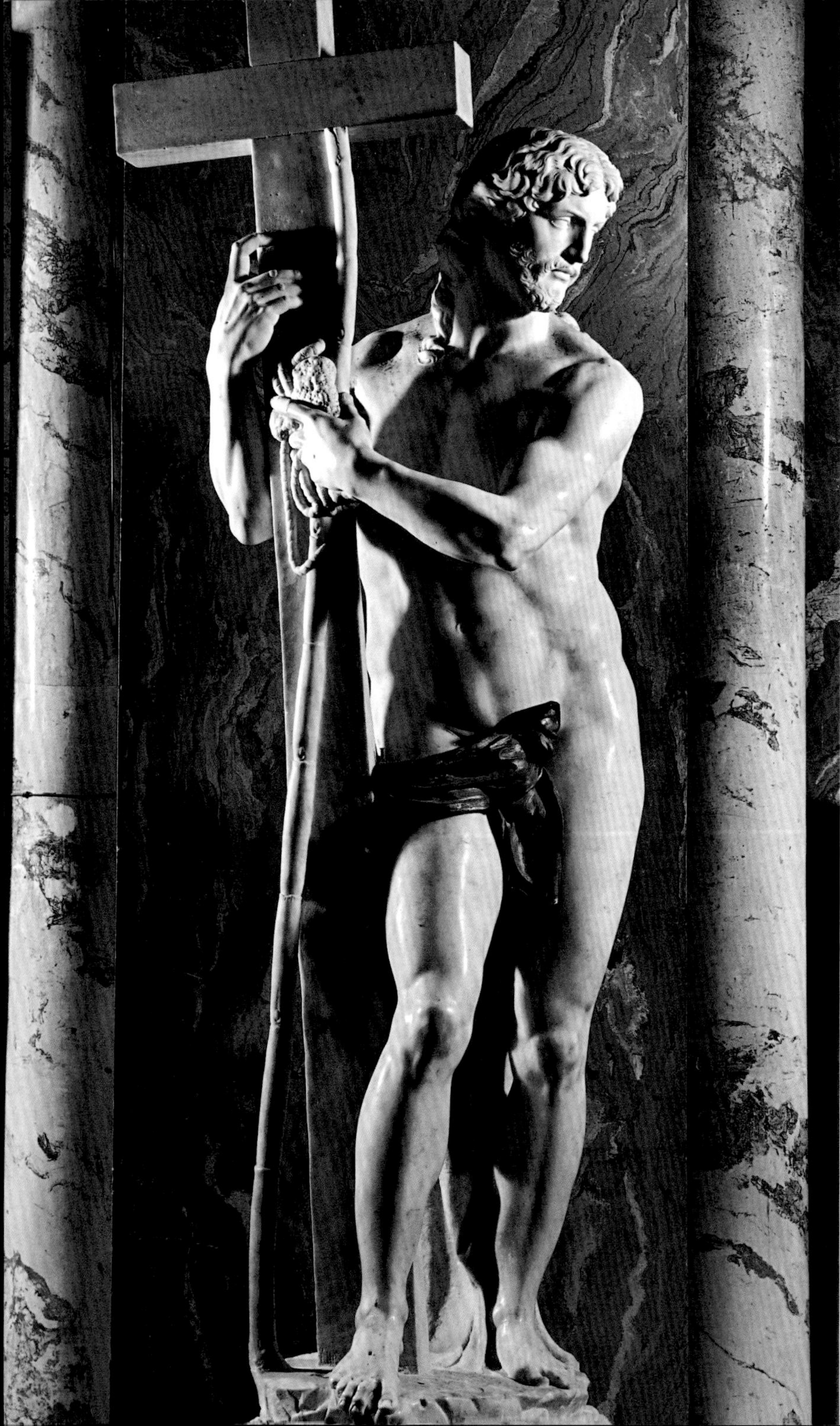

p. 203
Michelangelo,
Risen Christ
detail of the *contrapposto*
between the head and torso
Rome, church of Santa Maria
sopra Minerva

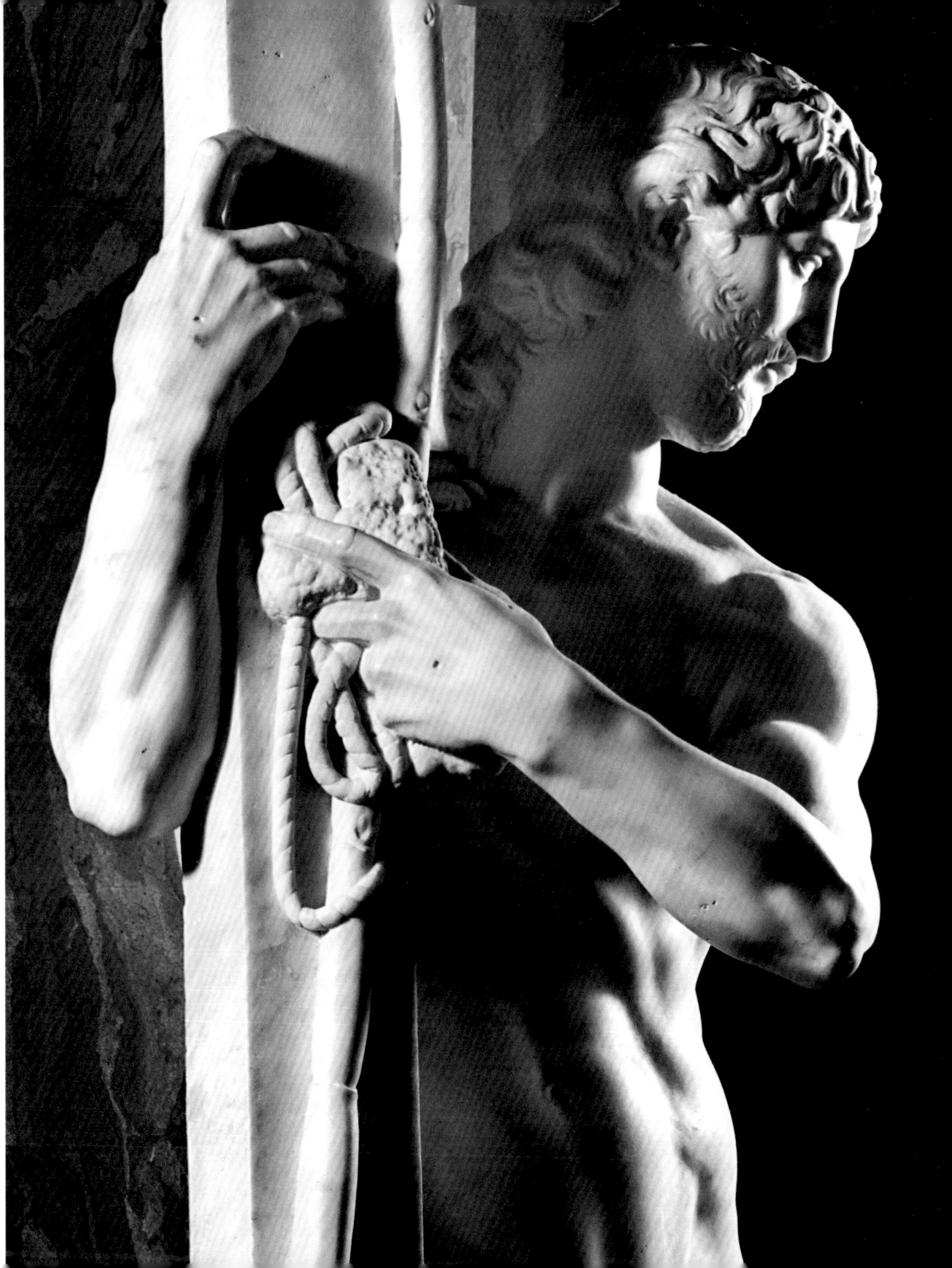

the autograph drawing on a sheet formerly in the Brinsley Ford collection.[4] These sketches reveal a sort of transition from the first to the second version of the statue. The *Christ* thus offers a variety of angles, which placement up against the partioning wall to the left of the high chapel allows the viewer to fully appreciate: from a frontal view the legs are spread apart, the torso twisted, the left arm crosses the body, the head turns above the shoulder in a direction opposite that of the arm; if observed from the side the space between the legs is clearly visible, as is the relief of the gluteal muscles, the forwards shoulder and arm movement, the sweet, knowing face turned towards the viewer. When Michelangelo shipped the statue to Rome it was not quite completed, so he asked Pietro Urbano to deal with the finishing touches. But in 1521 an alarming letter he received from his friend Sebastiano del Piombo warned him of the irreparable damage that had been made by his incompetent assistant.[5] A subsequent assignment had to be made to repair the damage and place the statue *in loco*, and this time Michelangelo turned to Federico Frizzi. The common belief is that the damage was mostly in the toes, but to my mind, other parts were also poorly made, such as the unoriginal way the base was shaped to make it resemble a pile of stones, not to mention the work done to accentuate the expression of the mouth by drilling two holes between the lips and the moustache. This was something that Michelangelo would never have approved of, let alone executed. On 27 December 1521 the *Christ* was installed; the cloth that was probably placed around the hips has now been replaced by gilded drapery.[6]

Although the statue was never much liked by its inventor, who even offered to make a third version for Vari,[7] it was nonetheless observed with much interest by the artist's contemporaries, for whom it represented a public example of the "figura serpentinata", the spiralling aesthetic which Michelangelo suggested creating in order to raise the number of excellent viewpoints in a sculpture.

The "kneeling" windows for the Palazzo Medici

The newly proposed dates for Michelangelo's work on the Palazzo Medici stretch from 1519 to 1521 (not 1517 as commonly indicated).[8] This consisted in closure of the open loggia on the ground floor at the south-western corner of Via Larga and Via de' Gori by means of walls in *pietra forte*. The two windows designed by the artist were so important that he submitted a model of them to his patron, Cardinal Giulio.[9] Their innovative shape was called "kneeling" because of the presence of long brackets below the sill – resembling the legs of a person kneeling. These brackets corresponded to the smaller pair under the projecting triangular tympanum unusually supported by an iron grill. The windows were a prototype and became very popular in palace architecture, bestowing on Tuscany's historic quarters one of its most typical features.[10]

The Tribune of the Reliquaries in San Lorenzo

The work Michelangelo carried out for the Medici popes was expressed in two other locations in the Medicean complex of San Lorenzo: the Tribune of the Reliquaries and the Library with the vestibule.

In 1525, Clement VII commissioned Michelangelo to design a "ciborium" for the church in order to display the precious antique vases made from rock crystal and semi-precious stone that had been converted into reliquaries. These had once belonged to Lorenzo il Magnifico, and the pope himself had reacquired them after the family's heirlooms were scattered in 1494. This was yet another Medicean project for San Lorenzo that bore the sign of the dynastic continuation from one generation to the next. Once the location of the counterfaçade was chosen,[11] construction began in 1531, and it must have been at a

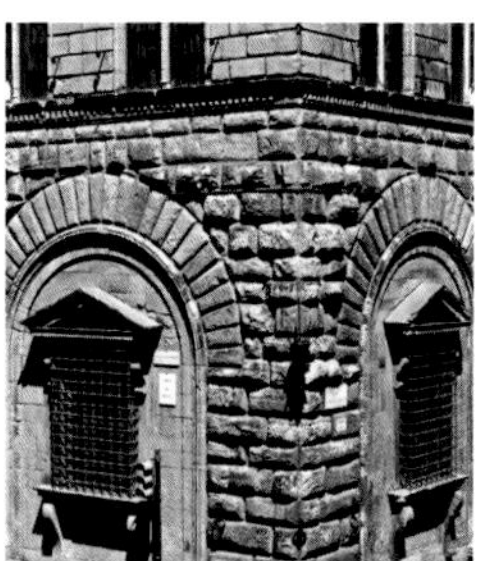

Michelangelo,
Kneeling Windows
for the corner room
(formerly the loggia)
of the ground floor
in the Palazzo Medici
Florence, Palazzo Medici

very advanced stage in December 1532 when, after Michelangelo's journey to Rome in September, the vase-reliquaries were donated to the basilica by two papal bulls and placed on display. The architectural structure designed by Michelangelo, and completed in July 1533, which reflects the 15th-century and post-Brunellesque inner façade, consists in a slightly overhanging balcony with a balustrade supported by two slender Corinthian columns. On the balcony three doors open into the depth of the façade[12] – with the central door crowned by a triangular pediment – each framed by a pair of pilasters carved with vegetal festoons in high relief. A private and ironic joke by the artist appears to be the only explanation for the otherwise mysterious difference between the capital of the left pilaster and its corresponding number to the right. It is likely that after requesting his distracted patron and impatient intermediaries to make a choice, Michelangelo personally made the provocative decision to install both versions of capitals, convinced that their distance from the ground would protect him against criticism.[13] The Tribune is an unusual architectural piece, plain and sober in appearance but in actual fact pervaded by numerous tense elements. Alongside its relationship with the preexisting counterfaçade is its twofold function: a kind of "closet" for precious relics and at the same time the "official location" where the much-cherished reliquaries were put on display.[14]

The Medicean Laurentian Library

When Cardinal Giulio decided to build the Library in 1519, he was actually resuming a project that had first been imagined by Lorenzo il Magnifico, when he put stone-cutters to work on the "marble, or rather the cut stonework" in the Sculpture Garden at San Marco, to erect a proper home for the "very noble collection of books that he and his ancestors had gathered from all over the world".[15] This return to the library project represented a strong sign of continuity for the Medici, as well as for Michelangelo. It was only after 1523 that Giulio, who had become Pope Clement VII, could finally devote his attention to the project, and through his secretary Fattucci the first thing he did was to designate a location for it in the vast space on the first floor of the San Lorenzo complex.[16]

The phases in which the long rectangular reading room was built, starting in April 1525 after the reinforcement of the underlying structures, were interspersed with a number of embellishments and modifications to the plans pursuant to the pope's ever-changing demands. The idea for a "secret library" for the *rariora*, visible in the wonderful drawings marked A79*r*. and A80*r*. at the Casa Buonarroti, which reveal the artist's visionary triangular plan (truly a stroke of genius), was given up so that the space was never built. The arrangement of the reading desks or "plutei", and consequently the design for the ceiling and corresponding floor, also continued to change. From 1526, construction began on the *ricetto*, the high entrance vestibule destined to accommodate the staircase leading from the upper level of the cloisters to the reading room. When he left Florence in 1534, Michelangelo had finished building the reading room, its walls punctuated by pilaster strips and hollowed out by wide tabernacle windows. He had also defined the scheme for the ceiling and the design of the reading desks. The vestibule was under construction, and the walls, excluding those of the upper floor, were complete, with pairs of mighty columns embedded within them and floating consoles on the lower level combining a number of architectural orders often pointed out as being "heterodoxical".[17] As far as the staircase was concerned, there were only "signs on the floor" and some sketches, together with "many stones" prepared but not installed.[18]

From 1548 on, construction of the ceiling in carved linden wood was begun under Tribolo's guidance by specialized artisans, who also made the terracotta floor in red and white *impasto* (plaster), and the reading desks, or "plutei" which had been designed by Michelangelo personally. The installation in 1568 of panes of glass decorated with grotesques completed the large reading room.

Once again, Duke Cosimo's attempts to make Buonarroti come back to Florence were in vain, despite the good offices of Tribolo who went

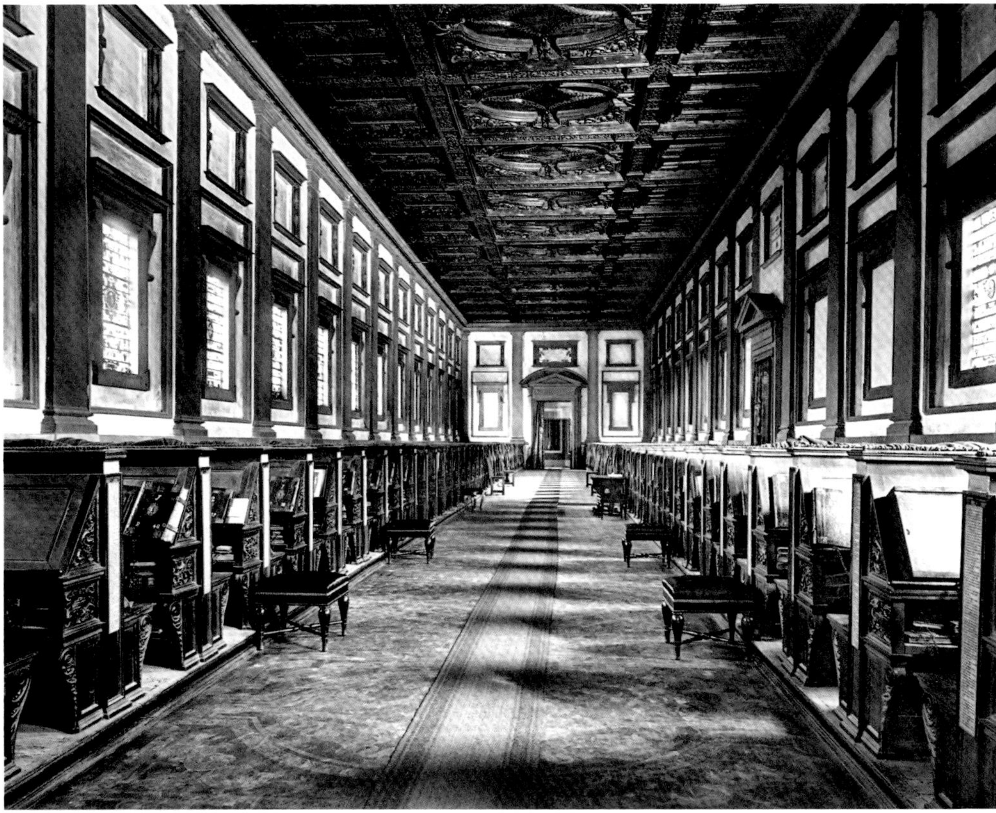

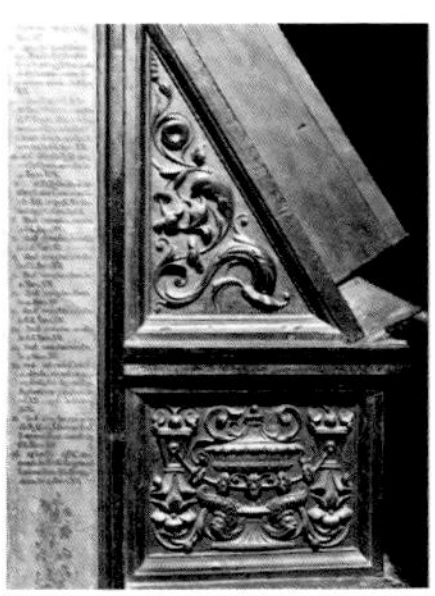

After designs by Michelangelo, one of the carved wooden reading desks used to consult manuscripts
Florence, Medicean Laurentian Library

Niccolò Tribolo, Santi Buglioni and other artists after a project by Michelangelo, Medicean Library reading room
Florence, San Lorenzo complex

p. 207
Michelangelo, Laurentian Library vestibule, detail of the corner construction for embedded columns, tabernacles, windows
Florence, Medicean Laurentian Library

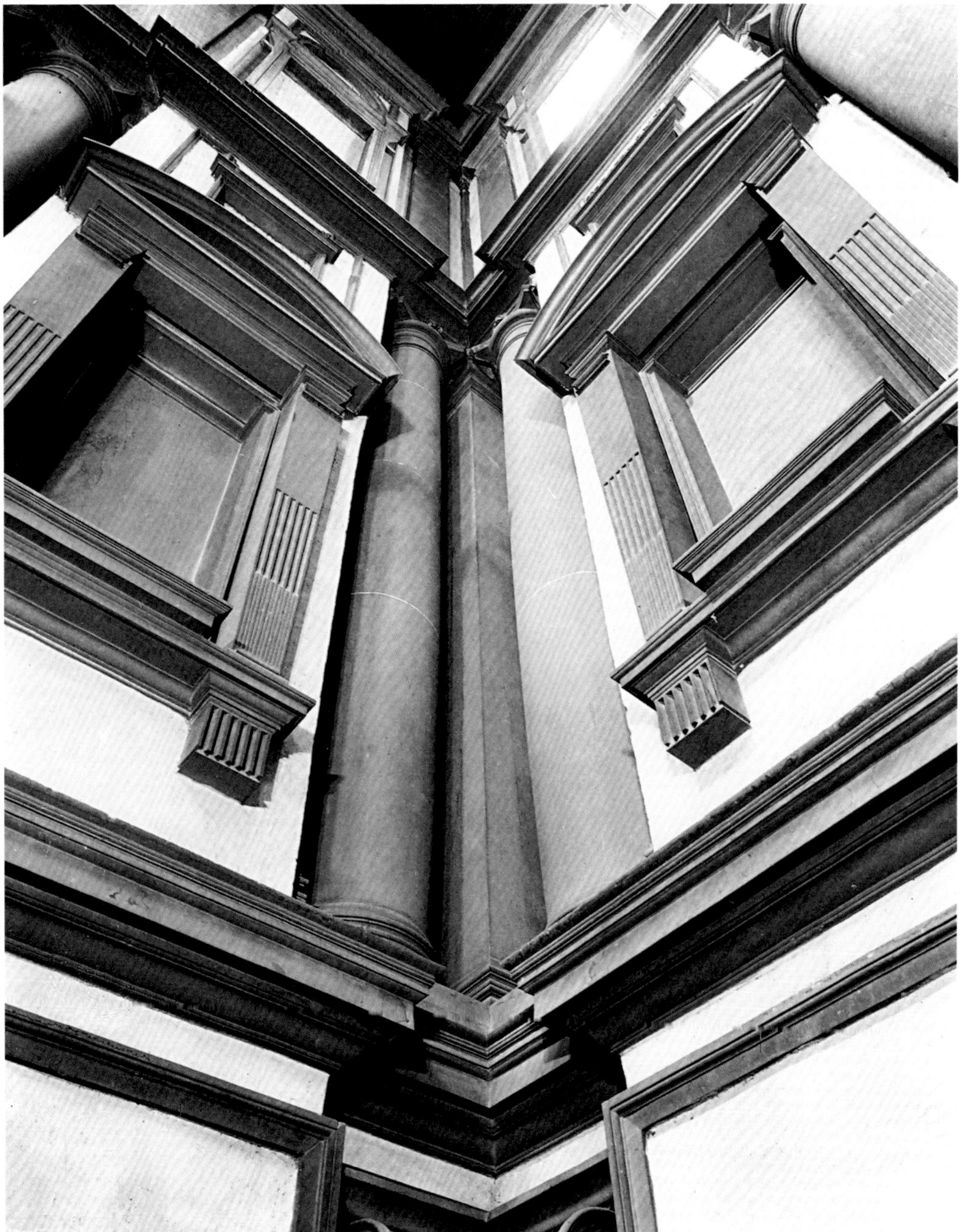

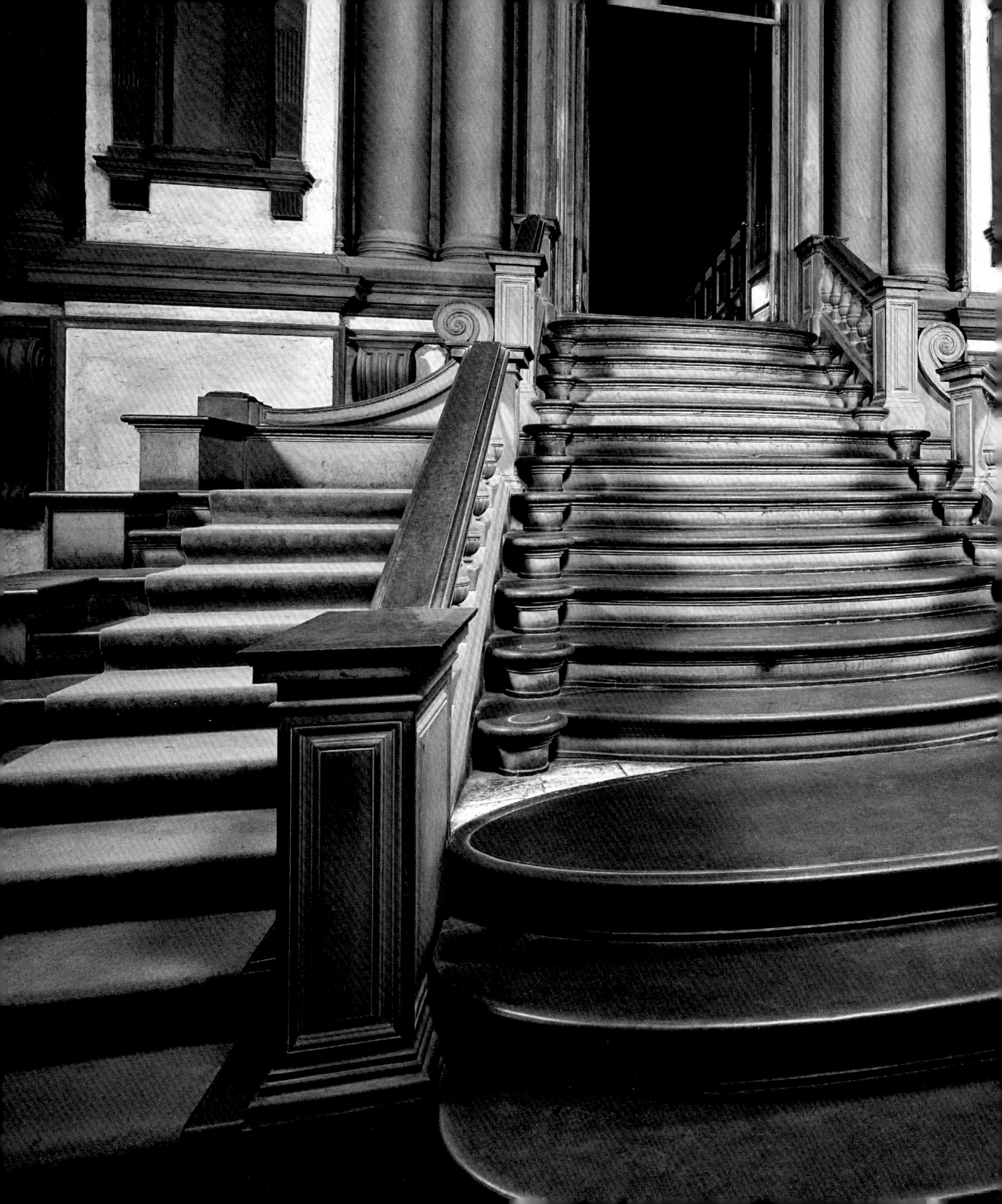

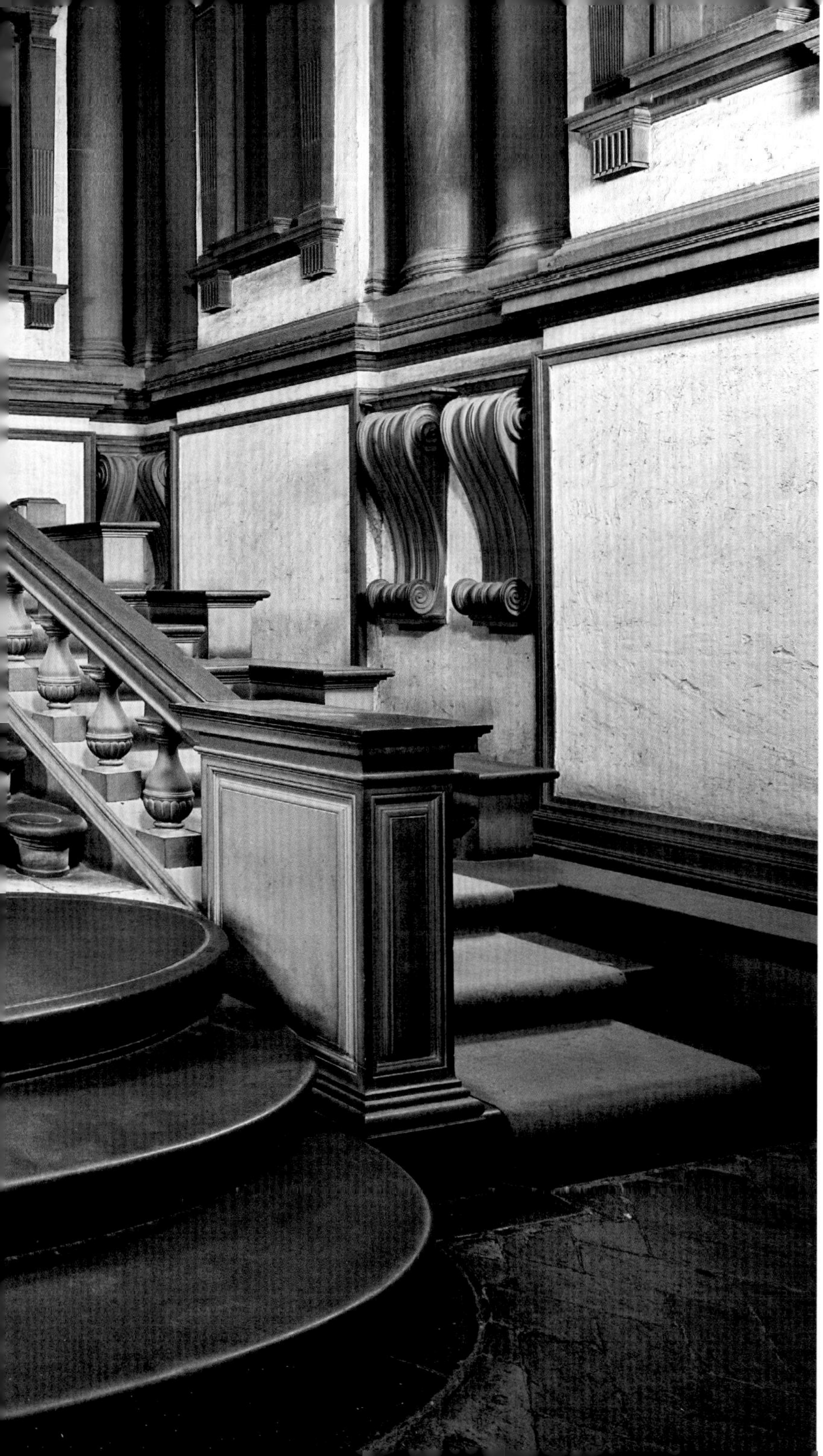

Bartolomeo Ammannati after what he remembered and a model by Michelangelo, tripartite staircase between the vestibule and the Library reading room
Florence, Medicean Laurentian Library

to Rome in 1549 for this very purpose. On that occasion, and in the following years, Michelangelo's answer was always "no", although from time to time he would provide some vague instructions.

Completion of the reading room and vestibule, or *ricetto*, with the staircase represents a unique case of an interpretative construction site. For the staircase in particular, the Florentine architects, Tribolo, Vasari, Ammannati took turns asking Michelangelo what needed to be done; but the artist was getting older and becoming increasingly irritable. At first, his description of the original project was hazy, but then he described it in greater detail ("I can clearly remember a certain staircase as if in a dream..."): a tripartite staircase with rectilinear steps on each of the sides and a central flight resembling a series of thin "oval boxes" of decreasing size set one upon the other. In 1559, he was finally coaxed into sending a small model to Florence ("a small terracotta model"), and thanks to this the staircase in *pietra serena* was finally completed.[19]

The Library was at last inaugurated in 1571 under the Grand Duke Francesco I.

Fantasy for a colossal statue of Clement VII

As a fitting crown for the general ferment produced by the presence of the Medici in San Lorenzo, Clement VII expected Michelangelo to make a giant statue of him for the piazza in front of the church, one that was to measure 55 Roman feet, or 40 Florentine *braccia*, in height, i.e. 16 metres or more.[20] The letter Michelangelo wrote back was filled with ridiculing wit, which tells us that he had no qualms about expressing his annoyance with the pope.[21] The pope quietly gave up the idea, once more manifesting the extent of his indulgence towards his trusted artist.[22]

The *Apollo/David*

Vasari briefly mentioned the statue as follows: "For Baccio Valori he then began a small marble figure of Apollo drawing an arrow from the quiver",[23] dating the onset of the work from the time of the artist's return from Ferrara and Venice (after November 1529), or rather, as historical circumstances would indicate, after August 1530, when the Florentine Republic fell. Because Bartolomeo, called Baccio Valori (formerly *gonfaloniere di giustizia* in Florence in 1524), returned to Florence as apostolic commissary for the papal troops and now governed the city ruled by the Medici, Michelangelo wanted to use the statue to curry favour with him, and make peace with Clement VII. Work on the statue was carefully reconsidered by Vasari in the second edition of the *Lives*: "... and carried it almost to completion [...] a very rare work, although it is not completely finished".

Valori was still waiting for the statue in 1531 or 1532; in 1537, he was decapitated as a *fuoruscito*, or political exile, and supporter of the republican restoration. One inventory records that in 1553, the statue – described as "David del Buonarroto imperfecto" – was located in Duke Cosimo de' Medici's apartment along with the two statues of *Bacchus* by Sansovino and Bandinelli. Whether or not the duke received the statue through confiscation of Valori's estate is unknown. In the second edition of the *Lives* (1568), Vasari related that it was in the apartment of the "prince of Florence".

It has often been hypothesized that the figure was begun as a *David* and only later converted into an *Apollo*. If this were the case the small mound on the base must originally have been intended for Goliath's chopped-off head under the shepherd and hero's foot, like in the lost bronze *David* that Michelangelo had made for the marshal of Gié. But the iconography of the figure may have been misunderstood by the person who drew up the Medicean inventory in 1553 (the only source for the biblical identity), who was probably more familiar with the Bible than with Greco-Roman mythology, and especially with the

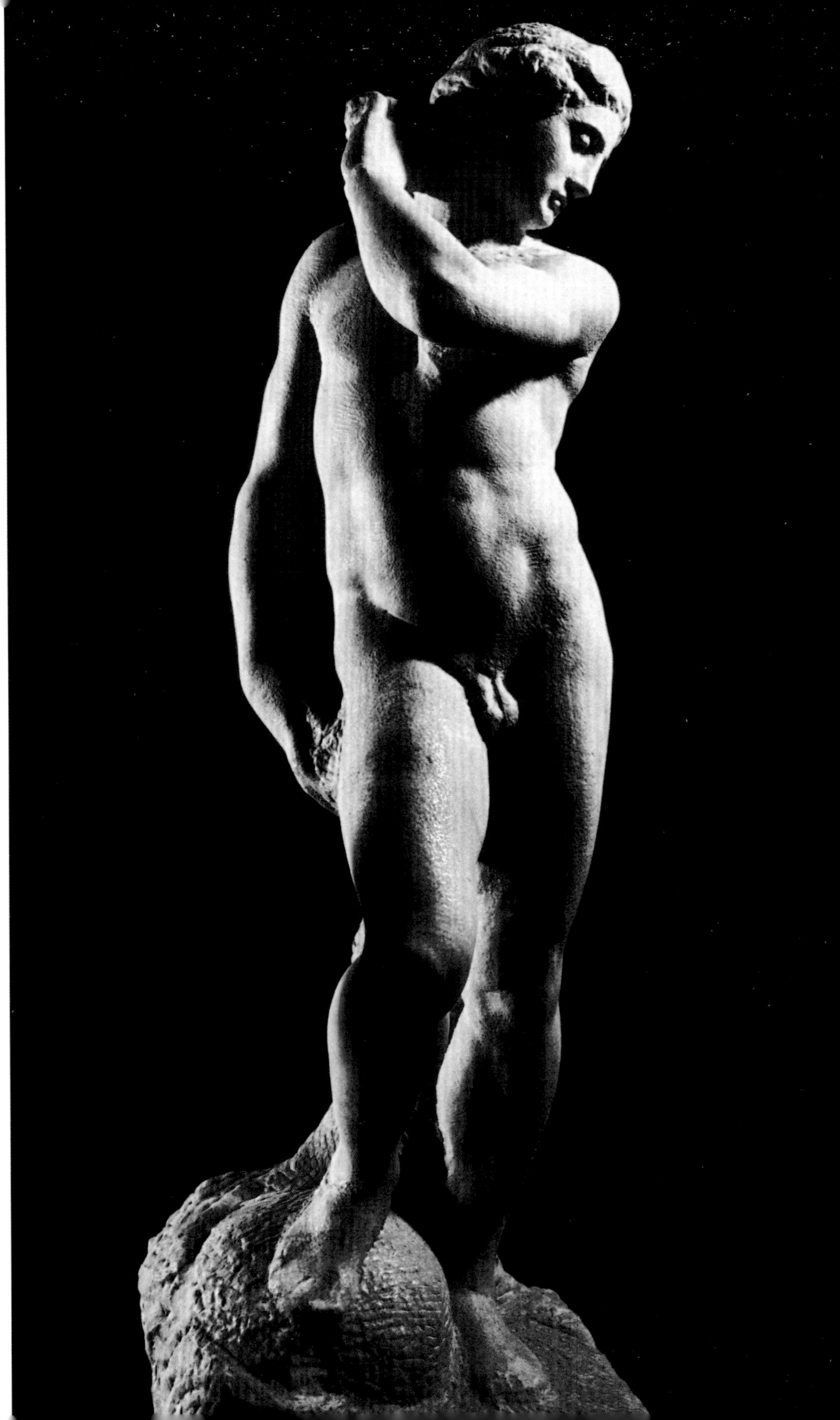

Michelangelo, *Apollo/David,*
statue of an unidentified
young archer
Florence, Museo Nazionale
del Bargello

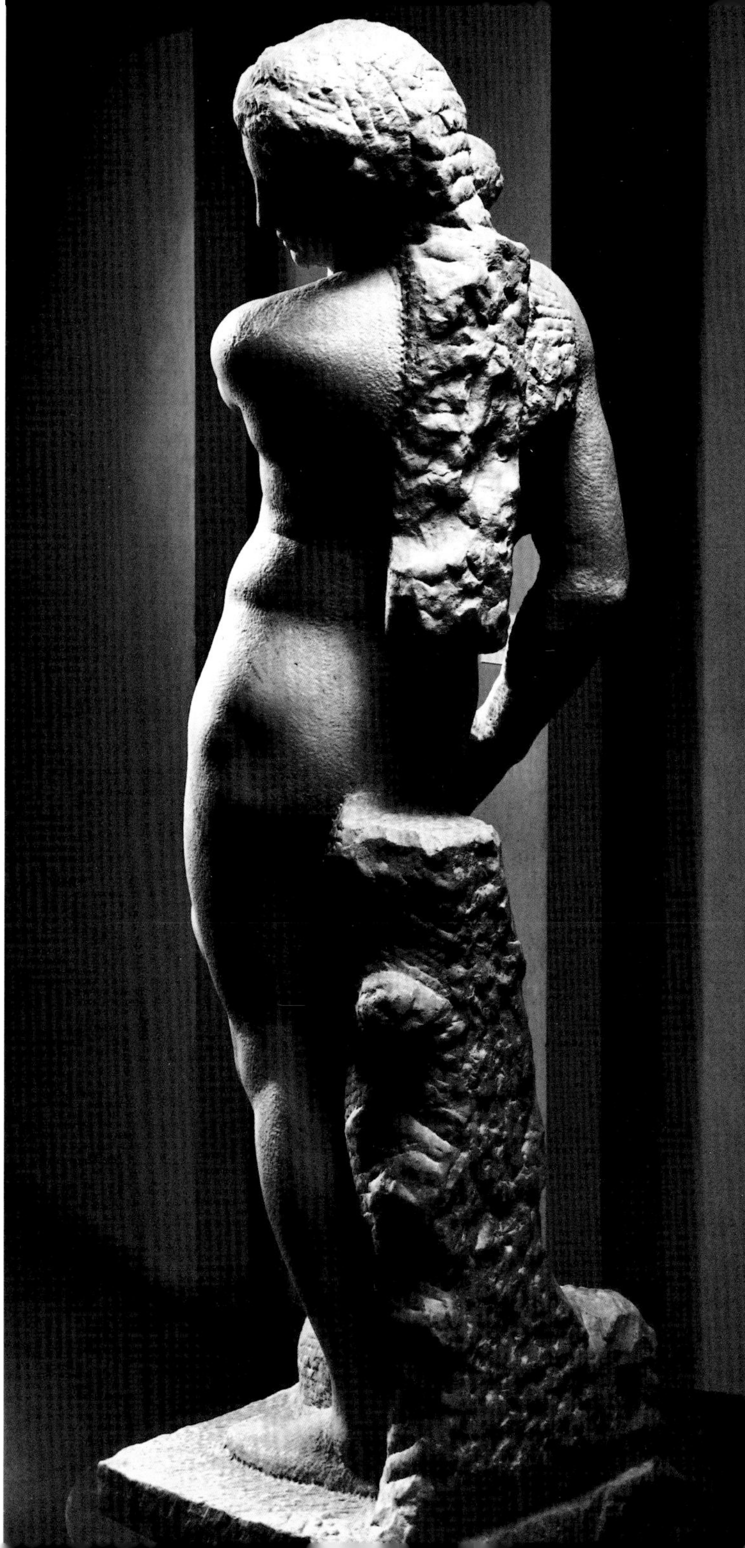

Michelangelo, *Apollo/David*
Made for Baccio Valori, the statue was never completed and eventually became a part of the Medicean collections
Florence, Museo Nazionale del Bargello

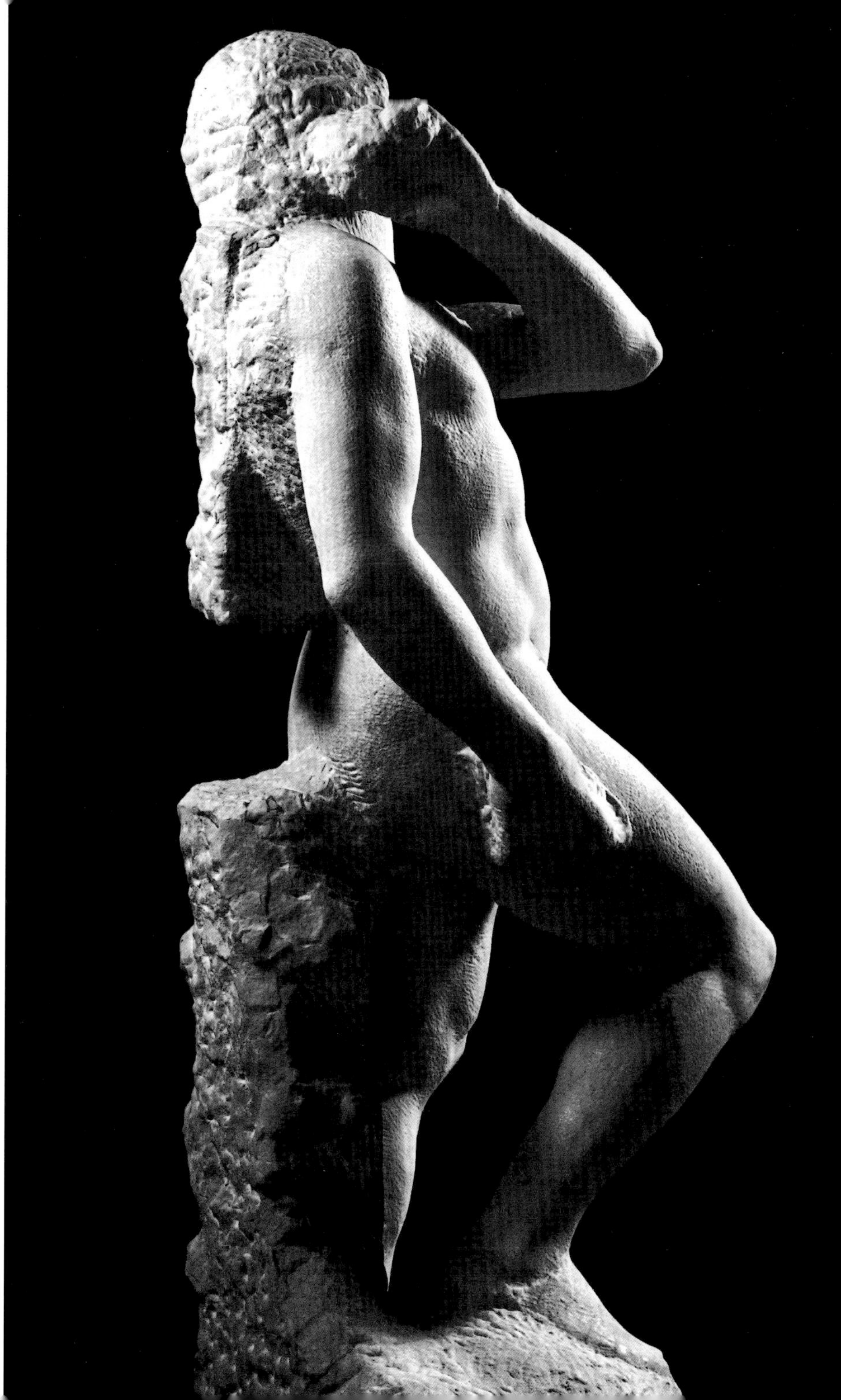

Michelangelo, *Apollo/David*
Its twisting movement is a perfect example of the "figura serpentinata" that Michelangelo encouraged other artists to use
Florence, Museo Nazionale del Bargello

image of the Old Testament character represented more than any other in Florence from the 14th century on, a symbol of the victory of the just protected by God.
The archer's movement as he draws an arrow from the quiver that hangs from his shoulder leads into an overall harmonious twisting, reminiscent of the solutions used in the *Minerva Chri*st and in other figures (one arm hangs at his side while the other is raised and bent, his legs are apart, his feet at different levels, he tilts his head at the same turning turning his neck); but what is achieved here, by way of the figure's vague, absorbed expression, is calm and unconstrained sweetness.
Although the sculpture is substantially complete, the nude youth does feature unfinished parts in the hair and limbs, while the coarse surfaces of the rock and trunk suggest naturalistic effects. The treatment of the skin, which never reaches a final polish, shows signs of the creative passage of the claw-chisel. This "foggy definition of the forms"[25] has inspired suggestive interpretations of the statue in a 20th-century psychological key, for which an excellent example is Tolnay's comment of Freudian inspiration: "it is conceived not as a body that is alive, but as the embodiment of a psychological state [...] the position is that of someone turning in his sleep. The gestures seem unconscious reflexes, like those of a person who is dreaming and wants to put an end to a nightmare".[26] Moreover, in light of considerations regarding the Bologna *Saint Proculus*, the New York *Young Archer* and the Florence *David*, I would be encouraged to draw attention to the unsteady, transitory nature of the stance. Like a cinematic frame, the action depicted corresponds to a precise instant, and it is so exact that it presupposes as follows: the arrow is drawn, the arm straightens, the figure gazes in the direction of an invisible bow. While the blurry softness of the unpolished limbs suggests dream-like slow motion – to use another cinematic term – if the statue had been finished, the organized sequence of bodily movements would have expressed a much more penetrating kind of latent energy, ready to spring.

The four Florentine *Captives*

The agreement stipulated with Leo X allowed Michelangelo to continue carving marbles for the figures – single ones and in pairs – for the lower storey of the Julius Tomb. The four *Captives* currently at the Galleria dell'Accademia in Florence thus date from the artist's Florentine period. They are: the *Young Captive*, the *Bearded Captive*, the so-called *Atlas*, the *Awakening Captive*, and the group known as *The Victory*, now called the *Genius of Victory*: the former are housed in the Galleria dell'Accademia in Florence, the latter is in the Palazzo Vecchio.
These sculptures continued to be considered of use to the tomb until a new contract, the fourth, was drawn up between the Della Rovere heirs and Michelangelo on 29 April 1532, also thanks to the intervention of Pope Clement VII, on the basis of a new idea. This act had been preceded by complicated negotiations, including an estimate of the parts of the tomb that had already been prepared by Sebastiano del Piombo, which Michelangelo had wisely had his friend send him a year before in order to deal with the Della Rovere family's agent with greater self-assurance.[27]
One of the reasons for redrafting the contract was the change in the location of the tomb: as the building for the new Saint Peter's was not yet completed, after considering – but then rejecting – Santa Maria del Popolo (which would have pleased Francesco Maria Della Rovere, Duke of Urbino), the final choice fell on San Pietro in Vincoli, where Clement VII gave his permission to have the altar with Saint Peter's chains, the "vincula", removed. This significant relic was translated to the high altar. When the contract was drawn up, the project for the monument was not final: it had by now become a wall façade, but Michelangelo would provide a design for it when the exact location had been chosen. The artist agreed to supply six statues by his own hand ("they will be incomparable" were agent Giovan Maria della Porta's reassuring words to the Duke of Urbino)[28] and the execution of the missing archi-

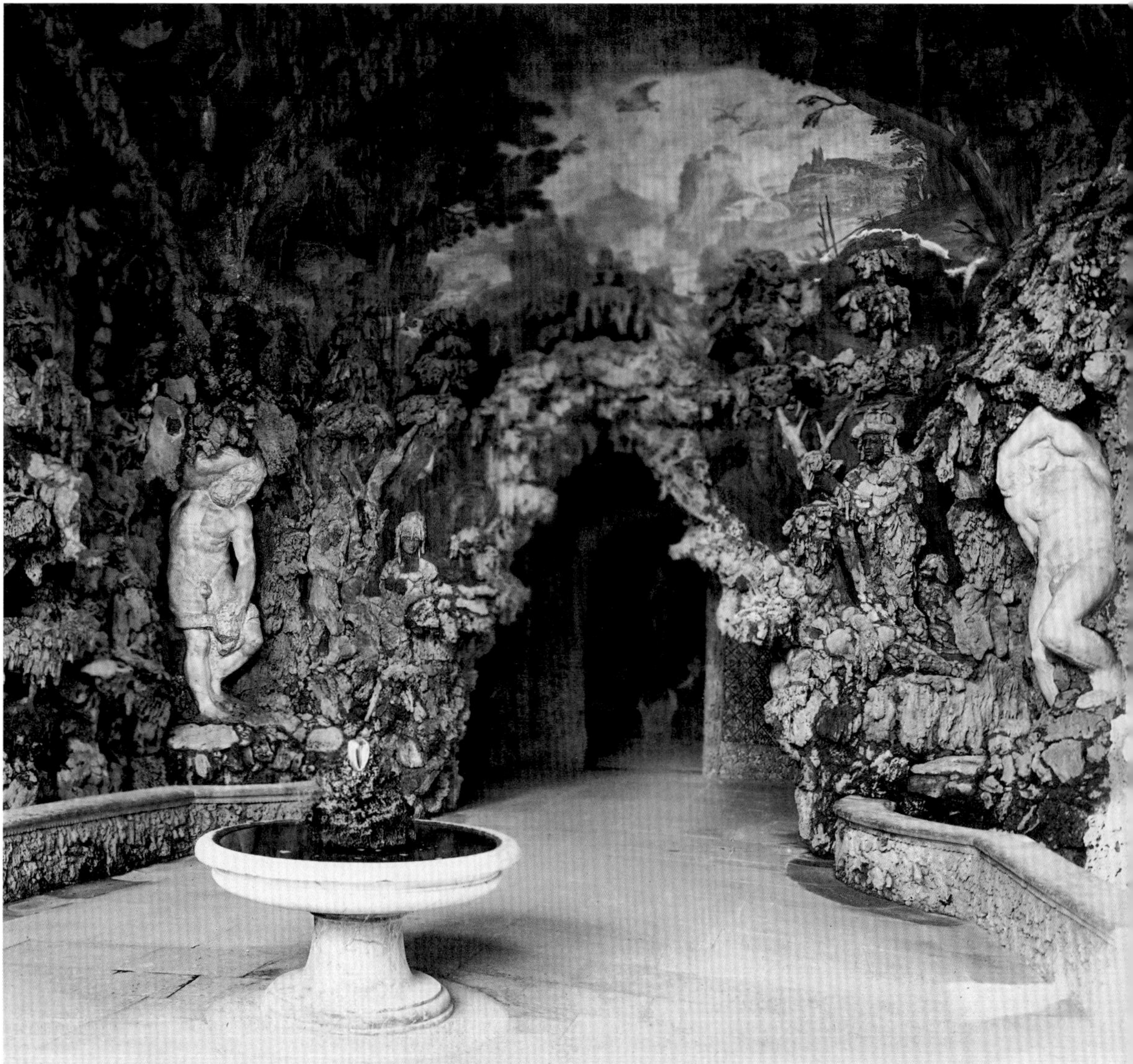

The *Grotta Grande* in Florence's Boboli Gardens, in the corners of which Bernardo Buontalenti set Michelangelo's four *Captives* (originally made for the *Tomb of Julius II*), as part of the rustic scenery

tectural framing, if necessary by the hand of someone under his direction.The contract states that in June 1532, Michelangelo had four of the six figures ready in Rome: these included the two *Slaves* currently at the Louvre (which could not have been completed at the time, however) and the *Moses*. It was recently hypothesized that the fourth statue was a reclining figure of the pope, but this shall be dealt with further on.[29]

At the time, in his combination workshop and home in Via Mozza, Michelangelo was working on other statues for the tomb. But all of these were incomplete. And since the contract only required that he make two statues to be added to the four that he already had in Rome, Michelangelo may have slowed down to concentrate on the two male figures making up *The Victory*.

The *Captives* were thus left in an endless "non-finito" state, ready, in just a few years, to become the exemplary expression of a new category of Florentine sculpture. This category was neither recommended as an example, nor practised, but it was ennobled and elaborated on from a critical standpoint. Despite the feature they all to varying degrees have in common, i.e. their "non-finito" state, visible, nonetheless, are postures and accessories such as chains and binding elements which bestow upon these figures attitudes of suffering varyingly interpreted as awakening, affliction, the struggle for freedom. Although their state cannot be compared to the artist's painting, which was brought to a "finished state" in the words of his biographers, these *Captives* can be compared to some of the resurrected figures in the *Last Judgement* that he would paint a few years later, protagonists of the weary exit from the Earth's hold, still bound by the ropes used to bury them and by sudaria.

Like for the statues at the Louvre, the name *Captives* is relatively recent and purely conventional.

The *Young Captive*

The statue was called the *Young Captive* because of the combination of soft, smooth facial features and a vigorous body. The figure recalls the Louvre *Slaves*: his right arm restrained behind his back is like the *Rebellious Slave*'s, while his left arm crosses his head like the *Dying Slave*'s (which he was probably supposed to replace). But the difference here is that his hand hangs down right in front of his bowed face, as if to protect it. The body, pervaded by rotations of the torso and bending of the limbs, is still a part of the original block of marble, just barely blocked out in the back and at the bottom. The portions of the statue that are more developed, such as one side of the breast and some of the passages in the arms and legs, nonetheless show signs of furrowing with a pointed chisel and a variety of claw-chisels. The position and development of the body tell us that the figure was intended to have a frontal position. A preliminary red wax model believed to be an autograph is now at the Victoria and Albert Museum in London.[30]

The figure's indistinct expression suggests that he is slowly awaking, but if we accept the idea that the *Captives* were meant to represent the affliction of the Arts and Disciplines for the loss of Julius II, then the forced and restrained must be interpreted as the effect of painful consternation.

The *Bearded Captive*

The tremendous suffering caused by the state of captivity is expressed here through the resentment of the body, which is crushed and as if collapsed under the weight of the arm and the portion of rough-hewed block attached above and behind the head. The figure was to be assigned a frontal position. The broad torso and powerful way the thighs are attached, their shapely muscles visible at the very surface, would suggest a derivation from the *Belvedere Torso* by the Hellenistic artist Apollonius. Bound to his native marble, by thick ropes as well, the *Captive* holds enough raw material in his left hand for an attribute to be fashioned.

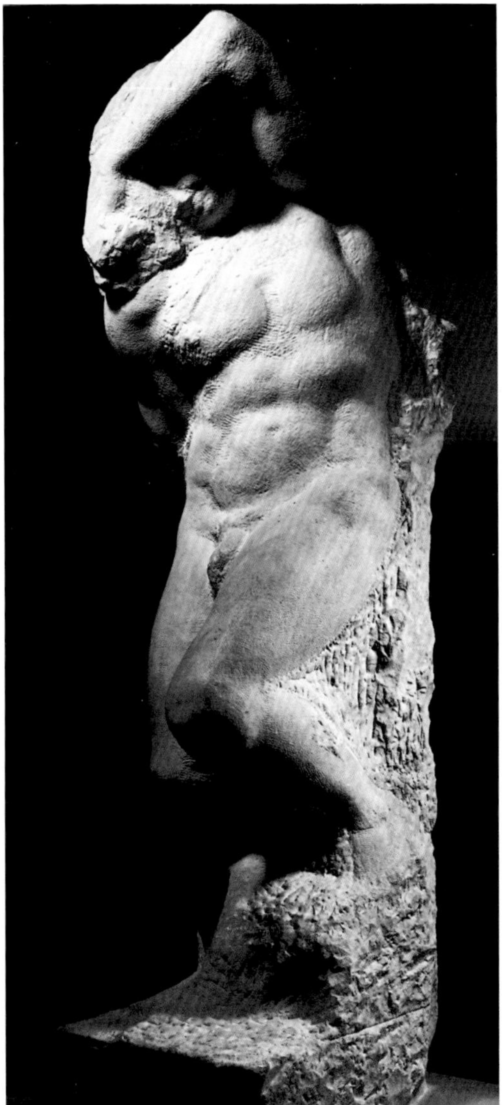

Michelangelo, *The Young Captive*, whose mighty body emerges from the marble block
Florence, Galleria dell'Accademia

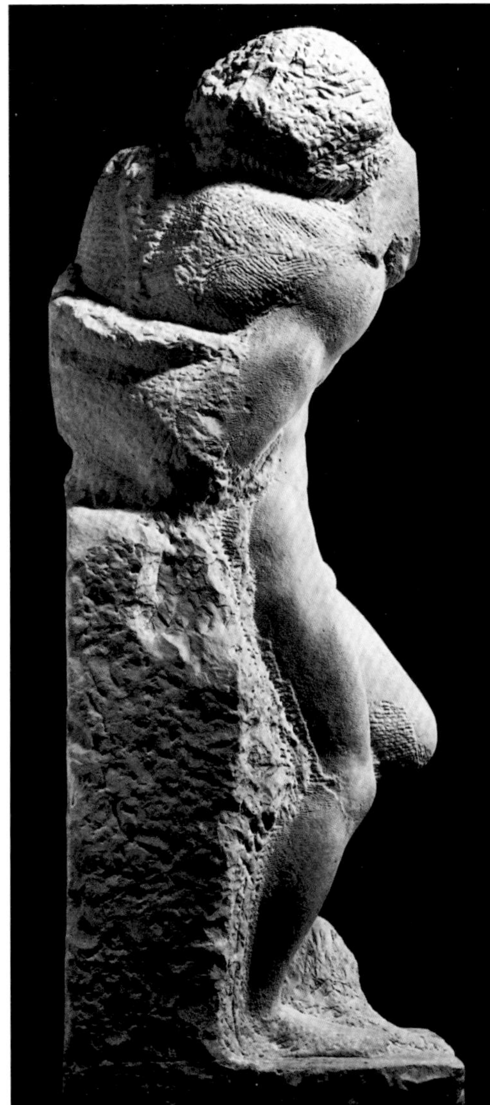

Michelangelo, *The Young Captive*, profile view showing the roughed-out mass
Florence, Galleria dell'Accademia

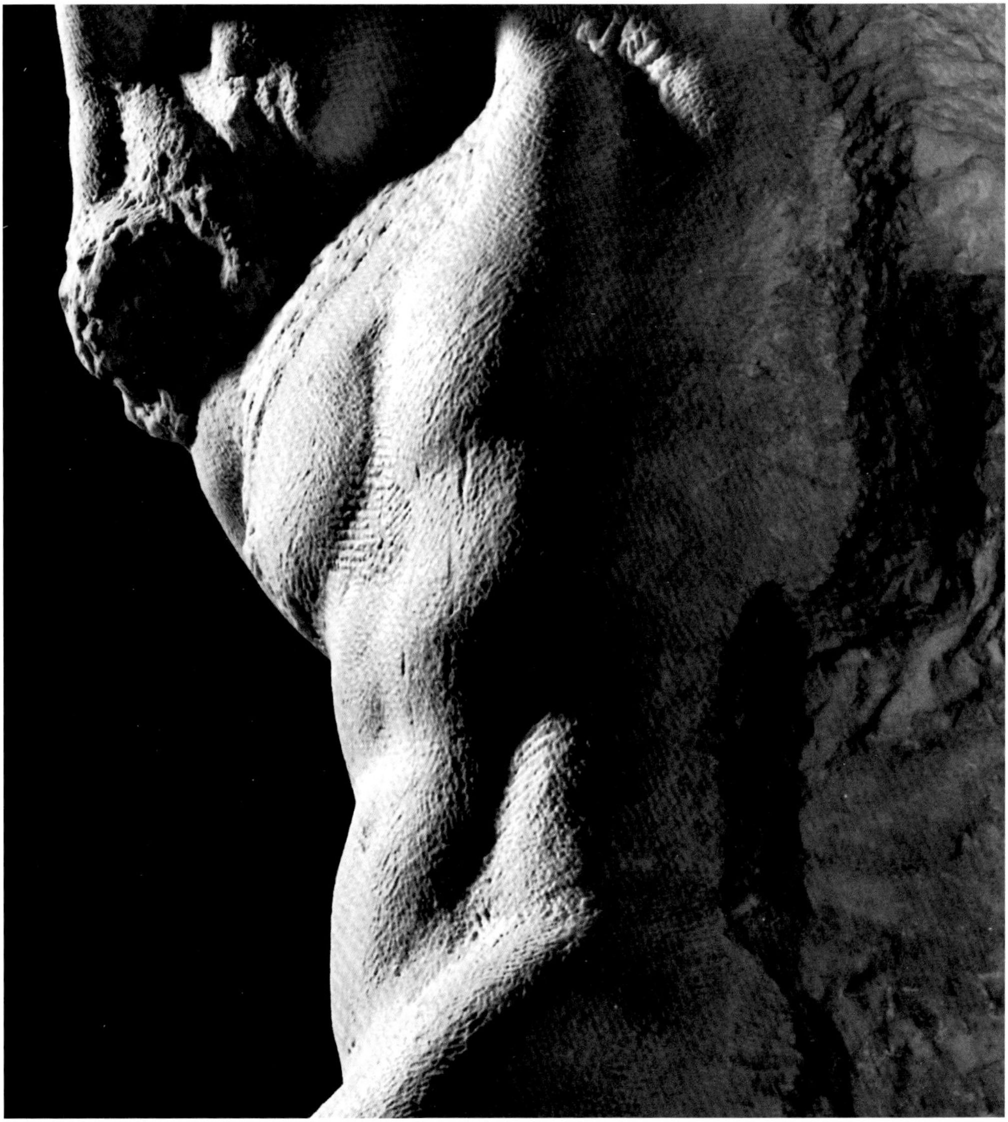

Michelangelo, *The Young Captive*, foreshortened view of the torso and hips
Florence, Galleria dell'Accademia

p. 219
Michelangelo, *The Young Captive*, detail of the arm crossing his forehead perhaps expressing the desire for protection from a disconcerting and painful view
Florence, Galleria dell'Accademia

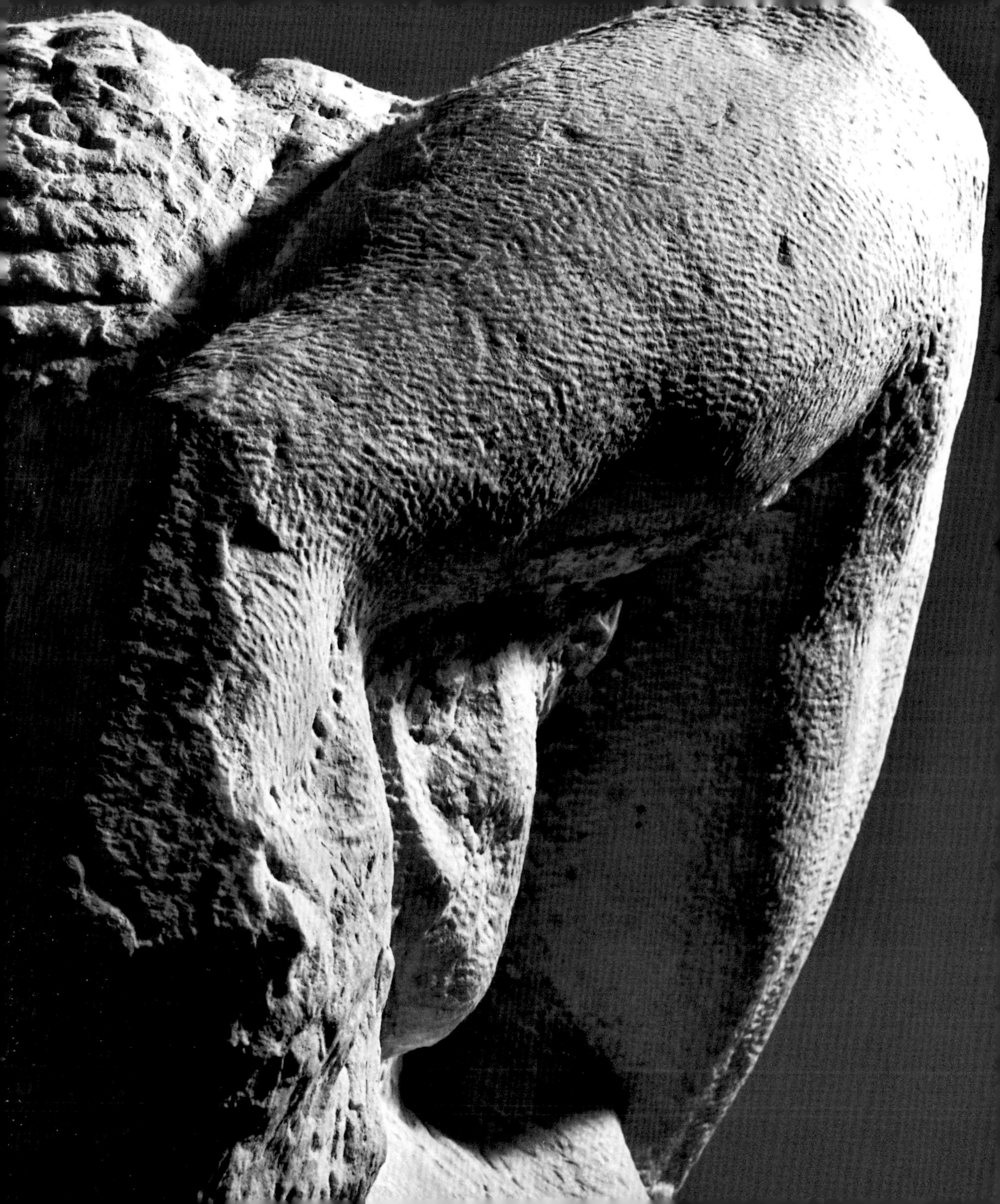

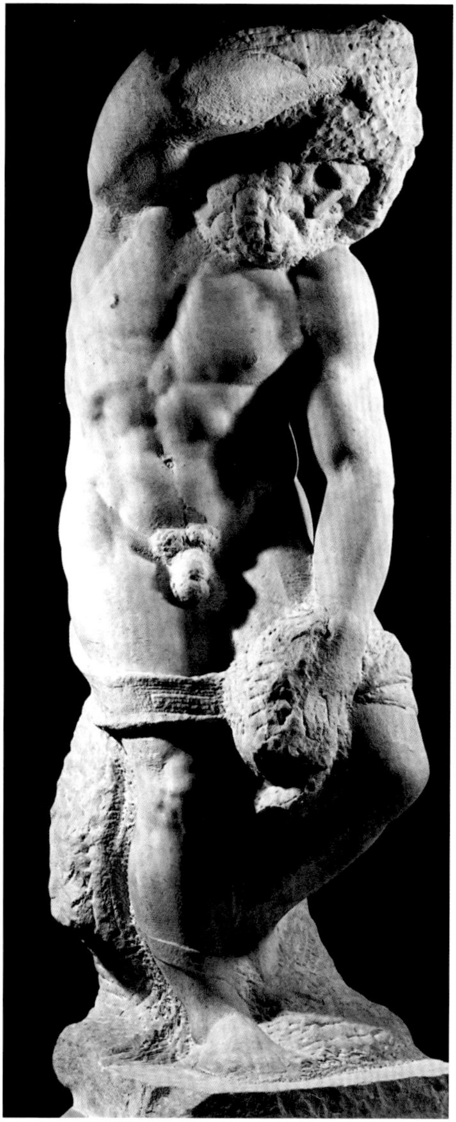

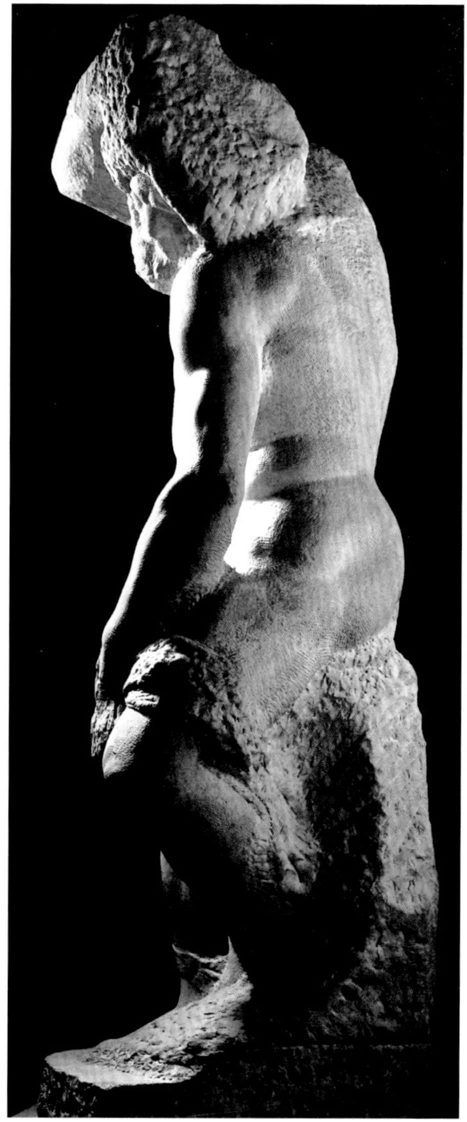

Michelangelo, *The Bearded Captive*. Whereas the central portion of the body was worked on, the remainder was left in a "non-finito" state
Florence, Galleria dell'Accademia

Michelangelo, *The Bearded Captive*
Florence, Galleria dell'Accademia

The so-called *Atlas*

This is the most impressive of all of the *Captives* owing to the effect produced by the laboured, partial emergence of the figure from the mighty depth of the block. Nor can his head be freed (released), imprisoned as it is in the piece of marble itself. The sculptor had imagined an image for the legs that he had used before, one straight and the other bent; the torso was instead meant to feature a gradual twisting that culminated upwards with the torsion of the shoulders and the oblique movement of the head. Designed to be placed on a corner, the figure conceals his right arm but brings his left one forwards, probably to express grief.
The statue's "non-finito" state is such that the upper portion of the marble still shows Michelangelo's identification marks and those of the quarrymen: three circles to indicate that the block belonged to Michelangelo, an inscribed "L" that stands for the quarryman Leone, a stylized boat, a three-pronged instrument. The block had been sketched out and and its size recorded by Michelangelo in the "book" he used for notarial purposes when the marble was already in the port area.[31] Especially interesting is the comparison between the blocked-out *Captive* and the original shape of the block, which was rather irregular and characterized by a very evident projection. The artist was not indifferent to this particular feature, which must have offered him ideas and suggestions.

The *Awakening Captive*

Like the *Atlas*, this figure was also roughed out from inside the block and worked on "di spigolo". It was evidently meant to be placed on one of the corners of the tomb. The posture of this probably bearded man is complex and sophisticated: bent backwards, his head brusquely tilted to the side, he hints at lifting his left arm and pulling his right one back. The figure crosses his legs with the same kind of emphasis that we saw in the New Sacristy's *Dusk*. The current interpretation of the figure, which is also where it gets its name, says that the *Captive* is the protagonist of a "violent struggle against sleep so that he may attain awareness".[32] Sleep of this kind is a metaphor for the brutal state of the earliest intellectual, religious and artistic life for which the just roughed-out marble tenaciously restraining the figure offers a visual equivalent. But in place of this undoubtedly fascinating reading, which combines Neoplatonic concepts with Freudian suggestions, I prefer to search for clues to explain the composition in Michelangelo's figurative corpus: perhaps the Sistine's *Jonas*, frightened by the monster on its way, reveals the same kind of sudden throwing oneself backwards in fear that we see in this *Captive*, who, like Jonas, is trying to escape from impending horror, although in vain.
Michelangelo may have formulated other ideas in relation to the theme of *Slaves* or *Captives*, but in a preliminary form that was never fully developed: this might explain the small autograph model made of dark wax and other materials currently in the Casa Buonarroti (inv. 542).[33]
The four *Captives* were left behind in the workshop in Via Mozza when Michelangelo moved to Rome in 1534. When the artist died, his nephew Lionardo offered them, along with the *Victory*, to Duke Cosimo de' Medici. While the Grand Duke Francesco I was in rule, a place was found for the four roughed-out statues, the highest possible expression of "non-finito", thanks to Bernardo Buontalenti, a versatile artist famous for his devotion to the memory of Michelangelo.[34] Buontalenti saw the four statues as a perfect device for the first chamber of the Boboli Garden's Grotta Grande (1585-1588) as an architectural and plastic scheme alluding to the primordial flood that led to the metamorphosis of inanimate matter into life. Set within these "spongy" walls with jagged protruberances, the *Captives* dramatically expressed the notion of human form struggling to free itself from the restraint of rough stone. This creative use of

p. 222
Michelangelo, *The Bearded Captive*, detail of his distressed and bowed face
Florence, Galleria dell'Accademia

p. 223
Michelangelo, *The Bearded Captive*, detail of the torso muscles, which express a vibrant dynamism, despite the "non-finito" state of the work
Florence, Galleria dell'Accademia

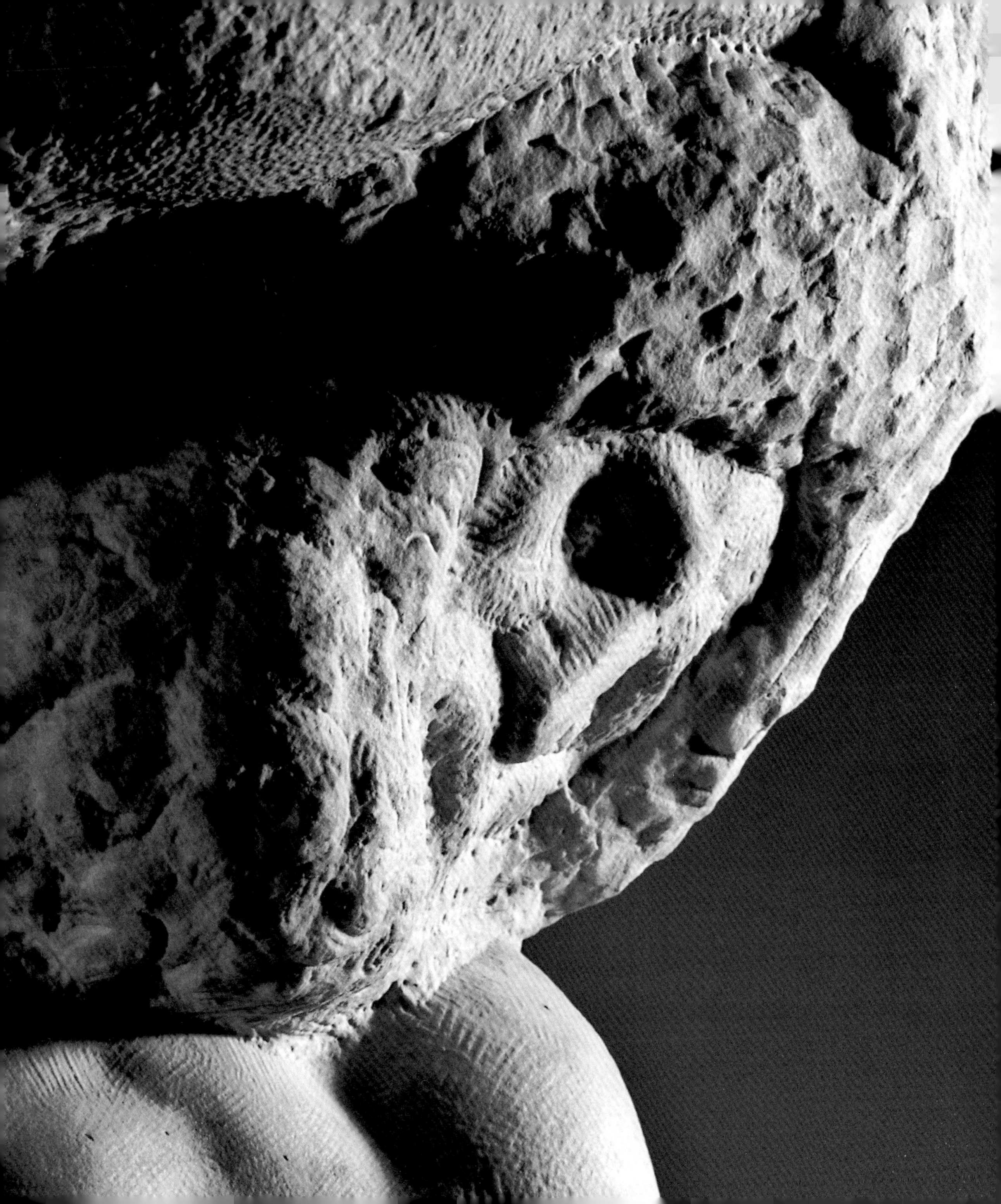

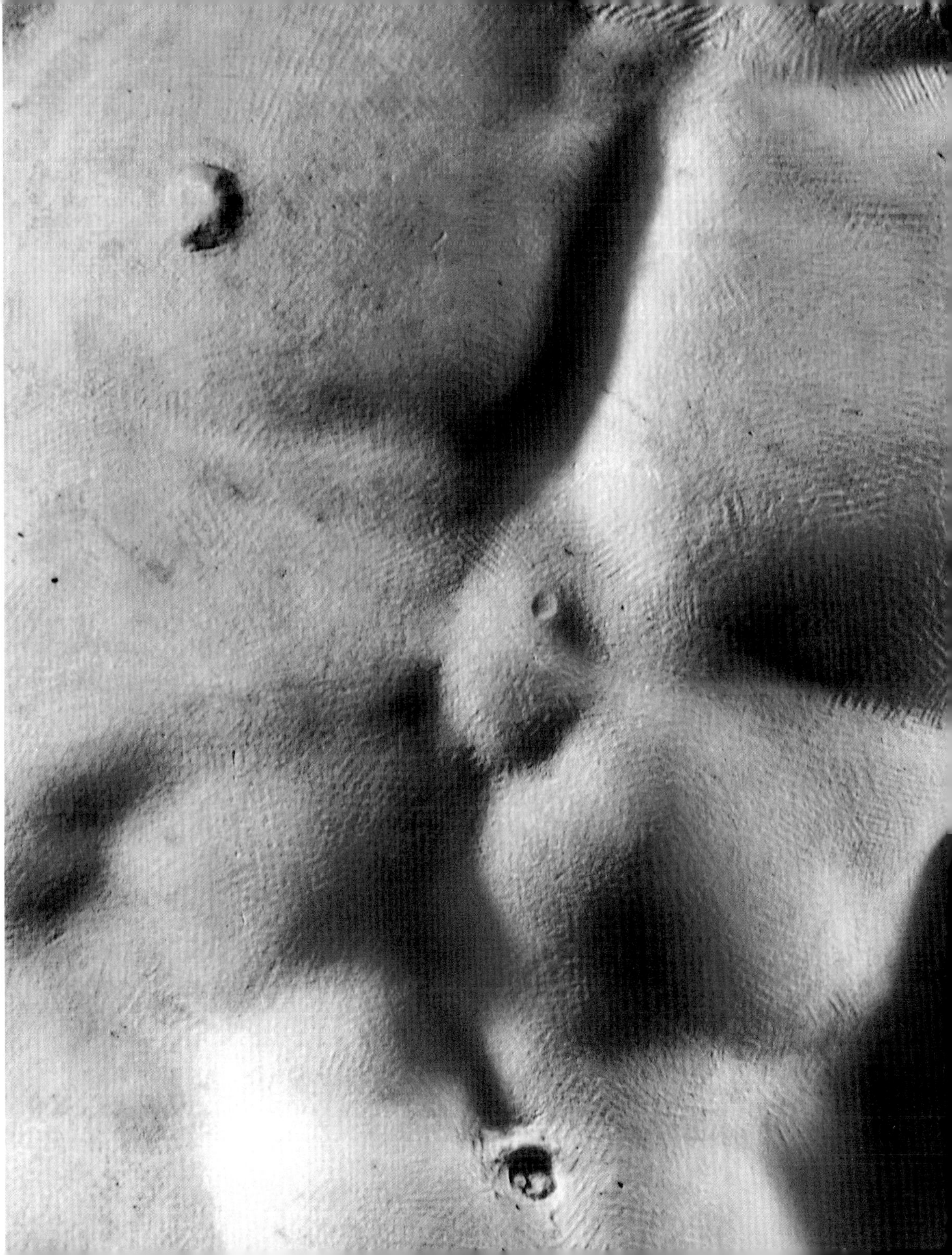

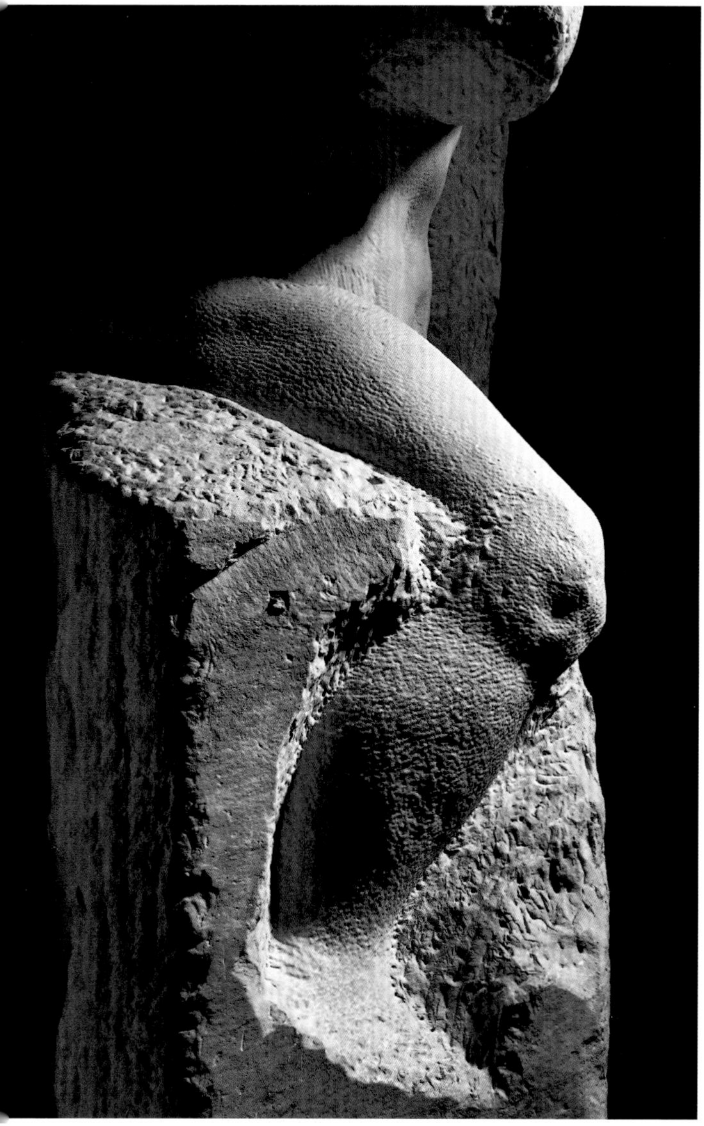

Michelangelo, the so-called *Atlas*, side view emphasizing its "non-finito" state
Florence, Galleria dell'Accademia

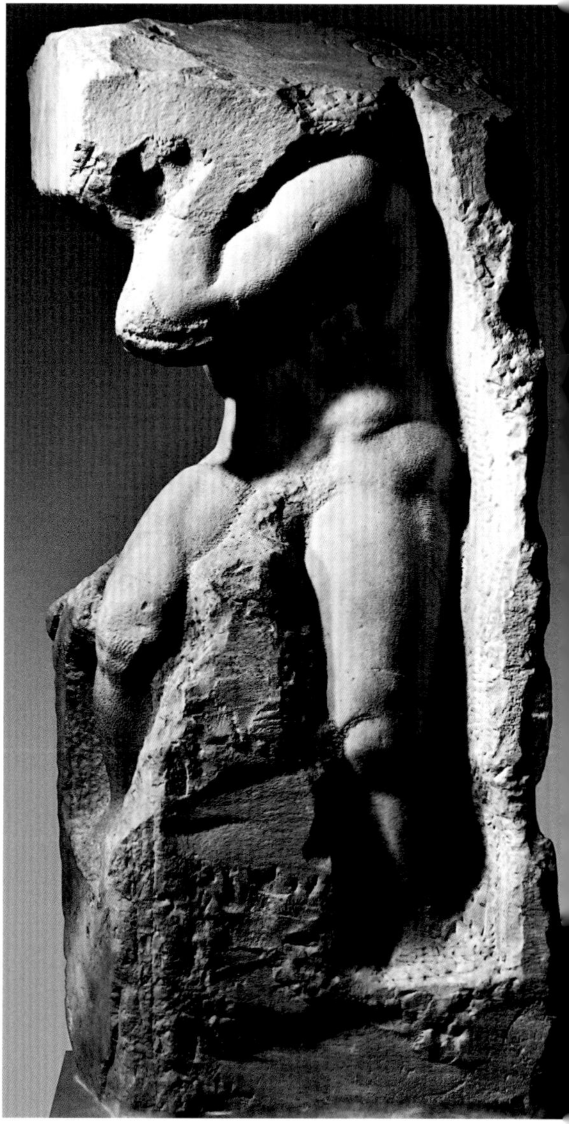

Michelangelo, the so-called *Atlas*
The work got its name of mythological inspiration from the "non-finito" of the head, a mass protruding from the block which the figure seems to struggle to support
Florence, Galleria dell'Accademia

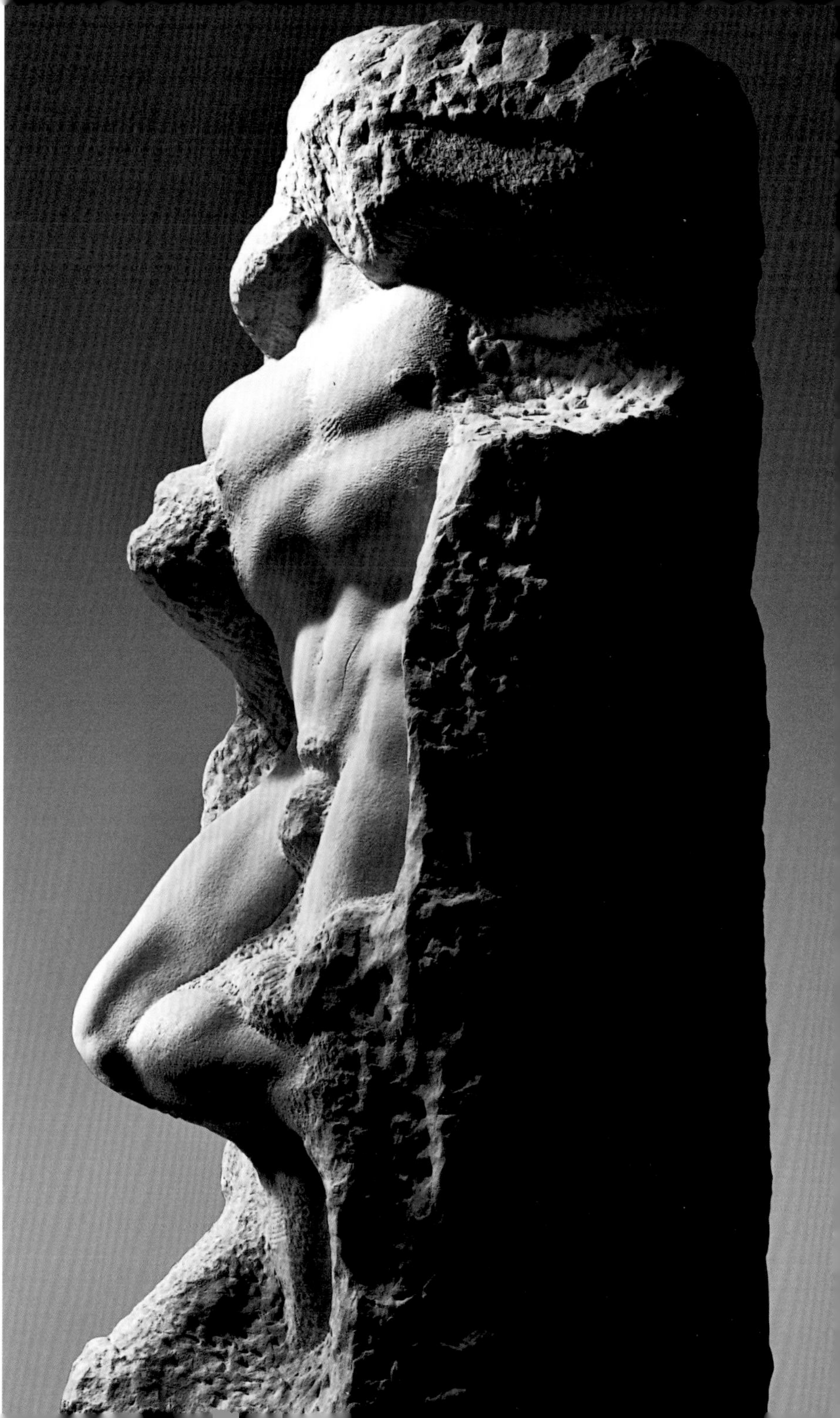

Michelangelo, *The Awakening Captive.* The conventional name is suggested by the idea of a gradual release from the burden of the material
Florence, Galleria dell'Accademia

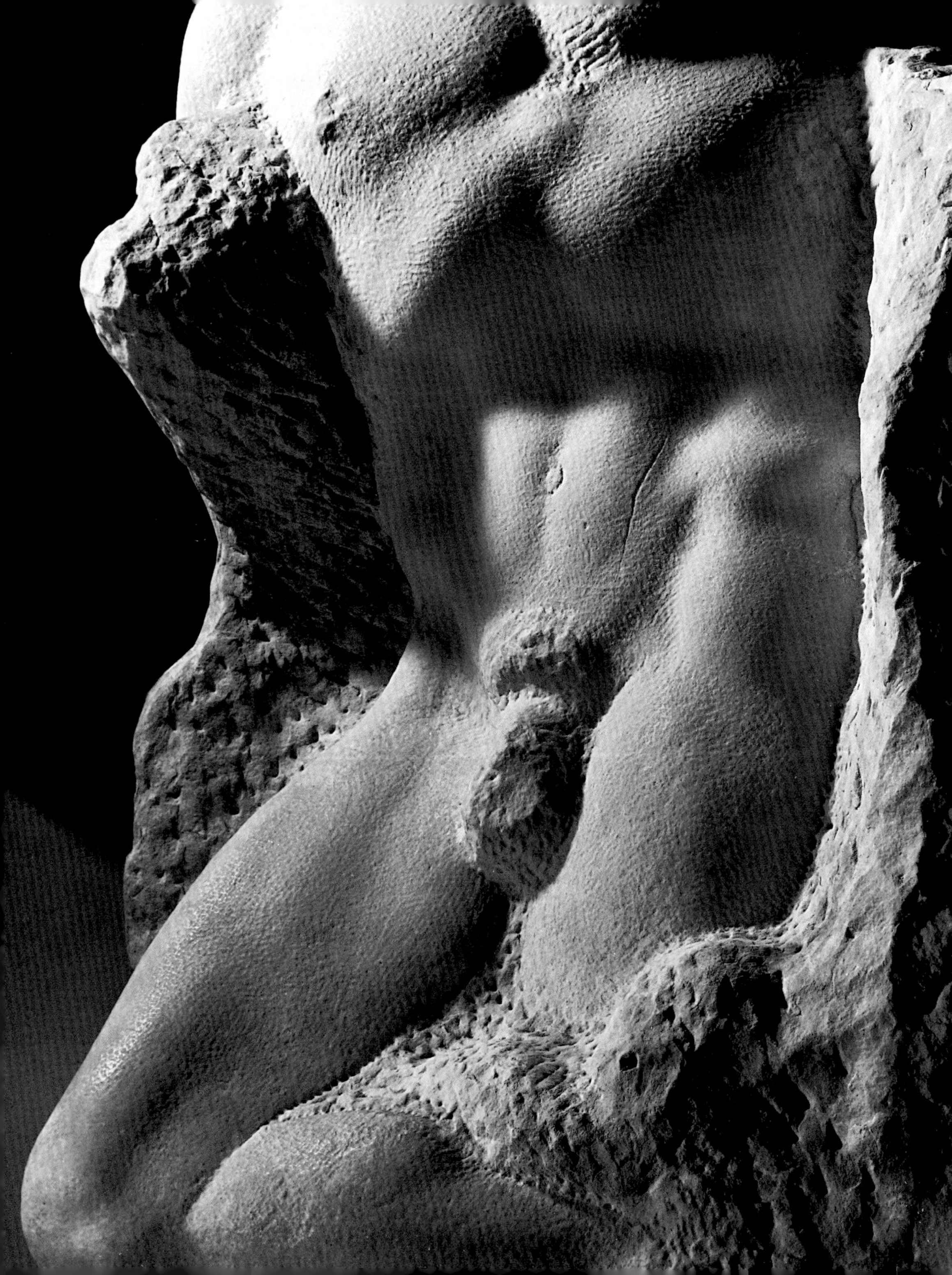

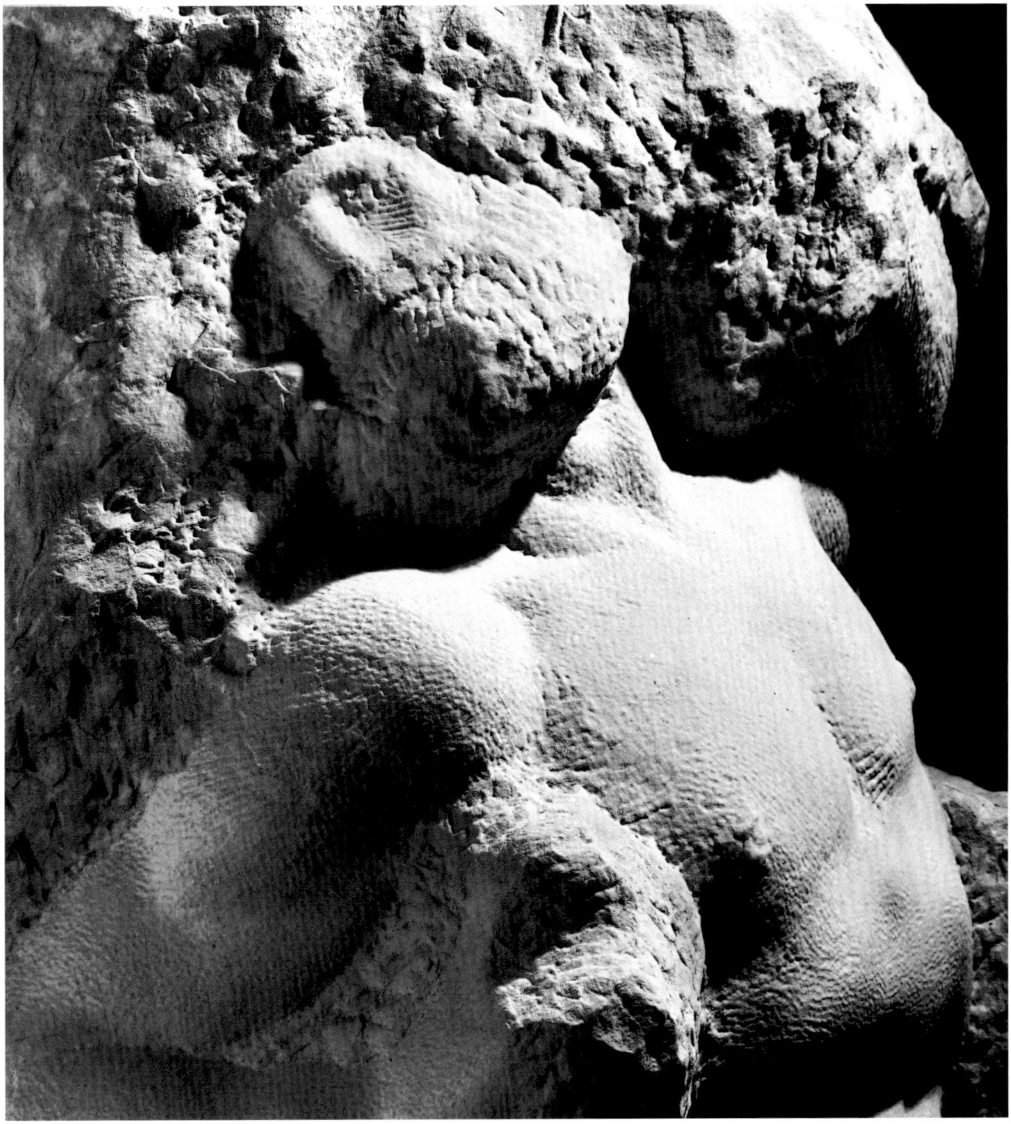

p. 226
Michelangelo, *The Awakening Captive*, central portion of the body
Florence, Galleria dell'Accademia

Michelangelo, *The Awakening Captive*. The pathetic twist of the head, with the face turned upwards, is a further allusion to the *Laocoön*
Florence, Galleria dell'Accademia

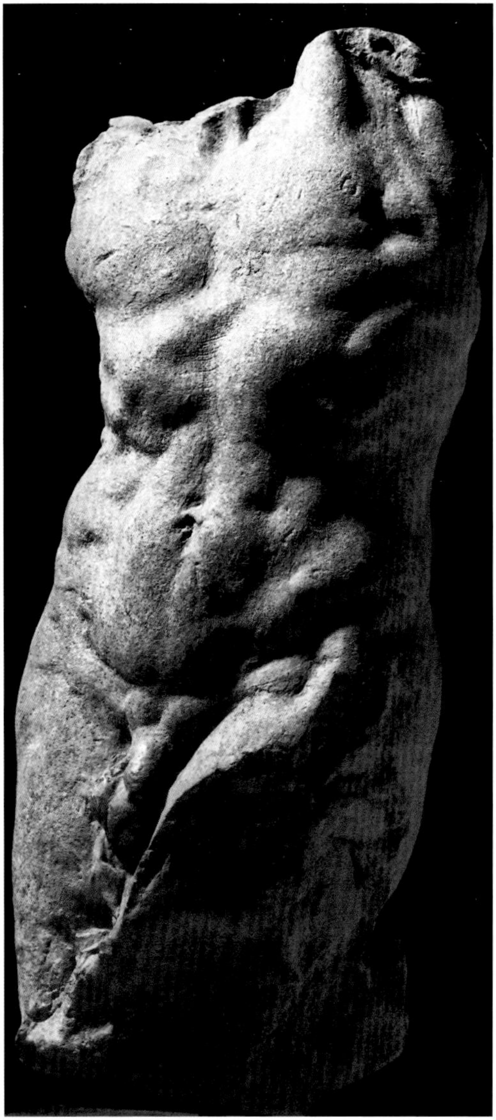

Michelangelo, light-coloured terracotta model for a *Male Torso*, associated with the project for the *Slaves* and *Captives* for the *Tomb of Julius II*
Florence, Museo di Casa Buonarroti

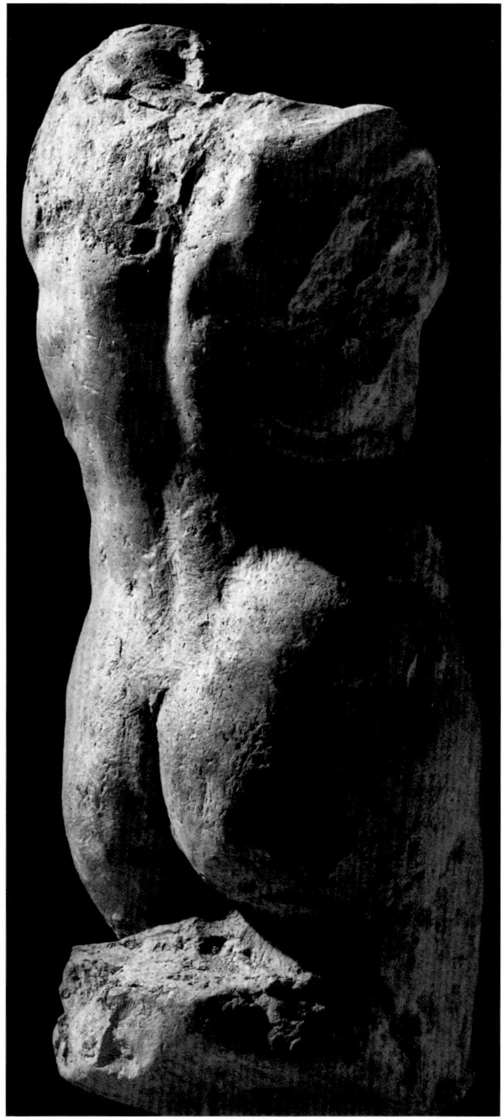

Michelangelo, light-coloured terracotta model for a *Male Torso*, resembling the *Dying Slave* at the Louvre
Florence, Museo di Casa Buonarroti

the statues represented a formidable interpretative contribution to the theme of Michelangelo's "non-finito", varyingly dealt with by biographers and contemporary experts, and still today at the heart of lively critical debate. The first explanation for the statues' symbolism was offered by Francesco Bocchi in 1591: "roughed out with incredible and marvellous artifice, these figures reveal with every effort their desire to be freed from the marble so that they may escape the ruin which is above them".[35] The critic's words are a reminder of the original iconographic programme for the *Captives*: the ruin of knowledge in the world caused by the death of Pope Della Rovere.
The statues were removed from the Grotta Grande in 1909 and placed in the Galleria dell'Accademia. The original *Captives* were substituted by copies.

The *Victory*

The group was conventionally named the *Genius of Victory* for the sake of genre, but the sources, beginning with Vasari, call Michelangelo's first invention a *Victory*:[36] this was indeed the meaning it was to have for the Julius Tomb, to which, along with other groups, it was to be inset in niches that were never executed. From the very few extant drawings for the tomb, it seems that the pairs of figures for the niches, which personified a positive principle defeating a negative one, originally featured females protagonists, the *Victories*, to be exact, but that these were later replaced by victorious males.[37]
This statuary group, situated in the Palazzo Vecchio in 1565, is the only one that was actually carved.
There is a tendency to consider the light-coloured terracotta model named *Two Wrestlers* now in the Casa Buonarroti, whose autograph has been firm for some time now, as a preparatory study for another pair with the same destination. Although the subject lends itself to other interpretations (*Hercules and Cacus*, *Samson Slaying a Philistine* or, although less likely, *Hercules and Antaeus*), its composition, made up of a victor and a vanquished figure, both violently entangled in a zigzagging dynamic of forced and bent limbs, would be suited to one of the *Victories* intended for the Julius Tomb.[38] Also compatible with the idea of the niche as a final destination is the missing right arm, which is not lost: believed to be unnecessary it was never made.[39]
Carved out of a single block of Apuan marble, the group in the Palazzo Vecchio portrays a youth with an elongated body in an act of heroism, who uses one knee to oppress the crouching, bearded man armed *all'antica* whom he has defeated. The leaves in the crown set on the youth's hair, recognized by experts to belong to a variety of broad-leaved oak,[40] is consistent with the idea of the Pope Della Rovere monument as the final destination.
It is likely that Michelangelo began to work on the group in about 1530 and abandoned the project in 1534 when he left Florence. When the artist died in 1564, the sculpture, parts of which were incomplete, was in his workshop in Via Mozza. The asymmetries of the group, as well as the presence of "non-finito" areas on the victim's left side, indicate the angular position required for the group's insertion in a niche.
On the basis of the advice he received from Giorgio Vasari, the artist's heir Lionardo did not use the group for his uncle's tomb, but rather offered it to Duke Cosimo de' Medici, who it is believed gave it to Vincenzo Danti so that he might continue to work on it.[41]
A close examination of the statue, made possible thanks to its restoration in 1998-1999, suggests that further work involved at least the victor's head in its entirety, the features of the face and perhaps the victim's hair. This would substantiate the attribution made to the sculptor from Perugia, who was another great admirer of Michelangelo.[42] Nor can we exclude further interventions by Danti to finish the statue, specifically involving the areas of the youth's body and hand which are now smooth. The manner in which the victor markedly spreads his legs from a frontal view in order to crush his cringing victim is brought to extremes here if compared to the same gesture in other statues by the artist. In the excessive length of the victor's legs the artist went beyond the

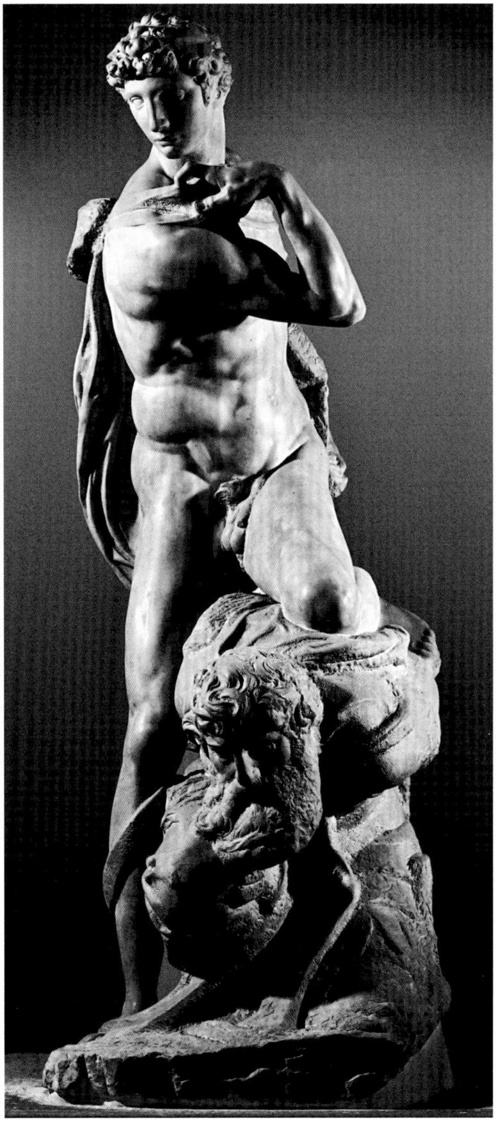

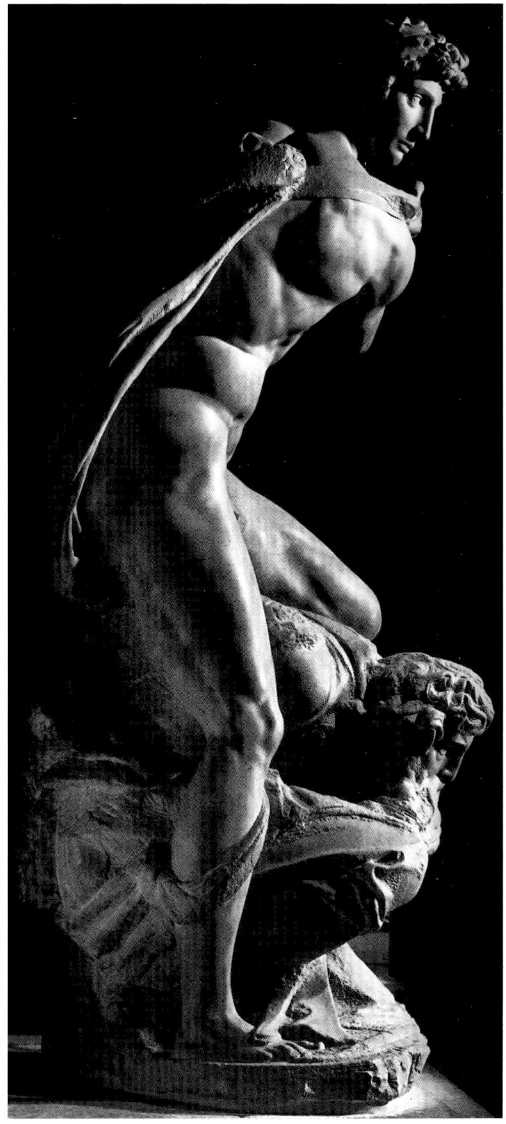

Michelangelo, *The Victory* (*The Genius of Victory*) group originally made for the *Tomb of Julius II*. When the artist died it became a part of the Medici collection, Florence, Palazzo Vecchio, Sala dei Cinquecento

Michelangelo, *The Victory* (*The Genius of Victory*), side view expressing the dramatic relationship between the triumphant victor and the vanquished figure crouching below him
Florence, Palazzo Vecchio, Sala dei Cinquecento

p. 231
Michelangelo, *The Victory* (*The Genius of Victory*), detail of the face and right hand, probably completed by Vincenzo Danti
Florence, Palazzo Vecchio, Sala dei Cinquecento

p. 232
Michelangelo, *The Victory* (*The Genius of Victory*), detail of the victor's brusquely spiralling torso
Florence, Palazzo Vecchio, Sala dei Cinquecento

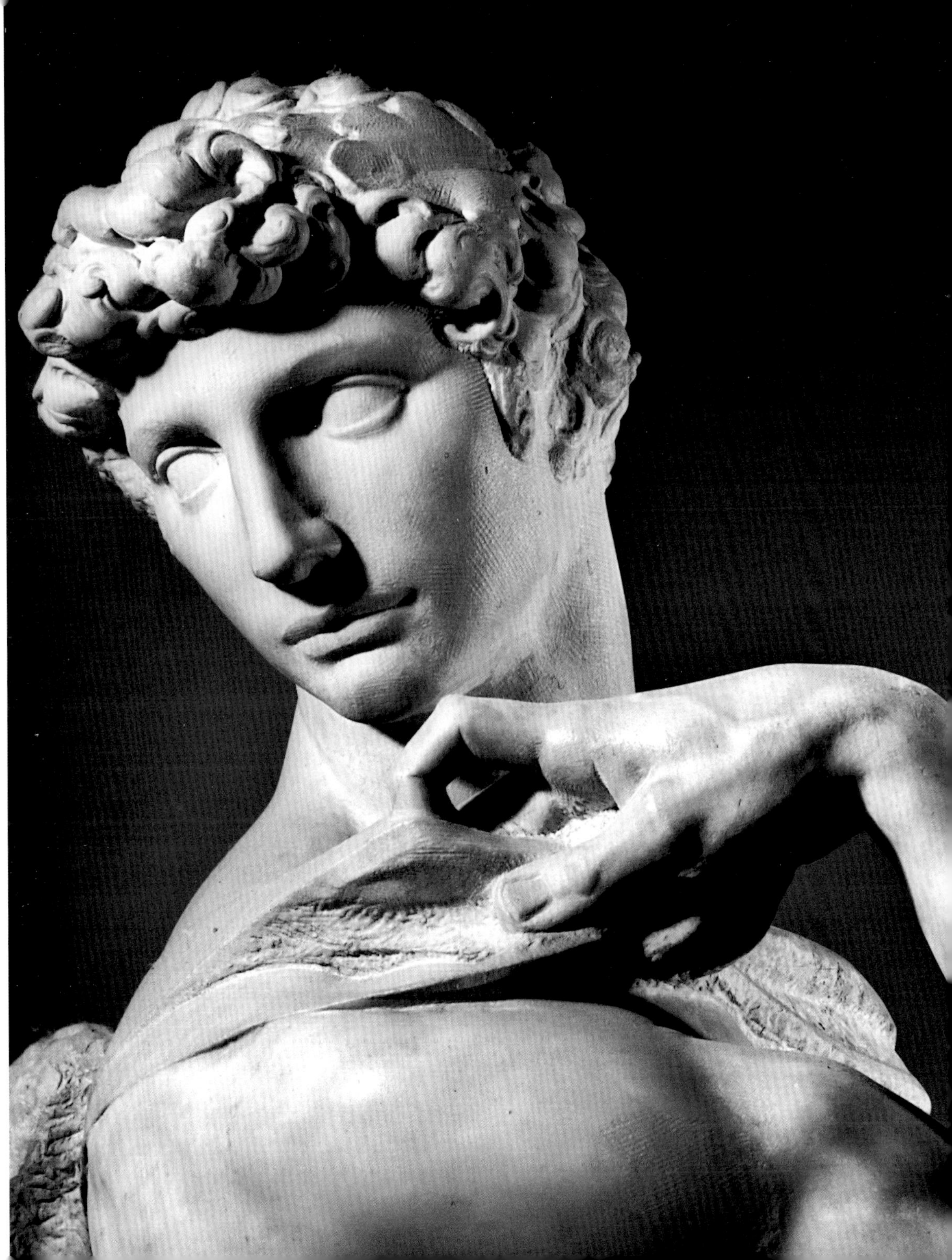

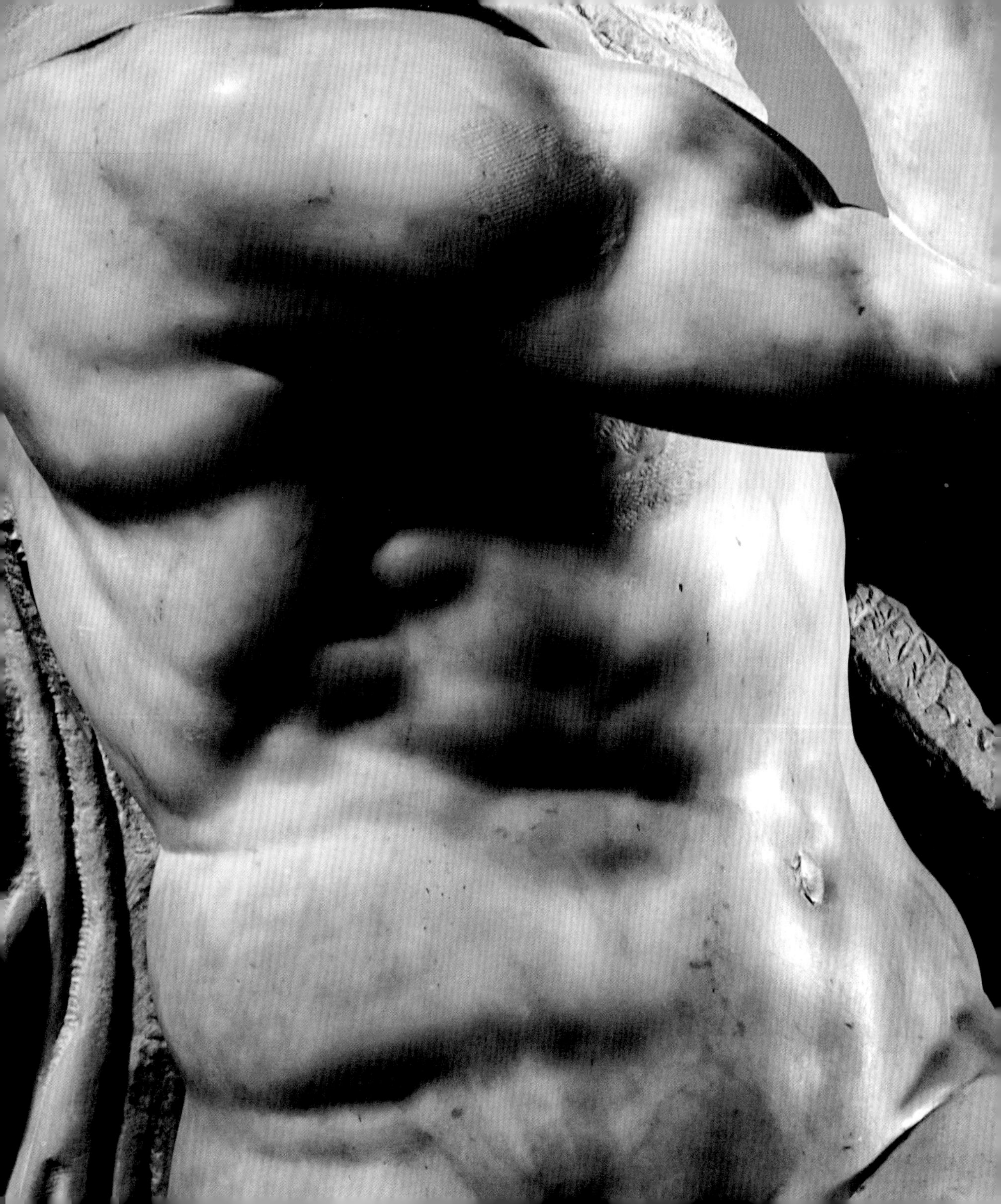

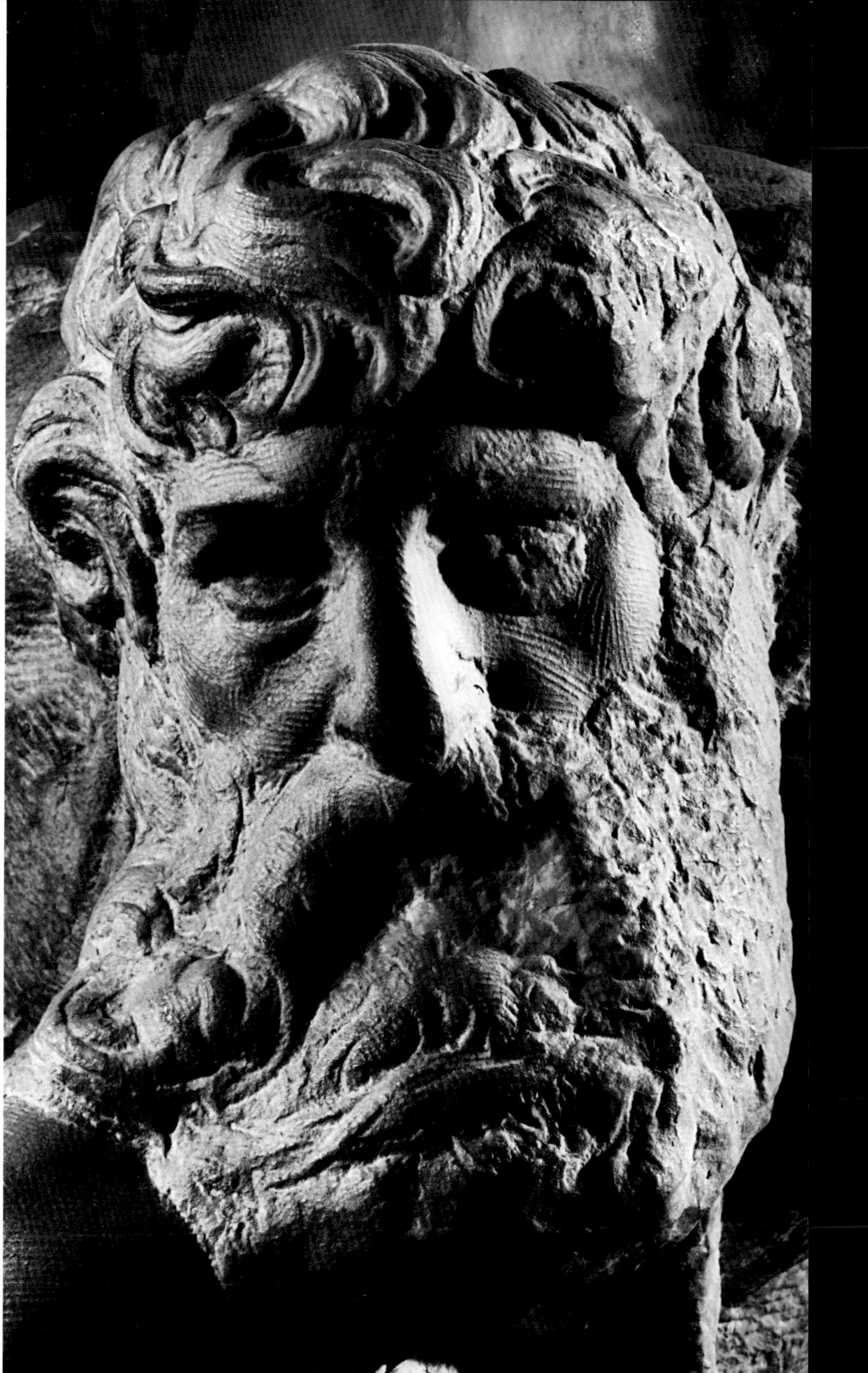

Michelangelo, *The Victory* (*The Genius of Victory*), the "non-finito" face of the vanquished figure
Florence, Palazzo Vecchio, Sala dei Cinquecento

Canons of Proportion, and the same may be said for the level extension of the victim's back. The torso with its contracted muscles spirals on the pelvis so that the right arm extends forwards and bends upwards, thus allowing the hand, poised elegantly, perhaps excessively so, to hold the cloak by its ribbon (a possible intervention by Danti); at the same time, the figure's head turns in the other direction for a sharp *contrapposto*. The reduction of the left arm behind the figure's back is explained by the fact that the work was meant to be a frontal niche figure. Michelangelo had already experimented with some of the most important solutions for composition we see here in other works: the sudden twist of the arm of the cloaked *Ignudo* situated right below Adam in the Sistine ceiling, the *contrapposto* of the *Minerva Christ*'s head, the way the colossal *David* moves his hand.
After generally setting aside Vasari's suggestion that the subject represented one of the provinces subjugated by Julius II, 20th-century criticism expanded on biblical, symbolic and autobiographical interpretations. Also in light of widespread reception of the composition motif by Florentine sculptors from the Cinquecento onwards (sculptors who were familiar with the work from when it was first created in Via Mozza) in statues, often meant for public display, that symbolized the prevalence of virtue over vice, order over chaos and Good over Evil in general,[43] the *Victory* group was probably an ethical expression of an overall political allegory for the virtues of Pope Della Rovere which prevailed over opposing negative principles.
This interpretation is confirmed by the fact that Duke Cosimo had the statue installed in the Sala dei Cinquecento in the Palazzo Vecchio in 1565, where it headed a series of sculptural works of allegorical and laudatory nature made by Giambologna and Vincenzo de' Rossi representing virtuous victors defeating iniquitous victims.[44]

The room in Via Mozza

When Michelangelo left Florence never to go back, he also left behind the room he used as a workshop. The need to find a spacious location not far from the San Lorenzo complex had arisen in 1518, while the artist was designing the church façade to be filled with statues for Leo X. On 14 July, he had purchased a piece of land close to the church of Santa Caterina delle Ruote (although the original church is no longer there, it is referred to by the street named "Via delle Ruote" as well as the recently built church of Santa Caterina d'Alessandria). But that was not where Michelangelo had his much needed workroom built: that was where he kept his kitchen garden until he agreed to sell the place in 1555. Back in November 1518, the artist had bought a piece of property one side of which was in Via Mozza, the old name of the stretch of Via Zan Zanobi that runs as far as Via delle Ruote. After having the work done in great haste, he had a large room set up (described in the documents as a "stanzone" a "stanza a tetto", "casa", suggesting it was very large) whose total area is said to have measured 200 square meters,[45] his idea being to be able to work on twenty statues at the same time[46] and store dozens of blocks of marble. A narrow kitchen garden was located at the back of the house.
It is generally believed that when Michelangelo wrote the word "canto" followed by a round sign in a letter dated around 1522-1523[47] he was alluding to Canto alle Màcine; but this location is on the corner between Via Guelfa and Via Ginori, in the same area but farther away. To my mind, he was actually referring to a Canto alla Ruota – whether or not it actually existed – either associated with the name of the street, or possibly as a kind of word play involving his own surname, at times paraphrased as "Buona Ruota", that is, "good wheel".
On 9 June 1519, the *carradori* delivered a "stone" there, which had been transported on a cart drawn by five pairs of oxen. From September onwards, this happened over and over again. In addition to the blocks he needed to make the tomb, others arrived to be used for his Medicean commissions: after they were roughed out, they were sent to Via di San Lorenzo.[48] When Michelangelo set off for Rome, he left behind countless drawings, cartoons and wax or terracotta models (some of which were stolen in the siege of 1529-1530, and later recovered), the four *Captives*, the *Victory*, probably the Hermitage *Crouching Boy* and blocks of marble, eleven of which Duke Cosimo purchased in 1544, followed by

another one, or several others, in 1555. The room was very popular with such artists as Daniele da Volterra and Leone Leoni, who were eager to get their hands on works by the master and others as well perhaps.
After Buonarroti died, his nephew and heir Lionardo gave the unfinished statues to Duke Cosimo and used the left over marble for his uncle's tomb in Santa Croce. Lastly, Michelangelo the Younger, heir to Lionardo Buonarroti, sold the room with all its contents in 1617.[49]
Michelangelo had left another example of his architecture not far from his workshop, which, after much controversy, was finally attributed to him: the portal for the church of the convent of Sant'Apollonia in Via San Gallo, where one of his nieces was a nun.[50]

Back to Rome

Although he was actually living and working in Florence, Michelangelo had not severed his ties with Rome. That was where he had met the young nobleman Tommaso de' Cavalieri, in 1532, a figure whom many say played a major role in helping the artist decide to move back to the capital. During that same period, Clement VII was thinking about giving him a most wonderful commission; Sebastiano del Piombo described it as something he could never have imagined.[51] In September 1533, the pope met Buonarroti in San Miniato al Tedesco, probably to outline the project, and in the winter of 1534, rumour had it that Michelangelo was preparing to paint the *Resurrection* above the Sistine Chapel altar. On 23 September 1534, Michelangelo moved to Rome; just two days later the pope died, but not before giving him the commission to paint the *Last Judgement* in the Sistine Chapel, which was strictly speaking a Medicean commission. The new pope, Paul III Farnese, lost no time confirming the commission. The works that followed, which included a growing number of major architectural commissions, kept Buonarroti in Rome until his death. He was also to benefit from the affection and close friendship of such figures as Tommaso de' Cavalieri and Vittoria Colonna, Marchioness of Pesaro,[52] along with solid, sincere friendships with Florentines (and others), who were either expatriates or doing work in Rome.

Michelangelo's artistic legacy in Florence

The consequences of what Michelangelo bequeathed to Florence's artistic milieu in terms of sculpture (painting was solely represented in that city by the *Doni Tondo*, private work, and the cartoon for the *Battle of Cascina* soon to be destroyed) is immeasurable. His excellence in sculpture, especially with marble, was the reason for the rise in the number of sculptors, over a period of one century or more, a number which was unequalled in other Italian cities, and turned Florence into a veritable museum of statuary, both in the open air and in covered environments.
Especially popular with Florentine sculptors was the motif of the victor subjugating a vanquished figure, which stemmed from Michelangelo's drawings, plastic arts and sculpture. The motif was used as laudatory allegory for the Medicean court, and fostered research into the complex spiralling movement of the figures it portrayed, with the goal of multiplying the number of viewing "angles". This was a recurring style, dubbed "figura serpentinata", or serpentine figure, by an elderly Michelangelo in a precept suggested to the painter Marco Pino and reported by Lomazzo.
The marble that Buonarroti just roughed out or actually worked on, which remained visible in many locations that were accessible to varying degrees,[53] became the material for study used by young artists, and when the Accademia delle Arti del Disegno was established in 1563, its didactic role was formalized. The inspiration accruing from Michelangelo's sculptures, with its many ways and forms, lasted throughout the long season of Florentine Mannerism, going well into the 17th century.[54]

Notes

[1] See, among others, *Disegni di fortificazioni...*, 1984, Marani, 1985, Brandi, 1988.
[2] Hatfield, 2002, pp. 156-158.
[3] Michelangelo is believed to have often hid in the labyrinthine Laurentian complex, and the drawings discovered on the walls of some of the rooms adjoing the Sacristy – the "lavamani", the apse, the "hiding room" under the apse – have been related to this clandestine sojourn. Published and critically analysed by Dal Poggetto (in *I disegni murali...*, 1979), the drawings led to heated discussion concerning attribution, which is still encouraging in-depth study and research.
[4] In 1936, the drawing went from the Henry Oppenheimer collection to that of Sir Brinsley Ford in London, and when this collection was sold (Christie's, 4 July 2000) it was purchased for a record-breaking amount by K. Bellinger.
[5] Letter from Sebastiano del Piombo in Rome to Michelangelo in Florence, 6 September 1521, in *Il Carteggio...*, 1965-1983, II, 1967, pp. 313-315, no. DXXVIII.
[6] For a time, the Christ wore a sort of gilded metal shoe on his right foot, not so much to hide its flaws as to protect the figure from being worn down by the hands of the faithful. For another period of time, even the drapery was missing, and the figure was completely naked.
[7] Vari was very understanding about the whole episode, but turned down the offer. Michelangelo gave him the first version, described previously, at no additional cost.
[8] Hirst, 2004b.
[9] Hirst's hypothesis (2004b, pp. 41-42) is that the model mentioned in the letters between Michelangelo and Buoninsegni is not, as commonly believed, the one for the New Sacristy (for which there are neither indications nor proof) but rather for the large, new windows.
[10] The perforated copper jalousies were executed by the goldsmith Piloto to a design by Michelangelo. For the closed environments, in late 1521, Giovanni da Udine and Domenico da Forlì made stucco work and paintings for the ceiling (Vasari, 1568, 1966-1987 ed., V. p. 452), which were subsequently lost; the same fate befell the lunettes frescoed by Vasari in the winter of 1534-1535 (see Cecchi, 1983 and then A. Cecchi, in *L'Officina...*, 1996, p. 284, no. 98 with bibliography).
[11] The pope had suggested building the ciborium above the high altar, but Michelangelo wasn't convinced. After an exchange of letters with the papal administrator Giovan Francesco Fattucci in 1525-1527, the negotiations were interrupted by war; when activity recommenced, the pope was coaxed into accepting its placement in the counterfaçade. For this architecture, especially see Argan, Contardi, 1990, pp. 198-200, Salvi, 1993b, pp. 115-118, Ragionieri, 2000, pp. 67-68.
[12] "The cavity in the depth of the wall for the reliquaries" according to the legend written by the artist in his drawing at the Ashmolean Museum in Oxford, no. 311*r*.
[13] The differences are clearly described by Salvi 1993b, p. 115, who explains them by pointing out a "multiplicity and variety" of the "heretic" sort.
[14] The ostension in the presence of the people took place on Easter Sunday and on the Sunday after All Saint's Day, while on 13 December, the anniversary of its arrival, a procession was held (Ciseri, 1993, p. 41).
[15] The citations are from Condivi, *The Life of Michelangelo* (1553), 2006 ed., p. 11; "library" obviously stands for collection of books, the books in the estate. It was precisely from one of those marble "stones" that the young would-be sculptor carved the "head of an old faun" which Lorenzo is said to have admired, not without some good-humoured irony. Inherent to the Laurentian project was the idea of emulating and surpassing Cosimo *Pater Patriae's* Michelozzian library in San Marco.
[16] See Tesi, 1993, pp. 135-140, for a summary of the events surrounding the project and the construction itself.
[17] In 1885-1886, Franceschini used the adjective "undefinable" to describe the Composite order of the vestibule (Barocchi, 1962a, III, p. 867). See the comment by Morolli, 1993b, pp. 127-136, for the observation that carved into the capital was the "protome of a monstrous bat peeking through the crescent of the abacus in place of the canonical flower". This was unusually similar to the "Germanic order" that had just been published by Albrecht Dürer (*Unterweisung der Messung*, Zurich, 1525, sheet h, figure 8), thus confirming Michelangelo's interest for art from across the Alps, which began when he was an adolescent.
[18] Tribolo used some of these stones to build "quattro scaglioni", and then gave up. The records support the hypothesis that the actual construction never commenced (cf. Argan, Contardi, 1990, p. 195). Five columns had been attached to the walls by June 1526, but a curtailment of funds had caused the work to slow down, and it was almost suspended until 1530 (Vasari, 1568, 1962 ed., I, p. 59, III, pp. 867-874).
[19] On the very long story of the staircase, see Vasari, 1568, 1962 ed., I, p. 59, III, pp. 878-887.
[20] The episode is not discussed by the biographers but news of it may be found in the first letter written by Giovan Francesco Fattucci in Rome to Michelangelo in Florence dated 14 October 1525, in *Il Carteggio...*, 1965-1983, III, 1973, pp. 170-171, no. DCCXVII, which was followed by various letters from the pope where he asked the artist for an answer.
[21] Letter from Michelangelo in Florence to Giovan Francesco Fattucci in Rome [early December 1525], in *Il Carteggio...*, 1965-1983, III, 1973, pp. 190-191, no. DCCXXX.
[22] Letter from Pier Paolo Marzi for Pope Clement VII in Rome to Michelangelo in Florence, 23 December 1525, in *Il Carteggio...*, 1965-1983, III, 1973, pp. 194-195).
[23] Vasari, "The Life of Michelangelo" (1550), 2007 ed., p. 175.
[24] Vasari, *The Lives* (1568), 1996 ed., II, p. 685. *Apollo* and his quiver are recognizable in a drawing attributed to Rosso Fiorentino (New York, Pierpont Morgan Library, formerly Janos Scholz Collection, attribution confirmed by Carroll, 1987, pp. 146-148, no. 49). There are those who say the drawing should be dated before 1527, thus anticipating the start of the Michelangelesque statue (cf. the entry by G. Bonsanti, in *L'ombra del genio...*, 2002, pp. 219-220). But Rosso may have seen the statue while it was being worked on during his long stay in Tuscany between the autumn of 1527 when he was in Sansepolcro, after arriving from Perugina when the Sack of Rome had already taken place, and Easter 1530, when he left Sansepolcro for Venice and then Paris. It is known he had business contacts in Florence.
[25] G. Bonsanti, in *L'Ombra del genio...*, 2002, p. 220.
[26] Tolnay, 1970, pp. 96-97, 181-182, op. cit. by G. Bonsanti, in *L'Ombra del genio...*, 2002, p. 220.
[27] Letter from Sebastiano del Piombo in Rome to Michelangelo in Florence dated 19 August 1531, in *Il Carteggio...*, 1965-1983, III, 1973, no. DCCCXXV, pp. 325 and ff. Sebastiano estimated the remaining figures to cost over 4,000 ducats, the architectural framing 2,000 ducats, and he exhorted Buonarroti to: "take heed of your interests, don't just impulsively accept the first offer of 2,000 ducats. The Pope is on your side".
[28] Letter from Giovan Maria della Porta in Rome to the Duke of Urbino in Urbino, dated 29 April 1532, in Gotti, 1875, II, p. 78.
[29] But Echinger-Maurach (2003) believes that the statue of Julius II was made between 1532 and 1533.
[30] London, Victoria and Albert Museum, inv. 4117-1854, red wax, height 16.7 cm, provenance Florence, it is believed to be from the Ignazio Hughford and after that Gherardini collections. Although held to be autograph in connection with the *Young Captive* by most of the critics, it was rejected by Tolnay (1954). After it was damaged in 1924, it was reassembled around a metal frame. Cf. O'Grody, 1999, no. 3.
[31] Archivio di Casa Buonarroti, I, 82, fol. 225, the second block from the top. Le measures annotated here might correspond to those for the so-called *Atlas* (Rapetti, 2001, p. 49).
[32] G. Bonsanti, in *Michelangiolo...*, 1989, no. 10.,
[33] It is now considered to be preliminary for a *River God*, so it is on display in a reclining position (*I bozzetti...*, 2000, no. 3, pp. 38-41), but until 1969 it was in a vertical position because it was linked to a *Captive* (Wilde, 1928 and others) or a similar figure (for example, a vanquished figure). For it to be a *River God* I find the hip area set on the ground to be too narrow, and the pose uncomfortable: the torso and stomach muscles are contracted and not relaxed as in the large model, also in the Casa Buonarroti. On the other hand, Andrea Commodi, in his enlightening series of drawings from models by Michelangelo, portrays the figure in an even more fragmentary state with the torso alone, in a vertical position (Florence, Gabinetto Disegni e Stampe degli Uffizi, inv. 18519 F).
[34] Vasari recounted that, while all of the artists who contributed to Michelangelo's exequies were paid, Buontalenti painted the apparatus depicting *L'anima di Michelangelo* etc. "not by commission like the others, but spontaneously and with such assistance as his own merit enabled him to obtain from his courteous and honourable friends" (Vasari, *The Lives* (1568), 1996 ed., II, p. 766).
[35] Bocchi, 1591, 1677 ed., p. 138. Not without contradicting himself, the scholar also suggested the myth of Deucalion and Pyrrha according to Ovid, that is, the generation of humanity that stretches from the Stone Age to after the Deluge.
[36] Vasari, 1550, 1986 ed., p. 890.
[37] Balas (1989) freed the *Victory* from the Palazzo Vecchio and instead considered it a private, secret work made by Michelangelo in 1532-1534, which alluded to his amorous captivity by the handsome Cavalieri. The link between the group and the Tomb was artfully introduced by Vasari with a moralizing intent after Michelangelo's death (letter to nephew Lionardo dated 18 October 1564).
[38] There is indeed some resemblance between the model and an autograph sketch at the Casa Buonarroti (inv. 63 Fr.). In linking the drawing to the commission for the *Hercules and Cacus*, Tolnay (1975-1980, I, no. 65) dated the drawing from 1508, the year at that time related to the project undertaken for Soderini, but which ended quite a bit later; also Barocchi (1962b, pp. 18-19, no. 10). Hirst instead ties it in with the statuary group by Baccio Bandinelli (2000, p. 491), especially as concerns the position of the vanquished figure.

[39] Florence, Casa Buonarroti, inv. 192. The relationship with the *Victory* was proposed by Springer, 1883, foreshadowed by Wilde from 1928, underscored in 1978. The model (which fell to pieces and was restored in 1926) was drawn whole in some three drawings in the Andrea Commodi series, after a number of Michelangelesque subjects leading back to the 1580s (Florence, GDSU, inv. 18524 F; 18665 F; 18666 F). Cf. *I bozzetti*..., 2000, no. 4, pp. 42-46).

[40] For the verification that was carried out on the statue, I am grateful to the representatives of the Accademia dei Georgofili di Firenze and to its president Franco Scaramuzzi.

[41] The hypothesis is not unanimously accepted by scholarship.

[42] After Danti returned to his native country, in order to contribute along with other local artists to the creation of an artistic academy in Perugia similar to the Arti del Disegno in Florence, he offered plaster casts of the *Times of the Day* from the New Sacristy, which arrived in Perugia in 1573 "perhaps made by him personally" (Fidanza, 1996, p. 21), which are still at the Accademia di Belle Arti in Perugia today. A small label on the back of the *Day* reads: "Gift of Vincenzo Danti 1573". The first seat of the academy was in Danti's workshop below the piazza del Sopramuro (Santi, 1989, p. 31).

[43] The contraposition between the manifestation of Good and the manifold forms of Evil is found in allegories of struggle between Justice versus Fraud, Loyalty versus Deceit, Wisdom versus Ignorance, Order versus Chaos, and so on.

[44] Heikamp, 1980, p. 208.

[45] Hatfield, 2002, p. 80.

[46] Letter from Michelangelo in Florence to Leonardo Sellaio in Rome [21? December 1518], in *Il Carteggio*..., 1965-1983, II, 1967, II, pp. 129-130, no. CCCLXXXII.

[47] Letter from Michelangelo in Florence to Giovan Francesco Fattucci in Florence [1522-1523?], in *Il Carteggio*..., 1965-1983, II, 1967, p. 344, no. DLII.

[48] In *I ricordi*..., 1970, pp. 123-124, no. CXVIII (12 January - 27 October 1524), mention is made of a piece of roughed-out marble carried by the stone-cutters from Via Mozza to San Lorenzo.

[49] It seems that since 1855 there has been an apartment building with several floors at number 39. Hatfield, 2002, pp. 82-84.

[50] Davis, 1975; Argan, Contardi, 1990, p. 201 (with the date of 1525-1535).

[51] Letter of 17 July 1553 from Sebastiano del Piombo to Michelangelo in Florence, in *Il Carteggio*..., 1965-1983, IV, 1979, pp. 17-19, no. CMX.

[52] See the catalogue *Vittoria Colonna*..., 2005.

[53] The rooms at the Opera di Santa Maria del Fiore, the Arengario of the Palazzo dei Signori, the New Sacristy in San Lorenzo, of course, the house in Via Ghibellina and the workshop in Via Mozza, later the Grand-Ducal collections.

[54] See the catalogue *L'ombra del genio*..., 2002.

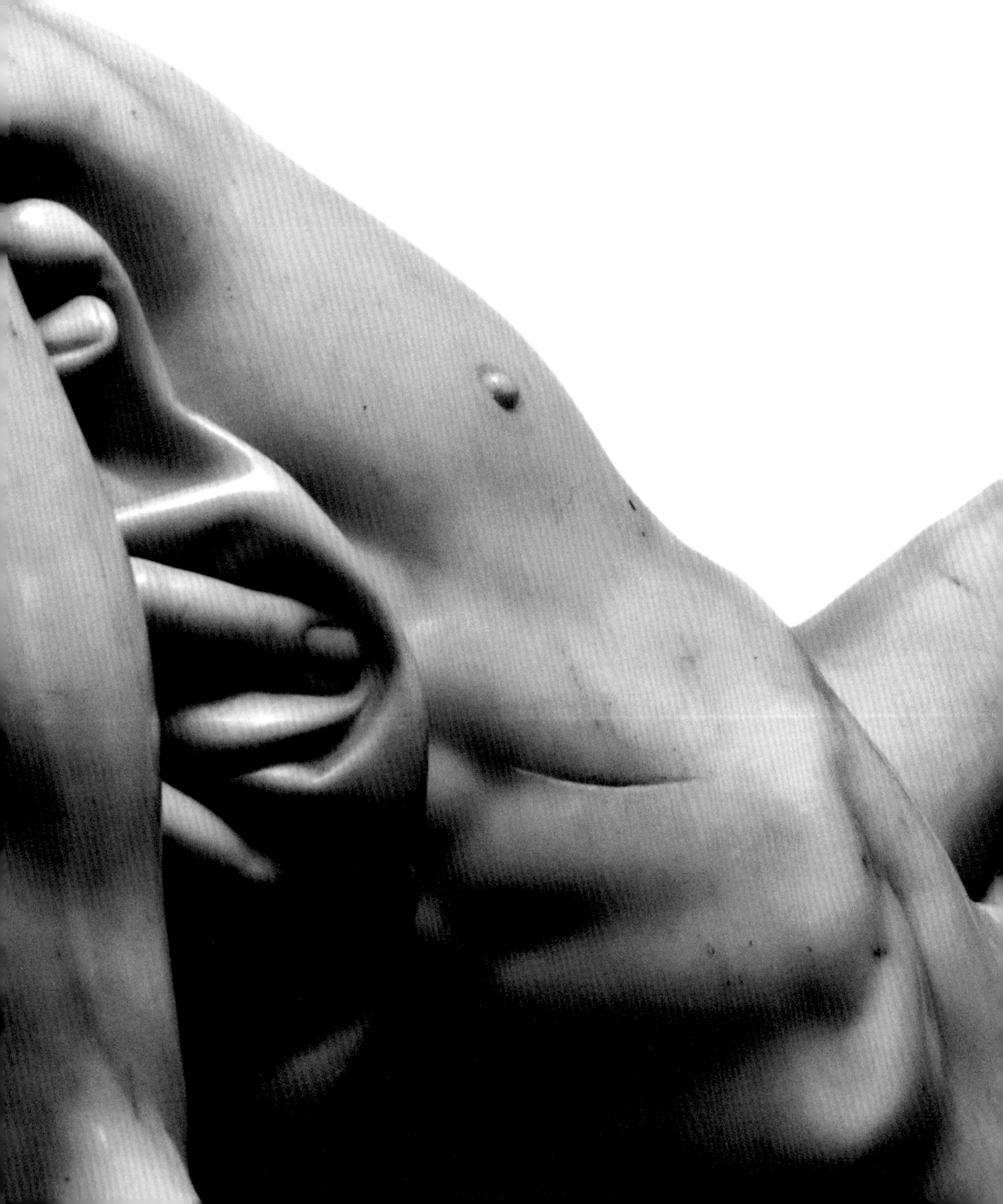

The final thirty years

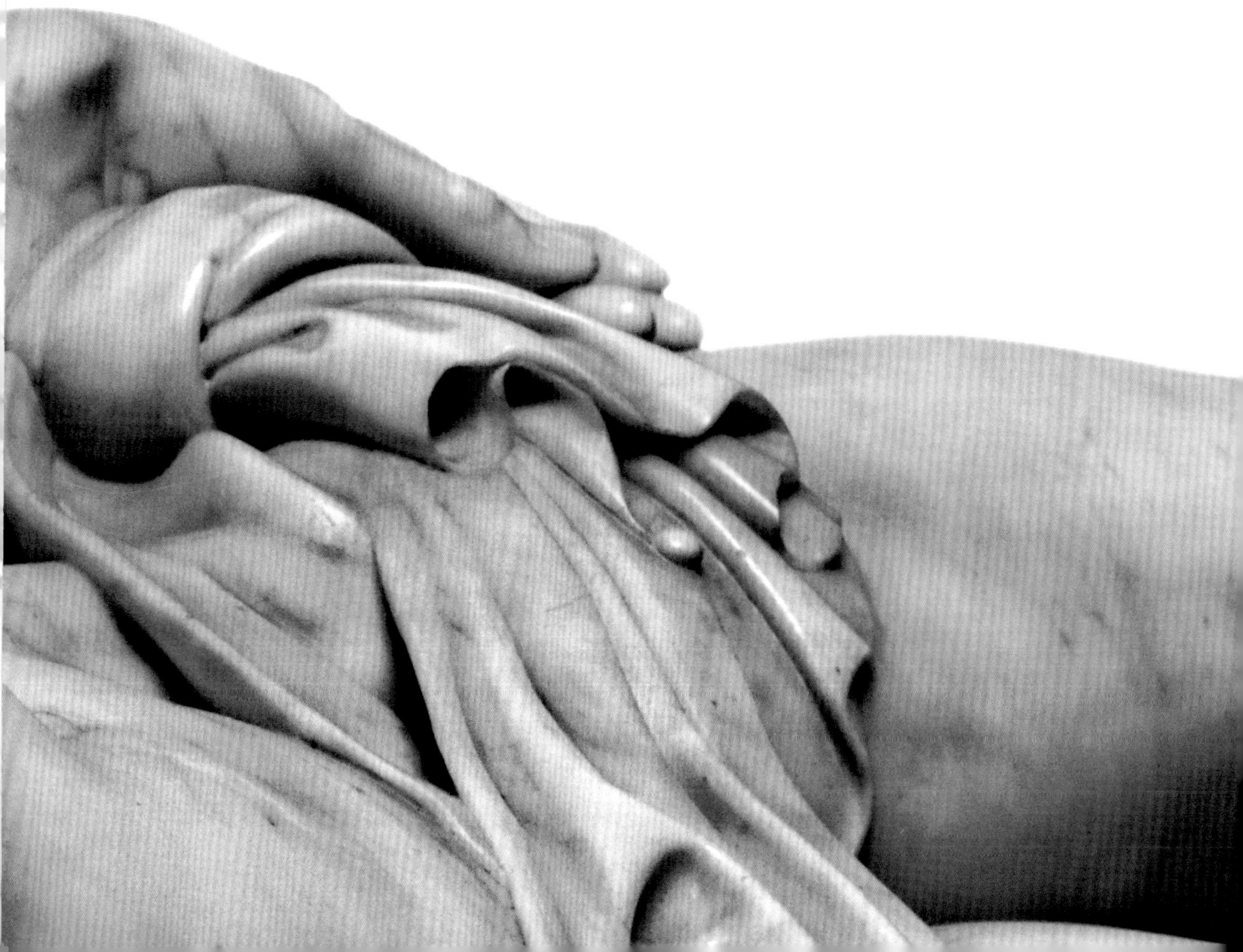

a vision already enjoyed a general consensus and it continued to gain ever-increasing acceptance. But the biography was resented by its subject, who was displeased at anything he believed to be an omission or a distortion, especially as concerned the embarrassing story of the Tomb of Julius II. For this reason he asked his modest collaborator Ascanio Condivi to transcribe his memoirs in a second biography, hastily published in 1553. Even this version, which he had personally overseen, failed to satisfy Michelangelo, so he had Tiberio Calcagni add notes of disagreement to it by hand. Vasari's second edition of the *Lives* was published in 1568, four years after Michelangelo's death and actually encouraged by the event. Vasari could at last complete the parable of the master's long life, collecting verbal recollections about him that circulated in Rome after his death and taking a personal satisfaction in reiterating and explaining in detail those facts that Michelangelo had denied through Condivi. The dedication of two biographies to a living artist and a third shortly after his death is in itself an astonishing reflection of the master's legendary status, reinforced during the following centuries, also with the help of records. Michelangelo, it has been rightly observed, was the first and foremost maker of his own myth, turning his life into a masterpiece that initiated, developed and perfected itself through a continuous dialectic between his biographers and himself. It is therefore not surprising, then, that Cosimo de' Medici tried on many occasions, indirectly, but also in person, to convince the prodigious venerable old man to come back to Florence. But Michelangelo either wouldn't keep his promise or he remained elusive. To no avail were the encounters of 1560 when several delegations arrived from Florence for the cardinalship of the cadet Giovanni de' Medici;[11] of no help was the homage of Prince Francesco, if it is true that when he went to see him in 1561 or 1562 he allowed him to sit in his very own chair, while he stood right before him. In one last attempt, Vasari informed Michelangelo of Cosimo's desire that he come back to personally finish work on the Sacristy or instruct the artists of the Accademia delle Arti del Disegno so that they could complete it with sculptures and paintings. The notoriously absent master occupied among the academicians the role of "second head" after the duke, in that he was "father and master of all", and the mark he left on marble – three intertwined circles perhaps the simplification of three rings with a diamond for the "old" Medicis – was made into an emblem for the academy with three crowns alluding to the three interrelated arts, all stemming from Disegno. Vasari's posthumous explanation for Michelangelo's refusal to return to Florence "for so many years [...] had been caused by no other thing than the nature of the air" is highly dubious.[12]

The *Brutus* bust

Michelangelo had not hesitated to place himself at the service of the Florentine Republic and had even gone so far as to invoke the help of Francis I of France with the aim of gaining it back after it fell.[13] Once he settled in Rome he became outwardly close to those who were known as *fuorusciti* or had been exiled from Florence because they were against the Medici regime. An example of this is the fact that he gave the cartoon for the *Drunkenness of Noah* for the Sistine ceiling to the great banker and staunch anti-Medicean figure Bindo Altoviti.[14]

Vivid artistic proof of the company he kept can be found in the marble bust of *Brutus*. Despite the story behind it, the sculpture is located along with an elaborate, late explanatory epigraph in Florence's Museo Nazionale del Bargello. This celebration of Brutus, Caesar's adoptive son and murderer, together with Cassius, tells us that Michelangelo was very well informed of the political ideals of the circle of Florentine exiles or *fuorusciti* in Rome, who believed that tyrannicide was legitimate, and, after the murder of Duke Alessandro de' Medici by his cousin Lorenzo also called Lorenzaccio (1537), actually praised it in no uncertain terms.[15] The *Brutus* bust was destined to be given to the exiled cardinal Niccolò Ridolfi as a gift from his secretary Donato Giannotti, a friend of Michelangelo from the time of the Florentine Republic. Giannotti had been the secretary of the

p. 243
Michelangelo, *Brutus*
Florence, Museo Nazionale del Bargello

p. 244
Michelangelo, *Brutus*
The drapery is probably the work of Tiberio Calcagni
Florence, Museo Nazionale del Bargello

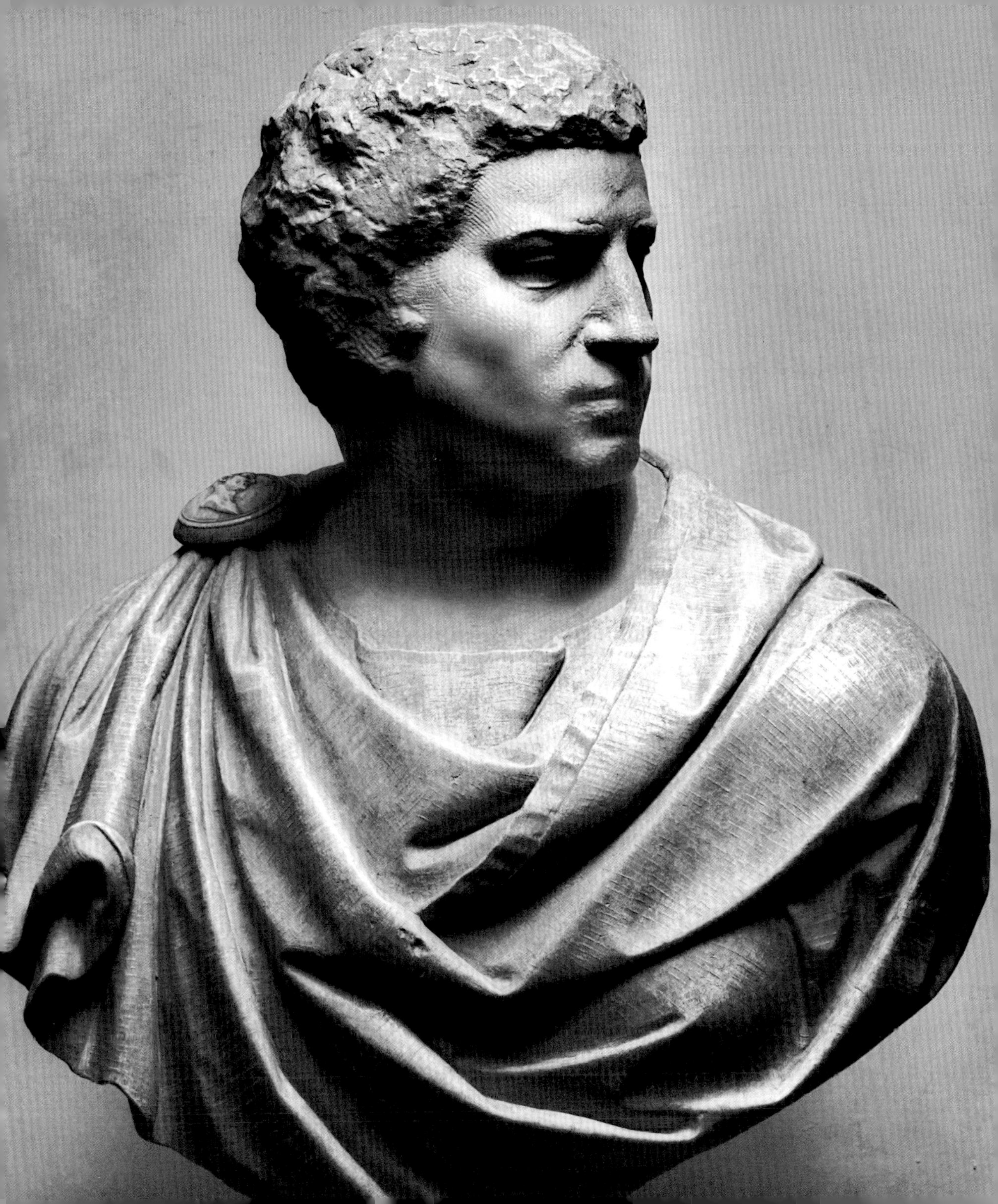

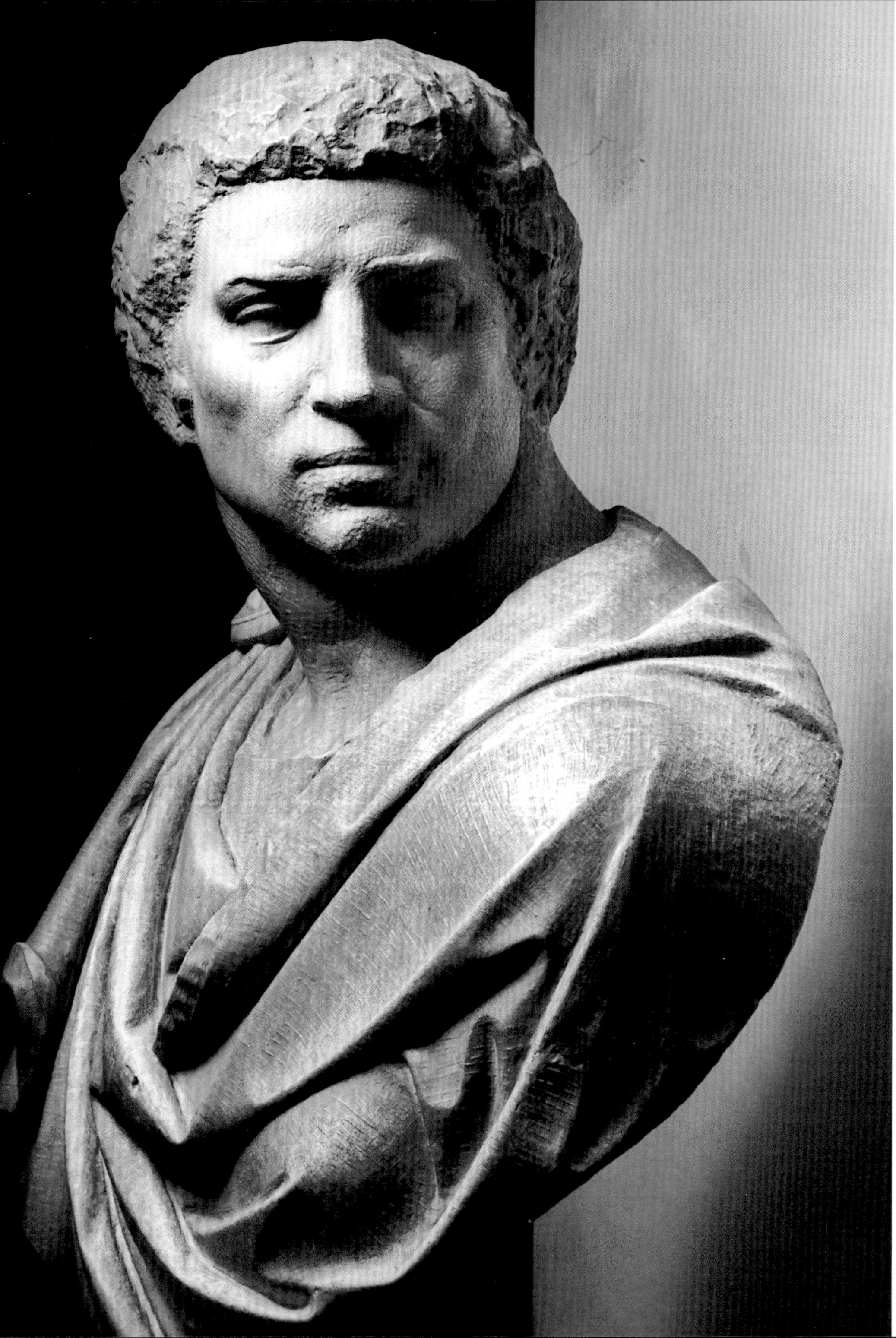

Cancelleria dei Dieci and was banished when the Medici regained power. But this is not the only evidence of the mutual friendship and esteem between the artist and the scholar: Michelangelo is in fact a speaker in Giannotti's book on the subject of Dante. The artist appears as an expert on the *Divine Comedy*, but he is also portrayed in the part of the text that defends Brutus and tyrannicide – perhaps a foreshadowing of the plan to murder Duke Cosimo – where the artist expresses his personal approval.[16] The fibula that holds the drapery still on *Brutus*' shoulder contains a portrait of Giannotti.
The date of the bust is controversial. Because Giannotti entered Ridolfi's services in 1539, the bust was dated about 1540, also in view of the murder of Duke Alessandro and subsequent exaltation of Lorenzino as a "Tuscan Brutus", a legendary figure for the Florentine *fuorusciti*. But for Hirst and Martin, the date of the bust should be brought closer to the death of Lorenzino, in 1548.[17] Michelangelo himself noted that the bust was not finished, and given to Tiberio Calcagni to complete. It is likely that Cardinal Ridolfi never received it.[18]
Inspired by the Roman iconography of Emperor Caracalla, in particular a marble bust from the II century A.D. now in the Museo Archeologico in Naples, Vasari's opinion was that the bust was also based on antique exemplars: the biographer indeed cited "a very ancient cornelian that was in the possession of Signor Giuliano Cesarino".[19]
The vital energy of the bust springs forth from the abrupt turn of the head on the neck, whereby the figure's gaze is directed above the shoulder: Michelangelo had previously experimented with this *contrapposto* in a number of male figures, for effects that were at times more subdued, other times more intense. The *Brutus* concentrates on a faraway vision from which the viewer is excluded, his brusque and severe attitude transmitting moral tension and political passion. This is enhanced by the austerity with which the face is treated: although the volumes are finished, the surface is not polished. The cap of close-cropped hair *all'antica*, the quick, frowning countenance just chiselled out, bestow the head with square, irrevocable resolution. Whereas Michelangelo is attributed the fibula, the archaeological citation coinciding with the discreet homage to Giannotti in the form of a portrait, and the group of folds just below it (skilfully wrinkled with the help of a capricious fold), it is hard to accept his authorship of the remainder of the drapery, so predictable in the volumes and so unlike Michelangelo in the handling of the claw-chisel. Calcagni's intervention has in fact been suggested for this part of the work,[20] although the artist's devoted helper probably didn't dare touch the head. An expression wrinkle to the left of the nose, which actually resembles a scar, could be Calcagni's, proving his difficulty at managing the carving tool. This might explain why he left it at that.
For a long time it was believed that the bust arrived in Florence because it was acquired by Francesco I de' Medici, but the truth of the matter is that his brother and successor, Ferdinando I, bought it in 1590 from the Diomede Leoni estate.[21] Although its anti-Medicean aura had diminished, it somehow still lingered, so at some unspecified moment, while the work was in the Uffizi Gallery, a distich was placed on it to explain its "non-finito" state as being due to the artist's horror upon learning of the murder while working on the sculpture.[22]

The Tomb of Julius II towards completion

In order to paint the *Last Judgement* Michelangelo had interrupted his work on the Julius Tomb, which he was not able to go back to until the autumn of 1541. Nonetheless, Paul III intervened with Duke Guidubaldo Della Rovere in order to get permission for the artist to delegate the execution of the parts that were still missing to others, under his guidance. Already in November of 1541 the pope had decided to commission Michelangelo to paint "his new palace chapel", i.e. the Pauline Chapel in the Sala Regia, which he estimated the sixty-five-year-old artist would take three or four years to finish. On Paul III's behalf, Cardinal Ascanio Parisani da Tolentino suggested to the duke of Urbino "that the six statues, which were to be made by the hand of the aforesaid M, should be made by the hand of another artist with his model and design, although everything will be done to see if one or more of these statues can be made or roughed out by his hand".[23]

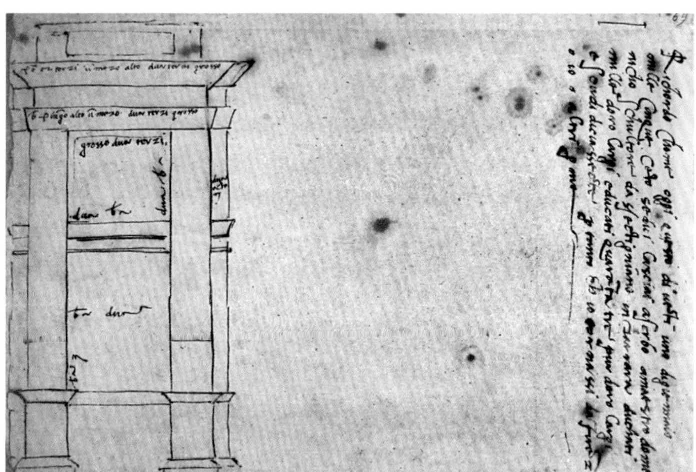

Michelangelo, *Lateral façade for the Tomb of Julius II*
Florence, Casa Buonarroti, inv. 69 A

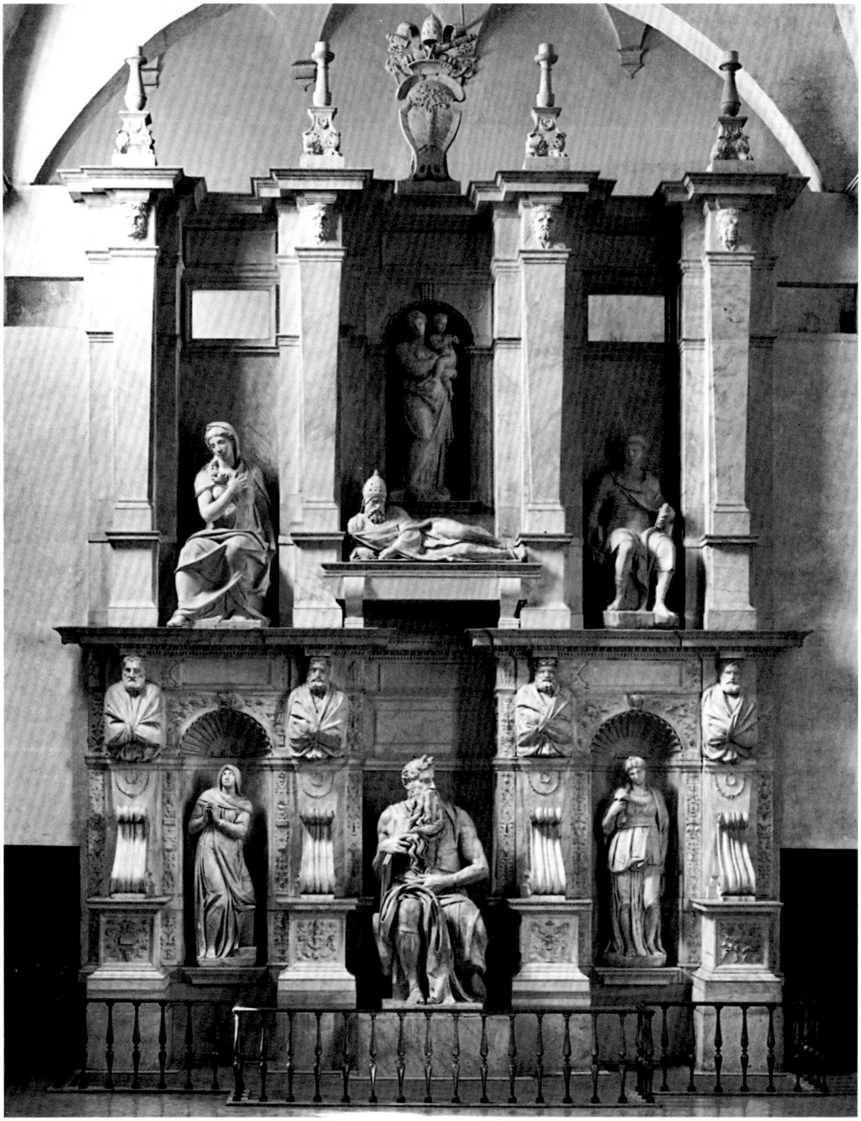

Michelangelo and collaborators, *Tomb of Julius II*
The monumental façade is actually a cenotaph
Rome, church of San Pietro in Vincoli

p. 247
Michelangelo and collaborator (Tommaso Boscoli?), *Julius II*
The figure of the recumbent pope suggests that Michelangelo made a drawing or model, which was then translated into sculpture by another artist
Rome, church of San Pietro in Vincoli

pp. 248-249
Michelangelo and collaborators, upper storey of the *Tomb of Julius II*, with the *Madonna and Child* and *Julius II* between a *Sibyl* and a *Prophet*
Rome, church of San Pietro in Vincoli

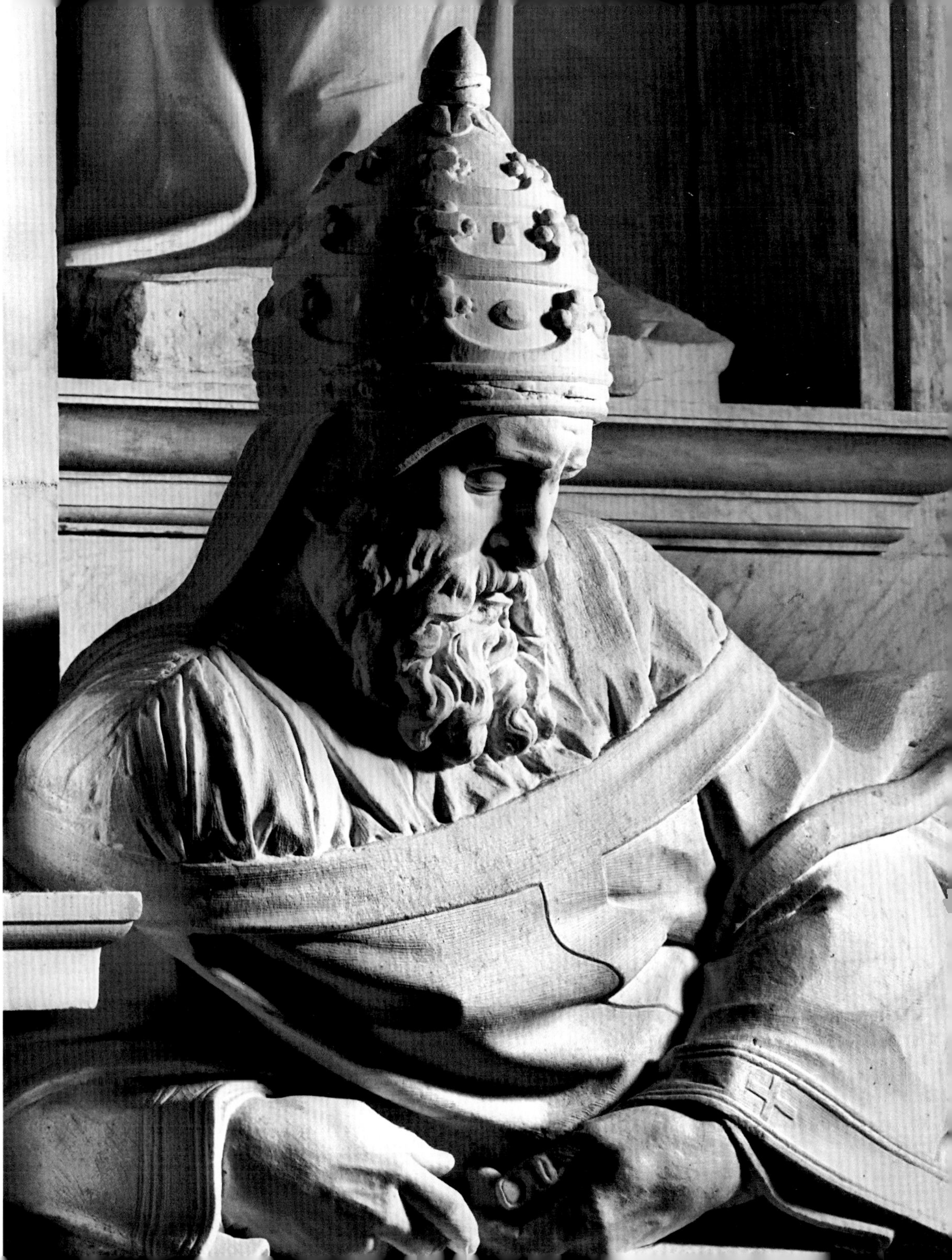

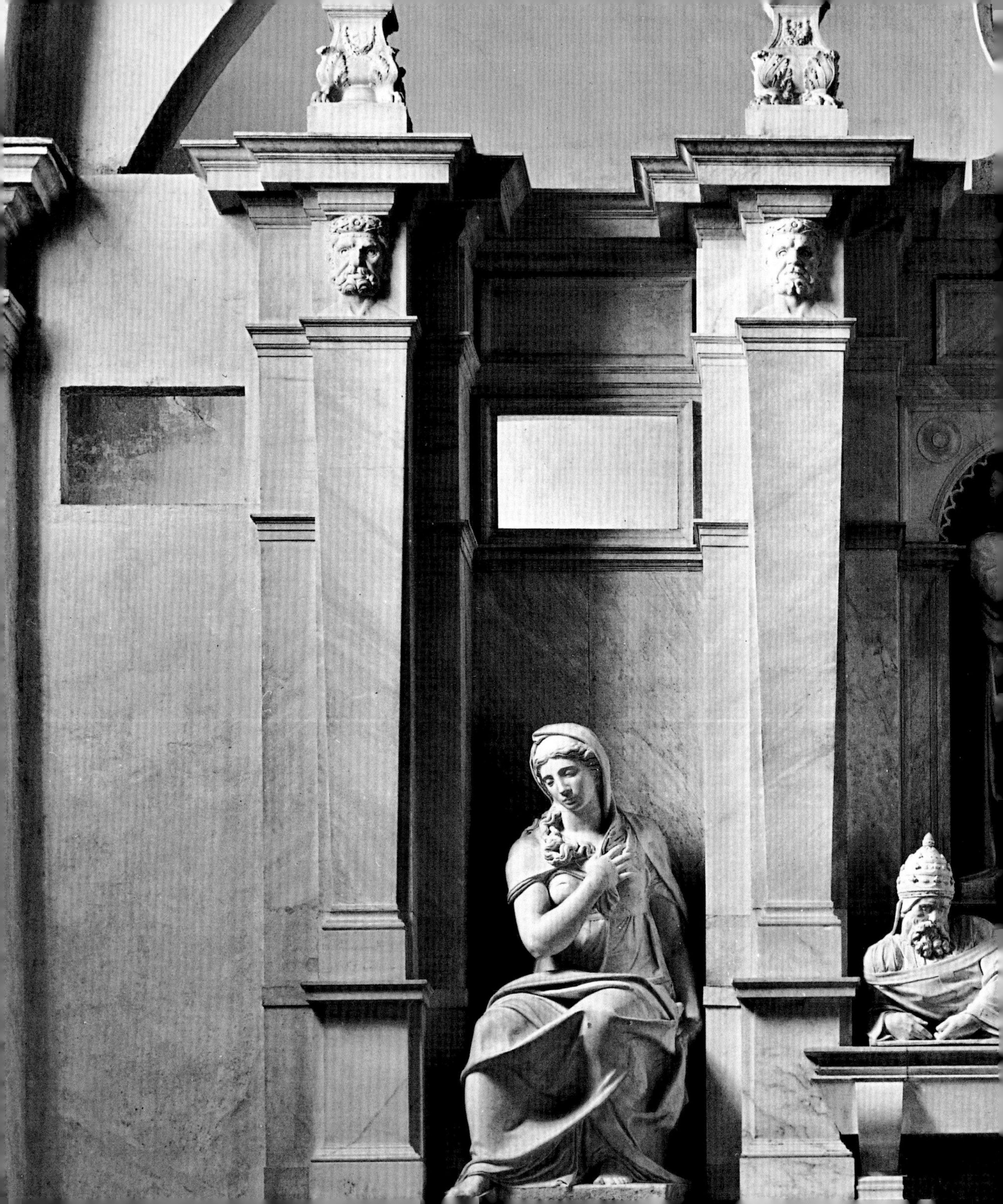

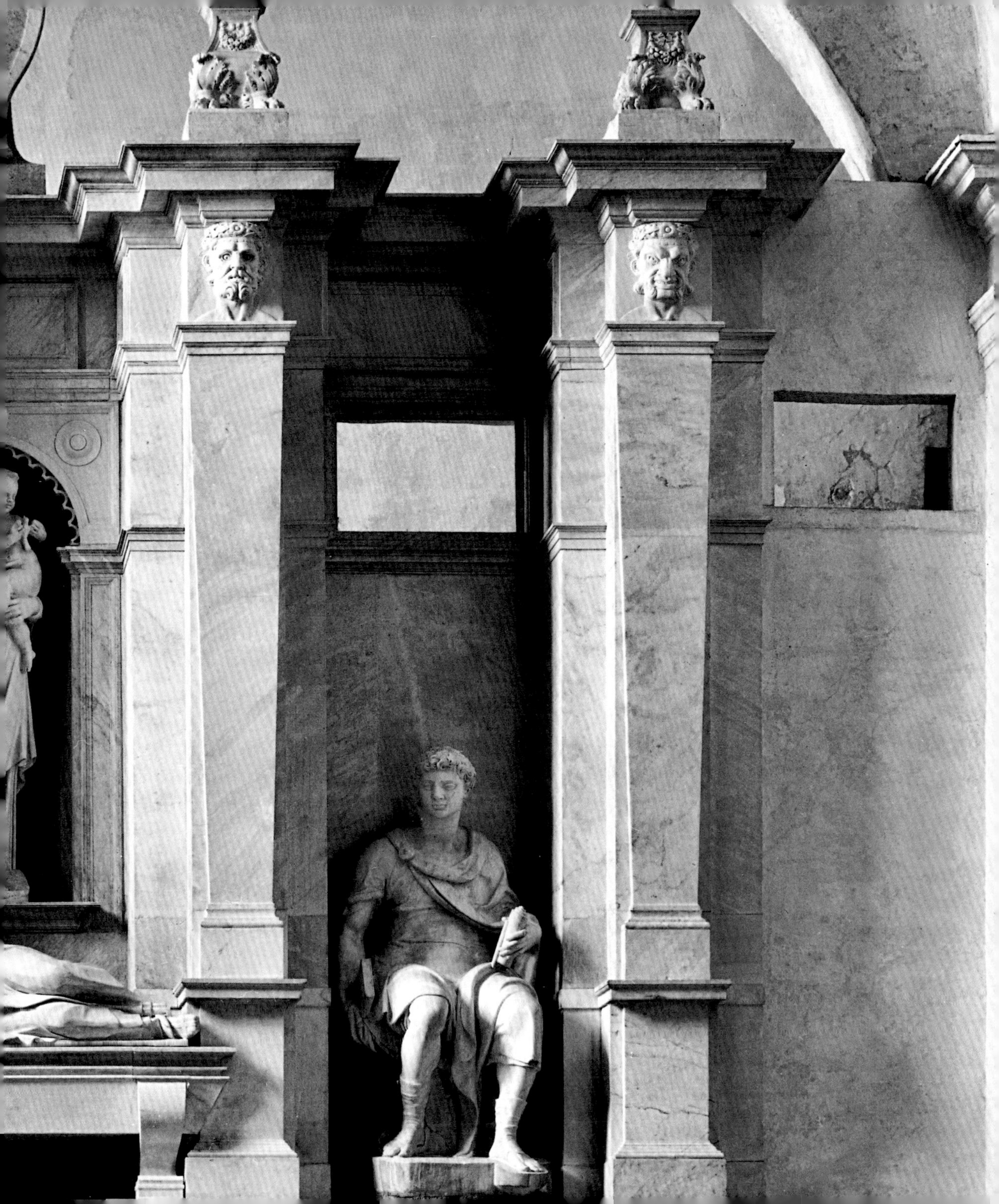

After further negotiation, an agreement was signed stating that Michelangelo would supply three autograph statues including a *Moses*, and that the remaining statues would be made by some other qualified sculptor.[24] Michelangelo thus gave three statues, a *Madonna and Child*, a *Prophet* and a *Sibyl*, to Raffaello da Montelupo, drafted in a contract signed on 27 February 1542. The other two autograph statues were to be two *Slaves*, undoubtedly the *Dying Slave* and the *Rebellious Slave*, which were in the artist's home in Macel de' Corvi. But while the work was underway, changes were made to this agreement as well, and as early as 20 July 1542 – at a time when the artist may have been distressed by the severe criticism of his *Last Judgement* – he gave up on the *Slaves* (which had been conceived for a significantly larger monument) and begged Paul III to speak with the Della Rovere and persuade them to accept the allegories of the *Active Life* and the *Contemplative Life*, also known by their biblical names *Leah* and *Rachel*. The statues were at a very advanced stage, and Michelangelo was counting on having them finished by Raffaello da Montelupo.[25]
Hanging over the elderly artist's head was the preparatory work for the Pauline Chapel frescoes scheduled to begin in autumn. But the pope's lack of interest in the problem persuaded Michelangelo to complete the two female figures himself. In the meantime, the stone-cutters and marble-carvers he had hired, namely Giovanni Marchesi and Francesco Amadori da Urbino, were busy working on what was left to be done for the architectural framework and ornamentation for the façade, except for the last tympanum. Giacomo or Jacopo del Duca, a stone-cutter of modest talent, worked on the four *Terms* for the upper register, while Donato Benti (son of a well-known procurer of marble in Carrara) sculpted the Della Rovere coat of arms. Michelangelo's collaborators also included Scherano, or Sandro de' Fancelli from Settignano. Vasari (1568) attributed the recumbent figure of the pope to Tommaso Boscoli, but a recent critical consideration put forth by Antonio Forcellino during and after restoration of the monument has strongly suggested, as we shall see, that this is really an autograph work by Michelangelo.
The funerary monument was finished in February 1545; the artist was seventy years old and had been intermittently occupied with it for forty years. As the pope had previously been buried in the Vatican Grottos, the monument was really a cenotaph. The extended, tormented story of the monument is clearly visible, for although it is truly a grandiose work it nevertheless contains numerous contradictions and inconsistencies. Initially conceived as a free-standing mausoleum with four façades to be filled with forty statues in the new basilica of Saint Peter's, the final result was a single wall façade with six statues plus the herms installed in the church of San Pietro in Vincoli. The signs of all of the changes in the project as well as developments in style over the four decades of its construction are clearly visible; moreover, some of the hastier solutions point to a situation that must have exasperated the artist, but also undoubtedly bored the patrons to death. To the extent that, as Hughes has observed,[26] there is not a single commemorative inscription on the Tomb, which would have been more than fitting for a papal tomb, despite the fact that enough space was left for a large inscription above the *Moses*, and that as many as six small panels are situated close to the terms.
Raised above a sober, smooth *basamento*, the lower register is an ensemble of Michelangelo's architecture and sculpture up until the 1520s. The shell-headed niches are flanked by pilaster strips, plinths and neatly elegant friezes that had been made by Antonio da Pontassieve thirty years earlier, examples thus of an ornamental repertory of erudite classicism that had seen its day. Boldly turned fluted volutes raised up on plinths that resemble dividing armrests hark back to the inventive freedom of the Chapel of Castel Sant'Angelo and the Laurentian vestibule.
The four cloaked *Terms* instead represent the style of the 1530s; their clothing and pose as defeated barbarians foreshadow the *Slaves* or *Captives* that had originally be planned and then abolished. The monument was already completed when, in 1546, Michelangelo donated the *Slaves* left unused and still in his workshop – the *Dying Slave* and the *Rebellious Slave* – to the expatriate Roberto Strozzi as a sign of his gratitude. In 1550, while exiled in Lyon, Strozzi personally paid to have the figures shipped to France. As stated previously, after changing hands on several occasions and numerous

arrangements – during which time they were occasionally likened to the traditional figures of telamons – these two sculptures were placed in the Musée du Louvre.
The upper register, probably raised to make it fit the above arch, is instead quite different in style and corresponds to the austere and less richly ornamented architectural language of the longer Tuscan order, the only ornamental elements being the four herm pilasters by Jacopo del Duca, and at the very top four rounded marble candelabra flanking the Della Rovere coat of arms. On closer inspection, the seated *Prophets* and standing *Mother and Child*, which were designed but not made by Michelangelo, are lifeless. Overall proportional harmony is never achieved here, neither between the statues themselves, nor between the statues and the architecture, which overpowers these two side statues despite the required perspectival correction *di sotto in su*.
Michelangelo was fully aware of the flaws in the solution, the outcome of drastic compromises, and he transmitted his feelings to Condivi who, although praising the *Moses*, the two biblical statues and the "corniciame", or framework, expressed himself somewhat callously: "... patched up and reworked as it is, it is still the most meritorious tomb to be found in Rome and perhaps elsewhere".[27] At a much later date, however, the artist himself, perhaps to rehabilitate the monument in light of the admiration surrounding it, corrected his biographer's limitative opinion by dictating to Calcagni one of his most striking annotations: "If everything that is patched up looked like this!".[28]

The *Contemplative Life* or *Rachel*, the *Active Life* or *Leah*

The two allegorical female figures from the original programme for the Tomb, so that they stand in the lower storey and are not seated in the upper one, were intended as a twofold model of the paths that can lead to God, a moral and philosophical motif which was deeply rooted in humanistic culture.[29]
The *Contemplative Life* is "... a woman of more than life-size, but of rare beauty, with one knee bent not on the ground but on a pedestal, with her face and both hands raised towards heaven, so that her whole being seems to emanate love".[30] Condivi used these words to describe the statue in the niche to the viewer's left of the *Moses*. Rachel's figure is to the extent possible anatomically elongated (visible in the distance between the groin and knee of the leg she stands on), and spirals upwards: from the three-quarter view of her leg, to her bust tilted frontally, to her arms bent and hands clasped together in *contrapposto*, all the way up to her head diagonally tilted upwards, she alludes to the spiritual ascent from prayer to vision. Her pose, like her garments of monastic austerity, hark back to the iconography of the theological virtue of Faith. Even more than her face lifted in rapt devotion (whose peaceful typology is reminiscent of the foreshortened view of the Madonna in the celebrated drawing of the *Pietà* with the lines "one does not think how much blood it costs" from just before,[31] what denotes the master's invention is the tense relationship between the powerful, tapering body and the light drapery it is wrapped in but not concealed by, expressed in layers of close-fitting, cascading and curving folds.
Rachel's reception (like *Leah*'s) has not undergone the in-depth study instead observed for the sculptures of the New Sacristy, also because the phenomenon is a more restrictive one. A miniaturized but rather faithful image of *Rachel* can be seen in the Uffizi Gallery in the portrait of Ortensia Montauti dei Bardi by Alessandro Allori, painted in 1559 in Rome, while the artist was studying antique and Michelangelesque statuary; embellished with a festoon featuring the head of a cherub at the bottom, within the context of the portrait of the matron, the figure symbolizes virtuous female devotion.[32]
Condivi described the *Active Life* "with a mirror in her right hand in which she examines herself attentively, meaning by this that our actions require consideration, and in her left hand is a garland of flowers".[33] He then added: "In this Michelangelo has followed Dante, whom he has always studied, who in his *Purgatorio* envisions an encounter in a field of flowers with the Countess Matilda".[34]

pp. 252-253
Michelangelo and others, lower storey of the *Tomb of Julius II*, with *Moses* between the *Contemplative Life* (*Rachel*) and the *Active Life* (*Leah*), and *Terms* above the brackets
Rome, church of San Pietro in Vincoli

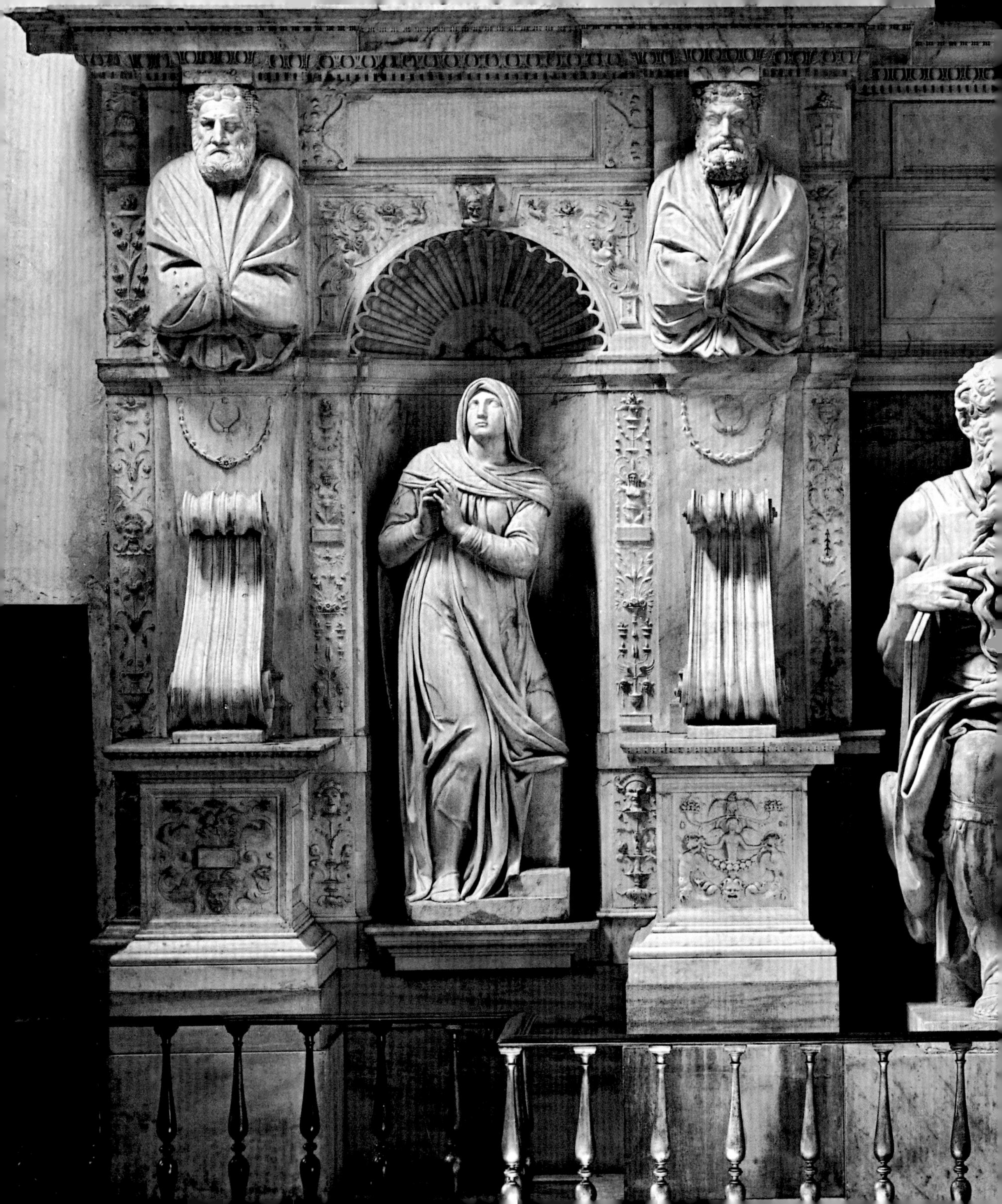

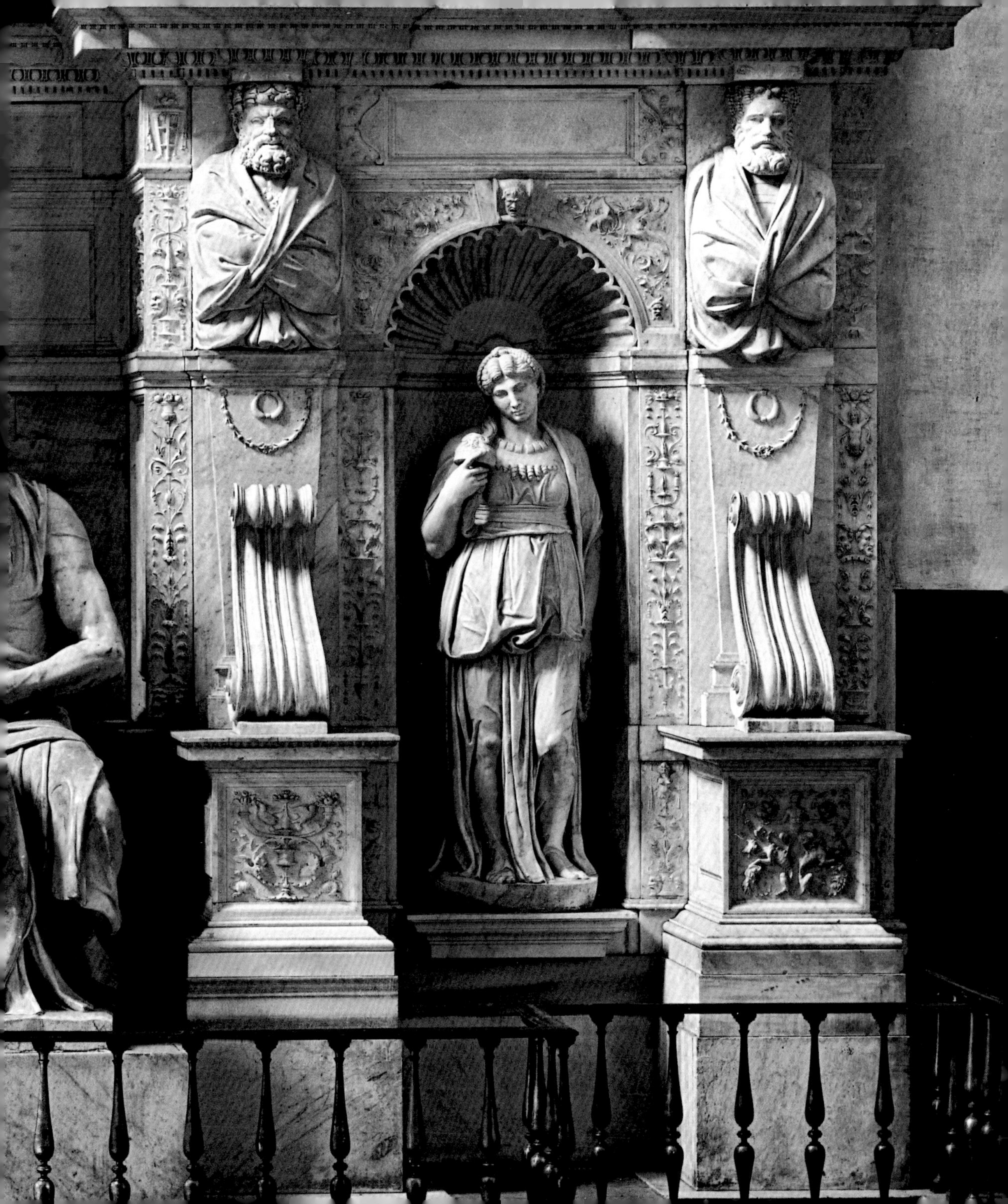

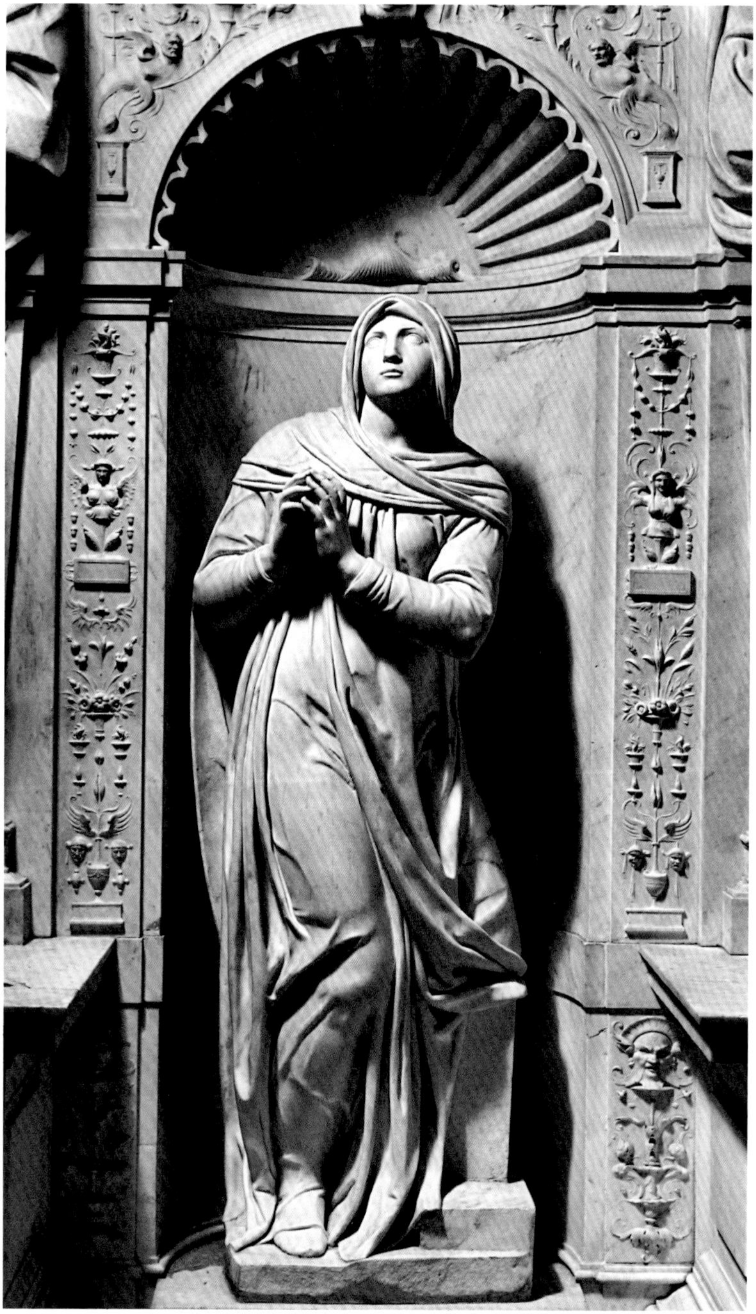

Michelangelo, the *Contemplative Life* (*Rachel*), a figure of intense spirituality transported upwards by prayer
Rome, church of San Pietro in Vincoli

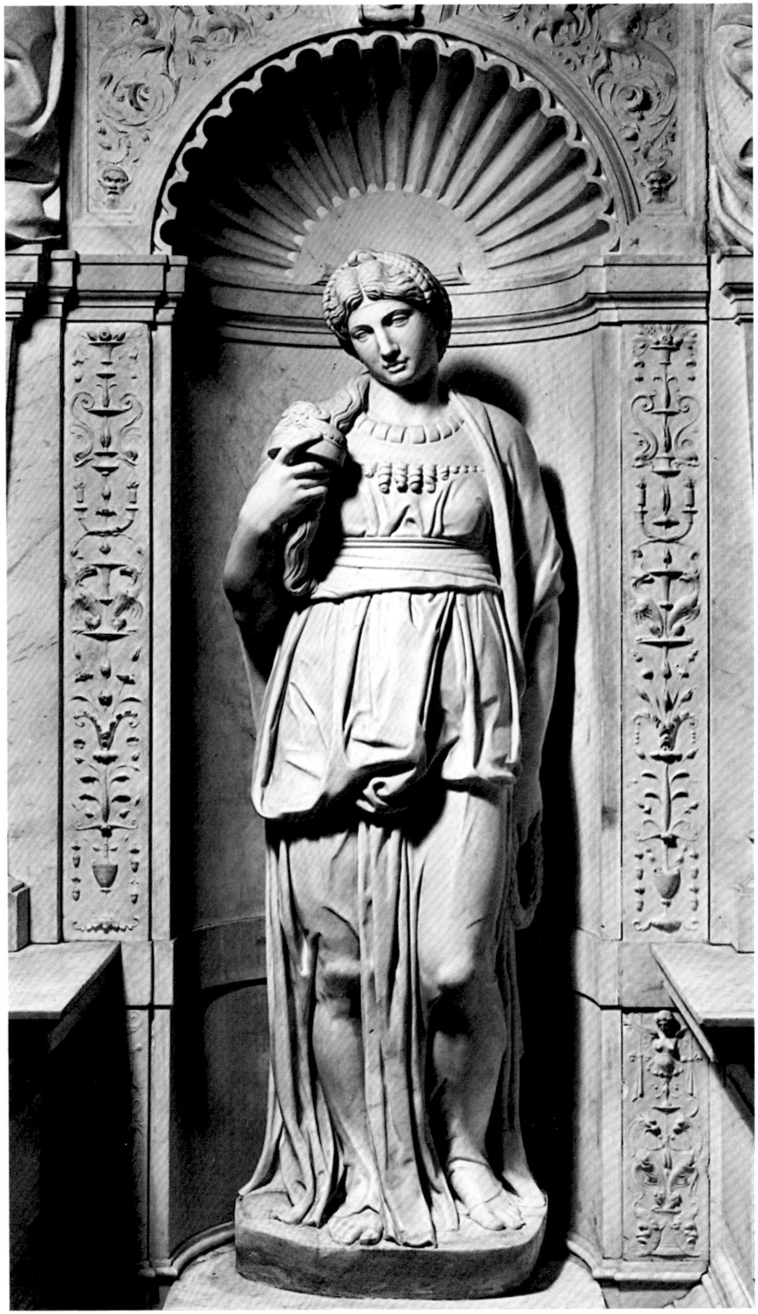

Michelangelo, the *Active Life* (*Leah*), an image of matronly beauty, with the attributes of the mirror and garland (as described by Dante) Rome, church of San Pietro in Vincoli

The biographer, who found himself having to briefly express his master's explanations on the basis of what he remembered from a few years earlier, seems to distinctly refer to Dante here. If, in fact, Matilde (Matelda) is present in the last scene of the *Purgatory* in the field of flowers where Beatrice receives Dante, it is nonetheless in another passage of the *Purgatory* that the two opposites, the contemplative life and the active life, are recounted in the temperaments of the two sisters, both of whom were the wives of Jacob, Rachel and Leah daughters of Laban.[35] The evocation of Matelda, the mysterious female figure who acts as Dante's guide to the Earthly Paradise, and whose flowers are the only thing she has in common with the *Active Life* (apart from the way she thoughtfully cares for Dante), actually contains an autobiographical element: Michelangelo unreservedly identified Matelda with Countess Matilde di Canossa[36] – a fact that all of the commentators of his day agreed upon – thus taking the opportunity to associate the sweet tomb figure with his own presumed ancestor, whose ancient and illustrious nobility reverberated in the artist's family.
Laden with allegorical meaning as the *Active Life*, biblical as *Leah,* and historically commemorative as Matilde di Canossa as Matelda – and inspired by the cardinal virtue of Prudence indicated by the mirror she holds in her hand – the attributes of and fashion worn by this female figure are more carefully wrought than in the other sculptures. The autograph is extensive, although portions of the mechanical repetitiveness in the braided hair have been linked to Raffaello da Montelupo.
Leah's standing and only slightly ponderated pose does not lend itself to the usual effects of the "figura serpentinata"; rather, it expresses unruffled, matronly solemnity, also suited to her conjugal role as the mother of three of Jacob's children. Rachel, who was sterile, has a more nun-like demeanor. The garment Leah wears, with folds and loops encompassing the figure, also features a thin bodice with a notched decoration. On her breast she wears a curious fringe of ribbons that shorten to either side, which recall the thin strips of leather in *Duke Giuliano*'s kilt, but also anticipate the hems with twisted buds that Vasari painted for some of his figures in the *Last Judgement* in the Cupola of Santa Maria del Fiore (1572-1574). Also quite unique is the mirror Leah gazes at: small and round, but enclosed in a deep frame topped with a grotesque mask. Although examples of round mirrors similar in size are familiar to us from the iconography, as well as in mirrors that have survived from that era, there are no examples of a frame as plastically fanciful and aggressive as this one: to be truthful, similar inventions indeed exist in the artist's own corpus of works, for instance, the monstrous protomes of the armour worn by the Medici dukes (moreover, in harmony with the friezes running all along the walls of the New Sacristy), and the head resembling that of a bat in the salt-cellar designed for Duke Della Rovere and visible in a drawing.[37]

Julius II Della Rovere

For centuries the recumbent statue of Julius II was ascribed to the sculptor from Fiesole Tommaso Boscoli, an attribution that Vasari seemingly authoritatively established with these words: "resting on projections of the cornice is a sarcophagus of marble with the recumbent statue of Pope Julius, executed by the sculptor Maso dal Bosco".[38] Owing to the distance and the qualitative intermediacy of the figure, the attribution never raised any doubts, also in consideration of some of Boscoli's other works, which include a number of very fine marble statues. But a closer examination of the statue while restoration that began in 1999 was being carried out led to further critical consideration, and persuaded Antonio Forcellino and Alessandra Risolo, who coordinated the work, to suggest ascribing the statue to Michelangelo instead. Vasari's syntax is ambiguous and would pose no obstacle: the word "fatta" (executed by) in relation to the statue might actually be a reference to the "cassa" or sarcophagus of rather simple, linear shape. After Forcellino made his case on several occasions in both oral and written form, the attribution was ac-

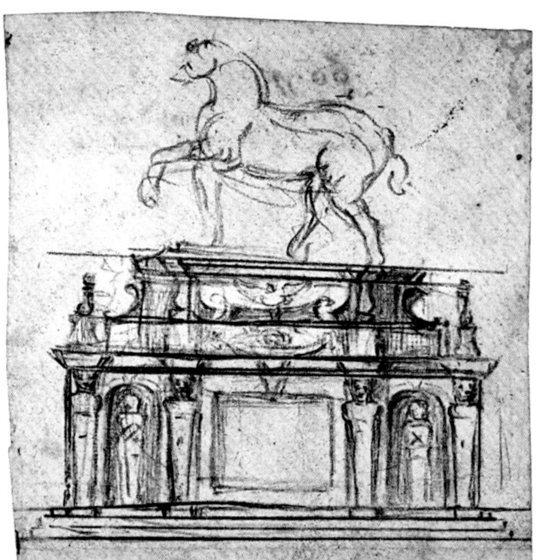

Michelangelo, *Project for an Equestrian Monument to Henry II of France*
Amsterdam, Rijkmuseum, Rijksprentenkabinet, inv. 53: 140

p. 257
Michelangelo, drum, cupola and lantern
Vatican City, Saint Peter's

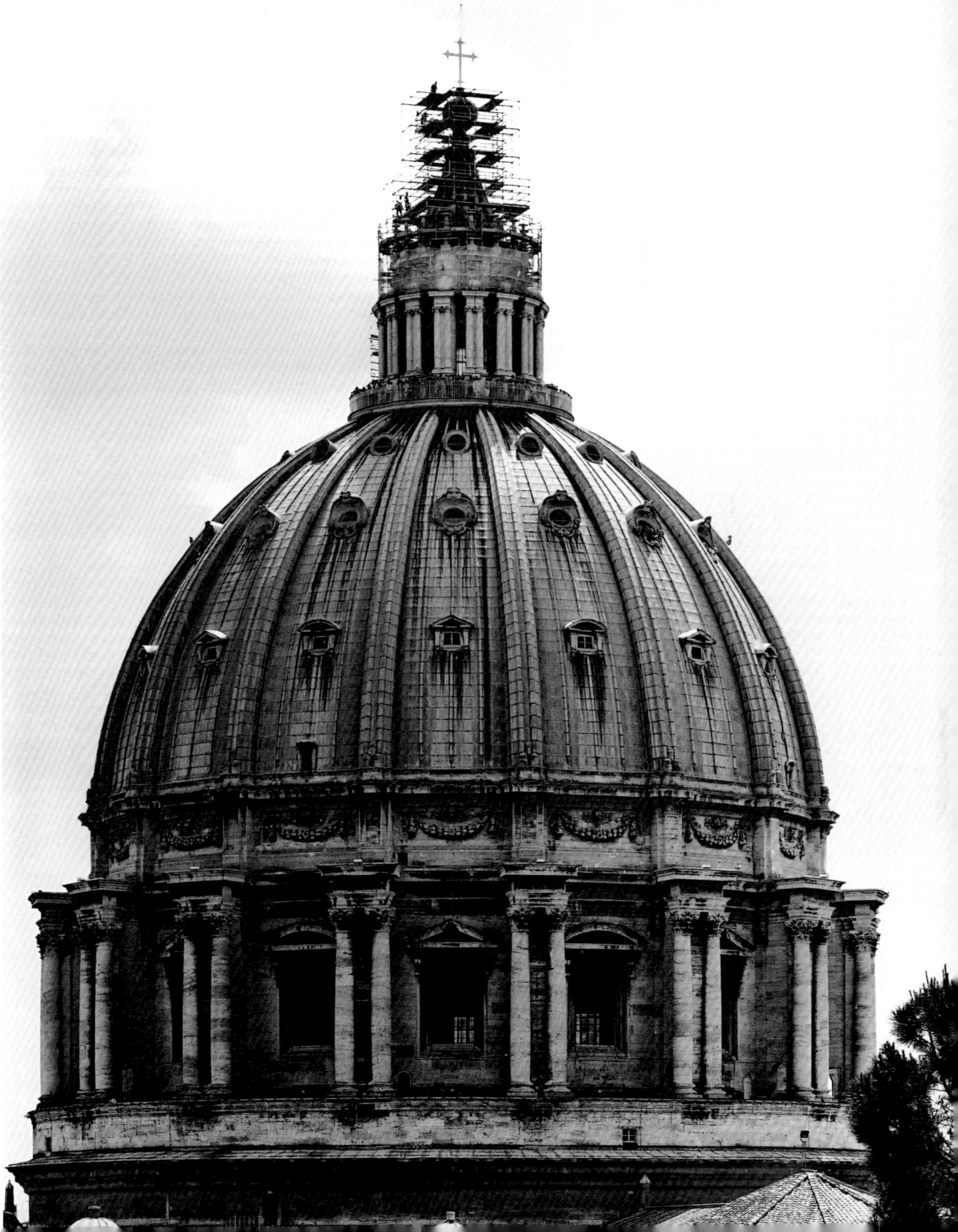

suspended in the background, the slender candelabra on the attic, the pediment made up of two volutes.
Also apparently of Florentine inspiration is the pavilion painted on the wall, which is more clearly visible in drawing no. 533 in the Casa Buonarroti than on the wall in its present state. Its scenographic function, to reveal the monument between curtains pulled to the sides, has both sculptural and painterly precedents, beginning with the tomb for Antipope John XXIII (Baldassarre Cossa or Coscia) by Michelozzo and Donatello in the Florentine baptistery, and continuing with the tomb of the chancellor Carlo Marsuppini in Santa Croce, where the beautiful vari-coloured pavilion crowning the carved pediment was revealed thanks to restoration work carried out in 1998.
Michelangelo's fondness and mourning for Cecchino Bracci have often been analysed in the literature on the artist's homosexual tendencies, as related to his interest in other men.[45]

The architect of popes, from Paul III to Pius IV

Michelangelo's work as an architect, at the head of fabrics, fortifications and other plans for urban renewal in Rome which were the result of commissions received or confirmed by some five popes in a row, took up most of his time and energy in the last twenty years of his life.[46] Because this book is concerned with his sculpture, like for the great cycles of frescoes in the Sistine and Pauline Chapels, this particular subject can only briefly be deal with here.
Michelangelo's design for the arrangement of the piazza or square of the Campidoglio was a unique experience for the artist, which combined architecture and urban planning with a sort of early open-air museology. The long story of the square began in 1537 when Paul III had the bronze equestrian statue of *Marcus Aurelius* relocated to the Campidoglio from the Lateran palace as a gift to the Roman people and to the secular authorities. Michelangelo's involvement over the years was so great that he planned the remodelling of the entire quadrangular space: this included the elevations and thus façades of the three palaces – the Conservators', featuring a powerful "gigantic" order, the Senators' and the Palazzo Nuovo – as well as the plan, for which he invented the extraordinary bichrome oval scheme at the centre of which a new pedestal, which he personally designed, with the statue of *Marcus Aurelius* was placed. Michelangelo also designed the stairway with two flights to the Senators' palace (1544-1552), which included two imposing statues of the ancient river gods, identified by 16th-century sources as the *Tiber* and the *Nile*, situated at the bottom. Also by Michelangelo is the impressive stairway leading up to the piazza, known as the "cordonata" (after 1559). The project was only in part carried out while the artist was still living: made known through two posthumous engravings based on his drawings, it is considered to have been completed only halfway through the 17th century.
The most difficult but also the most prestigious architectural commission was given to Michelangelo by Paul III in November 1546 when, upon the death of Antonio da Sangallo the Younger, he was nominated chief architect for the Basilica of Saint Peter's. The first thing Michelangelo did was to go see, rather visit the detailed model that his predecessor had had built by skilled workers overseen by Antonio Labacco beginning in 1539, and that being at a scale of 1: 30 could also be viewed from the interior. By 2 December Michelangelo had already rejected the project in a written note that contained scathing criticism, and proposed going back to the idea of using Bramante's central plan instead. After a brief phase during which terracotta and wooden models were produced, and some of the parts that had previously been made by Sangallo were demolished, construction began, to which the artist devoted every ounce of energy with frequent visits to the construction site. The apse area is where his intervention is most clearly visible, spanned by a gigantic order that organizes the magnificent window scheme and culminates with an attic for which the artist's paternity is likely. Michelangelo devoted an in-depth series of drawings to the cupola and lantern, and between 1557 and 1561 he produced four variations, and a

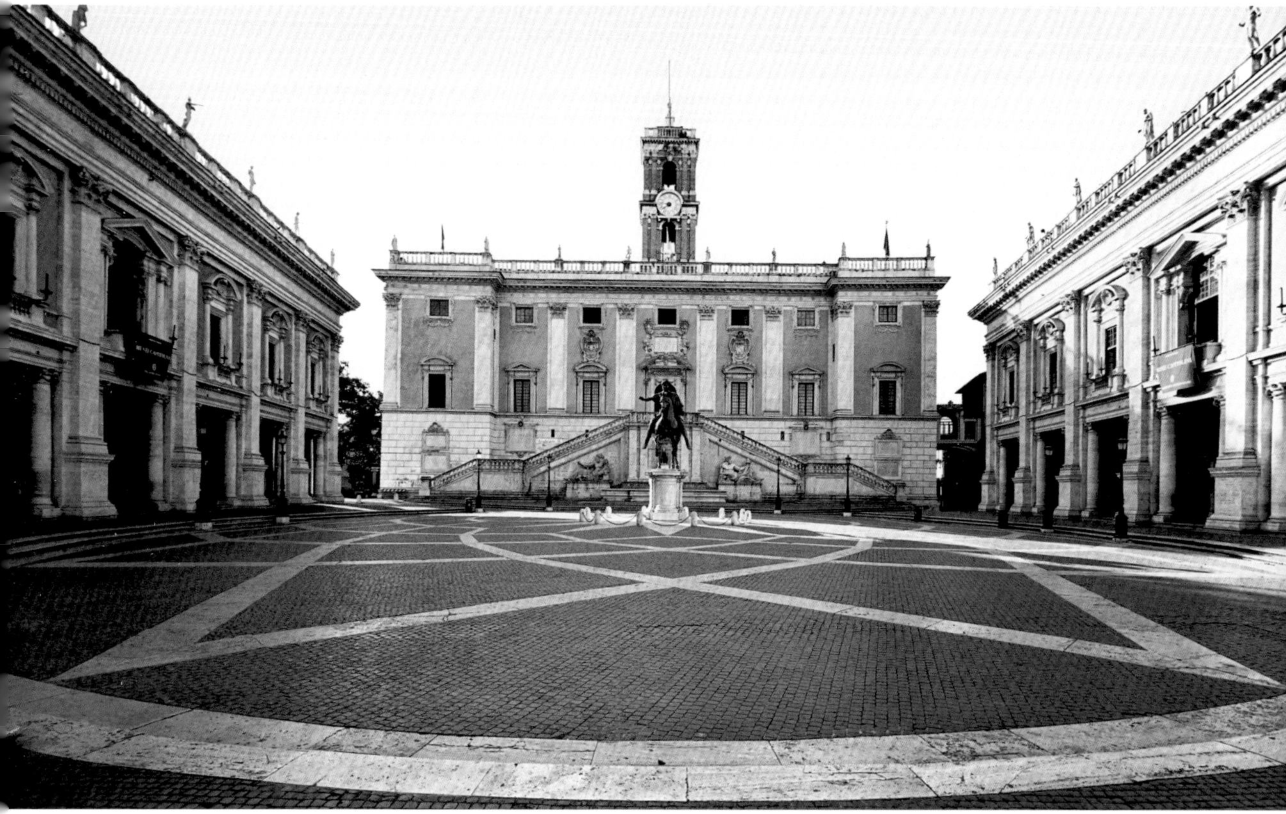

Project by Michelangelo,
Piazza del Campidoglio
Rome

pp. 262-263
Project by Michelangelo,
Piazza del Campidoglio
Rome

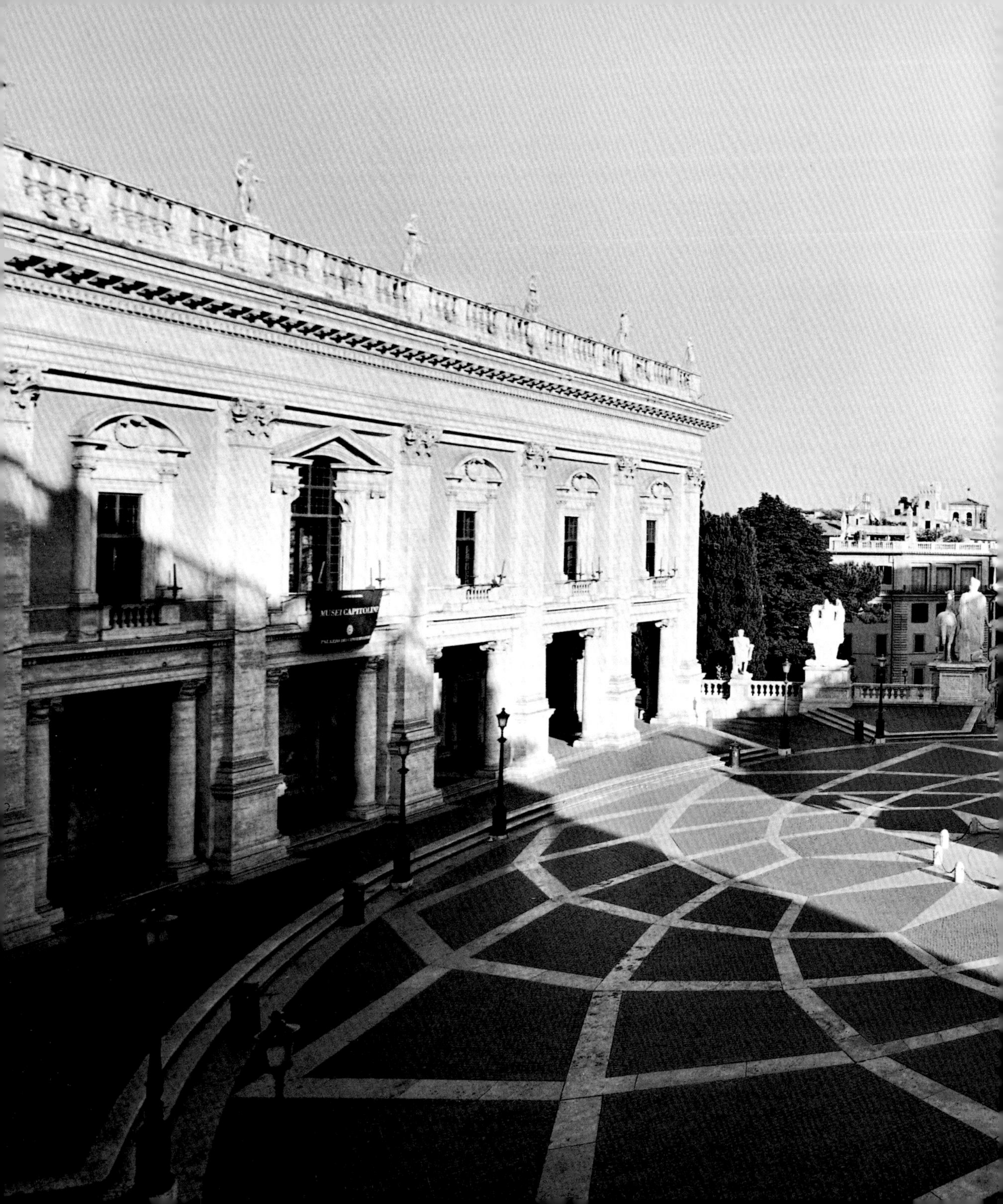
MUSEI CAPITOLINI

MUSEI CAPITOLINI

wooden model of the latter, which is still housed in the Vatican. Construction of the cupola ended in 1595, under the guidance of Giacomo della Porta. As the successor to Sangallo, Michelangelo had also inherited the continuation of the Palazzo Farnese, Paul III's family residence in Campo de' Fiori, which in 1546 had already been built up to the second storey. The artist completed the façade by raising the height of the upper storey and crowning it with an imposing cornice, as well as emphasizing the central axis by framing the middle window on the *piano nobile* in an elegant balconied structure that included the portal. Michelangelo also worked on the façades overlooking the inner courtyard, where the third order was marked by Corinthian pilaster strips set in between fanciful decorations, although the work subsequently carried out by Vignola makes it difficult to fully determine his contribution. Michelangelo seems to have wanted to continue this visual axis through the palace complex, which was already very imposing, and had proposed building a bridge crossing the Tiber River. The idea was to be able to see the palace at a glance, and to make it even more scenographic by installing the antique marble sculpture of the *Farnese Bull* in the second courtyard. But this part of the project was never developed.

In 1559, after a series of informal contacts between Michelangelo and the expatriate Florentine community in Rome, the artist was officially assigned – the request was made in a letter – the task of designing the church of San Giovanni dei Fiorentini which Duke Cosimo was having built. He gave the representatives of his compatriots in Rome, between 1559 and 1562, some five designs for a church with a central plan (three of which were found in the Casa Buonarroti) and from the one chosen by the representatives, no. 612 in Tolnay's Corpus, he made two models, one from terracotta, the other from wood. It has been observed that the artist's quick response was perhaps due more to his eagerness to build a majestic church at the top of Via Giulia from the ground up, than the desire to satisfy the repeated requests of the dukes. But he was soon disappointed as construction never progressed beyond the initial stages. Michelangelo's plans for San Giovanni dei Fiorentini constitute the most advanced example of his architectural inventions, and survived, with their radical innovations in the conception of space, well into the 17th century.

Pius IV, the last pope Michelangelo worked for, commissioned him to transform the Tepidarium of the Baths of Diocletian in the Carthusian church of Santa Maria degli Angeli starting in 1562. Out of respect for the original spaces and structures the artist made very few changes to the grandiose, ancient construction.

A fascinating and dynamic interior was designed by Michelangelo for the Sforza burial chapel in Sant Maria Maggiore, with an elliptical ground plan, altars housed in gently concave niches and a plastically articulated ceiling with four columns. Research carried out during restoration work (ending in late 2004) has shown that Michelangelo underwrote a regular contract for Cardinals Guido Ascanio and Alessandro Sforza in August 1562, which included the provision of a scale model, and that he oversaw the work until his death. Up until recently it was believed that the artist's contribution was limited to making a drawing, which he then gave to those actually working in the site.

In the very last years, Michelangelo also worked on an eccentric secular project for Cardinal Santafiora: a gateway known as Porta Pia, located at the end of the new Strada Pia that ran from the Quirinal Hill, with villas and gardens on either side. Preceded by fervent drawing activity, the architecture of the gate combines the morphology of several origins, while from a sculptural viewpoint, it hosts a fascinating repertory of transgressive and metamorphic forms. Even at an advanced age, the artist was setting himself extraordinary challenges, and the Porta Pia alone is sufficient to belie the image often associated with the late Michelangelo as someone exclusively interested in meditating on religious themes and inclined towards unimaginativeness. Here, the extraordinary ornamental inventions spring forth with the same energy and freedom as thirty years before when he was working on the San Lorenzo complex in Florence.

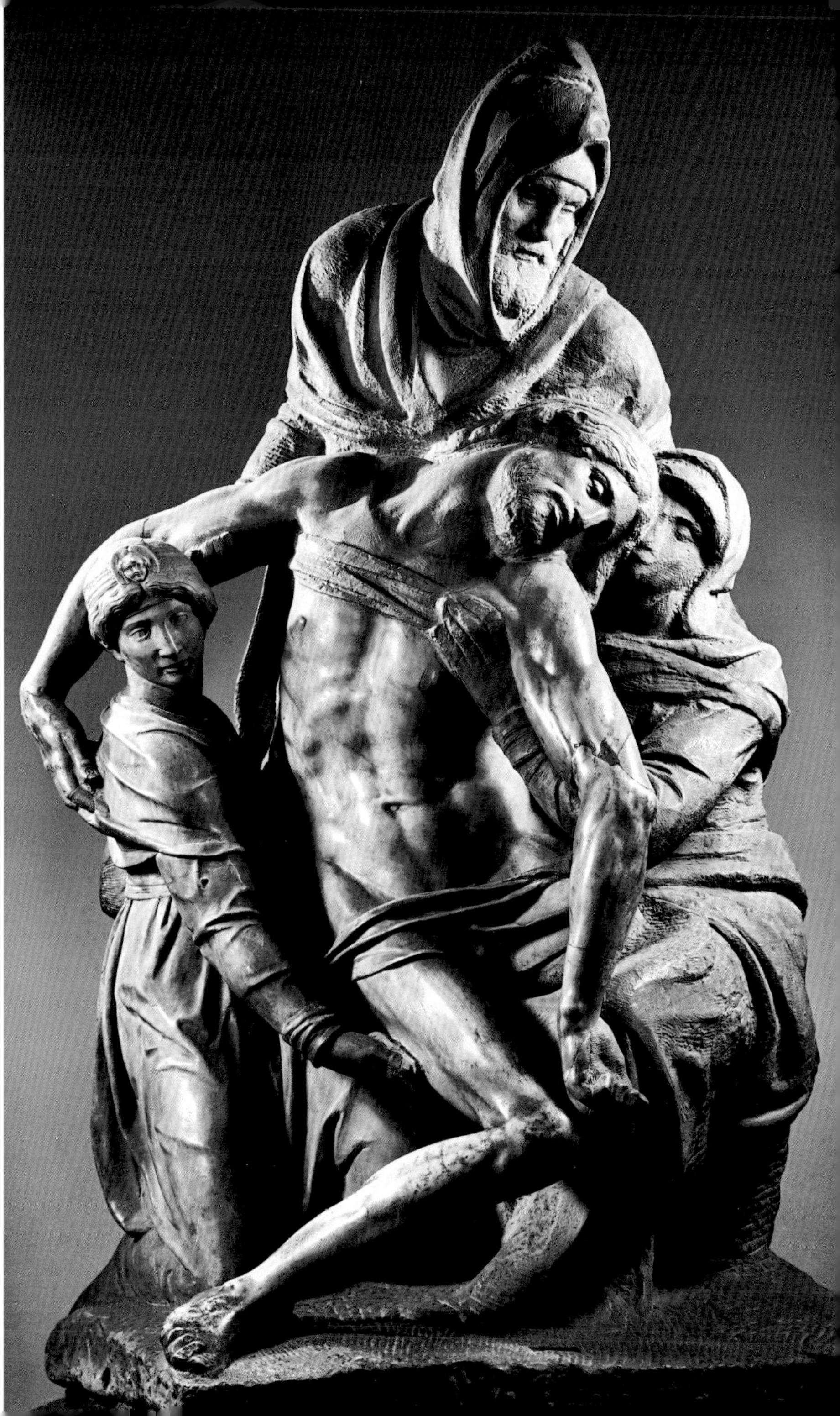

Michelangelo, *Bandini Pietà*,
acquired by Grand Duke
Cosimo III in 1671
Florence, Museo dell'Opera
del Duomo

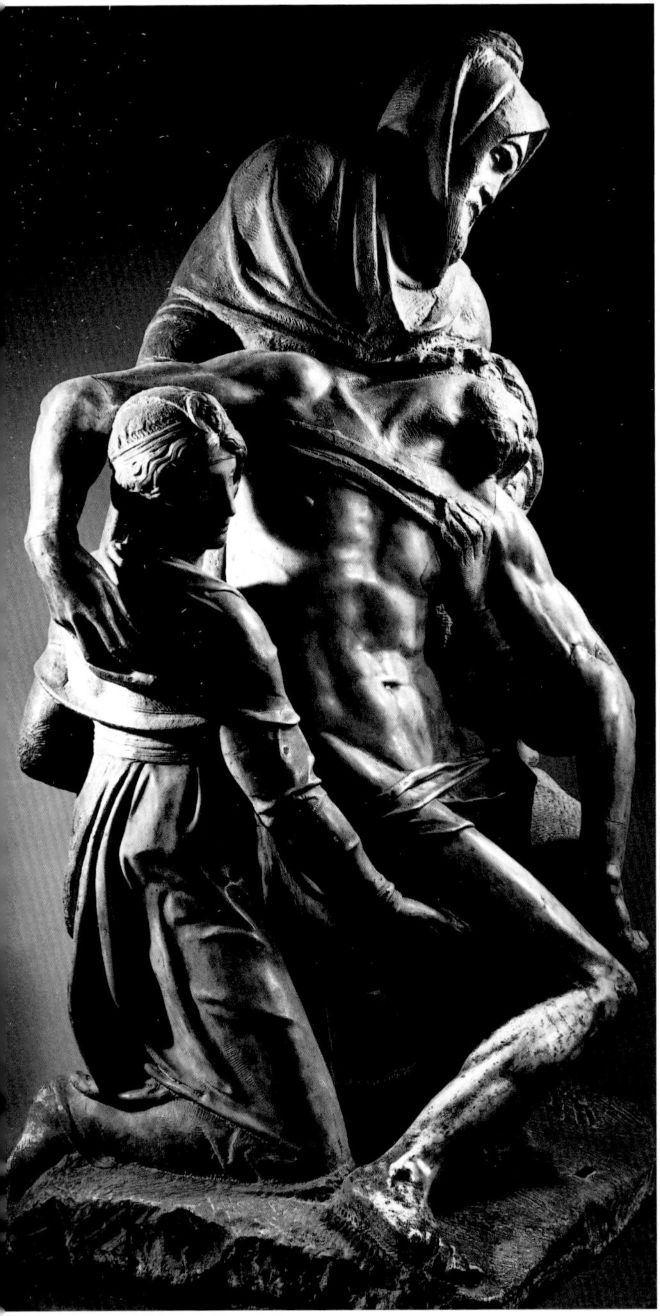

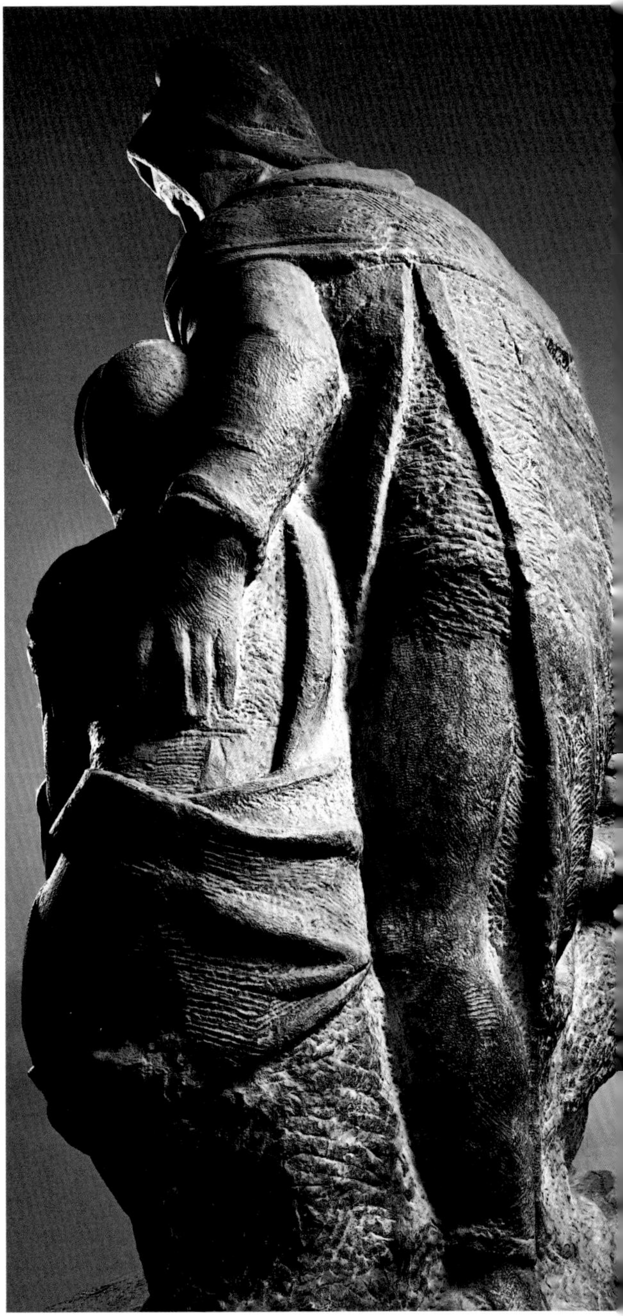

The *Florentine Pietà*

In the first edition of Michelangelo's biography (1550), just after he mentioned the *Contemplative Life* or *Rachel* and the *Active Life* or *Leah* for the Julius Tomb of 1544-1545, Vasari recalled a group of four figures "blocked out in a single piece of marble" meant to represent "a Deposition of Christ". The state of the work was such that it left a great deal of room for expectations and the imagination: "[o]ne may suppose that if this had been finished it would have surpassed every other work of Michelangelo, given the sheer difficulty of extracting so many perfect figures from that stone".[47]
In 1553 Condivi testified to the fact that Michelangelo had in hand "a work in marble which he is doing for his own pleasure; being a man who is full of ideas and energy, he naturally produces something every day". Condivi's description allows us to imagine the advanced state of the design of the over life-sized figures: the Christ coming down from the cross sustained by the Virgin with the help of an eager figure (Nicodemus according to Condivi) and one of the Marys. Despite the unfinished state of the work, every single expression and emotion could be intuited, that is, "the beauty and the emotions shown in the grieving and sorrowful faces of the anguished mother and all the others". Condivi added one more thing: "I really mean to say that it is something rare and one of the most exciting works that he has done to date, chiefly because all the figures are perceived distinctly and the draperies of any one figure are not to be confused with those of the others".[48]
In 1568, in the revised and expanded second version of the *Lives*, Vasari was able to provide further information on the fate of the group, by now defined the *Pietà*, a title that Gaetano Milanesi in the 19th century would begin to question, and suggest replacing with the "Entombment".[49] Intended to be placed on Michelangelo's own tomb, the *Pietà* "was broken" by the sculptor himself for a number of reasons that are still not clear, and donated to Antonio del Francese of Castel Durante, his servant. When Tiberio Calcagni, a young Florentine sculptor and the master's assistant, saw it,[50] he pointed it out to the banker Francesco Bandini, also from Florence, and his patron,[51] and in the end Michelangelo handed the statue over to Bandini, promising to allow Calcagni to finish it "with the assistance of models by his hand".[52] Tiberio was to have "put [the work] together again and reconstructed with I know not what new pieces",[53] but the death of all those involved in three years' time – Bandini in 1562, Michelangelo in 1564, Tiberio in 1565 – left the *Pietà* "imperfect" and as we see it today. It was installed in Bandini's garden on the Quirinal Hill and remained there until it was purchased by Grand Duke Cosimo III of Tuscany in 1671, and after three years it arrived in Florence. After many vicissitudes, it can now be viewed in the Museo dell'Opera of Santa Maria del Fiore.
Although the chronology of the marble sculpture remains controversial, it is likely that Michelangelo began working on it in 1549 or just before. This would mean that Vasari postponed sending the second edition of the *Lives* to the printer's so that he could mention it.[54] It is commonly believed that the artist stopped working on the sculpture in 1555, although proof is lacking of this. Weak and old, according to Vasari, Michelangelo did not so much devote his waning energy to sculpting marble for the purpose of keeping up his skills, as to prepare his own tomb with a subject alluding to the death of Christ and the power of imminent Redemption. The artist had perhaps first had the idea of creating not just a tomb for himself, but an entire burial chapel in the church of Santa Croce in Florence, close to his home and that of his family in Via Ghibellina, in the 1530s. He had suggested to the Franciscan friars that they have a building constructed, where he could then place "by his hand such Paintings, Statues, with such and so many ornaments, that Foreigners passing through Florence would have to see Santa Croce first to see that chapel, rather than behind the Palazzo della Signoria to see the Lions".[55] But the problems brought up by the *operai*, i.e. the lay overseers of the fabric, as well as their refusals so greatly irritated the sensitive artist that he gave up on his project, and deprived Santa Croce of a monument that he himself had imagined would be an excellent tourist attraction.[56]

p. 266
Michelangelo, *Bandini Pietà*
The kneeling Magdalene is the work of Tiberio Calcagni
Florence, Museo dell'Opera del Duomo

p. 266
Michelangelo, *Bandini Pietà*
the hooded man who takes pity, identified as Nicodemus, helps the women support the dead Christ's body
Florence, Museo dell'Opera del Duomo

p. 268
Michelangelo, *Bandini Pietà*, detail of so-called Nicodemus, whose face is the artist's self-portrait
Florence, Museo dell'Opera del Duomo

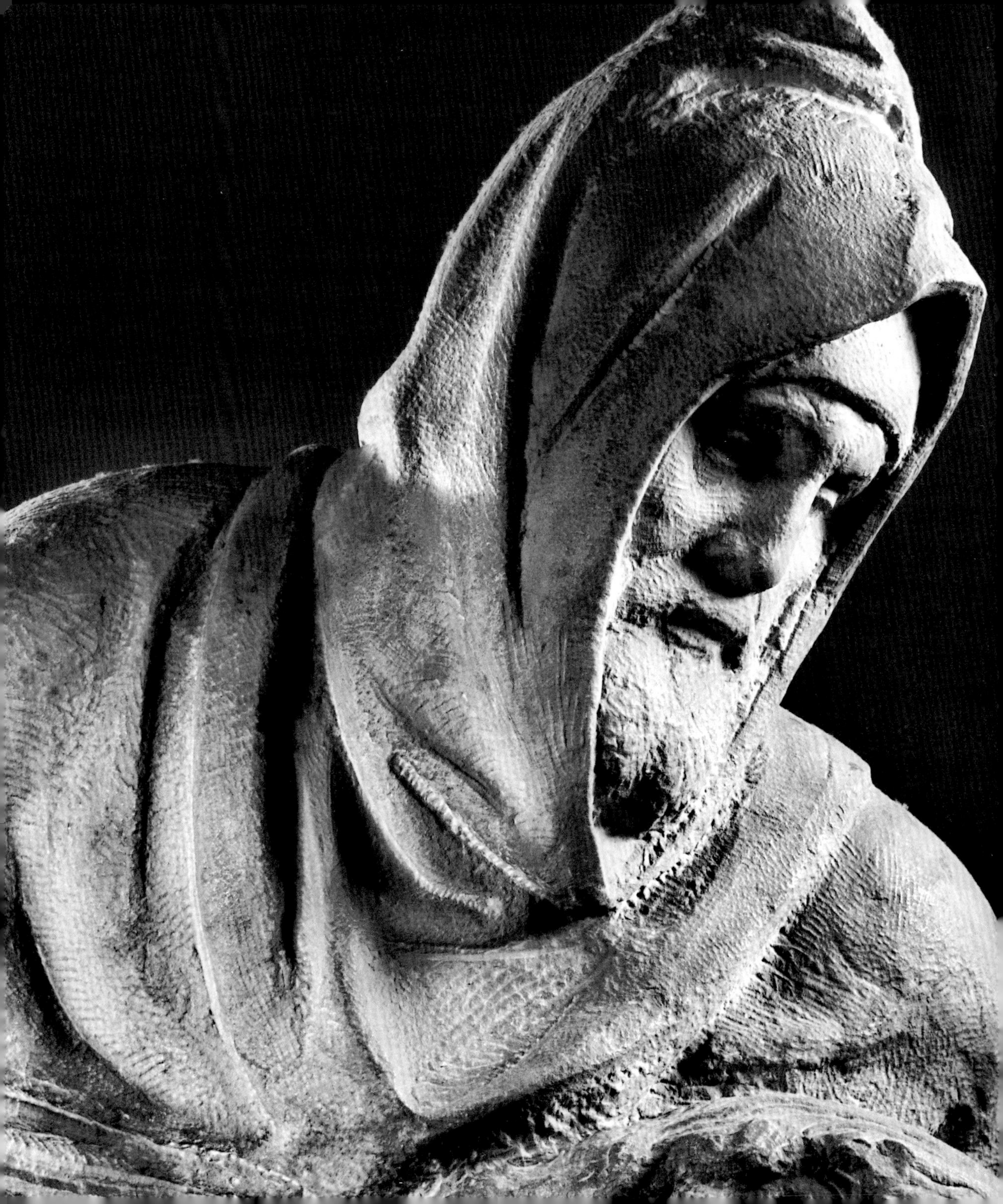

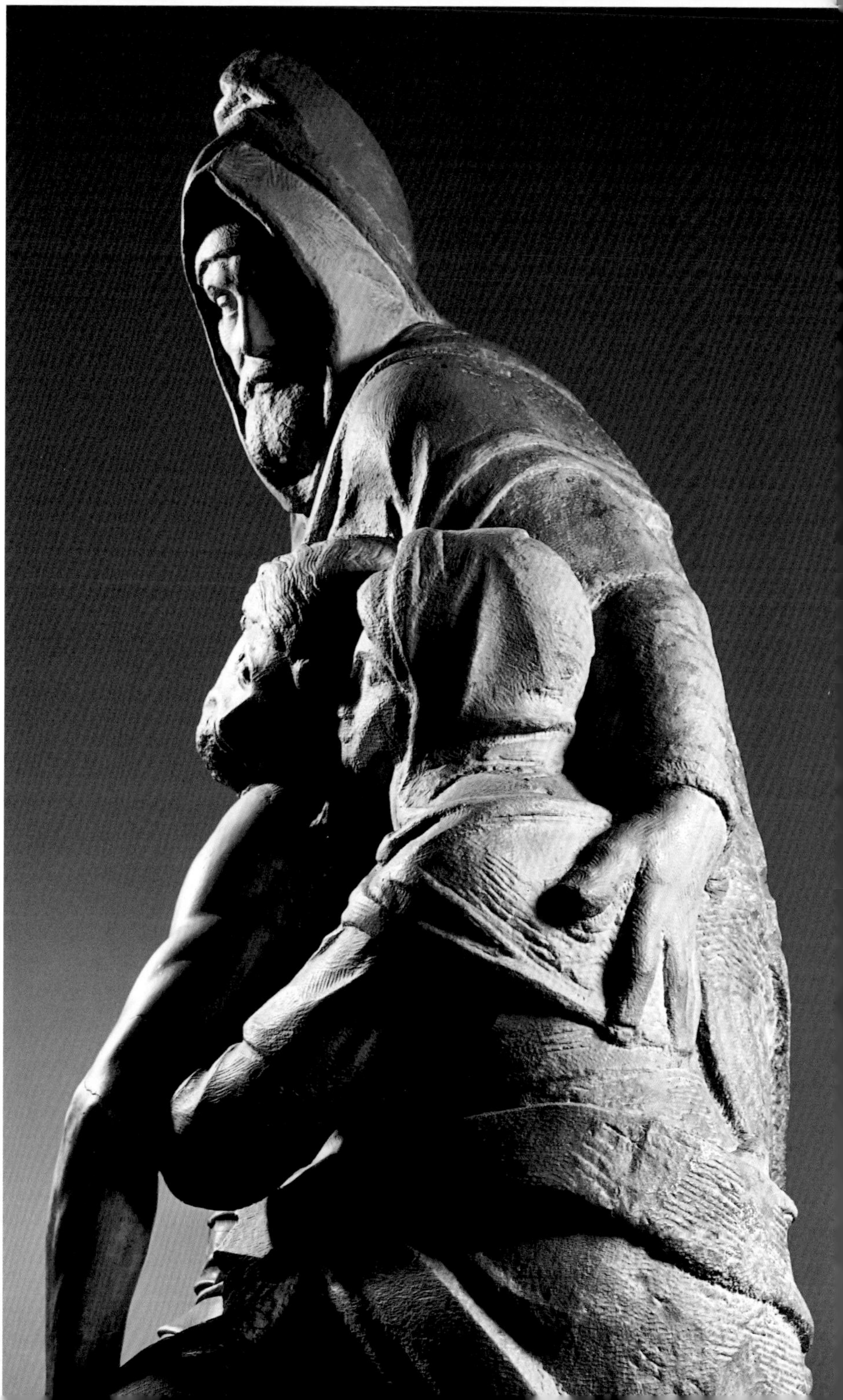

Michelangelo, *Bandini Pietà*
A side view shows the complex spatial relationship between the Michelangelesque figures
Florence, Museo dell'Opera del Duomo

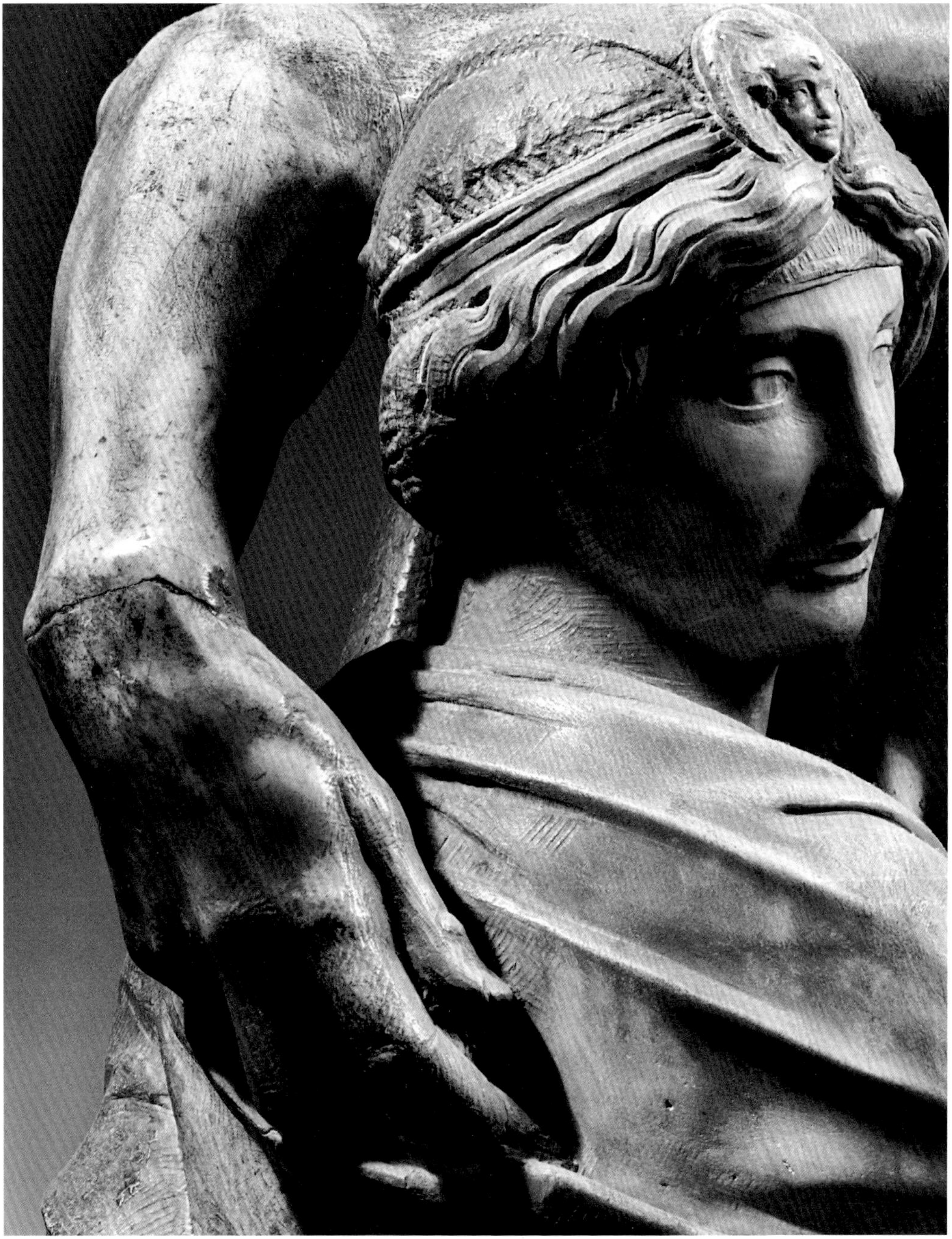

Michelangelo, *Pietà Bandini*,
with contributions by the hand
of Tiberio Calcagni
Florence, Museo dell'Opera
del Duomo

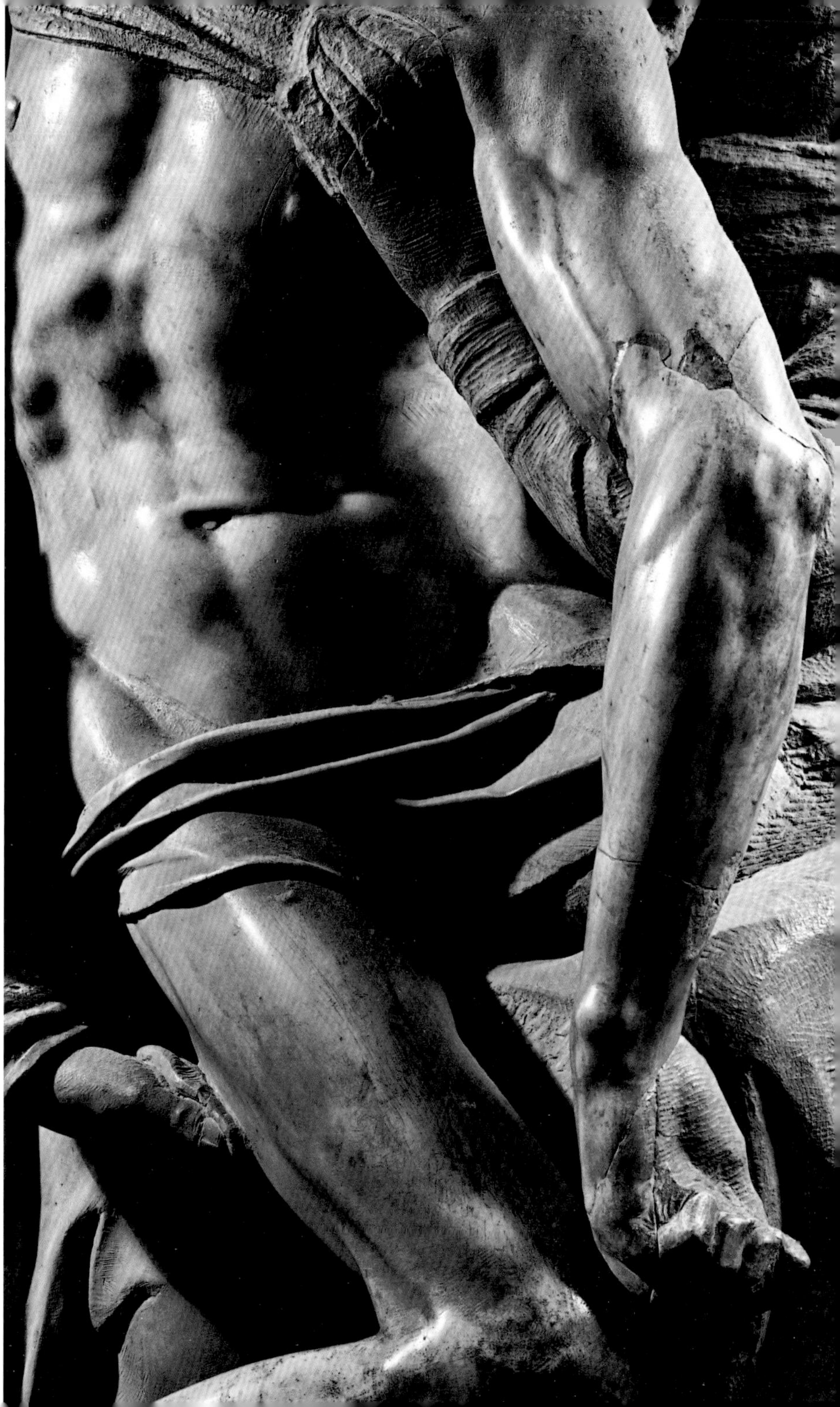

Michelangelo, *Bandini Pietà*, detail of the highly polished body of Christ
Florence, Museo dell'Opera del Duomo

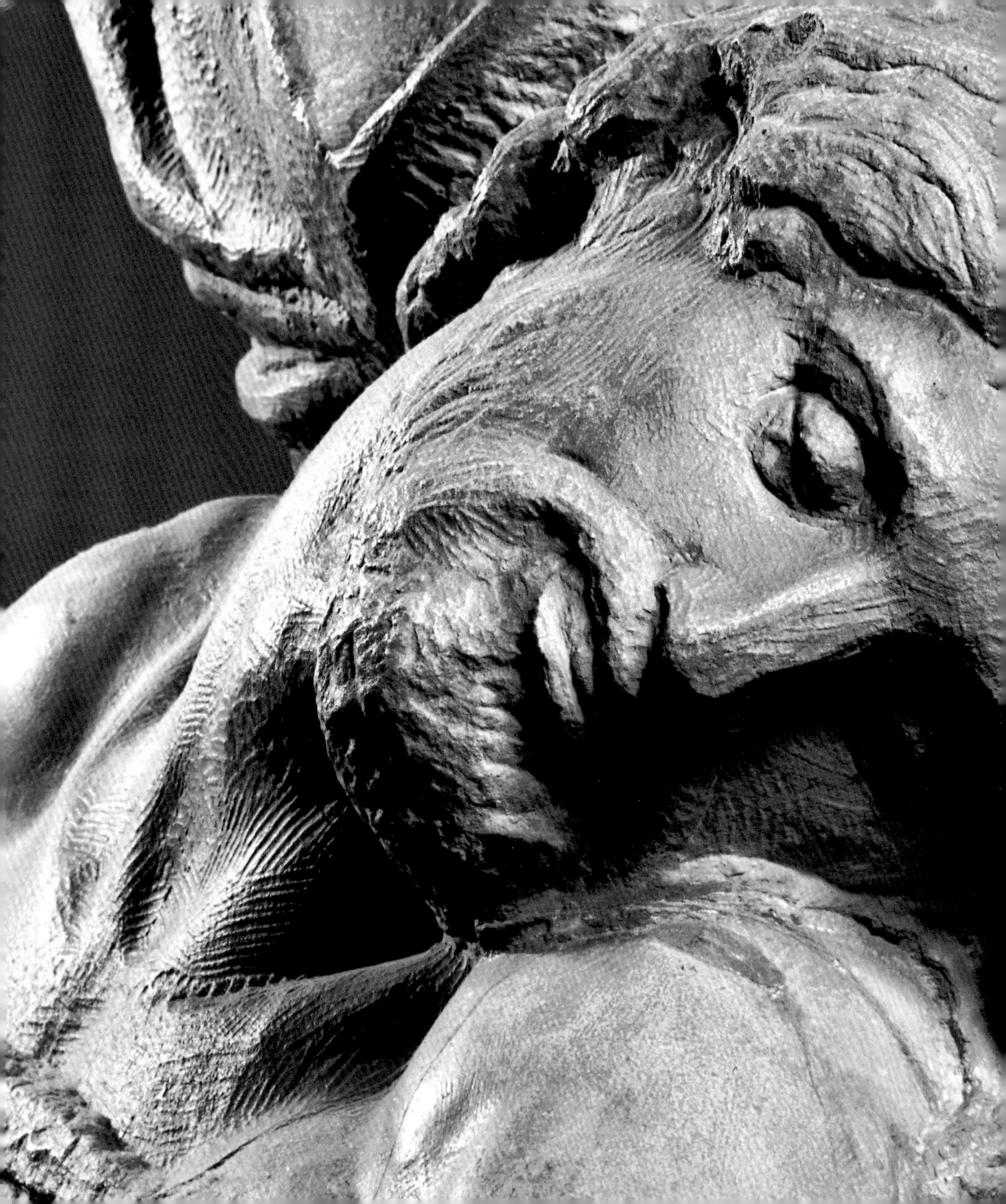

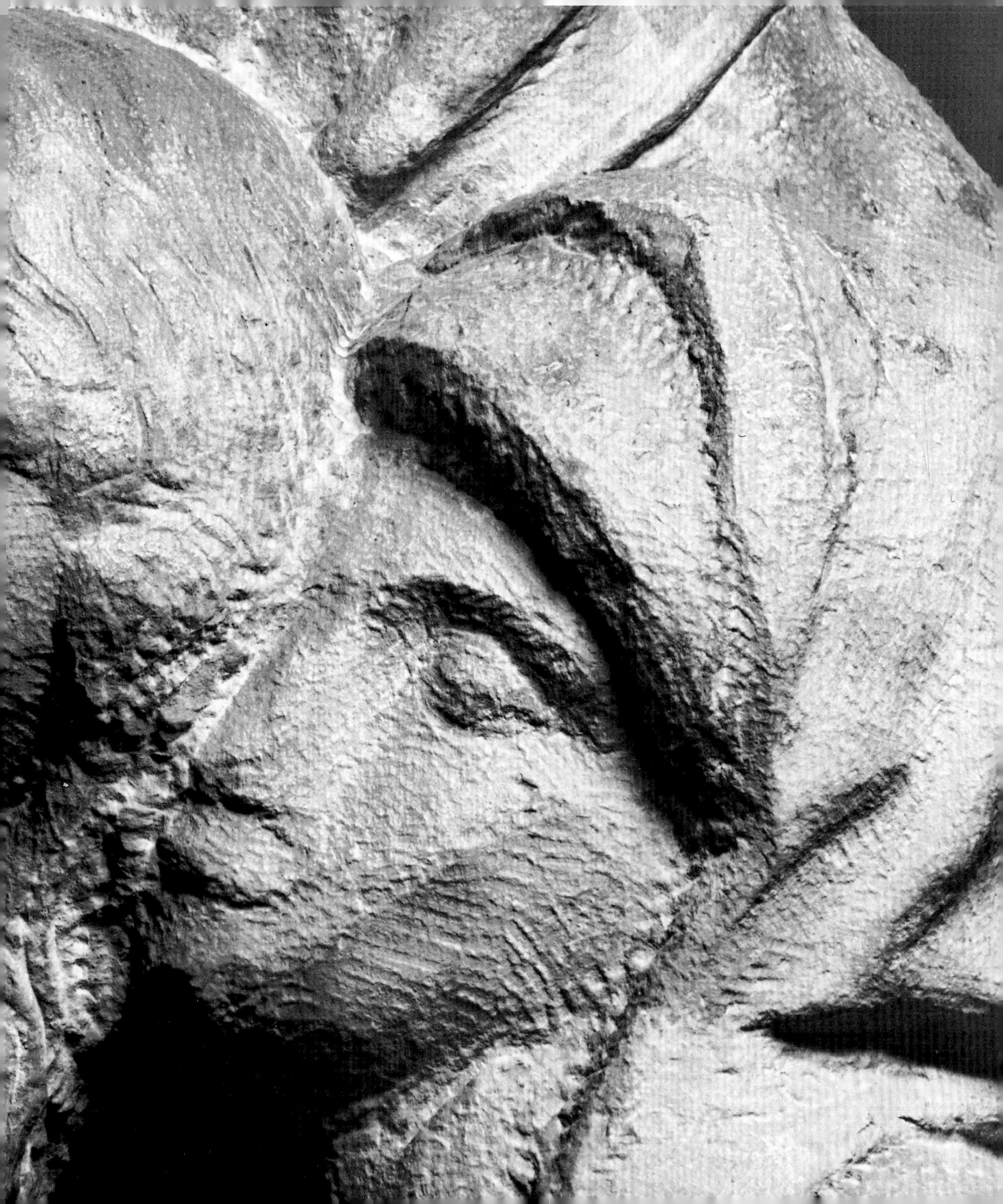

Michelangelo may have been considering placing the *Pietà* group – referred to as the "Bandini" *Pietà* because that was the name of its first owner, or the "Florentine" *Pietà* because of its presence in the city from 1674 onwards – inside a niche or above an altar.[57] We still do not know the name of the church where Michelangelo was considering being buried: nevertheless, it had to have been a Florentine church, for to the very end the artist insisted that his body be transported back to his native city.

The *Florentine Pietà* represents the sculptor's return to the theme of the celebrated Vatican *Pietà* of his youth; just how it relates chronologically to his other late *Pietà*, the *Rondanini* in Milan, still needs to be clarified. The Florentine group, conceived on a monumental scale, is the only one of the three that includes four figures, whereas in the other works the relationship is reduced to a very intense and exclusively intimate one between the sorrowful Virgin and the deceased Son slumped in her arms. Moreover, the iconography has an unprecedented narrative quality, as Michelangelo chose to portray the moment when Christ is taken down off the cross and given back to the Virgin, who bears his weight or at least tries to: "[his] dead body is sustained by His mother, as she slips her breast, arms, and knee under His body in a remarkable pose".[58] It is thus correct to acknowledge the group's dynamism, and consider the idea that the theme originally intended by the artist gradually evolved into another, "a Deposition at the point where it becomes a Pietà".[59] According to this interpretation, the bearded man wearing a hood, Nicodemus according to commentators of Michelangelo's day, Joseph of Arimathea according to others, guides Christ's descent from the cross towards his mother's embrace by holding his arm and using one hand to support her back. Michelangelo gave the merciful figure his own features, one of his last self-portraits, a fact that was already familiar to his contemporaries. The Virgin's embrace and the help of the pious woman, generally recognized as Magdalene (Michelangelo designed the arrangement for the figure, but Calcagni executed it) physically portray a resolute setting to the task. The members of the group interact by holding and moving their limbs and drapery: this is not a symbolic scene fixed in the atemporal dimension of the icon, but a coordinated sequence of actions, each of which corresponding to naturalistic effects that derive from the volumes of the marble. While the Son is being lowered into his Mother's lap, who is seated on a low rustic plinth, his body slips, and while his left leg (removed, however, by the artist himself) is imagined as resting on her legs, his right leg falls in between hers. Michelangelo even finds a passage for Magdalene's hands in the cloth crossing the figure's torso, typical of the iconography of the *Descent from the Cross*, thus anticipating its function as the sudarium for the burial.

Ancient precedents (although not monolithic) have been suggested for the composition: works like the *Laocoön* and the *Farnese Bull*, as well as medieval and modern pictorial sources such as Giovanni da Milano, Fra Giovanni Angelico, Albrecht Dürer, Filippino Lippi. Michelangelo had also worked on the theme of the *Pietà* in his drawings, in the famous sheet in Boston which he gave to Vittoria Colonna, in the sheet at the Louvre in Paris and in one at the Albertina Graphische Sammlung in Vienna dated from his last years in Florence (*circa* 1530-1534). The sheet at the Teylers Museum in Haarlem (*circa* 1540) shows that Michelangelo created a complex compositive paradigm for the *Deposition*, one that would inspire countless artists.

Like all of the statuary of Michelangelo's final years, close examination of the *Pietà* reveals many states of autograph "non-finito", from rustic rough-hewing, to fine-toothed claw-chiselling, to the highest possible degree of polishing in the Christ. Excluded from such considerations is the figure of the Magdalene, instead made by Calcagni. The gradual "non-finito" in the autograph portions allows us to see exactly how the artist used his tools: the *subbia da taglio* (pointed chisel) for the initial rough-shaping of the volumes, the two-toothed *calcagnolo*, the various types of claw-chisels all around, in some more specific areas the *scarpello* and *ugnetto*. Abrasives were used to polish Christ's torso, whereas the areas that were smoothed using a rasp are concentrated in the Magdalene and by another hand. The block itself, from the very beginning, must have forced Michelangelo to find a solution to the problems that Vasari pointed out when he spoke of the difficulty of working the "stone" that was very cracked and so hard that the chisel often struck sparks from it.

Observing the work from different angles reveals forced treatments, compressions and anatomical abbreviations, areas where, in any case, there was not enough marble to carve out complete forms.

pp. 272-273
Michelangelo, *Bandini Pietà*, where the contact between Mary and the Son is especially moving
Florence, Museo dell'Opera del Duomo

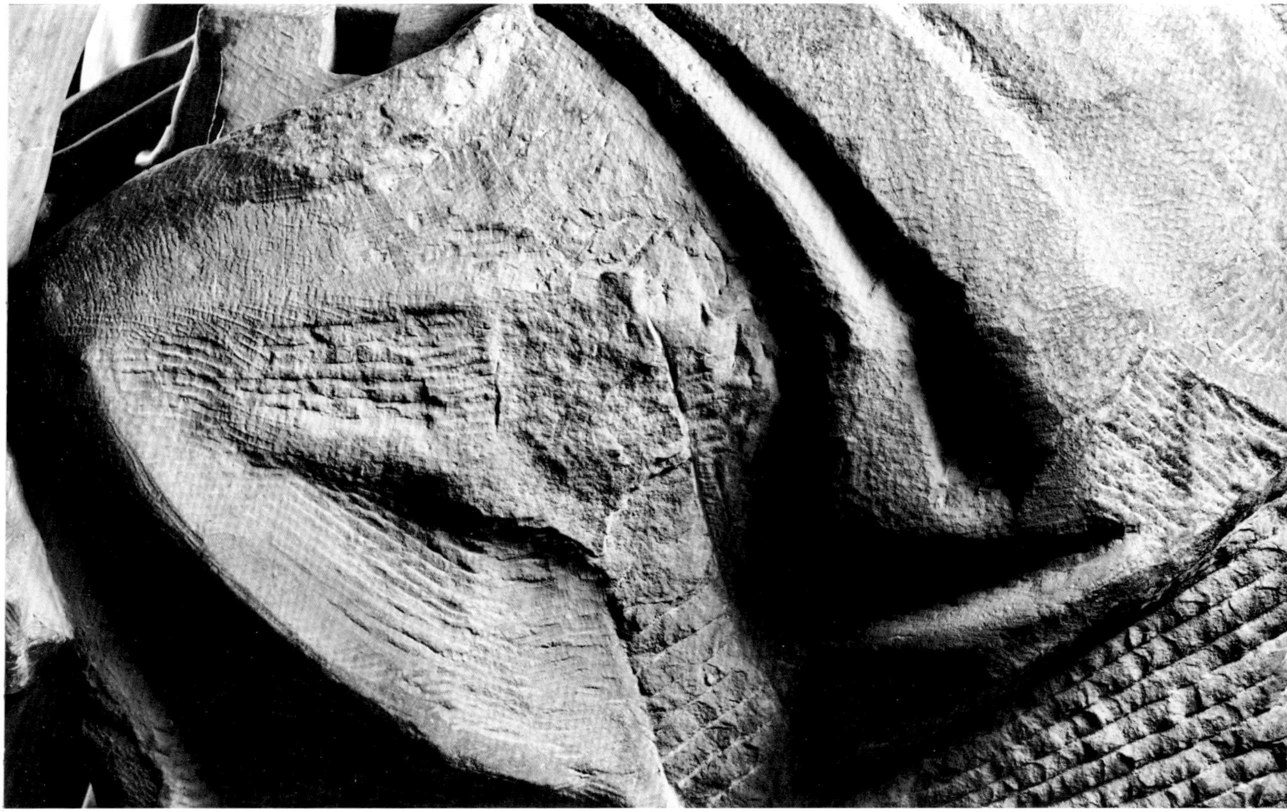

Michelangelo, *Bandini Pietà*, different degrees of "non-finito"
Florence, Museo dell'Opera del Duomo

The *Palestrina Pietà*, an attribution now rejected

Among the works freely inspired by Michelangelo's sculptural group (evidently not many, considering the complexity of conception and working) we need to include the Palestrina *Pietà*, which has the privilege of being on display in the room filled with Michelangelo's marble sculptures headed by the *David* in the Galleria dell'Accademia in Florence. This impressive sculpture[73] of two mourners holding up the body of Christ comes from Palestrina, to be exact from the church of Santa Rosalia that Prince Maffeo Barberini, from the eponymous family of Urban VIII, had built adjoining the family palazzo after they survived the plague, in 1660. The *Pietà* was located in the Barberini burial chapel and it has now been replaced by a copy.[74] Referred to for the first time as an "abbozzo" made by Buonarroti,[75] by 1795 a local publication had already shifted its attribution to a 17th-century sculptor: Niccolò Menghini or, even more ambitiously, Gian Lorenzo Bernini.[76] Eighteenth- and 19th-century scholars were divided on the attribution. Nonetheless, when the Italian government purchased the work in 1938 it was believed to be a sculpture by Michelangelo, and it was first displayed in Rome as part of the *Mostra Autarchica del Minerale Italiano*, and then in Florence at the *Mostra del Cinquecento toscano*. The latter exhibition was forced to close early when Italy entered the war in 1940. Triumphally showcased in the courtyard of the Palazzo Strozzi the Fascist regime intended it to be a contribution to the "Centro Michelangiolesco" undergoing construction at the time, but it was eventually assigned to the Galleria dell'Accademia. A scholarly examination of the work was carried out by the sculptor Quinto Martini, who reported that the sculptural technique used was incompatible with that of Michelangelo. Bonsanti, in the catalogue for the Galleria, attributed it to imitators of Michelangelo, confirming the opinion of the most eminent Michelangelo scholars.[77]

Further in-depth comparison with Michelangelo's entire corpus of works is still awaiting to be carried out, and could provide a solution and once and for all. At any rate, we cannot dismiss the extent to which sculptors of the Baroque Age admired the *Bandini Pietà*, that is, of couse, if what Paolo Falconieri wrote concerning Bernini's studies of it are true. Nor can we overlook the fact that the Barberini family were of Florentine origin, and may have found the idea of decorating the family chapel with a sculpture that had been specially commissioned and inspired by that magnificent group by the hand of the most eminent Italian sculptor to be a prestigious addition, even going so far as requiring that it be given a distinctive trait, its incompleteness.[78]

The *Rondanini Pietà*

Although the *Pietà*, called "Rondanini" in reference to the family that owned it for a very long time, and "Milanese" because of its current location in the Castello Sforzesco, of all Michelangelo's sculptures is perhaps the one that comes closest to manifestations of the tormented 20th-century sensibility in the arts, its fame is relatively recent, and only lately, with the publication of important studies[79] and the restoration work of 2003-2004,[80] has an in-depth historical and critical evaluation been attempted. Neither Vasari in the 1550 edition of the *Lives,* nor Condivi (1553) mentioned it, a sign that it was perhaps undertaken in 1553 or just after that date. Recorded in 1561 and 1564,[81] it was mentioned briefly by Vasari in the 1568 edition of the *Lives*, where he presented it as an indispensable occupation for the elderly sculptor after he had rid himself of the *Bandini Pietà* (Florentine), left unfinished and broken: "[...] it became necessary to find some work in marble on which he might be able to pass some time every day with the chisel, and another piece of marble was put before him, from which another Pietà had already been blocked out, different from the first and much smaller".[82] Vasari's anecdotic and for once reductive tone would seem to have been influenced by an association of ideas with the period that came just after, where a senile "second childhood" of the very old master was foreshadowed. This opinion was rebutted, however, thanks to a very clear-headed letter the artist wrote, where he also included one of his most famous sonnets, the one that begins: "Through stormy seas and in a fragile bark / my life has reached at last the common port ...", a touching, lofty meditation on death. Nor is the description of the Milanese *Pietà* as being "much smaller", in height, than the Florentine work correct. The belief can easily be explained, however, by the great amount of effort that was made to hollow out the volumes, which resulted in contracted and emaciated forms.

Michelangelo devoted time and creative effort to the marble group in two phases, from 1553 to 1564, if not three as has been conjectured, possibly beginning to work on it even before the *Bandini Pietà*, hence, before 1549. It is almost certain that this is the marble he was working on until he fell ill just shortly before his death, according to the chronology of his final days witnessed by Daniele da Volterra.[83] Like the other *Pietà*, it was a work for which Michelangelo was the sole

18th-century imitator (?) of Michelangelo, the *Palestrina Pietà* in its original place (church of Santa Rosalia at the Palazzo Barberini in Palestrina) in a photograph from before 1938
Florence, Galleria dell'Accademia

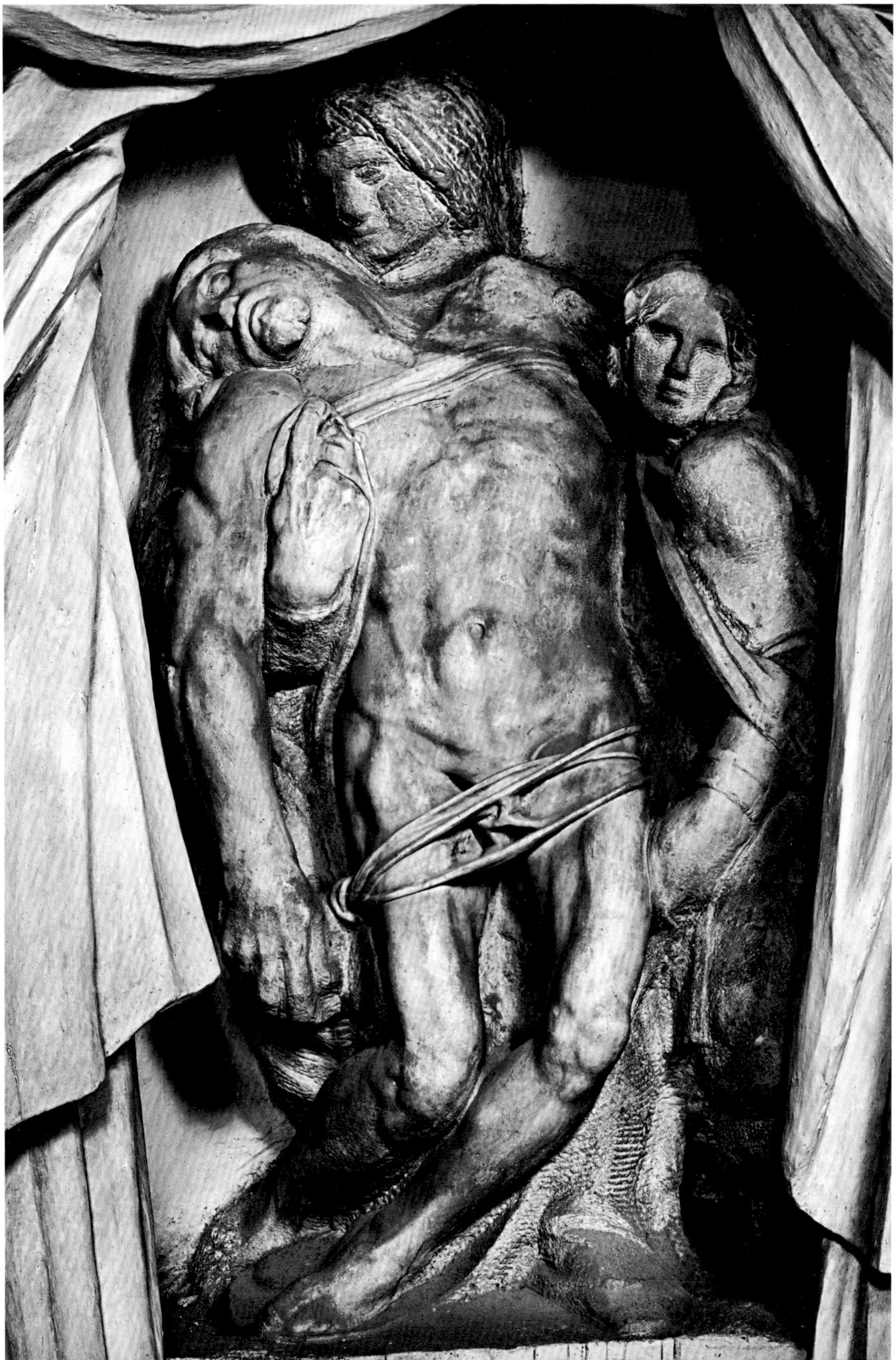

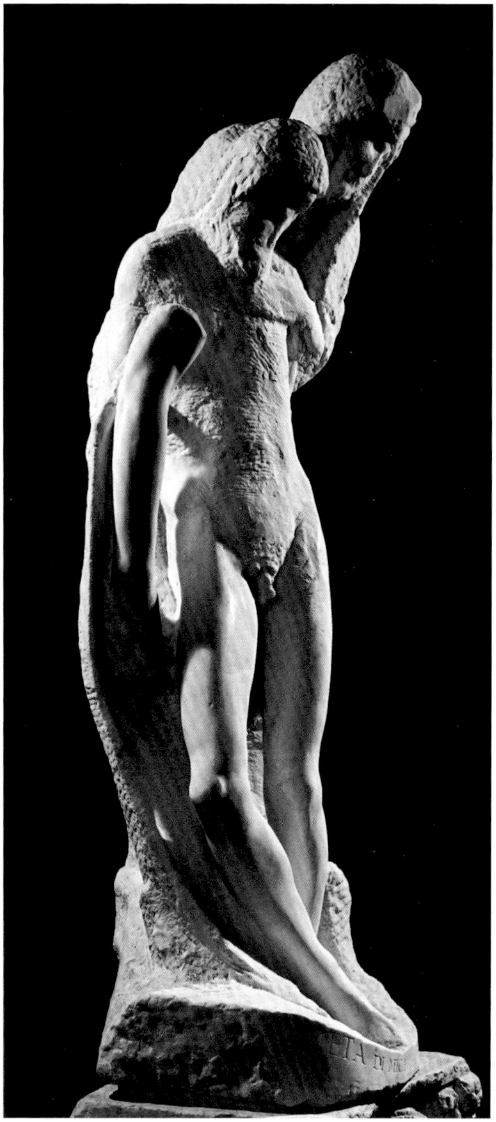

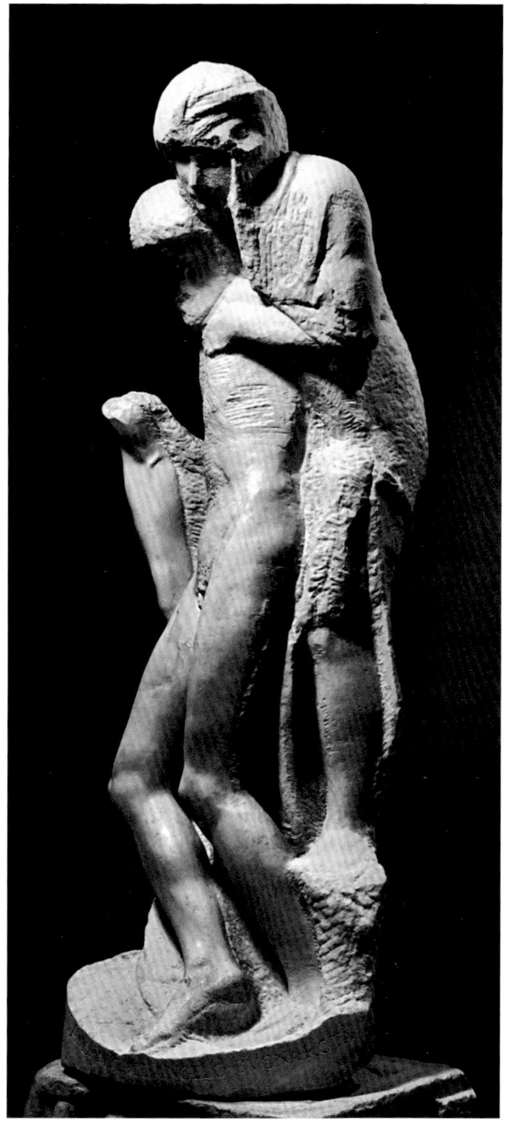

Michelangelo, *Rondanini Pietà*
The iconography suggests a moment of transition from a lamentation to an entombment
Milan, Civiche Raccolte del Castello Sforzesco

Michelangelo, *Rondanini Pietà*
The figure supporting the dead Christ, whose robe leaves one leg visible, must have been a male in the first version of the group
Milan, Civiche Raccolte del Castello Sforzesco

p. 281
Michelangelo, *Rondanini Pietà*
Michelangelo used a *scarpello* to reduce a first, more robust and probably more finished version of the Christ
Milan, Civiche Raccolte del Castello Sforzesco

p. 282
Michelangelo, *Rondanini Pietà*, areas of "non-finito"
Milan, Civiche Raccolte del Castello Sforzesco

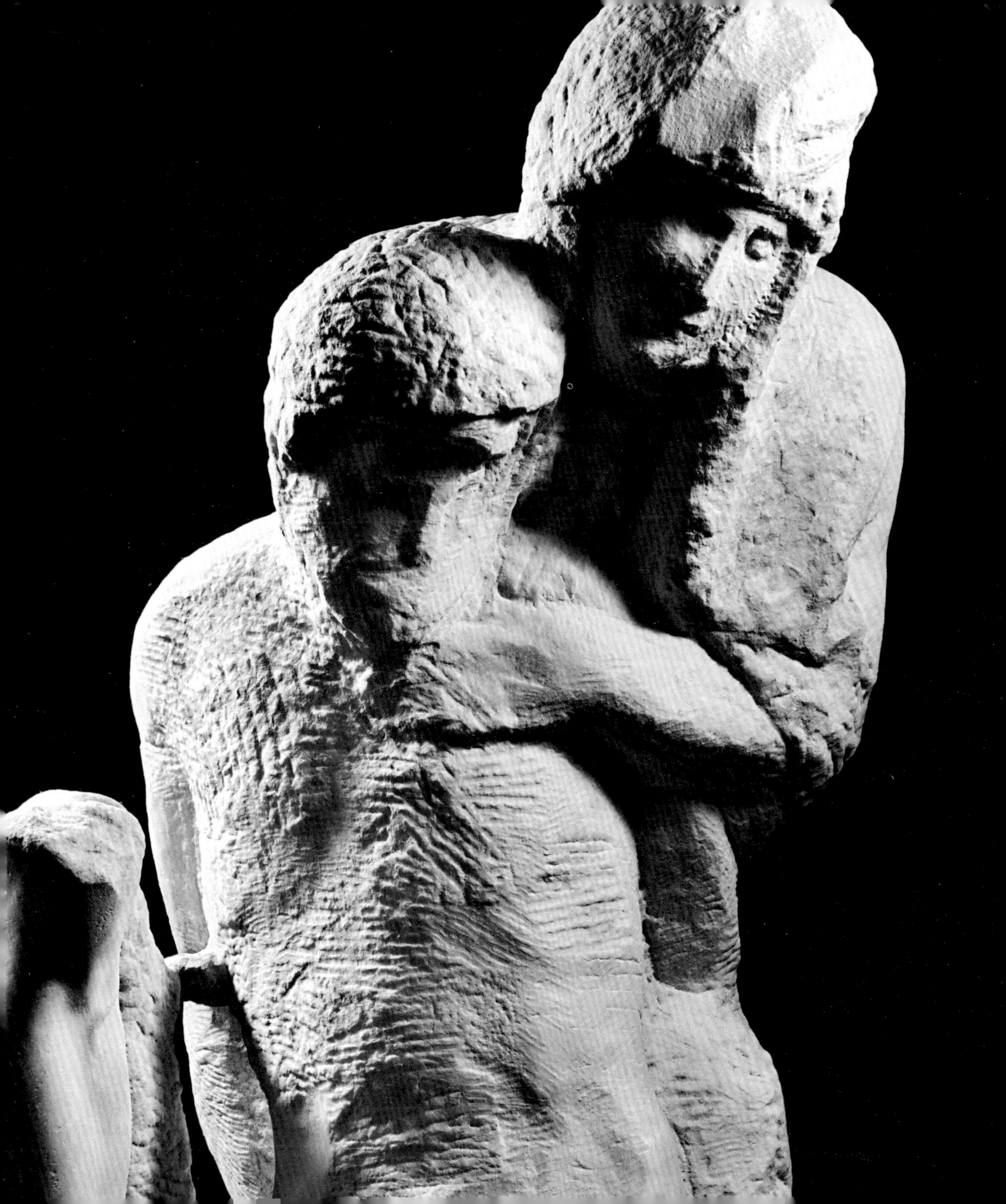

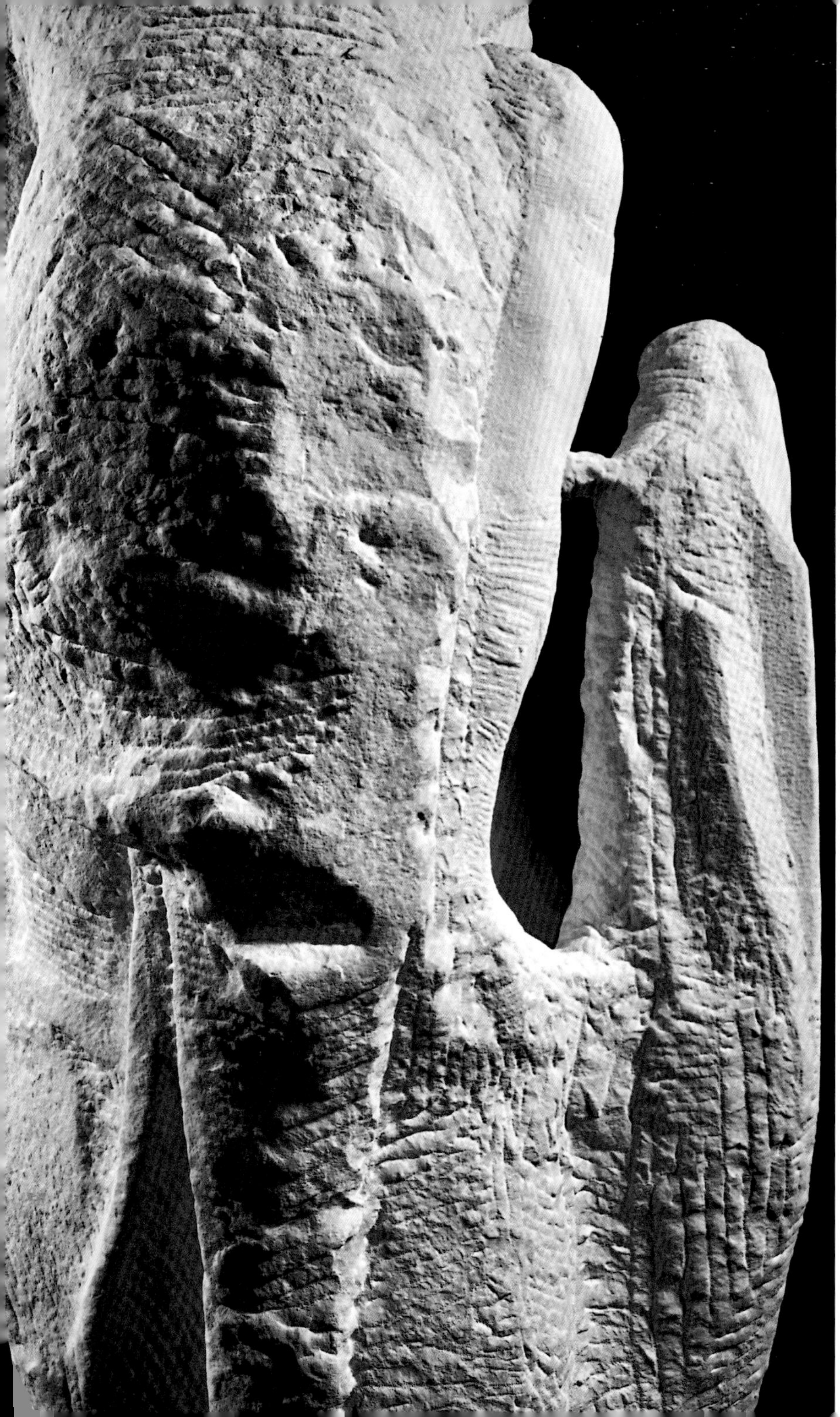

p. 283
Michelangelo, *Rondanini Pietà*, detail with the fragmentary face of the original figure, perhaps a male, visible in Mary's veil
Milan, Civiche Raccolte del Castello Sforzesco

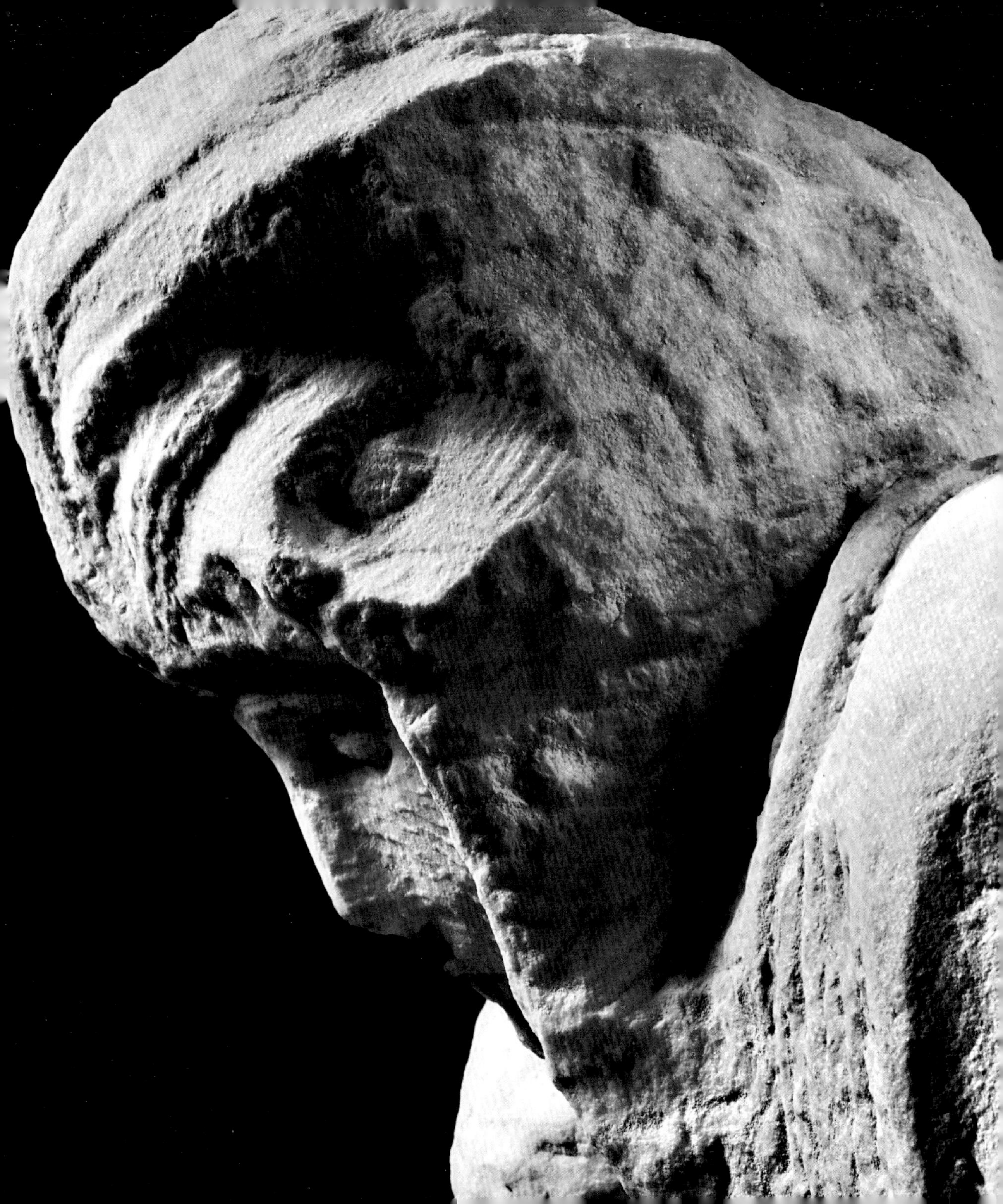

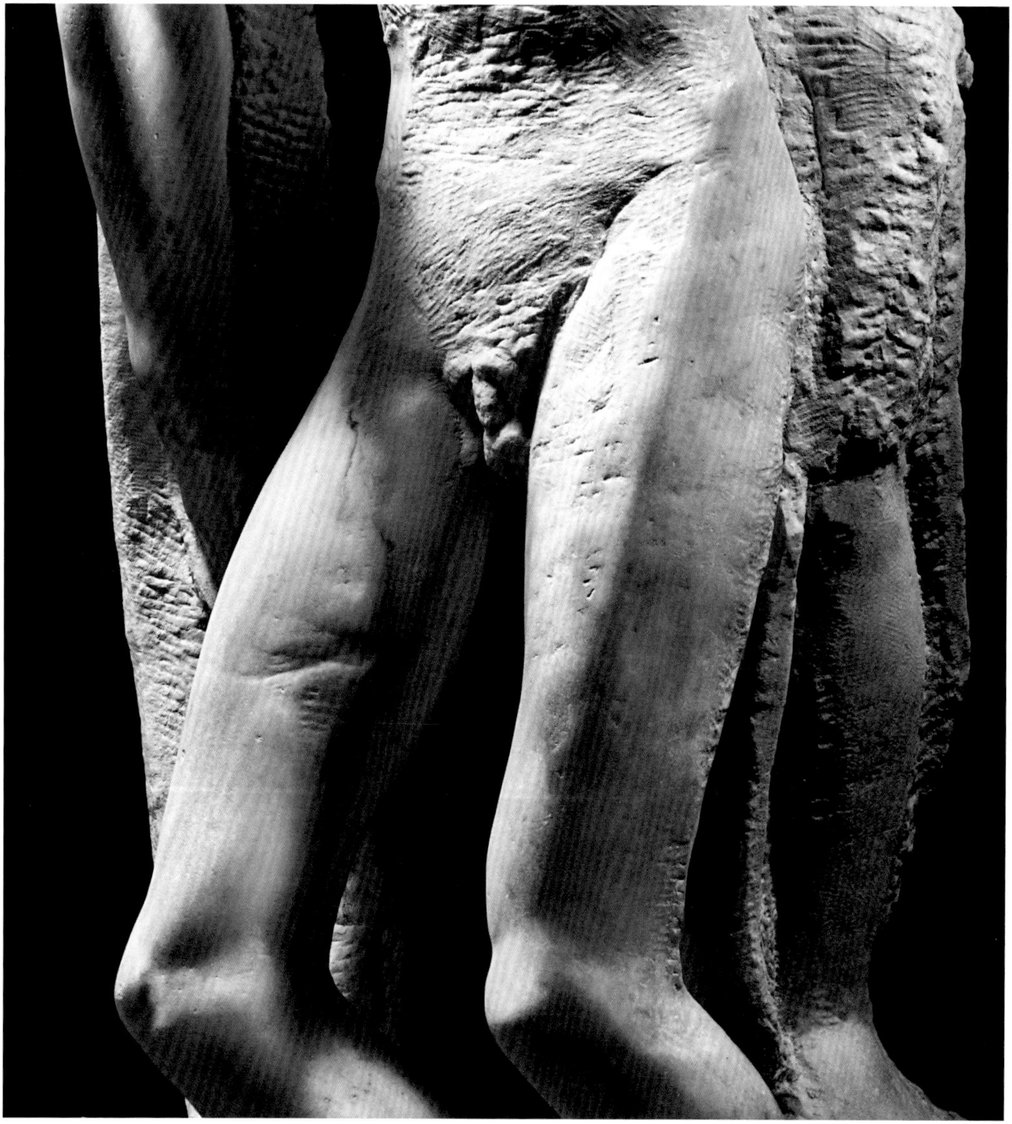

Michelangelo, *Rondanini Pietà*,
the legs remaining from the
first, fleshier version of the
Christ
Milan, Civiche Raccolte del
Castello Sforzesco

p. 285
Michelangelo, *Rondanini Pietà*,
traces where marble was
removed from the torso
in the first Christ
Milan, Civiche Raccolte del
Castello Sforzesco

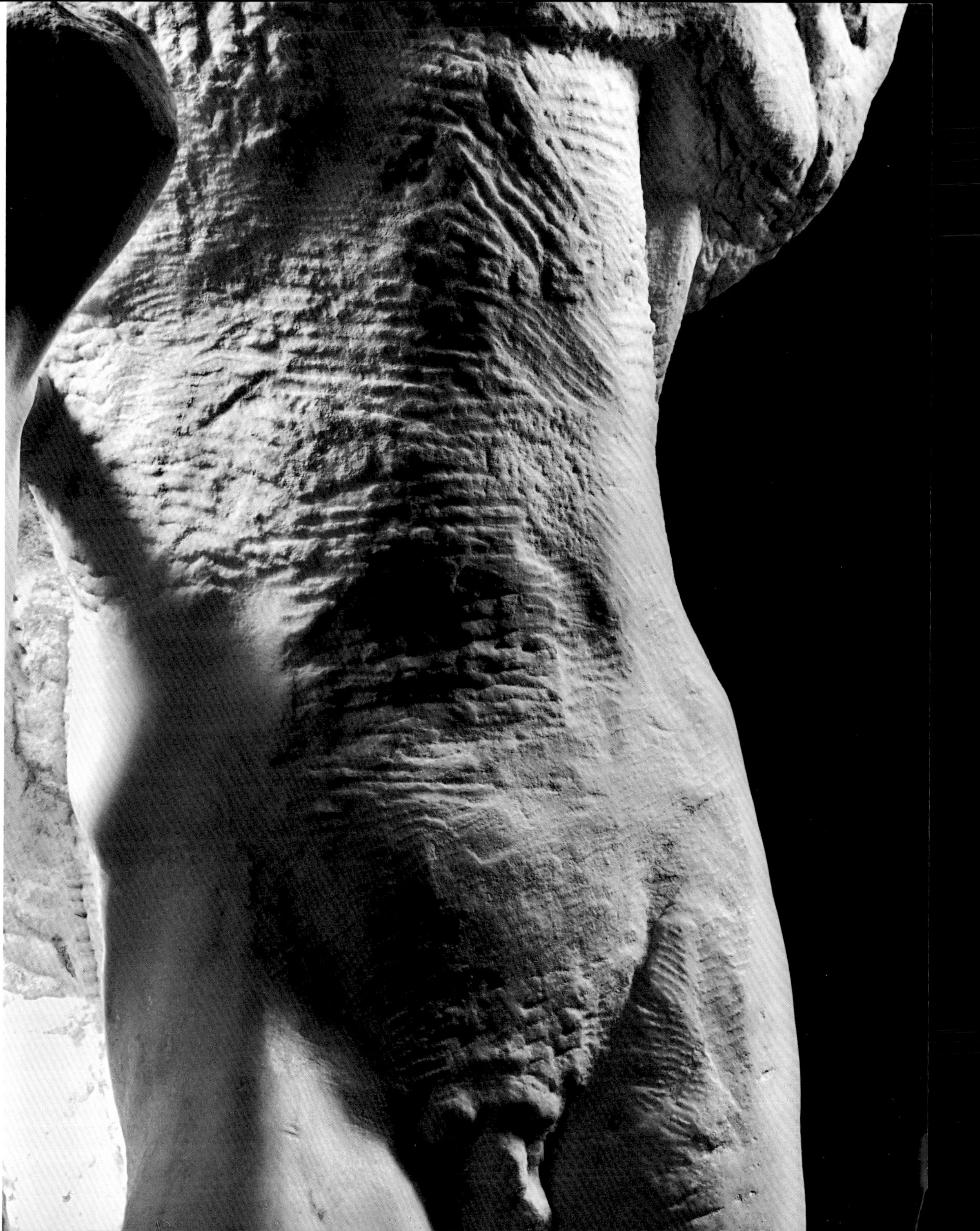

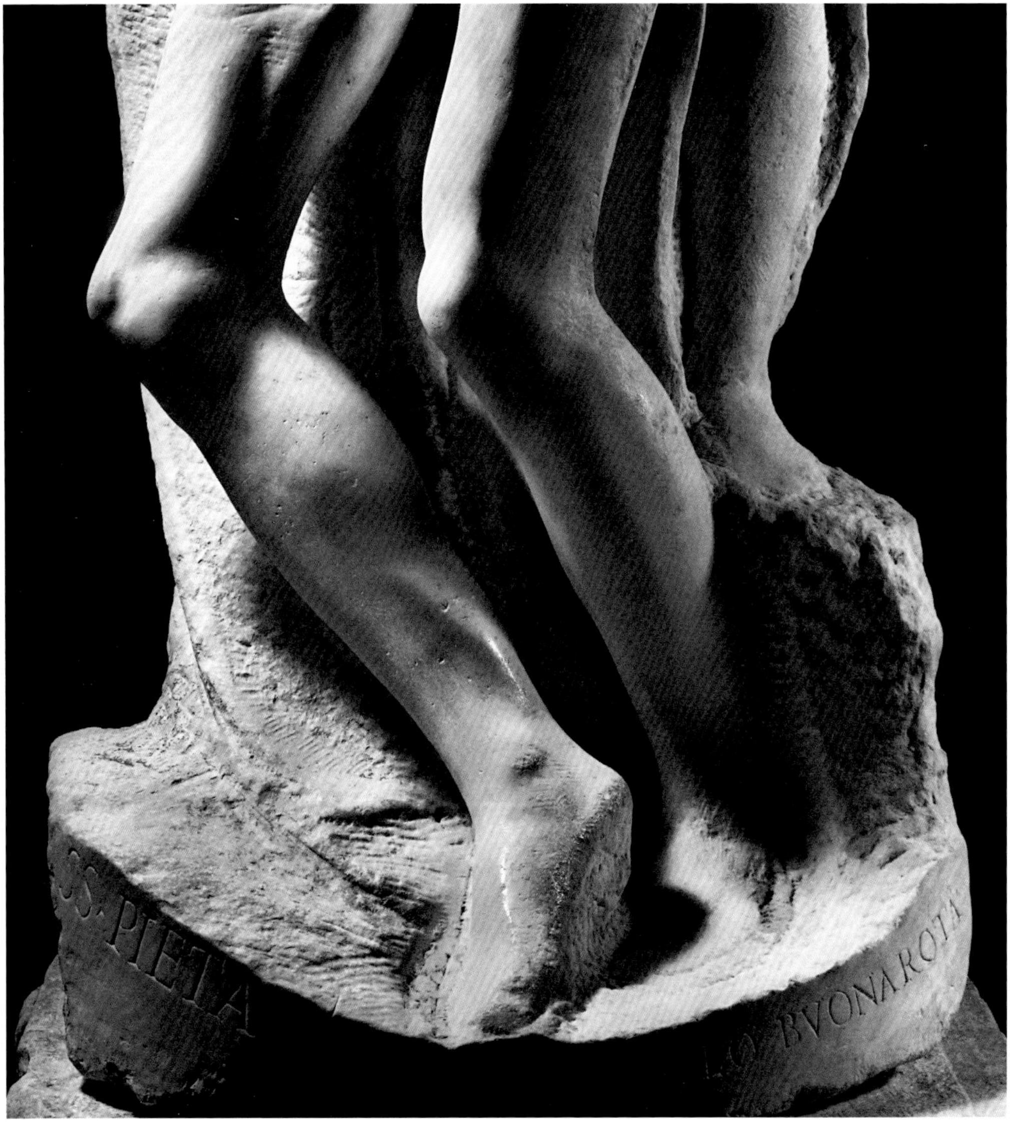

Michelangelo, *Rondanini Pietà*
The pose of the legs and feet suggests that Christ is slowly slipping into the cavity of the tomb below
Milan, Civiche Raccolte del Castello Sforzesco

p. 287
Michelangelo, *Rondanini Pietà*
The arm detached from the group is residual proof of the original Christ
Milan, Civiche Raccolte del Castello Sforzesco

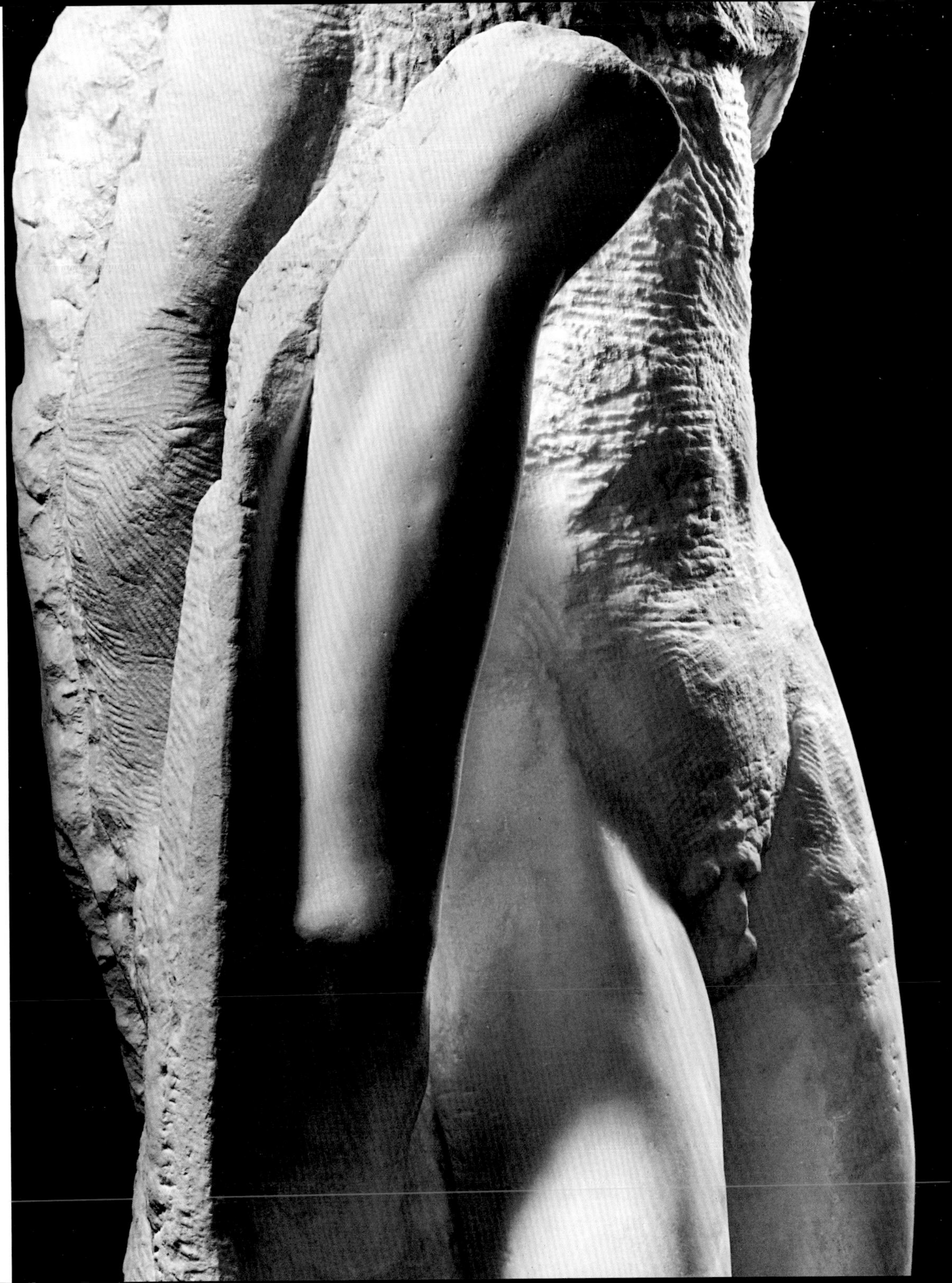

patron. The considerable changes made to the sculpture by the very hand of the author, which it would be too reductive to call *pentimenti* in that they constitute actual changes in design, have left us with a group that we might liken to a "palimpsest", where at least two variations in conflict with each other are present. A first idea and consequent sculpted version includes an athletic figure of a naked, deceased Christ, supported upright by the shoulders by a man wearing a turban as he lowers him into a depth that should be that of the tomb.[84] The figure supporting him is without the shadow of a doubt a man, also convincingly substantiated by John T. Paoletti, as the short tunic he wears that leaves his left leg naked from the knee down could not have been worn by a woman.[85] Still a part of this first phase are Christ's legs, his incomplete right arm detached from the body, the just roughed out mass of the supporting figure with the upper part of his face turned upwards, which now coincides with the veiled head of the figure itself. And, like Steinberg, we cannot exclude the idea that the first version included three figures.[86] A subsequent phase led to the semi-destruction of the Christ, reduced to a hollowed out torso on which the face with its features just roughed out rests, the sculpture of a second right arm, but this one in a backwards position and up against the other figure, and the transformation of the man into a woman – believed to be the Virgin despite the lack of proof – with the creation of a vaguely feminine veiled head that bends and attempts to touch the dead man's hair in a gesture of sorrowful affection. Daniele da Volterra must have been alluding to these final moments when he recounted that on the Saturday before the Sunday of the Carnevale, "he worked standing up, to study the body of that Pietà".[87] Such carefully chosen words, "study" and "body", summon up the artist's tormented labour around a torso that was by now fleshless.

It has been suggested that the original missing part could be a marble fragment, today at the Gallery Borghese in Rome, which features the head and upper torso of Christ; but this was ruled out when further scientific and stylistic analyses were conducted, which also included a recent comparison between marbles carried out in Milan (2002).[88] The original version of the *Pietà*, on the basis of the ample proportions and final treatment that reveal the limbs remaining from the first Jesus, can be related to a group of studies on the theme of the deceased Christ as he is being supported, considered preparatory for subjects that the artist was working on at the time, the object of fervent meditation in relation to his own imminent death and his eagerness for spiritual salvation: the *Descent from the Cross*, the *Lamentation*, the *Entombment*. In the foreground of a drawing in Vienna attributed to the master is the naked and abandoned body of Christ in his glorious physical fullness, supported by a seated figure that could be God the Father. His legs are crossed in a pose that – including the turn of the ankles and feet – seems to anticipate that of the *Rondanini Pietà*, but from the opposite view.[89] Five other variations on the theme of the whole body held up by one or two figures can be observed in a famous drawing in Oxford.[90]

The transformation of a male figure – Nicodemus or some other volunteer – into the female figure of the Virgin caused significant variations, not just in the composition but in the meaning itself of the group, blocking a dynamic and narrative vision to transform it into an immobile and symbolic one. While it was in fact legitimate to imagine the lifeless body, supported by a man, in the course of its slow and controlled descent to the tomb, the fact that the figure is now embraced with some difficulty by his elderly Mother signifies that it must now be interpreted as an iconic *imago pietatis*, thus, the object of meditation: most critics agree that Mary ought to be considered the allegorical image of Ecclesia, mother but also bride of the Redeemer. An elusive trace of fabric standing in for a sudarium recalls the "humeral veil",[91] in Catholic liturgy used to cover the ciborium containing the Blessed Sacrament, the *corpus Christi,* precisely.

Because of the "non-finito" state of the work, with its extensive areas of reworking, the *Rondanini Pietà* is a sampling of autograph structural and superficial treatments of the marble, which became even more comprehensible after it was cleaned in 2002. The marble, naturally furrowed by greyish veins, was generally sculpted in parallel stripes by a pointed chisel in its more rustic parts, but achieves a burnished smoothness (whose originality is not certain, however) in the limbs of the first Christ. At some point these were polished with an oily substance that seeped into the material so that now it is yellowish brown. Unusual traces in Christ's side, similar to long parallel furrows of varying depths, seems to offer proof that the elderly sculptor attacked the marble in order to

narrow the torso, which was presumably fleshier, and achieve its current state of tragic consumption.
Since 1956, the sculptural group, which went from the Rondanini estate in Rome to the City of Milan in 1852, is situated at the end of a row of antique sculptures in the civic collection of the Castello Sforzesco. For centuries, the Milanese sculpture was totally neglected by historiography and criticism, but in the 20th century admiration for the work grew. This was also due to its considerable harmony with the cultural themes of that age, and of the present time as well: a psychological and psychoanalytical interpretation that seeks, in formal rage, the tangible signs of the most intimate movements of the soul; the aesthetic of the fragment, which privileges the unadorned severity of the unfinished state as opposed to the harmony achieved or at least pursued in the completed work. Artistic movements such as Expressionism had created the sensibility to appreciate dramatic figurative manifestations that reached as far as anguish. A reassessment of Michelangelo's very last works, and especially of this *Pietà*, which until the early 20th century was relegated to the margins of his *oeuvre*, as it was considered to be the expression of senile decadence, presumes and reflects such philosophical and aesthetic orientations, to such an extent that one of the most penetrating comments – however much in the sphere of the total subjective perception – is that of the philosopher Georg Simmel, who observed therein Michelangelo's surrender in the long struggle between inner passion and its technical expression: "release is purely negative, nirvanic: the struggle is over, and there is neither victory nor reconciliation. The soul, freed from the weight of the body, has not begun its triumphal march towards the transcendent, but rather has collapsed at its threshold".[92] When classified as it dutifully and appropriately should be within the artistic activity of the great sculptor, the *Rondanini Pietà* represents the highest point of encounter between Michelangelo's thought, which, in the final years, incessantly and, in the end, with obsessive continuity, tended towards religious themes linked to salvation in Redemption, and his approach to the material, whose obvious natural resistance is ignored and overcome. The blocked out volumes, the inarticulate surfaces, the truncated limbs, the smoother passages of the *Pietà* are not the relics of a contradictory way of working, but rather the narrative elements of an extraordinary story. This work offers us a privileged view of Michelangelo's *modus operandi*. His unprecedented passion amazes us, a passion that would never again be surpassed, evident in the way he treats the marble as something that is forced to surrender to sudden changes in the overall design, if not total changes of heart. By expressing his personal quest – and it could only be thus – "per forza di levare", or "taking away", Michelangelo denied the fullness (despite the fact that it had just been achieved, and with great effort) of an enriched, complete form, to instead search, by way of deliberate impoverishment, for the ever-evasive essence of the concept.

The small wooden *Christ*

It was only forty years ago that the small, unfinished wooden *Christ* at the Casa Buonarroti in Florence was linked to Michelangelo's final activity, as the autograph work to which the master, by now almost ninety years of age, devoted his time with the intention, it is believed, of offering it to his nephew Lionardo.[93]
In August 1562 the artist asked his nephew to send him the "tools" he needed to be able to sculpt a wooden Christ, tools which he indeed received in September. He also insisted that his nephew have "someone from the trade, in other words, a wood-cutter" show him which tools were the right ones, and that they be "beautiful and good". In its apparent simplicity, the issue holds a number of interesting aspects: the artist did not have with him, either in Rome or Florence (in his home or in his workshop in Via Mozza), the tools he needed to carve wood, something he had not done in years, and as concerned tools and methods he trusted Florentine artisans and no one else. The purpose of the request emerges from a letter Tiberio Calcagni wrote to Lionardo on 17 July 1573, where he describes Michelangelo at work on the "wooden Christ" that he was making for him.
Whether the small wooden sculpture in the Casa Buonarroti was really meant to be a model for a larger figure has not be ascer-

p. 290
Michelangelo, wooden *Christ* (*Crucified?*), the last work of the great artist who was close to ninety
Florence, Museo di Casa Buonarroti

p. 291
Michelangelo, wooden *Christ* (*Crucified?*), albeit small in size, of bold anatomy and heroic proportions
Florence, Museo di Casa Buonarroti

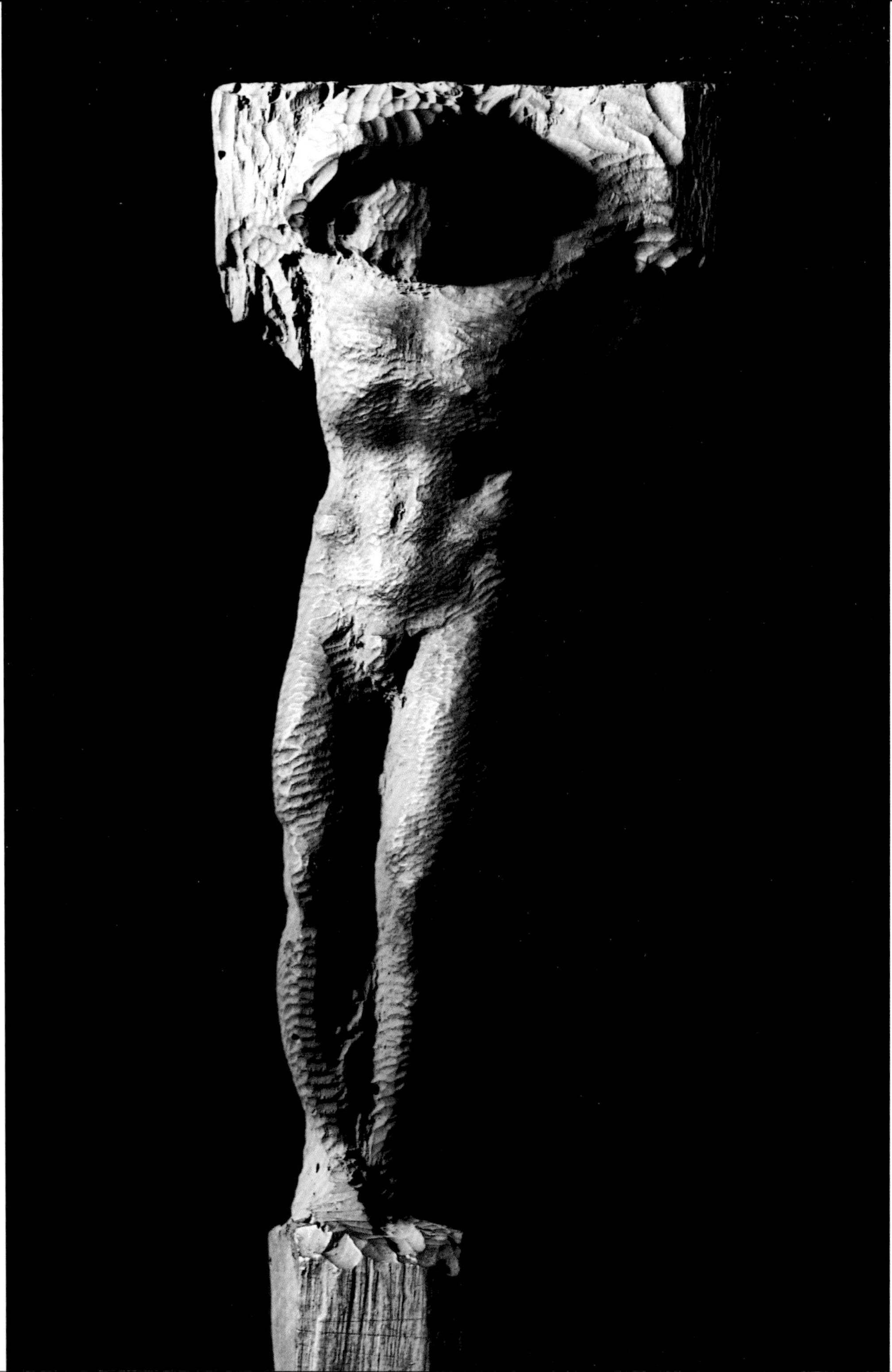

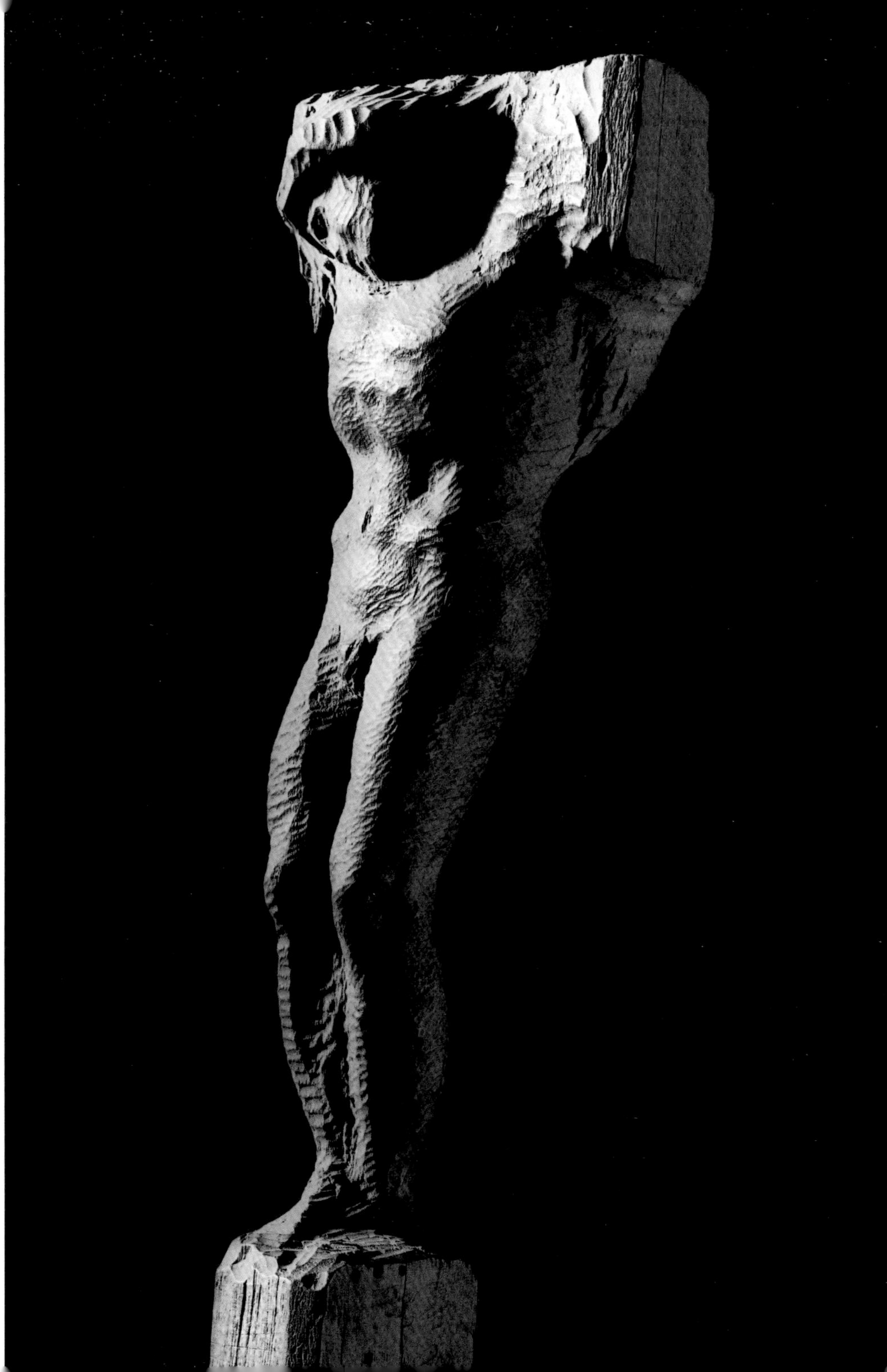

tained.[94] Tolnay suggested comparing it with the drawing for *Christ on the Cross* at the Louvre (DAG, inv. 842), whose proportions and sharp features of the torso it indeed recalls. But the abrupt rightwards drop of the head instead points to the linden wood *Crucifix* in a private collection, which was displayed as a youthful work by the artist in Florence's Museo Horne in 2004. The first impression is that Michelangelo was searching for a new interpretation of the subject, using the same technique of his early years but importing there the imposingness of the human figure, which the artist had developed over the years, and visible, for instance, in *Day* and *Dusk* in the New Sacristy. But the small wooden structure is not lacking in puzzling aspects, beginning with the title: at the state in which it reached us it is evident in fact that Christ's arms were not meant to be outstretched, unless added on, nor was one foot meant to overlap the other as is usually required in this particular iconography. The artist's final attempts to make sculptures – namely, the two late *Pietàs* – reveal just how much he laboured on the figure of the dead Christ, taken down off the cross, lamented and lowered into his tomb. Furthermore, in a letter he wrote to Lionardo Calcagni said that Michelangelo was working on a "Christ", which is a rather generic term. But leaving the unanswered question of the subject aside, it is worth stopping a moment to discuss technique, easily observed owing to the fact that neither primer, nor polychrome nor other types of finishing treatments were used on the figure. Not unlike marble, the wood seems to have been modelled by means of a series of strokes of the gouge, variable in number and results: the effect achieved in the head and legs is similar to chiselling, and to the use of the claw-chisel in the torso and stomach, which are more defined, the work having being done from the centre of the body outwards, likewise observed in other unfinished ("non-finito") statues by Michelangelo, for instance, the *Captives* at the Galleria dell'Accademia. The outcome here is a vibration of the surface that is characterized by movement, a wrinkling of the articulated and perceptible development of the volumes, with evident pictorial suggestions.[95]

The myth of Michelangelo

Michelangelo died following a brief illness on 18 February 1564; he was a celebrity who had become a legend. Shortly before, he had burnt an enormous quantity of drawings, leaving Duke Cosimo without the inheritance he had hoped for.

The artist's body was secretly transported from Rome by his nephew Lionardo, camouflaged as a bale of goods. The parish of the Santi Apostoli, where the body made a first stop, still preserves the memory of his presence in life, and his passage there in death: a statue of him in his work-clothes, inserted in the side wall of the cloister, a little-known cenotaph that is seldom visited. Giorgio Vasari openly rejoiced to see the body, as he, along with Cosimo de' Medici, saw the solemn exequies as a magnificent occasion to inaugurate the newly instituted Accademia delle Arti del Disegno, not just in terms of work for those enrolled, but as the "promotion" of the artist's role in society, whose champion had been Buonarroti. On 14 July 1564 a magnificent funeral was held in the church of San Lorenzo under Medicean patronage: it was a great public event, surpassing by far any of the ceremonies traditionally associated with San Lorenzo.[96] Only after Cosimo I de' Medici's funeral, exclusively reserved for grand dukes, their relatives, related European sovereigns or allies, was a series of such events initiated. This was the very first of such ceremonies, therefore, celebrated for an artist, who had on the one hand brought fame to the city and the ruling dynasty throughout the known world, thus taking on a public role so to speak, and on the other hand developed and adorned with magnificent architectures and sculptures the San Lorenzo complex itself. At the centre of the cerimonial apparatus spread to every corner of the church was the catafalque, a monumental terraced structure with a square plan (what we call a ziggurat today), ornamented with paintings and sculptures of an ephemeral nature.[97]

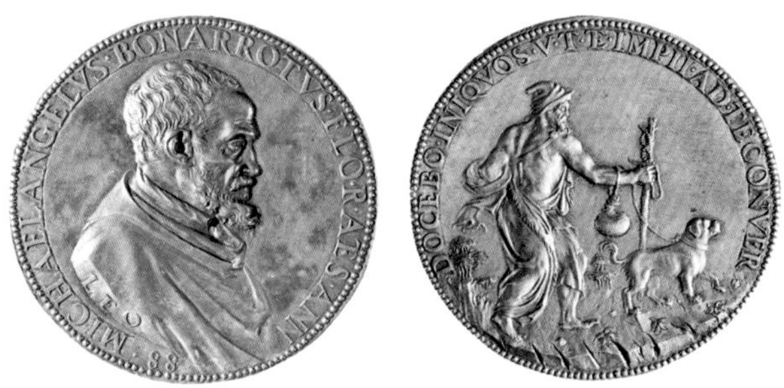

Leone Leoni, *Medal of Michelangelo*, with his profile on the *recto* and an allegorical portrayal as a pilgrim (Saint Roch?) on the *verso*
Florence, Museo del Bargello

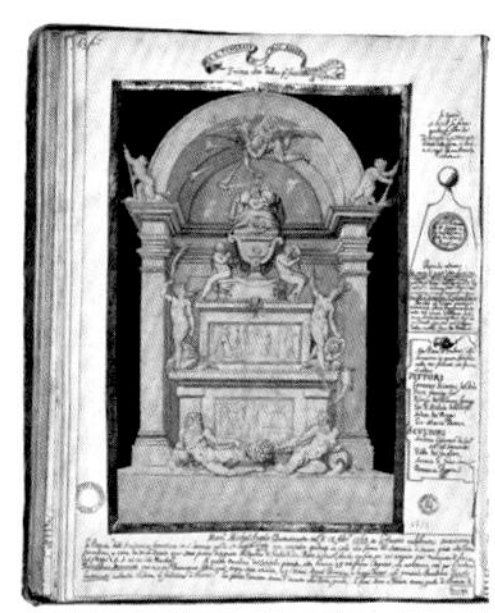

Zanobi Lastricati, *Project for Michelangelo's Catafalque*
Milan, Biblioteca Ambrosiana, Codice Resta, inv. 67/2, f. 65

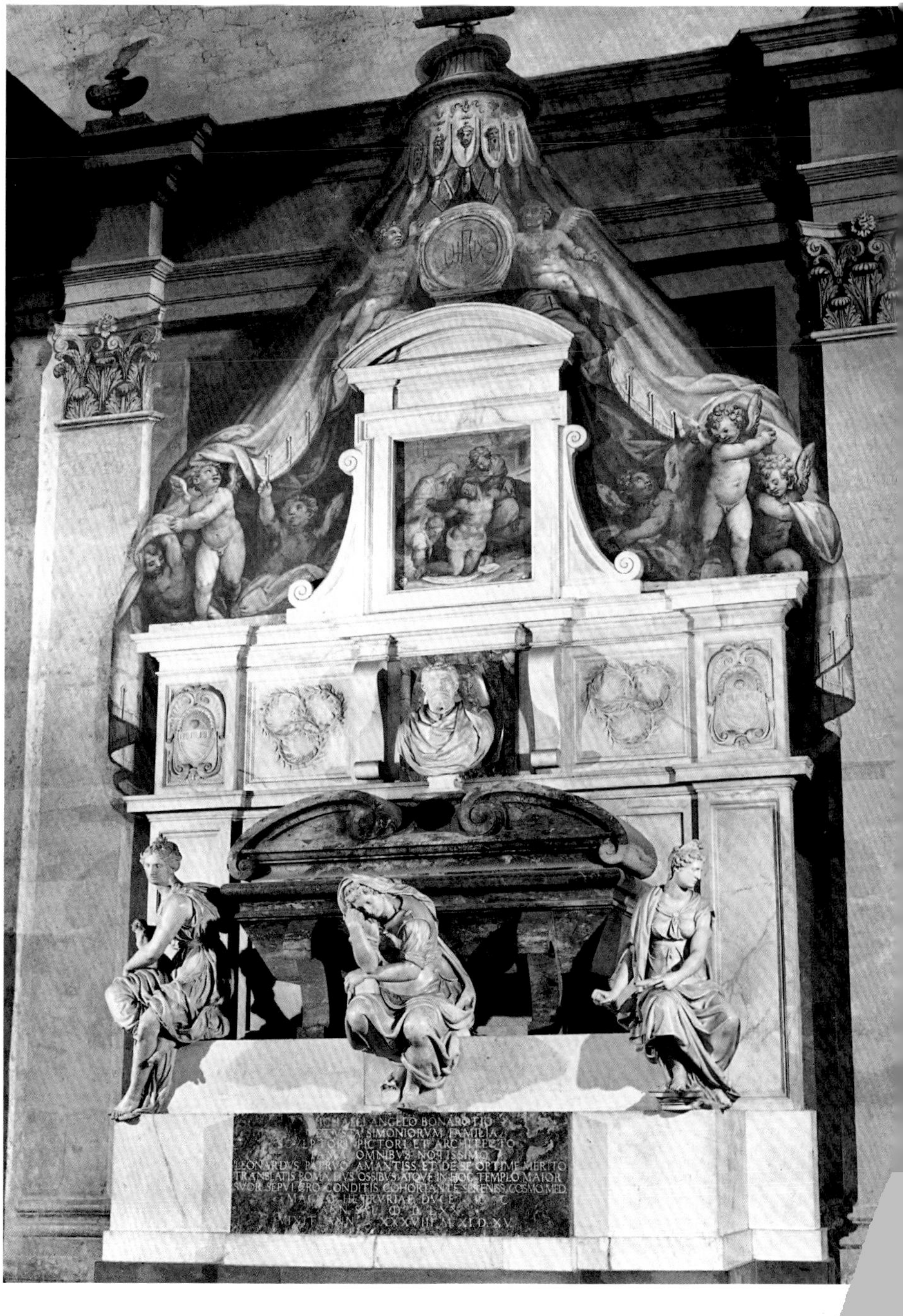

Various artists to a design by Giorgio Vasari, *Wall Tomb of Michelangelo* with the lamentation on the dead Christ and the mourning of the three sister arts
Florence, basilica of Santa Croce

Standing in one of Donatello's bronze pulpits, the scholar Benedetto Varchi recited the oration and claimed "the praises, the merits, the life and works of the divine Michelangelo Buonarroti" for the nobility and people who had flocked to the church.
Duke Cosimo de' Medici had made numerous attempts, with the help of diplomats and artists, to convince the prodigious old man to come back to Florence; he himself had tried to persuade him. But either Michelangelo wouldn't keep his promise or he remained elusive. Since he had not been able to have him while he was alive, we might say, to quote Vasari, "he did not hesitate to honour him with all manner of pomp", to exalt through this subject, universally acknowledged and divinized, the supreme role of the however small state of Tuscany in European art. On behalf of the city and ruling dynasty it was the initial act, a sort of cultural canonization of Michelangelo, the object of a lay veneration in that he was the father of Florentine and Italian art. But it was also, and no less, the anxious and nearly obsessive aspiration to fill the memory of a void, to repair his long absence with a posthumous reappropriation.
While preparations were being made for the exequies, proposals were also being put forth for a funerary monument for the artist in Santa Croce, where the tombs of illustrious citizens who had earned the honour of the Florentine state and where he himself, as well as his father, were buried. The wall tomb was designed by Giorgio Vasari and completed in 1578, but slowly because of nephew Lionardo's reluctance to provide the necessary resources, and misunderstandings between the various artists involved. Conceived as an apparatus of sculptures and frescoes, it develops around a sarcophagus dominated by a bust of Michelangelo by Battista Lorenzi, and surmounted by a fresco of the *Lamentation of Christ* by Battista Naldini. Around the sarcophagus three marble allegories stand in doleful attitude: *Painting* by Lorenzi, *Architecture* by Giovanni Bandini, and *Sculpture* by Valerio Cioli, representing the grief of the three sister arts.[98] All of the marble that had been left in Via Mozza was used to make it, and other marble was purchased as well, including marble known as *breccia fior di pesco,* which is purplish in colour and was the pride of the Medicean quarries of Seravezza in Pietrasanta, inaugurated by Michelangelo for Leo X.
Construction of the monument, a genuine "manifesto" of Giorgio Vasari's academic principles and of its inspirer don Vincenzio Borghini, was not the only tribute in Florence to the greatness of the artist. The Medici dynasty, imitated as much as possible by private experts, continued to search for his sculptures and drawings, and managed to bring back to Florence works from the artist's Roman period – the *Bacchus*, the bust of *Brutus*, the *Bandini Pietà* – which would otherwise have taken different paths in collecting. From the time of the artist's grand-nephew Michelangelo the Younger, the Casa Buonarroti in Via Ghibellina was transformed into a memorial to the great artist, where the pictorial apparatus of the finest 17th-century artists display his life and the events surrounding it. Letters, drawings, models, *bozzetti* and other memorabilia concerning Michelangelo and his milieu, that had either always been there or were retrieved, were kept in the Casa Buonarroti.[99] In 1875 the celebration of the fourth centenary of the birth of Michelangelo temporarily transformed the Galleria dell'Accademia, where the *David* had been relocated two years earlier to a specially built tribune, into a triumphal review of his sculpture. And this is only as concerns the events that took place in the city of Florence. When Michelangelo was still alive, his statuary, disseminated in the form of plaster casts, copies and drawings, was already included in the training of Italian artists, and in countries of European culture, and it constituted a benchmark for aspiring sculptors. The Novecento, with its vertiginous diffusion of static and moving images, critical bibliography, divulgative literature and inspired objects, consolidated the figure of Michelangelo into that of the greatest sculptor of all time. To the extent that he has become a world-class myth, with the power to attract the interest of millions of people and physically drive great floods of visitors. But what remains, despite developments in *media*, is the uniqueness of the personal experience when one approaches an original work by Michelangelo, rediscovering in the volumes and on the skin of that marble the signs of an immensely great creative processes, which continues to excite and inspire the men and women of this third millennium.

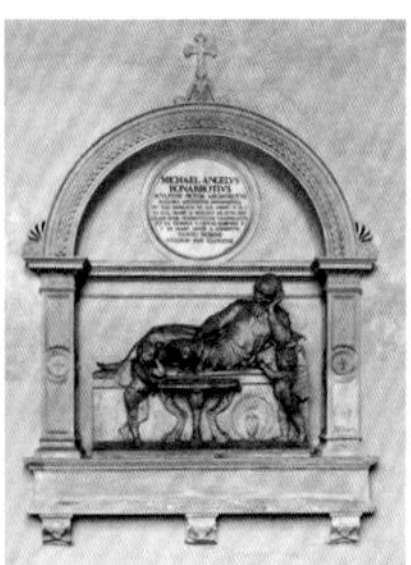

Commemorative monument to Michelangelo
Rome, cloister of the church of the Santi Apostoli

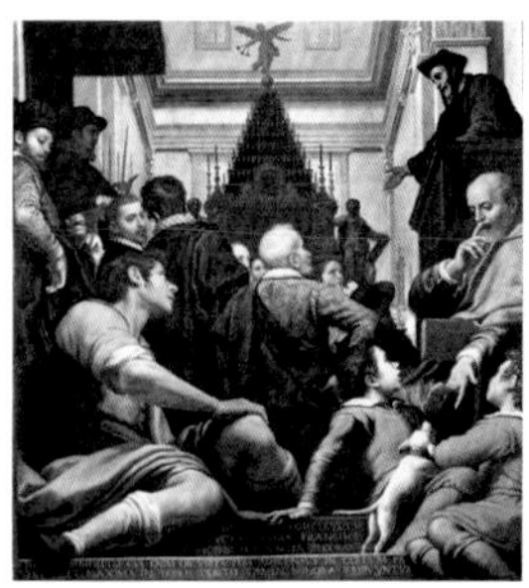

Agostino Ciampelli, *Benedetto Varchi Delivering the Funeral Oration for Michelangelo in San Lorenzo*
Florence, Casa Buonarroti

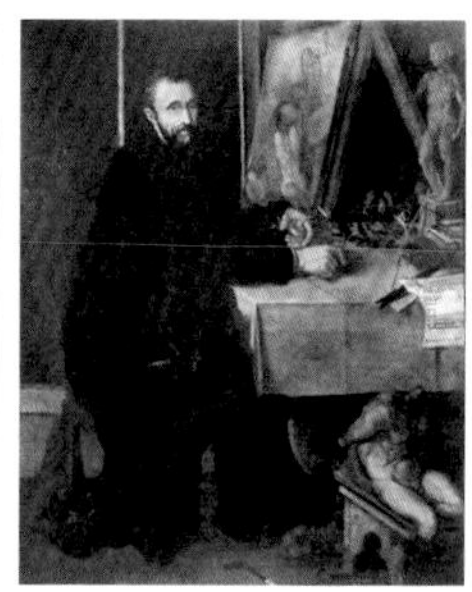

Pompeo Caccini, *Posthumous Portrait of Michelangelo in his Workshop*
Florence, Casa Buonarroti

Notes

[1] Romani, 2003, p. 50; E. Lombardi, in *Daniele da Volterra...*, 2003, pp. 162-165, nos. 51-52.
[2] Francesco di Bernardino d'Amadore (Amadori, Amatori) called l'Urbino mentioned the "buone lingue" (good tongues) of the stone-cutters; he said that they sounded like crickets ("cicale") and added that Michelangelo "never gossiped with any of them" (letter from Francesco di Bernardino d'Amadore called Urbino in Rome to Lionardo Buonarroti in Florence on 17 September 1552; in *Carteggio indiretto...*, 1988-1995, II, 1995, no. 265, pp. 40-41.
[3] Lionardo was kept up to date by Tiberio Calcagni, Daniele da Volterra, Diomede Leoni, all of whom were close to the elderly artist together with Tommaso de' Cavalieri, Federico Donati, physician of Cardinal Pio, and Antonio del Francese. On 13 February 1564, five days before he died, Calcagni recounts that he went out in the rain, and that when reproached Michelangelo answered: "What do you want me to do? I'm ill and I can't find peace anywhere". As he became weaker he wanted to see if he could still ride a horse. Then he withdrew to his home and hearth and was bedridden until he died. His death occurred on 18 February in the afternoon. For the Feast of Saint John, to express his gratitude, Lionardo sent Trebbiano wine to all of the friends listed above, of the kind that Michelangelo would have asked to be sent while he was still alive. The gift was much appreciated "because of where it came from, the remembrance of that blessed memory, and because of what it was, most perfect" (Letter from Daniele da Volterra to Lionardo Buonarroti dated 24 June 1564, in *Carteggio indiretto...*, 1988-1995, II, 1995, no. 372, p. 203).
[4] Letter from Michelangelo in Rome to Lionardo in Florence dated 30 July 1547, in *Il Carteggio...*, 1965-1983, IV, 1979, no. MLXXXVI, pp. 271-272. Along with separate measurements for the cupola-ground distance and for the lantern, the letter also contained the request that a third of a Florentine *braccio*, i.e. 19 cm, be "marked" so that he could then reliably convert the Florentine unit of measure into the Roman one. For the relationship between the two eminent artists, see *Brunelleschi and Michelangelo*, 1977.
[5] Conforti, 1993, pp. 22, 129 and ff. The work ended in about 1554. The relationship between Michelangelo and Ammannati was not the subject of recent studies and commentaries on the occasion of the meeting *Bartolomeo Ammannati...*, 1995.
[6] After several informal contacts between Michelangelo and the delegates of the Florentine "nazione", an official appointment arrived from Cosimo, in the form of an epistolary request for "a design in good taste and with the proper proportions" (letter from Duke Cosimo in Livorno to Michelangelo in Rome dated 26 October 1559, in *Il Carteggio...*, 1965-1983, V, 1983, no. MCCCIII, p. 181, this was followed by other letters on the subject). On 1 November, Michelangelo, who had probably started working on the project, had the drawings ready (three acknowledged in the Casa Buonarroti); one of these was chosen by the delegates, and he used it to make the two models, one from terracotta, the other from wood. Construction of the church never commenced (cf. Argan, Contardi, 1990, pp. 342-349).
[7] In the letter dated 25 April 1560 to the duke, written after the meeting with Vasari (in *Il Carteggio...*, 1965-1983, V, 1983, no. MCCCXXX, pp. 221-222), Michelangelo suggested raising the ceiling of the Sala dei Cinquecento, which is what Vasari did (Conforti, 1993, pp. 150-153). In the same letter he expressed his appreciation for Ammannati's project for the *Fountain of Juno* for that room. His thoughts on the bridge can be found in the letter Vasari wrote while he was in Rome to Duke Cosimo in Pisa dated 9 April 1560 (in *Der Literarische Nachlass*, 1923-1930, I, no. CCCIV, pp. 559-560).
[8] As concerns the success of the Horatian motif *ut pictura poesis*, the equivalence between Michelangelo's art and Dante Alighieri's poetry was already a *topos* in the 16th century while the artist was still alive (cf. Vasari, 1568, 1962 ed., VI, pp. 1983 and ff).
[9] Cf. Becker, 2002.
[10] A further example of Vasari's vision of Michelangelo as "national" and universal glory combined is a passage from a letter he wrote to Lionardo: "... the miraculous virtues of his chisel and paintbrush will always keep alive the memory of our house, which is immortal because of him, and the same may be said for Italy, Rome and Florence thanks to his works, but it is to the known universe that he gave light, life, and a name" (letter dated 1 September 1551, *Carteggio indiretto*, 1988-1995, II, 1995, no. 261, pp. 33-34).
[11] Vasari went to see Michelangelo on several occasions in April 1560, the two of them going together to visit the building site of Saint Peter's; Vasari requested and received opinions on the architectural innovations to be carried out in Florence (see the exchange of letters in *Der Literarische Nachlass*, 1923-1930, I, 1923, pp. 558 and ff.).
[12] Vasari, *The Lives* (1568), 1996 ed., II, p. 252. Vasari continued with his artful physiological interpretation of the artist's choice: "for the reason that experience had taught him that the air of Florence, being sharp and subtle, was very injurious to the constitution, while that of Rome, softer and more temperate, had kept him in perfect health up to his ninetieth year, with all the senses as lively and sound as they had ever been...". Despite his insistence on Buonarroti's "fiorentinità", however, it evidently hadn't seemed right to add his name to those of the artists encircling Duke Cosimo in the ceiling of the room dedicated to him in the Palazzo Vecchio.
[13] Proof of this can be found in the famous letter from Luigi del Riccio in Rome to Roberto Strozzi in Lyon dated 21 July 1544, also transcribed in *Il Carteggio...*, 1965-1983, IV, 1979, at no. MXXII, pp. 183-184.
[14] Vasari, 1568, 1962 ed., I, p. 118, IV, p. 1875. Pegazzano, 2004, p. 72; P. Costamagna, in *Ritratto di un banchiere...*, 2004, pp. 395-396, nos. 14-14a.
[15] See Piccolomini, 1991; Riklin, 2000. Giannotti dealt with the figure of Brutus from 1532-1533, after the fall of the Florentine Republic. More in general, the "myth of Brutus was alive in 15th- and 16th-century Florence like in no other place" (Riklin, 2000, p. 60).
[16] D. Giannotti, *Dialoghi sui giorni che Dante consumò nel cercare l'Inferno e il Purgatorio*, Rome, 1546. Giannotto also admired Michelangelo as a poet.
[17] Cf. Condivi, 1553, 1998 ed., p. XXXVI.
[18] Condivi, 1553, 1998 ed., p. XXII, annotation 20.
[19] Vasari, *The Lives* (1568), 1996 ed., II, p. 245.
[20] I agree with Wasserman (2003, pp. 95-96) when he observes that in the drapery for the *Brutus*, the long parallel furrows made by a claw-chisel with a lot of space between the teeth much resemble the pattern of regularly and definitely "non-Michelangelesque" stripes on the back of Christ's body in the *Florentine Pietà*, notoriously reworked by Tiberio.
[21] Starting with Tolnay (1954, pp. 76 and ff., 113) credit has been given to Francesco I for buying the bust, which is believed to have been in Villa della Petraia from 1574 to 1584 (cf. Barocchi, 1982); but the credit should really be shifted to his brother Ferdinando, supported by the document published by M. Hirst in his introduction to Condivi, 1553, 1998 ed., p. XX. Along with the *Brutus*, the Grand Duke purchased from the Leoni estate a bronze bust of Michelangelo. See the essay by E.D. Schmidt on Diomede Leoni, his vegetable gardens in San Quirico d'Orcia and the statuary he bequeathed.
[22] "DVM BRVTI EFFIGIEM SCULPTOR DE MARMORE DVCIT / IN MENTEM SCELERIS VENIT ET ABSTINVIT" (While the sculptor was carving the marble effigy of *Brutus*, the crime came to mind and he stopped [carving]). The lines were erroneously attributed to Bembo, Poliziano, Giannotti; perhaps the contents were instead suggested by Anton Maria Salvini (Florence, 1653-1729). With the 18th century – the age of new libertarian ideas – well underway, Lord Sandwich formulated a distich with a very different meaning: "BRUTUM EFFECISSET SCULPTUR: SED MENTE RECURSAT / TANTA VIRI VIRTUS, SISTIS ET ABSTINUIT" (Barocchi, 1982, pp. 27-29).
[23] Letter from Ascanio Parisani in Rome to Duke Guidubaldo Della Rovere in Urbino, 23 November 1541, in Gaye, 1839-1840, II, 1840, pp. 290-291.
[24] Letter from Guidubaldo Della Rovere in Urbino to Michelangelo in Rome, 6 March 1542, in *Il Carteggio...*, 1965-1983, IV, 1979, no. CMLXXXIX, pp. 128 and ff.
[25] Letter from Michelangelo in Rome to Pope Paul III in Rome, 20 July 1542, in *Il Carteggio...*, 1965-1983, IV, 1979, no. CMXCIV, pp. 138 and ff.
[26] Hughes, 1997, p. 268.
[27] Condivi, *The Life of Michelangelo* (1553), 2006 ed., p. 77.
[28] Condivi, 1553, 1998 ed., p. XXII, p. 17.
[29] Elements of historical identity have been suggested for the two allegorical figures: Vittoria Colonna for the *Contemplative Life* and Faustina Mancini for the *Active Life* (Guidoni, 2002).
[30] Condivi, *The Life of Michelangelo* (1553), 2006 ed., p. 79.
[31] Boston, Isabella Stewart Gardner Museum (inv. 1.2o/16.0; Tolnay, 1975-1980, III, 1978, n. 26r), datable to about 1538-1540, and on the basis of Condivi's recollections, dedicated to Vittoria Colonna.
[32] In the painting, where restoration work has made everything clearly visible again, other citations from Michelangelo are visible in the refined chair, called "dantesca", on which Ortensia is sitting (cf. Piccinini, 2005). It had been attributed to Bronzino in the past and was believed to be a portrait of Vittoria Colonna.
[33] The paraphrase may be found in the second edition of Vasari's *Lives*: "with a mirror in her hand to signify the con-

sideration that we should give to our actions, and in the other hand a garland of flowers, to denote the virtues that adorn our life during its duration, and make it glorious after death". Vasari, *The Lives* (1568), 1996 ed., II, pp. 689. The garland is not made up of flowers, however, but of round berries, so that it would seem to be from the laurel plant.

[34] Condivi, *The Life of Michelangelo* (1553), 2006 ed., p. 79.

[35] Dante Alighieri, *Divine Comedy*, "Purgatory", canto XXVII, lines 97-108: "a beautiful woman appeared in my dream, / And I saw her walking over an open plain, / Gathering flowers as she went; / and singing, she said: / If anyone should ask what my name is, / Let him know, I am Leah, as I go, / I move my beautiful hands to make a garland. / To please myself at the looking-glass, I adorn myself; / But my sister Rachel never stirs / From her mirror, and sits there all day long. / She is desirous of seeing her own lovely eyes, / As I am of adorning myself with my hands; / She takes pleasure in looking, and I in doing".

[36] Only much later commentators on the *Divine Comedy* observed the lack of coherence between Dante's sympathies for the Empire and the role of the Countess, in defence of the Pope and against the Empire, in the struggle for the investitures. Other identities suggested are Matilde di Hackenborn, a German nun and contemporary of Dante, and quite well known as the author of *Liber specialis gratiae*, which contained mystic visions; one of the women who appear in the *Vita Nuova*, or the *Rime*, or the *Convivio*. Observe how Condivi chooses to use the name "Matilda" here, closer in assonance to Dante's "Matelda", instead of "Mathilda", which he instead used in the first page of his bibliographical narration.

[37] London, British Museum, inv. 1947-4-12-161, recently reconsidered in Clifford, 2002. I don't see any reason for interpreting the object to be a diadem (Tolnay, 1954).

[38] Vasari, *The Lives* (1568), 1996 ed., II, pp. 690 (nothing in the 1550 edition).

[39] The attribution suggested by A. Forcellino, supported in authoritative sources by C.L. Frommel, K. Weil-Garris Brandt, in part by C. Echinger-Maurach, has been disputed in a number of journals and magazines by B. Agosti, V. Sgarbi, A. Pinelli, E. Guidoni, which resulted in Forcellino's strong reaction (2002b).

[40] Panofsky, 1939.

[41] Echinger-Maurach (who also recently referred back to some of the arguments in her article of 2003) suggests that Michelangelo worked on the recumbent figure from September 1532 to June 1533 making the model and probably intervening in the face and hands, while the rest was done by a collaborator, without excluding Boscoli. A persuasive defence of Boscoli as the author is in Guidoni, 2003.

[42] I don't find it necessary to hypothesize, as instead has been, that the two completely worked candelabra were made for the tomb in its temple version with three sides visible, while the other two were carved for a final version. The position of the monument, although featuring a limited three-dimensionality, would assume that the outer candelabra had to be visible from several angles, and not just from the front like the two in the middle.

[43] See the texts in Voelker, 2000.

[44] The drawing (inv. 533) passed through the collections of John Charles Robinson and Robert Ludwig Mond. Cf. the catalogue *Michelangelo: grafia e biografia...*, 2002, p. 73, no. 43.

[45] In addition to Tommaso de' Cavalieri, Andrea Quaratesi, Febo del Poggio, Gherardo Perini have also been mentioned. David Hockney, a declared homosexual, was inspired by the relationship between Buonarroti and the deceased youth for his painting *In Memoriam of Cecchino Bracci* (1962, Madrid, Thyssen-Bornemisza Museum).

[46] Paul III (1534-1549), Julius III (1550-1555), Marcellus II (1555), Paul IV (1555-1559), Pius IV (1559-1565).

[47] Vasari, "The Life of Michelangelo" (1550), 2007 ed., p. 181.

[48] Condivi, *The Life of Michelangelo* (1553), 2006 ed., p. 90.

[49] Milanesi, 1878-1885, VII, 1873, p. 244, note 1. Other interpretations suggested for the subject include the *Lament over the Dead Christ*, *Vir dolorum*, the *Deposition in the Sepulchre*, a combination of the *Deposition*, the *Lamentation* and other subjects.

[50] Tiberio Calcagni (1532-1565) came from a good Florentine family and was the son of Lucrezia Buonaccorsi, whom Michelangelo knew. Present in Rome from the late thirties or early forties, he was introduced to the artist by Francesco Bandini and Donato Giannotti, and worked as his discreet, courteous assistant after Urbino's death (1556). He brought Duke Cosimo de' Medici the drawings for San Giovanni dei Fiorentini, which he also explained to him, and then made two models, one from terracotta and the other from wood (the latter of the two is portrayed in a print). Calcagni was also the one to write down and transcribe Michelangelo's annotations to Condivi's *Life* (1998 ed.).

[51] Francesco Bandini (1496-1562) was a member of the old Florentine Bandini-Baroncelli family, with its own chapel in Santa Croce. Bandini may have been with Michelangelo in Ferrara in 1528. In Rome he was a banker and a delegate for the fabric of San Giovanni de' Fiorentini.

[52] Vasari, *The Lives* (1568), 1996 ed., II, pp. 716-717. The issue of whether or not a price was paid has been contradictory since Vasari's telling of it. The most recent reconstruction of the facts is in Wasserman (2003, pp. 75-76), according to whom Michelangelo gave the statue to Antonio del Francese and then authorized him to give it to Bandini; Antonio was compensated for the loss by Bandini, who paid him 200 scudi, and then received the *Rondanini Pietà* as a gift from the master.

[53] Vasari, *The Lives* (1568), 1996 ed., II, pp. 717.

[54] Wasserman, 2003, pp. 30-31.

[55] Varchi, 1564, pp. 37-38.

[56] Varchi (see previous note) supplied a vivid description of the episode, accusing the *operai* of want to prove, with their vetoes, their power over a figure like Michelangelo. The artist never once returned to Santa Croce; but he did write to Vasari to say that he wished to be buried close to his father, therefore in the cloister of the church. Varchi emphasized the artist's wishes, which ended up being instrumental to the Grand-Ducal and Florentine intention to honour the artist in his native city.

[57] Wasserman, 2003, p. 28. At the basis of this, as well as other observations made by Wasserman, reported along the way, is the critical use of IBM's digital model of the marble group.

[58] Condivi, *The Life of Michelangelo* (1553), 2006 ed., p. 87.

[59] Wasserman, 2003, p. 35.

[60] What is evoked for this twofold identification, which, in the absence of precise attributes for the male figure remains uncertain (although there is a predilection for Nicodemus), is a passage from Vittoria Colonna who exalted the roles of the two Evangelical figures, both glorious, the one for having guided Christ's descent from the cross, the other for donating his own tomb for his burial. To my mind, owing to the fact that Michelangelo chose to represent the deposition as something very close in time and actually not completed yet, the identification of Nicodemus by the two 16th-century biographers should be upheld.

[61] The topic is developed in Verdon, 2003, who underscores that fact that the decree on the Eucharist was published in 1552, thus confirming the bodily and not just spiritual presence of Christ in the consecrated host, contrary to Protestant theses.

[62] Steinberg, 1968, discussed by Verdon, 2003, p. 144 (also see Steinberg, 1989).

[63] Shrimplin-Evangelidis, 1989, pp. 63-65.

[64] Rockwell, 2003, especially pp. 63-65.

[65] Wasserman, 2003, pp. 69-72.

[66] The news that it had been identified with a small wax model of the group was published in the periodical *Le Arti del Disegno*, 5 January, 1856, Florence. After it became the property of Cavalier Gigli, the model was offered for sale to the Italian government, but it was not acquired (Milanesi, 1878-1885, VII, 1873, pp. 244-245, note 1, with reference to the publication *Documenti relativi al bozzetto in cera della Pietà di Michelangelo Buonarroti*, Florence, Pellas, 1873). The small model, which is now in a private collection in Florence (Wasserman, 2003, pl. 41), was probably one of those produced in the 18th century, made from wax or clay, after the group was placed on the high altar of the Florentine Cathedral. The drawing of the *Head* currently at the Boymans van Beuningen Museum in Rotterdam (inv. I 495*r*.; cf. Tolnay, 1975-1980, II, 1976, n. 324*r*., released as unpublished and dated about 1532) instead pertains to a preparatory phase and constitutes one of the very few testimonies, if not the only one, perhaps for one Maddalena (Wallace, 2000, note 71).

[67] Wasserman (2003, p. 84) cautiously advanced the hypothesis that Tiberio himself removed the left leg and was not able to replace it; this hypothesis obviously provides an alternative to the one that says it was Michelangelo who removed it. The differences observed in the type of stucco used would suggest different stages in restoration of the group, also keeping in mind that in 1671, as regards its sale to the Grand Duke of Tuscany, mention was made of "several small pieces".

[68] I agree with Wasserman's (2003) ascription to Michelangelo for Christ's torso, where others have instead chosen to see a minute and "feminine" trait suited more to his assistant.

[69] Paoletti, 2000, pp. 60-61 and Verdon, 2003, p. 137 are of the same opinion.

[70] [1] Now there was a Pharisee named Nicodemus, a leader of the Jews. [2] He came to Jesus by night and said to him, "Rabbi, we know that you are a teacher who has come from God; for no one can do these signs that you do apart from the presence of God". [3] Jesus answered him, "Very truly, I tell you, no one can see the kingdom of God without being born from above". [4] Nicodemus said to him, "How can anyone be born after having grown old? Can one enter a second time into the mother's womb and be born?" [5] Jesus answered, "Very truly, I tell you, no one can enter the kingdom of God without being born of water and Spirit. [6] What is born of the flesh is flesh, and what is born of the Spirit is spirit. [7] Do not be astonished that I said to you, 'You must be born from above'. [8] The wind blows where it

chooses, and you hear the sound of it, but you do not know where it comes from or where it goes. So it is with everyone who is born of the Spirit". [9] Nicodemus said to him, "How can these things be?" [10] Jesus answered him, "Are you a teacher of Israel, and yet you do not understand these things? [11] Very truly, I tell you, we speak of what we know and testify to what we have seen; yet you do not receive our testimony. [12] If I have told you about earthly things and you do not believe, how can you believe if I tell you about heavenly things? [13] No one has ascended into heaven except the one who descended from heaven, the Son of Man. [14] And just as Moses lifted up the serpent in the wilderness, so must the Son of Man be lifted up, [15] that whoever believes in him may have eternal life. [16] For God so loved the world that he gave his only Son, so that everyone who believes in him may not perish but may have eternal life. [17] Indeed, God did not send the Son into the world to condemn the world, but in order that the world might be saved through him. [18] Those who believe in him are not condemned; but those who do not believe are condemned already, because they have not believed in the name of the only Son of God. [19] And this is the judgement, that the light has come into the world, and people loved darkness rather than light because their deeds were evil. [20] For all who do evil hate the light and do not come to the light, so that their deeds may not be exposed. [21] But those who do what is true come to the light, so that it may be clearly seen that their deeds have been done in God". (The Gospel According to John, 3: 1-21.)

[71] From the sonnet "My eyes are saddened by so much they see" (301): "My wicked ways, the allure of vanity, / amid the shadows of the life I live, / Oh help me encounter these, help and forgive [...]". The contraposition between light and darkness, day and night, as metaphors for the condition of the spirit was certainly not rare for poetry of that time, but it was in any event present in Michelangelo's poetry. Just one more example, from "Why only at long last, why next to never" (257). "Those vacuities are the night, your glow's the day: / one turning the heart to ice, and one to fire / the love, the trust, of incendiary heaven". (Girardi, 1960, pp. 121 and 141).

[72] Paoletti, 2000, p. 63. Paoletti does not expand the subject beyond this nonetheless very significant indication; but the *topos* of the artist's self-portrait could be studied more in depth in secondary or servile roles (Saint Luke's errand boy, the servant in the *Last Supper*, at times the ruffian or bandit), which allowed him to humbly be among the figures of sacred scenes. As for Michelangelo, his sense of self-irony ever-present, he portrayed himself in the skin of the flayed Saint Bartholomew in the Sistine *Judgement*.

[73] Height 253 cm. The marble comes from a piece of ancient Roman cornice, also proven by the fragment of acanthus leaf visible on the back.

[74] Another copy, made from terracotta, was donated by the author Giulio De Angelis to the "Fondazione Giovanni Pierluigi da Palestrina".

[75] Cecconi, 1756, p. 309.

[76] Pope-Hennessy (1964, 1986) leaned towards Menghini, whose figure as a sculptor associated with Barberini and the author of statues in prestigious holy sites has been reconsidered: in Saint Peter's; in Santa Martina, where he executed the statue of the martyr and joint patron, whose remains were found during the papacy of Urban VIII. Lothar Nickel's contribution for the meeting *I Barberini e la cultura europea del Seicento* (Rome, 7-11, December 2004) was entitled *Niccolò Menghini. Uno scultore bolognese alla corte dei Barberini*.

[77] Martini, 1964; Bonsanti, 1987, pp. 22-23.

[78] Until 1671, the *Bandini Pietà* could still be seen in Rome, either in the Bandini vineyard or in the Capponi and after that Rusticucci-Accoro; Paoletti, 2000; Fehl, 2002; Fiorio, 2004.

[80] Completed in 2004, restoration work had been preceded by periods of study and diagnostic testing (for the restoration work, see Vedovello, 2004, pp. 107-113). See the foldout *Michelangelo ultimo. Riapertura della Pietà Rondanini, Museo d'Arte Antica*, Castello Sforzesco, Milan [2002].

[81] On 21August 1561 it was recalled as one of the two statues given by Michelangelo to his own servant Antonio del Francese of Castel Durante; it is listed with the property left by Michelangelo in his workshop as established in the inventory of 9 February 1564 (in Gotti, 1875, I, p. 356, II, pp. 148-156, no. 40) with the words "initiated for a Christ and another figure on top, joined together, roughed out and left 'non-finite'". The documentary sources required to reconstruct the history of the sculpture are collected, revisited and widely cited in Barocchi, 1962a, IV, pp. 1677-1678; Fiorio, 2004, pp. 13-16.

[82] Vasari, *The Lives* (1568), 1996 ed., II, p. 171.

[83] Lettere from Daniele da Volterra in Rome to Giorgio Vasari in Florence dated 17 March 1564 (in *Der Literarische Nachlass*..., 1923-1930, II, pp. 53-58, no. CDXXXV) and letter from Daniele da Volterra in Rome to Lionardo Buonarroti in Florence dated 11 June 1564 (in *Carteggio indiretto*..., 1988-1995, II, 1995, pp. 198-199, no. 370).

[84] For the identity of the male, Nicodemus, Joseph of Arimathea, an angel, God the Father have all been suggested. For a number of reasons, to a certain extent coinciding with the ones elaborated for the *Florentine Pietà*, there is predilection for Nicodemus.

[85] Paoletti, 2000, p. 63. The person who drew up the inventory of 1564 did not identify it, and described it in general terms as a figure (in Gotti, 1875, p. 356, II, pp. 148 and ff.).

[86] Steinberg, 1970.

[87] Letter from Daniele Ricciarelli in Rome to Lionardo Buonarroti in Florence, 11 June 1564, in *Carteggio indiretto*..., 1988-1995, II, 1995, pp. 198-200, no. 370.

[88] Mantura (1973) was the author of the proposal, which was supported by Parronchi (1980) and Paolucci (1997, pp. 139 and 145). But Schiavo (1977) and Hartt (1987) had already refuted the connection, the latter of the two even going so far as to consider the Borghese fragment a fake.

[89] Vienna, Albertina Graphische Sammlung, inv. 103*r*. Cf. Tolnay, 1975-1980, III, 1978, n. 432*r*.

[90] Oxford, Ashmolean Museum, inv. P. 339. Cf. Tolnay, 1975-1980, III, 1978, n. 433*r*.

[91] Paoletti, 2000, p. 72.

[92] Simmel, 1910, Italian edition 2003, pp. 46-48.

[93] Tolnay identified it at a meeting held in Bonn in 1964 (after which Tolnay, 1965 and 1967b). See J.A. O'Grody in the catalogue *I bozzetti*..., 2000, pp. 64-67, no. 8. For the link to the letters from Lorenzo Mariottini in Rome to Lionardo Buonarroti in Florence, see Bonsanti, in *L'ombra*..., 2002, pp. 220-221, no. 82.

[94] This was Tolnay's belief. I do not agree with Shell's observation (in *The Genius*..., 1992, p. 270), that since Michelangelo asked for a large assortment of tools then his plan was to make a larger statue. Firstly, we have no idea just how many and which "ferri" (tools) were acquired for him; secondly, we can't exclude the idea that he may have used all of them, considering the great care he took to create different effects, even when the object was a very small one.

[95] "The rough surface [...] strikingly recalls Titian's late paintings or, one century later, Rembrandt's" (G. Bonsanti, in *L'ombra*..., 2002, p. 221).

[96] See Ciseri, 1993, pp. 41-48, and related entries. An articulate tradition involved as many solemn funerals as there were feasts, especially for the Feast of Saint Lawrence, which became even more elaborate under the Medici.

[97] The catafalque was decorated with sculptures and paintings. Below the statues made of "terra", or clay, to imitate marble were depictions of the Arno and Tiber rivers signifying Florence and Rome, the two cities associated with the life and work of both Michelangelo and the Medici. On the corners of the upper register four groups of sculptures represented positive forces defeating their negative counterparts, for a contraposition between Good and Evil, which in 16th-centuruy Florentine sculpture gave rise to the figurative relationship between the victor and the captive, elaborated with elegant, refined *contrapposti*: Art and Envy, Christian Piety and Vice (or Impiety), the Arts (like Minerva) – Painting, Sculpture, Architecture – and Poetry. Depicted in two of the sides of the pyramid located above "in two ovals [there were] life-sized reliefs of Michelangelo's head". This was surmounted by the figure of Fame.
The stories painted on both the catafalque and the tables corresponding to the chapels illustrated the life of Michelangelo, from his artistic beginnings under the protection of Lorenzo il Magnfico, to his arrival in the Elysian Fields welcomed there by the great artists of antiquity and of his time. The high moments in the artist's life especially emphasized his relationship with the powerful, particularly the Medici; an "epitaph" in Latin composed by Pier Vettori expressed the gratitude of the Accademia. An elaborate composition on its own amended in Christian terms the allusion to the Elysian afterlife, removed from antique paganism; Michelangelo's soul was portrayed ascending towards a celestial light, while the Po, Nile and Ganges rivers were guided by Fame to present their condolences to the Arno. The scene was framed theatrically by way of curtains held open by Vulcan oppressing Hatred, and by Aglaia (Proportion) atop Disproportion. A painting on Donatello's pulpit, which hadn't been assembled on columns yet, portrayed Fame-Honour in the act of defeating Death and Time. Duke Cosimo ordered that the apparatus be left there as it was for several weeks, and it drew many visitors. Varchi's oration and numerous poems written for the occasion were published.

[98] See Cecchi, 1993.

[99] In 1616, Grand Duke Cosimo II gave back a part of the donation that his grandfather Cosimo I had received from Lionardo. Transformed into an institution in 1859 with the very last act of the Lorenese dynasty, the Casa Buonarroti is currently a very active research centre as well s an exhibition space dedicated to the great master, his family, and to art and culture as related to Buonarottian themes.

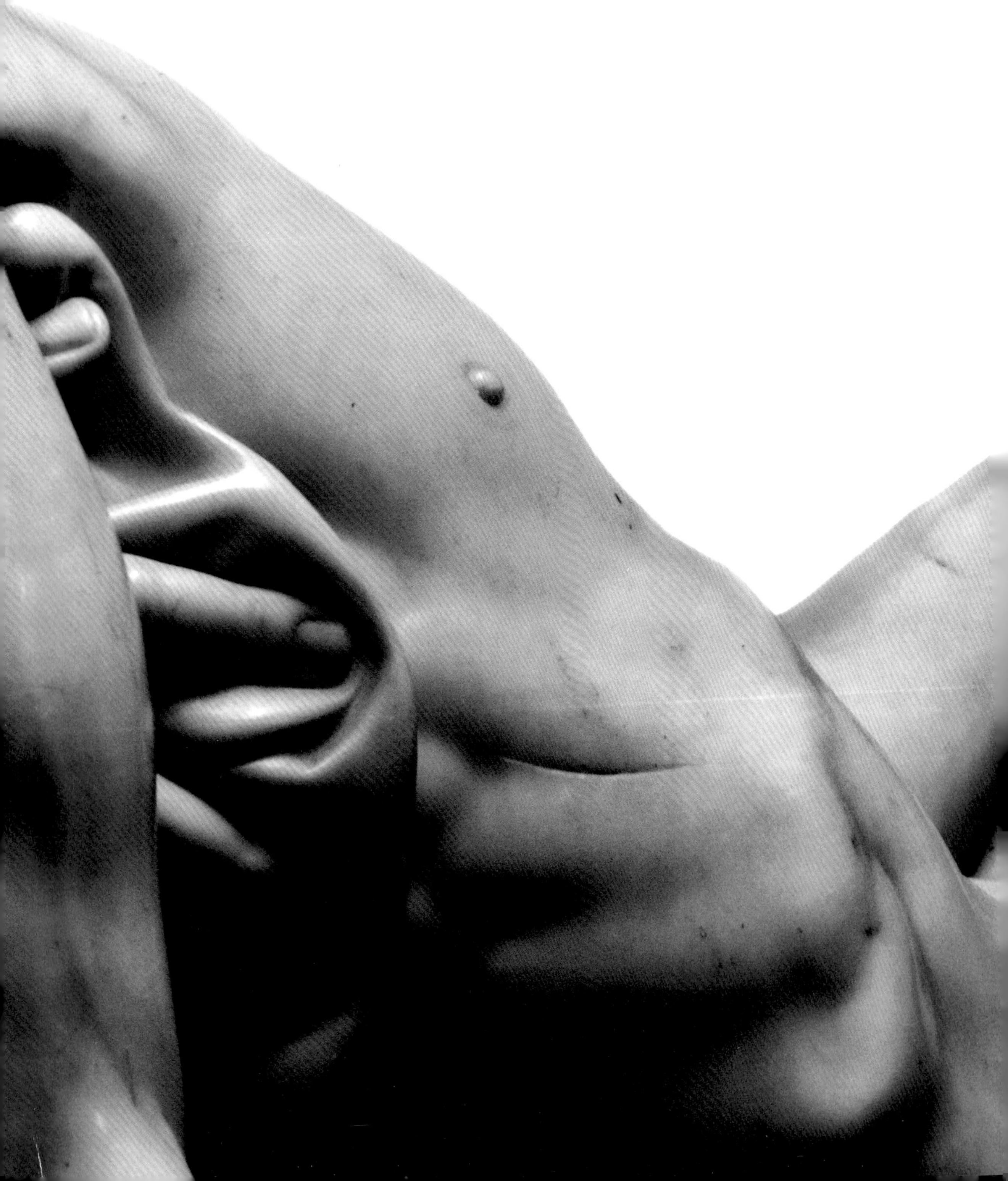

Entries

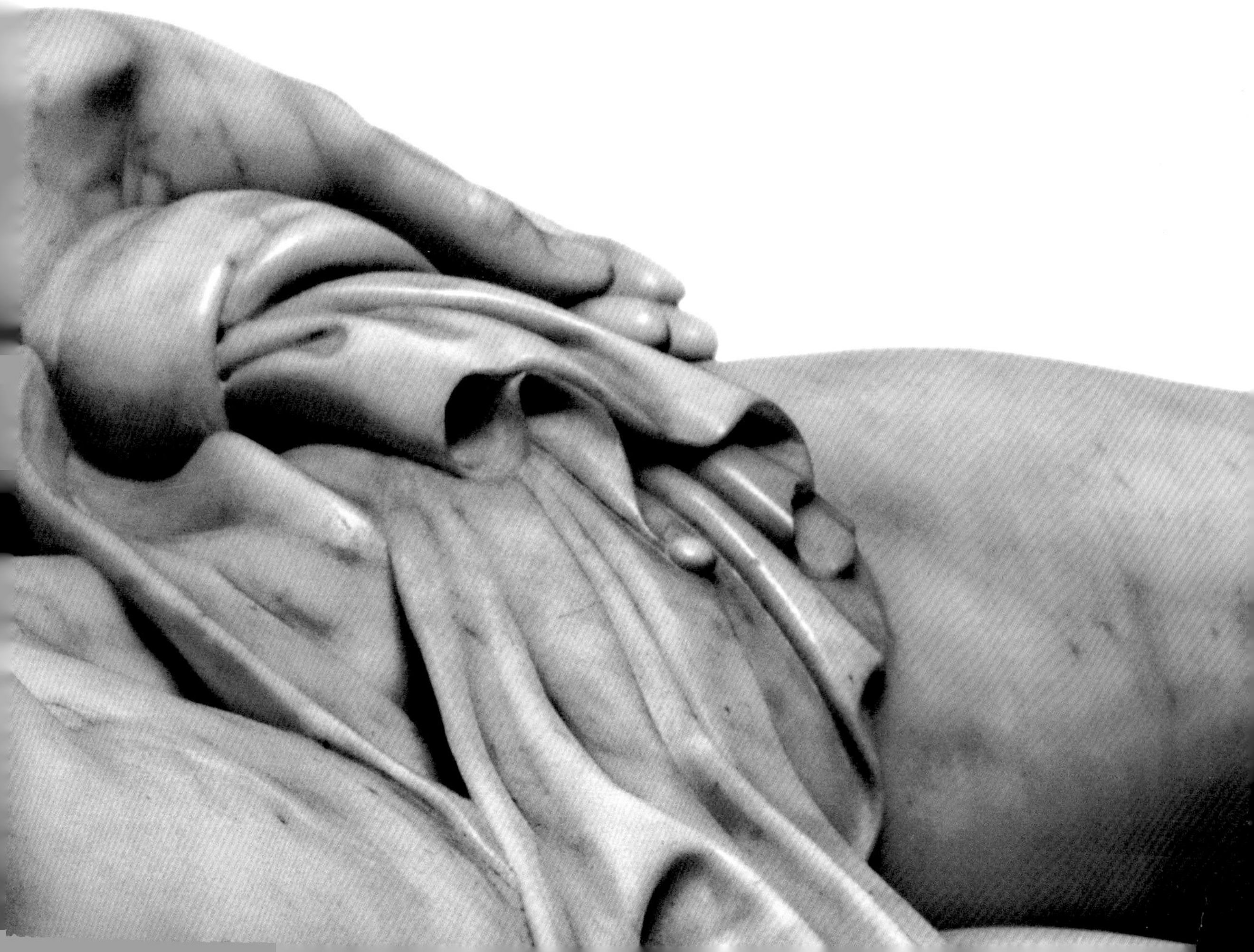

1. *Madonna of the Stairs*
about 1492
Marble, 57.1 x 40.5 cm
Florence, Casa Buonarroti, inv. 190

Lionardo Buonarroti kept the work in his home "in remembrance of his uncle" until he gave it to Duke Cosimo de' Medici before 1568 (the Giunti or second edition of Vasari's *Lives*). Grand Duke Cosimo II subsequently gave it to Michelangelo Buonarroti the Younger in 1616. In the meantime a plaster cast of the work had been made and a bronze copy executed. This copy is still preserved in the Casa Buonarroti, although doubt has recently been cast on its attribution to Vincenzo Danti. In the late 17th century the Madonna was in the "Camera degli Angeli" used as a chapel. Its state of conservation is good and it underwent mild cleaning in the late 20th century.

2. *Battle of the Centaurs*
about 1492
Marble, 84.5 x 90.5 cm
Florence, Casa Buonarroti, inv. 194

This high-relief marble sculpture is considered to be the second earliest extant youthful sculpture by Michelangelo, made when he was under the patronage of Lorenzo il Magnifico while at the Medicean Garden of San Marco, and left unfinished. Although at the time the artist's biographers indicated different subjects for the work, it should be a *Battle of the Centaurs and Lapiths* or the *Abduction of Hippodameia*; i.e. the moment at which the centaur Eurytus and his followers interrupted the wedding banquet of Pirithous and Hippodeamea, as told by Ovid in the *Metamorphoses*. The subject was suggested to the sculptor by the humanist Agnolo Poliziano. In the wild frenzy of the fight, the violent entanglement between the human bodies and those of the half-human, half-animal centaurs creates an articulation of volumes in the depth of the marble, the result of which is a spatially staggering effect handled by Michelangelo with great skill.
Although not of overwhelming importance, the artist was evidently inspired by ancient Roman reliefs, especially the sarcophagi still visible today in the Camposanto in Pisa.
The piece of marble remained "non-finito", with some of the parts actually rough, for example the strip running all around it. The recurring hypothesis that some of the figures were "reworked" is difficult to prove. Michelangelo continued to think back on the *Battle*, even when he was an elderly man, despite the fact that it was "imperfect". The sculpture remained in the Florentine home of the Buonarroti family. When Michelangelo the Younger began to work on the first-floor gallery of the palace, to be able to situate the *Battle* on one of the shorter sides he had a "slice of marble" sawn off from the posterior end of the relief (1614). In 1591 Francesco Bocchi described it in great detail (Bocchi 1591, 1677 ed., pp. 348-349).
During one of his Florentine sojourns (1600, 1603), the great Dutch artist Peter Paul Rubens copied a number of works by Michelangelo, including this one (Paris, Fondation Custodia, inv. 5422; Rotterdam, Boymans-van Beuningen Museum, inv. V7). Despite its accessibility, the relief was only reproduced for the first time in 1813-1818 (Cicognara, II, pl. LIX).

3. *Crucifix*
about 1492-1493
Polychrome linden wood, h. 139, w. 135 cm
Florence, church of Santo Spirito

Believed to have been lost, it was identified in 1962 by Margrit Lisner in a room in the convent complex, restored by Pellegrino Banella under the direction of Umberto Baldini in the Gabinetto dei Restauri of the Gallerie Fiorentine (cf. Lisner, 1963, 1964, 1966; Procacci, Baldini, 1966), and it became the object of controversy in the international community of art historians, divided between those who favoured the attribution and those who were against it. On display for the exhibitions that took place to commemorate the fourth centenary of the artist's death (Rome, Palazzo delle Esposizioni, and Florence, Casa Buonarroti, 1964), and presented at the meeting on Michelangelesque studies, it was then loaned to the Museum of the Casa Buonarroti. In view of the exhibition *Giovinezza di Michelangelo* (1999), Barbara Schleicher had it submitted to conservative analysis.
When the event ended, in compliance with the city of Florence's growing sensibility towards the work (of which it was the proprietor), as well as that of the Augustinian Fathers, the sculpture was once again placed in the church of Santo Spirito, and installed in the Sacristy (cf. R. Proto Pisani, in *Il Crocifisso... - The Crucifix...*, 2000).

4. *Crucifix* (attributed to Michelangelo)
about 1495
Polychrome linden wood, 41.3 x 39.7 cm
Private collection

The attribution of the wooden sculpture, supported by Giancarlo Gentilini with the consent of other experts (as well as the dissent of others, including M. Lisner) is a relatively recent one, and leads the way to an in-depth reflection on the theme of Michelangelesque works made for private patrons and not individually cited in the sources, datable to this period.
The quality of the invention, the high level of execution, the closely studied anatomical verisimilitude of the body of Christ require careful assessment, particularly as we are dealing with a technique – polychrome wooden sculpture – that does not easily lend itself to comparison in Michelangelo's corpus of works.
In what we might call a "family" of wooden crucifixes, which albeit to different degrees depend on this one, because of its particular likeness, mention must be made of a crucifix in a private collection in New York-Paris, which is similar in proportion, 1:1, and size.

5. *Angel Holding a Candlestick*
Marble, h. 51.5 cm with base, base 30.5 x 16.5 cm
6. *Saint Proculus*
Marble, h. 58.5 cm
7. *Saint Petronius*
Marble, h. 64 cm
1494-1495
Bologna, church of San Domenico, *Arca* of San Domenico

Michelangelo stayed in Bologna about a year, a guest of his patron the aristocrat Francesco Aldrovandi, and was commissioned to make sculptures to continue with the project to decorate the shrine, or *Arca*, of San Domenico; work on the notable monument had been interrupted upon the death of Niccolò dell'Arca. Although Leandro Alberti (1535) had previously ascribed the three statuettes to Michelangelo, both Vasari (1550 and 1568) and Condivi (1553) attributed the first two alone to the master. But today's scholarship generally accepts the *Saint Proculus* as also being an autograph work, whose Michelangelesque paternity was first advanced by Wilhelm von Bode in 1905. As for the *Saint Petronius*, on the basis of a report by Lamo (about 1560), in which the drapery alone was ascribed to the Florentine sculptor, the idea has been and is that the execution of the head is by another hand (Emiliani, 1999). To my mind, it is likely that the head, which is original, underwent reworking in the face in order to accentuate its physiognomic traits. We indeed need to consider the idea that while the *Angel* is clearly visible, the two *Saints* are located very high up on the monument, and were originally in semidarkness. The monumental *Arca* was moved from its first location in 1605, and the original location of the statues themselves is uncertain.
Fra Ludovico da Prelormo recalled that the *Saint Proculus* had been struck by a falling ladder on 4 August 1572, and seriously damaged. On display at the *Giovinezza di Michelangelo* exhibition held in 1999-2000, it was then sent to the Opificio delle Pietre Dure for conservative analysis and every inch of it was studied by the Stone Material Restoration Division. The marble was identified as Apuan white statuary. Optical testing revealed that the statue had broken and been reassembled by means of hinges, extensive reintegration and reconstruction with plaster and white cement.

8. *Bacchus*
1496-1497
Marble, height of figure alone 190 cm (for Condivi "palmi dieci", equal to 195 cm); with its base 209 cm
Florence, Museo Nazionale del Bargello, inv. S. 10

The statue remained in the Roman garden of the Galli family until 1572 when Francesco de' Medici acquired it for 280 scudi; the transaction was mediated by Diomede Leoni. In 1591, the date of Francesco Bocchi's description, the *Bacchus* was in the Uffizi Gallery situated close to an antique *Bacchus*, a further attempt (the same thing had occurred with the two *Sleeping Cupids* owned by Isabella d'Este in Mantua) to compare ancient and modern statuary, but in favour of the modern here. Between 1792 and 1798 it was removed from the east corridor and relocated to the west corridor in the vicinity of other modern statues: the *Bacchus* by Sansovino, Bandinelli's copy of the *Laocoön*, sculptures by Donatello. In 1871, together with the rest of the modern statuary, it was transferred to the new Museo Nazionale del Bargello where it can still be seen today (and where it was affected by the flood of 1966). Other works by Michelangelo from the same period are also on display in that area.

9. *Young Archer*
about 1496-1497
Marble, h. 100 cm (without the base)
New York, Cultural Services of the French Embassy

The provenance of the work is the Villa Borghese, where it appears it was already located in 1650. The work can be viewed as it must have been about halfway through the 18th century, installed in an outer niche and in a more finished state, in the drawings of the French painter Jean-Robert Ango (Musée du Louvre, DAG, RF4192 fol. 61r.; New York, Smithsonian Institution, Cooper

Hewitt National Design Museum, inv. 1977-110-1-4; cf. J.D. Draper, in *Giovinezza...*, 1999, pp. 380-381, no. 61). One hypothesis currently being examined concerns Cardinal Scipione Borghese's purchase of the Galli collection, which in addition to the *Bacchus* included an "*Apollo*" or a "*Cupid*" by Michelangelo.
The statue had been attributed to the young Michelangelo (or to his circle) at the Christie's auction held in London in 1902, where the Florentine antiquarian Stefano Bardini, who had acquired it from the Borghese prince, put it up for sale but without finding any buyers. It was subsequently purchased by the architect Stanford White, who in 1905 had it installed in the atrium of the Payne Whitney House on Fifth Avenue in New York, today the Cultural Services of the French Embassy. White placed it on a triangular base atop a fountain. Without knowing the statue's whereabouts, Parronchi reiterated its attribution to Michelangelo on the basis of a photograph, identifying it with the Galli *Apollo* or *Cupid* (1968). Draper, who had rediscovered the former Borghese-Bardini statue in New York, discussed it in his writings on Bertoldo di Giovanni (1992). But upon observing the statue under more favourable lighting conditions in 1995, Kathleen Weil-Garris Brandt reconsidered its ascription to Michelangelo (1996). This was followed by heated debate, which included refusal of the attribution, but none of the other hypotheses for attribution put forth, ranging from Bertoldo's authorship to the idea of its being a fake, have been persuasive. Several contributions on the subject were published in the two catalogues (Florence, 1999-2000 and Paris, 2000), as well as later; although not resolutive, Joannides' (2003) publication of the drawings in a sheet that went through Christie's (Paris, 12 March 2002, lot 122A) and now in a private collection does much to advance the question. The scholar used 16th-century copies of Michelangelesque projects to lead up to the entire figure of the *Young Archer*: the overlap between the invention and the statue in New York seems to indicate that although it is a very early and mutilated work, it is more than likely a youthful work by Buonarroti.

10. Vatican *Pietà*
about 1497-1499
Carrara marble, h. 174 cm, width of the base 195 cm, diam. 69 cm
Vatican City, Saint Peter's

Commissioned by Jean de Bilhères-Lagraulas, abbot of Saint-Denis, cardinal of Santa Sabina and ambassador for Charles VIII at the court of Pope Alexander (formerly a diplomat at the service of Louis XI) from 1497, the *Pietà* was undoubtedly finished in 1500 when the executors of the cardinal's will, who had died one year before, deposited the outstanding balance in Michelangelo's account at the Balducci bank. The actual contract had been stipulated on 27 August 1498 in the form of a private paper with Jacopo Galli as guarantor. Michelangelo himself went to Carrara to procure the beautiful piece of Apuan marble; it was the first time he went to the quarries to personally oversee the extraction and rough-hewing of the material on site. The cardinal's letter to the Anziani of Lucca (18 November 1497) described the group that the sculptor was to carve out of the marble as follows: "Virgin robed with naked dead Christ in her arms". The cardinal never saw the group installed: but he had undoubtedly determined its placement for his own burial in the chapel of the King of France, a building from Late Antiquity adjoining the transept of the old Vatican basilica where the relics of Saint Petronilla, daughter of Saint Peter and *auxiliatrix regis Francorum* were located, and rediscovered in the identification of 1474. A very unique engraving by Nicolas Beatrizet (1547), which presents the *Pietà* as a sculpture set in ancient ruins with a vault suggests instalment of the work in a niche or apse (*Michelangelo e l'arte classica*, 1987, pp. 109-110, no. 46). When the chapel was demolished from 1514 as a part of Bramante's plan for the new Saint Peter's, the *Pietà* was relocated to the *Secretarium*, also known as the chapel of Santa Maria della Febbre, an eponymous location in 16th-century commentaries. Later, the statue was translated to the choir called Sistine, the burial chapel for Sixtus IV, and from there to the "new choir"; it subsequently returned to the area of Saint Petronilla (in 1622 and on a new base) where it remained until 1749 when it was transferred to the first chapel to the right as you enter Saint Peter's (with a crucifix behind it) since then called "of the Pietà". See: Weil-Garris Brandt, 1987, Voci, 2001. A plaster copy of it was made for the new sacristy in Saint Peter's in 1933-1934.
A faithful copy, the work of the Florentine Nanni di Baccio Bigio when he and Michelangelo were still on speaking terms, arrived in Florence relatively early: the Florentine Luigi Del Riccio, a friend and collaborator of Michelangelo (Del Riccio died in 1546), had it executed in Rome for the chapel that had just been purchased in the church of Santo Spirito, where it is still visible today, although within a different context.
In 1964 the *Pietà* was temporarily relocated to New York on the occasion of the World's Fair. After minor repairs were made to damaged areas, some of which were the result of its being moved around so often, major restoration work was carried out in 1972 after it was attacked on May 21, the day of the Pentecost, by a man who used a hammer to strike it some fifteen times, and caused about fifty fragments to fly off. Casts and photographs from before were used to piece the fragments back together and place them in their original positions. Since then the group is protected by a glass plate. In 1964 in New York the Austrian recording engineer Robert Hupka, who had been asked to select the musical programme for the Vatican Pavilion and provide an image for a souvenir record album, took a number of splendid pictures of the marble. After the attack took place, these pictures were shown in a travelling exhibition. When the exhibition finally arrived at the Vatican in 2004 it was entitled *La Pietà rivelata* [The Pietà Revealed].

11. *David*
1501-1504
Carrara marble, h. 486 cm (the figure alone), 516 cm (with the base), 672 cm (with the plinth)
Florence, Galleria dell'Accademia

The colossal marble statue (volume 2,098 m³, total weight 5560 kg), which Michelangelo began to work on in September 1501 and finished before its unveiling on 8 September 1504, cost the consuls of the Wool Guild 400 florins, who paid on behalf of the Opera di Santa Maria del Fiore, which had actually commissioned the work. But the final placement of the statue at the foot of the Palazzo della Signoria underscored the "giant's" civic meaning. In the many years it was on display out in the open the *David* was damaged by both nature and man. The base of the statue was struck by lightning in 1512, after which it was unstable. Further damage was caused on 26 April 1527 during the citizen uprising that took place when the Medici were ousted from the city: objects were thrown from the windows of the Palazzo Vecchio and one of these, a heavy one, hit the statue's left arm breaking it into several pieces. Giorgio Vasari and Francesco Salviati, who were very young at the time, gathered the pieces together and gave them to Salviati's father for safekeeping, until 1543, when Duke Cosimo had them reassembled (the hinges are visible in gammagraphy) and restored to their original site by adding plaster; at the time, Michelangelo had been away from Florence for a decade. Other reworkings and treatments of the statue occurred over the centuries, particularly in the first half of the 19th century: in just a few decades the *David* underwent encaustic treatment by Stefano Ricci (1813), a drastic cleaning by Aristodemo Costoli (1843) who used a hydrochloric acid solution (50%) and sharp tools to scrape away the crusts that had formed on it, and, lastly, Clemente Papi executed a plaster cast of it in parts so that plaster copies could be made from it (1847).
Conservation of the statue, which by then tilted and was unsteady on its base, caused much concern in the second half of the century, and as many as three commissions in a row were appointed to study its stability and techniques to keep the marble from deteriorating: in 1852 (on the initiative of the Accademia di Belle Arti), in 1866 and 1872. One year later the statue was relocated to the Galleria dell'Accademia, but only after the idea (1866) of placing the statue in the recently founded Museo Nazionale del Bargello was shelved. The statue was carefully transported inside a wooden cart on wheels that moved along tracks specially installed in the centre of the city (a model of the cart is preserved at the Casa Buonarroti in Florence). The entire operation took from 30 July to 8 August 1873.
In its new location, set on a base somewhat reminiscent of the original one, the *David* came to be a part of an arrangement that responded to the needs of the 1875 celebrations commemorating the fourth cententary of the birth of Michelangelo (cf. *Michelangelo nell'Ottocento...*, 1994), and reflected the Galleria dell'Accademia's educational mission, which was identical to that of many other European museums.
Copies of the original statue, some of which actually preserved in Florence, were set up along the path that led to the *David*. The effect was comparable to that of the most celebrated plaster cast collections in museums such as the Victoria and Albert in London and the Pushkin in Moscow, and others too. A different museum arrangement, a prelude to the current one, was witnessed in 1909 when the superintendent and eminent scholar Corrado Ricci removed the plaster copies and set up all along the walls of the "nave" leading to the tribune the four *Captives* that were originally meant for the Tomb of Julius II, the *Saint Matthew* made for the Florence Cathedral; the *Palestrina Pietà*, whose ascription to the artist was controversial, was added later. Alongside the impressive parade of Michelangelesque statues, "a grandiose prelude" to accompany the visitor, a "further brilliant intervention to mythicize" the *David* had been accomplished (Paolucci, 2004, p. 10).
On 14 September 1991 a deranged man took a hammer to the statue's left foot; this was the part of the statue that stuck out the most and was therefore exposed and degraded. An analysis of the broken fragments from the toes resulted in a vast and differentiated campaign, organized by a number of Italian research institutes and coordinated

by the Opificio delle Pietre Dure in Florence, the results of which were gathered and interpreted beginning in 2002-2005 in view of conservative work to be carried out on the statue's surface. As part of the diagnostic campaign and the *Michelangelo Digital Project,* a laser-headed scanner was used to produce a digital image of the David, and thus a 3D computer rendering to be used in a number of ways: as a container to file data, news, findings; a base on which to make accurate calculations of the statue's centre of gravity; a starting point for simulations aimed at specific analyses, such as the depth of deposits or the unevenness of the surface.
Visual studies were carried out, which resulted in accurate mapping of the surface and the determination of four typologies: the original flaws in the marble, deposits on the surface, cracks, traces of working. The static stability of the *David* was also studied, with special interest in the cracks visible in the ankle and tree trunk at the base (see *Exploring David...*, 2004). Once it was ascertained that under normal conditions the statue's static stability was satisfactory, attention focused on its surface which, compromised by veining and pinholes inherent to the marble itself, presented signs of reintegration from various periods in time, the widespread presence of plaster, "black crusts" (deposits), residual wax and resin, stains and dust. A mild cleaning of the statue was conducted based on a technique devised by the Stone Material Restoration Division of the Opificio along with the scientific experts: this involved use of the deionized water poultice method supported on sepiolite and interposition of repair papers, with contact times that varied depending on the areas and the deposits. The stains were diminished. As a result of the intervention, completed by the conservator Cinzia Panigoni in 2004, conservation was safeguarded by removal of the plaster and dust that contained contaminants. From an aesthetic standpoint, the marble improved in luminosity and homogeneousness as it had been freed from the dark vertical stripes whose "zebra effect" had impaired the correct and complete perception of Michelangelo's work. While other studies have been concerned with the statue's stability (2005), a long-term monitoring and maintenance programme will be needed to ensure that the satisfactory conservative and aesthetic results achieved are preserved in time.

12. *Saint Paul*
13. *Saint Peter*
14. *Saint Pius*
15. *Pope Saint Gregory the Great*
about 1501-1504
Carrara marble, h. 127 cm, base 34 x 24 cm
Siena Cathedral, Piccolomini Chapel

The four statues of *Saint Paul, Saint Peter, Saint Pius* and *Pope Saint Gregory the Great* were installed in the lower side niches of Andrea Bregno's elegant marble façade for the Piccolomini Chapel (more often referred to as an altar).
Michelangelo's relationship with Cardinal Francesco Todeschini Piccolomini (for a very short time Pope Pius III) and with his successors was long and complicated, though it never amounted to a "tragedy" like for the Tomb of Julius II. The artist had agreed (on 5 June 1501) to make fifteen statues for the chapel, but he would only manage to deliver a total of four. He would continued to worry about this unsolved issue with the Sienese family for the rest of his life, and it was his nephew Lionardo who took care of paying off what the artist owed after he died. The statues were virtually neglected by 16th-century biographers and it was only in the 17th century that one of them was attributed to Michelangelo. The greatest critical interest was on behalf of Enzo Carli (1964) who, in referring to a similar observation made by Kriegman, pointed out the fact that the *Saint Paul* was the artist's self-portrait.
Nor has recent literature abstained from suggesting that ascription of the work to Michelangelo be removed, at times for *Saints Pius* and *Gregory*, other times for *Saint Paul*, and at times this has even been suggested for all four statues. The truth of the matter is that they are all compatible with Michelangelo's manner of working, although the role the artist played here, if compared with his much more important Florentine commissions at the time, was a more marginal one. On closer examination the works actually reveal Michelangelo's typical treatment of the marble, ranging from finished to rough, with intermediate and close-knit crossing of the claw-chisel.

16. *Madonna and Child and the Infant Saint John* (*Pitti Tondo*)
about 1503-1505
Florence, Museo Nazionale del Bargello

The tondo, which practically remained unfinished when the artist left in 1505, was made for Bartolomeo Pitti, an *operaio* for Santa Maria del Fiore, who left the marble to his son Miniato, an Olivetan monk, who in turn gave it to his friend Luigi Guicciardini in Vasari's time (1550, 1991 ed., p. 888). The tondo was acquired in 1823 by the Gallerie Fiorentine and in 1873 placed in the recently inaugurated Museo Nazionale del Bargello, where it is currently on display in a room on the ground floor. A well-known image, it can be seen reproduced in casts and copies in academic plaster cast galleries but also in more surprising contexts (for example, on the funerary monument of the physician and anatomist Girolamo Segato, who died in 1836, located in the cloister of the church of Santa Croce in Florence), as well as in private buildings. Likewise a source of inspiration for contemporary artists, it was transposed into thick blue glass by a British artist and there are plans to instal this unique derivation in the Cathedral of Our Lady of the Angels in Los Angeles (California).

17. *Madonna and Child and the Infant Saint John* (*Taddei Tondo*)
about 1504-1506
Carrara marble, diam. about 109 cm
London, Royal Academy of Fine Arts

After at least three centuries of undisturbed permanence in the Taddei home in Florence, the marble tondo was sold to the painter Jean Baptiste Wicar and taken by him to his home in Rome, where Felice Giani saw it and made a sketch of it (New York, Cooper-Hewitt Museum, with the autograph writing "Rome Michelangelo in the Wicar home". Cf. G. Ragionieri, in *Vita di Michelangelo...*, 2001, p. 129, no. 92). In 1822, thanks to the good offices of Antonio Canova, the piece was acquired by Sir George Beaumont and with much ado placed in his home in Grosvenor Square in London. The story goes that the sculptor Anne Seymour Damen offered to "finish it", but was discouraged from doing so by Henri Füssli; there is some doubt, however, that it may have been touched up after all. In compliance with the owner's will, his widow left it to the Royal Academy of Fine Arts, which received it on 14 June 1830. But before that Antonio Sarti, a pupil of Antonio Canova and friend of John Constable, had made a plaster cast of it for Sir George Beaumont, Jr. Constable immediately portrayed the tondo in an ink drawing and on 3 July published a letter in *Atheneum*. Valorized in exhibitions (Royal Academy 1950-1951, Victoria and Albert Museum 1960) and studies, the tondo followed the Royal Academy from the Somerset House to the Burlington House, and was moved around a number of times in the latter location until it was finally placed on display on the Sackler Gallery Landing, in a case designed by the company owned by Sir Norman Foster in 1991, after conservation which consisted in use of the poultice method on the surface was carried out.
The work is truly the symbol of the institution that owns it – being the only sculpture by Michelangelo on the other side of the English Channel, now that, as I was kindly informed by Mr. James Methuen-Campbell, the ancient attribution of the *Cupid* at Corsham Court has been resolved –, in 1979 the work was transformed into a silver medallion by Arnold Machin.

18. *Madonna and Child* (*Bruges Madonna*)
about 1501-1505
Carrara marble, h. 94 cm (with base, 128 cm)
Bruges, Onze-Lieve-Wrouwekerk

Purchased by the Flemish merchants Jean and Alexandre Mouscron (called Moscheroni in Italy), the statuary group was finally shipped to their successors in 1506, who donated it to the cathedral where the family's burial chapel was located. This is the only work by Michelangelo in the Netherlands, where the great German painter Albrecht Dürer saw it in 1521. In its most recent arrangement the group is situated inside the central niche of a complex façade prevalently made from "black Belgian marble", and flanked by the statues of Faith and Hope, thus investing it with additional religious meaning, as it now also represents the theological virtue of Charity.
The statue was taken to France during the Age of Napoleon, and given back to Bruges with the Restoration in 1815. The group was removed by Nazi troops on the eve of the Liberation of Belgium in August 1944, hidden with other masterpieces in the ancient salt mines of Alt-Aussee near Salzburg, and rediscovered by the allies. The sculpture was taken back to Bruges after the war ended.
The 1952 Florence exhibition of the group at the Museo Nazionale del Bargello, where it was on loan in exchange for the Uffizi Gallery's Portinari triptych by Hugo van der Goes, was an exceptional event. A life-sized copy is still in Flo-rence today, whose provenance is believed to be the 19th-century arrangement at the Galleria dell'Accademia, and after a long period of time spent on the ground floor of the Pitti Palace this copy is now in the nearby church of San Felice in Piazza.

19. *Saint Matthew*
about 1506
Carrara marble, h. 216 cm
Florence, Galleria dell'Accademia

The statue of the Apostle and Evangelist Matthew was the first and only one (unfinished) out of the twelve that Michelangelo had agreed to execute in April 1503 for the Florence Cathedral. The others were never even commenced, but Michelangelo devoted himself to the *Saint Matthew* in the few months he stayed in Florence in 1506, during the interval between his break and reconciliation with Julius II. Accurate chronology (Amy, 2000) has allowed us to affirm that the artist may have been inspired by the dramatic pose of the *Laocoön*, as suggested by numerous critics, the monumental statuary group having been discovered just a few months before. The roughed-out statue reveals the different stages of its working and the tools that were used (Giovannini, 1998). Owing to its educational value in the area of marble sculpture, which was already evident when Vasari wrote his comment on it, the work was moved from the Opera di Santa Maria del Fiore to the Galleria dell'Accademia in Florence in 1834. At present, it is situated near the *Captives* in the corridor that leads to the tribune with the *David*. In the late 20th century the statue was cleaned as part of a conservation campaign by the Stone Material Restoration Division of the Opificio delle Pietre Dure in Florence.

20. *Dying Slave*
Carrara marble, h. 229 cm
21. *Rebellious Slave*
Carrara marble
h. 215 cm
about 1513
Paris, Musée du Louvre

The two *Slaves* or *Captives*, perhaps begun on the basis of the initial idea for the Julius Tomb, but unquestionably continued according to the project that was modified after the contract was redrafted with the Della Rovere heirs in 1513, remained unfinished and unused in Michelangelo's Roman home in Via Macel de' Corvi after a final agreement for the design of the tomb was reached in 1542, at which point they no longer fit.
Out of gratitude for the hospitality he had received during several bouts of illness, Michelangelo donated the two marble sculptures to Roberto Strozzi after 1546. Strozzi, exiled to Lyon, had them transported to France at his own expense in 1550, after which they became the property of the Constable of Montmorency, and in 1578 were placed in niches in the courtyard of the Château d'Ecouen in Paris, visible in Jacques Androuet Ducerceau's *Des plus excellents bâtiments de France*, Paris 1578. In 1632, they were donated to Cardinal Richelieu, who relocated them to his own castle in Poitou, where, among others, Gian Lorenzo Bernini saw them (1665). Taken to the Pavillon de Hanovre in Paris in 1749, they were put up for sale in 1793, but the revolutionary government requisitioned them and the following year they entered the collections of the Louvre. The two *Slaves* in the form of plaster casts made from the actual statues were included in the display at the Galleria dell'Accademia in Florence celebrating the fourth centenary of the birth of Michelangelo in 1875.
Their current arrangement was designed by Catherine Bizouard and François Pin and inaugurated on 26 October 1994, so that the *Slaves* now head the Galerie Michel-Ange (formerly Mollien) in the museum's Denon wing.
For centuries now French culture has shown its great appreciation for the *Slaves*, recent proof of which is the display (2005) of the photography of Patrick Faigenbaum dedicated to the statues in the *Louvre et Chaussée d'Antin* series. Towards the end of the 20th century, the advertising campaign with black and white pictures by a famous Paris-based Italian fashion designer, which included the image of a model in an ambiguous and intriguing pose, was clearly inspired by the *Dying Slave*.

22. *Moses*
about 1513-1515
Carrara marble, h. 235 cm
Rome, church of San Pietro in Vincoli

Planned from the very first project for the Julius Tomb, the figure of the great "leader and duke" (Condivi's words in 1553), the fulcrum of the biblical epic of the Jewish people's liberation from Egyptian slavery, was commenced at the same time or just after the Louvre *Slaves*, as stipulated in the contract renewed with the Della Rovere heirs after the pope died on the night between the 20th and the 21st of February (common usage). Worked up to a point that is unknown to us, the statue remained for decades in Michelangelo's workshop in Macel de' Corvi, and it was not until sometime between 1542 and 1545, when a final agreement was reached regarding the placement of the monument in San Pietro in Vincoli, that it became the core sculpture in the monument, very visibly installed in the central niche of the lower storey. In that long interval of time, the statue was reworked, and that was when Michelangelo "turned" the Moses' head leftwards to make it fit its new location (two different procedures related to the statue's working have been observed in each of the parts). During the restoration work carried out in 1999-2003, the portion of a "belt" was observed at the back of the statue of which there was no trace in front. According to Maria and Antonio Forcellino, the changes suggested were based on the need to curtail expenses, and involved reutilization, to the extent possible, of the marble from the first phase of the project.
As the statue had originally been planned for a higher position and therefore to be viewed from below, it is disproportionate owing to the excessive development of the torso as compared with the legs. The position of the work today is not the one originally chosen by the artist: in 1816, the statue had to be moved forwards so that a cast could be made for the reigning prince of England, and future George IV. Earl Rosenthal exploited the plaster copy to develop his critical considerations concerning the possible correct positioning of the original much higher up than it is now (1964, figs. 16a, b, c, d).
There exist various copies of the statue from that period, not just in plaster but in marble as well, for instance the one by Edmonia Lewis dated from 1875 (for the fourth centenary of Michelangelo) now in the Smithsonian American Art Museum in Washington, D.C., as well as the more recent one made in Carrara, commissioned by the Open Air Museum in Hakone, Japan.

23. *Risen Christ or the "First Minerva Christ"* (attributed to Michelangelo and an unknown sculptor of the 17th century)
about 1513-1516
Marble, h. 201 cm (without the cross)
250 cm (with the cross)
Bassano Romano (Viterbo), San Vincenzo Martire, sacristy

Thanks to research and contributions by Baldriga and Danesi Squarzina from 2000 onwards this statue of Christ with the cross and the symbols of the Passion could be the "First Minerva Christ".
Commissioned by Metello Vari and others, in 1513-1514 Michelangelo agreed to carve a *Risen Christ* in memory of Marta Porcari for the church of Santa Maria sopra Minerva in Rome: it was to be "a large figure in marble of a naked, standing, life-sized Christ holding the cross". In 1516, Michelangelo stopped working on it when a black vein surfaced on the figure's face. Michelangelo gave the unfinished statue to Vari, who installed it in the garden of his home in Rome, and this is where Ulisse Aldrovandi saw it about halfway through the century before its owner died in 1554. According to the most recent reconstruction, the statue was offered to Francesco Buonarroti in 1607, but the Florentine painters Passignano and Cigoli advised him not to buy it. It is likely that this first *Christ* eventually ended up with Vincenzo Giustiniani, scholar and expert on art, who had it completed and installed in the family palazzo until 1644, when it was placed above the high altar of the church of San Vincenzo Martire in Bassano Romano. Shown at the *Caravaggio e i Giustiniani* exhibition in 2001, the statue was the cause of heated debate, but since it does contain a sufficient number of elements to denote the artist's lofty style, and because of the characterizing flaw of the black vein on the face, it has rightfully earned a place among Michelangelo's autograph works.

24. *Risen Christ* (the *Minerva Christ*)
1519-1520
Marble, h. 205 cm
Rome, Santa Maria sopra Minerva

While he was working on the New Sacristy Michelangelo prepared the second version of the *Risen Christ or Minerva Christ*, which Metello Vari and others were still waiting for in Rome. It was sent to Rome in 1521 and given to Pietro Urbano who was to complete it. But the assistant proved to be incapable of doing the work, and even damaged the toes. Urbano was replaced by Federico Frizzi. To my mind, the rocky base and some of the technical details, such as the two drill holes on either side of the mouth, are unlike Michelangelo's work and should also be attributed to the master's helpers. This powerful figure, built up by *contrapposti* generated by the rotation of the hips, features gilded drapery to hide its genitalia. For a certain period of time it also wore a sort of gilded shoe on the right foot.
The image inspired the Emilian Michelangelesque Prospero Sogari, and Taddeo Landini reproduced a copy of it in Florence in 1579 for Guglielmo Del Riccio, a friend of Michelangelo, which was installed in the second chapel in Santo Spirito (under the Del Riccio patronage from 1570, and coated in polychrome marble; cf. Capretti, 1996, pp. 316, 330). Landini also made a small bronze copy now at the Kunstmuseum in Düsseldorf; Pietro Simoni da Barga made the small bronze copy at the Museo Nazionale del Bargello in Florence (inv. Bronzi n. 70; cf. A. Capriotti, in *Via di Michelangelo...*, 2001, pp. 54-55, no. 29).

Statues for the Medici Tombs in the New Sacristy
1521-1534
Florence, Museo delle Cappelle Medicee in the San Lorenzo complex
Medici Chapel, called the New Sacristy

25. *Lorenzo, Duke of Urbino*
about 1525
Carrara marble, h. 178 cm
Florence, Museo delle Cappelle Medicee in the San Lorenzo complex
Medici Chapel, called the New Sacristy, Tomb of Lorenzo, Duke of Urbino

Although he is dressed as a warrior and even wears a helmet, because of his pensive attitude Duke Lorenzo has always been seen in contraposition to Giuliano. Vasari was the first to use the word "pensive" to describe the figure, which was thereafter interpreted as expressive of contemplative life or phlegmatic and melancholy nature. The way he holds his hand between his chin and mouth is indeed typical of allegories for "Melancholy" or philosophical meditation. His attributes remain a mystery: a pouch or a kerchief (the "map" to signal the start of horse races according to Trexler and Lewis, 1981, who then went on to suggest he might really be Giuliano), a box for coins, it has been suggested, with a bat's head on one of the shorter ends, a reference to the bees present in the Medici emblems, from Lorenzo il Magnifico to Ferdinando I. The lion's head in the helmet alludes to either the strength or the Marzocco of the city of Florence, or to Pope Leo X de' Medici.

26. *Dusk*
about 1526-1531
Carrara marble, h. 195 cm
Florence, Museo delle Cappelle Medicee in the San Lorenzo complex
Medici Chapel, called the New Sacristy, Tomb of Lorenzo, Duke of Urbino

Characterized by the way his knee bends sharply so that one leg overlaps the other, *Dusk*'s body is almost finished in the central areas, but shows evident signs of working towards the edges; the head is undoubtedly "non-finito". His face is rough and clearly reveals the traces left by the sculptor's tools. He emptily stares out into the central void, perhaps to suggest, within the allusive naturalism often featured in Michelangelo's work, the indistinct obscurity that gathers as the darkness of night is about to begin. The wax statue of the *Reclining Male Nude* at the British Museum in London is believed to be preparatory for this statue.

27. *Dawn*
about 1525-1526
Carrara marble, h. 206 cm
Florence, Museo delle Cappelle Medicee in the San Lorenzo complex
Medici Chapel, called the New Sacristy, Tomb of Lorenzo, Duke of Urbino

The statue had already been executed when it was portrayed in Sigismondo Fanti's engraving the *Triumph of Fortune*, Venice, 1527. Although every single part of the statue is finished, except for the rough mass on which it reclines, which I would interpret as clouds, it did not receive a final polishing. Of all of the *Times of the Day*, it is the one most appreciated by ancient commentators (Doni, Vasari) for its beauty, whose carnal sensuality drew a great deal of attention throughout the period that the statue lay on the ground: magnificent drawings, including those by Francesco Salviati in Edinburgh and in London (Rosenberg, 2000, pp. 248-249), depict the figure from points of view that were no longer possible after it was set on the sarcophagus. Its pose – torsion of the kind that expresses "bitterness" – implies a tormented awakening, symbolizing the painful disbelief that strikes the *Dawn* at the moment when she casts daylight on the Creation and is forced to acknowledge the death of Duke Lorenzo. Like for the other statues in the New Sacristy, actually more so, the *Dawn* has inspired drawings, engravings, paintings, small-scale copies (the clay model in the Caracas Pietri collection is now believed to be one such derivation) by countless artists all the way into the 20th century.

28. *Giuliano, Duke of Nemours*
about 1526-1532
Carrara marble, h. 173 cm
Florence, Museo delle Cappelle Medicee in the San Lorenzo complex
Medici Chapel, called the New Sacristy, Tomb of Giuliano, Duke of Nemours

Depicted in the guise of a warrior *all'antica*, Duke Giuliano holds the command staff as a sign, it has been said, of his role as papal leader, and coins to symbolize his munificence. His vigilant pose has suggested a link between his attitude and virtues such as pride, vigilance, the active life, as well as his irascible and quick-tempered nature. Tolnay's Neoplatonic reading of the work is that it expresses the contemplation of divine vision through desire. Trexler and Lewis, 1981, identified him as really being Duke Lorenzo. When it was pointed out to him that the statue for Giuliano did not particularly resemble the model, it was Michelangelo himself who observed that in time no one was going to remember what the deceased looked like, which tells us that he envisaged the projection of his work in the future, if not in all of eternity. The statue was accurately copied by Giovan Battista Naldini (1560s) in a drawing now in Princeton, and like all of the statues in the New Sacristy it was widely influential from both artistic and literary viewpoints (cf. on the subject, Rosenberg, 2000).

29. *Day*
about 1526-1531
Carrara marble, h. 285 cm
Florence, Museo delle Cappelle Medicee in the San Lorenzo complex
Medici Chapel, called the New Sacristy, Tomb of Giuliano, Duke of Nemours

The central portion of the body is finished, but the features of the face and head are just roughed out. *Day* turns his gazeless eyes in the direction of the viewer, "looking" at him from over the powerful muscular mass of the shoulder. Battista Franco made drawings after the statue (1536), but provided those areas of "non-finito", which he perceived to be disturbing, with a moustache and beard.

30. *Night*
about 1526-1531
Carrara marble, h. 194 cm
Florence, Museo delle Cappelle Medicee in the San Lorenzo complex
Medici Chapel, called the New Sacristy, Tomb of Giuliano, Duke of Nemours

One of the first statues to be executed for the New Sacristy, it is the only *Time of the Day* that can be recognized on the basis of its attributes: a diadem in the shape of a crescent moon, the monstrous mask of sleep, the owl, the bundle of soporiferous poppy capsules. The marble, brought to the height of splendour in the more polished areas, is characterized by its cold intonation, an allusion to moonlight. Owing to a significant change made while the work was underway, the figure's left arm was reduced. Famous from when it first appeared, it has inspired poetry (G.B. Strozzi, Michelangelo himself in his sonnet "Dear to me is sleep..."), it was copied in drawings (from Battista Franco onwards), transposed in painting (see the catalogue *Venere e Amore*..., 2002), fashioned in smaller scale models starting with Tribolo (derivations include the clay model in the Caracas Pietri collection, previously suggested as having been a model). Vasari (1568) wrote about Giuliano Bugiardini's paradoxical painterly derivation, who it seems added to the statue's attributes "a net for catching thrushes by night, with the lantern, and one of those little vessels [...] holding a candle, [...] nightcaps, coifs, pillows, and bats", which apparently made Michelangelo burst into laughter. The painting was given to Michele di Ridolfo del Ghirlandaio and is now in the Galleria Colonna in Rome, and features an abundance of invented attributes.

31. *River God*
about 1524-1527 (?)
Unfired clay, river sand, animal fur, plant fibers, wood, wire and wire mesh, 65 x 140 x 70 cm
Florence, Casa Buonarroti, inv. Gallerie 1890, n. 1802

This *Model of a River God* remained in the New Sacristy when Michelangelo left Florence. Duke Cosimo, who owned it, offered it to Bartolomeo Ammannati, who in turn gave it to the Accademia delle Arti del Disegno in 1583: shortly thereafter, in 1590, it was submitted to its first restoration. It was relocated from the Gallerie Fiorentine to the Casa Buonarroti. This is the only large autograph preparatory model for a sculpture that is extant. The statue, which was never begun, was to be placed at the foot of the Tomb of Lorenzo dei Medici, on the left side, in the recumbent pose prescribed by ancient Greco-Roman iconography for allegories of *Rivers*. For some time the piece was lost, perhaps owing to what may have appeared to be the modesty of a model made from mixed media, but its importance and paternity were critically reevaluated in the early 20th century. Together with the very few other autograph models, it has taught us about the style and technique Michelangelo used for modelling.

32. *Madonna and Child* (*Medici Madonna*)
about 1526-1534
Carrara marble, h. 226 cm
Florence, Museo delle Cappelle Medicee in the San Lorenzo complex
Medici Chapel, called the New Sacristy

For its instalment in the New Sacristy, overseen by Niccolò Tribolo and Giorgio Vasari under Duke Cosimo de' Medici during the thirty years that followed Michelangelo's sudden interruption in work at the building site when he left for Rome (1534), the *Madonna and Child*, also known as the *Medici Madonna*, was simply placed on the high marble "cassone", or marble sarcophagus, that held the remains of the Magnifici Giuliano († 1478) and Lorenzo († 1492). Seated to either side of the group in the act of pleading are the physician saints *Cosmas* (by Giovanni Montorsoli) and *Damian* (by Raffaello da Montelupo), the patron saints of the Medici house.
Michelangelo had planned to make an imposing marble façade with two sarcophagi placed side by side for the double tomb of the Magnifici, and the *Madonna* was to occupy the central niche located above. The Madonna of the Milk or *lactans* was an ancient and much-worshipped iconography, and together with the saints to either side it introduced the religious motif of a "double" intercession with the Eternal Father on behalf of the deceased. The Michelangelesque version is enlivened by powerful energy, transforming the relationship between Mother and Son, reminiscent of the *Tondo Doni*, in a reciprocal forwards movement pervading the bodies, and twisting them into unstable poses.
The *Medici Madonna* was copied in a drawing by Raffaello da Montelupo and others (cf. Rosenberg, 2000) and it was also copied on a smaller scale by Vincenzo Danti for a headless terracotta statue at the Casa Buonarroti in Florence, dated about 1570 (cf. *I bozzetti*..., 2000, pp. 68-73, no. 9).

33. *Crouching Boy*
about 1530-1534
Marble, h. 54 cm
Saint Petersburg, Hermitage Museum, inv. N.H. 154

The likely hypothesis has been made that the figure just roughed out for the *Crouching Boy* was meant for the upper storey of the *Medici Tombs* (along with others that were never even begun). Its crouching pose, inspired by the ancient *Boy with Thorn* type, expresses the defeat and pain of humanity before the mourning of the Medici house. The *Crouching Boy* probably remained in the artist's workshop in Via Mozza with other statues and marbles, and when Michelangelo died it ended up with Duke Cosimo de' Medici (Parronchi, 1981). From the Florentine galleries, where it was sold as a less valuable piece perhaps during the Lorenese era, it became a part of the John Lyde Brown collection in Wimbledon, where it was inventoried in 1779 as attributed to Michelangelo. Russian empress Catherine II purchased it in 1785 and had it placed in the grotto of the residence at Carskoe Selo with other sculptures. In 1818 it was in the Academy of Fine Arts in Saint Petersburg and, lastly, it was relocated to the New Hermitage. In 1876, after the fourth centenary was celebrated, a plaster copy belonging to the Duchess Marija Nicolaevna was placed on display in Florence. After scholarship generally agreed on Michelangelo's paternity, doubt was cast by Kriegbaum (1940); some critics saw the hand of Tribolo in the statue, others that of Tiberio Calcagni or the master's assistants in general. In the 1990s, after further study was conducted, the hypothesis of its being an autograph work prevailed once more. This was confirmed in studies conducted by Sergej Androsov, and reiterated on the occasion of the Florentine exhibition of 2000 (*L'adolescente...*, 2000). Since then in-depth analysis has been carried out on the treatment of the marble surfaces by Michelangelo, and on the basis of the cases examined, the master should be attributed the extraordinary invention of the dramatically compressed male nude, but not the monotonous and repetitive treatment of the "skin" with a claw-chisel, most likely the efforts of an assistant instead.

34. *Apollo/David*
about 1525-1530
Marble, h. 46 cm
Florence, Museo Nazionale del Bargello, inv. S. 121

"Begun", in Vasari's words, for the commissary to the Medici pope Baccio Valori, the statue was never completed. The biographer called it an *Apollo* in the act of taking an arrow from his quiver, but an inventory taken of Cosimo de' Medici's room in the Palazzo Vecchio in 1553 referred to it as an "imperfect" *David* "by Buonarroti". This explains why the work has two names, despite the fact that it is obviously an *Apollo*, recognizable as such also in the copy by Rosso Fiorentino at the Pierpont Morgan Library in New York. After a period of time spent with the other statues used to fill the niches of the Boboli Gardens Amphitheatre, in 1824 it became a part of the Uffizi Gallery and after that, in 1864, the Museo Nazionale. The "non-finito" treatment of the surface, which bestows softness to the forms and a vague gentleness to the features, has suggested that this inwards turned figure (truly a paradigm of the "figura serpentinata", or serpentine figure, in sculpture) is really the protagonist of a psychological state on the edge of the transient world of dreams. If the volumes had been brought to completion and cleaned up, however, his attitude would not be that of a dreamer, but of someone awake and accurately described.

Four Captives
35. *Young Captive*
36. *Bearded Captive*
37. *So-called "Atlas"*
38. *Awakening Captive*
1530 (about)- 1532
Carrara marble, h. 256 cm (*Young*), 267 cm (*Bearded*), 277 cm (*Atlas*), 267 cm (*Awakening*)
Florence, Galleria dell'Accademia

The four figures roughed out to different degrees of "non-finito" were carved by Michelangelo while the artist was in Florence for the Tomb of Julius II. Although the chronology is not firm, the work was probably done at the end of the period when the artist was in Florence at the service of Clement VII in the New Sacristy in San Lorenzo. Like the two *Captives* or *Slaves* now in the Musée du Louvre in Paris they were meant to allude, in a laudatory key, to the disastrous and painful decadence of the arts and knowledge after the death of Julius II. Planned from the initial, imposing project for forty statues (1505), Michelangelo probably interrupted his work on the *Captives* after an agreement was reached with the Della Rovere heirs in 1532, in which the artist was asked to make a much smaller number of statues, only six. The statues are so close to the original state of the blocks from the Apuan Alps from which they were roughhewn that one of the four, the so-called "Atlas", still has all of the identifying marks: the three circles for Michelangelo, an "I." for quarryman Leone, a ship, a three-pronged instrument.
When Buonarroti died, his nephew Lionardo gave them to Duke Cosimo de' Medici, along with the *Victory* group. Cosimo's son, Grand Duke Francesco I, had them installed to a design by Bernardo Buontalenti in a grotto at the Boboli Gardens (1585-1588), where they were incorporated in the four corners of the entrance to the gardens as part of the rustic decor of natural sponges and stalactites. In this excellent location they bore their original symbology related to the idea of imminent ruin, but they also lent themselves to a rereading of the pagan myth of Deucalion and Pyrrha, two just figures who survived the flood of the universe, and converted stones into people in order to give birth to a new humanity. In 1909 the four figures were removed from the gardens and substituted with copies; on the initiative of Corrado Ricci the originals were relocated to the Galleria dell'Accademia, where he had them placed in a gallery destined, in the 19th century, to host the collection's antique paintings, but later transformed into a trail of Michelangelesque works ending with the Tribune and statue of the *David* (Anglani, 1997). At the end of the 20th century the four *Captives* underwent mild cleaning carried out by Cinzia Parnigoni.
Owing to their expressive imposingness and tacit symbolic meaning the four *Captives* have also been used (as copies) in apparently distant contexts: for example, in 1959 Professor Fazzari of the Careggi Hospital in Florence had four copies after casts at the "Museo dei Gessi" in the Academy of Fine Arts made, to be installed as telamons at the entrance to the Division of Pathologic Anatomy.
For a *"fifth Captive"* recalled by Vasari, in 1965 Ugo Procacci suggested a *Standing Male Nude* roughed out in marble, 212 cm in height (base 234 cm), which at the time was situated close to the wall of the Palazzo Pitti's second courtyard, and then relocated to the Casa Buonarroti. Although the measurements, subject, some of the aspects concerning the way it was worked and the Medicean provenance would favour the hypothesis, because of the poor quality of the figure, scholarship has rejected the attribution to Michelangelo, suggesting that it is perhaps the work of a collaborator instead.

39. *Victory*, called the *Genius of Victory*
about 1530-1534
Marble, h. 261 cm
Florence, Palazzo Vecchio, Sala dei Cinquecento

The sculptural group portraying a young, athletic victor as he overcomes an elderly, bearded vanquished figure is generally viewed in relation to the lower storey of the Julius Tomb according to the second project, which was to include *Victories* in niches that alternated with *Terms* and *Captives* against projecting pilaster strips. Balas disagreed (1989) with this idea, instead seeing the group as being a sculpture undertaken by Michelangelo for himself, an allegory of the young and handsome Tommaso de' Cavalieri's amorous victory over the artist. With sides that featured areas of "non-finito" (planned, I believe, for its placement in the Tomb niche), the sculpture remained unfinished in the artists's workshop in Via Mozza.
When his uncle died, Lionardo Buonarroti was persuaded by Vasari to donate it to Duke Cosimo along with the *Captives* and the marbles that were left over. It is likely that the duke gave it to Vincenzo Danti so that he could do further work on it, traces of which are visible in the head and in some areas of the body of the vanquished figure. Later the statue was placed in the Sala dei Cinquecento in the Palazzo Vecchio, as one of the elements in a long parade of over life-sized marble statues expressing the moral-political idea of Good as opposed to Evil, i.e. the duke prevailing over his enemies. The *Victory* remained in the same room until 1868 when it was relocated with other statues to the Museo Nazionale del Bargello. But in 1921 it was moved back to the Sala, this time placed in a niche inside a Neo-Renaissance marble apparatus on the southern wall, decorated to celebrate Michelangelo's excellence. In 1980 on the occasion of exhibitions dedicated to the 16th-century members of the Medici family as patrons and collectors the entire room was rearranged as it once was (cf. Heikamp, 1980), and the Michelangelesque group resumed its original place in the sequence of 16th-century statues lining the walls. The campaign to clean the statues that took place in the 1990s ended with the *Victory*, and this allowed for a more in-depth analysis of the sculpture, including the relationships between the finished areas, those intentionally left rough, "non-finito" areas, and those which were reworked.
Many of Michelangelo's ideas for other groups of victors and vanquished figures that he had planned for the Tomb of Julius II intersect studies concerning other similar subjects, such as *Samson and the Philistines* and *Hercules and Cacus*. I believe that the model of the *Two Wrestlers* now in the Casa Buonarroti, discussed in this volume, is related to the group of *Victories*.

40. *Brutus*
1539-1540 or 1548?
Marble, h. 74 cm
Florence, Museo Nazionale del Bargello

The bust, the only one of its kind made by Michelangelo and one of the very few works directly inspired by Imperial Roman statuary (Caracalla, Museo Archeologico in Naples), was made for the anti-Medicean cardinal Niccolò Ridolfi on the initiative of his secretary Donato Giannotti, also an exile, who was a friend of the artist from the time when the siege of Florence took place. The fibula fastening the drapery on the shoulder includes a portrait of Giannotti. The date of the work ranges from 1539-1540 (when Giannotti first entered the service of Ridolfi) and 1548 (the death of the "Tuscan Brutus" Lorenzino de' Medici, also called Lorenzaccio, murderer of Duke Alessandro). Nevertheless, the work was undoubtedly conceived and in part made surrounded by the atmosphere of praise for tyrannicide that reigned among the Florentine expatriates in Rome at the time. Neither finished nor delivered, the bust went to Tiberio Calcagni, whose contribution is visible in the drapery. It was acquired by Ferdinando I de' Medici through the Diomede Leoni estate in 1590 (Hirst, 1998). For its display at the Uffizi Gallery it was given an inscription that explained how the "non-finito" state of the statue was due to the artist's sudden repulsion upon hearing the news of the murder: "DVM BRVTI EFFIGIEM SCULPTOR DE MARMORE DVCIT / IN MENTE SCELERIS VENIT ET ABSTINVIT" (While the sculptor was carving the marble effigy of *Brutus*, the crime came to mind and he stopped [carving]). Since 1874 the work has been on display at the Museo Nazionale del Bargello (cf. Rossi, 1932, pl. 46; Barocchi, 1982, who also suggests attributing the words to Anton Maria Salvini).

41. *Recumbent Statue of Julius II* (with Tommaso Boscoli)
Before 1532(?) - 1542
Carrara marble
Rome, San Pietro in Vincoli, Tomb of Julius II

It was not until after its restoration in 1999-2003 that critical attention was drawn to the recumbent statue of the pope, which – starting with Vasari – had always been attributed to Maso dal Bosco, or Tommaso Boscoli of Fiesole. The idea of this being an autograph work by Michelangelo was first suggested by Antonio Forcellino, with whom some of the most authoritative scholars concurred. This meant that Boscoli had only executed the "cassa" or sarcophagus.
The invention of the figure of Julius II lying on one side, the top part of his mag-ificent robe undone, would seem to re- ct the master's work, evident in the pressed dynamics of the contraction orsion of the limbs used to suggest nflict between the pope's authority e people while he was alive, and sary humility before God.

Nonetheless, the unoriginal execution of some of the areas of the work, as well as the use of the claw-chisel on the surface in a manner that is incompatible with the master's style, indicate a different hand, which could very well have been Boscoli's, therefore in agreement with Vasari. E. Guidoni (2003) passionately defended the idea of this being entirely an autograph work by Boscoli.

42. *The Contemplative Life*, or *Rachel*
Carrara marble, h. 209 cm
43. *The Active Life*, or *Leah*
Carrara marble, h. 197 cm
about 1542
Rome, San Pietro in Vincoli, Tomb of Julius II

Michelangelo carved the two female statues over a period of about a year on the basis of the last and final agreement for the Julius Tomb which was completed in 1545. The coincidence between the allegorical meanings of the statues, which had been planned from the first contract, and the biblical identities stands on the indications – which among other things are not perfectly clear – in Condivi (1553), who cites Dante's *Purgatory*. The statues, considered to be among Michelangelo's least successful works, nonetheless foreshadow other possible allusions as well: the theological virtue of Faith in Rachel, who prays, the cardinal virtue of Prudence in Leah, who looks at herself in a mirror, virtues leading to the spheres of transcendence and the earthly, respectively. And through the citation from the *Divine Comedy*, Michelangelo was also able to evoke his noble ancestor, Matilde di Canossa, whose overlap with Dante's Matelda was unquestionable for ancient commentators. The statues were perhaps finished with the help of some of the artist's assistants (Raffaello da Montelupo is mentioned), but they did not receive a final polishing.

44. *Bandini Pietà*
about 1549-1555
Carrara marble, h. 226 cm
Florence, Museo dell'Opera del Duomo

This impressive monolithic group with four figures (Christ, the Virgin, Magdalene, Nicodemus or, although less likely, Joseph of Arimathea) has been referred to as a *Pietà* since the second edition of Vasari's biography (1568), but the most recent criticism has especially shed light on the complex ambiguity and dynamism of the subject, definable as a *Deposition from the Cross* at the point when it becomes an *Entombment*. Michelangelo devoted himself to the work for which there was no patron, and was planning to have it placed in his own burial chapel, perhaps in Florence; Nicodemus' face is the artist's self-portrait. See the analysis in this volume of the troubled events of the statue that led to its mutilation and abandonment by the master, and to its further working (mostly in the Magdalene, but not only that) by Tiberio Calcagni, prior to 1565. Vasari also recalled that the marble group was located in the vineyard owned by Pierantonio son of Francesco Bandini in "Montecavallo", i.e. on the Quirinal Hill, along the Strada Pia, currently Via XX Settembre. After his father's death, through his inheritance Pierantonio had acquired both the vineyard and the *Pietà*, where it was perhaps already installed, so that in 1564 he was its sole owner. Perhaps this is why Lionardo Buonarroti was unable to buy it for his uncle's tomb, which was what Vasari had asked him to do as early as one month after Michelangelo's death.
An engraving by Cherubino Alberti would seem to substantiate the idea of the work's placement in the open air, as it shows the group in a meadow close to the tomb with the Golgotha in the background (in Paolucci, 1997). Thanks to the research conducted by F. Trinchieri Camiz (2003) the events that followed could be reconstructed. While in the vineyard, the *Pietà* was in a garden, inside a side niche at the centre of a loggia covered over by a terrace: the statue's position at the end of a pathway all along the wall must have been very scenographic. This was very much in keeping with Michelangelo's vision, if we think of his design to place the *Marcus Aurelius* at the centre of the square on the Campidoglio, or his project for the *Farnese Bull* in the second courtyard of the eponymous palace. At the end of the 16th century some thirty-two antique pieces, including sarcophagi and fragments of statues, were scattered throughout the vineyard, but the presence of the religious group must have conveyed the symbolic meaning of a Golgotha to the entire garden. The property, which had gone first to the abbot Giovanni Bandini, and then to his brother Cardinal Ottavio, went to Scipione Capponi in 1646. When the property was sold to the nearby Jesuit novitiate in the church of Saint Andrew in 1649, the *Pietà* was relocated to the Palazzo Montecitorio owned by the Capponi, and after that to the Palazzo Rusticucci-Accoromboni in Borgo. Through mediation by Paolo Falconieri, Scipione Capponi's son Piero sold the marble to Cosimo III de' Medici in 1671. While awaiting its problematic transportation by ship to Florence, the statue was placed in the Florentine citizen's place of residence in Rome, the Palazzo di Firenze in Campo Marzio. After a number of bureaucratic and technical complications, the heavy group was loaded onto the ship, left for a while in the Rocca of Livorno, and, lastly, transported (October 1674) to the *sottochiesa* of San Lorenzo in Florence. In 1722 the *Pietà* became the focus of work to restructure the choir in Santa Maria del Fiore, placed on marble from different locations ("marmi mischi") to a design by Giovan Battista Foggini, and with an inscription by Filippo Buonarroti which stated: "though it was disdained for its flawed marble by the artificer, it is nonetheless an excellent work of art". But despite the fact that the group's beauty was heightened by the location, it was handled incorrectly and damaged. In 1931 it was moved to the chapel of the Madonna della Neve, the first to the right in the northern tribune. In 1981 it was taken to the Museo dell'Opera del Duomo and placed on a landing of the main stairway. But this arrangement, not an ideal one, will soon be solved when the statue is relocated to the Museum's new wing, currently under construction.
To repair the damage made to the work by Michelangelo himself, as well as damage to the marble (currently made up of several pieces) which resulted from its having been moved so many times, the work has undergone restoration on several occasions. Tiberio Calcagni was the first to intervene, using metal hinges and stucco to repair the fragments that could be restored to their original state, and integrating the large gaps with five pieces that he personally carved. A number of substances have been applied to the surface of the statue over the years (wax, natural resin) for the sake of diminishing the visibility of the cracks; the colours of these substances have changed and turned yellow or brownish.
The small wax version formerly in the Gigli collection in Florence is believed to be a derivation and not a *bozzetto* (despite the fact that Christ has both legs). Lorenzo Sabbatini made a free painting of the group, which is now in Saint Peter's (*ante* 1576). For the influence of the artistic group over the centuries, see Wasserman, 2003. For information on the *Palestrina Pietà* at the Galleri dell'Accademia in Florence, which may be interpreted as a derivation from this one, but whose chronology and attribution are still controversial, see the comment in this volume.

45. *Rondanini Pietà*
1549 or 1533? - about 1564
Marble, h. 195 cm
Milan, Museo del Castello Sforzesco

The two figures in the *Pietà*, called "Rondanini" after the family that owned it for a very long time, were undoubtedly

the last on which Michelangelo used his marble carving tools. The date when the artist started to work on it, before the *Bandini Pietà* (1549) and after Condivi's *Life* (1553), is still unknown, although we do know that it is the sculpture on which the artist, close to ninety years of age, worked on until a few days before his quick death. Disconcerting if we consider the parameters of 16th-century sculpture, but very much in tune with the informal, symbolist, Expressionist movements of the Novecento, the *Rondanini Pietà* that has survived to our day is a "palimpsest" (Paoletti, 2000) revealing the passage from the one to the other of two distinct projects: the first characterized by one or perhaps two figures supporting a deceased Christ featuring a powerful, full body, the second characterized by only one figure to support Christ, whose body is emaciated and face is sunken. The figure embracing the lifeless body, perhaps guiding it into the tomb lower down, as we see it today is the Virgin: but the signs of a previous figure (a Nicodemus?), i.e a face half-carved in her veil and a naked leg, are still clearly visible. What is left of the first Christ are the legs, incompatible with the narrowed and reduced torso, and an extra arm, detached from the shoulder and isolated. A Christ's head with a portion of the shoulder now in the Borghese Gallery has been suggested as one of the missing pieces (Mantura, 1973), but despite the authoritative consent of Italian scholarship (Parronchi, 1980, Paolucci, 1997), international scholarship was skeptical. And the most recent analysis carried out in Milan, both stylistic and scientific (including petrographic testing), would seem to exclude its pertinence to the group.
The *Pietà*, which remained in the workshop in Via Macel de' Corvi and was inventoried there in 1564, was inherited by Antonio del Francese. The date when the Rondanini family received the statue is unknown. Perhaps it was purchased by Giuseppe (who died in 1801), a great collector of antique and modern marbles. The work was located in the atrium of his Roman palace in Via del Corso where, in the inventory drawn up by Albacini and Pierantoni (1897), it was described as follows: "a modern group just roughed out which is said to be by Michael Angelo Buonarroti, but this is commonly believed to be a mistake, the work represents a deposition from the cross" (Acidini Luchinat, 1983, p. 110).
The statue, whose subject was keenly defined, was nevertheless no longer believed to be an autograph work by the great sculptor; however, in 1875 a plaster cast was made of it. Perhaps the inscription on its base referring to the author as "BVONA ROTA", like in the past (see C. Negri, the *Gratie d'Amor*, rule LXVIII, in Fabrizio Caroso da Sermoneta, *Nobiltà di Dame*, Venice 1600, and other 16th- and 17th-century evidence), is perhaps dated from before the Rondanini period.
In 1904 the sculpture with the rest of the palace went to Roberto Sanseverino Vimercati, without the State exerting its right of pre-emption. The *Pietà* was relocated to the library, until it was acquired in 1952 by the city of Milan to be placed in the Castello Sforzesco. Display of the work in the Scarlioni Room was curated by Studio BPBR (1956), which also had the idea of using an antique *ara*, or altar, as a plinth. During conservation work carried out on the *Pietà* in 1998-2002, which was preceded by diagnostic testing, conservators observed that a patina had formed on the surface, which included residues of malt and plaster that had stratified on the marble and produced a colouring effect, in addition to the dust particles that had settled there, especially in the areas with more furrowing. The marble was restored to its original lustre, and the signs of subsequent working are now wholly legible (cf. Fiorio, 2004).
An international meeting of architects was held to discuss the museum display of the work, and while predilection was expressed for the project by the Portuguese Alvaro Siza, debate as to whether or not the work done by BPBR should be maintained (see contributions in Ceriana, 2002) has suggested that any decision be postponed.

46. *Christ* (*Crucifix?*)
about 1562-1563
Wood (linden?), h. 27 cm
Florence, Museo di Casa Buonarroti, inv. 195

In the very last months of his life Michelangelo began using gouges along with all his other carving tools. Gouges are employed to carve wood, and the master hadn't used one in a long time. In 1562 he asked that several of the finest quality be sent to him from Florence. It is believed that the wooden *Christ* he was working on in July 1563, which he intended to give to his nephew Lionardo, can be linked to the small sculpture in the Casa Buonarroti (*I bozzetti...*, 2000), pp. 64-67, no. 8). The frontal position of the body and the way the head falls sharply to the side recall the artist's youthful *Crucifixes*, but the vigour of the body is the same as that of the great nudes in the artist's most developed statuary. The only example of a non-polychrome wooden sculpture, the *Christ* reveals that Michelangelo used the gouge with great impetus in order to bestow a widespread vibration effect on the work's surface.

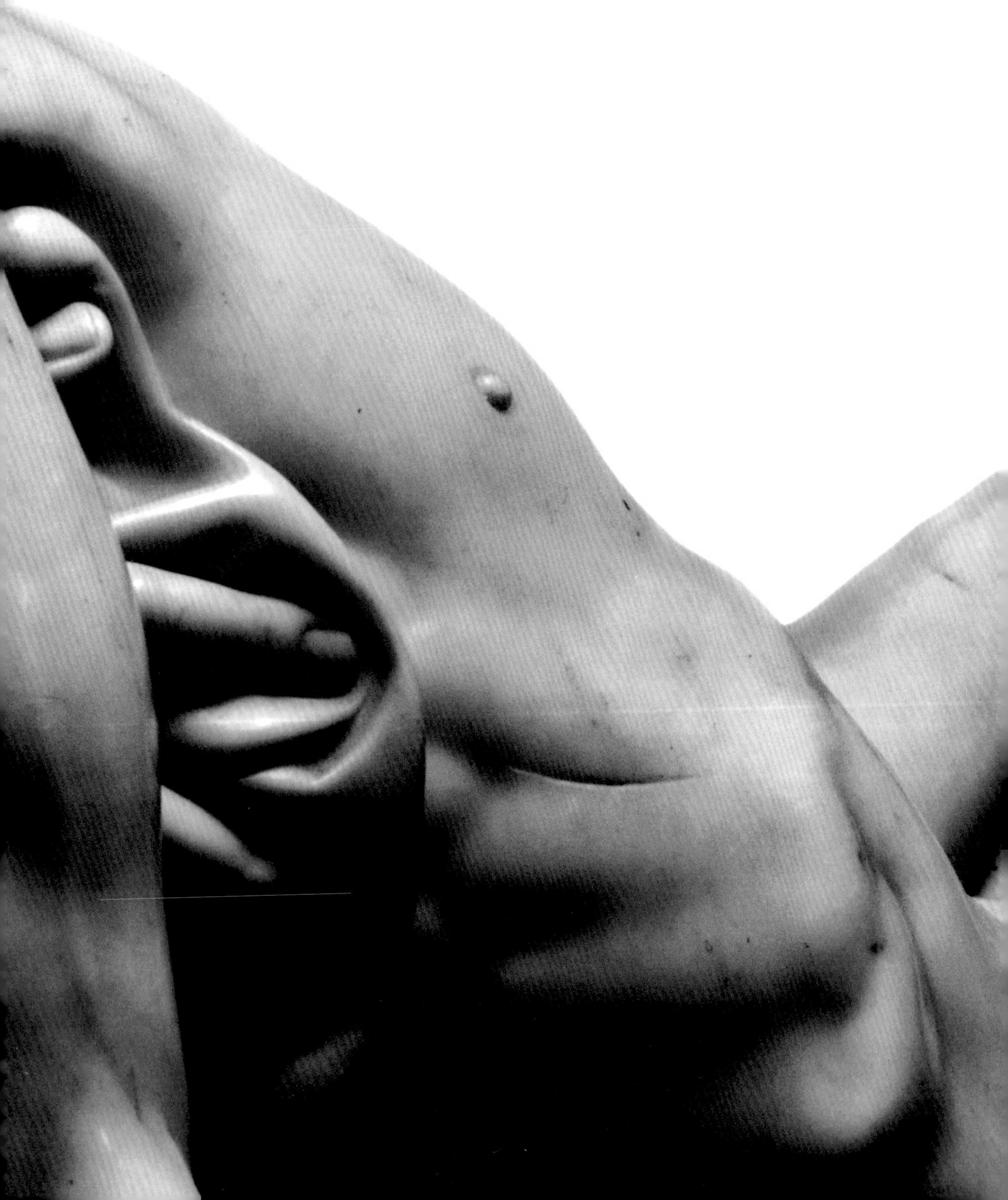